JET SET
CONFESSIONS

MAUREEN CHILD

RECLAIMING
HIS LEGACY

DANI WADE

MILLS & BOON

First Published in Great Britain 2020
by Mills & Boon, an imprint of HarperCollinsPublishers,
1 London Bridge Street, London, SE1 9GF

Jet Set Confessions © 2020 Maureen Child
Reclaiming His Legacy © 2020 Katherine Worsham

ISBN: 978-0-263-27917-7

0320

MIX
Paper from
responsible sources
FSC™ C007454

This book is produced from independently certified FSC™ paper to ensure responsible forest management.

For more information visit: www.harpercollins.co.uk/green

Printed and bound in Spain
by CPI, Barcelona

JET SET CONFESSIONS

MAUREEN CHILD

To my mom, Sallye Carberry,
who opened up the world of books to me.
Mom, you taught me to love reading and so much
more. Thank you. I love you.

One

"You've completely lost your mind." Luke Barrett stared across the room at his grandfather. "You said you wanted me to come over to really *talk*. This isn't talking, Pop. This is nuts."

Jamison Barrett stood up from behind his desk, and Luke took just a moment to admire the fact that, at eighty, the old man still stood military-straight. Fit and strong, Jamison was a man to be reckoned with—as he always had been. His steel-gray hair was expertly cut, and he wore a tailored navy-blue pin-striped suit with a power red tie. The look he gave his grandson promised a battle.

"You should know better than to tell an old man he's crazy," he said. "We're sensitive about that sort of thing."

Luke shook his head. His grandfather had always been stubborn—Luke was used to that. But a few months ago, the old man had dropped a bomb and, clearly, he hadn't changed his mind about it.

"I don't know what else to call this," Luke argued, feeling as frustrated as he had when Pop first brought this up. "When the president of a company suddenly makes a U-turn and wants to cut off its most profitable arm, I think that qualifies as nuts."

Jamison came around the corner of his desk, probably hoping to put this little meeting on a friendlier footing. "I don't have any intention of pulling out of the tech world. I only want to dial it back—"

"Yes," Luke interrupted. "In favor of wooden rocking horses, bicycles and skateboards."

"We're a toy company first," Jamison reminded him. "We have been for more than a hundred damn years."

"And then we *grew* into Barrett Toys and Tech," Luke pointed out.

"Grew in the wrong direction," his grandfather snapped.

"Disagree." Luke blew out a breath and tried to rein in the exasperation nearly choking him. He had always trusted Pop's judgment. But in this, he was willing to fight the older man because, damn it, the path to the future wasn't through the past.

"I've got studies to back me up."

"And I've got profit and loss statements to prove you're wrong."

"Yeah, we're making plenty of money, but is that all we want?"

Luke's jaw dropped. "Since that is sort of the whole point of being in business, I'm going to say *yes*."

Jamison shook his head in clear disappointment. "You used to have a broader vision."

"And you used to listen to me." Irritated, Luke shoved

both hands into his slacks pockets and gave a quick glance around his grandfather's office.

It was familiar and warm and pretty much fit the old man to a T. Jamison's desk was a hand-carved mahogany behemoth that dominated the huge room. If there was ever a tidal wave that swept this far inland, Pop could float on that thing for days.

On the cream-colored walls were framed posters of their most popular toys over the years, and family photos dotted the shelves that were also lined with leather-bound books that had actually been read. It was a prestigious Victorian office that seemed at war with the present times.

But then, so was Jamison.

"I don't want to argue with you about this again, Pop," Luke said, trying to keep the impatience he was feeling out of his tone.

He owed this proud old man everything. Jamison and his wife, Loretta, had raised Luke and his cousin Cole after the boys' parents were killed in a small plane crash. Luke had been ten and Cole twelve when they went to live with their grandparents as broken, grief-stricken kids. But Jamison and Loretta had picked up the pieces in spite of their own grief at losing both of their sons and daughters-in-law in one horrific accident. They had given their grandsons love and protection and the feeling that their world hadn't ended.

Luke and Cole had grown up working at Barrett Toys, knowing that one day they would be in charge. The company was more than a hundred years old and had always stayed current by leaping into the future—taking chances. When Luke was in college and convinced his grandfather that tech toys were going to be the next big thing, Jamison hadn't hesitated.

He'd gathered up the finest tech designers he could find, and the Barrett toy company got even bigger, even more successful. Now they were on the cutting edge. Counted as one of the biggest toy and tech companies in the world. For the last few years, Luke had been running the tech division, and Cole worked on the more traditional outlet.

Okay yes, Cole wasn't happy that Luke was the heir apparent, especially since he was two years older than Luke, but the cousins had worked that out. Mostly.

Now, though, none of them knew where they stood. All because Jamison Barrett had gotten a bug up his—

"I'm not talking about an argument, Luke," Jamison said, clearly irritated, "I'm talking about what I see every time I walk out of this office. Hell, Luke, if you weren't glued to your phone like the rest of humanity, you'd see it, too."

As irritated as his grandfather, Luke bit back his temper. He'd heard this argument over and over during the last couple of months. "Not this again."

"Yes, *this*. This is about the kids, Luke. As attached to their phones and screens and tablets and games as you are to your email." Jamison threw both hands high. "Used to be, children were running amok outside with their friends, getting into trouble, climbing trees, swimming." He glared at Luke. "Hell, you and Cole were in constant motion when you were kids. Making you stay inside and read was looked at like torture!"

All true, he thought, but he only said, "Times change."

Jamison scowled. "Not always for the better. Kids today, all their friends are online, and they wear headsets so they can talk to each other without actually having to see each other. Instead of getting outside, they build 'virtual' tree houses. They have carefully written adventures via game boxes."

"Hell, most kids probably don't even know *how* to ride a bike anymore."

Luke shook his head. "Bikes aren't going to teach them how to navigate what's becoming a completely digital world."

"Right. A digital world." Jamison nodded sharply. "Who's going to fix your cars, or air conditioners, or the damn toilet when it breaks? You going to pee digitally, too? It's going to get mighty hot in your house if you're only using virtual air-conditioning."

"This is ridiculous," Luke muttered, amazed that he had allowed himself to get sucked into Jamison's fixation. He had to wonder where his visionary grandfather had gone. Did this happen to *all* old people? Did they all start slipping into a hole and then pulling the hole in after them?

"Pop, you're making the same kind of complaint every generation makes about the newer one. You've never been the kind of man to look backward. You've always been more interested in the future than the past. This isn't like you."

"Times change." Jamison tossed Luke's words back at him. "And I *am* talking about the future," the older man argued. "There are all kinds of studies out now about what staring at screens are doing to kids' minds. That's why I wanted you to come in. I want you to see them. Read them. Open your damn mind long enough to admit that *maybe* I've got a point."

With that, Jamison turned to his desk and started riffling through the papers and files stacked there. Muttering beneath his breath, he checked everywhere, then checked again.

"I had it right here," he muttered. "Had Donna print it all out this morning." Facing Luke again, he said, "I can't find it right now and damned if I can figure out why—"

Luke frowned. "Doesn't matter."

"That's where you're wrong. Blast it, Luke, I don't want to be part of ruining a generation of children."

"Ruining?" Astonished, Luke stared at him. *"We're* giving kids a step up, helping them learn to read—"

"Their parents could do that by reading to them at night."

"Toddlers learn colors and puzzle solving with our games."

"They can do that with a box of crayons."

"God, you're a hardhead."

"First, I'm losing my mind, and now I'm just old and stubborn, is that it?" Jamison's eyes flashed. "Well, I can tell you I'm sharper than you are if you can't see the truth in what I'm telling you."

Luke shoved both hands through his hair. Maybe he hadn't really come to his grandfather's office. Maybe he was home in bed having a nightmare. Or maybe he'd taken a sharp left turn on the way here and had somehow ended up in hell.

His grandfather had always been on the current edge of everything. This about-face had really thrown Luke. He looked at Jamison's attitude now as not trusting Luke to take the helm of the company. As if he'd been indulging Luke and, now, was pulling the rug out from under him.

He took a deep breath, reminded himself that he loved the old man currently driving him bat-crap crazy and said, "You know what? We're just not going to agree on this, Pop. We need to stop hammering at each other over it. It's better if both of us just keep doing what we're doing."

Or at least what they had been doing the last couple of months. When Jamison first told Luke about his idea to scale back the tech division, Luke had argued until his head throbbed. He'd presented his case against the idea, which Pop had quickly dismissed. It hadn't been the first time they'd locked horns and fought it out, but somehow that argument had felt more…final than any of the others. When it was over, Luke had taken a stand and left the company to go out on his own. If nothing else, he was going to prove to his grandfather that he had faith in his own plans. Prove that tech toys really were the wave of the future.

"That's it? We just part ways? That's your final word on this?"

He met his grandfather's dark green eyes. It felt like the chasm between them was getting wider by the second. For now, Luke was going to concentrate on building his own tech toy company, Go Zone. "It is, Pop. The past can't build the future."

"You can't have a future *without* a past," Jamison pointed out.

"And the carousel keeps turning," Luke muttered. "Every time we talk about this, we say the same things, and neither one of us is convinced. We're on opposite sides of this, Pop. And there is no bridge. For me, it's better if I stay out on my own."

"Your grandmother cried last night. Over all of this."

Instantly, a sharp pang of guilt stabbed Luke but, then, he thought about it. Loretta Barrett was as tough as they came. His grandfather was sneaky enough to try to use his wife to win the argument. "No, she didn't."

Jamison scowled. "No, she didn't," he admitted. "She yelled some. But she could have cried. Probably will."

Luke blew out a breath and shook his head. "You're impossible."

"I'm doing what I have to do. You belong *here*, Luke, not running your own place."

And honestly, Luke had thought that Barrett Toys *was* his place. But things had changed with Pop's change of heart. With what felt to Luke as his lack of faith. His grandfather had always pushed him, believed in him. Trusted him. This felt like a betrayal, plain and simple. Luke's new company was small, but he had some great designers, just out of college, filled with ideas that would shake up the toy tech business. Luke was hoping to get manufacturing up and pumping out his new line by the end of the year.

This had all started because he'd been frustrated with his grandfather—but now, Luke was committed to making this work. Jamison might be willing to turn his back on progress, but Luke was greeting it with open arms.

"This is the *Barrett* toy company," Jamison reminded him. "A Barrett has been in charge since the beginning. Family, Luke. That's what's important."

That's what made all of this so much harder.

"We're still family, Pop," he reminded the older man—and himself at the same time. "And remember, you've got Cole here to run the business if you ever decide to retire."

"Cole's not you," Jamison said flatly. "I love the boy, but he hasn't got the head for the business that you do."

"He'll come around," Luke said, though he didn't really believe it. Hell, it's why Luke had been Jamison's choice to run the company in the first place. Cole just wasn't interested in the day-to-day of running a business. He liked being in charge. Liked the money. But he was a delegator, not a worker.

"You always were a stubborn one," Jamison muttered.

"Wonder where I got that," Luke said wryly.

"Touché." Nodding, his grandfather said, "Fine. You do what you have to do, so will I."

Luke hated having this simmering tension between him and his grandfather. Jamison Barrett was the rock in Luke's life. The old man had taught him how to fish, how to throw a fastball and how to tie a bow tie. He'd taught Luke everything about running a business and how to treat employees. He'd been there. Always. And now, Luke felt like he was abandoning him. But damned if he could think of a way to end it so that both of them came out winning.

"Give my love to Gran."

He left before his grandfather could say anything else, closing the office door behind him. The company headquarters was in Foothill Ranch, California, and most of the windows looked out over palm trees, more buildings and parking lots. Still, there was a greenbelt nearby and enough sunlight pouring through the lightly tinted windows to make the whole place bright.

Jamison's secretary, Donna, looked up from her computer screen. She was comfortably in her fifties and had been with Jamison for thirty years. "See you, Luke."

"Yeah," he answered, giving his grandfather's door one last look. He didn't like leaving the old man like this, but what choice did he have?

Still frowning to himself, he asked, "Is Cole here?"

"Yep." Donna nodded toward a bank of offices across the room.

"Thanks." Luke headed over to see his cousin. He

gave a brisk knock, then opened the door and stuck his head in. "How's it going?"

"Hey." Cole looked up and smiled. Even in a suit, he looked like a typical California surfer. Tanned, fit, with sun-streaked blond hair and blue eyes, Cole Barrett was the charmer in the company. He did lunches with prospective clients and took meetings with manufacturers because he could usually smooth-talk people into just about anything. "You here to see Pop?"

"Just left him." Luke braced one shoulder on the doorjamb and idly noted how different Cole's office was from their grandfather's. Smaller, of course, but that was to be expected. It was more than that, though. Cole's desk was steel and glass, his desk chair black leather minimalist. Shelves were lined with some of the toys their company had produced over the years, but the walls were dotted with professionally done photos of his wife, Susan, and their toddler son, Oliver—skiing in Switzerland, visiting the Pyramids and aboard the family yacht. Cole had always been more interested in playing than in the work required to make the money to do the playing.

Luke dismissed it all and met his cousin's eyes. "Wanted to warn you that he's still not happy about me leaving."

Cole leaned back in his desk chair and steepled his fingers. "No surprise there. You were the golden boy, destined to run Barrett Toys…"

Bitterness colored Cole's tone, but Luke was used to that. "That's changed."

"Only because you left." His cousin shook his head. "Pop is still determined to bring you back into the fold."

Pushing away from the wall, Luke straightened up. "Not going to happen. I've got my own company now."

Cole swung his chair lazily back and forth. "It's not Barrett, though, is it?"

No, it wasn't. A start-up company was fun. Challenging, even. But it wasn't like running Barrett's. He'd poured a lot of work and heart into the family business. But feeling as he did now, that his grandfather didn't trust him, how could he run Barrett's with any sort of confidence? "It will be," he said, with determination. "Someday."

"Right. Anyway." Cole stood up, slipped his suit jacket on and buttoned it. "I've got a lunch meeting."

"Fine. Just..." He thought about Pop, rooting around for those papers and looking confused about why he couldn't find them. "Keep me posted on Pop, will you?"

"Why?"

Luke shrugged. "He's getting old."

"Not to hear him tell it," Cole said with a short scrape of a laugh.

"Yeah, I know that." Luke nodded and told himself he'd done what he'd gone there to do—try one more time to get through to his grandfather. Make him see reason. Now it was time to move the hell on. "All right, then. I've got a plane to catch. So, say hello to Susan and Oliver for me."

"I will."

When he walked out, Luke didn't look back.

Jamison stood at his open office door and watched his grandson. An all-too-familiar stir of frustration had him falling back into the old habit of jingling the coins in his pockets.

"You're jingling."

He stopped instantly and shot a look at his assistant. "Didn't work, did it?" she asked.

"No one likes hearing 'I told you so,' Donna."

She shrugged. "I didn't say it."

"You were thinking it."

"If you're such a good mind reader," the woman countered, "you should have known telling him that Loretta cried was a mistake."

She had a point. No one who knew his wife would believe she'd given in to a bout of tears.

"Fine," he grudgingly admitted. "You were right. Happy?"

"I'm not unhappy. It's always good to be right."

He scowled at the woman currently ignoring him as she busily typed up some damn thing or other. Donna had been with him for thirty years and never let him forget it.

Shaking his head, Jamison shifted his gaze back to Luke as he walked across the room, stopping to chat with people on his way to the elevator. He was leaving, and Jamison didn't have a clue how to get him back. So it seemed it was time for the big guns.

"The woman you told me about. You still think she can help?"

Donna stopped typing and looked up at him. "Apparently, she's pretty amazing, so maybe."

Jamison nodded. He wanted his grandson back in the company, damn it. How the hell could he ever retire if Luke wasn't there to take over for him? Cole was good at his specified job, but he didn't have it in him to keep growing Barrett Toys. Jamison needed Luke.

"Well, I tried the easy way," he murmured. "Now it's time to put on the pressure."

"Boss…if Luke finds out, this could all go bad in a huge way."

He dismissed her warning with an idle wave of a

hand. "Then we'll have to make sure he doesn't find out, won't we? Make the call, Donna. I'll be waiting in my office."

"I've got a bad feeling about this," she said as she picked up the phone and started dialing.

Jamison turned to his office, but paused long enough to ask, "Where are those statistics I asked you to print out for me this morning?"

Frowning, she looked at him. "I put them on your desk first thing."

"You didn't move them?"

"Why would I do that?"

"Right, right." He nodded and tried to remember what he'd done with the damn things. Then something else occurred to him. "Okay, make the call. And Donna, there's no reason to tell Loretta any of this."

She rolled her eyes.

"I saw that."

"Wasn't hiding it," she countered.

"I am your boss, you know."

"Don't let it go to your head," Donna advised.

The next afternoon, Fiona Jordan walked into the restaurant at the Gables, a five-star hotel in San Francisco. The best part about owning her own business? She just never knew what would happen from day to day. Yesterday, she'd been working out of her duplex in Long Beach, California, and today, she was in a gorgeous hotel in San Francisco.

Smiling to herself, she took a breath and scanned the busy room.

White-cloth-draped tables and booths were crowded, and the hum of conversation, heavy silverware clinking against plates and the piped-in violin music streaming

from discreetly hidden speakers created an atmosphere
of luxury. There were windows all along one wall that
afforded a spectacular view of the Bay, where the afternoon sun was busily painting a bright golden trail across
the surface of the water.

But at the moment, the view wasn't her priority, Fiona
thought as she did a more detailed scan of the room. She
was here to find one particular person.

When she found him, her heart gave a quick, hard jolt,
and a buzz of something hot and potentially dangerous
zipped through her.

Luke Barrett. He had sun-streaked, light brown hair
that was just long enough to curl over the collar of his
dark blue suit jacket. Gaze focused on the phone he held,
he seemed oblivious to the people surrounding him and
completely content to be alone.

Fiona didn't really understand that. She liked people.
Talking to them, hearing their stories—everyone had a
story—and discovering what she liked about them. But
she'd already been warned that Luke was so wrapped
up in his work, he barely noticed the people around him.

So, she told herself, she'd simply have to be unfor-
gettable.

Luke sat alone at a window table, but he paid no attention to the view. Fiona, on the other hand, was enjoying her view of him a little too much. Even in profile, he
was more gorgeous than the picture she'd been given.

That buzz of something interesting shot straight
through her again, and she took a moment to enjoy it. It
had been a long time since a man had elicited that sort
of reaction from her. Heck, she couldn't even remember
the last time she'd felt a zing of interest.

Her gaze went back to his just-a-little-long hair and
realized that it was an intriguing choice for a corpo-

rate type. Maybe Luke Barrett was going to be much more than she'd expected. But there was still the whole wrapped-up-in-his-phone thing to get past.

Fiona watched as a beautiful woman strolled by Luke's table, giving him a smile that most men would have drooled over—he didn't notice.

"Hmm." Realizing that meeting Luke Barrett might call for a little extra punch, Fiona turned toward the long sinuous sweep of the bar. She ordered a glass of chardonnay, gave the bartender a big tip and a smile, took a deep breath, and studied her target.

Then Fiona tossed her long, dark brown hair over her shoulder and started for his table. The short hem of her flirty black skirt swirled around her thighs and her mile-high black heels tapped cheerfully against the glossy floor. Her dark green long-sleeved blouse had a deeply scooped neckline, and gold hoops dangled from her earlobes.

She looked great, even if she was saying it herself, and it was a shame to ruin the outfit, but desperate times...

A waiter passed in front of her; Fiona deliberately stumbled, took a couple of halting steps, and with a slight shriek, threw herself and a full glass of very nice wine into Luke Barrett's lap.

Two

Luke's first instinct was to grab hold of the woman who had dropped into his lap from out of nowhere. She smiled up at him, and he felt a punch of desire slam into his chest. When she squirmed on his lap, he felt that punch a lot lower.

"What the hell?" He looked into a pair of chocolate-brown eyes and realized she was laughing.

"Sorry, sorry!" She squirmed again, and he instantly held her still. "I guess I stumbled on something. Thank God you were here, or I'd have fallen onto something a lot harder."

He didn't know about that. He felt pretty damn hard at the moment. And wet. He felt wet, as the wine she'd been carrying now seeped into his shirt and pants. Even as he thought it, she half turned around, grabbed a cloth napkin and dabbed at the wine splashed across her blouse, then started in on his shirt. If she tried to dry his pants, he was a dead man.

"What'd you trip on?" He glanced down at the floor and saw nothing.

"I don't know," she admitted, then shrugged helplessly. "Sometimes I trip on air."

"Good to know."

She tipped her head to one side and long, dark brown hair slid across her shoulders. "Are you going to let me up?"

It wasn't his first thought. "Are you going to fall again?"

"Well, I'm not sure," she admitted with a grin. "Anything's possible."

"Then maybe it's safer if you stay where you are," Luke mused, still caught by the smile in those brown eyes of hers.

She started her fruitless dabbing at his shirt again. Not unlike trying to soak up the ocean with a sponge.

"Yeah," he said, taking the napkin from her. "Never mind."

"Well, I do feel badly about this," she said.

"Me, too."

"In all fairness, though," she pointed out, "I got plenty of the wine on my shirt, as well."

"And that should make me happy?"

She shrugged and her dark green off-the-shoulder shirt dipped a bit.

Instantly, his gaze dropped to the full swell of her breasts and he wondered if he'd get more of a look if she shrugged again. When he lifted his gaze to hers, he saw a knowing smile.

A waiter hustled up to them with several napkins, then just stood there as if unsure what his next move should be. Luke could sympathize.

Finally, the waiter asked, "Are you all right, miss?"

"Oh, I'm fine."

She was fine. He was being tortured but, apparently, no one cared about that.

"I'm so sorry, Mr. Barrett. Is there anything I can do?"

"No," he said grimly. "I think it's all been done."

"Well, there is one thing…" His mystery lap dancer spoke up. "My wine's gone." She held up the empty glass like it was a visual aid.

"And I know where it went," Luke muttered.

The waiter looked from Luke to the woman and back again. Still unsure. Still worried. Luke was used to that. He was rich. His family was famous. Most people got nervous around him. And he hated that. So he forced a smile and said, "Would you get the lady another glass of wine, Michael?"

"Certainly. What were you drinking, miss?"

"Chardonnay, thanks. The house wine's fine."

Luke frowned and shook his head. "I think we can do better than that, can't we, Michael?"

The waiter grinned. "Yes, sir."

When the man left, Luke looked into those chocolate eyes again. "So, since you're sitting on my lap, I think it's only right I know your name."

"Oh, I'm Fiona. Fiona Jordan." She held out a hand to him.

He glanced at it and smirked. "I think we've already moved past a handshake, don't you?"

"I think we have," she said. "And since your lap is being so welcoming, maybe I could know your name? Last name Barrett, according to the waiter. First name?"

"Luke."

She tipped her head to one side and studied him for a long second or two. "I like it. Short. Strong. Sounds like a romance novel hero."

This had to be the strangest conversation he'd ever had.

Nodding, he confessed, "You found my secret. By day, I'm a tech-toy developer. But at night, I'm a pirate or a lord or a Highlander."

She gave him a wide grin, and that punch of desire hit him harder. "How is it you know so much about romance novels?"

"My grandmother goes through a dozen every week. I grew up seeing books with half-dressed men and women on the covers scattered around the house."

"A well-rounded childhood, then."

Luke thought about that and had to say, she was right. In spite of losing his parents when he was just a child, Luke's grandparents had saved him. They'd given him normalcy again. Made sure that though his world had been rocked, it hadn't been completely destroyed.

His lips quirked. "I always thought so."

"I envy you," she said simply, and before he could comment, the waiter was back.

Michael hurried up, carrying a glass of wine for Fiona and a refill of Luke's scotch. He set both glasses on the table and said, "On the house, Mr. Barrett. And again, we're very sorry about—"

"You don't have to apologize, Michael," Fiona told him. "I'm the clumsy one."

The man winced. "Oh, I wouldn't say clumsy…"

"That's because you don't smell like chardonnay," Luke put in wryly.

Michael nodded again before he scurried away.

"I think you scared him," Fiona said as she watched the man rush back to the bar.

"I think you're the one who scared him. Pretty women can have that effect on a man," Luke countered.

She turned back and literally beamed at him. "But not you?"

"I'm immune."

"Good to know," she said, smiling. "Does that mean I should give up or try even harder to be scary?"

"Oh, definitely keep trying." Luke grinned. Hell, he liked a woman this sure of herself. Well, to be honest, he just liked women. But a strong, gorgeous one with a sense of humor was right at the top of the list. And this one was more intriguing than most. It had been a long time since a woman had made this kind of impact on him. He laughed to himself at that thought, because she had landed on him with both physical and emotional impacts.

He took a quick look at the whole package. Long, dark brown hair, those chocolate eyes, a wide mouth, now curved in a smile, and a body that filled his mind with all kinds of interesting images. That green shirt looked great on her, and the full black skirt was short enough to showcase some great legs. The mile-high black heels just put the finishing touches on the whole picture. Oh yeah, she could be dangerous.

Even to a man who had no intention of getting into a "relationship," Luke loved women, and the occasional date or one-night stand was great. But he didn't have the time or the patience to devote himself to two passions right now. All of his focus had to be on his budding company. So meeting a woman like this one could be problematic.

"So…" Fiona spoke again, and Luke told himself to listen up. "Now that we're so comfy with each other, what brings you to San Francisco?"

"I don't know if *comfy* is the right word," Luke said wryly, shifting position a bit.

She reached for her wine, but Luke was faster. He handed her the glass. He wasn't going to risk another wine bath.

"What's the matter?" she asked. "Don't you trust me?"

"Since my shirt is still wet from your last glass of wine, I'm going to say no."

She laughed. "Well, that's honest, anyway. I like honest. But I have to say, I think it's time I moved to a chair."

He reached for his scotch and took a sip. The aged whiskey sent a slow burn through his body that couldn't even compare to the current blaze centered in his lap. "Yeah, maybe you should." He knew everyone in the restaurant had to be watching them, and Luke didn't give a flying damn. Fiona Jordan had broken up his afternoon and brightened a long, boring day, and he was going to enjoy it. In fact, he hadn't felt this…light since the day before with his grandfather.

Something about her made him forget the things plaguing him and, for that, he was grateful. Just before she'd dropped into his lap, he'd been going over and over again that conversation with Pop. Wondering if he could have handled things better. Hating that the two of them were at such odds.

But this woman with the brilliant smile and the gorgeous legs had changed that—for however long the feeling lasted.

She hopped up, and Luke muffled a groan as she took a seat across the table from him.

He had to admit he was breathing easier, even when she took a sip of her wine, then ran the tip of her tongue across her top lip to catch a stray drop. His gaze locked on that movement and yet one more sharp jab of heat stabbed him. He couldn't remember the last time a woman had attracted him so completely. And while warning bells were going off in the back of his mind, Luke ignored them all.

She took another sip of her wine, met his gaze across the table and asked, "So, what should we talk about?"

His eyebrows arched. "You want to have a conversation now?"

She shrugged. "You want to sit here in silence?"

She had a point. "Fine. Let's talk."

"Great." She took a sip of wine. "You start."

All he could really think about was what she was doing to him. Hard to come up with a conversational starter beyond *Let's go upstairs to my room.* "No. You start."

"Okay." She shrugged, and the bodice of her blouse dipped again. "What're you doing at the hotel?"

"At the moment, trying to keep my mind busy."

She grinned. "Let me rephrase. Are you from San Francisco?"

"No," he said. "I'm from Orange County. Newport Beach, specifically."

She grinned. "We're practically neighbors, then. I live in Long Beach. So, why are you here?"

"Business," Luke told her. "I'm here for the tech conference." Though he hadn't been enjoying it until she had dropped onto his lap. With all the thoughts racing through his mind—his grandfather, Barrett's, his own new company, he'd been silently stewing. She'd interrupted all of that.

"Ah." She nodded and gave a quick glance around the restaurant. "A conference. That explains all of the badges, not to mention the fact that everyone I see has their nose glued to a phone or computer."

He took a look, too, and had to admit that almost everyone in the dining area was reading a phone or scrolling on a tablet. Even at a table with six people sitting around it, all of them were busy with their own phones. He frowned a little, then shrugged it off. This conference was, as he'd said, for business.

"Guilty," he said, turning his gaze back to her.

"So if you're here for the conference, you're in the tech business, right?"

"I am." One of the reasons he came to these conferences was that here, he was surrounded by other forward-thinking people like him. People who understood that the future was in binary. "My company makes tech toys."

"Tech toys?" She tipped her head to one side. "What kind?"

She actually seemed interested, and there was nothing he liked more than to talk about the latest in tech toys. If Pop hadn't changed his mind, Luke would be even more eager to talk about them. He'd imagined steering Barrett's into the future. Drawing on their already trusted name in toys to introduce kids to the what was to come. Still, his new company would do all of that. It would just take longer to take off. To get recognition. Luke took the conversational thread and ran with it. "All kinds. From tablets that are user-friendly for toddlers, to gaming boards, video games and miniature robots and drones." He took a sip of his scotch. "We've got a full line of tech toys for every age."

She laughed again and the sound of it was like champagne bubbles.

"I barely understand my computer *now*. I can't imagine a toddler on one."

"You'd be surprised. Our test groups do very well at color and spatial relations and problem solving on the screen." He hadn't been able to convince his grandfather of that, of course. Because Jamison was concerned about pumping too much information into growing minds. But Luke believed that a young, open mind was far more likely to absorb information. And how was that a bad thing?

"There have been dozens of studies to prove that in children as young as one, the brain is like a sponge, soaking up information far faster than it will in the future."

She shook her head. "My best friend has a toddler whose main focus is eating the dog's kibble."

He laughed. "Maybe he needs a tablet."

"Maybe," she allowed. "Still, I'm amazed at the idea of babies on computers. But maybe I need a toddler to walk me through running my Word program."

Luke smiled at her.

"So, I guess 'tech toys' means you don't make bikes and dolls and things?"

His last encounter with his grandfather was still fresh in his mind, so his response was a little sharper than it should have been when he said, "No. The future isn't made up of dolls and bikes and Frisbees. It's in electronics."

She held up both hands in mock surrender. "Whoa. Okay. You convinced me. I give up."

Luke took a breath and blew it out again, reaching for calm. Wasn't her fault that his grandfather was suddenly retreating into the past. "Yeah, sorry. Sore spot. My grandfather and I have been going around and around about this."

"That has to be hard, disagreeing with family." She sipped at her wine. "Why are you?"

No way was he getting into all of that right now. "Long story."

She nodded as if she understood he simply didn't want to talk about it. But then she asked, "All right. But I'm still not convinced that tablets for toddlers are a good idea. Even tiny sponges need a teddy bear."

He smiled again, glad she'd dropped it. Back on safe ground, ground he knew like the back of his hand, he said, "There are plenty of companies that sell stuffed animals or dolls or whatever else you think a kid should have. But the future for kids today will be in technology, so shouldn't they get a jump as young as possible?"

She still looked unconvinced. "But toddlers?"

"Sure. If we can get children as young as two involved with electronics, their brains will develop faster, and they'll be more inclined toward the sciences. That's a win. For all of us."

"The sciences." She smiled. "Like making mud pies in the backyard?"

"You're a hard sell, aren't you?" He stared into her eyes and liked the feeling of being pulled in. A damn shame, he thought, that he could have a real conversation about what was important to him with a stranger—but his own grandfather wouldn't listen.

"I'm just saying that being comfortable with tech at a young age will make them more accepting of it later." As an example, he said, "We use colors and shapes and sound to get their interest." He was warming to the theme, as he always did. "They learn without realizing they're learning. Studies prove out that children who are challenged rise to the occasion more often than not."

"But aren't there just as many studies saying that it's not good to introduce small kids to tech too early?"

"You sound like my grandfather," he said.

"Thank you?" She laughed a little. "Not trying to

argue, I just think that there are two sides to this and maybe your grandfather has a point."

Luke grumbled under his breath. It wasn't easy arguing for the future when everyone wanted to cling to the past. "My grandfather won't even listen to the arguments on this, so it's pointless to try any further."

"Have you listened to his side?"

Luke took another sip of his scotch and studied her. He was trying to decide if he should keep talking or change the subject. She took care of that for him.

"It sounds interesting," she said. "And a little scary."

Frowning, he sipped at his scotch. Now that too sounded like his grandfather's argument. "Why?"

"Because I like watching little kids pick dandelions or splash in mud puddles." She shrugged and took another sip of her wine. "They should be outside, running and playing. Seeing them staring at a screen instead just seems wrong. I mean, once you grow up, you're always on a computer. Why start before you have to?"

"Because it's fun?"

"If you say so." She shook her head and her gorgeous hair slid back and forth across her shoulders. "I have a love-hate relationship with my computer."

"You like email and the internet, right?"

"Sure. But I hate a full inbox. Drives me crazy."

"A full inbox means your business is doing well."

"Except for the spam."

He brushed that off. "Downside to everything."

He wondered why he wasn't as irritated with Fiona as he became with his grandfather when they had pretty much this same conversation. His phone buzzed, and Luke glanced at the screen before shifting it to voice mail. He wasn't in the position or in the mood to take a call from his grandfather.

"You don't have to get that?" she asked.

"Absolutely not."

"Okay, then." She set her wine down on the table.

His gaze dropped to her fingers sliding up and down the faceted stem of the glass.

Instantly, his body went rock hard again.

"So," he said abruptly, "since I'm pretty much trapped in this chair for a while, why don't you stay and have a late lunch with me."

She chewed at her bottom lip and with every tug of her teeth, Luke felt an answering tug inside him.

Finally, Fiona said, "I suppose that's fair, since I'm the reason you're trapped in that chair for a while."

"You are." He hadn't planned on company, but what the hell? Beautiful woman or doing email alone? Not really a contest.

"Okay, then." She crossed those great legs and swung her right foot lazily. Propping her elbows on the table, she leaned in and smiled. "Feeling better yet?"

He should have been. But he was still hard, and he missed the feel of her lush body plopped on top of his. That probably made him a masochist.

"Strangely enough, no."

A slow, wide smile curved her mouth. "Just what I was thinking."

Heat pulsed inside him and fed the flames keeping his dick at full alert. Hell, at this rate, he was going to have to hire someone to walk in front of him just to get out of the damn restaurant.

She picked up her wine, took a sip, then flicked out her tongue again to sweep away another stray drop from her top lip. Fire burning even hotter now, he thought.

"You're doing that on purpose, aren't you?"

Her mouth curved into a smile. "Is it working?"

"Too damn well," he admitted, and her smile spread further.

When the waiter brought menus, she flipped through hers until she got to the burgers.

Surprised, he asked, "A woman who's *not* going for a salad?"

She lifted her gaze to his and shook her head. "That's completely sexist. You know that, right?"

He shrugged the comment off. "Every woman I've ever taken to dinner ordered some kind of salad."

"Clearly, you're dating the wrong women." She closed the menu and folded her hands on top of it. "I'm an unapologetic carnivore. Burgers. Steaks. Love them all."

Nodding, Luke just looked at her, enjoying the view. "Good to know. And today? Burger or steak?"

"The San Francisco burger, hold the avocado."

"You don't like avocado?"

"Ew." Her features screwed up. "No."

"I don't know if I can have lunch with you after all," Luke said.

Her eyes sparkled. "So you have standards?"

"Doesn't everyone?"

"And avocado is one of them?"

"We live in California. Guacamole is a way of life here," Luke said.

"Not my life," she assured him. "I love Mexican food, but avocados are a deal breaker. It's a texture thing. They're too slimy."

"Have you tasted one?"

"God, no. I have standards, too." She grinned and Luke's insides stirred again.

The waiter came back, Luke gave him their order, then leaned back with his scotch to study the woman who had become the focus of his attention. Her bare shoulders made him think about sliding that pretty green shirt down her arms so he could feast on her breasts. His dick hardened even further, though he wouldn't have thought that possible, and his hands itched to touch her.

Fiona shifted beneath his steady stare and fought down the rise of heat threatening to engulf her. She seriously had not been prepared for the rush of something... *tantalizing* that she'd felt the moment she saw Luke Barrett. But how could she have been? All she'd had was his picture and a brief description of where she was most likely to find him.

No one had said his eyes were the color of the ocean on a summer day. Or that he was tall and muscular beneath that well-cut suit or that his hair was too long and sun-streaked. And there was no way she'd expected the deep timbre of his voice to rumble along her spine.

Mostly, though, she hadn't been prepared for the hot, throbbing ache that had settled between her thighs from sitting on his lap and feeling the hard press of him against her. Just remembering made her squirm a bit in her seat, as if to rekindle the sensation.

But she wasn't here to "kindle" anything. She was here because she'd given her word to someone. Taken a job. Made a promise. And Fiona always kept her promises.

She smiled because Luke looked at her as if he were trying to read her mind, and she was grateful he couldn't. Liking him was okay, liking him too much could jeopardize her job and that had to come first. She'd been offered a twenty-thousand dollar bonus if she succeeded. And she needed that money.

With an actual savings account, she could buy a car

that didn't run on hopes and dreams and invest in her own business to help it grow.

"What are you thinking?" His question shattered the thoughts he was asking about.

Fiona had to scramble. "Just wondering how a man gets into tech toys," she said, and silently congratulated herself on coming up with that so quickly.

He took a sip of his scotch and set the heavy glass tumbler down again. "Started in the family business." He shrugged. "Recently I went out on my own."

"Really. Why?"

He gave her a suspicious look. "Why do you care?"

"I don't," she lied. "Just curious. Is this about your disagreement with your grandfather?"

"And why should I feed a stranger's curiosity?"

"Oh," Fiona said with a slow smile, "after what we've already shared, I don't think we're strangers anymore."

He laughed shortly and inclined his head. "Point taken. Okay, you're right. My grandfather and I couldn't see eye to eye."

"Isn't there a compromise in there somewhere?"

"Not with Pop. He prefers the past, and I want the future."

Basically what she already knew. "Sounds dire."

"No." One firm shake of his head. "Just business."

"Even with family?"

"Family adds another layer, but it still boils down to business." Frowning, he said, "My grandfather and I had a plan. He changed his mind, so I'm going ahead with the plan on my own. Simple."

"Is it? Simple, I mean."

"It will be," he said, nodding to himself.

He clammed up fast after that, and Fiona once again silently warned herself to go slowly. Carefully. His eyes were closed off, shuttered as if he'd erected a privacy wall around his thoughts. And she had a feeling that she'd never get past that wall by using a battering ram. He was clearly a private person, so that would make getting him to open up to her more difficult. And despite what he'd just said, she knew there was nothing simple about his situation.

Yet she had to wonder how he could shut out a grandfather who loved him. Fiona didn't have family. She had friends. Lots of friends, because she'd set out to *create* a family. She couldn't imagine turning her back on a grandfather who loved her.

Wistfully, she wondered briefly what that might be like and wondered why Luke couldn't see how lucky he was to have the very family he was at odds with.

Their lunch arrived then and they both went quiet as the waiter set the plates in front of them, then filled water goblets.

Luke had ordered the same burger she had, but *with* avocado. "Sure you don't want to try it?"

She held out one hand in a "stop" gesture. "Way sure."

"You could look at this as an opportunity to expand your horizons."

She laughed. "With an avocado?"

"It's a start." His eyes flashed and a new jolt of heat swept through Fiona.

"I think we could find a better place to start expanding those horizons," she said quietly. "Don't you?"

He looked at her for a long moment, the heat in his eyes searing every inch of her skin. "I can work with that."

Three

Back in Laguna Beach, Jamison walked into his house and strode directly into the living room. As always, he was struck at the silence in the big house. When Cole and Luke were young, there was laughter, shouting, the dogs barking and dozens of the kids' friends running in and out. Now that it was just him and his wife, Loretta, sometimes the quiet became overpowering.

The muffled voices from the television pulled him into the big room. Loretta was curled up in the corner of a couch, watching a flat-screen TV hanging on the wall above a fireplace, where gas flames danced over faux logs. She glanced at him and smiled, and Jamison felt that hard punch of love that always left him feeling off-balance.

From the first moment they'd met, almost sixty years ago now, Jamison thought with a jolt, he'd loved Loretta. She was the best thing that had ever happened to him and, as the years passed, that only became clearer to him.

Young people might think love was only for them, but Jamison was here to testify that flames didn't burn out, they only got warmer, steadier, and the love that fanned them, richer.

"Hi, hon," she said. "How was your day?"

"Frustrating," he admitted with a scowl and gave a quick look around the room. Usually, he walked in here and felt better. Loretta had decorated the place in soothing tones of blue and greens that always reminded Jamison of the sea. Overstuffed couches and chairs, gleaming oak tables, and a stained-glass window on one wall that tossed colored patches of light onto the hardwood floor. It was a room made for relaxation but, today, he knew it wasn't going to help him.

Jamison walked to the wet bar across the room, poured himself a scotch and took the first gulp like it was medicine.

"Tell me what happened." Loretta hit the mute button and instantly, silence dropped onto the room.

"Still thinking about another fruitless argument with Luke yesterday."

"Oh, Jamie, for God's sake, let it go."

He stared at her. She was as beautiful as ever. Her short, stylish hair was a striking white now, but her blue eyes were as sharp as they always were. She wore the diamond stud earrings he'd given her for Christmas and some kind of loungy outfit of soft black pants and a pale gray top that was loose enough to hide what he knew was a body she kept in excellent shape. But the look in her pretty eyes was as frustrating as the rest of his day had been.

"How can I let it go?" He walked over, dropped onto

the couch beside her and fixed his gaze on hers. "That boy was supposed to take over Barrett Toys. He was my future and, now, he's turned his back on everything to get kids hooked on technology."

She laughed, reached over to the closest table for her glass of red wine and took a sip. "You sound like a man on a horse-drawn cart complaining that his son wants one of those newfangled cars."

"Not the same thing at all," he muttered, looking into his scotch glass as if searching for answers.

"Exactly the same." She straightened one leg and used her foot to nudge his thigh. "When you took over from your father, don't you remember how he lamented the end of the company because you wanted to make too many changes?"

He dropped one hand to her foot and lazily stroked it. That was different. His father had been stuck in the mud. No vision. No ability to *listen*. "Yes, but I didn't leave the company, did I?"

"And Luke won't either."

He snapped her a hard look. "He already has."

Loretta waved that away. "He'll be back."

"You sound damn sure of yourself."

"Not of me," she said. "I'm sure of Luke. Yes, he's off on his own right now, but that's not saying he'll stay there."

"If you'd heard him yesterday, you'd believe it."

"He needs to prove himself. Just as much as you needed the same thing about fifty years ago." She sighed a little. "He's as stubborn as you are. That's why the two of you butt heads so often."

"Thanks very much."

She ignored that and wiggled her foot. "Foot rub, please."

He snorted, but obliged.

Loretta sighed her pleasure, but then kept talking. "Like I said, Luke's proving something to you, I think. And until you can accept his ideas and trust him to do the right thing, neither of you is going to be happy. Meanwhile, until Luke comes back, you have Cole to help you out at the company."

"Cole." Shaking his head, Jamison said, "He just doesn't have the head for the company like Luke does. Today, Cole left early again. Took a lunch and then just went home rather than back to work. Said he had some to-do with Susan and Oliver." He paused before demanding, "What kind of activity does a two-year-old have that a father can't miss?"

She gave him a push with her foot. "That two-year-old is our great-grandson."

"And I love him, but Cole's not just that boy's father, he's a vice president of the company…"

"Spending time with his son is a good thing, Jamie."

"I know that, and it's not about that, really. In a family business, you should be able to take off time when you need to, to be with your kids. That's not what really bothers me." Shaking his head again, he muttered, "He doesn't give a flying damn about the business. Meetings at work, he's not paying attention. He's…indifferent. At the heart of it, he doesn't understand or care about what happens to the company and makes no effort to, either. He's just—"

"Just what?"

He looked at her and admitted the truth. "He's not *Luke*."

Studying him, she asked, "This isn't just about Cole's lack of vision and effort or even about Luke, is it? I mean, you're angry and hurt, but there's something else, too."

He scowled at her. "It's not easy being married to a mind reader."

"Thankfully, you have years of practice. So, stop stalling and spill it."

He rubbed at the spot between his eyes but didn't bother trying to ignore her. Jamison knew better than to evade anything as far as his wife was concerned. "I'm losing it, Loretta."

"What do you mean?"

He pushed her foot off his lap and stood up, clutching his scotch glass. "I mean, I'm forgetting things. It's been going on for a while, but lately, it seems to be getting worse."

She frowned a bit, but her voice was soft and easy as she asked, "What kind of things?"

One of the reasons he loved her as fiercely today as he had sixty years before was her inherent calm. Nothing shook the woman. Even when they'd lost both of their sons and daughters-in-law in one blindingly horrific plane crash, she'd been rocked only for a while. Because she had taken her pain and turned it into love she lavished on their grandsons, Cole and Luke.

Jamison was very glad of her stoicism today because by God, he needed it.

"Today, I couldn't find the statistics I had Donna print out for me on the new toy line. I put them on my desk and then a half hour later, they weren't there." Shaking his head, he muttered, "I must have moved them, but damned if I can remember doing it."

"Maybe Donna moved them."

"She said no."

"Well then, you were busy. Distracted."

"Maybe." Distraction only worked as an excuse for so long, though. And he'd been losing track of little things for weeks now. When would that change to the *big* things? Would he forget who he was? Forget Loretta? He ran one hand across the back of his neck and tried to still his racing thoughts. If there was one thing that terrified Jamison, it was the threat of losing *himself*. Of his mind slowly disappearing. At eighty, he'd prided himself on staying in shape, but there was nothing he could do about his memory. His ideas. His thoughts. If he lost all of that...

"You're worrying for nothing," Loretta said.

"It's not just the statistic reports," he countered. "Yesterday, after Cole and Susan went home, I couldn't find my damn car keys."

"That's not a new phenomenon," Loretta said wryly. "On our first date, you couldn't find them either, remember? You had to walk me home?"

He remembered and his smile proved it. "That was different. I did that on purpose to get more time with you."

"Jamison Barrett!" She slapped his arm. "I got in trouble for that because I was home so late."

"It was worth it," he said with a wink.

Her mouth worked as if she was biting back words trying to slip out. Finally, though, she admitted, "Yes, it was worth it. And, Jamie, you're worried now for nothing. You don't have Alzheimer's. You've just got too much on your mind."

"It's been happening for weeks, Loretta." He scowled at the admission. He hadn't wanted to worry her. Hadn't wanted to acknowledge that there might actually be something to worry about.

"You should have told me."

"I didn't want to talk about it. Now..."

"If you're that worried, go see Dr. Tucker."

His scowl deepened. "That's just admitting that I'm worried."

"You're driving yourself crazy over *nothing*, Jamie. I would have noticed if there was something wrong with you."

A splash of color from the stained-glass window fell on her, shading her hair and her features with pale, rosy light. He looked into her eyes and chose to believe her— because he needed to.

"You're probably right."

She laughed shortly, reaching up to cup his cheek. "After nearly sixty years together, you should know that I'm *always* right."

"True." He smiled. "What was I thinking?"

She moved into him, wrapped her arms around his waist and laid her head on his chest.

He tucked her in close with one arm across her shoulders and took the comfort she offered. And he thanked whatever lucky stars had given him this woman to go through life with. He'd needed this time with Loretta. This calm, soothing time when he could center himself again.

Which was why he didn't mention hiring the woman Donna had told him about.

Fiona stepped out of the shower the next morning and asked herself what the heck she was doing. She and Luke had spent the evening together, and then made plans to tour the city today.

"Shouldn't be doing this," she muttered. "Not supposed to be getting involved in a case. But how can I not? I have to talk to him, right?" And she really liked him, too. Which made all of this even harder.

"But at the same time, I have to get him to see his

grandfather's side of things. Get him to talk to me about this, so I can present arguments he might listen to. Make him want to go back to the business, and I can't do that if I avoid him, right?"

Fiona turned the hot water off and took a second to just rest her forehead against the tiled wall. She'd flown all the way to San Francisco to meet him. To convince him... She couldn't exactly do that if she didn't spend time with him.

She flushed, just thinking about what had happened yesterday at their first meeting. She'd never been so blatantly sexual in her life. And wasn't sure how it had happened, beyond the instant attraction she'd felt for him.

"This has the chance of becoming a real mess," she muttered as she reached for a thick white towel and wrapped it around her still-dripping body. She used another one for her hair, then swiped the steamy fog off the mirror. That didn't help, though. Now she had to meet her own gaze and read the trouble in her own eyes.

Her big plan had been to meet him here, at the conference, where he was away from home. Talk to him, get to know him. Not sexually, just...friendly. Then when they got back home, maybe become his friend and ease him into seeing that his grandfather and the family company needed him.

"But I shot that plan down myself." Frowning at her reflection, she said, "This is really not good."

He was her job, damn it. She was supposed to be resolving his life, not throwing her own into turmoil. This was her job, and she was going to be professional. She had no business at all fantasizing about the most gorgeous man she'd ever seen. God, it was just embarrassing what had happened earlier. She never should have fallen into his lap.

When her cell phone rang, she thought of it as a break from her crazy-making thoughts. Then she saw the call screen and sighed. No avoiding this, either.

"Mr. Barrett," she said, forcing a smile into her voice. "I didn't expect to hear from you so soon."

Actually, she'd been hoping she wouldn't. But in her short acquaintance with Luke's grandfather, she'd already learned the older man wasn't exactly patient. Still, she didn't have anything to report. Didn't have any news to give him. And she couldn't exactly share with the man that his grandson had set her body on fire.

"Ms. Jordan—is it all right if I call you Fiona?"

"Of course." She straightened the tower of a towel on her head, then with one hand, wiped the steam off the mirror again.

"Did you meet with Luke?"

"I did," she said, though she wouldn't be telling him how that first meeting had gone. She could just imagine. God, that would be mortifying. Yeah. That would be good.

Keep your mind off Luke. At least while you're talking to his grandfather.

"I'm meeting him in an hour. We're going to spend the day together." And she hoped to be able to get him talking about his grandfather again. Get this job back on track. Jamison Barrett had hired her to bring his grandson back into the family business, and she was going to do it. She'd never failed on a contract before, and she wouldn't this time, either.

Fiona's business, ICanFixIt, had been born out of her innate ability to solve problems. Not math, of course. Math was terrifying to her. But if someone lost a diamond ring, or a puppy, she could find it. If you needed tickets to a sold-out concert, Fiona could get them. Find long-lost relatives, she was your girl. Basically, Fiona could fix your problem, no matter what it was.

So, she wouldn't spoil her success record by failing this time.

"He's ignoring the conference in favor of you?" Jamison chuckled. "I'm impressed. Nothing my boy likes better than the technology business and being around others just like him. You must be a miracle worker after all."

"I wouldn't say that," she said, and frowned at her reflection.

"Well, from what my secretary, Donna, tells me, you accomplish the impossible all the time."

She winced. Yes. She had worked for Donna's sister Linda. Fiona had found the daughter Linda had given up for adoption thirty years ago, and she'd helped the two women reunite. Which was how Jamison had found out about Fiona in the first place.

At the time, she'd had no idea that finding a long-lost daughter would be considered easy compared to what she was supposed to do now. From what she'd seen of Luke yesterday, not only was he gorgeous, ridiculously sexy and funny on top of it…he was also stubborn and determined to make his own company take off. She was on his side in that because she knew just how much her business meant to her.

But Jamison was her client, so her loyalties had to be to him.

"Mr. Barrett, I don't want you to get your hopes up too high," she warned quietly. Yes, she'd never failed before, but what was it her foster mom had always told her? *There's always a first time.* "I'm going to do my best, but your grandson seems very stubborn."

"He is," Jamison grumbled. "Got that from his grandmother."

Fiona almost laughed aloud at that. It was clear to her that Luke was more like his grandfather than either man would probably admit.

"This is the last night of the conference," he said next. "Luke will be flying home tomorrow, so I'll expect another update from you tomorrow night or the following morning at the latest."

"Of course," she said, and silently hoped that she would have some good news to give him. But from what she'd seen of Luke Barrett so far, Fiona had the feeling he wasn't the kind of man to make hasty decisions. He'd left the family business because he was convinced that it was the right move for him.

How was she supposed to change his mind over the course of a single weekend? Answer? She couldn't. It was going to take more than this weekend, which meant that she'd be seeing lots more of Luke Barrett.

She looked into the mirror and saw eager anticipation in her own eyes. Oh, not good.

"Fine, then. I look forward to hearing from you. Get it done." Jamison hung up a moment later, and Fiona set her phone down.

Staring at the woman in the mirror, she said, "This is just another job, Fiona."

When her own reflection rolled her eyes at that, Fiona knew she was in deep doo-doo. "No getting involved. No letting your hormones drive the car here. Get Luke talking about his family. Make him realize what he's walking away from. And when it's over...*you* walk away. Because if Luke discovers you were hired to meet him, convince him, he'll never speak to you again anyway."

So, it would be better for her if she simply didn't get attached in the first place...

* * *

By that evening, Luke felt like he was standing at the edge of a very high cliff. His body had been tight and hard since the moment Fiona had dropped into his lap the day before. Ditching the conference and spending time with her instead hadn't helped the situation any.

They'd played tourist all day, taking a cab down Lombard Street, checking out Golden Gate Park and stopping for a drink at a tiny pub at Fisherman's Wharf. Hell, if anyone had told him a week ago that he'd be playing tourist, he'd have laughed in their face.

But Fiona had wanted to see the park and the wharf, so he'd gone along. She'd checked out the sights and he'd watched *her.* The night before, his sleep had been haunted by images of her and now he had even more memories to draw on. Fiona, standing at the rail on the wharf as a sea wind tossed her hair and lifted that short black skirt. Her grin as their driver took them down the most notoriously twisted street in the world.

Not to mention the way her tongue had caressed the ice cream cone he'd bought her at the park.

He briefly closed his eyes and muffled a groan at *that* thought.

To distract himself while he sat in the bar and waited for Fiona to arrive for their dinner date, he opened his phone and checked his email. There were twenty new messages to go through and as he did, Luke shut out the rest of the room as if he were alone on an island.

The truth was, if he hadn't met Fiona, he'd have been bored out of his mind.

This conference had nothing new to offer him. Luke had already chosen his path, knew his own plans and had no interest in making changes to what was, in effect, a newborn company. He'd only come to San Francisco because he'd felt that he should make an appearance, talk to a couple of old friends. Then he'd met Fiona. She'd shaken him and he had no problem admitting that—at least to himself. She was smart and funny and confident and all three of those things, combined with that body and those eyes, had his mind wandering even while dealing with email.

"Not good." Luke shook his head to clear it. He had enough going on in his life right now and definitely didn't need the distraction of a woman—even one as intriguing as Fiona. Hell, he thought, maybe especially not one as intriguing as Fiona.

He had to focus on his company. No time in his life at the moment for a woman like her.

Blowing out a breath, he read the message from his assistant, Jack.

We've hit a snag in early production, boss. Peterson says they're backlogged and won't get to do the run of our new tablets in time for a Christmas release.

"Well, damn it." Frustration roared through him. Yes, to anyone else, talking about Christmas releases in February sounded ridiculous. But these things were always planned out months, if not years, in advance. Usually for just this reason. Something always went wrong.

This wasn't the first time Luke had had to deal with wrenches thrown into the works. At Barrett Toys and Tech, they'd often had to pull off last-minute miracles. Yes, his cousin Cole had supposedly been in charge of taking care of their production partners, but more often than not, that job had fallen to Luke. He'd handle it this time, too. Quickly, he fired off an email to Jack.

Tell Peterson we have a contract, and I expect him to honor it. Tell him I said to find a way. If he gives you any crap, I'll take care of it myself on Monday.

That would probably be enough to keep the man on track. If it wasn't, Luke would find someone else to do the job and word would spread that Peterson's Manufacturing couldn't be trusted to honor its schedules.

Focused now on his business, he answered a few more emails from marketing, engineering and design, then skipped the one from his grandfather. He knew damn well that Jamison would be telling him again that he should come back to the family business.

A quick ping of regret echoed inside him, but he ignored it. He loved that old man, but damned if he'd go back where his opinions weren't trusted. His new business wasn't just a company but a matter of pride. Luke wasn't going to walk away from it.

"Excuse me?"

A woman's voice from right beside him. One of the waitresses had already tried to freshen his drink twice before. He waved one hand at the table. "I don't need a refill, thanks."

"Good to know," the woman said, then added, "So do I have to fall into your lap again to get your attention?"

He went still before turning his head to look up at Fiona. If he'd thought she was stunning earlier in that short, flirty skirt, it was nothing to what he was thinking now.

She wore a dark red, off-the-shoulder dress that defined every curve in her body like a lover's hands. The dress was nipped in tightly at her narrow waist and the short, tight skirt stopped midway on her thighs. The black heels completed her outfit and made her legs look amazing. Instantly, he had a mental image of those legs locked around his hips while she pulled him deeper inside her heat.

And...just like that, he was too hard to stand.

Her hair was pulled back into a low ponytail that hung between her shoulders and her coffee-colored eyes sparkled as if she knew exactly what effect she was having on him.

"Have you seen enough?" she asked, "or would you like me to do a slow turn?"

If he saw her butt in that dress, it would finish him off. "Not necessary. Have a seat."

"Oh." She glanced toward the dining room. "I thought we were going to dinner. I am sort of hungry."

"Right. Carnivore. I remember." He nodded and as she sat down, he signaled for the waitress. "But that's going to have to wait until I can walk again."

Her mouth curved and he wanted nothing more than to taste it. "Again?" She smiled. "You're really good for my self-esteem."

"Yeah. Happy to help..." When the waitress arrived, Fiona looked up at her.

"Vodka martini, please. Dirty."

When they were alone again, Luke finished off the email he'd been composing. Anything to get his mind off what his mind wanted to stay on.

"Are we having a phone date?" Fiona asked, and her voice was so soft and sultry, he had to look up and meet her eyes.

"Should I get mine out of my purse?" She reached for the small black clutch she'd set on the table a moment ago.

"What? No. Just a little business I have to take care of."

"Uh-huh."

The waitress returned, set a chilled cocktail glass in front of Fiona and left again. Taking the stirrer from the glass, Fiona ate one of the three olives, then took a sip. "So business, anytime, anywhere?"

He tore his gaze from the email and glanced at her again, just in time to watch her put the second olive in her mouth and slide the stirrer between her lips.

Luke took a deep breath. "It's important."

"Oh, I'm sure." She sat back in the black leather chair and sipped at her drink. "Do you always do business after business hours?"

A little irritated with himself at how easily Fiona affected him, Luke concentrated on composing the email. "When I have to."

"You were working yesterday afternoon when we met, too."

"Things have to get done, whether I'm at the company or away."

"But today, you almost never checked your phone."

"Making up for it now," he said. It had been years since he'd gone most of the day without checking emails. But he hadn't been able to take his eyes off of her. It wasn't just a sexual pull he felt for her. He actually enjoyed listening to her, talking to her. It had been a long time since a woman had captivated him like this.

And right now, for Luke, that was off-limits. Fiona wasn't the kind of woman you walked away from easily. So, it was better to not get involved at all, right?

"So, you're never really off duty?"

"Not usually." He hit Send, and a response to his earlier message to Jack arrived. Dutifully, he clicked on it and smiled in satisfaction.

"What's the point in having your own business if you never have any time off?"

He lifted his gaze to hers and reached for his drink. "Clearly, you don't know how much is involved in running your own business."

"Not true. I just don't let my business interfere with my *life*."

He snorted. "This business *is* my life."

"Well, that's just sad," Fiona mused.

Luke stared at her. "Sad? I'm building a company from the ground up. That's not sad. It's exciting. Challenging."

"And sucking up everything around it like a black hole?"

He laughed shortly, looked back at the email he was writing to Jack. He finished it off, hit Send and then set his phone on the table beside him.

"Amazing," he said. "For a second there, you almost sounded like my grandfather."

Her eyebrows arched. "What every woman longs to hear."

"Not what I meant." Luke shook his head. "It's just that he's suddenly anti-technology."

"Oh, then I'm not like him at all," Fiona said, sipping at her drink again. "I like technology. I love email and texting with my mom who makes hilarious typos, and I'm very fond of my washing machine, car and television."

Nodding, he smiled. "Glad to hear it. That's what people don't get—including my grandfather. Tech isn't just computers or robots or drones. More than a hundred years ago, tech was the first airplane. It's about the future. Seeing it. Grabbing it."

"What about the present?"

"What?"

"The present," she repeated, giving him a knowing smile. "As in dinner? Can you walk yet?"

"As long as you don't sit on my lap again, I think we're good." He stood up, then walked around the table to pull her chair out.

She slowly rose, took a deep breath that lifted the tops of her breasts to dangerous levels and said, "I'll try to restrain myself."

And it wasn't going to be easy. She didn't have to actually touch him, Luke realized. Just looking at her was enough to feed a fire that threatened to burn him to ash.

Luke steered Fiona toward the hostess, then followed behind as the woman guided them to a table by a wide window. His gaze dropped to Fiona's butt and the way it swayed with her every step. He wanted his hands on her. Soon.

Four

"We've spent the day together and I still don't know why *you're* in San Francisco," Luke said.

True. She'd managed for most of the day to steer the conversation around to him. To keep him talking about his own company and, every once in a while, to bring up the grandfather who was so desperate to get Luke back into the fold.

Because she couldn't tell him what he wanted to know. Couldn't reveal that she had been hired to meet him and ease him back into his family. So, she was left with half-truths and outright lies. Fiona wasn't comfortable with them, but sometimes, there was just no other way.

"I'm actually here on business," she said.

His mesmerizing eyes locked on her, and she just managed not to shiver.

"Who do you work for?"

"Oh, I've got my own business." Fiona reached for her purse. She dug inside for the brightly flowered, metallic card holder that had been a gift from her best friend, Laura. Opening it up, she pulled out a card and handed it to him.

He looked at it and a quizzical expression crossed his face. She couldn't blame him. Most people had that initial reaction.

"ICanFixIt?" He lifted his gaze to hers, and Fiona gave another little jolt. His eyes had a sort of power over her she hadn't really expected—or found a way to combat, yet.

"Fix what?"

She shrugged. "Anything, really. If you need it fixed, I can do it."

He tucked her card into his inner jacket pocket in a move that felt oddly intimate. "That's fairly vague."

"What's vague? Actually, it's a perfect description of what I do."

"Explain."

Well, it wasn't the first time she'd had to give an explanation of what she did. Her business card really said it all.

"If someone's lost something or if they have something they need and can't get, then they call me, and I fix it."

"Easy as that."

It wasn't a question, but at the same time, it was. "I didn't say it was easy." Fiona smiled at him because, honestly, he looked so dubious it was going to be fun to prove him wrong. Plus, she still had flames licking at her insides when she looked into his eyes. There was definitely something happening between them that she hadn't counted on. That she hadn't expected at all. Was it going to complicate the situation? Absolutely. Oh sure, he was paying attention to her and that would help with her goal of convincing him to go back to his family business. But she wasn't a one-night kind of woman and, once he found out she'd set him up from their first meeting, that's all she would be relegated to. Was that going to change how she was feeling? Nope.

"Tell me something you've 'fixed' lately."

"Okay." She did a quick flip through her mental file folders and came up with a quick example.

"About two weeks ago, a woman called me for help finding her son's letterman jacket."

He laughed.

Fiona scowled at him. She wasn't really surprised at his reaction, but she was a little disappointed. Just because it seemed silly to Luke didn't mean that it wasn't important to the kid who'd lost his jacket.

"It seems like a small thing to you, but that boy worked really hard to earn his varsity letter. And his mom paid a lot of money for that jacket. Money she couldn't spare."

"But she could afford to hire you?"

Fiona grinned. "She made her son pay my fee out of his savings."

"Okay." He nodded. "Good for her. So how did you solve the problem?"

Pleased, Fiona continued. "I backtracked. Found out where he'd been, who he'd been with, if he'd stopped anywhere along his route."

He frowned again. "Sounds like a lot of work."

She shrugged that off. "You work hard, don't you?"

"Of course."

"So do I. Anyway," she said, "I went everywhere that

Ryder went over a long weekend, because he couldn't remember where he was the last time he'd seen the jacket."

"Of course he couldn't."

She ignored that. "Really, it's amazing how many places a teenager can go in one weekend." Smiling now, she said, "I went to a hamburger stand in Bolsa Chica, a surf shop in Huntington Beach, a movie theater in Newport and a shake shack in Laguna. He was also applying for some jobs, so that took me back to Long Beach and then Palos Verdes, and I really hate driving over the Vincent Thomas Bridge."

He laughed again. "Why?"

"It's *huge*," she said. "Really long and really high, and I drive a Volkswagen Bug so when a truck gets close, I just picture myself sailing over the edge."

"You won't go over the edge. The railings are too high."

"Okay, then, being crushed."

"Reasonable," he admitted.

"Thank you." How very *kind* of him to admit she had a right to be nervous. A little irritated in spite of her attraction to him, she went on. "So, I talked to dozens of people, went through a lot of lost-and-found boxes, and finally found the jacket."

"I admit it. I'm intrigued. Where'd you find it?"

"At a girl's house." Grinning, Fiona picked up the martini she'd carried with her to the dining room and took a sip. "She'd seen the boy at a coffee shop in Long Beach where he was applying for a job. She goes to school with him, has a huge crush on him, and when he forgot the jacket after his interview, she picked it up."

"She just took it?" His expression said he was appalled.

"Well, she said she had completely planned to give

it back to him at school, but instead, she held on to it. I do think she was going to give it back eventually, she just liked having it."

"So she stole it."

Fiona held up one finger for correction. "She rescued it."

"And held it hostage."

Laughing, Fiona shook her head. "There was no ransom, and I really think you're missing the point of this."

"Fine. Clue me in."

"The point is, I found the jacket. I returned it to the boy and his very grateful mother."

"And did you tell him about the girl who had it?"

Fiona winced. "Since she pleaded with me not to, no. I didn't. She was embarrassed."

"She was a thief."

Fiona tipped her head to one side and studied him. This was a side of him she hadn't seen before. Until now, he'd been charming, funny and just sexy as hell. His response now, though, painted a hard, unforgiving picture that was a little startling. "That's cold."

"Just a fact." He shrugged. "She took it and didn't return it."

"She was going to." Fiona was sure of it. Heck, she remembered being in high school and completely infatuated with the star of the baseball team. Who had, naturally, not been aware of her existence. She had understood what the girl was thinking, and Fiona had believed her when she'd sworn that she was going to give the jacket back. "So to you, facts are all that matter? No straying from the straight and narrow?"

"Is that so unusual? You're okay with people stealing things?"

"Of course not, but I'm willing to admit that people do things they regret—"

"Everyone does." His features darkened for a moment before he said, "Doesn't mean you don't have to accept the consequences."

"I'm all about responsibility, but a little understanding wouldn't hurt, either."

"Right and wrong. Period." He sipped at his drink and looked completely at ease with that pronouncement.

Well, that didn't bode well for her, Fiona thought. She'd started this—whatever it was between them—with a lie. She doubted he'd understand that.

"So, no shades of gray in your world?"

He shook his head. "Not really."

"Must be difficult being perfect in an imperfect world."

His lips curved briefly. "I didn't say I was perfect. When I'm wrong, I own it."

Her guess was, he didn't consider himself wrong very often. "And do you confess it?"

He didn't say anything, and Fiona could guess what that meant. No, he didn't. She imagined that apologies didn't come easy to a man so sure he was right all the time. So she used that moment to drive home her point. "Then why should this girl confess? Or have what she did pointed out? Who would gain? I returned the jacket. The boy was happy. His mom was happy. And the girl doesn't have to be worried about being teased or bullied at school over it."

"And did she learn anything?"

"I think so." In fact, she was sure of it. Fiona remembered the horrified expression on the girl's face when she'd been tracked down.

"And that's your business?" he asked. "Tracking down jackets stolen by starry-eyed schoolgirls?"

"It's an example." This wasn't the first time someone had been dismissive of her business. But she bristled a little at his tone anyway. Feeling a little defensive now, she said, "I've helped people research their thesis, found a lost engagement ring, arranged for a band for a wedding and just a couple of months ago, I reunited a woman with the daughter she gave up for adoption thirty years ago."

And that case was the main reason she was here today. Of course, she couldn't tell Luke that. He might put things together if he found out that Fiona had done work for the sister of his grandfather's secretary.

His eyebrows arched. "That's impressive."

"Thank you. I know to some, my business might sound silly or not worth doing, even." Lifting her martini for another sip, she let the icy liquid cool the bubbles of insult in the pit of her stomach. It was ridiculous to take offense at Luke's remarks or outlook. It didn't matter what he thought of her business, did it? She'd faced the same thing from a lot of people over the years. It hadn't changed anything for Fiona.

She had a skill that she'd used in high school to make friends and, once grown, she'd honed her talents into a business that served a real purpose, and Fiona was proud of what she'd built. As proud, she was willing to bet, as Luke was of his tech business.

"But when it's your engagement ring that's missing, it's a big deal. Or when you manage to surprise your grandmother with tickets to a play she's been wanting to see." Fiona smiled at that memory. "It's not just the big things that are important, right? Sometimes, the small things in life mean the most."

"How did you get started in this 'business'?"

"You don't have to say it like that," she said. "As if it isn't a real company. I'm not as big as Barrett Toys and Tech, but I support myself and provide a service."

He gave her a slow nod. "Understood. So, how did you get started?"

"Kind of a long story..."

"I'll take my chances."

Fiona shrugged. "Okay, then. I grew up in a series of different foster homes." Before he could offer sympathy that she didn't want or need, she rushed on. "So that meant going to strange schools and always being the new girl."

"Rough."

"Especially for a teenager," she agreed, happy he hadn't gotten the pity gleam in his eyes that too many people did when learning about her background. It hadn't been easy, sure. But she'd survived. "So to make friends, I started offering help to people. Dog walking. Babysitting. Finding a pair of lost glasses. Tutoring football players. If it needed doing, I could do it."

He didn't say anything, just kept his gaze on her. She shifted a little uncomfortably under his steady stare but continued. "I went to community college, took business courses and turned my skill into a way to make my living."

"You still dog walking?"

"If someone needs it, sure. I also arrange for DJs for weddings, bounce houses for kids' parties, tours of movie studios..."

"And how do you pull that off?" He was curious, she could see it in his eyes, and she smiled.

"I've got a lot of friends with interesting jobs and we help each other out." She paused, then said, "I know that most of what I do doesn't sound important to you—or anyone else. But it's important to the people who hire me, and isn't that the point?"

He thought about that for a long moment, his gaze locked with hers. "Yes," he finally said. "You're right. It is."

His phone vibrated on the table and sounded like a rattlesnake in the brush. Fiona jumped, then frowned a bit when Luke reached for it. He glanced at the screen.

"This is business, just excuse me for a minute."

Times had changed, she reminded herself. Now no one thought twice about taking phone calls during dinner, or at a play or in the movies. And watching Luke, she could see his grandfather's point. Sure, technology was a great thing to have. It kept people connected—but it also had the ability to isolate them. If someone was more interested in a phone conversation than talking to the person he was with, why be with another person at all?

In spite of her annoyance, Luke's deep, rumbling voice sent shivers along her spine. His expressions shifted according to whatever the caller had to say. She could barely hear him, so she had no idea what the conversation was about. All she knew was that she was sitting opposite a gorgeous man who was more interested in his phone than in her. In the long run, that was probably best, she told herself. After all, she wasn't trying to make a romantic connection. She looked around the elegant dining room and saw that most of the people were staring at their phones.

It was a plague, she thought suddenly. And she was sympathetic to his grandfather's efforts to fight it... Strange that she'd never really paid all that much attention to people's dependency on technology until accepting this job from Jamison Barrett. She'd never paid much attention to people's love of technology simply because she was usually too busy. The evidence had been all around her all the time. Heck, she'd no doubt been guilty of it herself. Until today. As she sat there, waiting for Luke to hang up and look at her again, Fiona realized that she really liked him. Which had not been in the plan at all.

When Luke hung up, she said, "I propose a phone ban."

"Excuse me?"

"No more phones tonight. You took two calls earlier and now this one." Shrugging, she said, "I suggest we both put our phones on the table and the first one to reach for it loses."

"Loses what?"

"The agreement."

His eyes sparked and she saw a definite gleam there that kindled the fires inside her to burn hotter and higher. Apparently, Luke Barrett thrived on competition.

"And what does the winner get?"

"Hmm. Good question. The pride of knowing they won?"

"Not much of an inducement to get me to ignore business calls," he said.

What would be enough? she wondered. She couldn't offer a cash prize because he was a billionaire; he wouldn't need her twenty bucks. Then an idea occurred to her that stirred up the flames inside to make them bright enough to read by.

"Okay," she countered as a dangerous thought occurred to her. "A kiss."

Well, she had his attention anyway. Kissing Luke Barrett was more tempting than she wanted to admit even to herself. And maybe that's why she'd suggested the prize. After all, she knew very well, that whatever was between she and Luke now, it wasn't going to go anywhere, so why not a kiss?

"One kiss?" He lifted an eyebrow, and she wondered how he did that. "One kiss isn't much of a prize."

"It is if you know what you're doing," she said.

His eyes darkened until they were the color of a stormy sea. "A challenge. I like it."

"So you agree? No phone. Winner gets a kiss."

"Then the loser gets one, too."

"True, but—"

"But," he said, "the winner chooses where, when, for how long and how deep."

Just hearing him say those words set up a low, throbbing ache and made her heart quicken into a beat that was wild and fierce.

And that was just *talking* about a kiss. Maybe this wasn't a very good idea.

"Deal?" He set his phone on the tabletop.

Fiona had one last chance to back out, but somehow, she just couldn't. Instead, she laid her phone beside his and the challenge began.

Dinner was good, but Luke hardly tasted it. All he could think of was the kiss that was coming his way. He'd wanted to taste her since the moment they'd met, and now it was so close, his mind was completely fixated.

His phone buzzed again. Third time in the last half hour, and he didn't even look at it. Instead, he met her gaze and saw the smile in those brown depths. She fully expected him to cave. To take the call, because she'd been seeing him do just that too many times. But Fiona

Jordan had no idea just how determined he could be when he was focused on a goal.

And tonight, *she* was the goal. A temporary distraction? When he was back home, he could focus on his company. Here…

"I'm sorry to interrupt…"

Luke turned to look at a tall blonde woman in a slinky black dress standing beside a little boy clutching a stuffed green alligator to his chest.

After a brief glance at Luke, the woman looked at Fiona and smiled. "I'm really sorry, we'll only be a minute."

"It's no problem, Shelley," Fiona said, then looked down at the little boy. "Hi, Jake."

"Tank oo." He gave her a shy smile, snuggling up to his mom's leg as he rubbed his alligator across his cheek. "You find Dragon."

"Well, you're very welcome," Fiona told him with a grin. "He looks so happy now to be back with you."

Jake gave her a wide, two-year-old's smile and hugged the threadbare stuffed animal a little harder. "Me, too."

"I'm glad."

"He wanted to say thank you himself," Jake's mother said, "so when we saw you in the dining room, we had to come over."

"It's not a problem. I was happy to help."

"You have no idea how much you helped." Shelley smoothed one hand over her son's tousled blond hair. "He was heartbroken because Dragon was lost. He couldn't even sleep last night."

"Tank oo," the boy said again, then turned and scampered back to the table where his father sat, holding a baby girl with a bright pink ribbon in her hair.

"Seriously, thank you." Shelley shook Fiona's hand and left.

"Another satisfied client?"

Fiona smiled. "Jake lost Dragon yesterday somewhere in the hotel and, today, I saw his mom searching for it. But she was holding her baby and Jake was crying in his father's arms, so I volunteered to find it."

He frowned as he glanced at the happy little boy again. "We were together all day. When did you do this?"

She waved one hand. "When I went upstairs to change for dinner, I met up with them in the elevator."

Luke thought back. "You were only gone forty-five minutes. You found it that quickly?"

"This one was easy," she said. "They'd been at the pool most of the day, so I checked and found out the towels had been taken to the hotel laundry right after the family left the pool. Turns out, Dragon got lost in a bunch of towels. So, I went down there, and they let me look through the gigantic tubs of damp towels from the pool area that hadn't been washed yet and I found him." She shrugged. "No big deal."

Luke looked back to where the little boy was sitting, holding tightly to his alligator, and then turned his gaze back to Fiona. "To Jake it was."

She beamed at him. "You get it."

"Yeah," he said, now more determined than ever to win their bet because there was nothing he wanted more than to kiss her senseless. To lose himself in her. "I think I do."

Her phone rang, a medieval-sounding tune, and still smiling, she automatically reached for it.

"You lose," Luke said.

She stopped, hand poised above her phone. The music finally ended as the call went to voice mail, but it was too late, and they both knew it. "Not fair. I was distracted."

Luke smiled, looked her dead in the eye and whispered, "Not nearly as much as you're going to be."

The promise of a kiss hung over the rest of their dinner date, and by the time they were finished and the bill was paid, Luke was strung tighter than a harp string. He'd never looked forward so much to a damn kiss. Hell, he'd been torturing himself since the moment she'd dropped into his lap. Knowing that he was finally going to get a taste of her was pushing him closer and closer to the edge.

"You know, we should probably talk about this..."

He had one hand at the small of her back, and he could have sworn he felt heat pouring from her body into his. "You're not trying to back out, are you? This was your idea."

They walked out onto the wide flagstone patio and walkway that wended its way through a gigantic garden before winding around the hotel itself.

"Yes, but—"

"But you thought you'd win," he finished for her and saw her mouth work as if she were biting back what she wanted to say. "Admit it. You thought I'd cave and grab for my phone."

"Well, of course I did," she said, tossing a quick look up at him. "Who knew you could be so..."

"Determined? Strong? Single-minded?"

"All of the above."

He grinned and kept her walking until they were in the deserted garden. The wind was whipping in off the ocean, and February in San Francisco could be downright cold. It seemed no one else was willing to brave the chill and that suited Luke just fine.

"It was a silly bet," she said.

"And yet we made it."

She stopped, looked up at him and narrowed her eyes. "You're enjoying this, aren't you?"

"So much," he admitted. He smiled at her, but that smile slowly dissolved as he *really* looked at her. That long dark hair was lifting in the wind and her brown eyes looked almost black in the moonlight.

If Luke had been looking for a romantic setting, he couldn't have picked a better spot. Trees swaying, flowers scenting the air, and the moon, shining out of a cloud swept sky, painting shadows on the grass. There were a few old-fashioned lamps made to look like gaslights sprinkled throughout the garden, adding splashes of gold in the darkness.

But it wasn't romance he was after, he reminded himself. He wasn't looking for a relationship, just to quench the fires inside. Lust was driving him. Pure need and a desire so all-consuming, he'd never known anything like it before.

"Are you trying to back out of our deal?" he asked quietly, keeping his gaze locked on hers so he could see if there was the slightest hesitation there.

"That would be awkward, since it was my idea in the first place."

"Not an answer," he said, his voice deepening with the need clawing at his throat. Still watching her eyes, he saw desire, irritation at herself for losing this little bet, but he didn't see "no." *Thank God.*

"No, I'm not trying to back out," she said, and took a deep breath as if steeling herself for a challenge. "You won, so it's your call. Just as we agreed."

He reached for her and slid his hands up and down her arms until she shivered under his touch. Her tongue swept out to lick her bottom lip, and everything in Luke fisted tight.

"I suppose if I were a gentleman, I'd let you squirm out of this…"

"But you're not a gentleman, are you?" she asked, tossing her wind-blown hair back from her face.

"Nope," he whispered, bending his head to hers.

"I'm glad," she murmured just before his mouth took hers.

The moment their mouths met, Luke knew he'd never be satisfied with a single kiss. The taste of her swamped him, filling every cell, flavoring his breath, fogging his mind.

She swayed into him and his arms came around her, one hand sweeping up her back to cradle her head in his palm. His fingers threaded through her hair, he held her still so he could drown in the sensation of having her with him at last.

It had been the longest day or two in his life. Being constantly tortured at her presence and not touching her had driven him crazy. And now he was determined to make the most of the kiss she'd lost to him.

Their tongues tangled together, and he swallowed her sigh. He devoured her, feeding the need within and spiking it to heights he hadn't known existed. She was more than he'd expected. More than he'd thought possible. And a part of him realized that made her dangerous to a man who wasn't interested in anything that lasted longer than a couple of weeks.

Who would have guessed she would be so addictive? The taste of her. The feel of her body, pliant and giving, pinned to his. The slide of her hair against his hand and the sound of her sighs. Everything about her demanded that he take his time. Everything he was told him to stop now while he still could.

Regretfully, Luke drew his head back and stared down

at her. Her eyes were closed, her mouth still ready for the kiss to continue. Her breath heaved in and out of her lungs, and he saw her pounding pulse in the elegant column of her throat.

He couldn't seem to let her go. Her heat called to him. The need still gripping him erupted into a throbbing ache in his dick. All he could think about was sliding her dress down her shoulders, so he could bare her breasts to him. But damned if he'd act like a horny teenager in a public garden.

Slowly, she opened her eyes and looked up at him. Her tongue crossed her top lip, and she gave him such a sensuous, deliberate look, it was all Luke could do to keep from tasting her again.

"Wow."

He snorted. "Wow?"

Fiona took a deep breath, giving him a glimpse of her cleavage that only deepened the ache he felt. "Well, yeah. That was a really good kiss."

Luke grinned. No games. No playing or trying to pretend that kiss hadn't shaken both of them. Damned if he didn't like Fiona Jordan almost as much as he wanted her.

"Thanks," he said wryly, lifting one hand to stroke his fingertips along her cheek. "I try."

She patted his chest, then swept both hands through her hair. Taking another deep breath as if to steady herself, she blew it out in a rush. "It's appreciated. Seriously. So. Deal honored?"

Best bet he'd ever made. "Yeah."

"Then what do we do now?"

Images filled his mind, and heat roared through his bloodstream. He shoved them all aside, hoping she was thinking the same things. "Your call."

She looked up at him, smiled and said, "Ice cream."

"What?" That was so far off from where his mind was that he didn't know how to process it for a second or two. She went from a passion-fueled kiss hot enough to consume them both to...*ice cream*?

"I saw a great-looking creamery just a block or so from here."

Luke really didn't know what the hell to make of Fiona. He liked her. He wanted her. He worried about getting too close to her. But following her train of thought wasn't easy.

Still. Maybe ice cream would freeze the fires inside. Worth a shot.

Five

A couple of hours later, Fiona heard her best friend answer the phone and blurted out, "Help me."

"Who is this?"

Fiona choked out a laugh. "Laura, not kidding. I think I'm in deep trouble here."

Laura's tone changed instantly from teasing to worried. "What's wrong?"

Sighing a little, Fiona smiled to herself. She knew she could count on Laura Baker. Laura and her husband, Mike, owned the Long Beach duplex where Fiona lived. The Bakers had the three-bedroom unit and Fiona was up front in the one bedroom. From the moment Fiona had moved in a few years ago, the two women had bonded as if they'd known each other their entire lives.

And for Fiona that was a gift like nothing she'd ever known before. Oh, she had a huge circle of "friends" that she'd deliberately made along the way, to somehow fill the emptiness that never having a family of her own had carved into her heart. But finding Laura was like living her whole life alone and suddenly discovering she had a sister.

Like she'd told Luke, she'd grown up in a series of foster homes, bouncing like the proverbial Ping-Pong ball throughout Orange County. Until she was sixteen and was sent to Julie Maxwell. Julie was more than a foster mom. She had become *Mom*. She'd given Fiona the stability and sense of belonging that she'd always dreamed of. And when Fiona aged out of the system, Julie had insisted that she stay on at the house and go to school. Julie was the only real mother Fiona had ever known and she'd always be grateful.

She was just as thankful to have Laura in her life. Laura was short, blonde and, as her husband liked to say, *stacked*. She was also the most sensible human Fiona had ever known and the first one she went to with a problem. And she had a beauty to talk about this time.

"It's Luke Barrett. He's too sexy."

Laura laughed. "Is that even possible? Isn't that like too skinny? Too rich? Who ever heard of too sexy?"

Mike shouted in the background, "Thanks, babe!"

"Wasn't talking to you," Laura called back with a laugh, then asked Fiona, "What's going on?"

Fiona clutched the phone and paced aimlessly. Standing in this beautiful hotel room, all alone, she imagined that she was sitting next to Laura on her big leather sofa and immediately felt better. She stopped at the windows and stared out at San Francisco, draped in lights that made the city look magical at night. "This job. It's not turning out like I thought it would."

"Hold on." Then she called out to her husband. "Mike, bring me a glass of wine, will you?" Back to Fiona, she said, "I'm thinking I'm going to need one. Am I wrong?"

"Tell him to bring the bottle."

"Well, now I'm intrigued. Okay, I've got my wine. Travis is tucked into bed. I'm all yours. Talk."

So she did. While she continued to pace like a tiger in a too-small cage, Fiona told Laura everything that had happened from the moment she'd dropped into Luke's lap. Through it all, Laura only gave a murmured "Oooh" and a few sighs.

Finally, Fiona told her about the kiss that had singed every nerve ending she had and ended up with, "What do I do now?"

"Have sex?" Laura asked.

"Great idea!" Mike shouted, his voice coming clearly through the phone.

Fiona laughed again and felt the tight knot in her chest begin to dissolve. This is what she'd needed. To talk it all out with Laura. To be back in her "normal" zone. "I can't. It wouldn't be ethical. Would it?"

"Ethics, schmethics," Laura said. "Is he married?"

"No!"

"You're not either. So, what's the problem?"

"Um…" Fiona waved one hand in the air. "How about I'm lying to him? I'm working for his grandfather. This whole trip was paid for by Jamison Barrett just so I could convince Luke to go back to the family business."

"And did you take a celibacy pledge when I wasn't looking?"

"No, but—"

"Are you hoping that he's *the one* and you'll find happily-ever-after with him?"

Okay, she could admit that it wouldn't have taken much to imagine a perfect future with Luke as a gorgeous husband and father to a few beautiful kids. But that wasn't the point. Because the chances of anything like that happening were *way* out there.

"No, of course not, but—"

"Do you want him?"

Easy question to answer, given that her blood was still burning, and she could still taste his mouth on hers. "Oh, yes."

"So stop being so tortured. Go to bed with the man. Enjoy yourself." Laura took a breath, then said, "Let's face it. He's going to be furious when he finds out what's going on anyway. You've already said there's no future with the guy. So why not have the memory of great sex to help you through it?"

"Maybe he won't find out," Fiona argued. And really, if the job went well, he shouldn't. He should just go back to the family business and pick up his life without ever knowing that the woman he spent a long weekend with was the reason why he'd changed his life around.

"He'll find out, sweetie," Laura said. "If you want something to stay secret, that's practically a guarantee that it won't."

"That's helpful." Fiona frowned as she caught her own reflection in the window glass. She hated the idea of Luke thinking she was a liar. That she'd felt nothing for him. Because despite her best efforts to remain professional, she couldn't help being drawn to him.

Laura sighed. "I think I'm going to need more wine. Fiona, do you like this guy?"

"I really do," she admitted, thinking back over the last couple of days. Luke was funny and gorgeous and smart, and men like that didn't grow on trees. "That's the problem, you know? I really do like him."

"Then enjoy him. Stop overthinking everything. Just accept this for what it is and appreciate it while it lasts."

Could she do that?

"Stop thinking," Laura said as if she could see the indecision written on Fiona's face. "Just relax for once and go with it."

She wasn't the most impulsive person in the world. And she definitely wasn't the one-night-stand kind of woman. Heck, it had been nearly a year since her last date. She liked to take her time. Get to know a guy before she had sex with him. Color her old-fashioned. But her personal rules seemed to be flying out a window when it came to Luke Barrett. She was so far out of her comfort zone, she couldn't even *see* it.

Luke Barrett was the kind of man who came along once in a lifetime. Fiona thought about him. Remembered that kiss. The way he felt pressed up against her The fire in his eyes when he looked at her.

And she knew, trouble or not, she was going to risk it.

Late the next morning, Jamison Barrett was in his study at home. Church services with Loretta were finished and the rest of the day was his. He didn't quite know what to do with himself, though. In spite of his wife's assurances, Jamison was worried. If he was losing his mind, then he needed Luke back more than ever. And if Fiona Jordan failed at her task, Jamison didn't know how he'd manage it.

"Hey, Pop."

He looked up from his desk, startled to see his oldest grandson stroll into the room. "Cole? What're you doing here?"

"What do you mean?" Cole laughed a little uncertainly and tucked one hand into the pocket of his casual slacks. "We've had this planned for a week."

"Hello, Pop." Susan came in behind Cole, carrying

Oliver, a blond boy with big blue eyes like his mother's and a smile just like Cole's.

"Susan!" Jamison came around the desk and scooped Oliver into his arms. "I wasn't expecting you and this little devil."

Susan smoothed her perfect hair and gave him a curious look. "I thought we were set for brunch today after your meeting with Cole..."

Jamison felt a hot jolt that he hopefully managed to hide. Oliver slapped both hands together in excitement and shouted, "Papa!"

Grinning at his great-grandson, Jamison set the toddler onto his feet and said, "Go see Nana in the kitchen. She's always got cookies."

The boy took off like a shot and not surprisingly, Susan was right behind him. How the woman managed to run in three-inch heels was beyond Jamison, but if there was one thing you could say about his granddaughter-in-law, she was devoted to her son.

When she and the boy were gone, Jamison turned to look at Cole. "Not that I'm unhappy to see all of you... but why are you here and what's this about brunch?"

Cole just stared at him for a long minute. "We've got a meeting scheduled for today about the new Christmas line, Pop."

Jamison frowned and shook his head. "That's tomorrow."

"No," Cole said softly, carefully. "It's today. You said you wanted to get it out of the way on Sunday so you could talk to marketing tomorrow at work."

Jamison scrubbed one hand across the back of his neck. He didn't remember saying that. Or even thinking it.

"And you said since we'd be working at the house, I

should bring Susan and Oliver, and we'd do a Sunday brunch at the yacht club."

Jamison took a breath and held it. It was as if Cole were speaking Greek. He didn't remember anything about this. This didn't make sense. None of it did. A man didn't wake up one morning to find a giant hole in his metaphorical marble bag. Wasn't this something that slipped up on you? Weren't there small signs before big ones—like forgetting entire conversations?

"Are you okay, Pop?" Cole's gaze was steady and filled with the concern Jamison hated to see.

"Fine. I just forgot, is all." He was forgetting too damn much here lately, but he wasn't going to admit that to Cole. Or anyone else, for that matter—except Loretta, of course.

"You wrote it into your calendar last week."

Had he? Jamison searched his memory, but he didn't remember changing the meeting to Sunday. Worry coiled inside him like a snake. But just as quickly, he dismissed it. Damn it, he *knew* he'd set up that meeting for Monday. Irritated now, Jamison opened the calendar program on his computer. His home computer and his work unit were linked, so he could make changes or plans at either location.

Cole was the one who'd given him this program, telling Jamison that it would make his life easier. How in the hell going through a program was easier than a damn pen and paper was beyond him, but since it was a gift, Jamison had felt obligated to use it. "I know I wrote it down, boy. For tomorrow."

He scrolled through the program until he found what he was looking for and once he had, he felt worse than ever. There it was. *Sunday—Cole: Christmas line. Brunch with family.*

He swallowed back a knot of fear lodged in his throat. What the hell was happening to him? He never forgot a meeting. Hell, up until last year, he'd kept all of his appointments in his head and had never missed one.

Now he glared at the screen accusingly. As if it had somehow changed what he'd written.

"Pop?"

Cole's voice was hesitant, filled with distress, and Jamison hated it. He didn't need sympathy or concern. And he wanted it less.

"I'm fine," he insisted, in spite of the niggling doubts rattling through him. If there was a problem, he'd take care of it himself. The last thing he needed was people fluttering about him, treating him like a damn invalid— or worse. Pushing those thoughts aside, Jamison looked at his grandson and forced a smile he was nowhere near feeling.

Cole had his own wife and son to worry about. He didn't need to be thinking that his grandfather was on a slippery slope, balanced on one leg.

"Must have been too busy to notice," he said brusquely. "With Luke gone, I'm having to pick up a lot of slack in the company."

"You don't have to do it alone, Pop," Cole said stiffly. "I'm your grandson, too, you know. If you need help at the business, tell me. I can take over Luke's accounts. He's not the only one of us who grew up working at Barrett Toys and Tech."

Well, Jamison thought, he'd walked right into that one. It was a bone of contention for Cole that he wasn't stepping into Luke's shoes.

"I know that," he said, nodding. Cole was the oldest, but if truth be told, Luke was the more mature one. The one with the vision to see the company and where it could go. The fact that they were now arguing about that vision didn't matter. Cole was more about being in the moment rather than seeing the big picture, and that wasn't a trait that made for a good company president.

Still, he didn't need to get into all of that now. Looking at Cole, Jamison told himself that maybe he was being too hard on the boy. But he'd watched Luke and Cole grow up. He'd seen their personalities develop and though he loved them both, Jamison wasn't blind to their faults. Luke was always in the future, ignoring the present—and Cole was interested in a paycheck, but not the work.

"Maybe soon," Jamison hedged, "we'll have a talk about that." But if Fiona Jordan did the job he was paying her to accomplish, he wouldn't have to. Still, Cole knew nothing about that. "For right now, though, we'll go on the way we have been." He nodded and winked at Cole. "You never know, Luke might come back."

"Sure, Pop." Disappointment and frustration briefly crossed Cole's features, but an instant later, he'd buried whatever he was feeling beneath his usual smile. "We'll do it your way for now."

"That's good. So," Jamison said, sitting down at his desk again, "if you're ready, we can take care of this meeting right now."

"Okay." Cole took a seat, opened up his tablet and started talking.

Jamison listened. He really did. He even made notes when appropriate. But the back of his mind was filled with whispering voices, and none of them were comforting.

An hour later, Fiona somehow found herself on Luke's private jet, feeling like a peasant in a palace.

She was used to dragging herself through security, waiting at a crowded gate on uncomfortable chairs and then squeezing into tiny seats built for a butt a little smaller than her own.

This kind of luxury, she told herself as she looked at her surroundings, was going to make flying coach even more miserable in the future. There were two black leather sofas on either side of the sleek jet, and toward the front of the plane, a conversational group of six black leather chairs faced one another.

There were tables, reading lamps and a thick, plush white carpet on the floor. A flat-screen TV was on one wall and there were even fresh flowers in a copper vase that had been bolted to one of the tables. Slowly, she sank down onto one of the sofas and idly ran one hand across the cool, smooth surface, as if to convince herself she was really there and not dreaming.

Her gaze locked on Luke, talking with his own private flight attendant, the pilot and the copilot. She'd been introduced to all three of them when she'd come aboard and had even had a brief tour of the cockpit—an impressive and confusing wall of switches, lights and buttons.

And as distracted as she was by the plane and the luxury of not having to fight through a crowded airport, Fiona could barely take her eyes off Luke.

He wore a dark blue suit, pale blue shirt and scarlet tie. His hair, for some reason, kept capturing her attention. Too long for a businessman and too short for a surfer, and her fingers itched to touch it. His eyes were so blue, she felt as if she could drown in them. And when he turned his head to look at her, she felt a sharp jolt of electricity that set every nerve in her body sizzling.

It was that look that had kept her sleepless the night before. That *knowing* gleam in his eyes. Well, that and the memory of the kiss they'd shared in the garden. She had the distinct feeling she would remember that kiss even if she lived to be one hundred.

The feel of him pressed against her. The rush of his mouth on hers, his breath sliding into her lungs. The fire he'd kindled inside her had burned brightly all night, driving her half-crazy with an aching need that still throbbed with every beat of her heart.

Her gaze locked with his, Fiona realized she was sorry this weekend was over. It had started out as a job, but somehow it had become more than that. Now she was caught up in something completely different and she had no idea how it would end. Or where they would go from here.

When they were back in Orange County, she'd have to keep seeing him—that had been the original plan, after all. She still had to convince him to go back to the family company. But with that kiss, she had realized she wanted to keep seeing him because she simply wanted to. But sleeping with him was something else entirely. If she did and then he walked away at the end of the weekend, then she'd failed at her job. And there was still a big lie hanging between them that she really didn't want to think about. And what if he expected their weekend to end, well, with the weekend?

Too many thoughts were crashing through her mind at once and she instantly recalled Laura saying, *You always overthink everything.* Well, maybe her friend was right. Maybe it was time to stop thinking and just see what would happen.

A moment later, Luke walked toward her in long, almost lazy strides and Fiona's breath caught in her lungs. Honestly, the man was dangerous. Her heartbeat kept jumping into a fast gallop and that couldn't be healthy.

"We'll be cleared to take off in a few minutes."

"Okay." If she hadn't accepted his offer of a ride back to Southern California, right about now Fiona would have been sitting in the crowded airport waiting to be shuffled onto a jam-packed, uncomfortable plane. Not to mention, she wouldn't be with Luke. This was so much better. And so far out of her 'normal' world, she was a little off-balance. Of course, just being with Luke made her feel unsteady, so...

He helped her up, then drew her to one of the matching chairs. "We'll sit here for takeoff."

"A lot better than what I'm used to," she said, snapping her seat belt as she turned to watch him sit beside her.

He gave her a half smile that tugged at something inside her. "You can fly with me whenever you like."

"Well, that's a tempting offer," she mused, wondering if he meant it or if he was just being charming. Either way, it worked.

So strange, she thought, watching him. A few days ago, she didn't know him. Had never heard of him, really. And today, she was sitting beside him, feeling a tangle of emotions she'd never experienced before.

"I'm hoping so," he admitted, then turned to look at the woman approaching.

She was tall, wearing black slacks, a white long-sleeved blouse and a bright red scarf knotted at her neck. She was carrying two glasses of champagne and when she delivered them, she smiled. "Enjoy your flight. If you need me, Mr. Barrett, I'll be with the pilot as you requested."

"Thanks, Janice. We'll be fine."

So, he'd arranged for them to be alone. Oddly enough, that didn't make Fiona nervous at all. She took a sip of the bubbling wine and let the froth of it settle on her tongue for a moment before swallowing. Nope, not nervous. Eager, maybe.

The last few days had been so much more than she'd thought they would be. She'd gone there to do her job, but she'd never expected to be so drawn to Luke. So tempted by him. She'd never known a man who could turn her inside out so easily. Why did it have to be this man? They were separated not just by the lie that was hanging between them, but by the fact that she was in no way a part of his world. A world of private jets, for heaven's sake. No, sleeping with him would be a huge mistake.

Was it hot in the airplane, she wondered. Or was it just her?

Fiona took another sip of the cold champagne. "Oh yes. Definitely better than coach."

He grinned. "I told Janice we wouldn't be needing her after takeoff. It's only a ninety-minute flight, after all."

"Sure." Her mind was working, dancing, jumping from one thought to another. Ninety minutes could be a long time if you spent it wisely. Fly with him anytime? She doubted that would happen in the future. So why not take Laura's advice, stop thinking for a while, and just enjoy where she was and who she was with?

It wasn't like her at all to simply give in to her own wants and needs. She was more the type to think things through from every angle. Being impulsive was just counter to her nature. So why was she considering being just that?

Nerves rattled her, but Fiona tamped them down. If there were…consequences to pay, then she would pay them. Later. But if this weekend was all she would have of Luke Barrett, Fiona didn't want to waste it. For once in her life, she was going to leap without worrying about the fall. Just this once, she would take a chance. Risk it.

She felt the hum of the jet's engines as they revved, and the plane started taxiing to the runway. It felt as if she were doing the same thing. Moving inexorably forward.

"Once we're in the air," Luke said, leaning in closer to her, "I'll show you around."

She blinked at him. "There's more?"

He only smiled and then their plane was racing down the runway. Her heartbeat kept pace, thundering in her chest. Looking into his blue eyes was almost hypnotic. He could capture her with a glance. Her blood heated in her veins and she took another sip of the champagne to ease the fire. But nothing could do that.

The jet raced faster, then lifted into the air. As always, Fiona's stomach did a quick jitter, but this time, she had the feeling it was more being with Luke rather than her fear of flying.

A few minutes later, they were high above the banks of clouds she could see outside the windows. The jet's engines settled into a throaty purr that hummed in the background. Luke unhooked his seat belt, then held out a hand to her. She set her champagne aside and slipped her hand into his. He curled his fingers around hers and held on, and Fiona didn't mind in the slightest.

His skin next to hers made heat swarm through her and Fiona started a silent mantra, demanding that her hormones take a nap. They weren't listening to her, but she kept trying. Laura's advice aside, she couldn't help thinking that this connection she felt to Luke was not a good thing.

He was a job. He wasn't hers to care for or to dream about. If not for his grandfather, none of this would be happening. She still had to complete the job she'd been hired to do. What was she thinking even considering going to bed with him?

For heaven's sake, she'd known him about three days. Fiona couldn't remember a time when she'd been so willing to go with her instincts rather than planning something out. Still, it wasn't as if he was a complete stranger, was it?

A voice in the back of her mind said that the last three days, they'd been together almost nonstop. They'd talked more than most people did during weeks of getting to know each other. She liked him. A lot. And that worried her a little, because she had zero business building fantasies in her mind that centered on Luke Barrett. Just standing here, in his private jet, told her that much. They were from separate worlds. She had no place in the kind of universe he inhabited and no illusions about it, either.

Nothing in her life had prepared her for this man and she didn't think anything could have. He gave her hand a squeeze and her insides leaped into life again.

Take a nap, hormones, she thought to herself. *Take a nap.*

"And this is the bedroom," Luke said, opening a door to a room at the back of the plane.

"Handy," she answered, looking around. The room was small, but plush. A queen-size bed covered in a dark red duvet, twin tables and a television on the wall.

She looked up at him and knew there wasn't a chance in hell her hormones would be napping.

Six

His gaze was locked on her, and Fiona felt the heat of it bathing her. The power of his stare was like a touch. She could *feel* him looking at her.

"The bathroom's right here," he was saying. "Though there's another up front by the cockpit."

"Right." She laughed a little, shaking her head. This was so far from her normal life it was as if she'd landed on a different planet. "Of course. A one-bedroom, two-bath plane. Sure."

He quirked an eyebrow. "Are you okay?"

"Honestly? I don't know." She glanced around the room, taking it all in before turning her gaze back on him. Was he really so used to living like this that he didn't even see how weird it was?

"I'm fine. It's just—usually when I fly, I call it luxury if the seat next to me is empty."

He shrugged and tucked his hands into his pockets. "Yeah, I can see that."

"But you've always lived like this."

Nodding, he said only, "Pretty much."

The plane's engines hummed beneath their feet and set up a vibration that echoed in her nervous system.

"My father was a pilot, so he liked having his own plane."

"Does he still?"

Luke's features tightened. "No. He and my mom died in a plane crash."

"Oh God. I'm so sorry." She didn't know which was worse, the pain in his eyes or the matter-of-fact way he'd said it. Fiona hadn't grown up with a family, and she knew how awful that had been. The emptiness, the wish for more, for love, to be wanted. Needed. But she couldn't even imagine the pain of *having* a family and then losing them like that.

"I was a kid," he said softly. "My cousin Cole's parents were with them. They were headed to Florida on a vacation and went down halfway there. No one survived."

Fiona didn't question her instincts this time. She just went with them. Wrapping her arms around his waist, she laid her head on his chest and simply held on. There was nothing she could say. No way to help. But she could see old pain in his eyes and hear it in his voice, and it was in her nature to try to offer whatever comfort she could.

When his arms came around her and Fiona's heartbeat jumped, she knew the decision she'd just made was going to lead to more than comfort.

Luke threaded his fingers through her hair and pulled her head back. Looking down into her eyes, he shook his head as if in wonder. "You're...unsettling."

She stared up at him, gave him a small smile and said, "Thank you."

He laughed shortly. "Figures you'd see that as a compliment."

Her heart jumped into a fast rhythm. "You really do say the nicest things."

He grinned, bent his head and kissed her. Fiona's mind scrambled so fast, it was a wonder she remembered how to breathe. They were standing beside a bed. In a jet. Alone.

Sex was bound to happen. Right? She'd already decided to go for it…to surrender to whatever was happening between them. And she vowed to not regret it later.

He deepened the kiss, and Fiona eagerly matched him. Her breath was coming short and hard. Her heartbeat raced and the blood in her veins was like lava. Every square inch of her skin felt as if it were on fire.

When he lifted his head and looked down at her, Fiona could see the same reaction on his face that she felt sure was stamped on hers.

"Are we doing this?" he asked, voice deep, quiet.

"I think we really are." Fiona shut down all her doubts.

Because none of that mattered right now. The only thing she could think was that she needed to touch him and be touched. She wanted to feel him deep inside her. She needed Luke Barrett in a way she'd never needed before.

And today, she was going to surrender to her own needs. This wasn't about anything but the current sizzling between her and Luke and Fiona wanted more than anything to indulge herself in him. Whatever came next…she'd worry about that when she had to.

A half smile curved one side of his mouth. "Really glad to hear that."

Then he kissed her again, and Fiona stopped thinking altogether. With his mouth on hers, his tongue stroking against hers, all she could do was *feel*. And there was so much, it was as if her brain were short-circuiting and she didn't miss it at all.

He tore his mouth from hers, tugged the hem of her red-and-white-striped boatneck shirt up and over her head, then tossed it aside. The cool air touched her skin and only enflamed it further. He stared at her black lace bra and sighed before flipping open the catch in front. Then his hands cupped her breasts and Fiona groaned.

His thumbs and forefingers tugged and pulled at her nipples, and she felt it all the way to her core. She was hot, achy and filled with so many needs she couldn't have named them all even if she could have spoken. Which she couldn't.

"I've wanted to touch you since that first day," he murmured, bending down to kiss her again. It was a hard, fast, desperate kiss that Fiona missed the moment it ended.

"Yes," she finally said, when she could gather enough coherent thought to form a sentence. "I remember how 'happy' you were when we first met."

He grinned. "You're about to find out that I'm a hell of a lot 'happier' right now."

"Promises, promises," she muttered as his hands dropped to the hem of her short black skirt. She'd always loved that skirt. Today, she thought it just might be her favorite piece of clothing.

Because it gave him quick, easy access to the one part of her body that was screaming for attention.

In seconds, his talented fingers had found the strip of elastic at her black panties and sent them sliding down her legs so she could kick them off. Then he cupped her with one hand and she instantly began rocking into his touch. She couldn't stop herself. Didn't want to stop.

What she wanted was what he was giving her. A ride into oblivion. Release. And that thought alone kept her standing, moving into him.

One finger, then two, moved within her, stroking, caressing. His thumb found her center and rubbed that one, so sensitive bud until her eyes were wheeling in her head and breathing became an extreme sport.

If she had stood outside herself, she might have been embarrassed to be mostly naked, with a fully dressed man who was sliding his fingers inside her. But she wouldn't have changed anything.

Fiona felt as if she'd been primed for an orgasm from the moment she'd landed on his lap. So, it was no surprise when her body was suddenly on the broken verge of shattering.

Until he stopped.

Fiona blinked and stared up at him. "What? Why?"

"Nope," he said flatly. "You're not going there without me."

She watched him tear his clothes off, tossing his elegant suit to one side until he was naked and, she saw… *impressive.*

He unzipped her skirt and let it fall, then he tumbled her back onto the wide bed behind her and followed her down.

His hands claimed her body while his mouth took hers. Their tongues twisted and tangled together, breath sliding from one to the other of them. Fiona clutched at his shoulders and slid her fingertips down his muscular arms, loving the feel of him. The heat in his body that speared into hers.

She kissed him with everything she had and threw one leg over his hip, pulling that erection closer, closer. When the tip of him rubbed over her, she groaned and broke their kiss long enough to mutter, "For heaven's sake, do it. Do it now."

He reached to the closest table, opened the drawer and pulled out a condom.

"Handy," she murmured.

"I try," he countered.

In a blink, he had sheathed himself, and then he was kneeling between her thighs, holding her body open to his gaze. Fiona squirmed with impatience.

"I feel like we've been doing the whole foreplay thing for days," she whispered, looking up, into his summer-blue eyes. "Can we go for the big show now?"

He grinned. "Have I mentioned I really like your attitude?"

"Nope, but you can. Later."

"Right." He pushed into her body with one long, hard stroke.

She groaned. Fiona's head went back into the mattress and she stared blindly at the jet's ceiling as she adjusted to his size. He filled her completely, and she didn't know how she'd lived so long without having him inside her.

Then he rocked his hips against her, and everything got even better. A delicious friction built up between them as he moved inside her. He set a rhythm that she raced to keep up with. Her body was humming, her mind shutting down. She fought for breath, hoped her heart wouldn't explode and rocked her hips with his every movement. "More," she groaned. "More."

"Yes," he ground out. "Always more."

She was so close. So near the teetering edge of oblivion Fiona could almost taste it. Then he changed things up and threw her for a loop.

He sat back on his heels, drawing her up with him until she was straddling him. Eye to eye, they looked at each other, gazes locked as Fiona took charge of the rhythm. The pace. She moved on him, taking him deeper and deeper inside her and still it wasn't enough. She swiveled her hips against him, creating a new kind of friction that drove them both to the brink.

"You're amazing," he muttered, leaning in to take her mouth with his.

She licked her lips when the kiss was over, as if she could draw the taste of him into her.

His hands locked on her hips, guiding her, pushing her, helping her keep that wild, frantic rhythm at a breathless pace, because they were now caught together in a net of desperation. When the first splintering sensation jolted her, Fiona grabbed hold of him and kept moving, kept pushing herself higher and faster, riding that incredible pulse of pleasure that rocked her right to the bone.

While she shattered in his arms, she felt his release shake through him. His grip on her tightened; he clenched his jaw and kept his gaze fixed on her as if seeing her fed what he was feeling.

And when the crash was over, they fell to the bed, still locked together.

"Nice to keep a supply of condoms in the drawer," she murmured.

Luke grinned. "Yeah. I bought some this morning. Just in case."

She turned her head to look at him and Luke thought her eyes looked darker, deeper, somehow. Almost as if they were pulling him in. "So you thought I was a sure thing?"

"I hoped," he admitted, leaning in to get another kiss. God, the taste of her pumped through him with a life of its own. He'd just had her and he wanted her again. More than before because now he knew just how good it was.

"Good call," she said, and gave a lovely, long sigh. "That was…"

"Yeah. If we're this good in the air, imagine how good we'll be on the ground."

Her gaze snapped to his. "Will we?"

He smoothed her hair back, indulging himself by sliding his fingers through that soft, dark brown silk. "I'm not finished yet. You?"

She dragged her fingertips along his chest, and he sucked in a gulp of air. "No, I'm not finished, either."

"Like I said before. I like your attitude." He leaned over her and took one of her nipples into his mouth. He smiled against her at the quick catch of her breath. His tongue and teeth worked that dark pink bud until she was writhing beneath him and all Luke could think was how glad he was he'd bought the large box of condoms.

Then he lost himself in her again and stopped thinking entirely.

An hour later, Luke hooked one arm behind his head and said, "We'll be landing soon."

"Back to the real world."

"This isn't real?" he asked, turning his head to look at her. She was beautiful. Her eyes alone were enough to spellbind a man. And the minute that thought hit, he scowled to himself. Luke wouldn't allow that. In his world, the plan ruled all. And Fiona was definitely not a part of the plan. He wasn't spellbound and wasn't about to be, either. But he could appreciate a beautiful woman he'd just had the most incredible sex of his life with.

She grinned and he worried again. "This isn't *my* reality," she said. "It's a great place to visit, don't get me wrong. But when I get home, I've got to pay bills, answer emails and do some laundry. *That* is reality."

"I pay bills and do emails," he pointed out.

"And the laundry?"

He shrugged. "The housekeeper does it."

She laughed, and he liked the sound of it in spite of the fact that she was laughing at *him*.

"Of course she does."

Still frowning, he changed the subject, since he was suddenly *embarrassed* about having a housekeeper. If she found out he had a cook, too, she might laugh herself sick.

"Why don't you let me take you to dinner tomorrow night?"

"Really?" she seemed surprised, and frankly, so was he.

When they'd first boarded this plane, Luke hadn't planned on seeing her again once they got home. He wasn't interested in a relationship—he had way too much going on at the moment. But he didn't care for the thought of letting her go, either. Now, after that bout of incredible sex, he was even more interested in sticking around for a while. He didn't want to consider why. Refused to think of what that might mean. He wouldn't be distracted by emotional entanglements. This wasn't about emotion anyway. This was simple, beautiful lust, and he would stay with her until the desire for her had ebbed.

"Why not?"

"Well, for one thing, I've got a job tomorrow evening."

"Doing what?"

She studied him for a long second or two, then said, "Why don't you come over and you can go with me to my appointment? Then we can have dinner after."

Go with her. On what? A treasure hunt like she'd had the day before when she dug through wet towels to find a stuffed alligator? But even as he thought it, he realized he didn't care. "All right. It's a date."

"Great." She leaned over to kiss him, then smiled. "I'm just going to put my clothes on. Your flight attendant might guess what we were up to, but I'd rather she didn't see me naked."

He watched her snatch up her clothes and step into the attached bathroom. Luke wasn't sure why he'd agreed to go along on her job. He'd thought a nice dinner and then another great bout of lovemaking.

What had he gotten himself into here? And why didn't he care?

Late the next afternoon, Fiona and Laura sat in matching lawn chairs watching Travis chase a bright red ball across the lawn. The little boy's laughter spilled from him and floated behind him like soap bubbles on the air.

"So, he's coming over," Laura said.

"Yep."

"To go on your job with you."

"Yep."

"Okay, my question is, *why*?"

Fiona had wondered that, too. She'd thought it was going to be hard to stay close enough to him to complete her job for his grandfather. Instead, Luke himself had suggested meeting again. Was it the sex? Because it had been really great, but sex wasn't *everything*. "Because I'm irresistible?"

Laura laughed. "That must be it."

Fiona grinned. She looked at Travis, a two-year-old whose only problem at the moment was catching up to his favorite ball. Maybe Laura was right. Maybe she did overthink everything. Maybe she should take a clue from Travis and just focus on what was in front of her in the moment.

A soft wind swept over them and nodded the heads of the gem-colored pansies in Laura's flower bed. At the duplex next door, the Gonzalez girls sat on the porch, each of them playing on her own tablet. They, too, were focused on the moment. So the trick was to focus on what was *important* right now.

"I don't know why he wanted to see me again, but I couldn't say no. Not only is he gorgeous and funny and smart and *way* talented in bed, he's my job, too." She winced. "I can't believe I had sex with him."

"On a plane." Laura sighed and looked wistful. "I'm so jealous."

Fiona looked back at the Gonzalez kids again. They didn't talk to each other or laugh together or anything. They could have been twin statues for all the interaction happening between them. She sighed and shook her head.

Funny that she'd never noticed how many kids were glued to tablets before working for Jamison Barrett. The girls on that porch were ten and eight. Too young to be that wrapped up in a computer.

Frowning, Fiona made a mental note to point the girls out to Luke and to remember that he wasn't her "date." He was her job.

"This is crazy," she muttered. "*I'm* crazy."

"Yeah, probably," Laura mused. "But, Fiona, you never do anything wild or outrageous. Honey, you never take something for yourself. So maybe you were due."

She had a point, as much as Fiona hated to admit it. But that didn't let her off the hook, did it? Was doing something for herself enough of a reason to be with

Luke? Was that fair to him? And what happened when he inevitably discovered the truth about their first meeting? She was lying to Luke about who she was and how she'd met him. He thought it was all an accident of fate. What would he say if he found out his grandfather had paid her to be there? Had arranged for her plane ticket and hotel room just so that she could convince him to come back to the company?

Wincing, she silently admitted she knew just what he'd say. *Goodbye.* So she had to remember that whatever was between them, it was temporary. An anomaly to her daily life. No more permanent than a sunset... beautiful, but quickly gone.

"Oh my... You know I love my honey," Laura whispered beside her. "But damn, Fiona..."

She didn't have to look to know that Luke had arrived. Laura's glassy-eyed stare was enough to alert her to his presence. Fiona was pretty sure she'd had the same expression on her face the first time she saw him. Still, she turned her head to watch the man approach.

He was wearing a suit again. Of course. She idly wondered if he even owned a pair of jeans. The suit was black with faint gray pinstripes. He wore a white dress shirt with a dark gray tie, and his too-long hair was ruffling in the sea breeze.

It was late afternoon, so the neighborhood kids were home from school. Somewhere down the street, a basketball thumped like the heartbeat of the neighborhood. Skateboard wheels growled across the sidewalks, and the sounds made her smile. At least *some* kids were outside and not staring at a screen.

"Hi!" Fiona stood up and walked to him, suddenly feeling very underdressed. Her beige ankle pants, yellow long-sleeved shirt and taupe Skechers really didn't hold up against that suit.

He slipped one hand to the back of her neck and leaned in to claim a quick, hard kiss. A zip of something amazing shot through Fiona like a whipcrack. A job, she thought frantically. He was a job. But even reminding herself of that fact didn't change what she was willing to risk just to be with him.

"I've been wanting to do that all day," he admitted.

A job and so much more.

"Well, don't be shy," she said. "Do it again."

He grinned and took advantage of the invitation.

Her head was spinning even as she gave herself a mental talking-to. Hadn't she just decided that she had to remain professional? Why was it that her best intentions flew out the window the minute she was close to him?

When she came up for air, Laura was standing right beside her. Her best friend was five inches shorter than Fiona's five nine, and her body was substantially curvier. Her wide smile was friendly, and her blue eyes were sparkling with interest and curiosity.

"Hi, I'm Laura. Best friend. Neighbor. Landlord." She held out one hand and Luke shook it.

"Nice to meet you," he said. "Luke Barrett."

"Fee!" Travis came racing up, grabbed hold of Fiona's legs and turned his face to her. "Up, Fee!"

"Right." She lifted him, sat him on her hip and said, "Luke, this is my boyfriend, Travis. He's the jealous type, so watch your step."

"I'll keep it in mind. He looks pretty tough."

"Oh, he is. Able to destroy a living room in less than ten minutes," Laura put in and scooped her son from Fiona.

"Maybe he could use something to keep him so

busy learning he wouldn't have time for destruction," Luke said.

Now it was Fiona's turn to frown. Just the thought of this active little boy sitting in front of a computer tablet when he could be running in circles refocused her on the job at hand.

Fiona tugged at Luke's arm and pointed him at the house next door. The two girls were still there. Still staring at their screens. Still so absorbed with their tablets it was as if they'd forgotten they weren't alone.

"Busy like them, you mean?" Fiona asked. "That's Elena and Teresa Gonzalez. I'd introduce you, but they're zoned out. Being *busy.*"

Luke looked at the girls and frowned thoughtfully. Fiona thought that maybe she'd scored a point. But whatever he was thinking, he didn't say. He simply shifted his gaze to her. "You ready to leave?"

Fiona let it go. For now. But she'd be talking to him about the girls and their technology again later. "Sure. Let me get my purse. I'll see you tomorrow, Laura."

"Have fun," her friend said, and headed off to get Travis's ball.

Luke followed her inside and stood practically at attention in her small living room. He looked around and she wished she knew what he was thinking. Fiona had no idea where he lived, but she knew that wherever it was, his place was nothing like hers.

Fiona's living room was painted a deep maroon and she'd installed the white crown molding herself. Her windows didn't have curtains because Fiona hated them, but she had installed window shades that she pulled down at night for a little privacy. There was a green love seat and two club chairs covered in a fabric that boasted wild sprays of flowers, and a coffee table she'd found in a thrift shop. She'd sanded and painted the table a pale yellow, adding to the garden feel of the room.

"It's a nice place."

"Thanks." Her entire apartment was probably the size of his closet, but she loved the home she'd built for herself. Every room was a different color, and she'd filled the apartment with furniture she loved. So every time she walked into her apartment, Fiona felt satisfaction and a sense of…rightness she'd never known as a kid.

She reached over and turned on one of a pair of dented brass lamps she'd found at an auction, and soft light spilled into the room. "I just need to get my purse." She stopped and looked at him. "You don't have to wear a tie, you know. You could…loosen up a little."

He smoothed one hand down the gray tie and said, "I came straight from work. And my gray tie is my loose tie."

She grinned at the spark of humor in his eyes. He really was the whole package. Smart. Funny. And so sexy it took her breath away. "Is that right?"

"Oh yeah." He nodded solemnly. "Red ties? Power. Navy? All business. Gray? Casual and loose."

"Wow, I didn't know they made a tie for 'casual.'"

"Now you do." He checked his watch. "What time is your appointment?"

"Twenty minutes or so. But he's in Seal Beach. It won't take long to get there."

"He?" Luke lifted one eyebrow. "What're you doing for 'him'?"

"It's a secret." Fiona smiled, grabbed her purse and headed for the door. "Let's go."

Seven

Whatever Luke had been expecting, this wasn't it. The "him" in question was seventeen, extremely tall and gangly, with a hank of hair that kept falling over his eyes, and he was going to his first prom in a few weeks. He needed to know how to dance.

"Ow!" Fiona hopped a little after the boy stepped on her foot for the third time.

Luke winced. This was painful to watch. How the hell did Fiona make a living doing all of these short-term jobs? Teaching a kid to dance. Finding an alligator. Now she'd probably be limping for a week.

"I'm never getting this."

"You're doing fine, Kenny," she said to the boy, who towered over her. "You just have to relax."

"How can I relax when I'm worried about stepping on you? I can't do this. I'll break Amber's foot." He shook his head and held both hands up. "I'll just stick to the fast dances."

Luke sighed and shook his head. He'd been watching this disaster for a half hour now, and he had to wonder how this kid was the star of the basketball team. He had zero rhythm. He was too tense, too. He held on to Fiona like she was a live grenade about to explode. He was probably more relaxed on the court, Luke thought. Hell, he'd have to be.

"Okay." He stood up and walked to Fiona. "Let's try something else." Talking to Kenny, he said, "You just sit down and watch." To Fiona, he added, "We'll show him how to do it."

How he'd gotten into this, he wasn't sure. Luke had thought about Fiona all day. What he'd wanted was to get her alone on a flat surface somewhere. Instead, he was slow dancing for a teenager in his parents' den.

"Oh, good idea," she said, and gave Kenny an encouraging smile. "Watch us for a minute or two, then we'll try again."

"It's useless." He swung his dark brown hair out of his eyes and scowled.

"Only if you quit," Luke said. Taking Fiona in his arms, he looked into her eyes, but his words were for Kenny. "Hold her closer."

"I can't hold on to Fiona like that. It's too weird, man."

"You're practicing," Luke reminded him. "You'll want to hold Amber close, right?"

"Well, yeah…"

"Okay. Hold her close." He pulled Fiona in tightly to him. "Put your feet in place before the music starts—on either side of one of her feet."

Kenny studied him. "Okay…"

"You don't have to be fancy about it. Going in circles

will get the job done for you." Luke started moving and paid no attention to Fiona's bright smile. She was enjoying this. Well, surprisingly enough, so was he.

The music played and Luke moved with it. "Listen to the beat and keep up with it. Slow or fast, if you stay with the beat you won't look uncoordinated."

"Hey!" Kenny the basketball star was offended.

"And you'll notice, I'm not stepping on her feet because I'm barely lifting mine."

"Yeah. That works…" Kenny nodded and looked a little less defeated.

"Her steps will follow yours in the dance. It's just instinct. You act like you know what you're doing, and it'll be fine." Of course, teenage hormones would be soaring. And he knew that because holding on to Fiona like this with the slow music streaming from the speakers on the wall made him want to pick her up and carry her out to the car.

Which meant, he told himself, lesson over. Luke stepped back and motioned to Kenny. "You try it now."

Fiona grinned at him, then gave Kenny an encouraging smile. "You can do this. And you'll be glad you did."

Kenny shrugged. "It's your feet."

"I'll risk it."

Luke stood aside and watched as Kenny did just as he'd been told. Fiona smiled up at the boy and, as the music played and they began to dance, Kenny visibly relaxed. It wasn't exactly an old Gene Kelly movie, but it was good enough for prom, and now the kid knew he could dance with his girlfriend without permanently maiming her.

The song ended and Kenny dropped Fiona like she was on fire. "That was awesome." He grinned and flashed a look at Luke. "Thanks, man. That works."

"You did fine."

Fiona asked, "Do you want to try it again? Just to make sure you've got it?"

"Don't have to. What he said made sense and now I know I can do it. Just plant my feet before the music."

"Excellent," Luke said.

"Okay, then." Fiona reached up and gave the kid a hug. "Lesson over. Have a great time at the dance, Kenny."

"I will now. Thanks." He jerked his hair out of his eyes and looked at Luke again. "Thanks. Really."

"You're welcome." He held out a hand and the kid shook it with a hard grip. "Have fun."

After Fiona collected a check from Kenny's grateful mother, they were outside on the front walk. Streetlights were on, casting pale white glows into the darkness. A crisp sea breeze kicked up and Fiona shivered. Automatically, he dropped one arm around her shoulders and pulled her in close.

"That was nice," she said. "What you did for Kenny."

"It was more for Amber. And you." He snorted. "I couldn't take it anymore. If I hadn't stepped in, you would have ended the night in a cast."

"It wasn't that bad." She laughed, though, and he liked the sound. "It's hard to teach a guy the guy's moves, so thanks for helping out."

"You're welcome." He looked down at her and felt his body stir again. Hell, since the moment he'd met this woman, his body had been like stone. "Not hard to sway back and forth and move in a circle."

She grinned at him. "It meant a lot to Kenny."

"Uh-huh." He couldn't have cared less about Kenny and his plans for a night of dancing and who the hell knew what else. What he'd done, he'd done for Fiona. To see that smile he was currently basking in.

He didn't like knowing that she was becoming more important to him than he cared to acknowledge. But even if his mind shied away from that thought, his body had no trouble admitting it.

"So?" she asked, and Luke was ready for any suggestion that would get them alone and naked. "Dinner. How about a burger?"

Her eyes sparkled and her lips were curved in that smile that drove him crazy. Not the idea he'd had in mind, but it'd do. For now.

The next morning, Fiona called Jamison Barrett on the direct number he'd given her. She had to report in on her weekend with Luke. Of course, she has no intention of telling the older man about what had happened on the plane. Or last night in her apartment, for that matter. She shivered a little at the images flooding her mind and knew she'd never be able to sleep in that bed again without Luke's memory joining her.

Jamison answered and Fiona jumped.

"Yes?" He sounded distracted. Maybe that was a good thing.

"Mr. Barrett," Fiona said, rising to walk across her living room. "This is Fiona Jordan."

"Hmm? Oh. Yes. Yes. Fiona. Hello."

Frowning, she stared out at the sun-washed street. "I just wanted you to know that the weekend with Luke went very well, and I think I'm making headway."

"That's good."

His voice sounded odd to her. Less confident. The last time she spoke to him, Jamison had been brisk, impatient. Now it seemed as if he wasn't even interested in what was happening with Luke. Was he having second thoughts? Was he sorry he'd hired her in the first place?

Because Fiona could completely understand regrets. She regretted ever lying to Luke. But she couldn't be sorry she'd taken this job, because if she hadn't, she never would have met him, and she couldn't even imagine not knowing him.

How did this whole situation get so confused and tangled up? Luke loved his grandfather but couldn't work with him. Jamison loved his grandson but couldn't compromise. And Fiona? Fiona was in the middle, unsure which way to turn.

Still, she tried. "I'm seeing him again today and—"

"Right. You just get it done and we'll talk then. All right? Thank you."

He hung up and Fiona took the phone from her ear to stare at it. For a man who was so determined to win his grandson back, he seemed decidedly uninterested in hearing the report he had asked for. What was going on?

When Jamison hung up, Fiona went straight out of his mind. He had bigger problems at the moment. He stared at the contract in front of him and felt panic clawing at the edges of his soul.

His signature was on the bottom line, but damned if he remembered signing it. "Why the hell would I order skateboards from a new company when I've already got Salem's boards?"

Didn't make sense. But then, lately nothing was making sense, and Jamison felt a fresh stir of fear. And he didn't like that, either. He'd faced a lot in his lifetime. He lost his father in a world war, the loss of his sons. He'd fought his way through bad times before and he would this time, too.

He knew Cole was worried about him. And it wouldn't be long before he saw the same look of concern on Loretta's face, too. Jamison didn't think he could stand that. Maybe it was time to talk to his doctor. Get to the bottom of this. Bill Tucker was a no-nonsense kind of man. He'd be straight with Jamison. And maybe, he admitted silently, that was why he hadn't gone to see him yet. He was afraid of what Bill might have to say.

Loretta claimed it was nothing, but he couldn't help worrying. He'd seen friends diagnosed with dementia. He'd watched them slowly fade away until there was nothing of them left, and it terrified him to believe that might be happening to him.

"Pop?" Cole poked his head in the door.

"Yes." He looked up. "What is it?"

"I wanted to ask you about the order for basketballs you canceled."

"What? I didn't cancel an order." Did he?

Cole stepped into the room and his features were twisted into a mask of worry that ate at Jamison's insides. "I just got a call from Adam Carey, and he says he got the cancellation late last night."

"Last night?" Shaking his head, Jamison jumped to his feet. That should be proof that he wasn't doing this. That he hadn't lost his mind. "I was out with your grandmother last night. We went to the club for dinner…"

Cole winced and handed out the email he'd printed out. "Adam forwarded the email to me, Pop. It's definitely from you. Went out about ten last night."

Jamison studied it and an icy ball dropped into the pit of his stomach. It was from his email address. Canceling an order. But he didn't do it. Crumpling the paper in his fist, he looked at Cole. "I didn't send this."

"Pop…" Cole scrubbed one hand across his neck and looked as if he wished he were anywhere else.

Jamison knew the feeling.

"Damn it, boy, stop looking at me like I'm dying."

"I don't like this, Pop."

"Well, neither do I. Look, I don't know what's going on here, but I didn't send this." He tossed the offensive wad of paper into the trash, then sat down behind his desk again. "I'll call Adam. Set things straight."

"Good luck. He's pretty pissed."

"I said I'll take care of it." He looked back at the file on his desk, silently dismissing Cole. But his grandson didn't leave.

"Pop, do you think maybe we should talk to a doctor?"

"We?" Jamison speared his grandson with a steely look. Damned if he'd be treated like a slobbering old fool. "You having a problem you didn't tell me about?"

Cole took a breath. "Fine. You, then. Pop, you seem to be having some trouble lately, and I want you to know that I'm here." The younger man moved closer, leaned both hands on the edge of the desk and said, "I can take over for you. Handle things while you take a break. Maybe you just need a long rest."

If what he was hearing was simple familial concern, then Jamison should have been touched. But he knew that there was nothing Cole would like better than stepping into the CEO job. He'd been angling for it for years.

"How long a break, Cole? Forever?" Jamison loved his grandson, but he knew Cole's ambitions far exceeded his talents.

"You know, I'm not saying that." He pushed up from the desk. "But with Luke gone, I'm the one you can trust to take over. Pop, I'm here. Use me."

Irritation rushed in and was swamped by regret for thinking badly of Cole. Sure, he had a lot of ambition, but so had Jamison at his age. It wasn't Cole's fault now that his grandfather's brain was taking a vacation. "I know that. And I appreciate it. But I'm not ready to quit. And we don't know that Luke's gone for good, either."

Cole pushed one hand through his hair in frustration. "Luke isn't your only grandson, Pop. He isn't the only Barrett who's worked at the company since he was a kid. He's not the only man who could run this company."

There was a lot of bitterness there. More than he'd suspected.

"You're getting worked up for nothing, Cole." Jamison shook his head and tried to understand that Cole's jealousy of his cousin was probably Jamison's fault. He'd always favored Luke because he'd seen himself in the boy. He knew that Luke was the one to run this company into the next generation. Cole was good at what he did, but he wasn't qualified to be the CEO.

It was never easy to admit unpleasant truths, but Jamison had faced it years ago. Cole, though, would never accept his own limits. Then again, maybe he shouldn't. If a person started putting limitations on what he thought he could do, then he'd never do anything.

"Am I?" Cole threw both hands up in complete exasperation. "I'm tired of being overlooked in favor of the man who left the company. Luke left. He walked out on you, Pop, and you *still* prefer him? I'm *here*. I stayed. I'm the one who gives a damn about the company. And you."

"I know." Jamison forced a smile. Truth be told, he wasn't up for a conflict right now. There were too many worries riding his possibly failing brain. Plus, he was already at war with one grandson. Did he really want another one?

"You're a good man, Cole," he said, hoping to placate him. "And I know you'll be there for me if I need you to step in. I just don't need it yet."

Clearly still irritated, Cole said, "You sure about that? You're losing it, Pop, and we both know it."

"No," he said flatly. He wasn't about to share his worries with Cole and get the man even more worked up than he already was. "We don't. Now I've got work to do and I'm sure you do, too."

"Fine." Cole shook his head and blew out a breath. "Call Adam. Straighten it out. I'm meeting Susan and Oliver at the yacht club for lunch. I'll probably just go home from there."

Jamison nodded, unsurprised. But he couldn't help thinking, *there,* Cole. That's why you're not the one. You leave in the middle of the day. Nearly every damn day. Jamison was all for spending time with your family, but there were responsibilities to be taken care of as well. Cole ran himself ragged trying to make Susan happy and paid little if any attention to the business that's keeping them both living in their mansion in Dana Point.

Cole stormed out, and Jamison rubbed his aching temples. If Luke didn't come back, he didn't think the company would survive. Hell, at this point, he wasn't sure *he* would survive.

And on that happy thought, he picked up the phone, dialed a number and said, "Adam? Jamison Barrett here. What's all this nonsense about a canceled order?"

Fiona loved the beach in winter. The sand was empty but for a few die-hard souls and the waves only called to the most dedicated surfers. In February, the sea looked slate gray and the wind that blew past them was sharp and icy. The waves crashed on the shore, then slid back where they'd come from in lacy patterns they left behind on the wet sand.

She tipped her face into the wind and smiled. The

only thing better than taking a winter walk on the beach was having Luke with her.

"I can't believe this is your view. Every day." She took a deep breath, drawing the damp sea air deep inside her. Holding her hair down, she looked up at him. "If I lived here, I'd be down on the beach every chance I got."

"Don't have many chances." He tucked a piece of her hair behind her ear and trailed his fingers down her cheek. Fiona shivered at his touch and wondered if she always would.

"Work keeps me busy," he added with a shrug.

"And your phone…" Her tone was teasing, but her words weren't.

He scowled at her. "I left it back at the house, didn't I?"

"And is not having it driving you crazy?"

"No. *You* are."

She smiled. "There you go, saying nice things again."

"I don't know what it is about you, Fiona." His gaze moved over her features before settling on her eyes. "When I'm with you I have to touch you. When I'm not with you, I'm thinking about you."

"I feel the same way," she said softly.

He pulled her into his arms and Fiona went willingly. Being with him now was worth the price she would eventually have to pay. Reaching up, she cupped his cheeks in her palms and told herself that later on, she wouldn't regret this time with him. If memories were all she was going to have, then she wanted a lot of them burned into her mind so that she'd never forget a moment of the time spent with Luke. She'd never taken something for herself. Not like this. And when this time with Luke was over, she might never feel like this again.

He turned his face into her palm and kissed it, sending pearls of heat tumbling through her. Fiona was in such deep trouble, and she didn't care. What she felt for Luke was so unexpected, such a gift, she couldn't turn away from it.

"How about we go back to my house?"

They'd stopped at his house for a drink after seeing a movie she couldn't even remember. And now all she could think was, she wanted to be inside, where people couldn't see them. Inside, where she could touch him and be touched.

"That sounds good," she said, and turned with him to walk back across the sand.

At night, his home shone like a jewel. It was right on the beach and built as if it belonged in Spain. The arched windows, the red-tiled entrance, and the trailing vines and flowers that swept across the second story all spoke of sun-drenched days and long, warm nights.

"I love your house."

"I did, too."

"Did?" She turned her face up to his.

"Yeah, I'm moving," he said. "To a cliff view where thousands of beachgoers aren't in my front yard every summer."

He had a point. The beach in winter was secluded, quiet. But the same spot in summer would be noisy and crowded and—still beautiful. "I suppose I can understand that, but I would miss the beach…"

He pulled her in close, one arm around her shoulders. "At the new house, there's a path down to the sand. And the house is close to my grandparents. They're getting older and—"

She stopped, drawing him to a stop, too. "You won't work for your grandfather, but you'll move to live closer to him?"

He stepped back and shoved both hands into his pockets—he did own a pair of jeans and looked spectacular in them. Squinting into the wind, he said, "Just because I left the company doesn't mean I left the family."

Why couldn't he see that his grandfather was convinced that that was exactly what it meant? To Jamison Barrett, the toy company was an extension of the family. Having Luke walk away from it made Jamison feel he was leaving *them* behind as well.

"So why do you insist on staying away from the company? That *is* your family, isn't it? Why not just work through your problems with your grandfather?" Fiona looked at this conversation as an opportunity she had to take advantage of. "Like you said, they're getting older. Why not compromise?"

He seemed to think about it for a long moment before answering. The wind ruffled his hair; moonlight glittered in his eyes when he met her gaze. "Because I've got to prove this to Pop. And maybe," he said, "to myself, too. I'm right about the technological future."

"But it's Barrett Toys and *Tech*. Isn't he already compromising with you?"

"No." His features went hard and closed. "It's compromise on his terms. He'll toss me a bone, but we'd still be doing things his way. He wants to dial the tech back while I believe it should be expanded." He looked at the churning sea and talked almost to himself. "Kids today are hungry for more and more tech. Why wouldn't we want to get in on giving it to them?"

"Oh, Luke. Just because a kid wants something doesn't mean they should have it."

He whipped his head back to look into her eyes. Surprise etched on his face, he asked, "You're on his side in this?"

"I'm on nobody's side," she assured him, holding up both hands in a peace offering.

"Thanks," he muttered.

She wanted to sigh. Any other time, she'd be happy to be on his side. But in this case, Fiona thought his grandfather had a point. "I'm just saying that because something is new and shiny doesn't make it better. Like you said yourself, technology isn't going away. It's the future. Why do kids have to learn it when they should be out playing baseball or surfing or whatever?"

"Because tech is part of the society that they're growing up in. Adapting young means they'll be more flexible when tech keeps changing," he argued.

A couple holding hands walked past them but neither of them noticed. Fiona couldn't look away from Luke's eyes. This was her chance to talk to him about the rift between him and his grandfather. Yes, it was her job to convince him, but more than that, she knew what it was like to not have a family. She didn't want to watch him throw away what she'd never had.

"Did you know," she asked quietly, "that doctors are actually seeing cases of severe language delays due to screens?"

That statement caught him off guard. "What?"

Fiona had done a lot of reading on this subject, and there were studies that supported both Luke's and his grandfather's opinions. But if you were dealing with the *chance* of doing permanent harm to a child's mind, wouldn't you take the more careful route?

"You said it yourself, there are a lot of studies—good and bad—being done. Well," she said, "I saw an article about it, and I thought it sounded weird, so I read it. Apparently, small children who spend many hours a day on screens—phones, tablets—don't develop normal language skills. Their brains are being rewired."

Luke frowned and shook his head. Bracing his feet wide apart, he folded his arms across his chest and shook his head. "I can point you to studies that say the exact opposite."

"I guess," Fiona said. "But it's scary to think about, right? This article said some toddlers have had to seek speech therapy to make up their delays. And teenagers are spending eight to twelve hours a *day* online."

His frown deepened and she wouldn't have thought that possible. "Anything can be bad if overdone."

"True." Fiona laid one hand on his forearm. "But see, that's the thing. They're kids. They're going to overdo. And according to this article, most parents are unaware of the negative consequences for their kids spending so much time on screens."

His stance relaxed a bit, but his eyes narrowed on her in suspicion. "Fiona, what are you up to?"

Slow it down, she told herself. Shaking her head, she said, "Nothing. Honestly. It's just that we've been talking about this since we met, and I decided to research it. Some kids are being digitally distracted from the real world."

"And you think that's what I'm doing?"

"Not deliberately, of course not."

The wind slapped at them both, whipping her hair across her eyes, and she pushed it free. Luke stood in front of her like a glowering giant, readying for battle. "We're selling screens. Tablets. We're not even trying to get into the video game market."

"But you sell reading games and swirling color games for toddlers," she argued. "Isn't that priming them to want to play as much as they can, and to want more involved games later?"

"Maybe." That glowering frown deepened. "I hadn't considered it, but I guess there is a case to be made for what you're saying."

"Luke, why don't you talk to your grandfather about all of this? I'm trying to see both sides and maybe your grandfather is feeling that his company is about family. And that you're walking away not just from the business, but from him. You never know. He might be more willing to compromise now that you've been gone for a while."

"No. Pop knows I love him. This isn't about that." He snorted and started walking toward the house again. "I'm willing to give on a couple of points you made. And I'm going to look into the research more deeply. But when it comes to my grandfather, you're wrong, Fiona. You don't know him like I do."

Fiona had to hurry her steps to keep up with him. Had she pushed too hard, too fast?

"People change, Luke."

"Not him, Fiona." His voice was low and almost lost in the driving wind and the throaty roar of the ocean. "I'm not saying you're completely wrong."

That was something, she told herself, so she gave him more to think about. "That article I read, it had a lot of really interesting points. The doctor wrote that screens are bad for kids, because they *need* to communicate face-to-face with other people. That it's essential for their social and emotional development."

He stopped right outside his home's enclosed patio. Plexiglass panels lifted off what looked like adobe but was probably stucco walls, to allow the view while protecting people on the patio from the fierce wind. There were chairs and tables and even a pizza oven tucked into one corner of the patio. But at the moment, all Fiona could see was Luke.

He tipped his head to one side and stared at her. "Did you *memorize* this article?"

She winced. "Sounds like it, doesn't it?"

"Sounds like you're trying to convince me that my grandfather's right."

Fiona stepped in close to him and laid one hand on his chest. "In a way, I guess I am."

He curled his hand around hers and held on. The faint wash of lights from his house fell across them. From somewhere nearby, a stereo played, and music drifted almost lazily on the wind.

"He's not right to turn his back on the future," Luke said softly.

"No, he's not." There must be a compromise, but he and his grandfather had to really talk to find it. "I'm not saying you're completely wrong, or that he's completely right. I'm just saying that maybe the world has enough room for technology *and* teddy bears. Imagination is important, too, right?"

"Of course it is," he agreed with a half-smile. "But my toys don't destroy imagination."

"No, but your designers make such great games and tech toys, the kids don't have to use their *own* imaginations because your guys did it for them." She moved in closer and hooked both hands behind his neck. "Maybe there's a middle ground."

"If there is," he muttered, as his arms snaked around her waist, "I haven't found it yet."

Tipping her head to one side, she met his gaze and asked quietly, "Have you really looked?"

He stared into her eyes for what felt like forever. She couldn't read his thoughts, but the expression on his face clearly said he wasn't happy. Finally, he said, "No, I guess I haven't. I was so busy trying to prove I was right, I never really thought about meeting him halfway. Or even if there *is* a halfway."

She smiled at him and told herself not to celebrate. This didn't mean he'd go back to his family company. But it did mean he was willing to consider his options and maybe that was enough.

"You could talk to your grandfather…"

Nodding, he admitted, "I do miss that old hardhead."

She grinned. "I envy you your family, Luke. I never had that. When I was a child, I would have given anything for a family of my own. And, like you just said, he's getting old. Do you really want to let this keep you apart until it's too late to fix it?"

His features tightened, and she could see that she'd given him more to think about. She was glad. Everything she'd said hadn't just been to serve this job. After Jamison hired her, Fiona had done research on kids and electronics, and some of the statistics had worried her.

She knew Luke was excited about this road he was on, but she thought that maybe he hadn't considered all the ramifications of pushing kids too hard into a digital world. If he was going to rethink some of his opinions, that was a good thing.

And maybe, she thought wistfully, one day, he'd look back on this time with her and smile. Maybe he wouldn't hate her once he'd found out she'd lied to him. Maybe…

"Why am I listening to you?" he asked, shaking his head.

"Because you're brilliant and insightful?"

"Yeah," he said, bending his head to kiss her. "That must be it."

Eight

The taste of her put everything else out of Luke's mind.

He liked talking to her. Even liked arguing with her, because she wasn't afraid to state her opinion and then defend it. She made him laugh. Made him think. Even about things he didn't want to consider.

But there was nothing like touching her. The rush of heat that overtook him every damn time kept him coming back to her. He didn't want or need a relationship. But for now, he needed Fiona.

He'd never meant for this—whatever it was between them—to continue beyond that long weekend in San Francisco. But the more time he spent with her, the more time he wanted with her. That thought should have worried Luke, and maybe it would. Later. But at the moment, all he could think was to feed the need devouring him.

Luke lost himself in Fiona just as he did every time he kissed her. Her scent, her taste, the hot, lush feel of her body pressed to his. He wanted it all. Wanted her more every time he had her.

Even with the icy ocean wind pummeling them from all sides, even with the lights of the house illuminating them for anyone to see, even with the fact that she'd just shot down some of his theories on technology for kids, he wanted her.

This kiss in the night wouldn't be enough. Tearing his mouth from hers, he looked down into chocolate-brown eyes that were swimming with passion and the kind of need that was nearly choking him.

"Come inside with me," he said, voice low and tight.

"Yes." She leaned into him more fully. "Oh, yes."

He gave her a quick grin, then grabbed her hand and tugged her along behind him. Across the patio, through the front door, and locked it after them. Up the stairs on the right to the landing and then down the hall to his bedroom.

Luke pulled Fiona into the room, then kicked the door shut behind them. She was laughing. Damn it, she was laughing and something inside him turned over. That wide smile, her bright brown eyes sparkling with humor and heat.

Of course he wanted her.

"In a hurry?" she finally asked, moving into his arms.

"Damn right I am," he assured her, pulling her in tight, using his hands, up and down her back to mold her body to his. He held her against his aching groin so she could feel exactly why he'd nearly run her legs off to get to this room with its massive bed.

"Me, too," she said, sliding her hands across his chest until he grabbed those hands and held them in a tight grip.

While they stood there, she looked around quickly. "I like your bedroom."

He knew what she was seeing. Pale gray walls, bookcases, flat-screen TV, forest green duvet covering his massive bed, and wide windows that overlooked the ocean. Because of those windows, Luke reached over and hit a switch on the wall. Instantly, heavy, dark green drapes slid soundlessly across the windows, throwing the room into darkness.

"Wow. A housekeeper. A cook. And you don't even have to close your own curtains," she whispered.

He grinned. "I did flip the switch."

"You're right. You're practically a frontiersman." She laughed again and everything in Luke fisted.

"Enough talking," he announced, and picked her up. She was tall, which he liked, and curvy, which he *really* liked, and she felt great in his arms.

He dropped her onto the bed and that amazing laugh bubbled out of her again. He'd never been with a woman who laughed before, during and after sex. He liked it. It was somehow *more* because of that ease, that companionable laughter.

Luke switched on a bedside lamp because damn it, he wanted to see her. She lay stretched out across the bed like a beautifully wrapped present. Her black slacks and green long-sleeved shirt were like the wrappings, and he couldn't wait to undo it all.

As he watched, she undid the buttons on her shirt and then sat up to shrug it off, leaving behind only a pale pink lace bra that barely covered the breasts he wanted to indulge himself in.

"You're amazing," he muttered.

"I'm happy you think so," she whispered.

Luke tore his clothes off and tossed them onto a chair

in the corner. Her eyes widened as she looked at him, and the expression on her face only fed the fires building inside him. Reaching down, he unhooked her slacks and slid them down and off her beautiful legs. The pale pink panties were next, and she lifted her hips to help him get them off. And then she was there, spread out before him like a feast.

Luke didn't waste a moment. He dragged her closer, then took her with his mouth. She gasped, lifted her hips again and cried out his name.

Sweetest sound he'd ever heard. Luke took his time, tasting, licking, nibbling at the core of her. Her heat swamped him, her shrieks and groans fed the need to give her more. To take more. He drove her to the ragged edge, while her fingers threaded through his hair and held his head to her. His hands cupped her butt and squeezed, his tongue swept over her innermost depths, and when he felt her nearly ready to shatter, he stopped.

"No, don't. Don't you dare leave me hanging like this." She lifted her head and fired a hard stare at him.

He grinned at her, then with a quick move, flipped her over onto her stomach. "Just getting started, Fiona."

She whipped her hair out of her face and looked back at him over her shoulder. "You're making me crazy."

"Well, it's about time. You've been doing that to me since we met."

Amazingly enough, she laughed again, and Luke told himself there was no one else like her. But who had time for revelations now?

"Up on your knees, Fiona…"

She stared at him for a long moment, then licked her lips in anticipation and did what he asked.

Still holding her gaze, he inched back off the bed and stood there a second or two before pulling her back toward him. When her butt was close enough, he smoothed his palms over it, squeezing, kneading, until she was moaning his name and rocking her hips in a futile search for the release he kept denying her.

Luke grabbed a condom from the bedside drawer, sheathed himself, then pushed himself deep inside her. Instantly, he groaned, and she gave a soft sigh of completion. It wasn't enough. It would never be enough. Being inside her heat, a part of her, yet separate, felt right. But the aching need to shatter pushed at him and Luke responded.

Again and again, he took her. He held her hips steady and moved his own, claiming her body, giving her his. He set a rhythm that she eagerly raced to meet. The only sounds in the room were their combined groans and the beautiful slap of flesh against flesh.

Luke gave himself over to the sensations pouring through him. He looked at her, listened to her and let her reactions multiply his own. When her gasping cries and shuddering body told him she was about to climax, he pushed her harder, faster until she called out his name on a high, thin scream and shattered in his hands.

A moment later, Luke let himself find the same shaking release, and he knew that nothing else would ever compare to what he shared with Fiona.

And as he swept her up into his arms, then lay down on the bed with her cuddled in close to his side, Luke realized that that admission should scare the hell out of him.

Later that night, Fiona stopped at Laura's because she had to talk to someone. Having that argument with Luke, fighting to make him see her side—his grandfather's side—had been nerve-racking. If she didn't push hard enough, nothing changed. If she pushed too hard, she'd lose him—even before she'd managed to complete her job and get him to go back to his family.

Then being with him, making love in that beautiful beach house, wrapped in his arms, feeling her own world shatter again and again. The whole night had filled her with an anxiety she didn't know how to deal with. She wanted this to be forever. And she knew it wouldn't— couldn't be. Because to stay with him, she'd have to confess to her lie. And if she did that, she'd lose him anyway. His was a world of black-and-white, right and wrong. And lying was wrong.

Mike answered the door. "Hey, Fiona."

He was wearing worn jeans and a black T-shirt. His hair was rumpled and whiskers stubbled his jaws.

"Hi, Mike. Sorry it's so late." Not really all that late. About eleven, but she still felt guilty for showing up out of the blue. Especially since Mike worked construction and would be out of the house at the crack of dawn.

"No problem." He pushed the screen door open and waved her inside. "Laura's in the kitchen baking cookies."

When Fiona looked at him in confusion, he shrugged.

"I don't ask why anymore." Smiling, he said, "Go on back. Have a cookie."

"Right. Thanks." She walked through the living room and found Laura, as promised, taking a tray of cookies out of the oven. Fiona wasn't even tempted to grab one, which only proved how torn up she was inside.

Laura looked up and blew a lock of hair out of her eyes. "Hey, you're home early. Usually when you're with Luke it's a lot later—or even," she said with a grin, "the next morning."

"I've got an early job in Lakewood tomorrow."

Laura nodded. "Cookie?"

"No, thanks." She slid onto a barstool beneath the island counter.

"Uh-oh. If chocolate chip cookies can't tempt you, something is seriously wrong."

"Pretty much." Fiona braced both elbows on the granite counter and covered her face with her hands. Too many different emotions were stirring inside her at once. The memory of being with Luke made her blood burn, but the memory of talking to him, trying to make him change his mind about his family, his business, made her want to come clean. Her lie of omission was tearing at her. "It's a mess."

"Start talking," Laura set the hot tray onto the stove top to cool off, then went for a bottle of wine in the fridge. She poured two glasses, handed one to Fiona, took a sip of her own and waited.

"I don't even know where to start." She was in so deep now, she couldn't imagine a way out. Even if she told Luke the truth now, would it be enough to make up for lying to him for so long?

And wouldn't it put him and his grandfather at odds, too, if he found out the older man had hired someone to bring him back to the business?

Fiona stared at the sunlight-colored wine and finally drank some, if only to ease the tightness in her throat. "It's Luke."

"Yes." Laura leaned both elbows on the countertop. "I cleverly deduced that. What about him?"

Fingers absently twirling the stem of her wineglass, Fiona muttered, "I think I've about convinced him to make up with his grandfather."

"That's good news," Laura said, until Fiona's gaze met hers. Then she added, "Or not."

She gave her friend a strained smile. "No, it is. It really is. I mean, that is why his grandfather hired me. So that's good. But, Laura, there's a problem."

"You're in love with him."

Gaping at her best friend, Fiona could only nod. "I don't know how you know when I only just figured it out myself on the way home."

Laura patted her hand. "Oh, Fiona, it wasn't hard. You light up when you see him. You talk about him all the time. And you look at him like I look at Mike."

"Oh God." She scooped one hand through her still-windblown hair and took another drink of her wine. "This wasn't supposed to happen."

"Everybody says that." Laura took another sip of wine and shrugged.

"This is different, though." Shaking her head, she had another sip of wine and felt the cool slide through her system. "This started out as a job. I wasn't supposed to care about him, let alone *love* him. Plus, I've been lying to him, Laura. Right from the beginning."

She shrugged. "So tell him the truth."

"I can't do that."

"Why not? It's not exactly a wild idea."

Probably not to most rational people, but Fiona was feeling far from rational at the moment. "But if I tell him, I'll lose him. Not to mention that he'd be furious with his grandfather and how can I do that? Luke has hard lines between right and wrong, and a lie from me is going to fall on the 'wrong' side for sure."

"Hard lines get erased or moved all the time."

"Not by Luke."

Laura set her glass aside. "Sweetie, if you don't tell him, you've lost him anyway. You'll never really have him because you'll have that lie between you and it will make you crazy."

She was right, and Fiona really didn't want her to be right.

"Or worse, what if his family tells him what's been going on? What if he makes up with his grandfather and the old man brags about how he hired you to make it happen?"

Well, that was a horrifying thought. Fiona didn't believe Jamison would do that, because he wouldn't look good, either. But it could happen; her secret wasn't safe.

"Telling him the truth is really your only shot."

"And I really don't want it to be," Fiona admitted. God, she could still feel Luke's arms around her. Taste his mouth on hers. The thought of losing him now was almost more than she could take.

"Honey, I know that." Laura turned and grabbed two still-warm cookies off the tray and handed one to Fiona. "But at least once it's done, you'll know where you really stand."

Fiona took a bite because she felt obligated, but as good a baker as Laura was, the cookie tasted like sawdust. Fiona didn't have to find out where she would stand when she told Luke the truth. She knew exactly where she would be standing.

On the outside looking in.

By the following afternoon, Luke was more torn than ever. He left work early because he just couldn't concentrate. Fiona stayed in his mind all the time now. Not just images of her, or the memories of incredible sex. It was her words haunting him, too. Everything she'd said the night before kept echoing in his brain, forcing him to sort through too many thoughts at once, struggling to make sense of everything and find the right path to take.

It wasn't just Fiona, either. Since meeting her, he'd become more aware, somehow. He'd noticed how people were attached to their phones. He saw little kids in restaurants, eyes on screens filled with laughing cartoon characters or brightly colored patterns. He realized that technology, while a boon to civilization—which he still believed—also had a downside.

It could keep families from staying connected.

Standing on his patio, staring out at the ocean, Luke had to wonder if his brilliant idea to hook small children on technology was the right path to take. He still believed technology was the wave of the future and that he wanted to be a part of it.

But everything Fiona had said to him the night before had sparked enough concern that he'd done more research of his own—all morning. And what he'd found had him second-and third-guessing himself. She'd been right about all of it. Kids were getting more and more isolated. Teen anxiety and depression rates were up, and toddlers were turning up with language delays after spending too much time with screens and not enough time talking with the grown-ups caring for them.

Scowling now, he took a sip of coffee and watched a lone surfer grab a wave and ride it to shore. "Another thing Fiona was right about," he muttered. "I'm going to miss being right on the ocean like this."

But wasn't that quandary a lot like his other problem at the moment? To live on the beach meant putting up with thousands of strangers staring in his windows or tossing trash onto his patio. Like being too involved with electronics cost a kid his own imagination. His own dreams.

He was moving to a cliffside house to protect his privacy. He was giving up what looked great for the right to make his life what he wanted it to be. Shouldn't he give his customers the same chance? By pushing tablets and screens on small children, wasn't he metaphorically tossing trash onto their patios?

"Damn it, Fiona." He gulped at his coffee and felt the burn as it scalded its way down his throat.

Do you really want to let this keep you apart until it's too late to fix it?

Her words had been circling his brain for hours.

Of course he didn't want Jamison to die with this stupid argument between them. Hell, he didn't want Jamison to die, period. And Luke was half convinced the old man was immortal. He was always so strong. So confident. So totally in control.

And Luke had turned out just like him. No wonder they clashed. Neither one of them was willing to give an inch. Back either one of them into a corner and they'd fight like mad to hold on to what they thought was right. Which meant that neither of them had ever learned how to bend.

On that thought, Luke pulled his phone from his back pocket and hit speed dial for his grandfather's office.

"Barrett."

"Cole?" Luke asked, recognizing his cousin's voice instantly. "What are you doing answering Pop's phone?"

"Pop's not here today," Cole said. "He took a personal day."

"Has there been an apocalypse nobody told me about?" Luke frowned at the phone. "Pop never takes a day off."

Cole sighed heavily. "He's eighty years old, Luke.

For God's sake, can't the man take a nap without your say-so?"

"He's *napping*?" Something was wrong. Jamison lived on about five hours sleep a night. Always had. And he had more energy than any ten men. Naps? Personal days? This was not Jamison Barrett.

"Did you expect him to live forever?" Cole countered. "He's an old man. You left and that changed everything for him. But I'm still here so I'm helping out."

That stung. Mostly because it was true. "Fine. Is he at home?"

"Yes, and don't call him."

"Excuse me?" Anger buzzed around like a hornet inside his mind.

"He needs the rest, Luke. He doesn't need you calling to argue with him again." Cole took a breath and said, "Look, I didn't want to say anything, but Pop's furious with you. Feels like you deserted him."

Regret and pain tangled together inside him, but Luke didn't argue with Cole. What would be the point? Besides, it wasn't his cousin he had to talk to. It was Pop.

"Just leave him be."

More emotions gathered inside him, nearly choking him. Since when did Cole call the shots not only for the company but for the family? "Yeah, thanks. Think I'll talk to him anyway."

"You would," Cole said. "Never think about the old man. Just do what Luke wants. That sounds right."

There was more bitterness than usual in his voice and Luke wondered what else was going on. "What's your problem, Cole?"

"Same as always," his cousin said. "You." He hung up before Luke could say anything.

"Well, damn. Things have gone downhill fast." He'd talked to his grandfather just before the San Francisco trip and he'd been fine. Pissed off, but fine. A little more than a week later, to hear Cole tell it, Jamison was at death's door and Cole was the new sheriff in town.

Luke turned his face into the wind, hoping that the icy air would sweep away all the conflicting, troubling thoughts. Naturally, it didn't work. He had some things to do, but when he was finished, he'd be going to his grandparents' house to settle things.

Jamison had had enough. Damned if he'd sit back and wait for the proverbial ax to fall. He had always been a big believer that it was better to *know* something than to worry or guess about it.

And the last straw had been that contract that he'd supposedly signed. He knew damn well he hadn't. So what the hell was going on with him?

"I hate doctors' offices," he muttered. Impersonal, almost terrifying places that were cold, clinical, where the pale green walls seemed to have absorbed years of worry and then echoed it back into whoever happened to be in there. He shot a dirty look at the examination table and stayed right where he was in the most uncomfortable chair in the world. "I hate being here."

"Hey, me, too." Dr. Bill Tucker walked in, closed the door and then sat down on a chair opposite Jamison. "What say we blow this place?"

Jamison grinned in spite of the situation. Bill Tucker had been his doctor for twenty years. Somewhere in his sixties, Bill had gray hair, kind brown eyes and a permanent smile etched onto his face. Not one of those plastic *it'll be all right* smiles, but a real one. And today, Jamison needed to see it.

"What's going on, Jamie? Didn't expect to see you until your physical in a couple months."

"This couldn't wait." God, he hated this. Hated thinking he was losing his mind. Hated even more that someone might be trying to *convince* him he was going crazy.

Jamison had created what he'd always thought of as a family atmosphere at Barrett's. Had one of the people who'd worked for him for years turned on him? Why? It was the only thing that could explain what was happening to him, though he hated to consider it.

Bill gave him a rare frown. "Okay, tell me."

Jamison did, and as he told the story, he began to feel better. More in control. He wasn't being a passive observer to his own destruction anymore. He was finally doing something about it.

By the time he was finished, Bill wasn't smiling, but he didn't look worried, either.

"Jamie, that's a strange tale." He sat back and seemed to be mulling over his thoughts. "I don't think you've got anything to worry about, but we'll do some tests. Starting with the SLUMS cognitive test."

"Slums?"

Bill smiled again. "It's an acronym for the Saint Louis University Mental Status test. It's fast and will give us an idea of whether or not further testing will be necessary."

Worry erupted in his belly again, but this time Jamison pushed it aside. He was done agonizing without information. If there was something wrong, he'd fix it. Or find someone who could.

"Fine. When do we start?"

Bill nodded sharply. "I'll go get the test, and we can start right away."

Alone again, Jamison went over the whole strange story in his mind and tried to figure out exactly when things had started going badly. He couldn't pin it down to a specific day, but he knew damn well that he'd been fine a couple of months ago.

"And I'm fine now, too."

He needed to believe it, because anything else was just unacceptable.

Fiona had spent the morning tracking down a band that had once played at her client's high school dance, because the client wanted the same band to play at her wedding. In the last few years, that band had built an audience and, now, it spent a lot of time on the road, opening for bigger acts. Fiona's client knew the odds of making this happen were long, but she really wanted it because she and her fiancé had met at one of those school dances.

It should have taken forever, but Fiona had a friend in the business who gave her the number of the band's agent.

Once she explained the request to the woman, she put Fiona in touch with the band's lead singer. He was so flattered at the request, he not only agreed to do the wedding, but he wasn't going to charge them a thing. Especially after Fiona pointed out to him that a story like this was publicity gold.

The bride was ecstatic at the news, but once that call had been made, Fiona was left with her own troubling thoughts again. She had to tell Luke the truth. But before she did that, it was only fair that she let Jamison Barrett know what she was planning. She hoped he would understand, though she knew he might not, since Luke would be furious not only with her, but with his grandfather.

But there was no other choice. If she wanted a chance

at long-term with Luke, and she did, then she had to remove the lie standing between them like a solid wall.

She didn't have to meet her next client for an hour, so there was no time like now to get the chat with Jamison over and done.

Fiona dialed, took a deep breath and let it out when a familiar voice said simply, "Fiona."

"Yes." As usual, she paced aimlessly in her apartment and for the first time, wished for more space. Wished she were at Luke's house so she could simply walk out onto the sand and feel the wind in her face.

"Now isn't the best time." His voice was short. Tense. "But I'll be calling you tomorrow to talk about a new job."

"What?" She hadn't been expecting that at all. He sounded better than he had the last time she spoke with him, and she was glad of it. But it was the current job she had to talk to him about. "Mr. Barrett…"

"Sorry, Fiona, no time." He hung up and Fiona was left hanging again.

"Now what?" she muttered darkly.

He had "no time" to hear about the job he'd hired her for? That didn't make sense. And he wanted to hire her for something else? What was going on with Luke's grandfather? And oh boy, did she wish she could talk to Luke about all of this. But she couldn't. Because of the lies.

Which brought her back to: she had to tell Luke everything and try to explain. Just the thought of that turned her stomach and made her regret ever getting into this in the first place. Although if she hadn't accepted the job from Jamison Barrett, she never would have met Luke at all.

God, she had a headache.

If she didn't tell Luke soon, he might find out on his own. And that would be worse. But if she did tell him without first telling his grandfather, that wouldn't be fair to the older man.

She was still caught. Trapped. In her own lie.

Nine

"Mr. Barrett. I didn't expect you here today."

Luke glanced at the other man. One of his top marketing guys, David Fontenot, was tall, blond and tanned. As the head of market research for Luke's new company, Dave ran the focus groups brought in to try out their new products. He knew how to read the kids' reactions to the tech they were introduced to and knew exactly how to push those products in the best markets.

"I wanted to come and watch the focus group for myself this time." He'd been getting reports, of course, from Dave himself, the observers, designers, graphic artists. But given the conversation he and Fiona had had the night before, Luke had decided it was time to get some firsthand information.

"Sure." Dave waved one hand down the hall and started walking. "I'll show you where you can sit and watch. We've got a group of six kids for today."

"How old?"

Dave winced, then laughed. "This is the toddler bunch. I'll tell you right off that getting the younger kids to settle down and pay attention is a little like trying to herd cats."

Luke lifted one eyebrow. "Aren't the tablets supposed to do that? Engage young minds, get them to learn?"

"Of course. Sure." Dave spoke quickly, explaining. "But first, we have to get them to notice the tablets. And the truth is, I think the toddlers scare Andy—he's our guy in the room. They're a little overwhelming—"

"So get someone else in there."

He laughed and shook his head. "Yeah, that's the thing, Mr. Barrett, we can't get anyone else to volunteer to be in the middle of toddlers. The older kids? No problem. Plenty of volunteers." He shrugged. "Andy will get the job done, though. I promised him I'd buy his coffee for a week."

"Good bribe," Luke said, approving.

"Not for me, since I'll be paying, and he drinks a lot of coffee." Dave opened a door at the end of the hallway and showed Luke into a tiny room with four empty chairs. "You can stay here. This is one of three observation rooms."

"Thanks." Luke didn't usually come down here to the satellite office in Irvine. Marketing, research and design were located here but he was able to stay on top of everything through email and phone calls.

He checked his watch. "When does it start and how long will it last?"

Dave took his phone out to check the time. "The kids will be going inside any minute and with the toddlers, we don't go longer than a half hour." He shrugged and grinned. "By then they want a drink or a nap or a banana."

For participating in the focus groups, the kids would get a toy and their parents received gift cards for any restaurant they chose. And hopefully, Luke and his team would get the information they needed to perfect their toys and tablets.

Dave nodded. "There they are now."

Luke watched six tiny kids race into the room. The area was filled with beanbag chairs, small tables littered with paper and crayons, and of course, his company's toys and tablets. For toddlers, the tablets were practically unbreakable and came in cases that were in bright primary colors.

Andy, the volunteer who apparently wished he were anywhere else, did his best to steer the kids toward the tablets, and four of the six complied. They turned on the tablets, and bright patterns and storyboards sailed across the screens. Those four toddlers immediately sat down to study the program playing, and Luke watched as they settled down and focused on the screen pattern.

The other two kids, though, chased each other around the small play area while Andy tried unsuccessfully to corral them.

Luke smiled to himself at the sound of the giggles streaming through the speakers. Two out of six were playing, coloring, jumping onto the beanbag chairs. And he suddenly remembered Laura's son, Travis, running across the yard chasing a ball while the neighbor kids sat on a porch lost in their screens.

He could almost hear Fiona's voice in his ear, talking about kids playing, using their imaginations. He could see her eyes, staring up into his, and he heard her telling him to take a chance at compromise with his grandfather.

She was right, he thought, and felt a twinge in his heart he hadn't expected.

And as he continued to study the kids, he realized there was a stark difference between those four children, mesmerized by the flashing colors and dancing bears—and the two free spirits now trying to color Andy's khaki slacks.

He stayed through the whole half hour and when he left, he found Dave. "Tell Andy the company's buying his coffee for a month. He earned it."

Laughing, Dave went back to work, and Luke stepped into the afternoon sunlight. His mind was racing, bouncing from one thought to the next as he began to rethink his own opinions on kids and tech.

Maybe it was time to go see Pop.

Jamison felt better than he had in weeks.

Except for the fury.

"Loretta," he snapped, "*someone* at the company's been trying to gaslight me and doing a damn fine job of it."

It infuriated him that he'd bought into the whole thing. He should have had more confidence in his own damn mind. But whoever was behind this had counted on him reacting just as he had. As you got older, there was no greater fear than losing your marbles. Forget *anything* and the word *Alzheimer's* sailed into your brain along with the terror that word invoked.

"There has to be another explanation," his wife said from her chair in his study.

"Like what?" He tossed both hands up and shook his head fiercely. "Some stupid practical joke that nobody laughed at? What other possible explanation is there except that someone wanted me to think I was losing my mind?"

Since taking that SLUMS test at the doctor's office,

Jamison knew his mind was as sharp as ever. Bill hadn't even bothered with other tests once he'd seen the results. The doctor had sent him home with a clean bill of health, thank God. But now he was forced to get to the bottom of a mystery.

Idly, he jingled the change in his pants pockets until the sound began to rattle him. He stopped, stared into space and tried to get a grip on the anger surging through him. Even Loretta's calming nature couldn't quell it. Not this time.

"Jamie," she asked, "who would do it?"

"I don't know," he admitted, shooting a glance at his wife. The not knowing was gnawing a hole in his gut. At this rate, he'd have his mind but would soon gain an ulcer.

Outside, the winter sky was as dark as Jamison's thoughts. He'd been betrayed. By someone he trusted. And that was a hard thing to accept.

"By God, most of our employees have been with us more than twenty years," he murmured. "Why suddenly would any one of them turn on me like this?"

Loretta folded her arms across her chest and hugged herself tightly. Shaking her head, she said, "It can't be someone we know."

"It has to be," Jamison countered. He knew what she was feeling, because he was feeling the same thing. Neither of them wanted to believe that someone they'd known and trusted for years would do something like this. But it was the only answer. "Who else would know how to forge my signature? Or do any of the other things that were done to me? It's someone close to me."

He paused. "Donna?"

"Oh, please." Insulted for the woman who had been their friend for decades, Loretta said hotly, "You might as well suggest it's Cole as Donna. I'll never believe she is capable of this."

"But we can say that about everyone at the company." He scrubbed one hand across the back of his neck. "Tim in marketing? Sharon in accounting? Phillip in purchasing? I'll tell you the truth, Loretta. This is a damn nightmare."

Loretta stood up, walked to her husband and wrapped her arms around him for a quick hug. "We'll find out what's going on."

He patted her back. "It won't change anything, but damn right we will. Someone in my own damn company was trying to sabotage me. Get me thinking I was senile or something. I need to know who." He thought about it for a minute. "I can't come right out and ask anybody, because they'd all deny it. So, we'll have to be sneaky about it."

"I hate this," Loretta murmured, stepping back from him to stare into his eyes.

"So do I," Jamison admitted. "But it has to be done, and there is one person who might be able to get to the bottom of this. Fiona Jordan."

"Who's that?" Loretta asked.

"How do you know Fiona?" Luke demanded.

Luke stared at his grandfather and, to his credit, the old man didn't look away. But he knew his grandfather well enough to see the shock and shame glittering in his eyes. As if it were a living, breathing entity in the room, Luke sensed *guilt* hovering right behind his grandfather as if trying to go unnoticed.

"Luke, sweetheart, it's so good to see you!" Loretta smiled and gave him a hug.

"Hello, Gran." He held on to her for a moment, then

let her go and fired another hard look at the man who'd raised him.

Jamison Barrett was a law unto himself. He did what he thought was right and didn't care what anyone had to say about it. But Luke knew him too well to be thrown by the bravado in the old man's eyes. There was something here, and he wasn't leaving until he found out what it was.

"Good to see you, boy."

"Uh-huh. How do you know Fiona Jordan, Pop?" Luke kept his gaze fixed on the older man's. He saw the flash of unease in Jamison's eyes and knew that whatever was coming, he wasn't going to like it. In his own head, Luke was putting things together quickly and he didn't like what he was finding.

Meeting a gorgeous woman at a tech conference in San Francisco when she had no real reason to be at that hotel? She'd said she was there on business, but what were the odds of someone in Northern California hiring a woman from Long Beach to do anything?

He smelled a setup.

Betrayal snarled inside him. Were Fiona and Pop conspiring together against him? God, he was an idiot. Fiona had been lying to him all this time. What the hell else had she lied about?

"Well," Jamison said, and jingled the change in his pocket.

Luke frowned. The jingling was a nervous habit when Jamison was trying to think or when he was uneasy.

"Fiona did some business for Donna not too long ago. Found her sister's long-lost daughter."

"It's true," Loretta said, laying one hand on her heart. "It was lovely to see Donna's sister Linda so happy after all those years."

Fiona had told him about that job. She hadn't mentioned that she'd done it for his grandfather's secretary's sister. All the time they'd talked about Jamison and she'd never once mentioned that she had a connection through Donna?

Coincidence? Luke didn't think so.

"Right. So, you didn't hire her?" Luke asked.

The change jingling got louder. Jamison rocked on his heels and did everything he could to avoid eye contact.

"You did, didn't you?" Luke pushed one hand through his hair in frustration. "You hired her. You sent her to San Francisco to ambush me."

His grandfather rubbed his jaw.

"My God, Pop. What the hell won't you do to get your way?"

"Jamie?" Loretta asked warily, "Is he right? Did you do something you should be ashamed of?"

Jamison looked from one to the other of them and even through the anger spiking inside him, Luke could see the old man trying to find a way out of this.

Luke wasn't going to let him. "Damn it, Pop, just admit that you did it. You hired Fiona to seduce me into coming back to the company."

"What?" He looked genuinely shocked at the accusation. "I did not. I hired her to get you to come back, yes. If you were seduced, that's on you."

"Jamie, how could you?" Loretta gave her husband a smack on the arm.

"What else could I do?" he argued. Pointing at Luke, he continued, "The boy wouldn't listen to me. I was afraid he'd never come back, and I needed him."

"You're unbelievable." Luke could hardly talk. He was furious. He'd been used by his family, lied to by his lover. His stomach was in knots, and his heart was hammering in his chest.

What the hell was going on here?

"You left me no choice."

"The choice was to butt the hell out."

Jamison waved that away. "That wasn't going to happen."

"Of course not." Through the rage, the sense of betrayal, Luke could admit that he should have seen this coming. His grandfather would always do whatever he had to do to get his way. He'd been doing it his whole life. Hell, he'd taught Cole and Luke both to go after what they wanted and never take no for an answer.

It had never occurred to Luke, though, that meeting Fiona was anything other than a happy accident. Had she *planned* to fall into his lap? Was the sex all about the job? Did she sleep with all of her clients or targets?

Damn it, he'd fallen for her whole act. That laugh of hers. Her eyes. Her kiss. He'd *listened* to her. Respected her opinion, and it was all a lie. Hell, for all he knew, she loved the idea of tech for kids, and everything she'd said to him about it had been scripted by his grandfather. He'd actually been tempted to build something with Fiona. In spite of not wanting a relationship, he'd been leaning toward breaking that personal rule. And this is what it got him.

"This is low, Pop," he ground out, gaze pinning the older man. "Even for you."

Jamison didn't like that and scowled to prove it. "If you'd just listened to me."

"Jamie, you never should have done this," Loretta snapped, glaring at the man she loved. "Apologize this instant."

"Damned if I will. I did what needed doing." Jamison

shot a hard look at his grandson. "I'm eighty years old, boy. You think I'm going to live forever? If you don't come back, the family company will go under."

"Oh no," Luke told him. "You don't get to lay this on me. Cole is more than ready to take it over."

"We both know Cole couldn't do the job. It's *you* I needed, and you damn well knew it when you walked out." Jamison was just as mad as Luke. and the two of them stood there glaring at each other.

"I left to prove something to myself. And to you," Luke snapped. "I didn't do it to ruin your plans—"

"Well you did anyway."

"Jamie!"

"They were *your* plans," Luke argued. "Not mine."

"And that's what this is about? A tantrum? You don't like taking orders, so you just run off?"

"Jamie, stop," Loretta ordered.

"I didn't run. I left. You know the irony is," Luke countered, gritting his teeth and narrowing his gaze on the man he admired more than anyone else in his life, "I was actually coming here today to say maybe you were right. Maybe we should work together at the family company. Find a compromise."

Jamison's eyes lit up.

"*Then* I find out you set me up."

"Oh hell," Jamison argued, "that doesn't change what you've come to believe, does it? True is true no matter how you come to it."

Loretta sighed. "Jamie, I'm so disappointed in you. You can't run our boys' lives no matter how much you want to. What were you thinking?"

He turned on his beloved wife then. "I was thinking that I heard my wife crying in the shower when she thought I couldn't hear her over the water running."

Luke snorted. "Gran doesn't cry." Then he looked at her and saw the truth on her face. "You *cried*?"

Frowning at Jamison, she stabbed her index finger at him. "You shouldn't have said anything. That was private. And stop listening at the bathroom door, it's rude."

He went to her, rubbed his hands up and down her arms and said, "I was worried about you, is all. And I knew I had to get him—" he jerked a thumb at Luke "—back for both our sakes."

Luke shoved his hands through his hair. He was angry and regretful and furious and guilty and realizing that maybe he'd had a huge hand in all of this happening. He hated thinking that Gran had been brought to tears over what he'd done. He owed her better than that. And Pop had only done what he'd always done. Rush in to handle a situation the best way he knew how.

That might excuse his grandfather, but it sure as hell didn't excuse Fiona. She'd lied to him. He felt like a damn fool. Every minute of time he had spent with her had been bought and paid for by his grandfather.

She had come to mean a lot to him. Now he had to face the fact that all of that was a lie as well. Where that left him, he didn't know.

Shaking his head, Luke promised himself to take this up with her later. He would have the truth. Finally. From everyone. For now, there was his grandfather to deal with.

Taking a deep breath, Luke shoved his hands into his pants pockets and stared at the old man watching him warily. "Leaving all the rest of it alone, what are you hiring Fiona for now?"

Jamison eyed him. "Does this mean you're back?"

"God, you're a hardhead." Luke threw both hands in

the air. "Even when I find out what you've been doing all you're interested in is, *am I coming back?*"

"Well, why wouldn't I want to know? That's what it's all been for. So, are you?"

Blowing out a breath, Luke said only, "It means I'm here now, and I haven't left even though I'm so mad at you I can't see straight."

Clearly insulted, Jamison muttered, "Well, that seems an exaggeration."

"Jamie!" Gran slapped one hand to her own forehead in clear exasperation and, suddenly, Luke felt all kinds of respect for the woman who could put up with Jamison Barrett for nearly sixty years.

Scowling, Jamison admitted, "Fine. We'll leave it for now. As to your question, I need Fiona to find out who's been trying to drive me out of my mind." He was jingling again.

"What are you talking about, Pop?"

Jamison started talking then, words rushing together, and with every word his grandfather said, Luke's anger became cold as ice. Who the hell would torture an old man like that? Make him doubt himself?

Too many lies, he told himself. Too many people who couldn't be trusted. He'd find who had been trying to destroy Pop. He'd even use Fiona to get it done.

But first, he was going to have a talk with the woman who'd been lying to him from the moment they met.

Fiona finished typing up three résumés for new clients, then baked a pan of brownies for a neighbor's birthday party and ended the day by returning a lost dog to its very happy owner. Of course, she still had to design baby announcements and one save-the-date card for two other clients, but those jobs would be fun.

She loved the creativity of what she did and, mostly, she loved being busy. Because at the moment, keeping her mind occupied meant she didn't have time to worry about what would happen when she talked to Luke.

Fiona had tried to make plans for exactly *how* to tell him the truth. No matter what she came up with though, it didn't sound right. Over a drink? During dinner? After sex? She wouldn't want to tell him *before* sex, or it might not happen again.

The sad truth was, she didn't want to tell Luke at all. In her fantasies, her lies were buried, Luke loved her, and they lived happily ever after. But fantasy rarely had anything at all to do with reality. So, she was left with her only choice.

Confessing all and watching him walk away.

When she pulled into the driveway that afternoon, it seemed almost cosmic, then, to find Luke sitting on her front porch, waiting for her. Her stomach jumped and her heart gave a hard leap in her chest.

He wore one of his amazing suits, with the top collar button of his shirt undone and his dark green tie hanging loose. He had one arm resting on his upraised knee and as she approached, he narrowed his gaze on her until she felt as if she were under a microscope.

"Luke? I wasn't expecting to see you tonight."

"Yeah. Thought I should come by and tell you that I talked to my grandfather today."

Her heartbeat skittered into a frantic beat. She swallowed hard and forced a smile. "That's wonderful. Did you work everything out?"

"Not nearly." He stood up and loomed over her, forcing Fiona to tip her head back to meet his gaze. "But you'll be happy to know that Pop is planning on hiring you again since you did such a great job with *me*."

Did the earth open up under her feet? Is that why she felt that sinking sensation? Staring into his eyes, she wanted to look away, but didn't. She saw the accusation, the anger, there and knew this talk was going to be every bit as bad as she'd feared it would.

"Oh God. Luke... I wanted to tell you—"

"But you just couldn't find the time?" Sarcasm and a hard expression.

Fiona shook her head, dug in her purse for her keys and said, "Just let me open the door. Come inside. I'll explain everything."

She squeezed past him and he didn't budge an inch.

"Can't wait to hear it."

She felt him behind her. Judgment and anger were rolling off him in thick waves, and she couldn't even blame him. Her hands shook so badly she couldn't get the stupid key into the stupid lock. But maybe part of that was psychological. She knew that the minute they were inside, the argument would start, and the end of her relationship with him would arrive.

"Let me do it." Luke reached around her for the key. She gave it to him; he slid it home and opened the door. He was right behind her as she stepped into her house.

Fiona dropped her purse onto the closest chair, braced herself and turned to face him. "I know you're angry..."

"Oh," he assured her, "angry doesn't even come close to describing what I am right now."

One look into his eyes told her that. The cool blue was glinting with too many emotions to sort out. But his fury was obvious in the way he moved and stood.

"You have every right to be mad."

"Thanks so much."

She winced at the ice in his voice. "I was going to tell you myself tomorrow, Luke."

"Easy to say now."

"I know, but it's true." He wouldn't believe her, she knew. But then, why should he? "I hated lying to you."

"But you did it anyway. Impressive."

Fiona ignored that. "Yes, your grandfather hired me. I couldn't tell you that. Jamison was my client and I owed him confidentiality."

"And what did you owe me?"

"Luke, at first, it was just a job, but the moment I met you—"

"Let me guess," he said sarcastically. "Everything changed for you."

Helplessly, she threw her hands up. "Well, yeah."

"Don't, Fiona." He stopped her before she could say more. "Just, don't. My grandfather paid you to talk me into going back to the family business. Everything else was just part of the dance."

His voice was cold and hard, and she couldn't even blame him. But oh, standing here with him, so close, but so far away from each other, was even worse than she'd imagined it would be.

"Not everything."

"Right. So, do you sleep with all your targets, or was I just lucky?"

She sucked in a gulp of air at the insult. He was hurting. He was pissed. He felt betrayed. Of course he was going to strike back. "I'm going to let that go because I know you're furious."

"Tell me, just how much did you charge the old man for having sex with me?"

Her head jerked back as if she'd been slapped. "He didn't pay me to care about you. Didn't pay me to sleep with you."

"Good, because we didn't do much sleeping, did we?"

Okay, she was willing to give a lot here because she was the one who'd screwed this all up. As soon as she'd realized she was coming to care for him, she should have told him everything. Should have been honest with him no matter what it had cost. But there was a limit to how much offense she was willing to put up with. Her own anger started as a flicker of heat in the pit of her stomach and quickly spread until she was swamped with it.

"You know what?" she snapped, taking a step toward him. "Insulting me isn't the answer here. Yes. I lied. Yes, I'm a horrible human being. But I didn't have sex with you for money."

"And I should believe you because you're so honest." Sarcasm dripped from his tone and if anything, his eyes became even icier.

"Do or don't," she said hotly. "That's up to you. But I'm not going to keep taking this from you, Luke. Are you so perfect that you've never done anything you regret? Are your hard lines of right and wrong so deeply drawn that you can't see that other people make difficult choices and don't always make the right ones?"

"Are you seriously trying to turn this around on me?" he countered.

"I didn't say that. I'm willing to take the blame for all of this—even though *you're* the one who put your grandfather into a situation where he felt the only way to solve it was to hire a stranger to talk to his own grandson!"

She enjoyed seeing a quick flash of guilt in his eyes, but it was gone an instant later.

Fiona felt bad about this whole situation. She had all along, but she wasn't going to stand there and not defend herself.

"I didn't decide to sleep with you easily. I've never done anything like that before. Heck, I've never slept with anyone as quickly as I did with you." She'd known all along that this was coming. She'd taken something for herself, for her own needs and desires and now, the bill was due. She had to accept the consequences, no matter how difficult. "And I wanted to pretend, I guess, that there was more between us than there was. I only had sex with you because I cared about you."

"Right."

"Do you think I could fake that? What we felt when we were together?" That hurt. Looking into his eyes and seeing only anger flashing there might have made it a little easier. But she saw pain there, too, and that told her he was having as hard a time with this as she was.

"How the hell do I know? You're a damn good liar."

"Now who's lying, Luke?" She met his gaze and stared him down. "I was there. I felt your response to me, and I know you were feeling everything I did."

"You don't know anything about me, Fiona," he said, bending lower so their faces were just a breath apart. "If you did, you wouldn't have lied to me."

"Yes. I lied. But not about everything."

"I don't believe you."

"Was it so wrong for me to be with you? To let myself feel? Think what you want to, you will anyway." She moved in closer to him, tipped her head back and met that icy blue stare unflinchingly. "But I took that job from your grandfather because it was for *family*." Even saying that word had tears burning at the backs of her eyes. "I never had what you turned your back on. I had exactly one person in my life who loved me. One. That's more than I ever thought I'd have.

"But you had a whole family who loved you. You had everything I used to dream about having and still you walked away from it all. You crushed your grandfather."

He snorted, but his expression said he worried she was right. "That old man is indestructible."

Sadly, she shook her head. "No one is, Luke. Jamison depends on you. Loves you. He's proud of you."

"This isn't about Pop," he pointed out.

"Part of it is," she countered. "He didn't want you to know that he'd hired me because he knew you would never listen if you did. So, this is mostly about you, Luke. You walked out on the people who loved you most. Well, your grandparents want you to come home. And I think you should."

"I think what I do is none of your business."

"Yes, you've made that clear enough." His words were like another slap, only this time to her heart. Fiona loved a man who would always see her as a liar. He would never understand what had driven her to be with him, even knowing that it was impossible for it to last. So, it was over. And emptiness rose up inside her like an incoming tide.

But he was still standing there, staring at her, and she couldn't help wondering why he hadn't left. Why hadn't he stormed out, taking all of his righteous anger with him?

"Is there more?" she asked. "Have any other insults you'd like to toss around?"

"Quite a few, actually," he said tightly. "But I'll pass. Instead, I have another job for you from my grandfather."

"No, thank you. Go away." She wanted nothing more to do with the Barrett family.

"I think you owe me one," he said and that had her snapping him a look.

"How do I owe you anything?"

"Lies have a price, Fiona, and you told a boatload."

She took a step back from him because she couldn't

stand being so close and not being able to touch him. Even now, her heart yearned for him and everything in her ached to wrap her arms around him and hold on. So, a little space between them was a very good thing.

"Fine. What does he want?"

"Someone at the company has been trying to convince Jamison he's crazy." Luke scowled at the thought. "Hiding things from him, canceling orders, ordering other things. They had him convinced he was sliding into dementia. He wants you to look into it. Do what you do. Talk to people. Find out who's behind it."

That was terrible, and now she at least knew why Jamison had sounded so unsure of himself that time on the phone. Who would do something so vicious and heartless?

"I'll do it," she said. "Only because I like your grandfather."

"Fine. Let me know when you have something."

He couldn't have been more distant. His beautiful eyes were shuttered. His voice was clipped and raw. And still, she loved him. Knew she'd never love anyone else like this. Everything in Fiona ached to say the words. Just once, she wanted to say them and mean them and it didn't matter to her if he dismissed them, because he'd already dismissed *her*.

He opened the door, and Fiona knew she had to tell him because who knew if she'd ever have the chance to say those words again and really mean them. Her heart hurt because her best chance at a happily ever after was about to walk out her door. How could she not tell him how she felt?

"Luke."

He looked at her.

She took a breath and let it out again. "I only had sex with you because I fell in love with you."

His eyes flashed, and his mouth worked as if he were biting back words that were trying to tumble out.

"I just wanted to tell you that," Fiona said. "Because I've never said those words before, and I don't know if I'll ever have the chance again."

Still he didn't speak, but his gaze was fixed on her. It didn't matter if he responded or not. She hadn't said those magical words for his sake, but for her own.

"But when this job is done," she said quietly, "I never want to see you again."

Ten

Luke hadn't seen Fiona in a week, and he missed her, damn it.

He shouldn't. She'd become the very distraction he had been trying to avoid. She'd lied to him from the beginning. Every conversation. Every laugh. Every kiss. Every… It was all built on lies.

And still, he wanted her. Thought about her. Missed her.

"Where's your mind, boy?" Jamison's voice cut into his thoughts, and Luke could have kissed his grandfather for the distraction.

"Right here," he said, looking at Pop from across the dining room table.

His grandparents' house hadn't changed in years. And somehow that was comforting since everything else around him seemed to be a swirling vortex of chaos. For the last week, Luke and Jamison had worked here, at the house, coming up with a compromise. Luke believed that this time, they'd be able to find a way to walk a line between the past and the future, while encouraging kids to get outside and have adventures again.

It would have been easier to do all this at the office, but until they found out who was behind the mental attacks on Jamison, they weren't announcing Luke's return. Not even to Cole, because he'd never been very good at keeping a secret.

"Are you sure you want to keep your group of people working on the tech division?" Jamison shook his head and checked one of the papers strewn across the table. "Might be easier to fold them into the division we've already got."

"No," Luke said. He was willing to go back to Barrett. Thought it was a good idea, actually. But though the tech part of the business would be taking a back seat to more standardized toys, he wanted his hand-picked crew working on the technological side of things. Whatever tech toys they *did* produce would be top of the line.

"My people have some great ideas, and I'd like them to keep working on those right where they're at for now. We'll call it a research division of the company. Maybe later, we can revisit."

Jamison looked at him for a long moment, then nodded, satisfied. "All right, then. We can talk about next year's lineup."

"That's fine, Pop." Better to focus. To think about work—that way thoughts of Fiona couldn't slip in to torture him.

"Have you heard from Fiona?"

He muffled a groan because it seemed he couldn't avoid thinking or talking about Fiona. "No. You?"

"Nothing," Jamison muttered, and tossed his pen down in disgust. "I was hoping she'd have something by now. I need to know who was doing that to me, Luke. Need to get rid of them so I can move forward knowing that everyone working for me is really working *for* me."

"I get it." Luke wanted to know, too. And then he planned on having a long chat with whoever had tried to submarine his grandfather.

"Well, then, call her, boy. Find out what she knows."

Luke went still. "She'll call when she has something."

"Is there a reason you're suddenly not interested in talking to the woman?"

Luke just stared at him for a long moment. "Yeah. She lied to me."

"They weren't her lies, they were mine."

Snorting, Luke shook his head. "Not all of them."

"The problem here is, you care for her."

"Nope, that's not it." Luke picked up the graphic sample of their fall ads. "What do you think about this? I'm thinking my graphic designer could find a way to make this stand out more."

"I'm thinking you're avoiding the subject."

"Good call," Luke told him. "So drop it."

"I would, but I like the girl."

Leaning back in his chair, Luke glared at him. "This time I'm just going to say it. Butt out, Pop."

"Well now," Jamison said with a wink, "we both know that's not going to happen."

Reaching for the coffee carafe, Luke poured himself another cup of the hot black brew and tried to ignore the older man across from him.

"When I met your grandmother, I knew right away that she was the one." He smiled to himself as if looking back through the years. "You know how?"

"No." But he guessed he was about to find out.

"Because she made me laugh," Jamison said. "She

made me think. She made me a better man just by being around me."

Luke frowned at his coffee. He didn't want to hear this because it struck too close to home. Wasn't that exactly what Fiona had done for him? Hadn't she, just by being herself, made him reconsider everything he'd thought he'd believed?

Didn't her laughter make him smile? Her touch make him hunger? Her sighs feed something in his soul that had been empty before her?

He remembered the look on her face when he'd confronted her. Remembered the shock and the pain in her eyes when he'd suggested she'd had sex with him because it was her *job.*

Okay, yes, he'd been a colossal jerk, and she'd called him on it. But in his defense... Screw it, there was no defense.

Jamison was watching him, and the old man was way too cagey for Luke's liking. Whatever had been between him and Fiona was over. Whether it was her lies or his accusations, it was over and done now.

"Let it go, Pop. *Please.*"

"Fine," he said, nodding. "For now."

At this point, Luke was willing to accept that.

Two days later, Fiona knocked on the front door of Luke's home. The roar of the sea seemed to match her thundering heartbeat, and the icy wind was the same temperature as her cold hands. Her stomach was a twisting, swirling mess and it felt like every cell in her body was on high alert. She felt brittle. As if she might shatter into pieces at any moment.

She'd completed her job, and though they might not like the answers she was offering them, once this task was done, the Barrett family would be out of her life for good. And that thought chilled her far more than the wind could.

The door swung open and there he was, just inches from her. Fiona took a deep breath to steady herself, but it didn't do any good. How could it, when all she had to do was look at Luke Barrett and her knees got wobbly and her heart began racing?

He wore a tight black T-shirt and worn jeans that rode low on his hips. He was barefoot and his hair was rumpled, making her wish she had the right to run her fingers through it. But those days were gone for good.

Still, she was glad she'd taken the time to dress for this meeting. She wore a dark green shirt with cap sleeves and a scoop neckline and the kicky black skirt she'd been wearing when she first dropped onto his lap. She knew the choice had been a good one when she saw his eyes flare dangerously.

"Fiona."

His voice sent a whisper of sensation drifting along her spine.

"Hello, Luke. I finished looking into your grandfather's problem."

One eyebrow lifted. "And?"

"And," she repeated, "I want to talk to you about it."

His gaze felt like a touch. It was intimate and distant all at once.

He opened the door wider, and she walked inside, being careful not to brush against him. How strange this was, she thought. They'd been as close as any two people could be and, now, they were less than strangers.

She knew her way around, so she walked directly into the living room. There were moving boxes everywhere, and her heart felt a sharp stab of regret. He was getting ready to leave this house and though she knew he was moving, she had no idea where. So, she'd never be able to find him again. That thought was a lonely one, but at the same time, she supposed it was for the best. Now she couldn't be tempted to drive past his house like some sad stalker, hoping to catch a glimpse of him.

Turning to face him, she handed him a manila envelope and when he opened it, she started talking. "I have a friend who's a computer genius."

"Of course you do."

She ignored that. "With Jamison's permission, he hacked into the system at Barrett's and tracked everything he could. There were what he called 'footprints' left behind and when he followed them, he found the person responsible for hurting your grandfather."

Luke looked at the papers, then lifted his gaze and shook his head. "This can't be right."

"It is," she assured him. "We checked everything twice, to make sure. I'm sorry, Luke."

His gaze hardened instantly, and she was sad to see it.

"I don't want another apology."

"I'm sorry about *this*." Fiona straightened up, squaring her shoulders, lifting her chin. "As for the other thing, I've already apologized once, and I won't do it again."

"Is that right?"

"Yes, Luke." She moved in close enough that she could see every shift of emotion in his eyes. "Normal people screw up and when they do, they apologize, are forgiven and the world goes on."

"So now this is my fault." He snorted and shoved the paperwork back into the envelope.

"I didn't say that." Sighing, she shook her hair back behind her shoulders. He wouldn't bend. Wouldn't understand that what she'd done had been hard for her.

That it had torn at her. That it was more complicated than black-and-white. It wasn't that he *couldn't* forgive her. He chose not to. "I don't think you'll ever find anyone perfect enough to live in your idealized world, and that's a shame."

He stiffened, and his features went cold and hard. "I didn't ask for your sympathy, either."

"Too bad. You've got it anyway." She paused to steady herself so she could say and believe the hard truth. "It's over, Luke. No matter who's at fault, it's over. I know that and so do you. That's really the only thing that counts now."

She took one long last look into those summer-blue eyes of his, then left while she still could.

"I'm sorry about this, Pop." An hour later, Luke watched his grandfather read over the paperwork Fiona had given him, and he could have sworn he saw the old man age right before his eyes.

And Luke could have punched his cousin in the face for that alone.

"Can't believe Cole would do all of this," Jamison muttered. "I never would have guessed it was him. Which is why, I suppose, he was able to do it."

"There must be a reason," Loretta mused aloud, as if trying to reassure herself.

There was a gas fire dancing in the hearth against the February cold, but it didn't do a thing to mitigate the chill sweeping through his grandfather's living room. The cozy furniture, the warmth of the decor, all seemed covered in a thin layer of ice brought about by Cole's betrayal.

"It's his ambition," Jamison murmured, sitting back and rubbing one hand across his jaw. "His and Susan's. That woman's always pushing Cole for more. I'm not excusing him, mind you. What he did, *he* did. But I am saying he's probably been feeling some pressure."

He looked at Luke. "The way I treated you—favored you over him—probably had a lot to do with it, too."

"No," Luke said. He'd been going over and over this since the moment Fiona had given him the proof of Cole's deception. "You're not taking the blame for this, Pop. What Cole did, he did on his own. If he wanted more responsibility at the company, then he damn well should have earned it. You know as well as I do that he loves the paycheck, he just doesn't want to work.

"He doesn't get to slide on this. You should call the police."

"And tell them what?" Jamison countered with a choked laugh. "That my grandson was gaslighting me? No. This is family, and that's how we'll handle it."

"I agree, Jamie." Loretta's voice was soft but firm.

Luke looked at them both and didn't get it. Cole had hurt the man who'd raised him, loved him. Cole had done awful things, so how could he ever be forgiven for it? Fiona was wrong, he told himself. An apology didn't mean forgiveness, and it certainly didn't mean anyone would forget what had happened.

But this wasn't his call.

"Fine," he said finally. "We'll do it your way. What's the plan?"

"We'll be having a family dinner here tonight," Jamison said, with a glance at his wife to make sure the idea was all right with her. At Loretta's nod, Jamison said, "We'll talk then, and I'll handle Cole."

"I'm sorry it all went to hell. I liked Luke."

"Me, too," Fiona said with a wry smile. She'd re-lived that last argument, the one they'd had the week before, almost daily. She kept coming up with things she should have said, should have done. Would it have changed anything? Probably not, but he might have at least understood.

For a week, she'd tortured herself while gathering information for his grandfather. Now that job was done, and it was time to admit that whatever she'd had with Luke was just as finished.

"He might come crawling back," Laura mused.

"Luke? Crawl?" Fiona shook her head and laughed. "That would be something to see. But it would never happen. He's too proud. Too sure of himself and too wrapped up in his boldly black-and-white, right-and-wrong world. He'll never forgive me for lying to him.

"And though I'm sorry it was necessary, I can't completely regret it, because if I hadn't agreed to keep my identity and purpose a secret, I never would have met him in the first place. God. Isn't this a pitiful rant?"

"I've heard worse."

Fiona laughed a little. "That's something, I guess." She reached for a cookie, pulled off a few crumbs and said, "What am I supposed to do now, Laura?"

Her best friend reached across the table, patted her hand and said, "What you always do. Live. Work. Smile."

Fiona's eyes filled with tears. That all sounded impossible at the moment. "It hurts to breathe."

Laura cried with her. "I know, Fee. It's going to for a while. That's why we have wine and cookies."

Briefly, Fiona's lips curved. "And friends."

Then dutifully, she took a bite of her cookie and washed it down with wine.

When Cole and his family arrived, Jamison braced himself. He still didn't want to believe that the boy he'd loved and raised had tried so hard to convince him that he was losing his mind. That was a stab to the heart that was going to take some time to get past.

But he would get past it. This was family and, despite the current circumstances, Jamison knew Cole was a decent man. Underneath his jealousy of Luke, his blind ambition and desire to take over the company to prove to himself he was just as good as, if not better than Luke, Cole was just a man looking for something he couldn't find.

Jamison hurt for him, but his anger and disappointment were just as vibrant as the pain he felt. He needed to make Cole accept that actions have consequences.

Cole needed to be reminded of what was truly important.

Carrying his son Oliver into the room, Cole was followed by Susan, just a step or two behind them. Cole was wearing khaki slacks, a red polo shirt and loafers while Susan looked as she always did. As if she'd just stepped out of a fashion magazine—cool and beautiful. Oliver, of course, was the shining, smiling boy he was supposed to be. And Jamison meant to keep him that way. Damned if he'd destroy the boy's father to make a point.

Jamison noticed the moment Cole spotted Luke standing at the wet bar in the corner, and Jamison frowned to see the hard resentment on Cole's features. Yes, Jamison told himself. No matter what else, he had to take partial responsibility for this mess. He'd favored Luke and, in doing so, he'd shortchanged Cole. He hadn't meant to. He'd only responded to the boys as their nature—and his—had demanded. But that had been a mistake. Maybe if he'd expected more of Cole, Jamison would have gotten it.

What was the old saying? *People will rise or fall according to your expectations of them.*

In that, he'd let Cole down.

He was about to make up for that.

"Luke," Cole said flatly. "I didn't expect to see you here."

"I'll bet," Luke muttered.

Jamison shot him a quelling look, then said, "Susan, why don't you take Oliver back to Marie? She's made his favorite cookies today and that will give us all a chance to talk."

Their cook loved little Oliver, so Jamison knew the boy would be looked after while the adults had a serious discussion.

"All right." Susan did as asked, and Cole sat down on one of the sofas.

"Want a drink?" Luke asked from the corner.

"Yeah. Scotch."

Loretta took Jamison's hand and gave it a squeeze as he stood up and walked across the room to stand by the fireplace.

Luke delivered Cole's scotch, then took a seat in an armchair near his cousin. Jamison watched them all.

Luke was tense, Loretta was miserable, Cole was clearly uneasy and Susan, when she reentered the room, looked tranquil. That wouldn't last much longer.

Jamison had done plenty of unpleasant things in his life, but none of them, he thought, compared to this single moment. He loved Cole, but Jamison had been through a nightmare the last few weeks and his grandson was the reason why. That had to be addressed, like it or not.

Cole shot a look at Luke, then turned to his grandfather. "What's going on, Pop?"

"I know what you've been up to, Cole." He kept his gaze fixed on Cole's, so he saw when the man flinched, and it damn near broke Jamison's heart. Yes, he had known it was true. But seeing it on Cole's face just made it so much more painful.

"I don't know what you're talking about."

"Don't lie to him," Luke muttered. "Don't make it even worse."

Cole snapped, "Stay out of this. Why are you even here? You *left*."

"I came back."

"What?" Susan finally spoke and the shock in her voice said volumes.

Jamison knew she'd been counting on her husband taking over the company. Susan wasn't a bad person, but she was a social climber and having her husband as the CEO of a billion-dollar company would be right up her alley.

Cole ignored his wife and turned to Jamison. "You mean, he's back at the company? All is forgiven? Just like that?"

"Just like that," Jamison said, and lifted one hand to Luke, silently telling him to keep quiet. This was for Jamison to do, as much as he wished he didn't have to. "You have anything to say about this, Cole?"

"If you're talking about Luke sliding back into the fold, then yeah. I've got things to say."

"You should be more concerned with yourself than Luke," Jamison told him shortly. "I told you. I know what you've been doing to me."

"Pop—"

The room was so quiet it was as if everyone in it had taken a breath and held it. "I've got evidence, so don't bother denying it."

Eleven

Cole tossed his scotch down his throat, then set the glass on the table in front of him. "I won't. What would be the point?"

"You bastard," Luke muttered.

"That's enough, Luke." Jamison's heart was aching as he looked at his oldest grandson. "Why, Cole? Just so you could take charge?"

"Why shouldn't he?" Susan asked. "He's your grandson, too."

"He is." Jamison nodded. "But as of today, he's not a vice president at the company any longer."

"You can't do that." Susan jumped to her feet and faced Jamison.

"Yes, he can." Cole gave his wife a steely look, then stood up. He looked directly into Jamison's eyes and said, "I did it. And I swear a part of me thought it was for your sake, too, Pop. Force you to slow down. Retire."

"By making me think I was losing my mind?"

To his credit, Cole flushed and shifted his gaze.

Jamison wasn't nearly finished. "You gave me more than a few hard days. But you made your Gran worry *for* me and that I won't allow."

Cole looked at Loretta and even from across the room, Jamison could read the man's shame. "I'm sorry for this, Gran."

Sadly, she nodded. "I know you are, Cole."

"I don't know that," Jamison said brusquely and waited for Cole to look at him again. "But I'm going to believe that you mean it because I want to. And more importantly, because I need to."

Cole nodded and squared his shoulders. He never again looked at Luke and that, to Jamison's mind, was telling. He was standing on his own and taking it, maybe for the first time in his adult life, and Jamison was glad to see it.

"I am sorry, Pop."

In Jamison's eyes, Cole was still a young boy, devastated at the loss of his parents, coming to live with his grandparents, trying to find his way and failing more often than he succeeded. He'd never been as sure of himself as Luke and, after a time, that had begun to eat at him. Maybe if Jamison had tried to address what Cole was feeling earlier, none of this would have happened.

Loving Cole didn't stop just because he'd been a damn fool. But love didn't mean there'd be no consequences.

"You're not going to be running Barrett's, Cole. You're not going to be trusted with much of anything at the company. Not until you prove yourself to me."

"I understand."

"I don't." Susan nudged her husband, and Cole turned to glare at her.

"Quiet," he said tightly. "Just, be quiet, Susan."

"But it's not right."

"Stop."

Shocked, she closed her mouth, but her eyes were screaming.

When he had quiet again, Jamison said, "You'll be working with Tony in janitorial."

"What?" Susan exclaimed again, and Jamison almost enjoyed watching her stunned expression.

But Cole didn't even flinch, and Jamison gave him full points for that.

"You'll work there until Tony is convinced that you're ready to move up to research. From there, you'll move through the company, earning the respect of every one of our employees."

"I understand." Cole's teeth were gritted and his voice strained, but he didn't argue.

"I hope you do. But, so we're clear on this, Cole," Jamison said, "you'll take the time to learn everything there is to know about this company, to understand every detail *and* the big picture, or you'll be fired."

Stiffly, he nodded.

"This is my offer to you, Cole." Jamison looked only at Cole. It was as if the rest of the room had disappeared. He had to reach his grandson, and this was the only way he knew. "Work your way back up. Earn my trust again. But ultimately, the choice is yours.

"You can do this my way or you can leave the company and strike out on your own."

Cole turned to look at his wife, then slanted a look at Luke, who'd been so still, so quiet, Jamison had almost forgotten he was there.

"I'll stay," Cole said, and lifted his chin. "I'll do whatever I have to do, Pop. And I'll earn your trust again."

"I look forward to that." Nodding, Jamison walked

to Cole and stopped right in front of him. "Just so you know, no more yacht club memberships, and your salary won't be a vice president's."

"Oh, now—"

Cole simply ground out, "Susan…"

"I'll see that you can stay in your house," Jamison added, and that mollified Susan a bit. "For Oliver's sake. I don't want my great-grandson uprooted because his father was a damn fool."

"Thanks." Cole swallowed hard and nodded. "It's more than I deserve. And I know that."

Jamison looked into his grandson's eyes for a long minute and was relieved to see what he'd hoped for. Real contrition. Real shame. And a determination that he'd never really seen there before. This might turn out to be the best thing that had ever happened to Cole. Jamison hoped so.

"What you did was bad, Cole," Jamison said, and reached out to clap one hand on the other man's shoulder. "But I love you. Nothing you do can change that."

Hope shone in Cole's eyes before he said, "Thank you for that, too. I'll prove myself, Pop. Even if it takes a decade."

"Good." He squeezed Cole's shoulder and the gratitude in his eyes almost undid Jamison. "Now why don't you take your family home so you and Susan can talk about your new situation."

"I will." He walked to Loretta and bent to kiss her cheek. She patted his hand and gave him an encouraging smile.

When he passed Luke, Cole nodded. Finally, he took Susan's arm and steered her from the room. Jamison dropped onto the nearest couch and sighed, exhausted from the emotional turmoil. "That's not something I ever want to do again."

"I'm just going to the kitchen to see Oliver before they leave." Loretta hurried from the room, leaving the two men alone.

"That's it?" Luke asked. "Start him at the bottom and work his way back up?"

Still tired, Jamison slanted a look at his other grandson. "It's a lesson for him, Luke. The last time he worked janitorial was when he was sixteen. Just like you." Jamison rubbed his eyes trying to ease the headache settled behind them. "For a man like Cole, starting over is the hardest thing for him to face.

"The fact that he accepted it is a good sign. Of course we'll have to see if he actually follows through."

"I think he will," Luke admitted reluctantly.

"Why?"

"He was shocked when you called him on what he'd done. I don't think he ever considered that he'd get caught."

"True."

Frowning to himself, Luke added, "But once he knew you had him, he stood up to it. I'll give him that."

"Sounds like you're easing up on him."

Instantly, Luke shook his head. "Nope. For what he did, there is no forgiveness."

"Oh hell." Jamison pushed out of the chair and walked to the wet bar. He poured himself a scotch and took a sip. "All of us need forgiveness now and then."

"And then it's all good? Slate clean?"

"The slate's never clean," Jamison told him. "Hell, the slate doesn't even start out clean. There's always dust or something on it. And when we wipe away the bad stuff, there's a shadow, an echo of what's been there before. But that's all there is. Just a shadow. And we're free to write on the slate again—good or bad."

Luke stared into his glass and the expression on his face told Jamison he was thinking about his own "slate." Jamison had a feeling he knew what Luke was thinking about and being a man who always had an opinion and didn't mind sharing it, Jamison started talking again.

"Fiona's a miracle worker, I swear."

Luke's gaze shot to his. "I suppose. She came through this time, anyway."

"Came through with you, too," Jamison said.

"By lying? Sure." Luke took a sip of his scotch and sat there glowering like a gargoyle.

"Lies are slippery things," Jamison mused as if to himself. "I tell them and say your Gran looks good in that ugly blue dress she loves, and she kisses me. Cole tells them, and it destroyed what he most wanted. Fiona tells them, and you're back with the company where you belong."

Luke just stared at him. "You're not exactly subtle. You know that, right?"

Jamison chuckled. "Wasn't trying to be. What Fiona did, she did because I hired her. She couldn't exactly show up and tell you why she was there, could she?"

"She could have told me later. After—"

"Maybe she was afraid you'd take it badly," Jamison said wryly.

"Maybe," Luke allowed, still staring into his scotch as if searching for answers in that amber liquid. After a long minute or two, he said, almost to himself, "And maybe there's no forgiveness for what I said to her once I knew the truth."

"Both of my grandsons...damn fools. There's only one way to find out if she'll forgive you." Luke looked at him and Jamison blurted out impatiently, "For God's sake, boy, go and get her. Convince her to take a shot on you."

A brief smile curved Luke's mouth. "And start over with a clean slate?"

"Write a new story."

The next day, Fiona realized she was doing just what Laura had advised.

She lived. She worked.

She wasn't smiling yet, but she'd get there. Eventually.

"And you're helping, aren't you, George?" Fiona bent down to frame the giant dog's face. A Bernese mountain dog, George weighed a hundred and twenty pounds and was living under the delusion that he was a lap dog.

George lifted one huge paw and laid it on her forearm. Fiona staggered a little but found a small smile just for him. Dog sitting was one of the jobs she most loved doing. Having George in her house for the next week while his family was at Disney World would give her comfort and company.

"You're such a good boy," she said, and gave his big head another brisk rub. "You want to go for a walk?"

George barked and wiggled all over. Thankfully, Fiona had already taken all the breakables off low tables so his swishing tail couldn't do much damage.

"I'll take that as a yes," she said and picked up the leash. Hooking it to his collar, she grabbed a couple of poop bags, just in case, and opened the front door.

"Hello, Fiona."

Her heart stopped. Actually stopped.

When she took a sudden deep breath, it started again and almost made her dizzy. The one person in the world she never would have expected to find on her porch was standing there staring at her.

"Luke?"

As if sensing her distress, George stepped in front of her, looked up at Luke and growled from deep in his throat.

Luke took a step back. "Whoa. You have a pony now?"

A short, sharp laugh shot from her throat. "This is George. I'm dog sitting for a neighbor." Looking down at the big dog, she ran one hand over his thick neck and smooth, beautiful fur. "He's very protective. It's okay, George. Luke is a...*friend*."

The dog calmed down, but Luke said, "Am I? A friend?"

She shrugged, not knowing what to make of this. "He knows that word, so he'll calm down."

"You didn't answer the question, Fiona."

"I don't know the answer, Luke." She didn't know anything. Obviously. She hadn't expected to ever see Luke again, yet here he was. His hair was a little longer now, and his summer-blue eyes were locked on her. He wore one of his perfect suits and managed somehow to look both businesslike and dangerously attractive.

She was trying to get over him. To let go of him and everything that might have been. Having him show up at her house wasn't exactly helping.

"He needs to take a walk," she said, stepping outside with George and forcing Luke to step back farther. She closed her door and stopped again when Luke stood in front of her.

"Can I go with you?"

She wanted to shout *yes!* Because she'd missed him so much. Missed talking to him, looking at him, kissing him, laughing with him, kissing him, curling up next to him, their naked bodies still warm from the sex that haunted her with detailed, torturous memories.

Apparently, Luke saw her indecision, because he said, "I need to talk to you, Fiona."

That decided her. "What's left to say, Luke?"

Sunlight drifted through the branches of the trees and a soft, cold wind slid past them.

"A lot, I think. Will you listen?"

She looked into his eyes and tried to decide why he was there. What else he might want to say to her? And finally, Fiona realized that the only way to get through this was to get it over with.

"Walk and talk," she said, and let George pull her down the walkway to the sidewalk out front.

George was in seventh heaven, sniffing at every tree, every blade of grass. He turned his face into the wind, shook his head and kept going. Thankfully, he had been well trained for the leash because if she'd had to hold him back, Fiona never would have been able to.

"Pop settled the situation with Cole," Luke said, and she glanced at him.

"I'm glad."

"He didn't fire him." Luke frowned a bit at that. "I thought he should have, but Pop wouldn't hear anything about it."

She shrugged. "He's family." And Fiona, who had never had a family of her own, understood the importance of that relationship. Knew what a gift it was and how hard it would be to deny.

"Yeah. He's been seriously demoted, though. He has to work his way through every department in the company, earning respect along the way, before he'll be allowed back in completely."

"He'll do it," Fiona said firmly.

"You're so sure?"

"I am. He knows now what he almost lost. He'll fight to get it all back." That's what she would do.

"Can he?" Luke asked.

She looked up at him when George stopped to mark a tree.

"Of course. Your grandfather loves him. Love doesn't just stop one day because things get hard or ugly."

"I'm glad to hear you say that."

Luke took her arm and turned her to face him. God, he'd missed her. Just being beside her. Looking into her warm chocolate eyes. The only thing missing was her smile and he knew that *he* was the reason behind that. It killed him now to remember what he'd said to her. How he'd treated her.

And he knew how Cole must have felt standing before their grandfather. Unsure of whether he'd be forgiven— or even if he deserved forgiveness.

Suspicion flashed in her eyes. "Why?"

"Because I need you to forgive me, Fiona. I said some really crappy things to you." Which didn't even start to cover it. "I'm sorry for it. Maybe I was looking at things like you said, black and white, right and wrong, and I forgot—or didn't want to know that there are shades of gray, too. My view was so narrow I couldn't see what I was missing. I looked at my job, my family, my company in a single vision and didn't notice that other things were there, too.

"And I saw your lies and didn't look for more. I should have. You're the one who opened me up, Fiona. Taught me to look beyond the obvious and I should have done that with you, too. I want you to know I didn't mean a word of what I said before. I was just—"

"Furious? Hurt?"

"Both," he admitted.

"I understand that. So yes. I forgive you."

"Thank you." He smiled. "And now I can tell you that the main reason I came here today was to hire you for another job. I've lost something important."

"Oh."

Disappointment shone in her eyes, and Luke felt like an ass. At the same time, a flicker of hope rose up in his chest.

After a second or two, she asked, "What did you lose?"

"My heart." Luke watched her reaction and saw confusion there now, which was way better than disappointment. "My heart's been lost since the moment I met you."

Her eyes widened and her breathing quickened. All good signs. Then she asked, "Are you sure you had one to begin with?"

One corner of his mouth lifted briefly. "A fair question. And yes, I'm sure. It was a hard ball of ice in my chest and when I lost it, warmth came back." He kept his gaze locked on hers, searching for what he wanted, *needed* to see. "I didn't even recognize it for the gift it was," he admitted. "I didn't appreciate that warmth until it was gone, and the ice was back."

"Luke…"

He cut her off. "I'm not saying it'll be easy to find my heart. Might take years. Might take forever. Are you willing to take on a long-term job like that?"

George tugged on the leash, clearly impatient with the humans interfering with his walk. Fiona laughed and the sound swept through Luke like a warm breeze. He'd missed it. He'd missed so much.

"I don't know, Luke," she said, shaking her head. "I want to believe you, I really do."

"Then do it." He took the leash from her hand, looked at George and said firmly, *"Sit."*

Once the dog complied, he turned back to her. "I was an ass, Fiona."

"No argument."

He snorted. "I deserve that. I was wrong. If it weren't for the lies you told for my grandfather, I never would have met you and—" He shook his head. "I can't even imagine not knowing you. Not loving you."

She sucked in a gulp of air. "Love?"

"Yeah," he said, rubbing the backs of his fingers against her cheek. "Surprised me, too. And maybe that's why I was acting like such a jackass. I'd never been in love before, so I didn't appreciate it. Didn't really recognize it. But I do now.

"I love you, Fiona. I want you. I need you. But mostly, I can't even picture living my life without you."

Fiona sighed and he hoped it was with happiness. But he kept talking because he couldn't take the chance of losing her now.

"I'm asking you to marry me, Fiona."

"Oh my God." She staggered back a step, and he tightened his grip on her. "I can't believe this."

"Believe it. Believe me," he urged. "I want to marry you. I want us to have that family you used to dream of having. Kids, Fiona."

She inhaled sharply, her heart clenching as he offered her…everything.

"I want us to build something amazing together. And I really hope you want all of that, too."

Lifting one hand to cover her mouth, her gaze was locked with his and he saw what he'd hoped to see in those dark brown depths. Love. Acceptance. Forgiveness.

And Luke took his first easy breath in more than a week.

She reached up and cupped his cheek in her palm, and the heat of her touch slid through him like a blessing, easing away the last of the chill that had been with him since he'd sent her away.

"I want all of that, too, Luke. I do love you. So much."

He let out a breath he hadn't realized he'd been holding. "Thank God."

"I want you, too. I love you, Luke. Maybe I have right from that first day. And I'd love to build a family with you." Tears glimmered in her eyes, making them shine with hope and a promise for the future. *Their* future.

The big dog wandered over, leaned against Luke's leg and nearly toppled him. When he would have snapped at the beast, George looked up at him with adoration. Luke sighed and petted him before digging into his pants pocket for a blue velvet ring box.

Fiona saw it and gasped.

"I don't understand the shock," he said, smiling. "I proposed, you accepted. A ring is traditional."

She laughed. "I know, it's just…this is all so not what I expected to happen today."

Luke opened the box to show her the ring he'd chosen for her. A huge dark emerald surrounded by diamonds winked in the afternoon sun.

She looked up at him. "It's beautiful."

He took the ring from its perch and slid it onto her finger. "When I saw it, it made me think of that dark green shirt you were wearing the day we met. The day you fell into my lap and completely changed my world."

A lone tear escaped her eye to roll down her cheek. He caught it with a fingertip and kissed it away.

"This is the most romantic thing that's ever happened

to me," she said, lifting her gaze from the ring to the man who'd given it to her.

"Even with George here?"

At the sound of his name, George barked and looked from one to the other of them, a smile on his face as if he were in on the secret.

"Especially with George here," she said, laughing. "Which reminds me, I always wanted a dog."

"Deal," he said, then stroked the big dog's head. "Maybe George has a cousin who needs a home."

If not, Luke would find one. A dog like George. To always remind him of this day. This moment. When Fiona loved him.

"You're offering me everything I ever dreamed of," Fiona said softly. "Someone to love and be loved by. Someone to make a family with. Someone who will always be there, standing beside me."

"All of that and more, Fiona." He swore it to her and to himself.

She went to him and hooked her arms around his neck, holding on tightly as if afraid he might slip away. But she didn't have to worry, Luke told himself as he held her just as close. He'd never lose her again.

He pulled his head back then and grinned at her. "Oh, there's something else, too. Jamison wants to see you."

"About what?"

"Something about keeping an eye on Cole for a while to make sure it's all working out with him."

"Do you think it will?" she asked, still holding on to him, staring into his eyes.

"I know it will," Luke said. "He got a second chance. Pop loved him enough to forgive him. To start over. Cole won't blow that chance."

Still looking up at him, Fiona asked, "And we've forgiven each other, so the same thing holds true?"

"We've got a clean slate, Fiona," Luke said. "No echoes, no shadows. Just a brand-new story we get to write. Together."

She grinned. "What does that mean?"

It meant, he thought, that shades of gray were beautiful.

"I'll tell you later," he promised. Then he kissed her and his world came right again. Everything was good. Everything was...perfect.

* * * * *

RECLAIMING
HIS LEGACY

DANI WADE

This book is dedicated to my son, Riley.
Thank you for making me laugh,
for challenging me to be authentic,
for each and every hug.
May you ever find something in life that you love.
Go forth and conquer!

One

"What happened to the nanny, Father?"

For a moment, Blake Boudreaux thought his father wouldn't answer. Instead Armand Boudreaux adopted the inscrutable, haughty look that matched his perfectly fitted suit, manicured hair and highly polished shoes. All of which said he wasn't obligated to give excuses to anyone. Then one perfectly trimmed brow slowly lifted and he replied with dead calm, "My traitor of a wife cleaned out her bank account. A sizable amount, I might add. I had to recoup my investment somehow."

"By firing the nanny of a sick child? Are you crazy?"

"You never had a nanny and you were just fine."

Blake could say more than a few words on that subject, but this wasn't the time or place… Not that his father would care anyway. Besides, being back inside the Boudreaux plantation house was making his skin crawl already. This place left him chilled to his core, even after all these years away. "I didn't have epilepsy. This is a serious illness. Abigail needs to be supervised. Taken care of."

"That mess is all in her head. Obviously so, or her mother wouldn't have flaked off to Europe and left her behind."

Wasn't that sympathetic of him?

"So the doctors are lying?"

"They're making a mountain out of a molehill. Really, they should do what they do best. Give her a pill that will make it all go away. It doesn't need to be more involved than that, I'm sure. As long as she takes the medicine, she'll be fine. And more importantly, she will believe its fine. That's about all its good for."

Blake knew a lot of things about his father. He was cold and autocratic, and spent his life tearing holes in the people around him. Sometimes he was subtle about it... sometimes not. But this was the first time he'd known Armand to truly jeopardize someone's life. Blake truly believed this was not something to play around with.

Abigail, Blake's half sister, was seven years old and her symptoms had been severe enough for her "flaky mother" to take her to a specialist. Of course, the minute the diagnosis had been made, she'd packed her bags and headed out to less stressful pastures.

"The doctors aren't crazy. This could be dangerous," he insisted.

"It's not as bad as they make it seem. Besides, you sound like someone who honestly cares," his father pointed out with a smirk. "Considering this is the first time I've seen your face since you told me to shove my money and my parental rights seventeen years ago, I guess I should take you seriously."

The dig wasn't unjustified. This *was* the first time

Blake had set foot in his father's house since he was eighteen years old. If he had never again walked through the doors of the infamous Boudreaux plantation house, he would never have missed it. He could have continued to live in the most luxurious settings in Europe, rather than return to this arctic tundra of a house despite the sultry heat of the Louisiana summer outside.

He would never have met his father's much younger second wife, Marisa, and his then five-year-old half sister if said wife hadn't been on a trip in Germany at the same time Blake had been involved with the princess of a small, nearby principality.

That's when he'd discovered that Marisa loved to travel to exotic places and be seen by the most important people. Abigail's care was relegated to a nanny while her mother spent her days exploring her next big adventure. She'd only taken Abigail along because Armand had refused to let her leave the child at home. Marisa matched his father in narcissism, though she lacked his vindictive streak.

Blake had never thought he would ever care about children in any capacity that had an impact on his life. His playboy reputation was widely known and accepted by all but those women who tried—and failed—to change him. Children were something that existed and were cute...as long as they belonged to someone else.

But one charming afternoon with the little girl with soft ringlets, wide brown eyes and a keen curiosity about everything around her had this playboy hooked. Luckily, Marisa had facilitated his attempts to stay in touch with his half sister until a few months ago. Blake would have had no idea about the present situation if his half sister's former nanny hadn't called out of the blue two days ago

with the distressing news. Blake had rented a private jet
and gone to New Orleans immediately.

Thank goodness he had an inheritance outside of his
father's reach. His mother's exclusive gift had given him
the chance to live a carefree life without a thought to
money…or his father's opinion. The fact that he successfully supplemented that income with an avid interest in producing and distributing art was a bonus known
only to him.

"I do care about Abigail," Blake finally said. Better
to keep it simple than give his father any ammunition to
use against him. "Someone should."

"She's weak. Life will toughen her up."

His father turned his laser-focused gaze on Blake,
studying him in a way that made Blake want to squirm.
He resisted the urge, of course. He was long past the
point where he would allow his father to direct his actions in any way. Showing any sign of weakness would
be seen as a victory by the old man, and Blake wasn't
giving an inch.

"But since you're here, I might consider giving you
the job."

That wasn't what Blake expected at all. "Excuse me?"

"The job of looking after her. Though you're hardly
qualified for childcare, now, are you?"

At least I'm willing to try. Blake simply locked his jaw
and waited. If his father was willing to about-face, there
would be a price to pay. Might as well wait for the bill.

"I don't know," the older man said, fiddling with his
diamond cuff links as he pretended to consider the situation. "I haven't decided if I'll let you see her at all."

A sudden tiny gasp sounded from behind a chair
tucked into the far corner of the room. Unfortunately
it echoed off the vaulted ceiling, and was magnified for

the listeners nearby. His father's gaze swung immediately to the shadows.

"I told you to stay in your room," he yelled, his booming voice forcing Blake to suppress a wince.

A little girl slid out from behind the piece of furniture. Despite a little extra height on her, Blake would have said she was unchanged in the last two years. She had the same brown ringlet curls, though they were currently a tangled mess. The same vulnerable gaze. She hesitated before obeying, her brown eyes, flecked with green, seeming to memorize every inch of Blake as if afraid she would never see him again. Blake could certainly relate. His father was just enough of a jerk to forbid him to ever see her if he realized how much it meant to Blake.

So he hid his own emotions, gave Abigail the barest of smiles and motioned for her to go upstairs…before she heard more from her father about what a problem she was. Blake had grown up with a lifetime of those abusive rants stuck in his brain. He didn't want that for Abigail.

While her mother was here, Blake had thought she would be protected from the harsh reality of Armand Boudreaux's judgments. Now there would be no one in a position to protect her. The housekeeper, Sherry, might be able to check in, but she still had a job to do. Would that be enough?

Blake hadn't even had that much. He remembered long, endless days when he barely saw anyone except the cook, who would fix him a plate. He'd been healthy, but lonely. Except having his father take an interest in him had usually meant an hour of yelling about how horrible Blake was.

Blake couldn't allow that to happen to Abigail. Two years ago, he never gave his terrible childhood a second thought, but Abigail's situation was bringing a lot of bad memories to the forefront of his brain.

Turning his gaze back to his father, he continued as if they hadn't been interrupted. "You were saying I could help with Abigail's care?" Caution was the name of the game here.

"Sure. You care so much about her—" Armand narrowed his gaze on Blake, a thin smile stretching his lips. "It might be worth something for you to see her."

Oh boy. "Don't you have enough money?"

The seconds-long hesitation sent a spear of worry through Blake. Money had never been an issue for his father. Not growing up. And, Blake assumed, not now. But that hesitation made him wonder.

Then his father said, "Not money, son. *Freedom.*"

A pretty significant bargaining chip for Blake. It always had been. This would not end well. "I'm not following."

His father paced back and forth across the marble floor, the click of his dress shoes echoing off the vaulted ceiling. Blake's stomach sank. This was his father's move whenever he was plotting...planning. Definitely not good.

His father paused, tapping his index finger against his bottom lip. "I think there might be a solution to this situation that will benefit us both."

Hell, no. "I know how this works. Your solutions only benefit you."

"It depends on how you look at it." His father's smile was cold. "This could definitely benefit Abigail. Isn't that what you *say* you want?"

"I never said any such thing."

"Your actions speak loud enough for you."

And he'd thought he'd shown remarkable restraint... Remaining silent would keep Blake from incriminating himself further. So he kept his trap shut and his gaze glued to the man before him. Armand fitted in so well with the sterile beauty of the Boudreaux plantation. It was his perfect backdrop.

"Yes, I believe this will definitely work. I've waited a long time for this." Armand nodded as if confirming the thought to himself. His full head of silver hair glinted in the sun from the arched window behind him. "And you're gonna give me exactly what I want."

Blake turned away, panic running through him at the thought of going back to being that eighteen-year-old boy who had no defenses against his father. But just when he thought he would stride right over to the door and disappear through it, he caught a glimpse of tangled brown hair and pink leggings at the top of the stairs.

What choice do I have?

He could report Armand for neglect, but Blake doubted that would do more than dent his father's reputation. Armand knew too many people in high places for any charges to go far. Abigail probably wouldn't even be removed from the home.

He could take her with him now, but that would probably lead to him being accused of kidnapping…and she'd end up right back home.

He needed more time, more resources…but he could not let Abigail down, even if it meant turning his own life inside out to help her. Who would have guessed this playboy would grow a conscience?

He turned back to his father. "What do you want me to do?"

With a grin that said he knew he'd gotten his way, Armand slipped through the double doors at the far end of the room leading to his office, then returned with a file folder in his hand. Blake didn't dare look up the stairs and give away Abigail's continued presence. But he was conscious of her sitting just out of his father's line of sight.

"There is a woman here in town, Madison Landry. She has something that belongs to me. Something you will retrieve."

"Can't you get a lawyer to take care of that?"

"That route has proved…fruitless. Now it's time for a different approach."

The rare admission of failure was unheard of from his father, which piqued Blake's interest. "So you want me to convince a former…what, lover?…to return something to you?" Obviously legal channels hadn't worked, so his father didn't have a legitimate leg to stand on.

His father smirked. "Hardly." He pulled a photograph out of the file. "Have you ever heard of the Belarus diamond?"

"No." Jewels had never been a major focus for Blake.

"It's a rare, two-carat, fancy vivid blue diamond that was gifted to our family by a Russian prince before we settled in Louisiana after leaving France. When I was young and foolish, I had the diamond placed into a setting for an engagement ring. For a woman who did not deserve anything nearly so special."

Well, this was news to Blake. He studied a photograph of a brilliant blue oval-shaped jewel. "You were engaged before my mother?"

"To the daughter of a now nearly extinct family from Louisiana society, Jacqueline Landry. The engagement lasted less than a year."

"So she dumped you?"

If not, Armand would have taken steps to get back what was his before walking away.

Armand's back went ramrod straight, as if he were affronted by the assumption. His sigh indicated he had no high horse to sit on. "She made the foolish choice to leave, and took the ring with her. That diamond belongs to our family. It is mine to do with as I wish."

But not the ring? This wasn't about a piece of jewelry Armand could hand down to his children. It was about something else... Money? Pride? Surely not after all of these years.

"Then you shouldn't have given it away," Blake reasoned.

"I sent several letters through the years demanding the ring back, all of which were returned unopened."

"From my limited experience with broken engagements, that's her prerogative."

His father's snap to attention told Blake he'd touched a nerve.

"Dammit, this is not the time for your flippant sarcasm. I want that ring and I will have it." Armand smoothed down his hair and jacket in a move utterly familiar to Blake. Growing up, he'd seen it often after his father's rages. Blake steeled himself as a wave of unpleasant emotions washed over him.

"You will get it for me, Blake."

"How? You don't even know if Jacqueline's daughter still has it."

"There's never been any record of it being found or sold. Which means it's still in the family's possession somehow. You will find this woman and get it back from her. With her knowledge or without it."

"You expect me to convince her to just hand over a priceless diamond that belonged to her mother?"

"You'll find a way. I'm sure a man like you, one who has seduced and discarded numerous women through the years, will have no problem with this mission. It should be a perfect use for the very few skills you've actually cultivated in your lifetime."

Blake had to admit, that stung a little. Even if it came from his father, who wouldn't have a nice thing to say about him if he'd used his wealth to become a big-shot CEO, either. Of course, the other skills Blake had developed he kept well disguised behind the facade of his care-free lifestyle. "Those women knew the score going in."

"This one won't. And I forbid you to enlighten her." He narrowed his gaze on his son. "Until afterward, of course. If you want to tell her you stole from her to save your sister, that's your business."

Armand handed over a file with all the confidence of a man who would get his way. "Read it. Let me know."

"I can't do this." *Could he?*

"And there's one more condition," his father went on, as if Blake hadn't spoken. "Access to Abigail will be limited by me until the job is done. But afterward, you can have her all to yourself. I'll sign the paperwork to wash my hands of her, and you can give her the upbringing you claim she needs."

Bile rose in the back of Blake's throat. He wasn't sure what he'd expected when he'd walked back through the Boudreaux plantation's doors, but no part of this conversation had gone according to plan. What business did a man who'd spent his life deliberately avoiding any type of responsibility have raising a young girl with epilepsy?

As if he could read Blake's thoughts, his father smirked. "Are you sure a playboy like you is up to the challenge?"

"Sleepy?"

Madison Landry started awake, embarrassed at being caught sleeping by her boss at Maison de Jardin. "I'm so sorry," she stammered out, "I'm just not sleeping well right now."

"It's not a problem for me," Trinity Hyatt said with one of her trademark gracious smiles, "especially since you're here on your day off. Want to tell me why that is?"

Madison tried to shrug off the question with a lame excuse. "There's always plenty to do around here." And there was.

The charity, which provided a safe haven and life skills training for abused women and children, was in a constant state of managed chaos. If it wasn't laundry that needed doing, it was job applications or fund-raising or any number of things. The desk in front of her in the downstairs office was filled to overflowing with paperwork and records.

Not for anything would Madison admit she'd come over to Maison de Jardin, which shared a border with her family estate, because she needed a distraction. Not because work needed to be done.

The last thing she wanted to discuss were the sleepless nights. The memories of her father's last painful days. Dreams where she could hear him struggle to breathe with the pneumonia clouding his lungs, causing fear to tighten her own chest. Waves of gratitude over the old-fashioned doctor who would still come to the house to treat him after her father's refusal to be moved to a hospital. The stuff of her nightmares.

Though the understanding expression in Trinity's soft gaze said she probably knew already. And her boss wasn't one to shy away from the hard discussions. "Well, I hate to see you suffering from insomnia. I had the same issue after my mom died. Just couldn't turn my brain off for anything."

"That's definitely an issue," Madison agreed, fiddling

with her pen as she thought back over so many sleepless nights lately. It was one of the few things Madison felt comfortable discussing. She tried distracting Trinity from any deeper issues. "Besides, it's hard to retrain yourself to sleep well after having to stay alert during the night for so long."

Only her attempt at distraction just gave her boss more fodder for discussion.

"How many years did you take care of your dad?" Trinity asked, leaning against the doorjamb.

Her gaze swept over the room with familiarity, giving Madison a momentary reprieve. After all, the office had last been Trinity's. She'd only moved up to take care of Hyatt Heights, the company started by her late husband. He and his parents had established Maison de Jardin in New Orleans when he'd been a young man. But taking over his company meant Trinity didn't have time to run the charity, too, especially after her late husband's relatives had gone to court to fight over his estate.

Madison just happened to be in the right place at the right time. She'd known Trinity since she was a teenager, coming over to the shelter to help whenever she could. Unfortunately, her dad's illness had prevented that at times. But when Trinity had to move on, she'd trusted Madison to step into the role despite her age, knowing her life experience went way beyond her years.

Trinity's perusal of her old office ended with a look straight at Madison, who squashed the urged to squirm in her seat.

Madison cleared her throat. "Ten. But the sleeping and mobility issues were only a problem for the last five or so."

"Madison," Trinity said in a voice so gentle it eased

Madison's instinctive panic. "You realize that it's perfectly normal to *not* be okay. Right?"

Madison knew her answers were clipped, but the dread she'd felt for weeks was clawing at the back of her throat with each word.

Multiple sclerosis was a tough disease. One Madison didn't wish on anyone after dealing with it up close and personal. The thought of what her dad had gone through always made her sad. He'd lost his business when Madison was young, then been diagnosed with MS before losing the love of his life. But they'd had good times together, too, leaning on each other for comfort and joy.

Madison could barely respond above a whisper. "I know." With a hard mental shove, she locked all those roiling emotions away. The more she talked about them, the more power they had. It was better just to move forward. "It's really okay," she said, mentally reminding herself that her restlessness and fear and pain could be normalized. "Last night, I spent the time cleaning and reading some more of my mother's journals." After all, what else was there to do at three in the morning?

There was a gentle caution in Trinity's question. "Are you sure you're ready to clean out the house, Madison? Your father has only been gone six months."

As much as she sometimes wished it didn't, Madison was well aware that life had to go on. "The house has to go on the market soon. With only me to clean it out…" She shrugged, as if this wasn't a discussion she'd had with herself a million times over.

Shuffling the papers on the desk before her didn't distract her from the ache of knowing she would have to sell the only home she'd ever had. It was falling down around her, even after years of doing the best she could with it, but every one of her lifetime of memories involved that house somehow. Knowing she would have to part with it was only making her grief grow exponentially.

But who knew how long it would take to clean out the clutter and sort through her parents' possessions? She discovered new pockets of stuff all the time. Just a couple of months ago she'd found a collection of journals that had belonged to her mother. Reading them had brought her memory back in vivid detail. They brought her a lot of solace as she sorted through more and more stuff.

And she had no idea how she would afford to do any of the repairs the house would need, much less cosmetic work, before she put it on the market. Her job here paid her substantially better than the odd jobs she'd taken to keep her and her dad afloat after her mother's accidental death, but years of neglect had led to some significant damage in what had once been the most beautiful, stately home in New Orleans's Garden District.

Deep down, Madison just wished it was all over and done with. That the house was fixed, sold and being renovated by someone who could afford to return it to its former glory. It might hurt to rip the bandage off, but at least it would be gone.

I can only do so much...was the mantra she lived by. All of her life Madison had focused on one task at a time, because she was only one person, usually working without any help. Coming to Maison de Jardin had allowed her to be part of a team. But for much of her life, it had been her...or nobody.

"I'm so sorry, Madison."

"Don't be," she replied with a shaky smile. But at least she still remembered how to form one. "Coming to work here has been the best thing that's ever happened to me. Thank you, Trinity."

"Girl, I couldn't do it without you. Especially right

now. I know the women here are in good hands. But—"
She grinned. "Enough of all this emotion… I have an
exciting surprise for you."

"What?" Madison welcomed the change of subject,
relief easing her tense muscles.

"Your dress came in!"

For most women, the news would be exciting. For
Madison, it brought on another fit of nervousness. Next
week they would be attending a society fund-raising
event, a first for Madison. She'd never had cause to leave
her father's sickroom for such things, nor the funds. But
in her new capacity as director for Maison de Jardin, it
would be her job to mix and mingle with New Orleans's
best and brightest. Though their legacy from Trinity's
deceased husband should fund them for a long time to
come, it never hurt to have support from others who
could afford to help.

Thus, Madison found herself about to be presented to
New Orleans high society.

A generation ago, it would have been Madison's right-
ful place. Her parents both came from established families that had helped found this incredible city. The last
of their respective lines, the love merger should have ce-
mented them as a power couple.

But Madison only knew this from a few stories she'd
heard from her mother growing up. Her mother had been
very secretive about their marriage and choice to live a
more isolated life despite their prominent home in New
Orleans's Garden District. Something had happened
around the time of their marriage, but Madison had never
been able to figure out quite what the scandal had been.

Which was why she'd been reading her mother's journals each night after finding them in one of the closed-
off rooms on the upper floor of their house. Maybe there

she could find some clue to how her parents had met and married. After all, stories like that might replace the sad memories she currently fought off during her sleepless nights.

Trinity took her hand and led her through the halls of Maison de Jardin to the master suite up on the second floor. It was currently empty, having been Trinity's room before she moved out when she married Michael Hyatt a mere two months ago. Michael's tragic death and Trinity's current battle over his estate left her life a little unsettled. Since Madison lived nearby for the time being, she hadn't claimed the space as hers, wanting Trinity to still feel like she had a home here if she needed it.

Laid across the pale blue bedspread was a beautiful lavender dress. Madison gasped, letting her fingers train over the soft flow of material.

"It's an unusual color for a redhead," Trinity said. "I think it's gonna be a fabulous choice."

Madison hoped so.

This was how she would be presented to society. Her stomach churned, though her nerves were a welcome distraction from her earlier grief. First impressions were a big deal. While her family name had been well known in NOLA in the past, history had slowly erased it from the current consciousness. The South still prided itself on its history, and the history of its families, but money stood for a lot more. It was the way of the world. Madison knew that and knew she couldn't change it. With her father's illness, her family had drained its coffers until all they had was social security and what little she could eke out from various odd jobs. Her father's health meant she couldn't go to work full-time.

She had to remember, this was her job now. Making a good impression would allow her to be helpful to the charity—now and in the future. But that didn't ease her nerves.

Should she back out now? Give in to the fear and tell Trinity she would need someone who could better handle this part of the job?

"Let's try it on!" Trinity exclaimed, her excitement puncturing Madison's growing fears.

When she stepped back into the bedroom suite after changing, Madison didn't recognize herself in the mirror. The bodice was fitted, with only one strap made out of fabric flowers that went over her left shoulder. Multiple layers of chiffon allowed the skirt to swing around her legs to right above her knees.

"A killer set of strappy heels and you're all set."

Madison chuckled. "Let's just hope I don't break a leg in them."

"You'll be fine. It just takes practice."

Madison brushed her hands down over the gown, learning the shape with her shaking fingers. She didn't even look like herself. It was hard to take it all in.

"We can do your hair like this," Trinity said as she lifted Madison's mass of thick auburn tresses to the top of her head. "With some drop earrings and curls."

"I feel kind of like Cinderella," Madison said with an unsteady laugh.

"Well, maybe you will meet a Prince Charming at the ball. It's really just a good ol' New Orleans party, but you know good and well there will be dancing. Won't that be fun?"

The very concept was foreign to a practical girl like Madison, but the transformation hinted at in the mirror egged her on. After all, she'd never been someone who backed away from what needed to be done. Ever. "I could use a little fun."

Trinity gave her an exaggerated wide-eyed look in the mirror.

"Okay," Madison conceded, "I need quite a bit of fun."

"As long as it's safe."

And requires nothing that makes me think too hard. In fact, a Prince Charming might be a little too complicated for her right now. Her life had always been and continued to be full of responsibilities and organization and obligations… She needed some space from all of that.

Madison smiled at herself in the mirror.

And who knew? Maybe she could find a *Prince for Now* to have some fun with. A girl could dream, right?

Two

What the hell was he doing here?

Blake should have been perfectly at home at the party being held at the home of one of Louisiana's most famous power couples. It was the type of event where people with money gathered to discuss local gossip and politics, and generally impress others with their money and intelligence…or lack thereof. Blake frequented many such parties all across Europe. The only change was the language and food. The people were mostly the same.

While he usually anticipated getting lucky at such parties, he'd never gone to one for the express purpose of initiating a one-night stand.

Yes, casual sex was a part of his lifestyle, but the women he spent time with were always on the same page. He made sure of that up front. The fact that the only plan he could come up with—in terms of feasibility and expediency—was to get into the Landry home by way of a one-night stand brought on a completely foreign feeling of shame.

But for Abigail, he'd do what he had to.

Hell, even reporting Armand for neglect wasn't an option. His father had more than one city official in his pocket. Besides, could he risk the possibility that Abigail might be forced into foster care before he could get everything worked out? At least at home there was a sympathetic housekeeper to keep an eye on her. Sherry couldn't be with her all the time, but she was always nearby and looking out for Abigail. At least, that's what Blake had gathered from their phone conversations. Given the odds of her ending up some place worse than his father's house, Blake knew his best bet was to get the diamond as soon as absolutely possible.

So, as uncomfortable as the idea made him, his only choice seemed to be seducing Madison Landry to fulfill his father's demands…unless he wanted to resort to breaking and entering.

It hadn't taken him long to spot the woman he sought in the crowd, though she appeared much younger than he'd anticipated.

Even in the photographs in the file, she hadn't looked quite as old as her twenty-six years. Maybe it was her pale complexion or the dusting of freckles across her nose that she hadn't bothered to hide for tonight's occasion. But somehow he'd expected the hard life that had been briefly chronicled in the file to show on her face.

She'd also spent most of her time here barely speaking and rarely venturing from the table she was standing near. He'd been anticipating someone eager to display herself on the marriage market, rather than the quiet woman he saw before him. After all, she was young, single and had too hard of a life to be a party girl. She wasn't dancing, though she moved slightly to the music as if it intrigued her. There was no steady round of interested men introducing themselves. Certainly no flirting.

She appeared to be a species he had no experience with.

He had enough confidence to approach her while she was still surrounded by her friends. But now it looked like he wouldn't have to. She'd just returned from the restroom to her table alone, looking longingly out on the dance floor. A young woman who needed to have some fun…and Blake was the perfect partner in crime.

Glancing down at the napkin in his hand, he grinned. Now he had an interesting opening to approach her.

Blake crossed over to the table and paused beside Madison's chair. She glanced up, then did the double take he was used to. Her eyes widened as she got a good look at him, though she quickly tried to mask her reaction. He'd never been uncomfortable knowing he'd dressed to impress—but for some reason he was tonight; it made him feel like a used car salesman.

"Hello," he said simply.

"Hi there." Her smile wasn't quite firm at the edges.

Then she glanced around as if he surely must be looking for someone else. But he wasn't. Blake knew exactly who he was meeting tonight.

Slowly he slid the napkin in front of her on the table and gave her a moment to get a good look. Her brows went up, then she leaned in for a closer look. Step One accomplished.

He'd made a sketch of her on the white scrap. Her face was in profile, and dead accurate, though the drawing lacked the vibrant color of her auburn hair and the multihued strings of lights decorating the large room.

He pitched his voice slightly louder to be heard over

the music. "A woman this beautiful shouldn't be sitting on the sidelines."

The muscles in her throat worked as if she had to swallow a couple of times before she answered. "Is that a remark about my physical appearance or your artistic prowess?"

"Both?" he answered, surprised at her response. Most women would have gushed over the gift or been flattered by his remarks. He'd never been questioned over a drawing before.

Despite that, she rubbed her finger over the edges of the sketch. Finally she looked up with a small smile that seemed genuine. "How long did it take you to draw this?"

He shrugged. "About five minutes."

"At least you aren't too invested as a stalker," she said, raising a single brow as if in challenge.

Blake was shocked enough to laugh. Definitely not what he'd expected. Neither was her voice. On the deep side, slightly husky, it evoked images of mystery and sex. The opposite of her young, bright presence.

She ducked her face down for a moment, before glancing up at him through thick lashes. "I probably wasn't supposed to say that out loud."

"Definitely not." But she could keep talking all she wanted.

"I knew I'd never fit in here."

On their surface, the words could be taken as if she were teasing, just making polite conversation, but the way she worried her bottom lip with the edge of her teeth told him otherwise. "First time?" he asked.

She nodded, causing the colored lights to reflect off the glorious red of her hair. Blake had the sudden urge to see it down around her shoulders, rather than pulled back from the heart shape of her face. His lips suddenly felt dry. "Me, too," he murmured.

To his surprise, she leaned a little closer. "So you're not from around here?"

"Yes—" Suddenly the music cut out, making Blake's voice sound loud. "Yes, I am from here, but it's been a while. Care to be new together?"

Again her teeth pressed against the fullness of her lower lip, causing blood to rush into the curve as she released it. "My friends will be back soon."

Blake ignored the subtle rejection. "Good, then they can watch me *not* stalk you on the dance floor."

Suddenly the music started up again, this time with an exuberant trumpet player in the lead.

He moved in closer to make himself heard. Leaning toward her ear, he asked, "Would you like to dance?"

Her breath caught, trapped inside her throat as she swallowed once more. Then her body gave a quick shiver, though it was far from cold in the room. Blake should be grateful for her reaction, this confirmation that she wasn't immune to him, but instead he felt a strange mixture of grim determination and melting heat low in his belly. Did she feel the same attraction as he found trickling through his unprepared consciousness?

Madison's gaze swung longingly toward the dance floor. Until now, the lively sound of jazz tunes had filled the air all night but she hadn't once approached the dance floor.

"Well, I don't think so."

To his shock, she pulled back a couple of inches. "What's the matter? Part of coming to a dance party is to dance."

"I think people come to parties for a lot of different reasons," she said, glancing down as she ran her finger over the edge of the drawing once more. "To socialize, to drink, to eat, to be seen…" She paused, and he swore he saw a flush creep over her cheeks, even in the dim light.

A woman who still blushed? Blake couldn't remember the last time he'd dealt with one of those. Before he could confirm it, she glanced the other way. Maybe to look for her friends? Maybe to hide the evidence?

He wasn't sure, but part of him, the part that had been watching her tonight, wanted to know for sure. In fact, the more he watched, the more he wanted to know. And that interest made him even more uncomfortable with what he was doing here tonight.

"I'm Blake Boudreaux, by the way," he said.

To his relief, no recognition showed in her expression.

"I'm Madison." She seemed to relax a little before she asked, "Did you move away for work?"

Oh, she was gonna make him earn that dance, wasn't she? "More like life management."

"Seriously?"

"Yes. Leaving allowed me to have a life." He softened his unexpected answer with as charming a grin as he could muster.

Madison cocked her head to the side, awakening an urge to kiss her delicate chin. He straightened just a little. "I'm just visiting long enough to handle a family issue."

She nodded, the move containing an odd wisdom considering her youth. "Those aren't easy."

"Never, but they are the reason we drink and have fun."

The laugh that came from her surprised him. No giggles for this girl. Instead she gave a full-bodied laugh that made tingles run down his spine. She didn't try to hide her enjoyment of his little joke or keep her response polite.

"So how about that dance?"

Suddenly a strange look came across her face—a combination of surprise and panic and almost fear. This time her retreat was obvious. Blake sat stunned as she mumbled, "I… I don't think that's a good idea. I mean…" She waved her hand in front of her as if to erase her response but inadvertently bumped her drink and knocked it over.

"Oh, my. I'm so sorry."

"It's okay." Blake wasn't sure why, but he reached out to grasp her hands in his. "It's okay, Madison."

She started to smile, but then her face contorted and she jerked her hands away. "Good night," she said, then turned on her heel and ran into the crowd.

Blake stared for a moment in confusion. They'd seemed to be having a good time. She wasn't as comfortable with men coming up to her as he'd expected, but she hadn't shown any signs of hating him during the conversation. What had gone wrong? This was not at all how he'd expected tonight to turn out. But then again, not much about Madison had turned out how he'd expected.

Honestly, this hadn't happened since he'd passed his eighteenth birthday, and he had no idea how to handle it. Something had spooked her. Should he leave it for tonight and try to find another way in?

Thoughts of Abigail and what might happen to her in the amount of time it might take him to find another opening into Madison's life had his heart pounding hard in his chest. He clenched his fists. He would not let her down.

Reaching out, he righted the now-empty wine glass. The small amount of liquid that had been inside had already been absorbed by the tablecloth. Next to the stain lay the napkin with Madison's sketch on it and a small lavender bag.

A bag? As the realization hit that it must be Madison's, so did a renewed sense of purpose. A one-night stand might not be an option, but at least he could arrange a date? It would afford him a chance to impress her and possibly find another way into her house to do some digging.

Plunging into the crowd, Blake didn't give himself time to think or plan. Halfway across the room he saw Madison and her friends near the door, speaking to the hosts as if they were about to leave. Adrenaline quickened his step as he realized his window of opportunity was closing.

The opportunity to find the diamond and save his sister. To understand more about the unusual woman with her emerald green eyes. To explore the strange feelings she called up inside of him.

Blake called out her name when she and her friends were just steps from vanishing through the door into the warm Southern night.

"Madison."

She glanced over her shoulder, her eyes widening as she saw him. She turned back to her friends, but Blake wasn't going to let that stop him. He stepped into the circle without an invitation.

"Madison, I believe this is yours." He held out the lavender bag.

"Oh, yes." She frowned as she looked at the offering. "Yes, I'm so sorry—"

"I thought you might need it," he said, cutting off her words, which seemed to just compound her awkwardness.

"Thank you so much."

He glanced at the couple standing with them, but the woman simply gave a composed smile. "We'll meet you at the car, Madison," she said and they turned to leave.

Madison took the bag from his outstretched hand, then fiddled with the strap for a moment. "I really do appreciate this," she murmured.

Luckily, they were far enough away from the dance floor that he could hear her. "Look, Madison. I think maybe I came on too strong back there."

"No. No, it wasn't you. It's me. I'm just not used to—" She waved her hand around them. "Please don't think you did anything wrong."

He could almost feel her need to leave as the feeling came over her. Something about her body language told him she was ready to run. He couldn't let that happen.

"Tell you what, how about you make it up to me?"

Her gaze flicked up to his, and he gave her a teasing smile. "Or rather, how can I get a second chance… an opportunity to get to know you when I don't have to yell to be heard?"

Her muscles relaxed and she smiled, just a little. Why did that smile feel like a big victory?

So let's try this again… "Where can I pick you up?"

"Why in the world did I agree to this?"

Madison looked around at the array of clothes that she'd brought over to try on for Trinity. Never in her life had she done this. She'd never been the girl to worry over what she wore or what her makeup looked like or how other people perceived her outward physical appearance. Because her life didn't have anything to do with that.

It was about helping others and doing what needed to be done for her daddy. Not clothes and shoes. Her daddy had never cared about any of those things. And neither had Trinity. It was easier to do their job in jeans or yoga pants.

Even her mother's journals provided no blueprint for

how to date. Madison had found them oddly lacking in information from before her marriage. There were a few comments about a happy childhood but nothing about dating or her engagement.

Right now, it was easier to focus on clothes than to wonder whether she could sit across from a man as suave and charismatic as Blake Boudreaux and be comfortable and happy and…have fun?

The women at Maison de Jardin were grateful for a helping hand and a friend. That was what made Madison feel fulfilled.

Wasn't it? She had to admit to an unfamiliar restlessness since her daddy had died six months ago. It wasn't that she didn't enjoy helping people. But there was an aching need for something a little *more.* Something only hinted at on the nights she sang at a local nightclub—a hobby that she could indulge now that her father was gone. The pure enjoyment of losing herself in things that didn't require her to meet someone else's needs. That didn't require her to work, to figure out how to fix things. She'd been doing that stuff all her life.

Maybe it was the extra space in her life now that her last living relative was gone. Maybe it was her age, and the realization that most young women were starting to settle down or already had by now. Maybe it was just a quirk of her overactive imagination. But for once, she simply needed enjoyment without any responsibility attached.

Would she find that with Blake? Everything about that man made her nervous and excited and tingly in ways she'd never felt before. He made her feel emotions that weren't exactly comfortable enough to be called fun. He made her feel *too much.* Especially when he moved in close, smelling spicy and exuding heat.

Just thinking about it made her heart thud hard against her ribs.

She hadn't imagined two people could have that much chemistry outside of a bedroom. He made her think of magic and sin and heat all mixed together in the air. Incredible.

Which only made her more awkward, more anxious than she'd ever felt. Her life was built on a definition of success that had become uniquely hers through the years. Not money or fancy cars or expensive clothes, but days and hours and moments of achievement through sheer determination, hard work and action. Not this uncertainty that made her feel paralyzed.

"What am I doing, Trinity?" she asked, unable to resist nibbling at the inside of her lower lip. "Why did I say yes to this?"

But she knew why. It had been a combination of that tingly excitement and the fact that he'd tracked her down and given her purse back. She'd hastily surrendered her phone number, then rushed out the door with burning cheeks and butterflies in her stomach.

"Everything will be fine," her friend assured her. "Did he tell you what y'all were gonna do?"

"No," Madison huffed. "He said he wanted it to be a surprise. All I have is an address and that's about it."

"Which I know is driving you crazy. You're nothing if not prepared."

Trinity knew her too well. "The mystery should be perfect. It should help me step out of my comfort zone. Instead—" Madison pressed her fist against her stomach.

"I know, love." Trinity gave her a quick hug. "What's the address?"

Madison picked up her phone to review Blake's texts. "Looks like it's somewhere down near the river."

"Well, meeting him there is a smart move." Trinity's lips twisted in a small grimace, confirming Madison's belief that she needed to keep her own vehicle nearby. Better to take precautions and be safe than sorry later. "I guess working in this place makes me extra cautious."

Me, too. Madison had tried to be a modern woman—also something she didn't have a lot of experience in—assuring Blake she could get herself where they were going. After all, what did she really know about him besides chemistry? Except now the lack of information made her feel even more ill-prepared for the night ahead.

The array of clothes before her included a relatively small number of articles from her own closet and a few she'd just spent a meager part of her salary on at an upscale secondhand store. "So we'll be near the river, right?" she asked herself more than Trinity. With an impatient sigh, she grabbed a new pair of jean shorts and a casual blouse and forced herself to dress without thinking any more about how she looked.

Trinity offered an understanding smile. "If you need anything, keep your cell phone on you. I'll come get you if you call. No matter what time."

"I will," Madison said as she tried to breathe through her nerves.

"Text me anyway when you get there so I know everything is okay."

This time Madison smiled. "Yes, Mama."

But she was very grateful for Trinity's offer when she arrived at the address and found herself near a marina. She walked along the worn planks of the dock until she found Blake waiting for her halfway down. Next to him in the slip was a very smooth, very elegant boat.

Embarrassed heat washed over her immediately. Only sheer determination kept her feet walking toward him. He was dressed in a designer polo and dress pants, standing next to the nicest boat she'd ever seen—even on television. She tugged down on the hem of her shirt, wishing she'd opted for a summer dress at the very least.

What the heck was she doing here? she asked herself for the bazillionth time that evening.

Blake didn't seem to notice. "Good evening," he said smoothly.

Madison drew her gaze away from the craft, realizing her mouth had dropped open…just a little. But all that gleaming chrome sure was pretty…and way above her pay grade.

"I'm glad to see you made it," Blake said, as if he hadn't noticed her gawking.

Madison could barely meet his eyes. This wasn't a situation she knew how to handle or fix or arrange. What should she say? *Nice boat?* Was it even called that? Or was it a small yacht? *Ugh.* "I'll admit, I almost backed out." *Dang it.* Why did she say that?

But Blake chuckled. "I guess I understand. After all, I'm practically a stranger. Though why you wouldn't want to spend the evening with someone as heroic as me…"

"Heroic?"

With a sheepish grin, he offered a hand to steady her as she stepped onto the craft. "I did return a missing purse."

"That hardly qualifies," she scoffed.

"A guy can hope, right?"

She raised a brow at his begging puppy dog expression, then forced herself to glance around the boat. "The question is, can you pilot this thing without breaking it?"

"You'd be surprised how smooth she is in the water. A captain's dream."

Something about the way he said the words sent a tingle along her spine. The good kind…not the afraid-he's-a-serial-killer kind. To distract herself, she hurriedly took a picture of the boat's name on the prow and texted it to Trinity, much to his bemusement. Even though Blake didn't give her any creepy vibes, she wasn't taking any chances…and he needed to know that.

"A girl can't be too careful," she said with a shrug. "After all, if you are secretly a serial killer and I disappear tonight, at least my friends will know where to start looking."

His shocked expression made her laugh. Normally, Madison never censored herself when it came to laughter. There'd been too many sad times in her life for her not to cherish every happy moment. But here, on this beautiful boat with a beautiful man, her full bodied laugh suddenly seemed loud, obnoxious. She quickly smothered it.

"That's actually pretty smart."

To her surprise, he didn't seem offended that she might think he was dangerous. She hoped that proved he could handle the quirks that made Madison who she was. Not that she should care. She should have the attitude that if he didn't like her, she could easily walk away.

This was about fun. Not relationships or happily-ever-afters.

So why did her hand in his feel much more important than that?

Blake had clearly spared no expense when it came to tonight. The boat itself was brand-new, with a lot of bells and whistles from what she could tell. It had a large deck, covered access below and several leather-upholstered chairs in the upstairs driving area. It was the on-water equivalent of a luxury car.

Blake cast off, then joined her in the chairs up front. Now it was just the two of them. Maybe she should be happy that there wasn't a captain to navigate and watch their every move all night. She wasn't actually sure if that would have made her happy or not.

Only twenty minutes into this date and settling down seemed impossible. Blake guided the boat smoothly out of the slip and down the channel to where the shore spread out before them. The boat practically glided on the glassy surface.

At this time of year, the breeze at night was cool and comforting, a relief from the midday heat. A recent rain had lowered the humidity, though Madison knew from experience that in a couple weeks it would be uncomfortable no matter what time of day without a breeze and a cold drink.

That was life in the South.

Blake picked up speed as they gained open water, which was when the first bit of uneasiness hit Madison's stomach. Her focus turned inward as she tried to figure out the source. Maybe her nerves? After all, she had experienced plenty of anxiety over the past few days. No, this was something else. Something she couldn't quite put her finger on.

The queasiness rose with each passing minute, forcing Madison to swallow once or twice. She tried to concentrate on the feel of the wind on her skin, praying that the feeling would pass. Of all the things she'd anticipated tonight, feeling sick was not one.

Blake slowed, then stopped the boat out in the middle of the glassy gray water. The wake rocked the boat, sparking a quick surge of nausea. Madison breathed in deeply, then let it out slowly. Maybe she'd be better now that the boat had stopped.

Blake smiled over at her. "Good?"

She nodded with what was hopefully a steady smile.

The last thing she wanted was a double helping of embarrassment tonight.

"I'll set up dinner then."

Madison didn't move as Blake made his way to the back. At the press of a button, a portion of the deck floor retracted and a table rose out of the depths. *Well.* She guessed they wouldn't be eating off paper plates from their laps, would they?

She didn't have a lot of experience eating outdoors with formal silverware. More like fast-food wrappers and brown paper napkins.

Madison turned back toward the front of the boat, pretending to be absorbed in the view of the water. But her stomach continued to churn. What should she do?

Ask to go back? The thought of that trip had bile backing up into her throat. She definitely couldn't eat right now. So she simply breathed and prayed whatever this was would go away.

To her relief, the unease in her stomach subsided. She gave herself another minute, then two, but the ticking clock in her head told her he would start to wonder what was going on if she kept delaying. Finally Madison stood to make her way to the back of the boat. The world seemed to tilt as she walked, even though she could swear the boat wasn't rocking. What was wrong with her?

"I'm about ready," Blake said as she approached. Then he looked up from his task. "Are you okay?"

She tried to smile. She really did. Then she glanced down at the table and saw an open container of what appeared to be chicken or crab salad. Two seconds later, she was hanging over the edge of the boat to empty her stomach.

Three

"Are you okay now?" Blake asked.

The ultra-pale cast to Madison's skin worried him. Her freckles stood out even in the dim light from the dock. They'd made it back but the last thirty minutes had been a strain, as he knew the very thing he was doing to quickly get them to land was the thing that was making her sick. It had never occurred to him that she would suffer motion sickness.

He was used to drama like crying, yelling and feigned illness. One look at Madison, with her trembling and careful movements, convinced him this was real. His chest went heavy, filling with an unfamiliar mixture of responsibility and regret.

"No," Madison croaked, her hands tightening around the edge of the dock where she now sat. She swallowed hard enough for him to see. "Actually, I'm good. Just let me not move for a while."

"I'm sorry." Her sheer desperate need to stay still made his own stomach twist. Having ridden everything from a camel to a fighter jet in the name of adventure, Blake could only relate through sympathy. "Why didn't you warn me that you suffered from motion sickness?"

She cracked one eyelid open to peek at him. Even her brilliant green eyes seemed a paler color. "I didn't know. I've never been on a boat before."

That explained that. For the second time since meeting her, Blake found himself in the minor role of rescuer. Without an instructor in sight... "I'm gonna lock everything down. Will you be okay for a few minutes?"

She nodded but didn't speak. Blake left her to get her bearings on the dock while he secured the yacht and packed up their uneaten dinner.

He wasn't sure whether to laugh or rage at his current situation. His only thought when he'd chosen this adventure had been to impress her. He knew she didn't have a lot of money and probably had never seen a vehicle like this one. Add in the reflection of a full moon on the water at night. Instant romance! That was as far as he'd gotten.

He'd been searching for the quick and easy route to accomplish his goal of getting into the house. And maybe the current situation afforded him the perfect opportunity. He could kill two birds with one stone. By taking her home and watching over her, he could make sure she didn't suffer any ill effects from the motion sickness and get some time to search the house. The longer he spent with Madison, the more sleeping with her to accomplish his plan seemed wrong. Madison wasn't a casual girl and he simply couldn't treat her that way.

His frustration sparked as he thought back over the last few days and his father's refusal to let him see Abigail. He'd been worried about how she was, and anxious to do something the old man would see as "progress" so that maybe he could check on her. But looking over at Madison on the steady wooden planks, sunk in on herself to ease the pain in her stomach, made him feel guilty for that, as well.

Blake finished securing the boat, then stepped up onto the dock. "Here," he said, offering both his hands to help her up, "let's get you home."

"Oh, right." Madison pushed her hair back behind one ear. Was her grimace one of discomfort or embarrassment? "You don't have to do that. If you'll just call me a car…"

Blake scoffed. He may be a lot of things, but he wasn't the type of man to send a sick woman home all by herself. Besides, he still had a job to do. "Absolutely not. I'll take you home. Then we'll both know you're safe." He thought back to her insistence that she meet him here. "I promise I'll take you straight to your house."

With great reluctance, Madison put her hands in his and let him lift her to her feet. He waited a moment to make sure she was steady before letting go. He held her hands just long enough to feel the tremble in them. Was she nervous? Was it him? Or something else?

Part of him was intrigued at the myriad emotions she'd shown tonight. Most women just put the best face on things, presenting him with a facade. But not this one— she was very real.

And overly quiet as they started the drive back to New Orleans proper. Blake had to admit he found himself at a loss.

Which reminded him of exactly where he was and what he was doing. He glanced over at the woman in the seat next to him, who had her gaze trained solidly out the window. She probably was embarrassed by all of this, whereas he was completely focused on his own emotions and complications.

So he softened his voice when he said, "What's the address, Madison?"

He knew exactly where she lived. But taking her straight there would give away too much. Instead, he'd play this out like he knew nothing about her other than what she'd told him. Then he'd go to work on plan B.

"Just take me to Maison de Jardin."

The husky quality of her voice only heightened the panic racing in his veins. Nope, that wasn't a good idea.

"Are you sure? Wouldn't you be more comfortable in your own bed?"

She immediately shook her head. "No," she snapped.

Surprise had him gripping the steering wheel a little tighter. So she was more spirited than he'd thought at first. As he remained silent, she squirmed just a bit, causing her seat to squeak in the quiet. He glanced over at her, but she continued to face the window.

After letting the silence stretch out for a while, he took a deep breath and said, "Look, I just don't want you to be alone and sick." And that was true, despite his currently conflicted emotions and motives. "This is my fault. Let me drive you to your house. I'll stay with you until you feel better...rest will help."

Please let this work.

The barest sounds of a sniffle caused more panic to shoot through him. But another quick glance at her showed no evidence of tears. He'd dealt with a lot of in-sincere waterworks through the years, but something about the rawness of Madison's demeanor right now took it to a whole other level he wasn't sure how to handle.

"Just take me to Maison de Jardin. My friend Trinity is there this evening. She'll watch over me."

He felt a wave of disappointment. He actually wanted to be there with Madison. To make this better—though he had no clue how to do that. But he wanted to be there in a way that had nothing to do with his mission. At all.

Remember Abigail... Remember why you're here...

Right.

What could he do to salvage this? He glanced over at Madison, who was in almost total darkness. True sickness wasn't something he had any experience with. What should he do?

He stewed for a bit, tapping his finger against the steering wheel. By her deep and even breathing, he guessed she'd fallen asleep. Probably the best thing for her.

As soon as the lights of New Orleans appeared in front of them, Blake came up with plan B. Madison slept as he found the local coffee shop he wanted, and locked her inside the car. After a few minutes, he was back. Madison stirred when the internal lights flicked on.

"Where are we?" she asked.

"Not far from the house," he assured her. "I stopped to get you something for your stomach. It probably shouldn't be empty."

She glanced at the cup and frowned. "I don't think coffee is a good idea."

"It's not coffee. It's ginger lemon tea. Supposed to help settle an upset stomach."

Slowly she reached out for the cup, as if scared to believe him. "Thank you. I wouldn't have thought of that."

"Don't be impressed," he said, brushing it off. "You have just witnessed the extent of my knowledge of medicine."

She chuckled, ending with a sigh. Maybe he'd salvaged something of tonight.

A few minutes later, he pulled the car into the circular drive of Maison de Jardin, which he knew bordered her own family land. The house was lit up, assuring Blake that someone was inside.

He unbuckled his seat belt. "Let me just—"

Before he could finish, she had unstrapped herself and was out the door. "No need. Thanks, Blake."

Then the door slammed and she made a quick but unsteady trip to the front door. Blake remained frozen as she unlocked it and slipped inside. Before she did, he caught how the lights along the sidewalk glinted off the wet trails on her cheeks. So much for plan B. He thought about her having someone to look after her, then thought about Abigail, wondering if she was okay tonight.

Would he even be allowed a plan C?

"Oh, Lord. We are in trouble now."

Madison looked over her shoulder to see Trinity and one of the tenants, Tamika, come into the kitchen at Maison de Jardin. She wanted to grin at Trinity's facetious comment but instead turned back to the stand mixer on the granite counter to hide her embarrassment. She was nothing if not predictable. Another strike against her.

"Don't judge," Madison said as she continued adding flour to the mixture. "Besides, everyone benefits."

"Tell that to my waistline," Tamika complained.

"It's totally worth it," Trinity said.

Her boss at the charity completely understood where Madison was coming from. After several years of working together, she could usually recognize when Madison needed some downtime. And showing up here last night after her disaster of a date certainly qualified.

Trinity had been helping out the night before with some budgeting work, which thankfully meant Madi-

son hadn't had to take Blake up on his offer. But she suspected that Trinity hadn't wanted to be at her deceased
husband's mansion across town, hounded by memories
of her best friend and the business consultant hired to
make her an acceptable heir to Michael Hyatt's business empire.

One of Madison's indulgences was to bake in the
kitchen at the grand house. She could bake at home, but
there were a lot of sad memories associated with her
house, her kitchen. It had always been depressing to make
micro versions of her father's favorite sweets, because
there were only two of them to cook for, and there was
barely anything in the cabinets.

Here in Maison's kitchen with its original brick walls,
she could focus on the peacefulness of cooking for people
who appreciated it. All the amenities didn't hurt, either.

Trinity peeked over Madison's shoulder at the batch
already cooling on the counter. "Chocolate chip! My favorite!"

"I'm glad I could help," Madison mumbled.

Tamika said, "I should've known you'd be here baking
after your experience yesterday. I guess residual nausea
kept you from starting sooner."

Madison whirled around, slapping her hands on her
hips. Flour dust floated into the air. "Who told you about
that?"

Tamika's eyes went wide. "I guess a little birdie told
me," she said before glancing over at Trinity.

Great! The humiliation of her failed date would be all
over the building by noon, less than twenty-four hours
since the debacle. Word spread fast. Madison gave Trinity a pointed stare.

Her friend had a chagrined look on her face. "Sorry!
I was worried about you."

"*We* were worried about you," Tamika corrected. "That's why we're down here now instead of waiting until the cookies are completely done. Besides, we thought you might need somebody to talk to after those new posts."

"What posts?" Madison asked, confused.

Tamika shook her cell phone. "Your boy is the subject of today's *New Orleans Secrets and Scandals* blog."

Trinity groaned. "No, please, no more gossip!"

"Don't blame the messenger," Tamika said with a shrug.

Trinity stomped over to the fridge. "Right about now I could use a gallon of wine."

Unfortunately for her, the charity didn't allow alcohol on the premises. But Madison could fully sympathize. The anonymous owner of the *Secrets and Scandals* blog was in the process of making Trinity's life hell. The site posted all kinds of lies about Trinity's relationship with her late husband and questioned her involvement in his death. There had even been posts digging into Trinity's abusive childhood. The popular blog had made Trinity's current sticky situation even more complicated.

Madison wished she could help her friend as she sought to learn everything she could from the business consultant the company had hired to make Trinity a better candidate to run the businesses. She knew Trinity was afraid of losing the court case Michael's relatives had initiated to take the estate from her. Trinity didn't discuss it too much, but Madison had a feeling the situation with the consultant, who was living in the Hyatt mansion, had taken a personal turn that had Trinity more than a little unsettled.

When Tamika handed over her phone, Madison couldn't stop her gaze from scanning down the post. Its headline blared, Playboy Home for Good? Various salacious tidbits jumped out at her from there: *Last seen romancing a Greek princess... Making a splash in Rio de Janeiro...* Photographs of him looking like a Scandinavian prince with a blonde model in a bikini...

Feeling a little sick, Madison handed the phone back. That last picture especially left her feeling like a complete washout as a woman. Blake had spent his life surrounded by gorgeous women who were obviously more on his level...and could actually ride in a yacht without losing their lunch. Heck, they probably owned yachts themselves.

What in the world had he been doing with a down-on-her-luck charity director from New Orleans?

"This guy really lived it up in Europe," Tamika crowed. "He's been spotted skiing in the Alps with beautiful women, on all the best beaches, at all the fancy parties. And he doesn't seem to have a day job, so he's got to be loaded."

"Hey, he sounds like a perfect guy to just have fun with," Trinity mumbled around a bite of cookie.

Madison glared at Trinity for a second, who simply shrugged. Bitterness built up in her throat, roughening her voice as she said, "I have no idea what he was looking for on a date with someone like me, but I'm pretty sure it wasn't me hanging over the side of his boat vomiting. I seriously doubt I'll ever hear from Blake Boudreaux again."

Madison stared morosely down into the second batch of chocolate chip cookie dough, hating that she cared so much about this...hating that she couldn't shake it off... hating that she didn't seem to be the type of woman who could just have fun and not care when things went wrong.

Then she heard a slight giggle from her left, then from her right. She glanced up to find her friends desperately struggling to hold in the laughter. "I'm sorry," Trinity said. "But the visual your words call to mind is just…"

Tamika couldn't hold back any longer and burst out in laughter. Madison realized what she'd said and started to smile…then giggle…then laugh. The image of her hanging over the railing, backside in the air, while a sexy, incredibly rich man watched her ralph over the side of his yacht… If she didn't laugh, she was gonna cry.

Eventually they were all indulging in full-on belly laughs. A sense of gratitude for these good friends who understood her and weren't afraid of a quirky sense of humor warmed her up. All too soon, they were down to a few chuckles and wiping the tears from their faces as they indulged in another spoonful of dough.

"Thanks, guys," Madison said as she tried to catch her breath. "I needed that."

But as she slowly chewed a few chocolate chips, savoring the burst of flavor against her tongue, she sobered. What had a man like that been doing with her? He was obviously sophisticated, and according to the post, he'd been with plenty of women. Model types. Nothing like Madison's red hair and freckles.

Why had he picked the least likely woman at the party to ask on a date?

"Sometimes I wonder if I was being punked the night we met." And yesterday. Except she wasn't anyone anymore. No one would care enough to read about *her*.

Trinity scoffed. "Of course not! You're a bright, attractive woman…"

"With a tendency to fatten up everyone around you," Tamika said with a saucy grin.

"We won't mention that," Madison mumbled.

Trinity raised her voice. "Who bakes the best chocolate chip cookies around…"

Not to be outdone, Tamika added, "Along with chocolate chip Bundt cakes, macaroons, apple fritters…"

"So I like to feed people. So what?"

The teasing felt good, though. Madison had gone a long time feeling alone and unappreciated. Not that her daddy hadn't loved her, but she'd been taking care of him so long that it had become more habit than anything for him to say thank-you. She knew how precious it was to have people in her life who loved her, and she made sure she let them know. Even if it was just by delivering a plate of brownies.

Here, in this kitchen, was the place she'd felt most welcome in her lifetime. That was the most important thing. Not some guy she'd just met and embarrassed herself in front of.

Her phone lit up just then, causing her to glance over at it. Blake's name flashed on the screen. "I thought for sure I'd deleted that number…" she mumbled, remembering her middle-of-the-night intention.

That was wishful thinking. After all, it wasn't like she had that many numbers in her phone. She stared at it, trying to decide what to do.

Tamika leaned over the counter for a look. "Girl, he is interested! You'd better answer that."

With the girls goading her on, Madison reached out and connected the call. The phone was chilly against her ear as she gathered the courage to speak. "Hello," she croaked.

"Hi, Madison."

Wow. How could just hearing that deep voice make her chest ache for what could have been? If only she were a different type of person. The kind who went with the flow instead of diving deep into the tide.

"Uh, hi."

"How are you feeling?"

"Fine." Could she be any more lame? "I mean, everything's good. Just some motion sickness." That she hoped never to experience again. "Boats are definitely not for me," she said, trying to laugh it off.

A glance over at Trinity and Tamika made her cringe. They weren't even pretending to not eavesdrop. Instead they both nibbled on warm cookies, watching while she agonized over what to say.

"I don't blame you," Blake said, then paused. After a long minute of silence, he went on. "Listen, I wondered if you wanted to go out again tomorrow night. Something completely on land this time."

Madison worried the inside of her bottom lip, trying to decide what to do. Even though they couldn't hear him, Trinity had a slightly skeptical look on her face. Tamika, on the other hand, was giving her the thumbs-up. For someone who came to Maison de Jardin after being in an abusive relationship, Tamika had managed to maintain her belief that a happily-ever-after was somehow attainable. Or at the very least, that a couple of good nights could be salvaged from the situation.

"Madison? You there?"

Out of the blue, a wave of nausea hit her. It ebbed, then flowed, just as it had with the motion of the boat. Maybe she just wasn't ready?

She was shaking her head before the words tumbled out of her mouth. "No, I don't think so, Blake. Goodbye."

She stared down at the phone in her hand, wondering what the heck just happened. For a woman who had been determined a few days ago that she needed a little fun in her life, this had been the most stressful attempt at fun she'd ever known.

It reminded her of her attempts throughout the years

to carve out time for herself as a caregiver. She'd known she needed to renew her energy, to rest, but it had been too complicated to make it worth her while. By the time she'd hit on the one thing that brought her joy and was easy to fit into their lives, her father had fallen into a rapid decline. Death had followed not a month later.

A glance up showed a mixture of dismay and understanding on her friend's faces. Madison just continued to shake her head. "What the heck is wrong with me?"

Four

So Madison had forced him to move to plan C.

Blake couldn't believe it when Madison turned down his request for another date. What was he, the plague? She was nothing like any of the women he'd dated before, but he was realizing that that was part of what kept him intrigued.

He knew from being with her that Madison wasn't a typical woman, wealthy or otherwise. She'd had a very unique upbringing; she had an altruistic focus in her life. A unique woman called for a unique approach. Somehow he knew he wasn't giving her what she needed.

This was taking him a little while to figure out, because rejection was not his usual experience in life. It wasn't typical in his general daily dealings, in his business interactions and certainly not in his relationships. Not that he'd really call what he had *relationships*.

They were more like encounters, he realized.

Not one-night stands exactly, but his interactions with women rarely got too deep no matter how many times he saw them. He liked it that way. He kept it that way, because then he didn't have to deal with any ugly emotions or pain. The few tantrums or hissy fits he'd encountered had been surface-level, because the last thing he'd allowed was for any woman to get attached.

If there was one thing his father had inadvertently taught him, it was that the more you loved someone, the more they could hurt you.

Blake found a place to park his car, then got out and started to walk. To the casual onlooker, he was just strolling. Blake knew his destination, but he wasn't in any hurry to get there. He'd give Madison time to get settled in, and then he could show up. The edge of the Garden District at night was just as beautiful as it was during the day. The shadows of the stately homes created mystery and intrigue, showcasing a history that was barely hinted at in a casual glance. It was still early, but the heat had dissipated, allowing him to walk in relative comfort.

He was surprised he'd caught this little tidbit of Madison's life in the PI's notes. Though he'd read through the file his father had given him before, Madison's actions had sent him back to the drawing board. Another thorough read had shown him one line that he'd missed the first time around.

Sometime during the last year of her father's illness, Madison had managed to find herself a new side gig: singing. The little neighborhood pub was not too far from her house. As a matter of fact, it was within walking distance. She'd lucked out that it was so close, which had probably given her a chance to sneak away at night... maybe when her father was sleeping. There she spent a couple of hours creating atmosphere for those around her, and dreams for herself.

That little discovery had made having to reread the story of her sad upbringing worth it.

His father had been a big motivator, too. Surprise, surprise. After his continued refusal to let Blake see Abigail, Blake had confronted him to demand proof that she was okay. His father had once again refused, stating that Blake hadn't made any kind of progress that was worth rewarding him for.

He'd later called the housekeeper, who had loudly told him she could give him no updates, then whispered she was fine. But the ticking clock in his brain told him he had to do something soon, or else Abigail might not be there for him to see. He could only hope that Sherry would continue to keep an eye on her. He had a feeling that if time ran out, she'd either have a medical episode, or his father would end up sending her away.

Blake noticed his destination up ahead on the right. The little neighborhood hub was a hole in the wall that only locals would know about. The single door and dusty windows weren't enough to draw in tourists.

As Blake approached, he could smell a whiff of alcohol and a slight smokiness coming from the entrance, even though patrons were no longer allowed to smoke inside. He paused not far from the door, leaning against one of the support posts. A soft amber light glowed behind the milky windowpanes.

The voice hit him in a smooth, insistent way. He would have recognized it anywhere…but Madison's husky tone was enhanced somehow by the song. He closed his eyes and let the wave wash over him. The undertow was so smooth he would have willingly followed it anywhere. Suddenly Blake understood the stories he'd heard about sirens. He could feel himself falling under her spell; the words didn't even need to mean anything. It was simply a sound that filled empty parts of his soul he didn't even know he had.

In a moment of panic, his heart picked up speed. It felt as if something out of the ordinary was happening, and he might never be the same. Logically Blake scoffed at the idea. Still his heart and lungs continued to race.

"Incredible, isn't she?"

With a jerk, Blake realized he wasn't alone. In the dim light beneath the awning, he'd missed the grizzled bouncer seated on a stool on the opposite side of the doorway. His knee-length shorts, button-down shirt, leather vest and chest-length beard announced him as a biker all the way. His smile revealed a couple of broken teeth.

"Our Maddie is something else, right?" he asked again.

Blake nodded, still feeling a bit too unsteady to leave the support of the post. "Sure is," he said simply.

"The regulars love her, for good reason. I've heard a lot of talented voices in New Orleans, but hers is one of the best. Untrained, but still smooth as silk. She could tell you to go to hell and make you enjoy the ride."

Blake chuckled, then straightened up and paid the cover charge.

"Enjoy," the bouncer said.

Blake made his way through the tight quarters right inside the door. The bar was there on the left, the wood smooth and aged but still glossy. A couple of tables on the right were sparsely populated.

Several feet in, the room widened, opening into a much larger space with multiple tables. The crowd had gathered here to listen to Maddie sing.

Blake didn't bother with a table. Instead he slipped

along the back wall and stood in the shadows to watch the sexy woman in the spotlight. She wore a simple blue dress that revealed curves he remembered from the first night he'd met her. She barely moved, yet somehow she gave the impression of keeping time with the music. Her gorgeous auburn waves were pulled up and back from her face, revealing the smooth column of her neck.

Once again the words of the song rolled over him, tempting him to let his eyes drift closed so he could absorb every one. But he couldn't take his gaze from the woman on the stage. Her voice washed over him, luring him to stay, breaking through his barriers piece by piece.

"Can I get you a drink, hon?"

Blake realized he had indeed let his eyes drift shut. He glanced over at the waitress, whose expression was hard to make out in the dim light. He requested a whiskey, then turned back toward the stage, but the mood had been broken. He found himself a table and had a seat. The waitress delivered his drink. He sipped at it every couple minutes, letting the burn coat his throat.

Almost too soon Madison's set was done. He saw the waitress whisper to her and nod in his direction. He wasn't sure how she'd known he was here for her, but even from across the bar he could see the flush that stained Madison's cheeks.

She should be used to men being drawn in by her voice, so was the blush for him in particular?

She approached and slid into the seat across from him.

"Drink?" he asked.

She shook her head, and something inside him became impatient. The urge to hear her speak, to compare that voice to the one he'd heard from the stage, grew as the seconds slid by.

But when she did speak, her voice came out hard.

"What are you doing here? You aren't supposed to be here. No one is supposed to know—"

He leaned back in his chair. This wasn't at all what he'd expected. "I'm just glad I did."

"I'm not."

Blake frowned, surprised by the pushback. "Why?"

She drew in a deep breath, glancing around as she slowly released it. "I've just never shared this with anyone before. It's private."

Blake perused the people filling the small bar. But it was the room itself that helped him understand her protest. The stage was lit with a spotlight, but the rest of the room was cast in dusky shadow. Here Madison could have her own space, indulge in something she loved, practically anonymously, and be free of her burdens for a few hours.

"I know it doesn't make sense—"

"No, Madison. It's okay. I'm sorry for intruding."

She swallowed and dropped her gaze to the tabletop. "Why are you here?" she whispered, barely loud enough for him to catch it over the people speaking now that the music had ended.

"I've never explored much of New Orleans, so I decided to take a walk and happened by." Which sounded lame, even to him. "I got drawn right in. Your voice is incredible, Madison." *There you go. Distract her with the partial truth.* "I feel privileged to have heard you sing."

"No. Why are you here with me?" She patted the table with her palms in emphasis. "Why are you even interested in me?"

"Madison…" He wasn't sure what to say. The answer to that became more complicated with every minute he sat here.

"You shouldn't be. I'm not like them."

"Who?"

"The women in the pictures. I saw them online." She shook her head. "I'm not like them. I'm broke and awkward and a caretaker and have obligations. I'm just not a casual kind of person, Blake. I want to be…but I don't know how."

Every word rang in his head, confirming why he was here. She wasn't anything like what he was used to—and he liked that. The fact that her assumptions about him were so close to what he was like any other day made him angry. At himself, for being so shallow. At her, for buying into his public image.

True panic sizzled up until it popped like a champagne cork. "Damn it. Don't you think I know that, Madison? With all those women, nothing about them kept me coming back. But I can't stop coming back to you. Do you even understand what that means?"

Where had that come from? They stared at one another in silence. Blake breathed hard, his mind racing. His brain replayed the words he'd said, words he wished he could take back. It was a truth he hadn't wanted to face…much less blurt out to Madison like that.

But he couldn't take it back…so he waited.

His heart pounded as he kept waiting for her answer. As much as he wanted to convince himself that his nerves hinged on Abigail's fate, that it was about his father's demands, deep down he knew he'd just made it something more. Something personal.

Was that why this felt more real than anything he'd ever experienced before?

Then she spoke. "For something that was supposed to be *just fun,* this has sure gotten complicated."

Her words, so closely echoing his own thoughts, startled him. He quickly hid his reaction and asked, "What do you mean?"

"I don't understand why a guy like you is here with me. You're champagne and caviar. I'm—" she waved her hand "—just not."

"Maybe we need to explore that difference. No obligations."

This was it. This was the key he'd been looking for. So why wasn't he elated? Instead, anticipation and fear sizzled in his veins. "So what do you say?"

"I still don't understand."

He didn't want her to. The truth would be devastating—maybe to both of them.

"But yes," she conceded.

He lifted his glass in a toast, and was relieved when she nodded her consent. The burn centered him once more. He set his glass on the table, rimming the edge with his index finger. He needed this conversation back on a smoother track. "So I guess a hot-air balloon ride is out, right?"

Madison laughed, pressing the palm of her hand against her stomach. "Let's not risk it." She studied him for a moment. "So you haven't seen much of New Orleans? Not even as a kid?"

"No." The pressure of her gaze urged him to elaborate, but for once he kept quiet. His childhood was something he never wanted to relive, even in memories.

"Well, how about I show you my version?"

"Are you sure you want to walk?" Blake asked as he met her on a corner of the outer edge of the Garden District a few nights later. "I'm happy to drive."

"Don't be a baby. It's barely even summer here," Madison teased.

Besides, the June heat was starting to dissipate as evening fell on the Garden District. The only way to get a good feel for this town was to walk it.

"You can't experience the essence of New Orleans in a vehicle," she said, "unless it's a streetcar."

"Those are just tourist traps," Blake scoffed, but he fell into step beside her.

"Those are history," Madison corrected. "And a lot of people use them besides tourists."

"God forbid."

Madison paused to study him, one brow lifted. Blake either hadn't been exposed to the history of New Orleans, as he'd admitted, or he made a habit of not looking at a place too closely. "Just for that, I'm going to make you ride one. A lot of people commute on those things."

"I'm not sure I'd fit in with my designer shoes." He struck a pose, a grin forming on his too-perfect face. His words and actions were a reminder to keep things casual. A reminder she definitely needed.

How was she supposed to manage that?

"Pretty spiffy," she agreed, keeping her tone light, "but you'll be fine. I'm starting to get the feeling you didn't really see all these countries you claim to have visited. Not really."

He shrugged. "Maybe not." But the line that appeared between his brows told her he didn't feel as casual as he let on.

She didn't want to ask what he'd really been doing in them. All those pictures of him with supermodel types told her most of what she didn't want to know. Instead, she resumed her stroll along the sidewalk. As they walked, the tall, stately houses gave way to smaller, crowded buildings that contained businesses.

As they paused on one corner, a bus stopped at the

red light. Its door opened and the older man called from the driver's seat, "Hey, Madison."

"Hi, Frankie," she hollered back. "How did your granddaughter's soccer game go?"

"She scored the winning goal," he answered with a toothy grin and a thumbs-up before heading on down the road.

Not too much farther along, ol' Mr. Paddington rounded the corner, walking his golden retriever. Madison paused to say good evening and pat the dog's head as she passed.

At Blake's curious look, she said, "Mr. Paddington lost his wife recently to a stroke. I encouraged him to get the dog to give him something to do. He walks her every evening about this time."

A couple more blocks down, an elderly woman in a floral housedress paused while sweeping her front porch to wave. "Evening, Madison," she yelled.

Madison raised her hand in greeting but didn't stop this time. Maybe this hadn't been the best route. She hadn't thought about how many interruptions they might run into.

They crossed another street to a corner, where a familiar gentleman sat on a stool in the shade. His lovely saxophone blended with the sounds of traffic and commerce around them, and had for more years than Madison could count. She dropped a couple of coins in the open case at his feet. "Night, Bartholomew."

"Thanks, Miss Madison," he said.

They strolled along in silence for a few minutes before Blake glanced over at her. "Is there anyone you don't know around here?"

"I've been walking this area since I was a kid. So honestly, not many. We lost a lot of people during Katrina and afterward, but new ones have moved in and that's been a blessing."

The sights and scents around her drew her in, enveloping her in a cozy feeling that had nothing to do with the fading heat of the day. She nodded at a small bakery, then a hometown pizza restaurant across the street. "All these places have been here for years. My mama used to walk up here when she was busy taking care of my dad. One of the special adventures she would take me on when I was a little kid was to get a free cookie from that bakery. They gave one to every kid who came in the door, and sometimes they'd be nice and give me two. I'd always share with my mama. I think the owner knew that.

"After her death, it was my turn to take care of my daddy." Madison pressed her lips together for a minute. Was she revealing too much?

"What was wrong with him?"

"Multiple sclerosis. At first he thought he was in a severe depression after losing his business in a bankruptcy, but he progressively got worse. You never knew what a day would bring with him. My mother died when I was sixteen. This was the extent of her world, and mine for a long time." She didn't mention that they'd rarely had money for her to go anywhere else. Abruptly Madison paused, realizing just how much she'd said.

She'd intended to introduce Blake to her New Orleans…not spill the details of her sad and meager childhood. The sounds of the cars on the road and music coming from the stores covered their silence for several steps while she tried to figure out how to keep this conversation from getting too deep.

"Speaking of houses, when are you going to invite me over?"

Apparently Blake didn't have the same issues about boundaries. Or most likely, he had no idea what a touchy subject her home had become.

Having him over was the last thing Madison wanted to do. *So much for a modern girl's attitude...* As much as she hated how shallow it sounded, Blake was loaded. Money was not something Madison had ever had. Only now was she able to truly make a living with her job at Maison de Jardin.

The house that had once been a showplace of the area now had overgrown hedges to block the sight of it from the road. The disrepair from years of having to make do with a shoestring budget was something that embarrassed her greatly. She'd done what she could to keep up with the major fixes, but the broken windows, peeling paint, warped flooring and the lack of a new roof were sore issues for her right now.

The very knowledge that she would soon need to sell off her family home made her heart ache, but she knew it was for the best. It was taking every bit of her current salary to get it up to snuff. There was no way she could maintain the house in the glory it deserved.

A lot of people bought houses in the Garden District specifically to renovate them, and she was hoping her house would be lucky enough to have the same fate. Soon, but not yet.

"Are you staying far from here?" she asked, hoping to distract him.

He went along with it for now. "I'm in an apartment in the business district, but my family lives on one of the old plantations."

Madison smiled, taken back to her vivid daydreams of open spaces and old barns as a child. "I bet that was a magical place to grow up."

"It was a hell with no means of escape." A brief glance showed her a fake grin on Blake's face to go with his harsh tone. "But then childhood memories are often exaggerated in our minds, right?"

She wasn't so sure. Memories of the hard years of her childhood had softened with age, but they never went away. She reminded herself that that wasn't why they were here tonight; this was about fun, not digging deep. Luckily, the place she had planned for dinner was just ahead. That should steer the conversation in another direction.

They stepped through the door with its peeling paint and a jingle bell over it into a long, narrow galley kitchen.

"Madison!" An African American woman rushed from behind the counter to hug her. Bebe was old enough to be her grandmother but appeared timeless with her smooth, dark skin. "It's so good to see you. And who's your friend?"

"Bebe, this is Blake. And I told him he needed to have the best po'boy in the city of New Orleans for dinner."

Blake gave the dim conditions of the room the side-eye but seemed to be won over by the woman's smile.

Bebe's grin was contagious, as always. She pulled off her apron to give Madison a hug. "Girl, you are skin and bones. You need a po'boy and then some."

Madison just smiled. "All that mothering instinct coming to the fore."

"Yes, ma'am." Bebe's smile turned down at the edges. "And I'm happy to report Talia is doing better."

Madison gave her friend a little extra squeeze before turning her loose.

Bebe glanced over at Blake. "Love this one like a daughter. She's the same age as my own Talia, whose undergoing cancer treatments right now." She patted Madison's arm while Madison blinked back tears. "This girl can make me smile on the worst of days."

Then Bebe went back behind the counter. As soon as she put her apron back on it was all business. "What can I make you?"

Madison's throat had closed up so that speaking was impossible. Blake stepped up to the counter. "How about Maddie's favorite…times two?"

Bebe beamed her approval and got to work. Soon she handed the food back over the counter, then leaned over to give Madison a kiss on her cheek. "You have a good evening, darling," she said as they headed out the door with their heavy bag.

"This way," Madison said.

A couple of stores down, a narrow alleyway opened to the right. She led him down the space barely wide enough for his shoulders. As they walked, she took a few more deep breaths to try to clear her emotions away. Seeing Bebe was always a mix of happy and sad, but that was how they got through the tough times. Madison just hadn't thought about it before taking him in there. She'd just wanted to show him some of her favorite places.

Finally they reached the end of the alley to face a black wrought iron fence. Taking a few steps to the side, Madison reached for the latch to let them in. And this was her favorite place of all.

"What is this?" Blake asked as they stepped into a lush, overgrown garden.

The centerpiece was a beautiful cherry tree, surrounded by various ferns, hostas and an abundance of moss growing in the shade. Tucked into one corner was a small wrought iron table and chairs.

"This is one of my favorite places in the whole city,"

she said. "The garden is actually part of the St. Andrew's Catholic Church. My mother brought me here as a child, and we would eat our cookies while enjoying the cool and quiet."

She noticed Blake cock his head to the side like he was listening for something. Sure enough, the buildings and lush foliage blocked out the sound of the busy street not too far away. Despite living in the city, Madison had a deep love of nature and enjoyed these green spaces. Being here gave her a sense of peace and calm that everyday life seemed to withhold. But wasn't that the same for everybody?

Maybe not, but she'd take peace where she could get it. Even now her heart rate was slowing and those unwelcome tears were seeping away.

"The priests don't mind because they knew we would never leave a mess. The church allowed my mother's services here when she died."

"This is beautiful," he said simply.

"You should see the conservatory at Maison de Jardin. It's absolutely gorgeous."

She started to unpack their dinner, needing a distraction from the minefield of memories. How come she couldn't just have fun?

"How did you go to work there?" Blake asked as they settled in. "You're very young to be the director of that large a charity."

In years, maybe. She didn't want to talk about the experience that had made her qualified for her job. "Trinity, the former director, has known me for a long time. Knows what I'm capable of. But she's still very hands-on."

She paused to take a bite of the sandwich, enjoying the resistance of the bread and the crunch of the fried crawfish. "What do you do?"

He immediately popped off, "According to my father, nothing."

Whoa.

Blake jumped to his feet and paced in the small space. Madison held really still. Should she say something? This went way beyond their surface chatter tonight. Not that she'd stuck to her goal of keeping it light very well herself.

He was quiet for so long the back of her neck tightened. Was he looking for a way to blow the statement off? Then she realized she didn't know enough about Blake to counteract his bitter statement in any way. Just as panic set in, he turned back toward her and leaned against the tree trunk behind him.

"Is he right?" she asked, blowing off all of her angst and going with her instincts.

"Partly." He offered a half smile. "But less than he knows."

A lightbulb went off. "Your drawings?"

"How did you—of course, you noticed. You see a lot, don't you?"

"Is that a good thing?"

"Probably not." He pushed away from the tree and crossed to her side. "Definitely not."

Before Madison could blink, Blake had her in his arms, his lips barely meeting hers. But he didn't rush. He waited for her to open, granting him permission to press forward. Then he sampled, testing and tasting her lips in smooth, slow strokes. Madison's spine lit up. The spicy taste of him on her tongue left her ravenous for way more than food.

After long moments he pulled back, leaving her dazed and a little unsteady on her feet. She opened her eyes, blinking once or twice before focusing in on the golden, angular lines of his face. Only to see them softened by his smile as he said, "I'm not comfortable with you seeing things, but I think it's more than worth it."

Five

Blake dove back in for another taste, leaving Madison breathless and gasping. The feel of him intoxicated her. She had the resistance of a rag doll as he pulled her into his lap. More naturally than she would have imagined, she found herself straddling his thighs. Belly to belly. Face to face.

As his mouth traveled from her lips, over her jaw, to her neck, she struggled to pull air into her lungs. The excitement of his touch, the racing of her pulse, the need to press herself closer to him despite the heat in the air… how was this happening?

Something tickled the back of her mind, something she should remember, but nothing intruded on the sensations evoked by the man beneath her. She clutched at his shoulders, kneading the well-defined muscles, not sure whether she was trying to steady herself or imprint him with her touch. A fire rose inside her, forcing her to squirm, needing relief from the intense sensations pooling low in her belly.

Madison rocked forward. Blake gasped against her skin, his hands squeezing her arms. "Madison," he groaned.

Her pulse pounded at the base of her throat. After one last hot, openmouthed kiss, he pulled back. "We have to stop. Right now."

"Why?" she whispered. She should know the answer, but right now it was as far from her as possible.

"We have to," he said. He rested his forehead against her collarbone, breathing heavy in the hush of the garden. "I had no idea how addictive you would be."

Well, no one had ever called her that. She drew in a deep breath, searching for equilibrium. How had this gotten so out of hand?

"May I help you?" a voice asked from the shadows.

Madison started, realizing they weren't alone. Instinctively she jerked back, and lost her balance because she was on Blake's lap. With a cry, she fell, landing on her backside on one of the stone pavers surrounding the table. She ignored the pain. Instead she focused in on the source of the voice. "Father Stephen... I'm so sorry."

The younger of the priests here—at forty-five—gave her a soft smile. "I see that."

Blake reached out and helped Madison to her feet. "Honestly, Father," he added. "I apologize for—"

He broke off and a flush of red tinged the skin right above his magnificent cheekbones. Madison would have giggled if she wasn't aware that her entire face was on fire, too.

"Yes, well, maybe it's time to finish your dinner? Yes, Madison?" the man asked.

Madison guessed it was a good thing he knew her, or

else she'd probably have been arrested for…something. But that thought made her embarrassment burn even hotter. "Yes, sir. I'll—we'll do that."

"See that you do," he said. "And I'll see you at mass Saturday night."

Madison choked on her emotions as the man retreated around the corner to the back door of the church. She only dared to glance over at Blake when he chuckled. He shook his head as he said, "Well, that was embarrassing."

"He hasn't known you since you were a baby. Imagine how I feel."

Blake held out her chair for her to sit back down at the table. "Oh, I don't have to imagine."

The suggestive comment should have put her back up. Instead, she covered her face with her hands and let laughter release her tension. Now that her head had cleared somewhat from the kiss, she could finally put her finger on what had been bothering her…they were in public.

It was the first time she'd ever managed to forget that…

Blake simply picked up his sandwich and continued to eat.

"How can you—" Men were obviously very different from women. Or maybe it was just her and her lack of experience with these things.

She simply stared at him until he met her gaze once more. It made her feel a little better when his smile had a sheepish tinge. "Well, I'm not about to let a little embarrassment keep me away from the rest of this po'boy. You weren't wrong about it being the best in New Orleans."

She recognized his attempt to return things to normal, and did her best to relax. "I hope you mean that, because I eat at Bebe's all the time."

"I'm on board for that."

They ate in silence for a few minutes. Madison preferred not to think about the last few minutes. Maybe later tonight, alone in her room, she would. But if she thought about it now, she'd never be able to carry on a conversation. Instead she cast her mind back to what they'd been discussing before.

"I'm sorry that your father can't see the value in your art," she said.

As hard as her life had been, Madison's father had always made his appreciation plain. He'd hated what she had to do to keep them afloat, but he'd always expressed gratitude for her hard work and dedication.

"My father is not an easy man." Blake's smile wasn't as convincing as he probably wanted. "And I would have said that was no longer an issue for me. But, well, family is never easy."

Instantly the picture he'd drawn that first night came to mind. "So you draw for a living?"

He shrugged. "I wouldn't necessarily call it a living. I had a lot of help from my inheritance from my mother, which would have let me live a careful existence without working for the rest of my life. But I'm rarely careful…"

"But you are a very talented artist." Even in her inexperience, she could see that.

"Some people think so, and they are willing to pay for my drawings." He glanced away, studying the lush foliage around them for long moments. "That was a very complicated answer to an easy question."

"Sometimes the easy answer isn't the best." She couldn't keep the words from slipping out. "I'm sorry, Blake."

He studied her for a moment. "Why?"

She shook her head. "I tried to keep whatever this is

between us on the surface, just fun, but everything about tonight has run completely counter to that. I don't feel comfortable, like I'm lying to you. This just…isn't me." Her smile was sad, apologetic. "I realize that now. And I'm sorry. I know that's not what you want."

"Are you sure?"

They both seemed equally surprised by the question. Then he cocked up one blond brow. "Quite frankly, I'm willing to hang around until we find out what it *is*. Not what it *should* be."

"Really?"

He winked at her. "Really."

That should be a good thing…so why was she shaking over the prospect?

"Let me see Abigail. Now."

Blake's father offered him a smile that had nothing to do with being happy. "Slow down," he cautioned. "You didn't seem to be making any progress the last time you checked in. Did you bring me some proof?"

For a moment, Blake just stared in disbelief. Arguing the way he wanted to would probably get him nowhere.

"What kind of proof are you looking for?"

"A pair of panties?"

Gross. Why would he—? "I don't have to sleep with Madison to get the diamond."

"But you do have to spend time with her, and get invited into her house. Which as far as I can tell, hasn't happened, either…"

His father's straight back and braced arms told Blake he wasn't backing down. So instead of saying more, Blake pulled out his phone and offered up a picture of him and Madison together in the garden at the church. His father nodded slowly as he studied it.

"Not the most efficient method in my book, but good job."

Those words grated over every nerve, forcing Blake to clench his teeth. His father had often told him "good job" as a child, usually after berating him for making a choice he wouldn't have, then forcing Blake to do things his way.

His father leaned closer, staring at the phone. Blake was surprised to see his lips tighten. "Let me guess," he finally said, his tone now clipped. "The garden behind St. Andrew's?"

Blake nodded slowly. "How did you know?" After all, he couldn't imagine his father being anywhere near that part of town.

"Her mother and I met there a couple of times."

Whoa. That wasn't what Blake had expected.

Then again, he couldn't imagine his father meeting a woman anywhere other than at a fancy party. There he could easily disguise his narcissistic attitude with fancy clothes and jewelry. Polite small talk. And offers of fancy outings.

That brought Blake up short. Wasn't that exactly what he had tried to offer Madison? To impress her? To keep things polite and on a superficial level?

Well, that approach hadn't lasted with this particular woman, had it? All it had taken was one physical touch to shake him. Madison's response hadn't been practiced or lukewarm. It had been real, full-bodied passion.

And Blake had found it amazing.

His father and a woman anything like Madison? He just couldn't imagine it. "Why are you doing this? Her mother is dead. Revenge is going to accomplish nothing."

Familiar rage seemed to make his father grow larger and more menacing. At least this time Blake was too big to be intimidated. "She should have been mine," he growled as he strode across the tile floor, his dress shoes clicking as he moved.

"And since you couldn't possess her, you now have to take back what didn't belong to you? After all these years? Come on… I'm not buying that."

He stopped abruptly. "Desperate times call for desperate measures."

"You're never desperate," Blake argued. "Cold. Calculating. But not desperate."

"In this economy, everyone is desperate."

"Money?" He should have known. But his father had always been more than solvent. What had gone wrong?

"Isn't it always about money?"

"No. Usually it's about people." Even when it seemed to be about money, for people like Madison, that money was necessary for keeping her family fed, housed, clothed. Not for fancy cars and travel.

"I made a few bad investments," his father said with a too casual shrug. "With that diamond, I'll be set."

"But it doesn't belong to you."

"I'll take whatever I have to. I did before, and I will continue to as long as necessary."

Suspicion filtered through Blake's consciousness. "Father? I know that tone. You couldn't have had anything to do with her father's illness. And I certainly hope you had nothing to do with her mother's death. What's the deal?" he demanded.

His father brushed at a nonexistent spot on his jacket. "No, unfortunately those issues were beyond me. But I made sure they didn't have the money to do much about them, now, didn't I? I set out to ruin Jacqueline's husband, and that was one goal I managed to accomplish."

Blake held silent. So this steady downward spiral of Madison's father's business, the bankruptcy that killed his spirit, had been his own father's fault? Why wasn't he surprised?

"So your only plan for pulling yourself out of the red is to steal from a young woman who deserves no punishment whatsoever?"

"She'll never miss what she's never had."

Blake should be surprised, but even after all these years, he remembered that the only person his father cared about was himself. If his finances were in that dire a state, he wouldn't hesitate to strike out, no matter who it was. If it wasn't Madison, it might just be Abigail.

His father turned away, cutting the conversation off. "I guess you deserve a little reward, for what progress you've made. Just make it quick. Abigail might be in her room. She's as slippery as you were when you were a kid. Always where she doesn't belong."

Blake heard the patter of tiny feet as he stepped onto the first stair in the foyer. He moved slower than he should have, considering the concern that had built over the last week. What did he know about talking to a child?

The few times he'd been with Abigail before, her mother and nanny had been present. She'd been cute and engaging, but children were completely out of Blake's league. He moved down the hallway to an open door and glanced inside. The pale pink walls, frilly pictures and a large silver monogram of the girl's initials hanging over the headboard showed that her mother had at least decorated before she left. Abigail sat in a puddle of fluffy blankets on the bed. The dim light in the room didn't reveal much about her, so he reached out to flick on the light switch.

She blinked in the extra brightness.

Those big brown eyes, so reminiscent of her mother's,

made her look vulnerable in a way Blake wasn't comfortable with.

What should he say after not seeing her for two years? "How are you, Abigail?" he asked. Lame, but he had to start somewhere.

She shrugged, but Blake remembered that response from his own childhood. He wasn't going to be brushed off.

"Tell me, Abigail." He made sure their gazes met. "I really want to know. Miss Sherry said you'd been sick."

"Those pills make me feel tired."

Was that normal? Blake wasn't even sure whom he would ask.

"But my head doesn't feel funny anymore."

So maybe the medicine was working? Her color looked healthy. Could you tell anything about epilepsy from just watching her? He needed to investigate that more.

"I'm sorry," she whispered.

Distracted from his obsessive worrying, he came closer and sat beside the bed. "Why are you sorry?"

"If I hadn't gotten sick, none of this would've happened."

Blake's heart sank. No child should have to feel responsible for the actions of the adults around them. Blake should not have had to feel responsible for his father's anger, for his mother's incompetence, for the string of stepmothers who moved in and out of his life. "Abigail," he said, searching for the right words. "You don't have to be sorry. Scratch that. You should not be sorry. None of this is your fault."

"But Mommy left me."

"And that's her fault." Blake didn't bring up the fact that her mother simply wasn't strong enough to handle anything outside of his father. He didn't want her more fearful that she already was. "You being sick, it just…is."

"Why?"

"I'm not sure." Man, saying that made him feel inadequate. He was probably screwing this up royally, but he didn't know how else to proceed. "I have to go, but if you need me, you just need to tell Miss Sherry to call me, okay?" The housekeeper had given him frequent updates, even though they'd been short to avoid detection from her boss.

Abigail nodded slowly. The move was solemn enough to make Blake's chest ache. "Look, I don't know when he'll let me come back. But I want you to remember, I *will* be back."

Her deep brown eyes filled with tears, but she blinked them back in an all too familiar move. Blake remembered that vividly from a time or two during his childhood. "Promise?"

"Promise." Even if he had to walk over hot coals. Which would actually be preferable to complying with his father's demands.

Six

Madison took a deep breath, trying to calm the nerves in her stomach.

She always had butterflies at the beginning of a performance, but this was different. This was her first time knowing she was singing in front of Blake. The first time she wasn't craving that chance to close her eyes and lose herself in a different world.

Normally when she was up here on stage, she didn't see the crowd. She didn't hear the clapping. She didn't pay attention to any hecklers. She lost herself in an inner world of melody mixed with darkness. A place where she felt happy and safe.

Tonight she felt the glare of the spotlight. But she needed it, wanted it. She could no longer deny that she wanted to see where this thing between her and Blake would go. The only way to find out was to dive in deep, and stop questioning every single stroke.

And he'd given her the perfect opportunity by showing up tonight.

Madison caught her cue and opened her mouth to sing. Tonight, instead of losing herself in the darkness, she sang for Blake alone. Every rhythm, every note was for him. As if they were alone in the room.

She braced her heels against the wooden planks of the stage. The mic stand felt cool between her palms.

She couldn't see him, but she could feel him. Feel his gaze as it roamed every inch of the silky green dress she wore. Her blood raced through her veins, as if the very act of singing were foreplay. She was amazed at how good this felt…and at her ability to let go and embrace what she realized she wanted.

A real relationship. Yes, she wanted it to be fun. But she wasn't capable of living on the surface. And if he was okay with it being more, then they'd see where this would go.

If it ended, it would hurt more. But Madison's life had been a series of endings, and she knew she'd survive.

This time when her set was over, she met Blake at his table with a drink of her own and slid into the seat opposite him as if they were strangers. The glass between her hands steadied her. "What brings you here?" she asked with what she hoped was a sexy smile.

His half smile sped up her heartbeat. "I heard there was a very sexy singer that I just had to see."

"I hope she didn't disappoint."

"Never," he said, his tone dropping an octave.

Even in the dark she could see his gaze dip down to the V-neckline of her dress, tracing the arrow down to her cleavage. Secretly she'd wanted to show off and had chosen this dress for that very purpose. Hoping he'd be here. Hoping he'd want more.

It looked like her hope just might turn into reality.

"You look beautiful tonight, Madison."

"You're not so bad yourself, Blake."

"How late will you be—"

A gravelly male voice interrupted. "Well, I should've known you'd be here, sugar."

Blake looked up, but Madison kept her gaze trained on him. Her teeth clenched.

She recognized the voice. One she'd dreaded hearing ever since her daddy had died. The man was a nuisance at best. His visits to their house had always upset her father. As an adult, she'd realized the man had been trying to buy the house out from under them. But he'd never wanted to pay a decent price for it. Or maybe her daddy had been like her. It really didn't matter who the house went to, as long as it didn't go to this obnoxious, self-entitled boob.

Finally Maddie looked away from Blake's enticing blue eyes up at the man's face. His overtanned skin and calculating look repulsed her. "Hello, John Mark. How are you?"

Not that she really wanted to know, but it was polite to ask.

The middle-aged, heavyset man pulled over a chair from another table and turned it around backward so he could straddle it. He held out his hand to Blake. "Hi there, I'm John Mark. I don't think we've been introduced."

"I don't guess so," Blake said, glancing back and forth between the two of them.

Madison had been raised to have manners, to be accommodating of other people even when you didn't care for them. But somehow she couldn't summon it tonight. Her greeting had used up her store of politeness. She could feel a frown pulling down the edges of her mouth and eyebrows. The energy to lift them just was beyond her. This man was associated with so many irritating memories from when her father was alive, and that gloom settled over her like a weighted blanket.

She didn't bother to contribute to the expected introductions. Hopefully the dim lighting would hide the animosity in her expression.

"I don't think I've ever seen you in here, John Mark," she said instead. That was one good reason to keep coming to the club. It had always felt like her safe place. What was with the sudden invasion?

"Oh, but I knew you would be here," he said. "And it's long past time we talk some business."

"I don't really think this is the time or place—"

"Of course it is," he said with a grin that was too wide. "Besides, you're a hard woman to catch. Always here or there. And nobody's returning calls from the house. In the meantime, that place is gonna fall down around your ears."

Blake cleared his throat. "I don't really think…"

"Oh, she knows what I'm after," John Mark replied with a careless wave of his hand. "I begged her father to sell me that house for years. Now it's time."

The audacity of his words hit Madison the wrong way. Heated pressure grew deep inside her. "Actually, I don't think there's anything for us to talk about."

John Mark wasn't listening. "I will take that house off your hands real easy, young lady. You just sign over the paperwork and the headache is no longer yours."

Madison knew she needed to sell the house, but not to this man. *Never* this man. "The house isn't ready…"

"There's no need to do anything to it. I'm pretty sure I know how bad a shape it's in. I might have to tear it down and start over, but that's a prime piece of land. It's a shame your daddy let it get that bad, but he wouldn't get out when his body gave up on him, would he?"

Madison felt the tips of her ears start to burn. The pressure rose, mixing with grief for her father and anger over this man's casual words. The last thing she wanted was for Blake to find out the true state of affairs with her family like this.

"When I am ready, I'll—"

"You'll never be ready. Just sign the papers."

"No." The pressure erupted. "And do not talk over me."

Madison stood, feeling more in control on her feet. She wasn't sure where the steel in her voice came from, but she wasn't being railroaded into anything she didn't want to do. "Do not come to my house. Do not call on the phone. I'm not selling my place to you. Ever."

John Mark glanced back and forth between them, a smile spreading across his face. "Now, there's no need to get into a tizzy, little lady."

"Ev-ver."

Something in her face or tone must've finally told him she was serious. His thin lips pressed together, a scowl curving his brows. "Beggars aren't in a position to be choosers. Don't be stupid."

"Back off," Blake said, a growl underlying his tone.

"Why? She's not going to get a better offer. And she desperately needs one… I could tell that with one glance around that place. I always did wonder how you kept it up." He gave Blake the once-over, clearly taking in his fancy watch. "Guess now I know, huh?"

Instantly Blake was on his feet, crowding John Mark away from the table. There was a flurry of activity as the bouncer headed their way, and a low exchange of voices between the men that she couldn't quite catch. But

Blake's advantage in height seemed to make an impression on the bulky man. He raised his hands in surrender.

The bouncer grabbed John Mark's arm. "This guy bothering you, Miss Maddie?"

At first she just nodded, not trusting her voice. As John Mark started to protest, she stepped in close. "My daddy was always a good judge of character. He had you pegged as slimy from the beginning. I do believe I agree." She nodded at the bouncer, who strong-armed him away.

For a moment, Madison stood still, stunned at what had happened, until Blake led her back over to the table. "Are you okay?"

Madison melted into the seat, the starch in her spine washing away. "I just can't catch a break. Every time I'm around you something stupid happens." She plopped back in her seat, trying hard not to let the tears well up. That would just be the icing on the cake.

"It's not stupid. You have no control over him showing up," Blake insisted.

"But why did it have to happen right now, right in the middle of—"

"It's okay, Madison."

She smacked her palm against the table, her voice rising. "It's not okay. I didn't want you to find out about that."

Blake tilted his head to the side in question.

"On the good days, I can handle the fact that I'm going to have to sell my family home. I've done the best that I can. My father did the best that he could. And I know it has to go. That's the way it is, but that doesn't make it hurt any less."

She stared down into her drink. For a moment, she was at a total loss. Her normal go-to was to get up and do something to fix it. And there was no fixing this.

She could walk away, and leave Blake sitting here by himself. She could hang around and let him convince her that it was all okay. He didn't need to—she knew her own worth. The state of her house embarrassed her, but considering the state of their finances when she was growing up, she knew she had done the best that she could. And if Blake couldn't understand that, then she needed to walk away.

Or she could do what her body and soul had been telling her since she'd met him. She could walk toward him, and let happen whatever happened. Accept his decisions and make the memories she wanted so badly.

She glanced back at him and saw his blue eyes trained steadily on her. No hint of embarrassment, no signs of anger or irritation. Just watching her. Maybe he was looking for the next clue?

Just then the waitress interrupted, drawing Maddie's attention to her with a hand on her shoulder. "Hon, are you going to finish the night out?"

Normally Madison would never walk away from her gig under any circumstances, but tonight she simply couldn't continue. "No, I need to go home."

The waitress squeezed her shoulder before walking away. It was wonderful to work with people who were so understanding.

With a pounding heart, she glanced back over at Blake. "Would you like to go with me?"

Blake stared up at the house as he turned off his car. The silence that surrounded them had almost an echo to it, as if there were unspoken words surrounding them. The history of the place, maybe? Blake wasn't sure, and he was hesitant to look too deeply.

This was what he'd wanted all along. To be inside this

house, to be given an opportunity to search through it. Hell, he'd even prepared himself for a one-night stand in order to do it.

But what he was walking into tonight wasn't a one-night stand. He was walking through those doors in an emotional state that he'd never anticipated. Because Maddie was real; she was more real to him than any woman he'd slept with before. And he had a feeling there would be no going back after tonight.

"Everything okay?" she asked.

He could hear the slight tremble in her voice. She was nervous. Blake knew that she was opening herself up in a way that she wouldn't ever have with someone else. That vulnerability, that choice humbled him.

He tried to remind himself about Abigail. He tried to remember his purpose, but all he could think about was Maddie. He glanced over at her in the dark. "Yes," he lied. "I'm fine."

Blake let himself out of the car and crossed around to her side to open the door. The driveway was tight, crowded on each side with an overgrowth of bushes. The oddly planted tree here or there. Was the overgrowth on purpose? Or simply one of those things that hadn't registered in the list of tasks that Madison faced every day?

He gave her just enough room to slip out the door, then closed it behind her. He pressed in close, trapping her between the vehicle and the hardness of his body. "Madison," he whispered, in deference to the quiet surrounding them. "I want you to remember something."

He could feel the shiver that went through her, and knew it had nothing to do with the temperature. The heated night closed in on them, but still her body responded. "Yes?"

That deep huskiness in her murmur shot straight down his spine. "Just remember, I want to be here."

Those simple words felt like more of a commitment than he could ever have imagined. Then he turned quickly toward the house, catching her hand in his.

Madison led him around the back and put her key in the door. The bushes surrounding the house were also out of control, some of them flowering crape myrtles, some overgrown hydrangeas. The heavy scent of flowers on the night air was intoxicating.

The door opened smoothly, to his surprise. A small mudroom opened up into a large kitchen. It was obvious that a lot of time was spent here. It gleamed with scrubbing. A meticulously maintained work surface that could possibly be original to the house gave the room a warm feeling that Blake could honestly say he'd never experienced in any house he'd lived in.

It wasn't until they moved on to other rooms that the wear and tear begin to make itself known. Bits of peeling paint. Cracked floor tile. Dim lighting where the bulbs in the chandeliers were obviously blown. Some rooms were closed off completely.

Madison kept her head down, as if she could ignore the signs of age if she didn't get a close enough look. Moving through the foyer, she did an abrupt turn to go up the stairs. Through the open doorway on the opposite side, Blake caught a glance of multiple pieces of furniture in various states of repair.

"What's this?" he asked, leaning into the doorway.

Madison paused about a quarter of the way up the stairs and looked back down at him. Her reluctance to return was clear, even in the shadows. After a moment's pause, she slowly came down one step at a time before reaching his side.

"What's this?" he asked again, not acknowledging her hesitation.

She stood next to him in the doorway but didn't glance into the room. "It's just a hobby," she said in a rush.

"It's a pretty expensive hobby…" The room had to contain at least ten pieces of furniture that were being refurbished. "That's a lot of elbow grease."

He glanced to the side to see Madison's arms crossed tightly over her rib cage. Apparently he'd waded into another touchy subject. But he really did want to know. This was obviously important to her, which spoke to him on a level he'd never experienced with other women.

"Come on, Maddie," he coaxed. "Tell me the truth."

She shot a quick glance up at him, her pupils wide and searching.

Finally she said, "John Mark wasn't wrong when he said times were tough. My father used to be a very affluent businessman, before he married my mama. But something…went wrong. He never would say what. They lost most of what they had. She did her best, and kept things fairly on track. But after she died, he just couldn't keep it together anymore. He was sick, and hurting, and grieving, and for a while, he just dropped off the grid. At fifteen years old, I learned just how deep in the hole we were."

Blake's chest ached at the sadness in her voice.

"We were eking out an existence on his disability checks. But he refused to let me sell the house. It was the last place he'd had a home with her. So I did the best I could, supplementing his income by running errands for Trinity, and turning my hand at anything I could find. I discovered I had a knack for refinishing furniture. He would help me sometimes when he was feeling better, and I'd sell the pieces to local antique stores. Sometimes they call and let me know when they have pieces that I can refurbish for them. I've gotten a bit of a reputation for it now."

"That's wonderful, Maddie." Blake had taken so much in his life for granted. He couldn't imagine realizing his family was on the brink of ruin as a teenager and knowing it fell on him to keep them from going over the edge.

"I'm sorry," she whispered.

"Why?" His chest ached at the somber expression in her eyes. They should be happy and smiling, instead of sad all the time.

"I wanted tonight to be special. And it's been nothing but complicated. Everything about us has been complicated."

Blake pushed everything aside in that moment—his own selfishness, shallowness, Abigail, even his own lust for the woman in front of him.

Instead he looked at Madison and really saw her. "No, Maddie. Tonight has really opened my eyes."

She immediately dropped her gaze, but he raised her chin back up with gentle pressure. "I've seen a lot, and I've learned a lot. And it has all told me what an incredibly strong and driven woman you are. That is something to be proud of. And if some guy can't handle it, you kick his ass to the curb."

She gave a huff of laughter. "Yes, sir."

Maddie was a woman to be celebrated. And Blake planned to do just that.

Burying his hands in her hair, he pulled her closer for his kiss. When he came up for air, he whispered, "Don't be sorry, Maddie. You're way more than I ever expected."

This time, he crowded his body close against hers, pressing her into the doorframe. Slowly he rubbed her, up, then down again, imprinting on her just how much he wanted to be with her. Her lips were supple and welcoming, parting in need to invite him in. He dove deep, intent on tasting every inch of her tonight.

In, out and around, he explored her mouth. Nibbled on her lips. Eased his body close to her and away, mimicking the very dance they rushed toward. He felt her hands roam up his arms, massaging the muscles as she too explored.

She reached his shoulders and dug her fingers in deep, igniting a surge of power that struck hard at the base of his spine. He groaned, needing action. Needing more. He lifted her and almost wept when her legs encircled his waist. "Maddie," he growled. "Please."

"Upstairs," she murmured around kisses that fed the flames.

He took the steps slower than he planned, partly to keep her safe, partly because he couldn't stop kissing her. Maddie's mouth was addictive. Her response egged him on.

She pressed against him, spreading heat through his body in waves, ramping his urgency sky high. He wanted to take his time, wanted to care for her, but he knew the moment was fast approaching when he wouldn't be able to control himself anymore. First, he had to make it good for her.

Maddie deserved more than he could ever give her.

At the top of the stairs, she pointed to an open door down the shadowy hallway. Blake had the barest impression of pale blue walls before he laid her out across the bed. Her face fell into the darkness, but her body was illuminated by the beam of light coming from a lamp left on in the hallway. The green dress she was wearing teased him, leaving him aching for the womanly soft skin it concealed.

With extra care he unbuckled her wedge sandals, and kissed each ankle bone, celebrating its delicacy. His body screamed at him to hurry, but he clamped down tight and focused on the woman before him.

Maddie.

Lifting one of her leanly muscled legs, he watched as the skirt fell to her waist. He caught a brief glimpse of glittery black material between her legs that had him opening his mouth and brushing his teeth against her calf. Very soon he would taste more of her. She gasped, her muscles twitching beneath his mouth. He repeated the movement closer to her knee, then her thigh, then her inner thigh. Each time she jerked harder, her fingers fisting the pale blanket beneath her. The sound of her gasps in the air was almost as intoxicating as her singing.

Then he buried his face in the heat between her thighs, listening to her cry out as he dragged in her scent with a deep inhale. His brain lit up, sending urgent directives to his body that he struggled to ignore. But his impatient hands grasped the edge of the flimsy material that covered her, ripping it from her hips. He wasn't moving away from her for a single second, not even to remove her panties.

The flesh now laid bare for him was crowned by soft auburn curls. They smelled of musk and some floral scent he couldn't place at the moment. With extra care he parted her lower lips, which were slick with a moisture that had his mouth watering. He opened his lips and pressed against her. Her knees jerked up as if to close off his access, but her hands clenching in his hair sent a different message. Her gasps grew louder, echoing in his ears. Her body throbbed against his tongue. Blake felt himself slipping into a world that was all about Maddie, that revolved around her reactions and his utter need to pull the ultimate high from her.

Her hips lifted against him. He rode her motions out, licking and sucking, instinct taking over. His body throbbed in sympathy to her cries of need.

When her moans reached a fever pitch, he pressed hard, growling his command that she come. Maddie broke against his mouth, one long scream echoing off the walls. It had to be the most satisfying sound Blake had ever heard.

Seven

Maddie lay for long moments, unaware of anything but the pounding of her heart in her ears and the excited throb that dominated her body in this moment. She clutched at the soft blanket beneath her, needing something solid to ground her.

Her very limited experience before hadn't prepared her for the havoc a very focused, very determined man could wreak upon her body. But as satisfied as she was right now, underneath she could feel the return of the urgency. The need to experience the same thing *with* Blake. To return the favor he'd so graciously given her.

He pulled back a little, causing a protest within. He couldn't leave. Not now. Maybe never.

Opening her eyes, she could see him crouched between her legs. He made no further move away, just silently watched her in the darkness. Slowly she sat up, connecting with his gaze in the dim light. Then she rolled around until she too crouched on her knees. With shaking fingers, she grasped the hem of her dress, lifting it and tossing it to the side. The stream of light from the doorway illuminated her bare body. Only a simple lace bralette covered her breasts. Blake's groan was one of the most gratifying things she'd ever heard. Reaching out, she unbuttoned his shirt, taking her time, letting her fingers brush against his skin. He gasped as she pulled the shirttails loose from his slacks, then ran her fingernails over his chest and belly.

"Please, Madison," he said, breathing as hard as a racehorse.

He made quick work of his belt and zipper, then eased her back against the pillows. To her surprise, he didn't jump right in. Instead he slipped the bralette over her head. Burying his face between her breasts, he squeezed them and played with the pink tips until the fire burned high between her thighs once more. Only then did he take one nipple between his lips and worry the flesh until she squirmed and raised her hips in a plea for more. She cried, clutching at his back through the fine cotton of his shirt. With a growl, Blake tore it from his body and tossed it aside, then pressed down against her.

Flesh to flesh. Heat to heat.

With an urgency that signaled he'd reached the end of his control, Blake used his thighs to press hers even farther apart. She felt him fumble on the condom. Then the blunt tip of him searched and found her core, easing slightly inside. He braced his arms above her shoulders, breathing so hard his chest rubbed against her with every huff. He played for long moments, easing in and out until she thought she would scream in need. He was trying to make it good for her, she knew. But if he didn't enter her soon, she might explode.

Madison needed this to be about them.

Sliding her hands down beneath the edge of his pants, which were miraculously still on, she grasped his clenching muscles and dug deep. At the same time she lifted her hips to him. The feel of him sliding inside her took her breath away. He let himself go all the way to the hilt, then froze. She could feel her body ripple around him, on the cusp of something incredible, something she wouldn't be able to control.

Blake eased his upper body down, letting their skin touch. Then he tucked his mouth against one of her ears. "Hold on, Maddie," he groaned.

Then he started to thrust.

Madison only thought she'd been breathless before. Now every movement forced the air from her lungs. Her body lit up like fireworks. Blake grunted every time their hips met. They strained against each other for that ultimate high. Snapshot sensations imprinted themselves on Madison's mind: the slickness of his skin beneath her fingers; the sound of his voice in her ear; the exquisite pressure of him filling her full. Then he twisted against her and her world exploded.

In the quiet aftermath, listening to the sound of their breathing, it seemed cliché to say she would never be the same again. But Madison knew it to be true.

After long moments, Blake rolled to the side, pulling her with him. In those moments, she had no defense against him. No way to close herself off from the incredible fullness in her heart. Just as she drifted into sleep, she felt the warm pressure of lips against her temple. Blake's words floated around her. "I'll make sure everything is okay, Madison."

Consciousness came slowly to Blake. Normally, he awoke with a start and was out of bed in seconds. Today, the dim light of dawn peeked through the windows as he blinked once, then twice. It took him a moment to realize that Maddie still lay in his embrace.

A first for him.

Usually, as soon as the sex was over, Blake was putting the boundaries back into place. Even if he had to manhandle them back into the grooves. But last night he'd barely slid off Madison, unwilling to get too far from the unbelievably silky skin and the delicate scent of her. He'd pulled her close enough to get the blanket out from under them, covered them with it, then hugged her against his chest in a way he didn't want to acknowledge.

He could tell himself it didn't mean anything, but that didn't change the truth. He was royally screwed.

She still slept deeply. He smoothed back the jumble of her auburn hair so he could see her face, long lashes resting against freckle-sprinkled cheeks. Her lips seemed redder, swollen from their kisses the night before.

He wondered what other evidence he'd left behind. He sure as hell wouldn't be showing any of that to his father.

The memory of his old man left a bitter taste in his mouth. He could go for a cup of coffee…or three…or more. Maybe just the task of fixing it in an unfamiliar kitchen would help him to obliterate the thought of his father demanding proof of his progress?

He might need something stronger, he was afraid.

On his way downstairs, more things than he wanted to think about grabbed his attention. The cracked mirror behind the lamp on the little table in the upper hallway. The closed doors along the hall. Even though he didn't want to, Blake forced himself to open one. All of the furniture had been pushed into the middle of the room and draped. The back wall, which should correspond to the back of the house, had old water stains running down the flowery wallpaper.

He closed the door with a quiet snick and continued downstairs.

A quick glance into a living area opposite the refurbishing room stopped him in his tracks. A worn sofa, rug and coffee table were pushed to one side of the admittedly large room. The other end was occupied by a hospital bed. Bile rose in the back of his throat as Blake took in the area that had been stripped of linens and personal effects, but still bore all the markings of an end-of-life experience. There was a stripped-down bed, a pole to hang fluids on, and what looked like a heart monitor machine on an otherwise plain end table.

While she'd gone to the trouble of cleaning up, Madison hadn't dealt with the bare bones of her father's last days. The thought of her having to deal with this with no support, no helping hands, devastated him. Granted, he hadn't had a true "loved one" in his life, ever, but how had she continued to push forward, day after day, year after year, knowing that she would lose her father?

How devastating.

He forced himself on to the kitchen. Here the true extent of neglect showed in the daylight. Paint was peeling from the walls and windowsill. There was rust on the faucet and inside the sink. Cracks formed a latticework on tile countertop. Blake wasn't an expert in such matters, but he would guess that the house hadn't been properly maintained for a long time and had once been in impeccable quality.

That tile was Italian. The chandeliers were Toso. The kitchen faucet was originally an Axel. No one let that stuff go unless they had to…or strippers came in to take it.

Which could only mean one thing: Madison's family had never sold the Belarus diamond.

Blake crossed over to the budget-brand coffee maker, contemplating the evidence literally before him. Why? Why in the world would her mother keep that diamond and not sell it when they obviously needed the money so badly? Selling that thing on the open market would have set them for life, even if her father's illness had lasted thirty years. Why would she do this?

And what was he supposed to do about it?

This was the last thing he wanted to deal with after last night. As juvenile as it sounded, he wished he could spend his morning sipping coffee and thinking about how good last night had been. Especially if he wasn't going to be allowed to repeat it this morning. But he couldn't.

He had to think about Abigail, about what she was going through, about the fact that she needed him. How did he do that, rather than obsessing about where he went from here?

He hadn't meant for whatever this was between him and Maddie to go this far. He'd planned to get what he needed with as little collateral damage as possible. It was the least risky way of saving Abigail. Despite that, he would never use Madison's body against her.

He wandered back down the hallway to the living room, staring at the large expanse of empty floor between the pieces of furniture.

But now all he could think about was whether she would believe that was exactly what he had done, when the whole story came out. Because he had no doubt it would. He might hope that his father would keep his mouth shut, but that wasn't likely to happen. Especially not if he couldn't have his way.

"What are you doing?"

Blake whirled around to find Madison standing at the foot of the stairs. She had on a thin robe, thin enough for him to tell that she hadn't put on her underclothes. Did that mean she was still open to being vulnerable to him? That was a precious gift Blake wasn't sure he would ever get over.

"I was going to make coffee, then I got distracted."

He knew it sounded lame but it was all he could come up with at the moment. The last thing he wanted to do was make her feel uncomfortable by talking about the empty hospital bed in the room behind him.

She looked so small and frail with her arms wrapped around her ribs like that. He wanted to touch her, to hug her, but her posture was like one big Keep Away sign. She held herself stiffly, her body wound tight. Angled slightly toward him. He noticed she looked everywhere but at the bed.

He wasn't sure how she could even stand to have it in the house, except she probably had no way of moving it. Madison was strong and capable, but not that strong... not strong enough to move that single-handedly...or without a truck.

And he found that he cared, he wanted to help her. Man, he was fully invested.

"Are you ready to go?" she asked.

"Not...really." Blake didn't understood where the odd question came from. Yes, he'd put on his clothes from last night. He simply wasn't comfortable walking around her house in his birthday suit. He hadn't come prepared for anything else.

She turned and started down the hall, her voice echoing behind her. "I'm sure you're ready to get on the road," she threw over her shoulder. "Clean clothes, a hot shower."

Blake trailed down the hall behind her. What was up with all the questions about leaving? Was she really that eager to see him go?

He stepped through the doorway into the kitchen, where she had turned to face him, her arms crossed tighter than ever across her chest. He struggled not to look down at the effect that had on her breasts, instead focusing on her face.

"Is something wrong?" he asked.

"No." The word was more emphatic than it needed to be.

"You're not going to offer me coffee?" Not that he cared, but he might as well test the waters.

"My father always said my coffee was horrible. You'd probably do better to stop somewhere on your way home."

He was not buying this. He took a step closer to her. Then another. A broken tile shifted beneath his shoe. Madison glanced down, and her lips tightened.

So was it the house that was her problem? Or *him* in her house?

Blake took another step. Only this time, Madison stepped back.

He crossed his arms over his chest, mimicking her position. "What's going on, Madison?"

Outwardly he projected calm, seeming in control of this entire situation. But inside, his temperature rose and his heartbeat sped up. He clenched his teeth on a jittery burst of panic. But he wasn't about to walk away. Instead he moved closer.

He should walk away. He knew it. Without a doubt, he should obey the Keep Away sign and leave Madison to herself. He should walk out of this house and never think about her again, and never think about that stupid diamond. But he couldn't.

So he locked away all thoughts of that beautiful jewel and focused on the beauty in front of him. He could divorce himself from his feelings, but then he wouldn't know the pleasure that came with her touch, the comfort that came from her listening ear.

Selfish bastard that he was, he couldn't leave her alone. "Madison, what is it, hon?"

As he came within arm's reach, Blake couldn't resist touching her. He smoothed his thumb across one high cheekbone. Excitement ratcheted up inside him, rapidly overtaking the panic.

Yes, he was definitely a bastard.

She turned her head to look away, only to flinch at whatever she saw. He followed her gaze to see the door to the pantry hanging crooked in its frame. As they stared in silence, the refrigerator struggled, its mechanical hum sounding strained. Blake let his eyelids drift closed for just a moment, wondering if somewhere in his shallow soul he had the words to make her feel better.

He used his hand to turn her head, guide her eyes back around to his. "Madison, it's okay."

She bit her lip, worrying it for minute before releasing the plump flesh. "No, it's not." She glanced up at him through her long, thick lashes. "You're the first person to be in this house since the day my father died."

"You know, if you don't let anyone in, then no one can help you."

"My father always told me we had to help ourselves. We couldn't expect someone else to come in and bail us out."

"But you're only capable of so much, Madison."

"It's amazing what you can be capable of when you're desperate."

He cupped her cheeks between his hands. "You don't have to be desperate anymore."

Her eyes went wide for a moment with a flash of surprise that cut through his shallow soul like a hot knife through butter. If he lived to be hundred, he hoped he never saw that pain in her expression ever again.

But he knew only one way to erase it right now. Holding her still, he bent to capture her lips with his. How could Madison taste so sweet? Last thing at night, or first thing in the morning, she was sweeter than pie. And he was desperate for dessert.

He sampled her lips, their breaths mingling as they gave themselves over to the sensations. He felt Madison's hands against his back, pulling him closer. To know she wanted him as much as he wanted her sent his spirit soaring. He let his own hands wander down, feeling the heat of her through the thin robe she wore. He groaned against her lips. He needed her. Right now. Not after a walk down the hall to the couch. Not after a walk upstairs to the bed.

Right. Now.

With what little brain he had left, Blake pictured the room in his head. Then he lifted Madison off her feet with his hands around her ribs. Her squeal echoed in his ears. He sat her down on the nearby empty space on the countertop.

He didn't think about where they were. He only thought about her, and the urgency driving him to take her once more.

To his infinite gratitude, she spread her knees wide, making space for him. Blake fumbled in his pocket for a condom, then reached around to lower his zipper. His glance down revealed the shadowed valley between her breasts, visible where her robe had slid open.

Blake drew in a hard, deep breath, easing off the brakes on his drive to be inside her once more. He trailed his fingers along the edges of her robe, sampling the plumpness, feeling her gasp, seeing her nipples tighten beneath the sheer fabric. Slowly he slid one panel to the side, revealing her firm, round breast with its pink-tipped nipple. His mouth watered as he leaned over and licked the turgid tip. Madison arched her back, her breath releasing in a hiss. He licked again. And again. Loving the reaction of her body. Knowing that she'd be wet and ready for him.

He dropped his pants and covered himself for their protection. His fingers found her slick and needy. His heart pounded in his throat as he eased himself through her tightness.

"Oh, Maddie," he moaned. "So good."

Then he felt her legs circle around his waist, trapping him close, pulling him closer. He forced his way in to the hilt, both of them shuddering. He ground against her, his entire body tightening with the need to lose control.

"Please, Blake," she begged.

Holding back was no longer an option. That simple request swept aside his hesitation. He dug deep, gathering every ounce of energy he had, desperate to share something special with her, something he'd never felt with anyone but her. He had a need for her response that would send him over the edge.

He smoothed his hand up her body to her breast, palming, then squeezing it. Tweaking the tip in a way that made her body clamp down on him. She gasped with every thrust but refused to let go.

Blake strained, desperate for release. His hand slid around to her bottom, jerking her against him with every thrust. In his need to impress himself on her, to draw out her response, he buried his mouth against her neck, and sucked on her flesh to make the pounding of her heart match his. She cried out, the sound vibrating against his tongue. Her body squeezed around him, sending his need into hyperspace. He ground against her as they both exploded with an intensity that almost knocked Blake out.

He wanted to crawl inside of her arms and never leave, an idea that at once felt overwhelmingly right and oh-so-wrong in a panicky way. The thought of staying just like this, forever, tempted him.

All too soon, Madison began to shift. He stilled her movements with his hands on her hips. Just a minute more…

"Blake," she murmured. "Your phone."

He blinked. Sure enough, a low metallic ringtone came from his phone, not far away on the countertop. On the display, Blake could see that it was his father's housekeeper. Alarm quickly pushed out the euphoria.

"Blake, it's an emergency." He barely recognized Sherry's shaking voice. "I had to take Abigail to the ER."

Eight

Madison could barely comprehend Blake's mad dash for his clothes. Her brain was still swimming in lust and satiation. Then she got a really good look at his face.

"What's going on?" she asked.

"I've got to go," he murmured. He tried to put a button through the hole on his shirt once, then twice. Finally he swore, then ran his fingers through his hair.

Did she hear him right? "What? Why?"

Who had called? Blake was as unattached as anyone she'd come across, seeming to exist in a strange ecosystem that had no one else living inside of it. Yet after one short conversation he was buttoning his shirt crooked in his haste to leave.

"Blake?"

Still he ignored her, as if his mind were already elsewhere. The switch from having his full attention five minutes ago to being completely tossed aside had her reeling. Not that she expected him to ignore an emergency for her, but what on earth had him switching gears faster than a race car? At least his preoccupation covered her awkward dismount from the counter. She might never look at her kitchen the same way again.

After calling his name a few times, she went to stand between him and the phone he had set back down on the counter while zipping up his pants. "Blake? What is happening?"

"I've got to leave right now." His tone didn't indicate he realized he'd already said this to her before.

"Why?"

He blinked, as if no one had ever asked him that. "They've taken my sister to the hospital."

Sister? "Okay. I'll go with you."

"No."

The vehemence encapsulated in that one word took her aback. "Excuse me?"

"No," he said with a hard shake of his head. "I need to leave now."

The hand he waved at her seemed to indicate it was her lack of clothes that was the problem. But was it? "Blake, you shouldn't go alone. Give me three minutes to throw on—"

"No. Just. Not now."

Hurt shot through Madison with the same speed that lust had earlier. She was a smart girl. It didn't take her too many tries to realize when someone didn't want her around—whatever the reason. But this wasn't something she could let go. Blake did not look like he should be behind the wheel. Besides, if there was one thing she had experience with, it was hospitals.

She doubted Blake could say the same.

This time she placed her hand over the phone as he reached for it. "Blake."

"What?" he asked, the word sounding short and clipped. He never lifted his eyes from the phone.

"Do you know which hospital?"

That had him glancing up. He gave a short shake of his head.

"When you do, do you know how to get there in the quickest way possible?"

"No," he admitted through clenched teeth.

"Then why don't you find out while I get some clothes on?"

She could actually see the gears start to turn before he gave a quick nod. Madison left him to his phone while she ran upstairs. A quick splash of water on the face was all she dared take the time for, then clean clothes and a ponytail holder she would put her hair in on the way. To her surprise, he was still in the kitchen when she ran in with her tennis shoes in her hand.

"She's at Children's Hospital. Her doctor was already there."

Madison paused for a mere second, then forced herself to finish putting on her shoes. "Let's go."

As much as it hurt, she wasn't surprised when he started to argue on the way to the car. "Just tell me the shortcuts. I'll get myself there."

"And get in a wreck because you're upset behind the wheel."

"I'm perfectly capable of driving right now."

Madison glided around the car until she reached the passenger door, then swung around to face him. "But you are upset, right? Shaken, maybe? In need of a friend?" She grimaced, feeling her anger slip the bounds of her control. "If you don't actually consider me as one, I get it. But I still feel some responsibility to fill that role, since ten minutes ago we were still having sex on my countertop."

Without waiting for an answer, she gave the car hood a quick slap, then slid around the door and into the seat. As she buckled her belt, she called herself every kind of fool. Blake still stood beside the car. Had all of this been just about the sex? If she got any more mixed signals, she wouldn't know which way was up.

Maybe he didn't, either.

Madison tried to hold onto that thought while dragging in a deep breath. For a moment, surprise streaked through her. She'd dealt with any number of medical emergencies in her lifetime…none of which had caused her to lose her cool. Of course, she was usually the person in charge. Not simply along for the ride.

Still, she shouldn't have struck out at him like that.

Thirty seconds later, he slid into the driver's seat. "I'm sorry, Madison—" he started.

"Don't be. Let's just go."

Maybe that wasn't the way to handle this. But she just couldn't go through with helping him if he actually said again out loud that he didn't want her.

She wanted to be a good person who would help him regardless. But she couldn't. Better to just do her part, then deal with the fallout later. After she'd had time to process her own emotions over sleeping with him, then discovering he had a whole family she wasn't aware of. And what man his age had siblings young enough to be treated at Children's Hospital? Was this child really a sister? Or something else?

Madison quickly cut off that line of thinking. She was here. She needed to focus on the job at hand. Speculation would get her nothing but upset.

Madison directed him toward the least busy streets she

could think of at this time of the morning. The only saving grace was the absence of school traffic. She watched him closely for any signs that he wasn't in control, but those few moments by himself outside of the car seemed to have calmed him.

She only wished she could get all of her suspicions under control just as easily.

Blake locked down his emotions as tightly as he could, just as tightly as he held the steering wheel. He executed the turns with precision, utilizing every ounce of experience he'd gotten on the autobahn, to maneuver the vehicle without slowing down.

"Call Father's housekeeper," he said, not daring to take his eyes off the road. His phone automatically rang the number, which went straight to voice mail.

Blake wanted to hit something, but he refused to slow down long enough to do so. To his surprise, Madison didn't complain. No gasps, no quick grabs for the door handle. She was just a solid, quiet presence in the car who gave the occasional direction to turn.

"Call Father's housekeeper."

When this call also went to voice mail, he let out a string of expletives that would've had a sailor blushing. Still, Madison remained silent.

"Where is she?" he growled.

Madison pointed out the entryway for the parking deck, and Blake pulled squarely into the valet spot.

Madison waved him through to the ER entrance while she paused next to the valet podium.

Blake felt a flash of gratitude, tossed her the keys, then stepped up his pace to get to the ER desk.

"I need to see my sister. Abigail Boudreaux," he told the nurse at the desk.

A part of him was surprised by the shaky, out-of-breath quality of his voice. This wasn't a Blake that he knew. But he didn't have time to think about that right now. The nurse nodded and calmly asked to see his ID. Her entire demeanor was a counterpoint to his.

Madison arrived as the nurse clicked away on the computer.

"Blake?" she asked. "Isn't there a parent you can call?"

"Good luck getting through to him," Blake murmured. Luckily the nurse looked up before he had to explain his words.

"Sir, I'm afraid I can't help you."

Blake froze. "What do you mean you can't help me? I know my sister was brought here."

Madison tugged at his shirtsleeve, but he ignored her. He focused entirely on the nurse, the person who would get him to his sister the fastest. "I want to see my sister. Abigail Boudreaux."

"I'm afraid I can't help you, sir."

For a moment, Blake was almost certain he was going to climb across the counter. What the hell was going on with him? All he knew was he had to make sure his sister was okay.

Just as Blake opened his mouth to start yelling, Madison intervened. "Blake." Her tone was firm and hard enough to catch his attention. He turned her way.

"Blake," she said in a softer voice. "Let me speak to you for a moment, please."

He gave the nurse a hard stare before following Madison over to the side. "I don't have time for this. I need to see my sister."

"I realize that," Madison said. "The thing is, if you're not listed specifically as someone who should be told she's here, they can't tell you her information. They can't let you up to see her."

"What?"

"It's considered an invasion of privacy and it's against federal regulations. Why don't you try the housekeeper again? Or maybe your father? Your mother?"

He ignored the question implied in her words, and tried to dial Sherry again. The call went straight to voice mail.

Blake felt scattered, like his racing heartbeat was pulling him away from information that was very important but he couldn't focus on. Instead he did the only other thing he knew: he dialed his father again.

"Yes?"

The calm sound of his father's voice only raised his irritation even higher. "Where is Abigail? Are you here at the hospital?"

"Hospital? I don't know what you're talking about."

"The housekeeper called me. Abigail had to be taken to the emergency room but they won't let me see her."

"Well, why would we list you as family? Until recently, I hadn't seen you in nearly twenty years. But I guess that's what the message on my phone is for. I haven't had a chance to listen to it yet."

"She called me almost two hours ago. How come you're not down here?"

"I'm in New York. Besides, it's probably just a fake episode to get attention."

"Abigail's epilepsy is not fake."

Blake knew he was yelling at this point but couldn't control himself. Beside him he sensed Madison shift on her feet. Then a warm weight settled at the small of his back. In all the chaos that raced through his mind and his body, that warm contact became a focal point. Her touch sent a wave of peace over him.

His father was in New York. He wasn't here—not that he would care if he was. Instead of trying to understand that, Blake just hung up the phone. He stared at it in his hand for a moment, wondering if throwing it across the room would make him feel any better. Except it was the only way he could find out any information about Abigail.

"What do I do?" he moaned, bending over to press his palms against his knees. How did he find his baby sister?

"Blake."

The softly spoken word brought his attention back to his surroundings. Blake straightened up, drew in a hard breath, then looked at her. "I need to find her, Madison."

"I know. Let me help you."

Just as she had been since they'd gotten in the car. Her words centered him, just like her touch had. "I don't know what to do."

"What kind of episode did your sister have?"

"She has epilepsy. All the housekeeper said was that she was unresponsive this morning. Maybe some kind of seizure?"

Maddie nodded. Her hand ran down his arm, only stopping when she reached his hand and curled her fingers around his. "Come with me."

As she headed out the door of the emergency room, he glanced back at the nurse at the desk who watched them walk away. "Wait a minute," he said. "Where are we going?"

Madison paused once they reached the other side of the automatic doors. Then she looked up at him. "I know of another waiting room for pediatrics that might be helpful. Let's go in the front of the hospital and see if we can possibly find the housekeeper there. That'll be the quickest way," she said, "even though it doesn't seem like it. Badgering the nurse will get us nowhere. I know—I have plenty of experience."

He walked with her along the sidewalks outside the huge buildings. Impatience bubbled up inside of him, but there were no other options for him at this moment. "How do you know this?" he asked.

"The staff at Maison de Jardin sometimes has to come to the hospital to help residents who've been injured, whose spouses have abused them. And their children." She tossed him a quick glance. "I've been here quite a few times."

She maintained a quick pace, not letting her shorter stature keep her from matching his longer strides. "Plus some of our residents actually come to work here."

Blake paused a step. "Can't you ask one of them to help us?"

"Unfortunately no. I can't ask them to risk their jobs when they've worked so hard to get into a better place."

As much as the logic made sense, Blake could only see as far as his needs in this moment.

Madison led him in the front door proper and took him around to a large bank of elevators. No sooner were they in one than she hit the button for the third floor.

"Has your...sister...always had epilepsy?"

There it was, the guilt that he couldn't figure out how to shake. "I don't know. I know this particular diagnosis is recent, but I'm not sure how long her symptoms have been occurring."

He shifted on his feet, uncomfortable with the knowledge that he had no idea what was happening, he had no control over the situation, and if he ever found that blasted diamond, he would find himself completely responsible for a child with an illness that could land her in the hospital. What the hell was he even doing here?

They came out of the elevator to a long hallway. Madison rushed down until it opened into a nurses station. "Tamika," she exclaimed. "I wasn't sure if you were working today."

Blake paused behind her as the young black woman in scrubs gave him a good eyeing.

He simply stared back.

"What are you doing here, Madison?" she asked.

"We're looking for... Blake's sister. I was just going to take him across to the waiting room."

Hearing her words, Blake turned abruptly and saw a waiting room behind them. He strode across the hall into the doorway.

"Mr. Boudreaux!"

Blake was so relieved to see Sherry rising from one of the chairs that he thought he might melt into a puddle. "Where is she?" he asked, rushing over to help her. "Is she okay?"

"Oh, Mr. Boudreaux. They haven't come to tell me anything." Tears overflowed the woman's eyes to trickle down her cheeks. "I can't imagine that little poppet all alone."

So he was one step closer but still knew nothing. Soon Blake found himself with an armful of weeping housekeeper, and his fear for his sister was even higher than ever.

Nine

"Is that really him?" Tamika asked, straining her neck to see behind Madison into the waiting room.

"Stop it." Madison wasn't sure how she felt about Blake in this moment, but she certainly didn't feel comfortable with her friend ogling him. She drew in a calming breath, only to wince at the antiseptic scent of the hospital halls. "We're just trying to find out where the little girl is. The housekeeper brought her in. All I know is that it has something to do with her epilepsy."

"Why would a housekeeper bring her in? Where are the parents?" Tamika asked, bracing her hands on her hips. Tamika's passion lay in caring for the children on this floor—and making sure none of them were mistreated.

Madison shook her head. "Blake tried to call someone while we were downstairs. I guess his father? I'm really not sure. It sounded like he might be out of town."

"How could he not have any information about his child? Are you sure this little girl is his sister?"

Madison did not want to go there. "I've been told very little."

Tamika looked sideways at her for a moment, confirming Madison's own fears.

"That's all I know. He tried to call the housekeeper and couldn't get her on the phone."

"Cell reception up here is terrible," Tamika said. "Her phone probably wouldn't work in that waiting room."

"That's what it sounds like." Madison glanced over her shoulder to see Blake holding a woman wearing a maid's uniform in his arms. "But I'm guessing he's found her now."

Her friend grumbled beneath her breath as she watched them. Then Madison and Tamika shared a glance. Madison felt awkward. She'd done what she told Blake she would. Should she join him now? The housekeeper appeared to be crying, definitely distraught. Should she offer some kind of help?

"I don't know what to do," Madison said. *About any of it*, but she didn't say that part out loud. She guessed maybe she could have gone online and looked into his family, but the excruciating effect of the gossip surrounding her friend Trinity had left a bad taste in her mouth. Besides, she hadn't wanted anything else to mess with her self-esteem. Guess she'd shot herself in the foot there?

"Should I go in there? Should I ask if I can help?"

"Girl, I'd help him all day long," Tamika teased with a saucy wink. "He's very pretty. Even prettier in person than he was online."

"Tamika!"

"Well, he is." She offered her typical shrug when she

was misbehaving, then glanced over her monitors for a moment.

"Don't you have a job to do?"

"Not at the moment. All's quiet."

"We need to find you a boyfriend," Madison grumbled. Then maybe she would stay out of Madison's love life.

"Well, if Blake has any friends…"

She'd walked right into that one. She gave her friend a quelling look. "I'm serious, Tamika. I had no idea he even had a sister. He hasn't spoken much about his family."

"What do you talk about?"

At first Madison thought she was being facetious again, but then realized her friend was serious. "We've talked about my family, the house, my job."

"But he's giving no information about himself?" She shook her head. "Girl, you'd better be careful."

Madison knew that. She just didn't know if she was in a position to be careful anymore. Blake's possession of her body had sealed what her spirit already knew. But was he on the same page?

He'd said he wanted to be with her. But he hadn't *really* shared himself with her, had he? Other than his art, and hints that his childhood had been quite bad, he hadn't really shared much. It was all about the present…and her. Looking back, that didn't seem right.

"I recognize that expression," Tamika said. "I see more cookies in our future."

Madison arched an eyebrow at her friend but was afraid Tamika wasn't far from right. "Any requests?"

"You know I'm good with any chocolate, and I've got finals coming up."

"I'm glad my pain can feed your success." Madison

could already feel the depression sinking in. She should have known that last night was too good to be true.

"I hope not," Tamika said, a frown between her brows. "I know I tease you a lot, but you're the last person who deserves any more grief."

Madison wished she could hug her friend, but the nurses station desk between them prevented that. "Thank you, Tamika."

"My pleasure."

Then a patient pressed a call button in one of the rooms and Tamika went to answer it. Madison stared after her friend for long moments. She'd been so blessed in her life. Yes, she'd lost both her parents. But they'd been a blessing to her while they'd been alive. And her friends, they helped keep her going. She drew in a deep, long breath. She could only do what she knew, which was to help people, including Blake. That was what she would do for now. The rest could be worried about later. She turned back toward the waiting room, only to find it empty.

She glanced up and down the hallway, but it too was empty. The faces at the nurses station were now unfamiliar, as Tamika had left to answer the call.

Madison stood in confusion for long moments. Where had Blake gone? Why didn't he let her know?

Of course, he hadn't wanted her here in the first place. Maybe taking her with him was more information than he wanted to let her in on. This was definitely a new one, and only magnified her impression from earlier that he'd been holding parts of himself back. Possibly hiding his true self on purpose.

What reason could he have for doing that? No good ones that she could think of.

She'd never heard of being dumped at the hospital.

Then again, she'd served her purpose, hadn't she? She glanced at her phone. Sure enough, no reception.

So calling him was out. She could stand around and wait for him to get back, but did he want her here? Somehow the thought of sitting here for hours on end while Tamika was working and knew she'd been dumped was just more than she could handle. She'd be more productive at home, where she knew her place and had things to do.

So she headed downstairs. As she stood in the lobby, she called for a cab.

The debate raged within her as she waited. Should she tell him? Should she not tell him? Should she let him make the next move? In the end, she couldn't not say something. Just disappearing without a word wasn't a responsible action on her part. So she typed out a text letting him know she'd gone home.

By the time she'd pulled into the driveway, the screen of her phone was still empty. Just as empty as she was.

Madison put a little extra effort behind her sandpapering. Normally she would have used an electric sander, but she'd chosen to do the manual work on the details simply to keep herself from thinking. It had been twenty-four hours since she'd walked out of the hospital, and Blake had still not contacted her.

She'd gone to work and kept herself busy with files, calls and orders. No one had been hanging around, so she didn't see the point in baking. She'd be tempted to just eat all the cookie dough herself. So by midafternoon, she'd come home and tried to keep herself busy on a new antique dresser that she'd gotten from one of the specialty stores in town. Unfortunately, it wasn't wearing her out as much as she'd like.

But she was too wound up to settle into reading her mother's journals, and nothing on TV interested her. So she'd rather get her hands roughed up and be productive at the same time, instead of spending her time pining over someone who couldn't care less about her.

She did recognize the selfishness in her thoughts. Blake was really concerned about his sister, and she hoped that the little girl was okay. She hoped that his not contacting her didn't mean that something terrible had happened to the child. But how long did it take to send a simple text?

Caring about someone meant you let them know you were okay. She could take the hint.

So she scratched and scraped, going with the grain to preserve the wood underneath the tacky finish and layer of old paint. She knew in the end she would create something that was really beautiful, and that kept her going.

She just wished she could shut off her brain for a few minutes.

Just then her phone dinged. Madison glanced over at it for a moment, not sure if she really wanted to see what was on it. All this time she'd been mentally complaining that he hadn't contacted her, and now she wasn't even sure she wanted to see if it was him, or what he had to say.

Finally, she dropped the piece of sandpaper, and wiped the dust from her arms. Then she took the few steps to pick up her phone and read the screen.

I'm at the gate.

Well, at least Blake was being considerate. The lock on the gate was so old he probably could've pushed it open without even worrying about letting her know. Instead he'd at least given her a heads-up.

Madison wasn't sure what she wanted. This whole relationship had been like a roller coaster. Did she want to let him in? She knew she cared, or else she wouldn't have spent the last twenty-four hours obsessing over him not contacting her. But was this a matter of too little too late?

Curiosity finally got the better of her, and she stepped outside to unlock the gate. They'd never been able to afford a fancy electronic version, so she had to manually pop the lock to let him in.

By the time he drove through, parked the car and got out, she'd closed the gate behind him and was standing at the entrance to the kitchen. The heat outside caused sweat to bead along her hairline. But she wasn't about to let him in this house without a really good reason.

"Hey, Maddie. How's it going?"

For a moment she simply stared at him. Did he really think he could leave her hanging for twenty-four hours and just waltz back in with a hearty how-you-doin'?

"You don't get to call me Maddie anymore."

That wasn't what she'd expected to come out of her mouth, and apparently he hadn't, either. The surprise on his face was clear, and for a moment she felt ashamed. What she'd said hadn't been polite, but then she realized at least it was true. Maddie was a nickname that came with intimacy. Intimacy meant relationship. Relationship meant including someone in your life.

"I'm sorry," he said, and it actually seemed true. "I didn't mean to upset you."

"Then why would you completely blank me out for twenty-four hours? Why wouldn't you at least send a text letting me know if you were okay, if your sister was okay?"

For a moment, his entire expression shut down. His

body stiffened as if he would pull away from her. *This is it. We're done.*

Then he took a deep breath and said, "Maddie, um Madison." He shook his head. "You're right. I'm going to go out on a limb and be honest here and say it didn't occur to me that you would want me to hear from me with an update."

"Why?"

Blake wiped the sweat off his forehead. "I know this doesn't reflect well on me but frankly, I've never been in a relationship before. I've never been involved with a woman who would want to know those things. And even if she did, I wouldn't have a clue how to give them to her." He took a step back. "And I also haven't been involved with my family in many years. Dealing with a crisis like this is out of my realm of experience, and it never occurred to me that you would want to be involved, either."

Well, at least he'd been honest. As the seconds ticked by, Maddie just stood there, numb as she tried to understand what living like that could possibly be like. How could you go through life with no one around who cared anything about you? How could you not have contact with your family? Blake seemed to care a lot about his little sister. How had that happened?

One thing at a time. "Blake, it wouldn't matter if we weren't involved. I would still want to help you. I would still care about what happened to your sister. I would still want to help support you. I thought I'd made that clear."

"That's because you're a much better person than me."

"I'm not an angel. I'm just human."

"Then we'll agree to disagree."

"So I don't know what to do here. What is it that you want me to do? Back off?"

Because that really was not in her wheelhouse. Thankfully, he was already shaking his head.

"Do you want me to not ask questions?"

"I'm guessing that might be impossible for you." His grin had a touch of smirk.

Time to bring her fears to the fore. "Well, I don't really think it's fair that you get to pry into my life and I don't get to pry into yours."

The widening of his eyes told her she'd hit a nerve. Then he gave a short nod. "I'm gonna try, Madison."

"Would you rather walk away now?" Because he obviously wasn't comfortable with this.

As if something inside him was unleashed, Blake sprung forward to wrap her in his arms. He buried his face into her neck. "No. No. No," he murmured against her skin.

Madison's resistance melted away. Blake was different than anyone she'd known, and she just had to work with that. Not accept it. But figure out what that meant for both of them.

She pulled him into the semi-cool house, which was a bit of a relief after the heat of the Louisiana sun outside. He closed the door behind him, then sank to his knees in front of her. He buried his face against her belly. Madison wrapped her arms around his shoulders, the weight of her heart telling her she was seeing him in this moment like no one else ever had.

"I thought I was going to lose her," he said. He didn't look up. He didn't say anything more. And she knew he was admitting something he might not have to anyone else.

"Is she going to be okay?"

He nodded against her. "I never thought I'd get this

attached to a child. But she's so small, so fragile. Seeing her in that hospital bed…"

She felt the tremor that shook him and rubbed his back. "How long has she been sick?"

"From what I understand, she was diagnosed several months ago with the epilepsy. Her mother never said anything about it before."

So she had a mother and father, but the housekeeper took her to the hospital? "Where were her parents?"

"My father was in New York. He and my mother divorced long ago. Abigail's mother is who knows where in Europe. How she could leave a seven-year-old like that is beyond even me."

Madison clutched him a little closer, disbelief sweeping over her. How in the world could they do that? Blake's horror made a little more sense now. Wait—

"Blake, is this the family business that brought you home?"

He nodded but didn't say more. Madison imagined this little conversation was the most Blake had shared with anyone, ever. While she should probably be nervous about that, she couldn't help but be grateful that she was someone he felt comfortable sharing this burden with.

After a few long moments, Blake stood and pressed a soft kiss against her lips. "Madison?" he murmured.

She knew what he was asking, without him having to say the words. And she knew what she wanted, without needing any promises.

So she once more took his hand in hers and led him up the stairs to her room. There she pulled her dusty T-shirt over her head and unsnapped her bra so it could fall away. She peeled off her khaki work pants and the plain pair of panties underneath. The whole time Blake watched her, his gaze ravenously devouring every new inch of bare skin she revealed. His fingers played over her, as if using his fingertips to memorize every curve and valley. Her breath caught as he lingered at the tips of her breasts, at the curve of her hips, at the apex of her thighs.

He tore his own clothes off with more haste than decorum, slid on protection and covered her body with his. As he slipped inside her, Madison squeezed her eyes shut, hoping to hide the sheen of tears caused by the emotions welling inside her. Somehow she knew she'd made a choice tonight. There were no guarantees for how it would turn out. But with every thrust he made her his. There was no turning back, only going forward. She didn't know how to do that. But she guessed she'd take it one day at a time.

As he took them both over the edge, she squeezed her arms around him, hugging him close, and silently accepted that despite all the craziness, this was the man for her.

Still she couldn't stop herself from asking, as they lay entwined on her bed, "Blake, is there anything else I need to know?"

Why didn't the shake of his head make her feel any better?

Ten

Blake was surprised when Abigail let him lift her from the car and into his arms. Sherry stood nearby as he carried her to the door. It was amazing how light she felt against him, how fragile. The doctor had said that she wasn't in any more danger, but that didn't take away the fear.

Blake knew the minute they stepped through the front door that his father was home. Yes, it could've just been the cold feel of the house after decades of being possessed by his father, but somehow he knew the concentration of his father's essence when he was around. It was an awareness he'd never get rid of.

Blake ignored the movement in his peripheral vision as he crossed the foyer, and continued toward the stairs. Abigail deserved to be at home, in her own bed, happy and safe. At least he could provide that.

He settled her into her bed and covered her with a comforter. The trusting expression in her brown eyes reached into his chest and squeezed. "It's going to be okay, Abigail." He hoped he sounded more confident than he was. Either way, Abigail got the short end of the stick.

"Thank you, Blake."

"Sleep well, sweetheart." Blake tucked the blanket in around her again, not sure if that was actually how this was done. Then he left the housekeeper to supervise bedtime.

He came back down the stairs with a feeling of dread. But this time it wasn't just about seeing his father. It was the knowledge that he couldn't keep either of the girls in his life safe from Armand. And he had no idea what to do about that.

"Blake, I see you found your way home again."

For a split second, Blake considered walking straight out the door. Not pausing. Not acknowledging his father in any way. But the memory of that little girl in his arms stayed his steps.

"Well, for now I don't have any choice, do I?"

His father inclined his head as he stepped farther into the foyer. "So how much did this hospital visit cost me?"

Even for his father, that seemed like a crass question. So Blake didn't bother to suppress his sarcasm. "Don't worry, Dad. I took care of it for you."

"I'm amazed they let you, considering they didn't want to give you access to her at all."

That gave Blake a little jolt but he said, "They'll take money under any circumstances."

His father nodded; obviously Blake had finally learned to speak his language. He took a few steps toward the front door.

"At least it wasn't an inconvenience to you," Blake said, looking back over his shoulder at his father.

"That's right."

That smirk made Blake want to wipe it off his face. But his father was ready to move on to new sport.

"So you finally bagged her, did you?"

Blake stopped dead in his tracks, struggling to keep his face completely blank as rage swept over him. To hear Madison spoken about in the same way teenagers would talk about a girl in a locker room was infuriating. What they had shared had nothing to do with bagging and everything to do with discovering who they each were. Blake couldn't even believe he thought about it in those terms, but it was true.

Then he realized the implications of what his father had just said, and swung around to face him head on. "What do you mean? What have you heard?"

Blake knew that his father had no friends who were close to Madison or her family or the charity. So who would be gossiping about them with him? Especially since his father had been in New York. "What did you do, Father?"

"The same thing any father does when his son cuts him out of his life. I hired a private detective."

"What the hell? Who spies on their child? What happened to 'show me proof'? Like my last visit."

Armand shook his head. "Your proof is not very reliable. And I know the closer you get to the girl, it will be even less so. Or the closer you get to Abigail. So I went with an unbiased source."

"Hell, if you're going to go to those lengths, why don't you just have someone break into her house and steal the diamond?"

Blake quickly bit his tongue, even though it had to have been an idea that his father thought of long ago. But the thought of Maddie being subjected to someone breaking into her house freaked him out.

"Stealing is illegal," his father said matter-of-factly, as if every machination he'd imposed since Blake had returned home wasn't in some way evil. But it was legal, and thus acceptable. Then Armand went on, "If the diamond is obtained through illegal means that can be tracked back to me, it will be difficult to sell."

"So you want me to steal it instead?"

"Actually, I figure she'll just hand it over to you. Or, if you take something she never knew she had, then is it really stealing?"

Blake shoved the completely insane reasoning behind his father's words away, and focused on the most pressing issue. "I can't believe you had someone spying on me."

And that person had been spying on Madison, too. The sheer weight of that understanding hit him hard. The things he was bringing into Maddie's life weren't just unfair to her. This was an invasion of massive proportions. He just hoped he could live with the results.

"You will stay away from Maddie," he insisted. "Do you understand me?"

His father only answered with another smirk. In that moment, a large part of the old Blake reappeared. The urgent need to run, to escape, just as he had when he was seventeen, was overwhelming. The only thing that kept his feet planted right where he was was a little girl upstairs and a woman across town, neither of whom he could abandon. When he'd walked out of here as a teenager, he couldn't give a rat's ass about anybody else. There was no one to care about. Every person in his life had disappeared, just like they had out of Abigail's life. But now he refused to run out on her like others had.

But he just wasn't sure how to help her.

"Don't worry, you bastard. You'll get what you want."

But as he walked out, Blake knew he was biding time.

He had to find a way out of the situation and quick. And that way out couldn't involve stealing a diamond, even one Madison didn't know she had.

I had options. When I chose to be with my husband, I knew what I was giving up. But not the pain that would follow.

I knew the man I was leaving behind would be vindictive, and I knew I would be punished, but I had no idea he would take it out on my family like this.

Madison read the lines once more. Many times her mother had mentioned making choices, but for the most part her words were about routine decisions. This was the first Madison had read about a vindictive *man*. What did that mean?

A quick glance over at the clock told her that Blake would be here any moment. He had offered to take her to an event at the ASTRA Museum that Trinity hadn't been able to attend. Madison wanted to make a good impression. To represent the charity in the best way possible. Hopefully, with Blake by her side, things would go smoothly. They'd be no embarrassment or fumbling.

She needed to get her shoes on before he arrived. She set the journal on her bedside table and crossed to her closet. Just as she reached it, she heard the book tumble to the floor. Crossing back, she picked it up to return it to the table, only to have something fall from the back.

It looked like several pieces of paper folded together. Madison could see her mother's handwriting on the back of the outside sheet. That was odd. She'd never found anything more than bookmarks stuck into her mother's journals. Only she didn't have time to look at it right now. She laid the packet on top of the journal and returned to the closet for her shoes.

When she went outside a few minutes later, Blake's wolf whistle made her smile as she crossed over to the car. She slid into her seat and was surprised when he leaned across for a quick kiss. This felt more like a real date. So far she and Blake seemed to only have out-of-the-ordinary times together. But this felt real and good. Madison would be more than happy to have a quiet, normal date.

"So," he said as he got them on the road, "I was wondering how you would feel about meeting my little sister."

For a moment, Madison felt like a bomb had exploded in the car. She glanced over at him as if to say, *Did you feel that?* The only indication that his request was unusual even for him was his super tight grip on the steering wheel.

So he knew what he was doing, and the fact that he was willing to still do it filled her with excitement. She also felt a touch of nervousness, because what did she know about spending time with a seven-year-old? Granted, she'd spent plenty of time with children at Maison de Jardin. But she had a feeling that, like Blake, his little sister would be a whole different breed of people.

"What did you have in mind?"

Blake chuckled. "I was hoping you could tell me. I've rarely spent time with her except overseas and then we weren't really doing kid stuff. She seemed fascinated by me probably because everything else about being in Europe bored her."

Madison laughed. "I doubt that. I find you fascinating all the time."

Her heart sped up when he reached over and squeezed her hand. It felt so normal, so right. Madison wondered if she had a right to be this happy.

"What does your sister like to do?"

"I have no idea. I think she likes animals? She seems pretty girlie. Likes dresses and the color pink."

"Maybe we could take her to City Park? It's not too hot if we go in the morning. They have some animals, playgrounds and lots of shade there." Was that too mundane for this child? It was going to be a long day if Madison worried herself over everything. She just had to stop and treat Abigail like any other kid she was taking on an adventure.

"Sure. Then maybe lunch out?"

"Good." Madison tried not to sound out of breath. This would be good.

She was really starting to relax and enjoy their time together after checking in at the museum and talking with a few people she already knew. Blake's ability to carry a conversation in a social setting really helped her relax. She knew she shouldn't be dependent on having a wing man, but it wouldn't hurt for these first few events, right?

She reminded herself of that as he excused himself to go make a call to check on Abigail. Sherry had been scared enough by the events the other day that she now gave him regular updates, despite whatever her boss might say. Madison's mind was just boggled by the thought. Blake hadn't come right out and said it, but Madison could tell that his father had to be emotionally abusive or highly manipulative. She had too much experience with these types of situations to not have a strong suspicion about what was going on.

She strolled around the rotunda in the museum, studying the various paintings highlighted here. It was a gorgeous space, one that she enjoyed standing in for a while whenever she visited the ASTRA. As she stood in front of one particular painting, a voice interrupted her thoughts.

"I never realized how much you look like your mother."

Startled, Madison whirled around to find herself facing a man of average height, looking slick in a black suit and blue tie that matched his vividly hued eyes. She was startled, because his eyes were exactly like Blake's, except cold where Blake's were heated.

The man studied her a moment more, then said, "Remarkable." He held out his hand. "My name is Armand."

"Madison, Madison Landry." She sounded out of breath to her own ears, and quickly tried to regain her poise.

"I am aware. Your mother was a beautiful woman, in a class by herself."

Madison shifted on her heels. Though the man was smiling, she felt uneasy. "How did you know her?"

All that Madison knew about her mother's life, outside of her own interactions with her, was from her journals. Which didn't touch on anything before her marriage, except her relationship with her elderly parents. Curiosity swept through her despite her nerves. After all, no one that she'd met at these events had mentioned knowing her mother, despite their pretty strong resemblance.

"Your mother was well known in my social circles," he said, his slight Cajun accent making the words sound exotic. "Before she…removed herself."

Again the man's intense gaze gave her a slight sense of déjà vu. Where was Blake? Suddenly she wanted him with her right now.

"Her beauty would have lit up any social setting, her grace a complement to any household."

Why did it sound like he was talking about Jacqueline as if she were an object? "My mother was a very gracious, caring woman."

With one elegant brow arched, his expression turned almost cold. "That I wouldn't know."

"Then you must not have met her in person." So many people's lives had been touched by her mother's authentic nature. But she also knew that those types of interactions didn't really make themselves known in this kind of social setting.

As if he read her mind, he said, "Circumstances often dictate what we learn about a person."

True, but that was kind of a strange thing for him to say to her. Madison found herself unconsciously taking a step back and forced herself to be still.

She'd been curious about her mother's life before her marriage for so long that she wanted to ask questions. She'd never met someone who knew her mother then. But something about the man's demeanor, the cold way he spoke, kept those questions locked inside.

Out of the corner of her eye, she saw Blake pass through the doorway into the arch. Relief swept over her.

Blake's eyes widened as he approached. She hadn't been mistaken. His blue eyes matched the colder ones of the man in front of her, who was staring her down as if she were a subject to be studied rather than a person to be known.

"Father!"

The steel behind Blake's voice startled her.

Armand turned slowly to face his son. Madison was surprised to see Blake's expression go from anger to almost a total blank. As if he completely locked himself down in his father's presence.

"Son, how could you leave such a beautiful woman unattended and vulnerable?"

There it was. That sense that though the words were innocuous, the meaning behind them was almost a threat. Why was that?

As Blake approached, he stepped right up to Madison's side, closer than he had all afternoon, and placed his hand squarely at the small of her back. The connection helped steady her skyrocketing emotions.

Given her knowledge of Blake's family, she had no doubts that Armand was an abuser. Whether he'd physically attacked the children, she wasn't sure. But the rise of the hair at the nape of her neck meant she sensed danger in his presence. Instinctively she braced her legs and straightened her back, as if she expected him to fly at her at any moment.

"I was checking with Sherry on Abigail. Remember her?"

It was hard to imagine this man as the father of a seven-year-old. It explained a lot about Blake. And made her heart ache for Abigail.

"Oh, yes. She's been most…helpful."

Madison felt like she was listening to a conversation where half the dialogue was missing. As if father and son were communicating telepathically. She could feel her hackles rise despite the innocuous words. What was happening here? It almost seemed as if they were silently challenging each other in a quest for dominance she didn't understand.

Alarms were going off in her head despite how calm everyone was. She knew without a doubt this man should not be left alone with the child.

She wasn't sure why, but that was why she had instincts. Something they taught the tenants at Maison de Jardin to never discount. Her heart raced. She wanted to be anywhere but under this man's gaze.

Blake didn't even look in her direction. He kept his eyes trained on his father, as if one look away might allow him to strike. Somehow Blake's watchfulness kept his father in check.

"She is indeed beautiful," his father said.

Suddenly Madison realized he was talking about her, but as if she weren't really here.

"I can understand your fascination with her. Just remember your duty. And that bloodlines tell a much bigger story," the older man continued.

Then Armand turned abruptly away and walked back down the gallery to disappear out the doorway. Madison shivered. As her instincts continued to ping and prod, she knew one thing for certain: she hoped she never ran into that man again.

"Family is something, huh?" Blake said.

"A little strange." That was the nicest way Madison knew how to put it. But she couldn't just go around insulting his father.

"Oh, he's an odd bird all right."

But she couldn't shake the feeling that Blake had been trying to protect her somehow. Especially when he'd put his hand against the small of her back. It could've just been a polite gesture, but the firm pressure of the contact seemed to have a different meaning. He wasn't trying to direct her somewhere. Instead, it was almost as if he were trying to reassure himself that she were okay.

It echoed her own uneasy intuition around his father. A high adrenaline rush, as if she'd had a face-to-face with one of the abusers Maison's tenants sought shelter from.

"Abigail isn't safe with him," she said, murmuring almost as if to herself.

Blake jerked to a halt, turning to her and stepping close. "What did you say?"

She looked up into his eyes and wondered if he would accept the truth. A lot of people who had abusers in their lives didn't. But she didn't do what she did every day to make friends. "Blake, I know he's your father, but there's something not right about him."

"You're not telling me anything I didn't already know."

Relief slipped through her. "So you know Abigail isn't safe there. Especially without her mother."

She felt his hand go tense on her back, the fingers digging in on either side of her spine. Not in a painful way, but almost as if he were having a reaction he couldn't control. "I'm working on that."

As she stared up at him, and realized he was a thirty-something playboy with no experience of children trying to do what he could to help his seven-year-old half sister, pride swelled within her. He didn't have to help. He wasn't Abigail's primary caregiver. She had parents. He could've just walked away and ignored it.

"I'm proud of you," she said.

The breath seemed to almost whoosh from his body. He swallowed hard, and his eyes darkened with emotion. The frown that appeared was sad in and of itself. How few people had said thank-you to him that it would upset him?

"I'm just trying to do my best," he said.

Just then they were interrupted by the waiter asking if they wanted a drink.

Madison kept her gaze on Blake, letting a small smile play at her lips. Her protector. She couldn't be in better hands, could she?

Eleven

Blake eased back into Madison's bed, pulling her close up against his chest when she shifted in her sleep. Dawn was just lightening the sky behind the window shades, but he'd been up for hours.

He'd done his best to do a thorough search of the house. Every step felt like a betrayal, after Madison had asked him to stay the night following their trip to the museum.

He felt like his entire conversation with Madison after his father left had been a big huge lie. He was worried about Abigail; he was trying to find a way to help her, but he couldn't come right out and tell Madison that after his father had been sending him a warning earlier.

Don't get too close to Madison. Because I will take her out one way or another. All over what her mother did to me. Or maybe his father was just being like this to prove that Blake could not control him in any way. Madison would never be safe. So he'd done the very thing he didn't want to do, and searched her house during the night.

Of course, he hadn't found anything. No secret cubbies, no safes. Nothing that would indicate a multi-million-dollar diamond was hiding somewhere on the premises. He'd searched every room, looked into every crevice. All the while his heart pounding, afraid Madison would walk in and he'd have to explain himself.

He was already sick at the thought that someday soon she'd know why he was here. Or rather she would assume she knew the real reason, though it had changed for him. Because if the last couple of hours had taught him something, it was that he didn't want to hurt Madison. He loved her. And that knowledge had sent him straight back to her arms. He didn't know what else to do, just like he didn't know what else to do with Abigail.

He'd searched his mind for ways out of the situation. Hell, he'd even made a phone call in the middle of the night to Abigail's mother. To no avail, because the woman wasn't answering…just like she hadn't any time in the last week as he'd tried to contact her. She probably figured he would deride her for walking out on her child. But he just needed a solution.

One that didn't involve the Belarus diamond. Because time was running out. And Blake had no more leads.

So instead he buried his head in the sand. Or rather, in Madison's fragrant hair. He breathed her in, and even though his body stirred, he was content to lie there with her in his arms. Right now he had no way to delay the inevitable, but by God he'd find a way to leave her with something good.

By the time the sun had fully risen, and Madison began to stir in his arms, he knew exactly what he wanted to do with his day. He gave her a chance to wake up, and felt his whole body react when she blinked at him with sleepy eyes.

"Good morning," she murmured.

"Yes. Yes it is," he replied. And he planned to make the most of it. "Want me to make you some coffee?"

She nodded, and he slid from the bed. The glance over his shoulder as he walked to the door revealed a warm, sleepy woman stretching beneath a light sheet. He almost turned back, so that he could explore the soft curves and erect nipples beneath the thin covering. But he knew then he might never get back out. So Blake headed down the stairs with a chuckle.

He waited until she had a whole cup of the chicory brew in her before he broached the subject. "So what are the plans for today?" he asked.

"Oh, I don't have to be over at the charity today. I figured I'd putter around with the furniture."

"I have something a little different in mind."

She lifted a brow as she stared at him over the rim of her newly refreshed cup. She took a sip before asking, "And what would that be?"

"What exactly do you want to do with that hospital bed?"

He knew the question was unexpected but didn't realize how much until she set her mug down on the counter with a hard *thunk*. Coffee sloshed over the side and unto the marble tile countertop. Her voice was huskier than usual when she asked, "Why do you ask?"

Blake knew he had to tread very carefully here. "I'm just wondering. Has it not been moved because you need it for some reason? Or because you need help with it?"

She turned her gaze over his shoulder to stare out the kitchen window. The way her lips tightened for a moment he thought she wouldn't answer, but then she said,

"I certainly have no need for it anymore. I know what I want to do with it, but I just…"

Her voice trailed off in a way that made him sad for her. He knew she didn't want to admit that she wasn't capable of something, but they both knew the truth.

It was right there in her sad smile when she returned her gaze to meet his. "So I just cleaned it up as best I could, and I'll get around to it when I get around to it," she said with a shrug.

"Well, how about we get around to it today? What is it you want to do?"

She quickly let her lashes fall, covering the expression in her eyes. "I don't understand. Why would you want to do this today? Or at all? We could do anything. Take your sister to the park today. I could bake. Any number of things that wouldn't be—"

"Hard?"

She glanced back up at him, her teeth worrying her lower lip.

"I know it's hard, Madison. And I just want to help." He held up hands that had no callouses or signs of manual labor. "I can't paint. I could get up on the roof, but I wouldn't know what to do when I got there."

He was encouraged by her small smile.

"But this, I can help with. I just want to lighten the load a little bit."

To his surprise, she covered her face with her hands. Panic whittled its way through him as her shoulders shook. *No. Not crying.* That was the last thing he knew how to handle.

He stood awkwardly for a couple of seconds, unsure what to do as her sobs got louder. Was he totally out of line?

In the end, he just couldn't bear to see her standing

there, sobbing and holding herself upright on her own. It seemed to be the epitome of Madison's life. That she handle every emotion, every circumstance *alone*. So he stepped forward and put his arms around her shoulders. He didn't know if it was the right move, he only knew he had to do it.

She leaned into him, her body seeking him out. Her hands dropped from her face and encircled his back. She buried her face against his chest, and the noise slowly subsided. With no other direction, Blake simply rested his hand on the back of her neck and held her. All too soon she pulled away, keeping her face averted as she walked over to grab a paper towel and blow her nose.

"Well, that was attractive," she said.

Blake appreciated her desire to brush off the whole emotional episode. But he felt he had to say, "I'm sorry."

"Don't be."

She turned back around to face him, revealing red-rimmed eyes. "No one has offered to help me with anything in this house. Even my friends. I don't know if they just don't feel like I would want them here, which I probably wouldn't. Or if they just don't want to be involved in such a morbid task. But I've done it all on my own."

She cleared her throat, then went on. "I can't tell you how much it means to me that you would offer, especially since you probably expected me to refuse."

"I had a feeling it might go that way."

"That's because you're a smart man."

Yeah…not. "I don't know about that, but I am persistent."

The laughter they shared broke the tension for a moment, but Blake wasn't about to let this go. "So you might as well tell me, what do you want to do with it?"

She swallowed. "I want to donate it. There's a nearby

resident facility that assists elderly, end-of-life patients. I've wanted to donate it to them since my father died, but I have no way of moving it."

"I do believe I can handle that."

"*Then* maybe you can climb up on the roof for me," she teased.

"Only if there's an ambulance nearby."

It made Blake feel really good that he could help her smile through this task. He did his best clown impression while they packed everything up, and the two guys he called showed up with a truck to move it all. Madison only tensed up when they had to come into the house, but he was proud to say that she pushed through. She really wanted this to happen, and he felt sad that it had taken all this time for her to find a solution to this problem. That even though she had friends to help her, she didn't feel like she could call on them for that help.

The director of the facility knew her well, and was grateful beyond measure for her donation. They had a recently renovated room but hadn't managed to afford the furniture for it yet. Before he left, Blake slipped the director a check for a couple of thousand dollars to cover the rest of the furnishings. Now they could open the room for a new patient.

The fact that Madison thought to help someone during this time of grief humbled him beyond measure.

"You're my hero," she murmured against his lips as the truck pulled out of the driveway.

But Blake wasn't a hero. He was a wolf in sheep's clothing. She just didn't know it yet.

I love my husband so much. I would do anything for him, and even though I know his decision is stubborn and hurtful, I don't understand where he's coming from.

He wants no part of my past. He wants to give no more power to a man who valued me only for my face and social graces. But I look at how much we need, how much we're hurting, and I know that selling that ring would make it all better. Why are men so stubborn?

Out of respect for him I've never mentioned this. Never so much as thought about it. Never wrote about my previous engagement in my journals and never talked about it with my daughter. I wish I could sometimes. Talk to her about the hard choices I made, how I knew my husband was the right one for me, how I chose love instead of money.

But I'd hate for her to know that my choice left our family ruined.

Madison reread the passage in confusion, burrowing down against the cushions of the chair in her bedroom. At first, it didn't even register what her mother was talking about. What previous engagement? But as she read through the passage once more, she realized the important part. Her mother had never spoken to her about this. Never spoken to anyone. The reason Madison couldn't find any hint of her previous life in these journals was because her mother chose not to talk about it out of respect for her husband.

Something had happened. Something that made her mother have to choose, and while she knew that her father had been over the moon for his wife, that choice must have caused this traumatic thing that he'd never wanted to remember.

Selling her ring? What ring was she talking about? Madison couldn't remember her mother having any kind of ring except her wedding band set. It was the only thing of value that Madison had refused to sell. Despite how hard times became, she'd never sold them, even though it would've brought a modest amount. But it was her mother's wedding and tenth anniversary bands. Money could never replace that.

Had her mother kept a ring from a previous engagement? It had to be pretty substantial to be worth agonizing over the selling of it. Why had her mother not just given it back?

She scanned the entries right before that and found nothing relating to the ring. In the entry for the day before she mentioned it, she had lamented over the struggle to pay her husband's never-ending medical bills. Her father had recently been diagnosed with MS, she believed. At least the date looked close.

Then farther down in the entry for the same day, her mother wrote, *My husband says it will get better, but I fear the damage is permanent. He told me he would have his revenge, and he did. My husband's business will never be the same. My husband will never be the same. I hope the sacrifice was worth it for him, now and always. It would kill me to have my husband resent me in the end.*

So yeah, whatever happened was really bad. Madison felt a burning curiosity to know what it was. All this time her mother had written about daily life, the joys of motherhood, her love for her husband, and some of her deepest thoughts. But she'd never written or spoken of this matter and it was obviously a huge deal for her.

For them all.

Madison stood up and paced around her room. She wanted to talk about this, to tell someone. Her normal go-to would be her girlfriends. But Trinity's life was upside down enough already right now. She didn't need anyone butting in. And a glance at the clock told her that Tamika was still at work.

So who could she… How much would this kind of speculation annoy Blake?

She felt like they'd grown much closer, and his help the day before had touched her on a level that nothing else ever had. No one had ever helped her like that. Who else would see beyond a superficial need for food or companionship and go out of their way to help with something that she hadn't asked for? Frankly, she'd been floored.

Heck, he could have simply focused on the attraction between them and Madison would have been none the wiser.

But she'd done her best not to cry over him again, because he'd been obviously uncomfortable with her appreciation. She smiled. Her father had always been the same way. Tears made him panic. So she'd kept a stoic facade the entire time she'd known she was losing him.

Madison glanced back at the journal. But this was something fun, something mysterious. Something that intrigued her.

What could be the hurt in calling?

"Hey there," Blake said when he answered the phone.

The sound of that huskiness in his voice, so similar to the way he sounded when they were together, sent shivers down her spine. "Hey to you, too."

"What's up? You having a quiet day today?"

"Too quiet. I had to find ways to occupy myself, since you weren't coming over today."

"Well, if you're that desperate…"

She laughed at his teasing. "I got tired of sanding, so I've been reading my mother's journals, and you won't believe what I found out."

"Wait a minute. Your mother's *journals*?"

"Yes. She kept them for as long as I can remember.

Although the oldest one I can find dates back to the first year of her and Dad's marriage."

The connection between them went oddly silent: no words and no breathing. Madison just figured it was a technical glitch and continued on.

"Anyway, today I was reading a passage from right after my dad got sick, and my mom talked about being engaged before."

Blake cleared his throat. "Engaged?"

"Yes! She said she was engaged and something terrible happened and my dad forbade her to ever talk about it."

"So that would mean…"

Again one of those weird silences, so she asked, "Are you there?"

"Hold on just a moment." She waited, until he finally said, "So do you think she left this guy for your dad? Do you know who he is?"

"She never says his name. She just says that she could sell the ring to help pay their medical bills, but my dad wanted nothing to do with it. Mysterious, right?"

Madison got excited just thinking about it. Who had the man been? What kind of ring was it? She started asking all these questions out loud to Blake, then realized after a few minutes that he hadn't responded. She paused.

"Blake?"

"Listen, Maddie, I need to go. Can I call you back in a little while?"

Disappointment had her dropping back into the chair in her bedroom. "Sure. Just whenever you're ready."

"I'll call you soon." *Click.*

Madison stared at her phone in consternation. That had been strange, and a tingling feeling of unease rippled through her once more. Even though Blake had said he wasn't keeping anything else to himself, she still felt

like there were a lot of things about him that she had no
clue about. Was this one of them? She didn't know what
it could be… He could be conducting business. Seeing
someone about his art. He never told her how that worked.
But New Orleans was filled with some very prestigious
art galleries.

Was Abby okay? Madison bit her lip. It could have
just been he was in a place that didn't have good reception. There was no sense worrying about this. And she
knew she shouldn't, but that didn't stop her mind from
running down the rabbit hole.

He would call her back. She just had to remember that.

Still, she was disappointed that he hadn't seemed too
interested in what she found out about her mother. Maybe
to other people it wasn't interesting, and Blake had never
had strong familial connections. So it wasn't surprising.

But Madison had loved her mother to death, and been
old enough to be really close to her before she passed
away in a car accident. It was so unexpected, and Madison had grieved at night in private, but by day she had
to continue on the work that she helped her mother with.
She was still going to school, because her father had
been functional enough that he could be left alone at that
point. But the rest of her waking hours had been spent
taking care of him or finding ways to financially support their family.

The ring sparked her curiosity. It seemed so tangible,
this link to her mother's past. But she'd never seen one.
Would her mother have hidden it? Gotten rid of it some
other way? Sold it and just not told her dad where the
money came from?

Madison's curiosity got the better of her, and she
walked down the hall to her mother's room. Though her
parents had shared a bed for a long time, the need for

extra equipment and furniture for her dad, to accommo-
date his disability, had necessitated her mother moving
her stuff into a separate room. In this big house there
were plenty to choose from. They had gotten rid of a lot
of things over the years after her mother passed away.
That included most of her casual clothes, a few odds and
ends other than those Madison had appropriated through
the years, like her brush. All that had been left of her
jewelry was costume pieces and her wedding set. Other
than a few quilts her mother had made, the only things
Madison had left were contained inside her mother's old
chifforobe. She opened the doors, and was immediately
met with the smell of lavender. It had been her mother's
favorite scent. She'd often kept lavender sachets around
the house.

Oddly, even after ten years, the scent still lingered
on her clothes. Madison had chosen to keep some of her
mother's more elaborate formal clothes. Dresses made
from expensive materials. Her mother's favorite dress-
ing gown—she would never call the beautiful piece of
lace and satin a robe. A few pairs of heels that now fit
Madison, but she'd never had occasion to wear them until
recently. Madison searched through the clothes, though
very few of them had pockets. Then she pressed against
the back of the chifforobe, checking for any drawers or
hidden compartments she might not have been aware of.

Finally she sat down in front of it and pulled out her
mother's jewelry box. It was a gorgeous piece that her father had actually made, using beautiful cured maple and
mother-of-pearl inlay. She could remember the Mother's
Day he had given it to her. Madison was maybe ten or
eleven? Her mother had been so happy. And genuinely
shocked because he'd managed to keep the secret so well.

Her father had been a builder. He'd come from a

modestly wealthy family himself, and he'd multiplied his fortune doing custom builds for the rich and famous of Louisiana. Madison had seen pictures of some of his houses, but he hadn't been able to keep it up and then he got sick. Losing his ability to work had eventually muted her father's love for life.

What had her mother meant about revenge and her husband's business? Madison had so many questions and so few answers.

But the beautiful box held nothing more than what Madison had seen over and over. A few costume pieces that her mother had let Madison try on through the years. But no true jewels. This used to surprise Madison, but now that she was an adult and knew just how much her father's illness had cost them, it didn't surprise her as much. She just assumed that whatever true jewels her mother's parents had given her had been sold through the years. Her mother had always been way more attached to people than things.

She set the jewelry box back into the bottom of the chifforobe and closed the doors.

As much as the mystery intrigued her, she would probably have to face the fact that her mother's secret had gone with her to her grave. Unless there was something later on in her journals. Madison thought she only had about six more months' worth to read.

She raced back down the hallway to pull the next journal from the box in her room. Money didn't matter. But her mother did. She might not find anything, but it was exciting to think the mystery could be solved.

Twelve

Blake watched nervously as the housekeeper settled the booster seat into the back of his car. Then she strapped Abigail in and turned to him.

"All ready," she said with a smile. "I know Abigail was looking forward to this. Thank you for taking her."

Blake just smiled and walked around to the passenger side. The smile masked a pool of unease in his gut. His father hadn't blinked when Blake had mentioned taking Abigail out with Madison. Instead he'd given simple consent.

Blake didn't trust that for one minute, but he couldn't divine any hidden motives and he didn't want to disappoint Abigail by going back on his word.

He hoped she would have a good time, because he had absolutely no clue what he was doing. Which was why he'd broken down and asked Madison to help him. He felt guilty about terminating their call the day before, but he simply hadn't known what to say. He let her think that he had something else going on, because knowing that she'd been in the dark about her mother's previous engagement, and had no clue what kind of ring she was looking for, made him sick to his stomach.

He had no idea what to do and no idea what to say. Which was becoming a theme in his life right now. But he'd promised Abigail when he brought her home from the hospital that he would take her to do something fun. Why he had done that he wasn't sure, but he wasn't going to let her down. He refused to make her beg like her father did. He remembered what it was like to live the life that she had, where promises had been few and far between, and often broken.

He wasn't going to do that to her.

In the meantime, he hoped he could sidetrack any conversations about Madison's mother. His current plan was to just nod and say *uh-huh*. And offer absolutely no information whatsoever.

He could do that, right?

"Ready, kiddio?" he asked as he pulled out onto the highway.

He caught Abigail's nod in the rearview mirror, her grin infectious, her excitement palpable in the way she swung her little legs.

They stopped by to pick up Madison on their way to City Park. "Are you excited, Abigail?" she asked as she buckled herself in.

Abigail nodded enthusiastically.

"I think you'll have fun. There's lots of stuff to do at City Park."

"But only until lunch," Blake cautioned. If it was one complaint he'd heard about kids, it was that they expected to do something forever. He didn't think he was up to a marathon on his first outing with her. Nor was she after her recent hospital stay…especially in the summer heat.

Madison grinned at him, sharing a little secret. "Definitely lunch."

Blake had to admit that City Park was an excellent choice. Abigail especially liked Storyland Castle and the Puff the Magic Dragon slide. Madison chased the little girl around the play area, so that her giggles filled the air.

Then they headed back to see the frogs and birds and turtles in the conservatory before strolling under the live oaks with their hanging moss. Having met her mother once after she had taken Abigail to a zoo, Blake had known this would be a big hit. Abigail enjoyed watching the animals for a long time, and getting to take pictures of them with Blake's phone. The only heartbreaking moment was when she asked, "Can I send these pictures to my mommy?"

Madison turned away. Blake wished he had the opportunity to do the same. "Absolutely, kiddio."

They didn't stop for lunch until Blake had taken them on a bike ride and paddled Abigail around the lake in a kayak. The whole time, Blake thought he must be incredibly lucky. Abigail was laid-back and easygoing, and he didn't have a single issue with her. He did suspect that she was on her best behavior. He'd had more than enough of those moments when he was a kid.

By the time they headed to lunch, he was feeling much more comfortable. Maybe he didn't know how to relate to Abigail as a child. But he related to her the only way he knew how. He talked to her the same way he would to anyone else. He didn't baby-talk her or cater to her every whim. He simply urged her to do things that looked fun, and when it was time to move on to something else he was firm but polite. It seemed to work well with this particular child.

They had lunch at a little kid-friendly café, where Abigail got a grilled cheese and chips, eyeing the cakes for later.

Madison talked about wanting to try one of the recipes, and Abigail got all excited.

"Can I help? Sometimes Miss Sherry lets me help her stir things. She says I do a good job."

Madison glanced his way before she said anything and he gave a quick nod. He appreciated her checking in with him before offering anything, but how could he say no to such a sweet little face?

Abigail was occupied talking about the different type of cakes she would like to make for quite a while before she started to run out of steam. Her eyelids got heavy, and she leaned against Madison despite still having part of her sandwich left.

Blake sat in silence for quite a while, just enjoying the shade and the slight breeze in the courtyard.

Madison plucked a thread from the little girl's shirt as she finally said, "So I went through all of my mom's stuff yesterday."

Blake should've known it was coming, but still it was a stock. Even in his surprise he was able to murmur, "Yes?"

"I didn't find any kind of ring. Of course, I got rid of most of her stuff ten years ago. But you never know when there might be a hidden drawer, or a locked box somewhere."

Blake returned her smile, even though inside he felt slightly ill. It was only a few days ago that he himself had spent the night going through her entire house looking for just such a thing.

"I just wish I knew more about what happened. My

mom's life at that time is such a blank for me. I think it would just be interesting to know."

And if she knew, she would be entitled to what she could find. But Blake had searched all over that house and found nothing. What the hell had happened to the Belarus diamond?

"For all I know, my mom could've sold an old engagement ring a long time ago. The only rings I could find were her wedding band set."

"So you kept them?"

Madison looked slightly surprised. "Of course. Granted, she could've sold them for a little bit of money. The diamond inside *was* worth something. But my mother was always more interested in people than things. She wouldn't have wanted to get rid of something my father gave her."

Abigail stirred slightly against her and Blake glanced down to see her lift sleepy eyelids. "Is she talking about Father's ring?"

Only years of having to hide himself from his father and present himself as someone he wasn't in society kept Blake's expression neutral. But inside, he was cursing up a storm.

Madison looked down at the little girl in question, but Blake quickly intervened. "No, sweetie. You just rest."

Who would've guessed that a seven-year-old listening from the top of the stairs could have absorbed so much? She was too smart for him to completely brush it off. Otherwise she would start asking more questions, he just knew it. "That was about something else, sweetheart."

Luckily, Madison kept right on, not really paying Abigail's question any mind. "I know it's a silly mystery, but I'm just curious."

Of course, she had no idea of the significance of what

Abigail had asked. And her curiosity was something Blake couldn't relate to. After all, neither of his parents had ever been real people to him. Just evil dictators who should be avoided at all cost.

He'd thought that was all behind him, but look at him now.

Any minute, that very dictatorship was going to crush the most precious thing Blake had ever found in his life, if he didn't find a way to stop it.

Tonight he'd try to reach Abigail's mother one more time—and hope his luck held out for an alternative ending.

Madison took Abigail's hand in hers and led her away from the table with a smile at Blake. He'd really done well and handled way more things than she'd thought he would, but taking a little girl to the little girls' room might be asking a bit much.

The restrooms were in the far back of the little café. They paraded past the sandwich counter and the goody counter on their way. "I think I might have to ask Blake for one of those big Rice Krispies treats," Madison said. "Doesn't that look good?"

Abigail paused to look at the huge confection. "He won't want me to have that. My father says sweets rot your teeth."

Not an uncommon belief among older people. "Well, maybe if you only eat sweets and never brush your teeth. But you take good care of your teeth, right?"

"Sure do. See?" Abigail gave her an overly wide smile.

Madison dutifully inspected her teeth and pronounced them perfect. "I think we're safe to ask Blake anyway."

Abigail looked up at her, then asked, "Do you think my brother likes me?"

Madison glanced down with a frown. "Of course he does. Why wouldn't he?" She ruffled one pigtail. "After all, look how cute you are."

Abigail giggled but quickly sobered. "My father said that if I don't behave myself, Blake will leave and never come back. Just like my mommy."

Just the thought of anyone telling that to a small child took Madison's breath away. *Bastard.*

She led the little girl through the door to the restroom, and let it slide closed behind them. She knelt down next to Abigail. "Honey, I don't know what your father told you. But Blake is not going to leave if you misbehave. All children misbehave at some time or another. It's just a moment for them to have a learning experience."

Abigail's doe-brown eyes widened. "Really?"

"Really. It's just part of growing up. You'll get in trouble, but that doesn't mean that the people in your life don't still love you."

"Like you love Blake?"

No way was she going to admit that out loud to a child who might repeat it. "Blake is a very special man. And I think you'll find, if you give him a chance, that he will love you lots."

Abigail smiled, seeming satisfied, then went on to do her business. Madison knew her words were true. Blake might not have felt himself capable of it, but this last week had proved he had more than enough love to give. He'd just never known how to access it before.

Abigail took her time washing her hands, as she had plenty more questions for Madison. It seemed that her little nap had revived her energies quite well.

Some were as innocuous as, "Did you like the tree frogs, too?" and "Can you bring me to the park again?" Then the uber serious, "Are you going to marry Blake?"

"Give it time, kid. Your brother and I haven't known each other that long."

Besides, the time they had been together had been quite tumultuous. Madison knew how she felt about him, but she was used to loss. Used to people leaving. And Blake had made no mention of emotions, though his actions spoke pretty loud. Still, she wasn't in any hurry to tell him her own feelings.

Abigail continued to chatter, which stopped the sweat from breaking out on Madison's brow. Hopefully she'd dodged a bullet there. She seemed to be handling the girl talk situation pretty well.

An unusually high number of the children who came through Maison de Jardin were boys. That was who Madison had the most experience with. She knew nothing about fixing hair or playing with dolls. A couple of teenage girls had come with their mothers to the shelter, but they weren't nearly as easy to befriend as the smaller kids.

"What is your mother's name?" Abigail asked.

Madison was a bit taken aback, and paused for a moment before answering. "It was Jacqueline."

"Was?"

Madison wasn't quite sure how much experience Abigail had with death, but she didn't believe in lying. "My mother died when I was younger."

"Were you a little girl like me?" Abigail asked, standing at the sink while the water ran over her hands.

Madison wasn't sure how much she should tell a child this age. "She was in a car accident when I was sixteen."

"So she didn't leave you like my mommy?"

"No," Madison couldn't believe how horrible that must be for Abigail. She waited a moment before saying anything else to see what the little girl was thinking.

"My mommy left because I was too much trouble."

Damn. "Oh, Abigail, that's not true."

"Oh, it was. My mommy told me so a lot of times. I tried to be good, but I guess I wasn't good enough."

Pure rage swept over Maddie. How dare someone tell a child that. She was sure Abigail had been on her best behavior during this trip, but she still couldn't imagine a child being so bad that you would outright tell them you were going to leave because of them. She was sure many parents thought it during the course of a stressful day, but they would never say it out loud, because they honestly loved their children.

"I'm really sorry, Abigail."

"Father said Mommy is fragile." She tilted her head so she could look at Madison in the mirror. "What does fragile mean?"

Selfish was what Madison wanted to say, but instead she said, "It just means that someone might crack easily, like a glass."

"I knocked a glass off the table once and it shattered on the floor."

"Yes, that is fragile."

"Do you think I broke my mommy?"

Man, talking to kids was a minefield. "Absolutely not. That is not what I meant at all." She knelt down beside Abigail. "Your mommy being fragile has nothing to do with you. It has everything to do with your mommy. And I hope that she can find something while she's gone to make her stronger."

"You can become stronger?"

"Of course. You just have to exercise and eat your veggies." Madison pumped her arm to make a muscle, which caused Abigail to giggle.

Abigail finally finished with her handwashing, or what

Madison would consider playing in the water, and got herself a couple of paper towels. As she dried off, she said, "I like you, but I do wish your ring had been Father's ring."

"How come?" Madison asked.

"It's what Blake needs. Father told him to get it."

"I don't think I understand," Madison said with a frown.

"I was listening on the stairs. Father didn't know, but I think Blake did. He and Father were arguing. Blake was mad because Father wouldn't take care of me."

She brushed her hands down over her little dress in an imitation of an adult. "Father said Blake could take me home with him, if he got the ring back. Otherwise Father would ignore me, or maybe send me away."

Madison could not wrap her mind around the horror of what she was hearing. Surely Abigail had to be mistaken.

"Your father told him to get the ring, from me?"

"I don't know." Abby scrunched her brows together. "That's what I thought he said. But he wasn't sure where it was."

"Maybe he was talking about someone else." *Please let him be talking about someone else.*

"Maybe so." Abigail looked up at Madison. "But I really want to go live with Blake. I can be really good and he won't want to send me away."

Since she wasn't sure what had been promised, Madison heard this hope with a touch of alarm. "Abigail, you realize Blake hasn't ever had children."

"I know." She shook her head vigorously. "But I can teach him how to have a little girl. I won't misbehave… much. Do you think he will help me learn?"

Madison blinked, desperate to not show tears in front of this girl who had been through so much in such a short amount of time. "I think you and Blake could teach each other a lot."

She gave Abigail a quick hug, then took her hand to lead her back to the table. Along the way, she had to wonder about the ring the little girl had mentioned. There was no way that could have anything to do with her.

But as she thought about those first days together, and her confusion over why Blake would want to be with her at all, the question wouldn't leave her. What ring had he and Armand been talking about?

Thirteen

"Quit blowing up my phone!"

For a moment Blake just looked at his cell phone, shocked. He'd called Abigail's mother, Marisa, over a dozen times, to no avail. Apparently she'd finally gotten tired enough of the noise to answer.

"Well, since I've run out of other options, I didn't know who else to call."

"Why are you calling me at all?"

Um, your child might need you?

That didn't seem to occur to her, as she went on, "The last thing I need to hear is how I have to come home. I am not coming home to that psychopath, and I can't find a new husband with a kid in tow."

Blake kept his mouth closed for just a moment. He wanted to lay into her about parental responsibility and how scared Abigail was and that she was really behaving like a child herself, but he couldn't. He had to help

Abigail. He couldn't find the diamond. *Marisa* had to help him.

"Look, I'm just trying to figure out what's the best course of action. You left a very sick child in the hands of a man who couldn't care less about her."

"He doesn't need to care about her. That's what nannies are for."

Wow. How cavalier could she get? "He got rid of the nanny."

"Why?"

"You didn't see that coming? He let the nanny go. He said there was no reason to pay someone to watch out for her, because he doesn't believe that Abigail is really sick."

"Well, when he gets tired of dealing with her as much as I did, he'll get someone else. Doctor appointment after doctor appointment…"

"He's not going to take her to a doctor. He doesn't believe there's anything wrong. Your daughter is being neglected."

"She'll be fine," Marisa insisted. "He'll eventually hire a new nanny, and he'll take care of her. He's in a much better place to take care of her than I am. I'm broke."

"You just emptied your bank account. How can you be broke?"

Blake knew that wasn't the right question to ask. He just needed some answers.

"Look, I don't care. I don't care why you left. I don't care that you're not coming back." Although he did care for Abigail, he just didn't want to get into that with Marisa now. "I just need to find out anything you can tell me so that I can take over Abigail's care."

"Don't bother. He's got more money than God. She's going to be much better off in his hands than her other options."

Blake had firsthand experience that said otherwise. The volcano of the emotions inside him erupted. "Really? An old man with a narcissistic personality disorder about to go broke is the best parent for a sick seven-year-old child?"

"What do you mean, *broke*?"

"Broke. No money. So if you think you're going to get a very nice settlement in the divorce, you can forget it."

Marisa was quiet for so long, Blake thought she might be reconsidering her actions. But no…

"I'm not supposed to get anything based on the pre-nup. Why do you think I'm out here trying to find somebody new? But Abigail is supposed to be taken care of."

There was no getting through to this woman. Blake insisted, "Well, there's nothing to take care of her with. He's basically housing her and that's it. She's already had one episode that landed her in the hospital."

"Well, if that's how it's going to be, she'd be better off with her real dad."

Blake held very, very still. It took him a minute to absorb what she had just said. "Are you telling me…that Abigail is not his?"

"Well, she should be. I mean, we were married."

So? "Is she biologically his daughter?"

"Well, no."

Blake couldn't believe it. Of all the things he'd thought she might tell him, this was not one of them. He sat for a moment in stunned disbelief. He wasn't sure exactly how this would fix everything, but he knew it would. And he would make sure that it did.

"Why didn't you tell him?" he finally asked.

"I needed him to keep her. Besides, you know how he is. The minute he found out that I slept with somebody else, we'd both be out the door. He wouldn't put up for that kind of humiliation. And I'm too good to be a chauffeur's wife."

What should I do? What should I do? Blake racked his brain for an answer.

"Look, Marisa. Will you fill out paperwork that lets me take care of her?"

"Well, she's not gonna be in a good place with me. I just can't deal with that stuff. As a matter of fact, the first time I get the chance I'm closing this baby factory."

Nice. "But Abigail? Will you let me take care of her if I can find a way to make it happen? And before you ask, there's nothing in it for you. I'm all about Abigail right now."

"I guessed. Better double down over here if I'm gonna find a new man before Armand cuts me off. Take her."

Blake wanted to rail at the harshness of the conversation he just had as she clicked to disconnect. But he couldn't. He couldn't get lost over what Abigail did or did not have. He had to look to the future. He had to figure out how to use this new information to get what he needed. Without the diamond, this was his only option.

If he lost Maddie in the process, so be it. But at least she wouldn't have to know that he got involved with her under false pretenses. He didn't want to hurt her like that, even though walking away from her would leave him out in the cold for the rest of his life. He'd never found anyone like her before, and he doubted he ever would again. But he couldn't worry about that right now, or he'd be paralyzed with indecision.

Instead he needed to figure out what he had to do to take over parental rights. He had a feeling his father wouldn't want to be humiliated by having Abigail's true paternity made public. Not to mention his lack of funds for a lawyer to fight for custody once her mother handed her rights over to Blake.

He just had to hope in the end Abigail would have him. He wasn't that much of a catch as a father, but he'd at least try. Which was more than his own father had done.

Madison strode back and forth across her bedroom, the sound of the squeaking floorboards more than a little satisfying. She wasn't sure why; she wasn't accomplishing anything. And she wished she could. She wished that she could stomp her way right over to Blake's apartment and demand the truth. Even if her only source was a seven-year-old child.

She just wanted to know: Was Abigail right? Had Blake and Armand been talking about her? Had Blake honestly met and dated her to try to get something out of her? And if they wanted something from her mother, why had they waited all these years? She wanted answers, not more questions.

But she was also afraid to get those answers.

Madison paced furiously, anxiety sending her energy into hyperdrive.

Why had her mother told her none of this? She may have felt she owed her husband something, but what about her daughter? What about the life she left her to? And even though she knew her mom hadn't left willingly, she had chosen to delay the inevitable until it was too late, leaving Madison with an adult-size responsibility and very few resources.

How could she find the answers? She hadn't missed a journal. Out of desperation, she walked over to the box and glanced over the half dozen, leather-bound journals. As she ran her hand over the spines, she suddenly remembered the pieces of paper that had been stuck in her mother's journal the other day.

Shifting the books to the side, she found the papers in the bottom of the box where she'd dropped them before leaving last week. Excitement caused her to breathe hard as she unfolded them. There was more of her mother's handwriting on the pages, but this was different than the journal entries. This was addressed directly to her.

Dearest Madison,
I'm hoping you never have to read this. I'm hop-
ing that the lawyer never has to give you this in the
event of my death.

What lawyer? Had her mother planned to take this to the lawyer to go with her will, and never made it?

But I need to tell you a story. One that I should
tell you in person, but I would do anything to not
hurt your father. If I'm gone, you need to know this.
When I was young, before I knew my own mind,
I went along with what my parents told me to do.
That was the acceptable thing in that time, for girls
of my class. That you obey your parents, learn
how to talk and act, not be too smart, or too sassy.
Marry well and be an asset to your spouse.
And I tried. I tried to make my parents happy.
They were elderly, as I was a late-in-life baby, one
that they never really expected to have. They al-
ways seemed frail in my mind and they didn't live
very long past my marriage to your father. Anyway,
when I was finally of marriageable age, I was pur-
sued by a man named Armand Boudreaux. He was
well known in our social circles, and his family was

very wealthy. He was slightly older than me, and well on his way to making his own fortune.

Armand was mostly charming, but I quickly learned that he hid an often subtle cruelty. He wasn't in love with me but seemed to want to acquire me because I exceeded his qualifications for a wife. And I think, on some level, that he thought I would counterbalance what he knew he was lacking in himself: compassion and a genuine interest in other people. Which would help cement his social status.

At the same time, my parents were building a house, and I met a new young man. He was a very well-known architect and builder, rising quickly in fame and wealth. Handsome and articulate. I'll admit, I became obsessed. Your father was smart and charming, and he understood me in a way that neither my parents nor Armand ever had. He brought out the best in me, and didn't ridicule me for wanting to do things that didn't seem to fit with my social status. He taught me to refinish furniture, build things. He encouraged me to paint and take pictures—lots of things that my parents didn't understand.

It didn't take long before I was completely in love and stuck in a place I didn't know how to get out of. Though my parents loved me, they were quite old-fashioned. I'd made a promise to Armand, and they expected me to fulfill it.

There was also the social pressure of knowing that their peers would be there to judge the decision that their daughter made, and thus it would reflect on them. Every generation has peer pressure; it just comes in different forms. But in the end I couldn't walk away from your father, so we eloped. On the eve of my wedding to Armand, I ran away with your father and left my parents and Armand letters telling them that I was sorry, but I could not go through with the wedding.

I had every intention of returning the ring. The engagement ring that Armand gave me was more than special. The diamond was a rare oval blue diamond called the Belarus diamond. Quite famous, and quite expensive. But upon my return, I found that Armand had embarked on his own form of revenge. I'd known he would be upset, and I suspected he would lash out. But I never anticipated what actually happened.

Armand went out of his way to ruin your father's business. The one time I approached him, he called me some quite inappropriate names, and honestly I was afraid of him, so I never approached him again. As time went on it became clear that your father might have to relocate to save his business, so I decided to hold onto the diamond as insurance for my family to hopefully save us from the ruination that I brought upon them.

Only we never had the chance to leave. Your father became ill and I thought the diamond would be the only thing to save us. But your father refused to allow me to sell it. He wanted no part of Armand and refused to listen to me.

I could not go against his wishes, but I kept the diamond and hid it, so that you, my daughter, would have it should you need it. It is yours to do with as you wish. After all, it was a gift, and it would be my wish that you should never be so destitute that you feel like you cannot sustain yourself or your

loved ones. I know that feeling well. And never ever
want that for you.

   I'm sorry that I couldn't make things easier. I
love you and your father more than I can ever tell
you. Be well, my child.
Love, Jacqueline

Madison flipped to the next page to find directions
on where the diamond had been hidden. She stared for
a moment, uncomprehending, then blinked. Her mother
had put the diamond in a place no one would ever have
looked for it. *Genius.*

Without hesitation, she grabbed her shoes and ran
out the door. Her jog across the back trail to Maison de
Jardin was familiar and yet felt longer than she could
have imagined. Her heart pumped from the run and in
anticipation of what she might find. Would the diamond
still be there?

The house was quiet during the day, with everyone
gone to various jobs or school. Madison made her way
to the conservatory without running into anyone who
might still be home, and quickly found the statue that
her mother had indicated.

Madison stared at it. She had always seen the statue
as a representation of this place's purpose. It was a little
girl and her mother with their hands clasped and arms
raised in dance. The purpose of this home had always
been to bring happiness and joy to women and children
who had been mistreated. To help them get back on their
feet and find their dance again.

Finally Madison moved around to the back of the
statue and started to dig at the mound of dirt around
the base.

It took a couple of inches before she found the little

compartment. Her smile felt like it lit up her whole body. Who knew there'd been a secret compartment all her life in the base of this statue?

Unfortunately she couldn't get it open, and had to go get a screwdriver to pry the edges apart. Finally it popped open, and Madison was able to work the little drawer out. Inside was a metal box, which she opened to find multiple layers of protective wrapping.

But as she pulled away layer after layer, Madison could not believe her eyes.

The fact that the diamond had an actual name should have been her first clue that it was something extraordinary. But that had kind of flown under Madison's radar. The oval-shaped jewel was a brilliant blue color, so brilliant it made her gasp. It shone against her dirt-stained fingers. The size would have made it very uncomfortable to wear, in her opinion, but she could see why someone like Armand would give it to his future wife. By doing so, he could prove he was the best husband in the world.

Only he didn't realize money wasn't everything.

Suddenly she understood what her mother meant. Selling this particular ring, this particular diamond, would have taken care of them for life, no matter how many medical bills her father had. Madison wouldn't have a house falling down around her ears. She wouldn't have had creditors banging on her front gate.

She wouldn't have had to spend her high school years working after school, or taking on other jobs while caring for her father.

Suddenly her elation faded. She could also now understand why someone might falsely portray himself, pretending to like or love her in order to get his hands on this.

Was Blake really capable of that? Was every moment they'd been together a lie? Madison had to know.

I know what you did. Meet me at ASTRA.

Blake clenched his fingers around his phone as he remembered the text he'd received from Madison last night. So he'd had an entire night to agonize over what had happened, wondering and worrying until he'd been sick to his stomach. She refused to answer her phone, which made him suspect she had turned it off after telling him when and where to be.

That wasn't like Madison at all, so he knew this was bad. Very bad. Which meant she'd found out something about the ring…and its connection to his family.

Had it been Abigail's innocent remarks over lunch that had alerted her? Had she found something in her mother's journals that made the connection with his family? Had she put two and two together and come up with the original plan his father had put into place?

Blake knew he couldn't change what had happened before, but if she'd found out part of the truth, would she listen to him when he told her what he was trying to do *now*? His true role in this entire mess? What he hoped worked—for both her sake and Abigail's?

He stepped into the rotunda to find her staring at a painting across from him, her arms wrapped tightly around herself. If he needed any evidence of her defensiveness, that would've been it. It wasn't a position he'd ever wanted to see her in again. It reminded him that too much had been thrown Madison's way.

She deserved the best—much more than life had dished out to her.

He approached cautiously, giving her a chance to see him out of the corner of her eye before he reached her.

"Madison, what's going on?" he asked.

He expected tears or a defeated attitude. Instead she seemed to almost closed down. Only her eyes seemed sad. "I know what happened. Abby told me."

"Abby told you what?"

Blake wished they weren't in the rotunda. All of a sudden he desperately needed something to lean on, to support his shaky legs, but even touching the walls in here would set off an alarm.

"When we went to the restroom, Abigail told me more about the ring. She recounted the conversation between you and your dad." She waved her hand in the air as if to erase her words. "In a roundabout kind of way. She didn't really know that it was about me. But it made me curious, so I went looking."

She reached into her purse and pulled out a box. A very expensive jewelry box. Blake held his breath as she opened it. Inside was the ring.

Of all the things Blake had expected to see today, that was not one of them. He stared for a moment, almost bemused. It was incredible, just like all the reports had said.

But he quickly moved his gaze back up to hers. There was no point in pretending anymore. "How did you find it?"

Madison sucked air into her lungs, blinking away tears at his implied admission. "My mother left me a letter. One that she never got a chance to give to the lawyer. I found it in one of her journals. She explained all about Armand. And quite frankly, after hearing that, I'm not surprised that she kept the ring."

"She was well within her rights to keep the ring," Blake insisted. "My father is…not an easy man."

"If he had just left them alone, she would've given it back."

"But he feels like he should have his cake and eat it, too. Which means being a major league asshole, and still getting his way."

Madison looked away, and he could see her bracing herself. She took a deep breath and straightened her back. "Why?" She glanced back at Blake and he could see the crack in the calm facade. The grief he'd never wanted her to experience again. She'd had enough loss. "Why would you do this? Why would you take it this far?"

He wished he could give an answer that left him looking squeaky clean. But he didn't have one of those tucked into his back pocket. "Maddie... Madison," he stumbled over the nickname after remembering her assertion that it should only be used by those who'd earned the privilege. "I just want you to understand that I never meant to hurt you."

"And you think finding out that you met me and dated me under false pretenses wouldn't hurt?" She stared at him for a moment. "Unless you never intended for me to find out?"

"There's really no way for me to defend myself against that," he said, utter defeat a physical weight on his chest. Because if he'd had his way, she would never have found out about any of this. He searched for a way to tell her the story that would not make him look like an insensitive jerk, but there really wasn't one.

"There's no point in me lying anymore," he conceded with a grimace. "I went into this knowing that I had to hide my motives from you. I thought it would be a date, maybe two, and then I'd be out of your life. It would all be over. No harm done, and no lasting repercussions for anyone but Abigail, who would have a better life. But that's not how it played out." He stared at her, aching to take away the hurt that bowed the lines of her body. "I knew with every move, every choice, that this wasn't right. But I simply could not stay away."

"And how I felt didn't play into it?"

"It did. But by that time I was in too deep and desperately searching for a way not to hurt you."

He didn't want to offer excuses, but she deserved more of an explanation. "It was obvious that you did not have the ring yourself and didn't know anything about it. I kept searching to keep my father at bay while I desperately tried to find some way to help Abigail."

"So what she said was true? Her father is going to… what? Trade his child for this?" She lifted the box once more.

He knew it was unbelievable. But having Armand as a father convinced Blake his father spoke the truth. "I told you he was a bastard. That's exactly what's happening. He wanted me to find the ring and get it back for him, and in exchange I will get full parental rights to Abigail."

She stepped closer as a couple of women walked into the rotunda and began discussing the paintings. "Why would a parent do that?"

"Madison, I've spent a lot of time with my father. And I've finally figured out that if you try to understand his motives, you're just going to spend a lot of time banging your head against a wall." He sighed. "No one can understand that, because we're not like him. He is his own selfish, narcissistic self. That's not going to change and the only option is to stop him at whatever cost. That's what I've been trying to do. Why I tried to keep him away from you before." But Blake feared he was fighting a losing battle. "Right now, I have to keep Abigail safe. Regardless of what I want, and regardless of the fact that I love you."

Madison's whole body jerked. Her eyes squeezed shut for a moment. "Please don't say things you can't mean."

Well, he hadn't meant to say it but... "I did mean it, Maddie, and I will always mean it. But I fully accept why that would mean nothing to you."

He reached out to grasp her arms in an effort to get her to look at him. The touch was bittersweet, as he knew it would be his last. "I'm more sorry than I can tell you. I didn't intend to get involved, I didn't intend to fall in love, and I had no idea what an incredible person you really are. But I have to save Abigail. I've lived that childhood, and I will not allow her to live it, too."

Madison nodded, though whether his words made sense to her, he wasn't sure. Then she explained. "I love you, too. But that's not why I am doing this. I'm doing it for Abigail, too, because no child deserves to live neglected and unloved. I've fought against that my entire life, and it's more important to me than anything."

She raised her hand between them. "That's why I want you to take this."

Blake blinked. He glanced down at the box, then back at her face. "I...don't...understand..."

"I want you to have this, so that Abigail will be taken care of."

Blake was already shaking his head. "Maddie, this was your mother's. It should take care of you for the rest of your life. Especially after you've given your life to take care of others."

She stared down at the box for a moment. "Taking care of others is not something that requires a reward. I did it out of love," she said, then pressed her lips together hard.

As her eyelids drifted down, a single tear rolled over her cheek. "Just take it."

"I believe that belongs to me."

Heated fear washed over him as Blake turned to see his father walking across the rotunda, which was otherwise empty now.

"Thank you for finding it for me, Madison," Armand said. "That seems to be more than my son was capable of."

Madison began to extend her arm, and Blake quickly stepped in front of her to face his father. "Absolutely not. You are not taking this from her."

"But I thought you said Abby could live with you if I give this back?" Madison said.

"No, he said I can have her parental rights, if I *stole* this from you."

"I believe I have a claim," Armand insisted.

"It was a gift to Madison's mother. It doesn't belong to you anymore. If it did, your lawyer would have been able to get it back for you long ago."

Armand's practiced smile grew wider. "But I'm the one who would benefit most. Unless you count Abigail."

Madison gasped.

"I will fix this, Madison," Blake insisted.

His father studied him for a moment. For once, Blake felt no urge to shift in his shoes. This wasn't about meeting his father's expectations. This was about two different scales, and the fact that Blake was looking out for more than just himself.

"I never thought you would defend a woman," his father said.

Blake was a little taken aback. Why wouldn't he defend another person? He just didn't know a lot of people who needed defending. But then again, his father's mea-

surements were based on his own warped standards, and
Armand had never gone out of his way to defend anyone but himself.

"Some people grow up, Armand, and learn to deal
with the consequences of their actions. That's what's happening here. As a consequence of my actions, I'm going
to lose Madison. She's fully justified in walking away
from me. And I'll let her because I betrayed her. You, on
the other hand, have just lost your free ride."

"I have no idea what you're talking about."

"Madison doesn't need to give you that diamond. It
will have no effect on Abigail. Because you have no claim
to her."

"That doesn't even make sense. I'm her father."

"You *thought* you were her father, biologically at least.
But you're not. She's not even yours. I can get a DNA
test to prove this and have her taken away. Or you can
sign over your rights."

He should've been satisfied that his father looked
stunned, but it didn't make him feel good to take the
old man down. It only felt good to know that Abigail
would be safe. "If you sign over your rights, I'll pay you
enough to get back on your feet, and you can dissolve
your marriage with no contest." He straightened, hoping
his height advantage would convince his father he wasn't
to be messed with.

"If you refuse, I'll make sure everyone in your social circle knows that your wife cheated on you with the
chauffeur. That you've raised a child who wasn't yours
all these years, and blackmailed your son into stealing
from another woman for your benefit."

Behind him Madison gasped, but Blake couldn't stop
now. "I have nothing to lose," he said. And that was true.

Without Madison, he would never be truly happy again. "You do. So are you going to take the easy way out, or lose your reputation along with your fortune?"

Only someone who'd lived with Armand all these years would know just how much his reputation meant to him. Not to mention the fact that it was his only way of getting his business back on its feet. His connections within Louisiana society, and the country as a whole, were his only source of revenue.

"Do you really expect me to give up a fortune to the daughter of my enemy?" he asked, his genteel facade slipping even further with his sneer.

"He wasn't your enemy," Madison said from behind him. "He was just a man who actually loved my mother. Not one who wanted her to enhance his reputation and social status."

"And that, Father, is the problem with your life in a nutshell. You just want to keep up appearances. Not to mention the fact, if you walk away now, Madison won't have to take out a restraining order against you."

For a moment, Blake thought his father might burst an artery. His entire face flushed and he practically shook with anger.

"So what will it be, Father?" Blake prodded. "Should I contact your lawyer?"

Armand visibly pulled himself together. "Of course," he said in a clipped, controlled tone. No yelling would be allowed in public today, Blake guessed. Then Armand turned on his heel and walked away, ever displaying the calm veneer of a wealthy gentleman, hiding the snake lurking beneath.

"How much is that going to cost you?" Madison whispered.

"It doesn't matter. As long as I can support Abigail,

we'll be good." He turned back to face her. "I'm so sorry, Madison. You didn't deserve that. Any of it."

Reaching out, he wrapped her fingers around the jewelry box. "Take this to Trinity, and ask her to find you someone reputable to sell it." He swallowed hard. "I need to know that you're taken care of in the way you deserve."

Madison stared down at the box for several moments before she glanced back up with tears in her eyes. "What makes you think I deserve the money from this?"

"Life. You've had a raw deal, Madison. You deserve far more than life has given you."

"And yours wasn't just as bad? At least my parents loved me. I didn't have to live under that guy's thumb my entire life. That was a close call, I'd say."

Blake cocked his head to the side. Was she actually joking? "Um, yes. I'd agree."

"Blake." She drew in a deep, hard breath. "I believe I've come to a decision."

This is it. Here comes the goodbye.

She held up the jewelry box, staring at it. "I believe that I'm going to need help taking care of this incredible piece."

"Yes?"

"I think you and Abigail would be perfect for the job."

What? "I don't understand."

"Well, I can't ask just anyone. I need someone who really knows me, knows what I believe in. It has to be someone I can trust."

"That would not be me." *It couldn't be me.*

"Are you sure?"

Blake swore as he broke out in a cold sweat. "What are you saying?"

"Yes, you lied to me. You met me under false pretenses and kept secrets from me."

"Yes, I did, Madison. I'm sorry."

"And I know you really are. Do you know how I know that?"

Blake shook his head, not trusting his voice.

"Because you just volunteered to give up a fortune to take care of a child who isn't even yours."

Her dark green gaze made his head swim. Was she really saying this?

"I know better than to think that your father will let you off cheap. And I know better than to think that raising a young girl alone doesn't scare the pants off you." She stepped in closer, bringing her heat to mix with his. "Those are the things that are important to me. That's the Blake I fell in love with—the man who isn't perfect but is trying his best…" She brushed her lips over his, pulling a heartfelt sigh from him. "And his best feels pretty darn good."

Blake struggled to keep his wits about him. "How do you know I wasn't lying? That I'm not lying now?" Maybe he was a fool to ask, but he'd rather know for sure before he fell too deep to dig himself out.

"It's quite simple, really," she said. "All I need is your response to my plan."

"You have a plan?"

"I do. And only the best of men would go along with it."

Blake wouldn't consider himself the best of men, but somehow he knew he'd support Madison in anything she wanted to do. He couldn't hold back. He wrapped his arms tightly around her and buried his face in her neck. "I love you, Madison."

"I love you, too," she whispered.

Then he pulled back. "You know we come as a package deal now—Abby and me?"

"Absolutely…" She waited for a moment, then asked, "So, don't you want to know the plan?"

"It doesn't matter. I got the girl…girls. That's all I need."

Epilogue

Madison watched as Abigail charmed an older couple who had come to the exhibit. This might be the little girl's "debut," but without a doubt, in her frilly dress and hair ribbons and curls, she was stealing the show from the main attraction.

Blake stood at the entrance to the rotunda at the ASTRA, ready to answer any questions people might have. In the past year, he'd become an expert on the Belarus diamond and its caretaker of sorts. Madison couldn't believe that he'd gone along with her plan. But he'd not only supported her, he'd embraced the purpose behind it and spent every day helping her fulfill her goal.

To use the Belarus diamond to create funding for those in need.

To that end, they'd arranged with the museum to exhibit it here for special functions. Part of the ticket proceeds would go to fund Maison de Jardin and charities like it. Ownership had been officially established with the charity. Madison didn't need or want the jewel. She had all she needed with her fiancé and the half sister who was now legally his child.

Trinity stepped up to her, resting her arm around Madison's shoulders as she took a sip of her sparkling water. No champagne for the mom-to-be.

Trinity's happy-ever-after had come around the same time as Madison's. The chaos and suspicions surrounding her first marriage and husband's death had been tough, but she'd been rewarded with a new husband…and a family of her own. Michael Hyatt's estates were in good hands, Trinity's hands, and Maison de Jardin was protected from vultures like Michael's relatives.

But even more important, the business consultant they'd hired was now Trinity's new husband. He'd rocked the Secrets and Scandals blog with his revelations, and come out on the other side as Trinity's biggest supporter and the father of her unborn baby. Their story was still a source of extreme interest from New Orleans' society.

"How's the second attraction of this little charity exhibit doing?" Madison asked with a chuckle.

Trinity grimaced. "Who knew so many nosy people would want to stare at a pregnant lady?"

"Only if said pregnant lady was the most talked about heiress in all of Louisiana…"

Trinity arched a brow in her direction. "You haven't done so bad yourself. I thought the phone would never stop ringing once your story broke."

"We both ended up with some pretty spectacular legacies, didn't we?"

Trinity smiled. "Funny how they weren't as important as the people that came with them, huh?"

Even if they weren't still here. They'd dedicated tonight's event to Madison's parents and Trinity's late husband, Michael, who had helped found Maison de Jardin.

But those legacies had brought other people into their lives: for Trinity, her new husband and the baby she was expecting, and for Madison, Blake and Abigail. For the first time in a long time, Madison's life felt full. Full to overflowing.

Blake's gaze caught hers from across the room. The intensity of his feelings reached her even though they weren't speaking. Not a day went by with him that wasn't her best. But tonight...tonight was special.

Somehow they both knew it.

Tamika sidled up to the girls, smiling over her champagne flute. "Ladies, I'm getting lucky tonight."

Madison and Trinity exchanged a glance. Tamika ignored them. "I figure all of this good luck has to rub off sometime. Trinity is married. Madison is getting close. We think. Surely it's my turn next."

"Go stand next to Blake."

"Why?"

"He's the lucky one."

"I didn't need to know that," Tamika said with a laugh.

"No, really. Today's the day."

Tamika and Trinity leaned in close. Madison smiled, unable to resist letting them in on the secret. She wiggled her fingers. "Because tonight, I think I'll let him put a ring on it."

* * * * *

COMING SOON!

JOIN US ON SOCIAL MEDIA!

Stay up to date with our latest releases, author
news and gossip, special offers and discounts, and
all the behind-the-scenes action
from Mills & Boon...

 millsandboon

 millsandboonuk

 millsandboon

It might just be true love...

Quick Start in 1946.
Italian design revs up.

Vespa for **PIAGGIO**

DESIGNDIRECTORY Italy

Claudia Neumann

DESIGN**DIRECTORY**

Italy

PAVILION

Successful Series.
SAPPER and **ZANUSO** design boxes
with global appeal.

Algol for **BRIONVEGA**, 1964

6

About this book

There are perhaps more designers per square mile in Italy than anywhere else on earth. And nowhere else have so many companies so consistently defined themselves through design. Design Directory: Italy tries to make the enormously diverse Italian design landscape accessible to the reader, through a simple alphabetical structure and numerous illustrations. The directory's main focus is individual profiles, with an emphasis on furniture and product designers. A number of major fashion and graphic designers are included, as well as discussions of important styles and currents in Italian design. And this book is the first of its kind to include portraits of companies both big and small involved in the business of design. The Interni Guide, a directory of the Italian furniture industry, lists about 1,000 design-oriented furniture makers and no less than 200 lighting manufacturers. Out of this immense number a selection was made that reflects the companies' historical significance as well as their relevance to contemporary design. An annotated index contains many additional entries; throughout the book, names and terms in bold in the main text refer to the index.

The Authors

Paola Antonelli is a curator at the Department of Architecture and Design at the Museum of Modern Art in New York. A graduate of Milan's Polytechnic, she is a frequent contributor to such publications as *Abitare*, *Domus*, and *Nest*. Exhibitions she has curated at MoMA include Mutant Materials in Contemporary Design. She lives in New York.

Fulvio Ferrari is a writer and world-renowned dealer and collector of Italian design as well as one of the leading experts in the field. The owner of an important private design archive, he has a particular interest in Radical Design. He lives in Turin.

Claudia Neumann is a freelance writer and editor and owner of the Design Archive agency. A copublisher of the Design Calendar, she has published numerous articles on design. She lives in Cologne.

Translated into English by Jürgen Riehle. 745.44945 NEU

Classics for the Masses.
ARTEMIDE molds plastic into serial
seating.

Toga by Sergio MAZZA, 1969

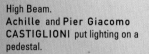

High Beam.
Achille and **Pier Giacomo**
CASTIGLIONI put lighting on a
pedestal.

Taccia lamp for **FLOS**, 1962

Above and beyond any romantic declaration about Italians and their secret recipe for success stands the exceptional effectiveness of Italy as a twentieth-century design case study. Nowhere else in the world can one find so many varied examples, both in terms of conception and of formal outcome; so many applications of diverse technologies; such a complete representation of all applied design forms, from fashion and graphics to product and set design; such an extensive and multifaceted documentation recorded in literature; and such an international resonance. By engaging the best industrial and cultural forces of the country in a single-minded and spontaneous operation of national image-building, Italian design has become an icon in itself, almost independent from its products.

Moreover, different national design cultures have reached their zenith at different times during the century, thus becoming temporary international symbols in the history of design. While it was France's turn in the teens and twenties, Germany's in the thirties and forties, and the United States and Scandinavia shared the fifties, Italy seems to own most of the sixties and early seventies, a period particularly dear and positively meaningful to the world.

Legend has it that during the 1950s in Italy, several talented but unemployed architects fortuitously met some enlightened industrial manufacturers in search of products; in the background, the mechanical and chemical industries were bubbling with innovations waiting to be grabbed and applied.

Together, they established the collaborative formula, based on sharing technical knowledge, dreams, and goals, that bore them great fruits in the sixties. The best examples of Italian design reflect this tight collaboration, a relationship that to this day provides designers from all over the world with exceptional support for experimentation.

Before World War II, only a few companies, concentrated in the food and mechanical industries—**Campari, Pirelli,** and **Olivetti** among them—shared this attitude. In the fifties, the model became contagious. **Achille** and **Pier Giacomo Castiglioni, Vico Magistretti,** and **Marco Zanuso,** to name just a few, might never have achieved their success without this receptiveness on the part of manufacturers. Likewise, many existing companies that relied on big contract commissions, yet also on trite imitation of eclectic styles, like **Cassina,** would have never become pioneers of design. The family-based companies, located primarily in northern Italy, in the region north of Milan and in Veneto, and in pockets of central Italy, reacted positively both to these architects' sophisticated culture and to the technology transfers provided by the idle war industries.

The postwar economic boom provided fuel for numerous new companies. Some of them were created from scratch to take advantage of new technologies, like **Kartell,** founded in 1948 by engineer Giulio Castelli to exploit the invention of polypropylene. Others, like **Arteluce,** were begun by designers who wanted to manufacture their own ideas, and who therefore approached technology in a more thought-out fashion. Meanwhile, the architecture and design community sparked a lively dialogue with the rest of the world and fostered the spectacular edge of Italian design through publications like *Domus, Abitare,* and *Casabella,* and international events, like the Milan furniture fair, established in 1961, and the *Triennali.* Italy felt like the epicenter of the design world.

This golden moment of Italian design culminated in the 1972 *Italy: The New Domestic Landscape* exhibition at the Museum of Modern Art in New York, also considered by some its swan song. The oil crisis and the "lead years" of terrorism took a toll on designers' optimistic attitude, yet could not defeat the profession's visionary soul. The **Memphis** phenomenon and the postmodern activity of companies like **Alessi** exemplified a new Italian way to design, more attuned to the fashion industry—companies started using the word "collection" in their catalogues—and focused on the designers' signature styles, supported by the companies' well-studied images.

To this day, Italian design companies have been able to maintain their status and their experimental verve and, in a time short of great indigenous designers, are attracting the best talents from all over the world. They keep the flag of Italian Design flying high.

Paola Antonelli
Museum of Modern Art, New York

Model for a Decade.
While the furniture objects remained
prototypes the **MEMPHIS** mosaics by
SOTTSASS & Co. were ubiquitous in
the 80s.

Carlton shelf unit, 1981

Red Wedding.
VALENTINO finds his signature color.

Couture, 1965

14

Dissolving Quotes.
In 1978 **Alessandro MENDINI**
proclaims the end of design history and
dismantles it with a saw and a
paintbrush.

Poltrona di Proust
for **ALCHIMIA**

Bicycle Thieves.
In 1957 Achille & Pier Giacomo
CASTIGLIONI steal the show with a
wobbly seat.

Sella, produced by ZANOTTA since 1983

Soft Calculator.
Mario BELLINI's soft-keypad
adds a sensual touch to arithmetic in
1972.

Divisumma 18 for OLIVETTI

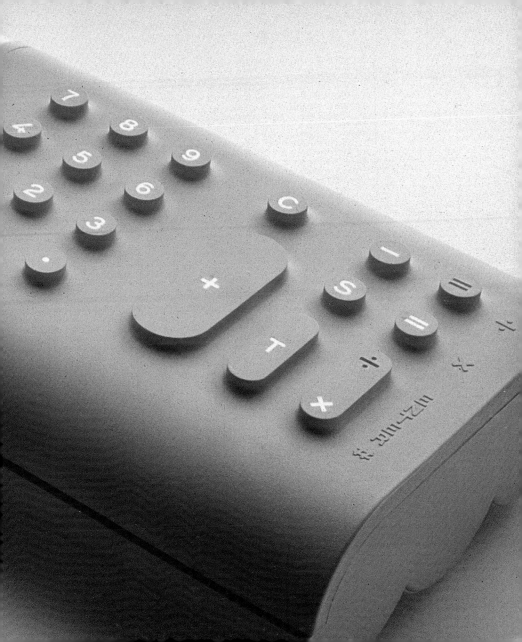

Interactive Mattress.
Years before Ikea, **Joe COLOMBO** invites furniture buyers to assemble their own beds.
Additional System for **SORMANI**, 1967

Cool Presence. In 1954
Bruno MUNARI brings
a smooth new style to
cocktail culture.

TMT ice bucket, produced by
ZANI & ZANI

"PRATONE

Plastic-Provocation.
GUFRAM'S designs create
pop icons out of foamed plastic.

Pratone artificial turf by **CERETTI,
DEROSSI, ROSSI,** 1971

High Contrast.
SAWAYA & MORONI give
seating a racy edge.

Bine by **Marcello
MORANDINI,** 1991

Piccolo Teatro di Milano
Ente Autonomo

Direzione Paolo Grassi - Giorgio Strehler

Milano - Palazzo del Broletto - Via Rovello, 2
Telefoni: 896915 - 803464 - 867206 - 867208 - 873585
Biglietteria 872352 - 877663

Ufficio Abbonamenti e Propaganda
Via Rovello, 6

stagione 1964/65 diciannovesima dalla fondazione
al Piccolo Teatro

da sabato 28 novembre

lunedì, mercoledì, giovedì, venerdì, alle ore 21,10 precise
sabato alle ore 15,30 e 21,10 precise
domeniche e festivi alle ore 15,30 precise
termine spettacoli: pomeriggio: ore 18,10, sera: ore 23,50
martedì (esclusi festivi e prefestivi) riposo

Sul caso J. Robert Oppenheimer

2 tempi di Heinar Kipphardt
prima rappresentazione in Italia

allestimento di Giorgio Strehler e Cioni Carpi,
Luciano Damiani, Gigi Lunari, Virginio Puecher,
Fulvio Tolusso

Distribuzione:

J. Robert Oppenheimer, fisico — Renato De Carmine

La commissione d'inchiesta:
Gordon Gray — Raffaele Giangrande
Ward V. Evans — Ferdinando Tamberlani
Thomas A. Morgan — Gastone Bartolucci

Gli avvocati della commissione per l'energia atomica:
Roger Robb — Franco Graziosi
C.A. Rolander — Ugo Bologna

L'avvocato della difesa:
Herbert S. Marks — Mario Mariani

I testimoni:
Boris T. Pash, ufficiale del servizio segreto — Corrado Nardi
John Lansdale, ex ufficiale del servizio segreto — Ottavio Fanfani
Hans Bethe, fisico — Antonio Meschini
Edward Teller, fisico — Luciano Alberici
David Tressel Griggs, geofisico della Air Force — Attilio Duse
Isadore Isaac Rabi, fisico — Giulio Girola

Assistente alla regia: Paolo Radaelli

Le scene sono realizzate dal Laboratorio di Scenografia del Piccolo Teatro
pittore scenografo Leonardo Ricchelli,
costruttore Bruno Colombo

Direttore di palcoscenico: Bruno Martini
Capo elettricista: Mino Campolmi
Rammentatore: Giuseppe Lelio
Vice direttore di palcoscenico: Luciano Ferroni
Primo macchinista: Fortunato Michieli
Attrezzista: Aldo Dal Santo
Sarta di palcoscenico: Lea Gavinelli

Prezzi:
1600 Poltrona di platea / **1100** Poltroncina di platea / **800** Balconata

Le prenotazioni si ricevono alla biglietteria del Piccolo Teatro (tel. 872352-877663)
ogni giorno dalle ore 10 alle ore 19.
La vendita e la prenotazione dei posti vengono aperte con quattro giorni di anticipo.
I posti prenotati telefonicamente si ritengono rinunciati.

I prezzi su esposti includono ingresso e tasse.
Posteggio autorizzato per automobili.

Vale il tagliando n. 2 degli abbonamenti

Biglietteria 872352 - 877663

stagione 1964/65 diciannovesima dalla fondazione
al Piccolo Teatro

da sabato 26 dicembre

lunedì, mercoledì, giovedì, venerdì, alle ore 21,
sabato alle ore 15,30 e 21,10 precise
domeniche e festivi alle ore 15,30 precise
termine spettacoli: pomeriggio: ore 18,10, sera
martedì (esclusi festivi e prefestivi) riposo

Il Signor di Pourceaugnac

commedia in tre atti di Molière
nuova traduzione di Ruggero Jacobbi
regia di Eduardo De Filippo

Distribuzione:

Il Signor di Pourceaugnac — Tino Buazzelli
Oronte — Armando Alzelmo
Giulia, figlia di Oronte — Manuela Andrei
Nerina, ruffiana, finta moglie di Pourceaugnac e finto ufficiale — Gabriella Giacobbe
Lucetta, altra finta moglie di Pourceaugnac — Narcisa Bonati
Eraste, innamorato di Giulia — Umberto Ceriani
Sbrigani, napoletano raillemestieri — Franco Sportelli
Primo medico — Sandro Merli
Secondo medico — Ivan Cecchini
Un farmacista — Sandro Dori
Un contadino — Giancarlo Cajo
Una contadina — Narcisa Bonati
Primo avvocato — Ivan Cecchini
Secondo avvocato — Pietro Buttarelli
Primo svizzero — Giancarlo Cajo
Secondo svizzero — Paride Calonghi

Infermieri, Bambini, Magistrati, Secondini, Arcieri — Giorgio Biavati, Pietro Buttarelli, Giancarlo..., Paride Calonghi, Piergiorgio Menegazzo

Musicisti — Antonio Baldini, Giuseppe Bova, Augusto C..., Antonio Esposito, Mario Sarria

L'azione si svolge a Parigi

Scene e costumi di Mino Maccari
Musiche di Fiorenzo Carpi
Pantomime di Rosita Lupi
Regista assistente Virginio Puecher

Le scene sono realizzate dal Laboratorio di Scenografia del Piccolo Teatro
pittore scenografo Leonardo Ricchelli,
costruttore Bruno Colombo

I costumi sono realizzati dalla Sartoria del Piccolo Teatro
Capitecnici: Angelo Bocenti, Tina Nicoletti, Ines Rezzonico
e dalla Sartoria Maria Consiglio di Napoli

Direttore di palcoscenico: Luciano Ferroni
Capo elettricista: Mino Campolmi
Primo macchinista: Fortunato Michieli
Rammentatore: Ildebrando Biribò
Attrezzista: Aldo Dal Santo

Prezzi:
1600 Poltrona di platea / **1100** Poltroncina di platea / **800** Balco

Le prenotazioni si ricevono alla biglietteria del Piccolo Teatro (tel. 872352-877663)
ogni giorno dalle ore 10 alle ore 19.
La vendita e la prenotazione dei posti vengono aperti con quattro giorni di anticipo.
I posti prenotati telefonicamente si ritengono rinunciati se non vengono ritirati entro le ore 18 del giorno successivo alla prenotazione.

I prezzi su esposti includono ingresso e tasse.
Posteggio autorizzato per automobili.

Vale il tagliando n. 2 degli abbonamenti

Servizio di recapito a domicilio dei biglietti o dei posti in abbonamento prenotati telefonicamente.

Di tutti i poeti comici che subirono, in Europa, le influenze della Commedia italiana dell'arte, il più grande e insieme quello che più direttamente ne proviene è Molière.

Beautifully Banal. **KARTELL**
brings plastic elegance to the humble
chore of straining pasta.

Gino **COLOMBINI**, 1959

Dramatic Red and Black.

For thirty years, a two-tone alphabet
has been **VIGNELLI**'s unmistakable
hallmark.

Playbill for the
Piccolo Teatro in Milan, 1964

Ample Charms.
Gaetano PESCE's
duvet-lined chair gives
comfort in the hectic 80s.

I Feltri for **CASSINA**, 1987

Nude Machines.
DUCATI radically
strips down its
bikes in the 90s.

Ducati *916 Biposto*,
1998

Street Style.
In the 70s **FIORUCCI** launches
fashions for the urban catwalk.

Collection 1997/1998

Gentle Waves. **Carlo SCARPA**
meditates on glass in 1940.

Battuto Bicolore vase for **VENINI**

Translucent Objects.
Marco FERRERI's stacking
bowls make a soft landing in the
kitchens of the 90s.

Antipodi for **DANESE**

Friendly Invasion.
Giorgetto GIUGIARO'S Golf
puts Italian Design on German roads.

VW *Golf* by **ITALDESIGN**, 1974

Serpentine Vertebrae.
Cini BOERI's modular rubber seats
turn 70s sitting rooms into comfortable
snakepits.

Element from *Serpentone* seating system for
ARFLEX, 1971

Furniture Aerobatics.
Stunt pilot Carlo MOLLINO
puts bold curves into hard wood.

Table of the series *Arabesque*, 1949

32

Streamlined Calculator.
Marcello NIZZOLI borrows a look
from car design for **OLIVETTI**.

Elettrosumma 14, 1946

Marketing Discovers Art.
The **FUTURISTS** turn into poster
designers and boost the sales of
beverage companies.

Poster for **CAMPARI** by
Fortunato DEPERO, 1920s

Illuminating Geometry.
Vico MAGISTRETTI'S
brings a sense of proportion to 70s
tables.

Atollo for O LUCE, 1977

Triangulated Sitting.
In 1969 **ARCHIZOOM** takes formal
reduction to parodic extremes.

Mies for **POLTRONOVA**

The Fast Lane.
Bodymaker **BERTONE**
tailors metal for speedy living.

Alfa *Giulietta Sprint Coupé*, 1954

Packaging Art.
Erberto CARBONI
makes a convincing
case for pasta.

Packaging for
BARILLA, 1956

Suspense.
In 1989 **LUCEPLAN'S** luminous UFO
enters into the office atmosphere.

Titania by **Paolo RIZZATTO**
and **Alberto MEDA**

Liquor or Learning?
Piero FORNASETTI
pastes books on **Gio PONTI**'s
cabinet.

Prototype, 1950

40

Slouch Zone
In 1968 the Flower-Power
generation gets mellow on
ZANOTTA's beanbag.

Sacco by
GATTI / PAOLINI / TEODORO

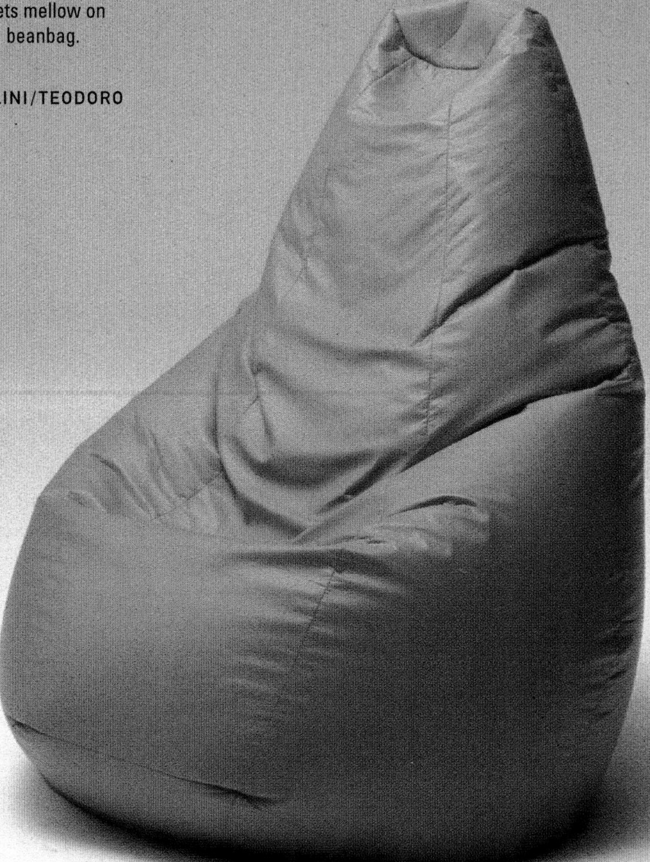

Bright White. In the 1960s **VALLE** and
ZANELLO establish order in Italy's
motley kitchens.

P.5 compact washing machine
for **ZANUSSI**, 1966

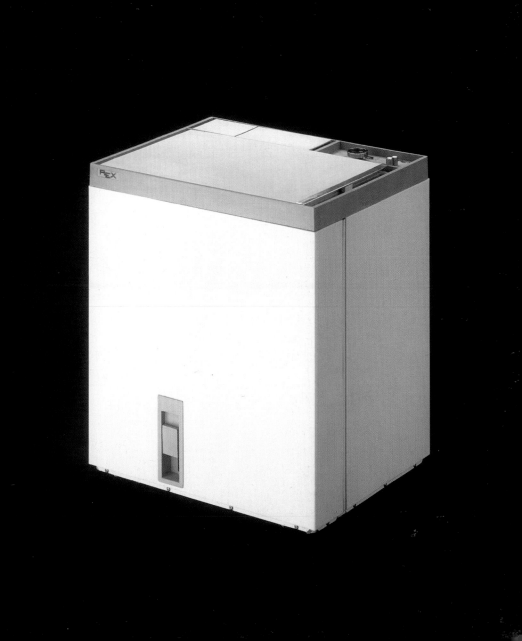

Auto-Erotic.
Enzo FERRARI and **Battista PININFARINA** lend sensuous form to combustive power.

Ferrari *250 GT Berlinetta SWB*, 1960

Iron Maiden.
MENDINI'S corkscrew ushers in
ALESSI'S colored period.

Anna G., 1994

Poster à la mode **Albe
STEINER** dresses up a
department store.

L'estetica nel Prodotto, poster for
LA RINASCENTE, 1953

Eye-Catcher.
With their gargantuan mitt
DE PAS / D'URBINO / LOMAZZI
pay homage to Joe DiMaggio.

Joe for **POLTRONOVA**, 1970

Plastic Elegance. **Enzo MARI**
gives high style to a lowly material.

Pago Pago vase for **DANESE**, 1969

Mother of all minicars.
Dante GIACOSA's little Fiat is
nicknamed "mouse"—and multiplies
accordingly.

Fiat *500*, 1936

Page 49

Timor calendar by Enzo Mari
for Danese, 1966

Decades

Italian Design History
from 1860 to the Present

1860 - 1945

From Single to Series:
Pioneers and Prototypes

Pioneers and prototypes

Italian design did not grow out of specialization. From the *Vespa* scooter to the *Sacco* beanbag, from the inflatable *Blow* chair and **Olivetti's** red *Valentine* typewriter to **Alessi's** *Conica* espresso maker, most of Italy's design classics were created by self-taught designers. None of the people responsible for Italian design's mythic aura had ever studied "design," a field that didn't even exist in Italy's schools until the 1980s. Instead, they are architects, artists, engineers, chemists, aircraft builders, and race car drivers.

Less surprisingly, all of those icons of Italian design were made after 1945. After the end of Fascism, every part of Italian culture was swept with the desire to build a new, democratic country. The architect **Ernesto N. Rogers** set the tone for the era when he demanded that everything in the human environment—"from spoons to cities," from the monumental to the utilitarian—be treated as objects worthy of design. This democratic spirit released an enormous amount of design creativity. Even a simple bucket could now transcend its basic use and win its creator Italy's highest design prize, the *Compasso d'oro,* awarded to **Gino Colombini** in 1955 for his plastic pail.

The history of industrial development and the history of industrial design are tightly intertwined—a fact often overlooked when the focus is fixed on aesthetic judgments. But it was only with the comprehensive industrialization of Italy

"And though there are philistines here, they're at least Italian orange philistines and not clumsy German potato philistines."

Heinrich Heine

Page 50
Fiat factory in Lingotto, Turin, with spiral ramp to rooftop test track, 1921

from left:
Pirelli, tire assembly, c. 1920
Cobra chair by Carlo Bugatti, 1902
First Olivetti factory in Ivrea, c.1910

and the economic boom of the 1950s that the conditions were created in which Italian design could rise to global pre-eminence and, in the 1960s, break the dominance of Scandinavian design.

The Industrial Revolution did not reach agrarian Italy until the 1870s, decades after it had transformed the economies and cultures of England and France. Even then, there were only a few adventuresome entrepreneurs willing to take a cue from abroad and build factories for the mass-production of consumer goods. One of these early pioneers was Camillo **Olivetti,** who in 1908 founded a typewriter company. Typewriters, he believed, shouldn't be "parlor items with ornaments of questionable taste," but objects distinguished by their utilitarian value. His vision took shape in his design for the *M1* typewriter of 1911, whose simple, clean lines were entirely derived from the industrial manufacturing process.

The Italian automobile industry developed more rapidly, though its output of luxury limousines and race cars was reserved for a small, wealthy clientele. **Fiat** was founded in 1899, followed by **Lancia** in 1905 and **Alfa Romeo** in 1909. These companies combined progress and tradition in a peculiar mix: while technological achievements and division of labor in the manufacturing process pointed forward into the new century, their cars' interiors displayed the pompous opulence the old

century had felt at home in. The Fiat *Zero,* introduced in 1912, marked a turning point. The Italian answer to Ford's *Model T,* it followed the American principle of lower cost through mass production.

The manufacturing industry's lingering reluctance to embrace formal experiments affected even its most ardent cheerleaders, the Futurists. Enthusiasm for the thundering Machine Age may have run high, but not high enough to integrate the furniture concepts or boldly patterned textile designs of Futurist artists such as **Giacomo Balla** into industrial production, or into everyday life.

The end of the First World War meant the end of the huge government contracts that had been fueling the country's industry. In Italy, as in the rest of Europe, the consequences were social unrest and a massive economic crisis. The situation became so desperate that Mussolini's promises of leading the nation back to its old grandeur found a receptive audience. When the Fascists rose to power in 1934, they immediately began subsidizing domestic industry, introducing the average consumer to mass-manufactured and, occasionally, well-designed products. Olivetti, now headed by the founder's son, Adriano, was again among the pioneers of functional design. The elegant typewriter models *MP 1* (1932) and *Studio 42* (1935) and an innovative, eye-catching advertising program all came out of the company's creative

"Look for your competitors' best parts and then combine them better than they do."

Fiat motto

from left:

M 1 typewriter by Camillo Olivetti, 1911

Fiat Zero, 1912

Table and chair for Gualino office by Giuseppe Pagano and Gino Levi-Montalcini, 1928

Alfa Romeo RL Super Sport, 1925

department, whose staff included the Bauhaus alumnus **Xanti Schawinsky,** architects **Luigi Figini** and **Gino Pollini,** and graphic artist **Marcello Nizzoli.**

Efficient industrial production after the American model became increasingly common, particularly among the large automobile manufacturers. Adopting the streamlined look, car-body designers such as **Pinin Farina** and **Bertone** applied it to such luxury models as Lancia's *Aprilia Coupe,* the Fiat *1500,* and the Alfa *6 C 2300 "Pescara"* Coupe. In 1936, Fiat took a more important step, introducing a car that had been designed for social reasons, not spectacular looks. The Fiat *500,* priced at a widely affordable 8,900 lire, was the world's smallest car and quickly became ubiquitous on Italy's roads. By 1948, 150,000 of the *"Topolini"* had been sold.

While cars conquered the roads, another technological achievement, the radio, invaded Italy's homes. At first they came encased in stately wooden cabinetry. That changed in 1940, when **Luigi Caccia Dominioni** and **Livio** and **Pier Giacomo Castiglioni** caused a sensation with the introduction at the Milan *Triennale* of their Bakelite radio for Phonola, designed with the functional aesthetics of the telephone, another symbol of progress.

These innovative designs bore the marks of European Modernism, which in Italy was known as **Razionalismo.** Originally a movement within architecture, the principle of form following function soon permeated product design. The

Fascists supported this movement through the mid-1930s; in 1934–36, **Giuseppe Terragni** built their party headquarters, the Casa del Fascio in Como, in the rationalist style. Mussolini eventually favored as the "true" Fascist style the architectural movement of the **Novecento,** which tried to integrate and modernize, rather than overcome, neoclassical traditions. In furniture production, the modernist influence was strongest in Bauhaus-inspired tubular steel and chrome pieces such as **Piero Bottoni's** *Lira* chair, whose frame had thin stainless-steel inserts, which stabilized the chair and formed the backrest. (The chair is now produced by **Zanotta.**) Many other rationalist designs never went beyond the prototype stage because Italian factories lacked the technology to manufacture them.

The effects of global politics were more acutely felt in 1936, after the League of Nations imposed sanctions on Italy for its invasion of Ethiopia. With its businesses cut off from international markets and suffering from shortages of raw materials, the country was now largely dependent on its domestic production. For all the hardship this caused in daily life, it also spawned a spirit of improvisation. **Salvatore Ferragamo,** a shoemaker, made a virtue of necessity and, instead of leather, used materials such as metal, raffia, and cork for his shoes, inventing a signature style that would later make him famous.

"Art has fallen in love with industry (...), and industry has become an intellectual phenomenon."

Gio Ponti

from left:

Fiat *Ardita* by Bertone, 1927

Serliana urn by Gio Ponti for Richard-Ginori, 1927

Luminator floor lamp by Luciano Baldessari, 1929

Desk for design studio by Annibale Pecorelli, c. 1930

Poster by Xanti Schawinsky for Olivetti's *MP 1* typewriter, 1935

Tea set by Nikolai Diulgheroff for Mazzotti, 1930

Ferragamo was a gifted artisan, a representative of the "other" side of Italian manufacturing. Cars, radios, and type-writers made up only a fraction of the products designed in Italy. Outside of the growing industrial sector, the country had countless small enterprises and workshops, each with a history that went back decades or even centuries. By the end of the nineteenth century, for example, cabinetmakers such as **Carlo Bugatti**, Eugenio Quarti, and Carlo Zen had established enormously successful businesses, while Venetian glass man-ufacturers such as Salviati and ceramics workshops like **Richard-Ginori** were on their rise to fame. Bugatti was renowned at home and abroad for his highly original interpretation of Stile **Liberty,** as Art Nouveau was called in Italy. By the early twentieth century, furniture manufacturers in the Brianza, northeast of Milan, had begun adopting industrial production techniques. (It is still the center of Italian furniture design.)

Well into the twenties and thirties, however, most utilitarian household objects were still manufactured by traditional methods, and the bulk of Italy's furniture production continued to be stylistically conservative and manufactured in small quantities. This was true even of a company like **Cassina,** whose products would epitomize modern Italian design only a

few decades later. In the meantime, adherents of the Novecento movement gently but decisively revolutionized the arts-and-crafts industry. Celebrated Milan architect **Gio Ponti**, for one, redesigned the venerable ceramics manufacturer Richard-Ginori's entire product line and prepared it for mass production.

Yet the word "design" was not yet part of the Italian vocabulary; "industrial design" was a mission, not a job description. At the 1936 Milan *Triennale*, for example, the architect **Franco Albini** designed *"A Room for a Man"* as a comprehensive environment that included not only furniture but also an extremely functional, habitable structure built around basic human needs. Design as a profession emerged casually, without a name and largely unnoticed. And for most Italians, the achievements of design's early pioneers were of rather marginal interest.

Of course, the central aspect of the period between the two World Wars consists in the fact that it was almost entirely defined by Fascism and its introduction of aesthetics into politics (a tendency as pronounced in Italy as in Germany; though Italian Fascists were remarkably open to Modernism). It is an aspect that still awaits comprehensive critical reflection by Italian art and design historians.

"An object is much harder to design than a building."

Luigi Caccia Dominioni

from left:

Lancia *Aprilia Aerodinamica* by PininFarina, 1936

Chair from Carlo Scarpa's *1934* series, reproduced by Bernini

Moka Express espresso maker by Alfonso Bialetti, 1933

Interior by Ottorino Aloisio, Exhibition, Turin, 1934

Giuseppe Terragni

Novocomum apartment building aka "Transatlantic," by Giuseppe Terragni, compl. 1929

1946 - 1965

Bel Design
From Basics to Beauty

In 1946 the first *Vespas* rolled off the assembly lines of the **Piaggio** factory. An aircraft engineer named **Corradino d'Ascanio** had designed the little scooter, with its voluptuous curves and innovative integral body. Cars weren't within the means of many Italians, but most could afford this relatively inexpensive vehicle, which after two decades of totalitarianism symbolized a new sense of free living. Like Gregory Peck and Audrey Hepburn in the 1953 movie *Roman Holiday,* more and more Italians buzzed through the streets on their "wasps," celebrating a modern style of *La Dolce Vita.*

In 1948, Olivetti introduced the *Lexikon 80* typewriter, designed by **Marcello Nizzoli.** Critics and buyers alike responded enthusiastically to its sleek form and smooth lines. The Museum of Modern Art in New York soon acquired it for its permanent design collection, noting, "The *Lexicon 80* office typewriter is **Olivetti's** most beautiful. The hands of a sensitive designer have turned its bright metal shell into a sculpture."

Both products—and many more after them—became emissaries of a totally new, modern Italian style distinguished by organic or "sculptural" forms, high functionality, and a complete absence of ornamental detail. In the 1950s, this so-called **Linea Italiana** established itself as an internationally

"Italy is a democratic republic based on labor. Sovereignity is exercised by the people within the forms and limits of the Constitution."

Article 1 of the Italian Constitution, 1947

Page 58

Salvatore Ferragamo presents Sophia Loren with a shoe, 1954

From left:

Vespa by Corradino d'Ascanio for Piaggio, 1946

Liù slipper by Salvatore Ferragamo, 1945

Vase from the *Battuti* series by Carlo Scarpa for Venini, 1940

admired paradigm of good design. The scooter and typewriter, too, were designed for mass production, their aesthetics reflecting the "democratic" cause of making desirable products affordable for all people.

After the deprivations of the war, Italians longed for such products. Everything was in short supply: food and housing, transportation, furniture, and clothes. Many architects, committed to the social causes of the Left, increasingly devoted themselves to the design of everyday objects. **Rationalists** such as **Franco Albini** and the members of the architectural firm **BBPR** employed the ideas of European Modernism in the service of building a more humane society that addressed everyone's needs. The time of vainglorious architecture was finally over—architects became designers, their motto, "new forms to shape a new society." Initially that meant a return to basics. In 1946, a furniture exposition organized by the Riunione Italiana Mostre per l'Arredamento (RIMA) showed works by such architects as Franco Albini, **Ignazio Gardella,** and **Vittoriano Viganó**. Their furniture designs were simple, inexpensive pieces for small apartments, most of them made of wood, since other materials were still scarce. In 1947 the first Triennale since the war opened. Its theme was L'abiatazione—the home. Its curator, the communist architect

Piero Bottoni, emphasized the need to tackle and solve "the problems of the least privileged classes."

Despite the sharp disappointment caused by the exclusion of the Left from Italy's government, which was led by conservatives, designers stuck to their agenda of reform. But their rigid adherence to the utilitarian value of designed objects softened considerably. At the end of the 1940s, new trends in contemporary art and American product aesthetics began to influence Italian design. With the economy slowly improving, a younger generation of designers emerged, among them the brothers **Achille** and **Pier Giacomo Castiglioni, Marco Zanuso, Ettore Sottsass,** and **Vico Magistretti.** These seminal figures, who have remained defining forces in Italian design, established a new design formula: "usefulness plus beauty."

While all of them agreed on this principle, they implemented it in vastly different ways, with each designer developing a highly personal formal language. For that reason, the history of Italian design is best reflected in the careers of individual personalities, rather than trying to arrange their achievements under specific "schools" or "movements." The creative freedom Italian designers insisted on, even when dealing with industrial clients, fostered a rich variety of forms not found in

"The real and the ideal home must both be considered part of the same problem."

Ernesto N. Rogers

From left:

Murrine opache glass bowl by Carlo Scarpa for Venini, 1940

Franco Albini

Table lamp by Gino Sarfatti for Arteluce, 1951

Casino in San Remo by Gio Ponti and Piero Fornasetti, 1950

Laminati plastici tables by Lucio Fontana, 1954

Palladiana porcelain jar by Piero Fornasetti, 1950s

other countries. There were individualists and eccentrics like the Turin architect **Carlo Molino,** whose *Arabesque* furniture of 1950 featured oddly distorted plywood shapes, or the Milan artist and designer **Piero Fornasetti,** who covered the surfaces of countless utilitarian objects with strange architectural, sun, and fish patterns.

Other designers established close working relationships with industrial companies. At the suggestion of the tire manufacturer **Pirelli,** the young architect Marco Zanuso developed a piece of furniture to be produced in a new kind of foam rubber called gommapiuma. The result was the *Lady* chair, equipped with kidney-shaped armrests, which became famous as an icon of fifties design. Zanuso's experimental design turned out to be so successful that he founded a new furniture company, **Arflex,** in 1951. He went on to design other classic pieces, such as the *Sleep-o-matic* convertible sofa of 1954, a pragmatic response to the tight living quarters in the public housing developments that began to go up all over Italy.

Another successful partnership evolved between **Gio Ponti** and the furniture manufacturer Cesare **Cassina.** The company had been around since 1927, but it was Ponti who supplied its first clear design strategy. His designs—including

the elegant *Distex* easy chair of 1953 and the famous *Superleggera* chair of 1957, which harmoniously synthesized traditional form and modern style — secured Cassina's place in design history.

There were many other examples of crossover between design and industry. The lamp manufacturer **Gino Sarfatti,** who had founded his own company in 1939, also designed all its products and pioneered modern lighting design. Dino **Gavina** was committed to a fusion of modern furniture design and fine art, and invited architects such as **Carlo Scarpa,** the Castiglioni brothers, and Marco Zanuso to work with his firm. All these entrepreneurs were willing to take stylistic and financial risks, to employ modern production technologies, and to experiment with new materials. Ever since, the principle of collaborating with both a pool of small workshops and large industrial suppliers has enabled Italian manufacturers to be flexible in their production and use specialized knowledge to realize seemingly impossible designs.

By the early 1950s, the public had become interested in design. In the competition for buyers, a product's aesthetic appeal became increasingly important. The Milan *Triennale* of 1951, 1954, and 1957 focused on the new field of industrial design. In 1954, a department store, **La Rinascente,** instituted its own design award, the

"I needed to make our mission and purpose transparent to our workers. This wasn't simply a matter of being an ›enlightened employer‹; it was my responsibility to society."

Adriano Olivetti

From left:
Wood-and-crystal table by Gio Ponti, 1954
Gio Ponti
24 ore overnight bag by Giovanni Fontana for Valextra, 1953
Supernova Bu sewing machine by Marcello Nizzoli for Necchi, 1953
Sleep-o-matic sofa by Marco Zanuso for Arflex, 1954
Cicognino side table by Franco Albini for Poggi, 1952

1953 **Tecno** founded

1954 first *Compasso d'oro* awards; *Stileindustria magazine* founded; *Sleep-o-matic* sofa by Marco Zanuso; **Olivetti** Showroom in New York (designed by **BBPR**); **Carlo Mollino** wins Le Mans race; **Pirelli** tower in Milan by **Gio Ponti**

1955 Italy joins U.N.; Vanoni Plan (economic program); *P 40* chair by **Osvaldo Borsani**

1956 **ADI** founded

1957 Italy joins EEC; *Superleggera* chair by Gio Ponti; Fiat *Nuova 500*; **Poltronova** founded; **Danese** founded

Compasso d'oro, which is still the ultimate measure of achievement in the profession. Since 1959, the awards program has been run by the Italian association of industrial designers, **ADI,** which was founded in 1956. The standards are famously high: in 1957, the judges, who included Franco Albini, Pier Giacomo Castiglioni, and **Ignazio Gardella,** gave the award to just five products, out of 1,200 entries. Only **Gino Colombini's** plastic bowl for **Kartell;** Marcello Nizzoli's *Mirella* sewing machine for Necchi; Benso Cesarino Priarollo's *Dolomite* ski boots; Ruth Christensen's *Alta Marea* fabric design; and a few colored glass vases by Vinicio Vianello met their strict criteria, which demanded that the objects display "a singular expressive power in their technical, functional, and aesthetic characteristics."

Across the industrial spectrum, the relationship between designers and manufacturers gradually became closer. In 1953 Marcello Nizzoli took charge of the design of *Necchi* sewing machines; he also put his stamp on Olivetti's products of the 1940s and 1950s. **Gino Valle** oversaw the design department at Zanussi, where he gave the firm's elettrodomestici—small household appliances—their elegant, purist look.

Unlike their peers in other countries, designers in Italy usually worked as independent consultants. Unhampered by

corporate structures, a designer like Ettore Sottsass could, in 1959, create the design for Italy's first domestically developed computer, the *Elea 9003,* and at the same time show his ceramic objects in small art galleries.

The automobile industry was another major client for the country's designers. With their genius for elegant and occasionally spectacular details, the car body designers **Pinin Farina** and **Bertone** were celebrated as the automobile's haute couturiers. Cars like Pinin Farina's 1947 *Cisitalia,* with its voluptuous curves, and the sleek 1956 **Alfa Romeo** *Giulietta Spider* became the embodiment of motorized luxury. While the former racecar driver Enzo **Ferrari** focused on producing speedy sports cars, **Fiat** concentrated on building mid-sized and compact models. Fiat's 1957 introduction of the *Nuovo 500,* an updated version of the old *Topolino,* turned countless Italians into motorists. "Italians wanted cars, and would have accepted the smallest space, as long as it was on four wheels," **Dante Giacosa,** the little vehicle's creator, wrote in his memoirs.

When Italy joined the European Economic Community in 1957, many export restrictions fell away. The effects fueled an economic boom that finally turned the country into a full-

"If people are afraid of the new, let's give them something even newer."

Giulio Castelli, Kartell

From left:

Marco Zanuso

Zerowatt V.E. 505 fan by Ezio Pirali for Fabbriche Elettrotechniche Riunite, 1953

Erberto Carboni and Pietro Barilla, 1960

K.S. 1146 plastic bucket by Gino Colombini for Kartell, 1954

Torre Velasca by Studio BBPR, Milan, compl. 1958

Kosmos chair by Augusto Bozzi for Saporiti, 1954

Poster for *Cinturato Pirelli* by Bob Noorda, 1956

fledged modern consumer society, and Italian design finally came into its own. By the early 1960s, Italian products were so successful internationally that their **"Bel Design"** broke the dominance of the Scandinavian aesthetic. In 1961, Milan hosted the first *Salone del Mobile,* still the most important international furniture fair. Design turned even common, aesthetically indifferent devices such as washers and sewing machines into desirable objects. Italians were proud of their design and celebrated it as a cultural achievement.

Close cooperation between design and industry had become the norm by the 1960s, when a second generation of creative consultants came to prominence—among them **Gae Aulenti, Rodolfo Bonetto, Cini Boeri, Mario Bellini, Afra** and **Tobia Scarpa, Anna Castelli Ferrieri,** and **Joe Colombo.** As different as these designers' personal styles were, they all realized a common motto, "Success through design," in bold, memorable forms. The products of radio and TV manufacturer **Brionvega** provide striking examples. Working with such designers as Marco Zanuso, **Richard Sapper,** and the Castiglioni brothers, Brionvega encouraged spectacular formal experiments and created products that stressed the playful aspect of design. For example, the purpose of Zanuso and

Sapper's cubic *TS 502* radio, designed in 1964, remained hidden as long as it was closed; only when opened did it reveal itself as a radio.

If the designer's basic mission consisted of giving function a clear form, it could now be expressed in imaginative ways. This was true even in the plastics industry, where Italian designers were instrumental in presenting new technology in an appealing package. Working with firms like **Kartell** and **Artemide,** they developed their own material aesthetics, liberating plastic from its negative connotations as a cheap, inferior material, and highlighting its advantages—its low cost, durability, lightness, and flexibility in terms of shape and color.

By the late 1950s, however, there were also some critical voices within Italian design, led by a group of Milan and Turin designers that included Gae Aulenti, **Roberto Gabetti, Aimaro Isola,** and **Aldo Rossi.** Calling themselves the **Neo-Liberty** movement in an ironic homage to the Italian version of Art Nouveau, they criticized what they saw as a conformist and increasingly dogmatic fixation on the Modernist tradition. The *Cavour* chair by **Vittorio Gregotti, Lodovico Meneghetti,** and **Giotto Stoppino,** with its "old-fashioned" curved lines, was

"People 'wear' their cars like jackets or coats."

Gillo Dorfles

From left:
Carlo Mollino
Card table by Carlo Graffi, single piece, 1950
Engineer Dante Giacosa with Fiat *500*, 1936, and *Nuova 500*, 1957
Plastic tub by Gino Colombini for Kartell, 1956
Mirror by Ettore Sottsass for Poltronova, c. 1960
Divisumma 24 calculator by Marcello Nizzoli for Olivetti, 1956

a statement of their dissent. Though the group did not find many followers, it did inject a dose of doubt in any single style's claim to ultimate truth.

There was soon controversy not only about stylistic issues but also about content. At the Eleventh *Triennale,* held in 1964 and centered around the theme of "leisure," a younger generation questioned whether the functional design of objects could or should be their profession's only goal. What, they asked, was the social context in which products existed. In numerous debates, participants queried the absorption of design into the cycle of production and consumption. One thing was clear: design had lost the social commitment that had driven it after the war. The renewed focus on social context led some designers to broaden their scope to include office environments and to develop flexible, modular furniture solutions. Other designers began to pursue holistic approaches.

1963 Aldo Moro forms leftist government, stabilizes economy, deficit and tourism; migration of workers to the north

1964 *TS 502* radio by Sapper and Zanuso

1965 Merger of Edison and Montecatini to form Montedison;
C&B Italia founded (later **B&B Italia**);
Cassina starts *I Maestri* series with reeditions of furniture by Le Corbusier et al.

Methodical organization and planning were stressed, and there were calls for a systematic approach to design education.

The principle of exploring the social implications of product design, first developed at the Hochschule for Gestaltung in Ulm, Germany, strongly influenced Italian designers throughout the 1960s. **Tomás Maldonado,** the Ulm design school's president from 1964 to 1966, became a leading figure in the field. In Italy, he developed a unified concept for the La Rinscente department store, which included the design of the salesrooms, merchandise display, and the store's graphics.

By the mid-1960s, Italy's economy had sunk into a deep recession. Struggling with high inflation and pressured by the country's unions, it had to abandon its low-wage policies. Workers and students took to the streets. Design, too, was part of the general upheaval and experienced fundamental changes in how it defined its role and function.

"Each object is a message that requires responses. The fact that tens of thousands of it are produced is very stimulating because it puts you in contact with the world at large."

Anna Castelli Ferrieri

From left:

Static table clock by Richard Sapper for Lorenz, 1959

Elea 9003 computer by Ettore Sottsass for Olivetti, 1959

Doney TV set for Brionvega by M. Zanuso and R. Sapper, 1962

BMW *3200 CS* by Bertone, 1961

Spinnamatic beer tap for Splügenbräu by Achille und Pier Giacomo Castiglioni, 1963

Cavour chair by G. Stoppino with V. Gregotti and L. Meneghetti, 1959

1966-1979

Design on the Barricades
Between Revolt and Marketing

In 1972 an exhibition that has since become legendary opened at New York's Museum of Modern Art. *Italy: The New Domestic Landscape* reflected the contradictory impulses of contemporary Italian design. On the one hand, the show's presentation of furniture and living environments showcased the aesthetics Italian design was known for. Visitors flocked to pieces like **Giancarlo Piretti's** *Plia* Plexiglas chair, **Anna Castelli Ferrieri** and **Ignazio Gardella's** *4997* plastic table for **Kartell,** and **Marco Zanuso's** *Grillo* telephone for Siemens, which combined dial and handset in one compact unit.

Other exhibits, however, did not fit in with the accustomed image of **Bel Design.** There was **Mario Bellini's** *Kar-a-sutra,* for example, an experimental vehicle that seemed to have sprung out of a science fiction movie. Encapsulated in glass and fitted with thick, soft cushions, it was a kind of mobile abode for modern nomads. Another "micro environment," **Joe Colombo's** *Total Furnishing Unit,* consisted of a modular container system with living area, kitchen, and bathroom tightly compressed but flexible in their arrangement—a futuristic vision of a home. Other exhibits explored public space in drawings, collages, and texts, and investigated alternative forms of living and dwelling.

These contributions showed that parallel to Italy's commercial production a new, subversive design culture had emerged. Clearly, there was no longer one unified Italian design

"There is no urban form that hasn't failed or else isn't about to fail."

Andrea Branzi

Page 70
Lassú, performance by
Alessandro Mendini, 1974

From left:
Ricerche individuali di design
(design research) by
Enzo Mari, 1967
Dondolo seat by Cesare
Leonardi and Franca Stagi, 1967
Frine table lamp by Studio
Tetrarch for Artemide, 1969

philosophy. In the years since 1965, Italian design had experienced a deepening identity crisis as social unrest and workers' protests shook the country. If the pioneers of Italian design had been preoccupied with function and beauty, the young rebels pointed out the dead end this approach had led to. In their view, design had become enslaved to industrial interests.

As in the rest of Europe, Italian universities—including the architecture departments—were in turmoil. Florence especially became a spawning ground for activist architectural groups like **Archizoom, Superstudio, UFO,** and **9999,** who, with the support of established figures such as **Ettore Sottsass,** the critic and filmmaker **Ugo La Pietra**, and the artist **Gaetano Pesce,** produced an endless stream of utopian designs, manifestoes, and exhibitions. The rebels' main targets were the cult of the product, the unchanging cycle of production and consumption in capitalist society, and the naive faith in functionalism. Their movement became known by two names: **Architettura Radicale** and **Radical Design.**

The young radicals drew inspiration not only from similar movements abroad, such as the Archigram group in England, but also from Pop Art, Arte Povera, Conceptual Art, and other contemporary countercurrents to traditional aesthetics. Their goal was to change society through design and architecture. If

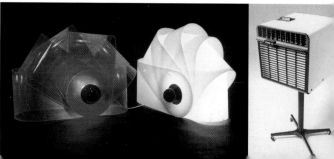

the movement became influential, though, it was not because of the few projects that were actually realized. Their most important designs, like Archizoom's *No-Stop-City*, a dystopian vision of a highly artificial future city, were never meant to be built. In a more ironic vein, the *Mies* chair by Archizoom members **Andrea Branzi** and **Massimo Morozzi,** had a seat so steeply angled that its purported function—rest—turned into an apparent threat. A sarcastic comment on the constructivist elements of modern furniture design, it served as a kind of shock therapy.

Manufacturers, for their part, continued to rely on Bel Design's innovative impulses in order to survive the recession. Among the memorable designs that came out of the economically strained mid-1960s were Kartell's elegant plastic furniture, Ettore Sottsass and **Perry A. King's** *Valentine* typewriter for **Olivetti,** and luxury limousines from **Alfa Romeo, Lancia,** and **Ferrari.**

It is a purely Italian phenomenon that the two divergent movements in design—classic industrial design and its utopian counterproject—occasionally ran together in the work of individual figures. Sottsass, for one, reflected on alternative design processes in various experimental projects while at the same time continuing his work as a consultant to Olivetti. At the 1972 MoMA show, Mario Bellini exhibited not only the cocoon-like *Kar-a-sutra,* but also an elegant leather chair designed for **Cassina.**

> *"When I started designing machines it occurred to me that they can influence not only physical states but also emotions."*
>
> Ettore Sottsass

From left:

Ribbon chair by Cesare Leonardi and Franca Stagi, 1961

Gherpe lamp by Superstudio for Poltronova,1967

Air conditioner by Joe Colombo for Candy, late 1960s

CUB 8 seat by Angelo Mangiarotti for Poltronova, 1968

Orio light by Sergio Mazza for Quattrifolio, 1973

Plia folding chair by Giancarlo Piretti for Castelli, 1969

Enzo Mari

A number of open-minded, adventurous entrepreneurs took on the challenge of integrating the new trends into designs for production. Around 1970, illustrious visitors from Milan began to turn up at the Archizoom studio in Florence. One of them was the furniture magnate Cesare Cassina, who came to discuss the possibility of putting the group's antiestablishment designs into commercial production. When he left, he had agreed to give them a monthly check in order to secure their creative output for his company.

Radical designers transformed the look, feel, and very definition of furniture: **De Pas/D'Urbino/Lomazzi's** 1967 *Blow* chair for Zanotta was inflatable like a balloon; **Paolini, Gatto** and **Teodoro's** 1969 *Sacco,* also produced by Zanotta, was just that: a sack to sit in; while Gufram's cartoonish *Cactus* of 1971 served as a clothesrack. But the furniture industry's embrace of the new design culture also took some of its edge off. And in any case, there were limits to what design's radicals could achieve; their built-in antagonism and obsession with theory

helped the movement run out of steam by the mid-1970s. Surprisingly, radical design returned only a few years later, and this time took hold. Its first center was the **Alchimia** design studio in Milan, which held its first show of small objects in 1978. **Alessandro Mendini** emerged as the leading theorist of the reborn movement, which before long included **Michele De Lucchi,** Ettore Sottsass, the UFO group, and several other young designers. Through the unconventional use of different design "languages," cultural pluralism, and ironic redesign (Mendini covered period furniture and classic Bauhaus pieces with colorful laminates and ornaments), the movement rigorously questioned the doctrines of good taste, correct form, and functionalism. Although Alchimia did not reach a wider audience, its work marked a progressive turn, a fresh approach that was taken up in the early 1980s by the **Memphis** group and would lead to a comprehensive transformation of Italian and international design.

"Alchimia believes in the importance of memory and tradition."
Alessandro Mendini

From left:
Asteroide lamp by Ettore Sottsass for Poltronova, 1968
Massolo table by Piero Gilardi for Gufram, 1974
Logos 50/60 calculator by Mario Bellini for Olivetti, 1972
Chiocciola chair by Studio 65 for Gufram, 1971
Paramount lamp for Alchimia by UFO, 1979
Mario Bellini

1980 - 1999

Memphis, Mode, and the Market
From Avant-garde to International Standard

There was a traffic jam in front of a Milan showroom at the edges of the 1981 Salone del Mobile in Milan. Here, the recently established **Memphis** group presented its first collection. More than 2,000 people came to examine pieces like **Ettore Sottsass's** *Beverly*. The object was made of a rather unconventional mix of wood, laminate, and metal and kept viewers guessing at its function—the doors indicated a wardrobe, an angled console on top of it suggested a shelf, and a red lightbulb screwed to a metal bow turned the whole thing into a lamp. Other designers, including **Michele De Lucchi, Andrea Branzi,** and **Mattheo Thun,** showed similarly undefinable objects and, presumably, furniture. Martine Bedin had designed a small cart spangled with little lights, **Marco Zanini,** a throne-like sofa called *Dublin*.

What got lost in the fuss—the press finally had something to write about—was the fact that the objects were not intended for industrial production, even though the ideas behind them would, in time, revolutionize the design culture of Italy as well as many other countries'. Memphis had unceremoniously and irredeemably slaughtered a holy cow—the doctrine of correct form. The focus of design now shifted toward colorful, sometimes exotic surfaces and patterns; multifunctionality; and the communicative aspect of products.

"The industrial sector doesn't realize that consumption can also mean pleasure and that pleasure can never be entirely controlled, not without consequences."

Barbara Radice

Page 76
Showroom for Artemide
by Vignelli Assoc., New York 1987

From left:
Piece from an experimental series of household appliances by Michele De Lucchi for Girmi, 1979
Beverly by Ettore Sottsass for Memphis, 1981
Ettore Sottsass

1980 *L'oggetto
banale* exhib. at the
Biennale di Venezia;
1,502 terrorist attacks;
Fiat lays off
14,469 workers

1981 **Memphis** founded; first
Memphis exhib. in Milan;
Carlton shelf unit by
Ettore Sottsass;
assassination attempt
on Pope John Paul II
at St. Peter's in Rome

1982 Second Memphis exhib. in
Milan; Italy wins its third
soccer world cup; Dalla
Chiesa assassinated;
intensified fight
against the Mafia

1983 **Alchimia** exhib., *Il grande
metafisico,* in Milan;
Craxi, a socialist, forms
government

1984 **Baleri** founded; *La
Casa Calda,* book by
Andrea Branzi; *La conica*
espresso maker by
Aldo Rossi for **Alessi**; **Zeus**
founded

The group showed a new collection every year. Soon a Memphis cult arose. When the fashion designer Karl Lagerfeld furnished his entire apartment in Memphis, the media made sure everyone knew about it. Inevitably, the movement devolved into fashion, and it was already past its peak when a second Memphis generation, which included **Massimo Iosa-Ghini,** appeared on the scene in the mid-eighties. Countless copies "in the Memphis style" began to flood the market. By that time, most of the movement's original founders had lost interest in what they had started.

Still, it is hard to overestimate the group's influence. Memphis unleashed a fresh wave of bold experimentation in form and color. The lighting manufacturer **Artemide,** the furniture companies **Driade, Zanotta, Cassina, Bieffeplast,** and many other firms worked with Memphis designers. And a slew of new firms emerged, including the furniture manufacturer **Alias,** which commissioned Mario Botta's architectural chair sculptures and **Carlo Forcolini's** archaic-looking *Apocalypse Now* table and lamp. Early in the 1980s Alessi hired **Alessandro Mendini** (who rarely worked for Memphis but remained committed to **Alchimia)** to develop the *Tea and Coffee Piazza* project, for which contemporary architects designed small utilitarian objects, such as **Aldo Rossi's** *Conica,* an espresso

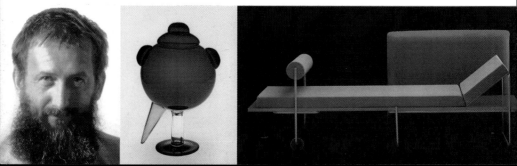

maker with distinct architectural elements. At the end of the decade, Alessi introduced a collection of playful products such as **Stefano Giovannoni's** *Merdolino* toilet brush, which is planted in a flower pot, and Alessandro Mendini's *Anna G.* corkscrew, shaped like a stolid woman who raises her arms each time a bottle is about to be uncorked. The emphasis in all these objects was on their communicative abilities, their humorous connotations, and their tendency to ironically reflect on recent design history. Without the liberating example of Memphis, this would not have been possible. Italy now was a hotbed of a diverse, open, playful design, which also had a strong impact in Germany, France, Spain, and England. **Nuovo Design**, as it came to be called, decisively shaped today's notion of "designer" objects. Formal eccentricities, once thought unacceptable, were increasingly identified with the very idea of design. And unlike the practitioners of the 1960s and 1970s—or even the early Memphis members—the new designers and firms, such as **Edra** or **Baleri,** worked with one eye firmly on the market.

Design's cult of personality, which made celebrities of people like Philippe Starck, developed during the 1980s. The distinction between less expensive "regular" products and pricier "designer items" was made more visible. And design became synonymous

"The eighties were an ecstatic era, obsessing about form and language. Today we are trying to overcome this fever by returning to things that make more sense."

Alberto Meda

From left:
Michele De Lucchi
Rigel glass object by
Marco Zanini for Memphis, 1982
Century daybed by Andrea Branzi
for Memphis, 1982
Riviera chair by Michele De Lucchi
for Memphis, 1981
Asoka lamp by Ettore Sottsass for
Memphis, 1983
D 7 lamp by P. Rizzatto and
S. Colbertaldo for Luceplan, 1981

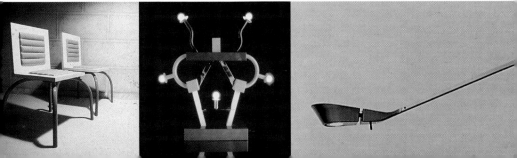

with "lifestyle," taking on a crucial role in any marketing strategy. It is not surprising that the same decade also gave birth to "signature" ad campaigns designed by high-profile agencies, and to an unprecedented emphasis on corporate image and identity. "Memphis is unusual," commented Michele De Lucchi, "because it gathered, concentrated and defined the essence of the eighties."

The boom in advertising also benefited Italian fashion. While designers like **Giorgio Armani** and **Gianni Versace** had gained a certain degree of fame in the 1970s (Armani through his "invention" of casual business attire), the media frenzy around fashion's stars and supermodels didn't fully set in until the 1980s. And as the decade drew to a close, a number of young designers had emerged to assert Italian influence on international fashion. **Romeo Gigli** counteracted the image of the power-suited business woman with visions of ethereal creatures in flowing robes made of velvet and lustrous golden fabrics. **Dolce & Gabbana** updated historic Italian peasant costumes into icons of early-nineties chic. The 1990s also saw the comeback of traditional fashion houses such as **Prada** and **Gucci** (which introduced new, luxurious designs by the American Tom Ford).

In product design, Memphis and Nuovo Design were largely confined to furniture and housewares. In the automotive industry, where high production costs demand a certain predictability of success, design followed other criteria. **Giorgetto Giugiaro** was representative of a new generation of car designers. Progressive and service-oriented, his focus was not on luxury models but, after the oil crises of the 1970s, on lower-priced compact and mid-sized cars. The stripped-down 1980 Fiat *Panda* and the 1983 Fiat *Uno* still displayed a distinctively Italian flair and were hugely popular with young, upwardly mobile Europeans, a testament to Giugiaro's subtle instinct for stylistic details and trends.

At the beginning of the 1990s, the cult of the spectacular designer object had exhausted itself, and gave way to a countermovement. With their raw, black chairs, the **Zeus** group, founded in 1984, explicitly dissociated itself from Memphis. "If the Memphis object is an affirmation of the transitory, the luxurious, the superficial, a costly and amoral object . . . the Zeus object is a modest, moral object with transcendental tendencies. As such, it reaffirms an absolute quality," **Paolo Deganello** wrote. Zeus thus anticipated the gradual shift of values that characterized the economically troubled 1990s.

"Designers must have taste but also be able to break the rules we, as their industrial clients, confront them with."

Alberto Alessi

From left:
Apocalypse Now table by Carlo Forcolini for Alias, 1984
Steps container system by Cini Boeri for Estel, 1982, with Laura Griziotti
Artifici tables by Paolo Deganello for Cassina, 1985
Studio set for TV show, *Obladì Obladà*, by Massimo Iosa Ghini, 1985
Tatlin sofa by Roberto Semprini and Mario Cananzi for Edra, 1989
Alberto Meda

Design lost some of its bluster in the nineties. After pieces like Philippe Starck's *Juicy Salif* lemon squeezer for Alessi and **Capellini's** flamboyant "auteur" furniture had successfully flaunted their "anything goes" attitude, many manufacturers, including **B&B Italia** and Cassina, returned to a more classically elegant approach. In 1995, the renowned avant-garde company Driade tried to reach out to a young generation of sophisticated "nomads" with its *Atlantide* collection, a line of blond wood furniture created by younger designers such as **Marco Romanelli,** Konstantin Grcic, and **Rodolfo Dordoni.** The lighting manufacturer **Luceplan,** founded in the late 1970s, experienced its greatest sales since the late eighties when it focused on transparent, minimal designs.

But while its aesthetics seemed out of favor, another trend associated with Memphis has prevailed: Italian firms have increasingly cooperated with international designers. Capellini, always a trendsetter, produces furniture by the British designers Jasper Morrison and James Irvine; Driade's catalogue features designs by Konstantin Grcic, a German, and Philippe Starck, a Frenchman; **Moroso** markets designs by the Spaniard Javier

1992 **Brionvega** liquidated; Assassination of Mafia prosecutors Falcone and Borsellino; beginning of *Mani Pulite* (clean hands) investigation into high-level corruption

1993 Fiat *Cinquecento*

1994 *Bookworm* bookshelf by Ron Arad; Silvio Berlusconi forms government, resigns the same year

1995 Opening of **Ferragamo** Museum in Florence; exhib. *Krizia. Una storia*, Milan

1996 *Fucsia* hanging lamp by **Achille Castiglioni** for **Flos**; Prodi govenment

1998 Opening of Archivio Storico **Olivetti** in Ivrea; Prodi loses parliamentary vote of confidence giving way to Italy's fifty-fifth postwar goverment

Mariscal; **Sawaya & Moroni** relies on the ideas and expertise of international architects; Ron Arad and Danny Lane have designed glass furniture for **Fiam**—and so on.

The work of today's young designers can no longer be characterized as specifically Italian. The famed **Linea Italiana** of the 1950s has made way for a Linea Internazionale, whose contours are much more difficult to make out. Innovation in design has moved to new arenas: the media, consumer services, and environmentally sensitive design. On the verge of the new millennium it is becoming harder to identify a country by its design; and Italy, in recent years, has not particularly distinguished itself compared to England or Scandinavia. So it is not too surprising that at the close of the 1990s, nostalgic reeditions are all the rage: Piaggio has revamped its old Vespa; Fiat has introduced yet another retread of the *Cinquecento;* and the Dutch Philips Corporation, under the direction of Italian designer **Stefano Marzano,** has produced a fifties-style collection of kitchen appliances. All these objects borrow their aura from design's great icons, so abundant in Italy's past.

"The first rule for every designer is to find the right client."

Massimo Morozzi

From left:
Merdolino toilet brush by Stefano Giovannoni for Alessi, 1994

Denis Santachiara

Angel Chair by Terri Pecora for Bieffe, 1990

Architectural model for ICE train station, Limburg, by Studio de Lucchi, 1997

Bellini Chair by Mario Bellini for Heller, 1998

Ducati *916 Biposto*, 1998

A bocca aperta mirror by Ugo La Pietra for Toppan Barbara, 1997

The Rediscovery of Beauty
Italian Design: La bella bionda

The long, wonderful period of Italy's economic boom, which lasted from the postwar years into the early 1970s, was pervaded by a pagan cult of beauty. A sense of freedom and optimism, economic success, and rising standards of living characterized this time whose aesthetic spirit can be aptly expressed by the image of a beautiful young woman.

Italian design was the era's golden-haired girl everyone was happy to see and be seen with—a radiant symbol of privilege and taste and, above all, beauty. For beauty was considered the ultimate goal of formal expression as well as a sure means of success.

The period before the Second World War was monotonous and creatively barren. After the conflict ended, Italians wanted to break with that, and to get away from the misery of the war—ideal conditions for the beginning of a time that favored everything new and applauded those who could design it. People literally and figuratively wanted to rebuild their home, to furnish it in a completely modern spirit tied to no tradition. And they eagerly followed the aesthetic criteria given by the blonde, blue-eyed girl.

There was color, lots of color: red, yellow, blue, green, purple, in a patchwork expression of existential bliss. And there were rich new forms inspired by the smooth lines of the human body. The form of the automobile was plastically reshaped; and plastic shaped a whole new world of forms. A tremendous number of new developments in transportation, aeronautics, graphic design, and material technology were promptly absorbed and transformed into objects, which were often minor masterpieces.

Design, the blonde, blue-eyed girl that had taken us by the hand, was growing up, and in the 1960s became interested in new technologies and the opportunities offered by a rapidly expanding market. The results were more sophisticated, a bit bourgeois, perhaps a bit boring. But our lively blonde rediscovered art, and pop culture began its joyful and massive invasion of Italian design. It was a restless, intense time. The blonde got caught up in its struggles and at the end of the decade discovered the first wrinkles in her face. But she did escape the ever-present danger of becoming trapped in a past no one is interested in anymore.

At the Milan *Triennale* of 1968, she asserted herself by shifting her focus from design to the politics of design and its "sociocultural implications," in the parlance of the time. Then, in the 1970s, an economic crisis temporarily cut off the financing for the development of her ideas. Toward the end of that decade, Mendini, Sottsass, and friends began to revitalize Italian design with their projects for Alchimia. And by creating Memphis in 1981, Sottsass and friends made sure that the blonde, now a mature lady, remained as alluring as ever.

The eighties also introduced the idea of "Italian Design" as a style and historical period. An archaeological hunt for design products of the previous decades turned up a wealth of objects that had been gathering dust in factories, workshops, showrooms, basements, and warehouses. In the process, numerous prototypes were discovered, single pieces that had been designed for presentations at the Salone di Mobile in Milan or the Eurodomus fairs in Milan, Turin, and Genoa. Discontinued products that had failed on the market were unearthed and in many cases turned out to be authentic avant-garde objects. Names of forgotten designers reappeared along with abandoned materials (such as burnt enamel) and objects that couldn't easily be classified as either art or utilitarian artifact. There were lamps with mysterious halogen bulbs or equally mysterious remote controls, and there were large sculptures made of foamed polyurethane and dyed a fluorescent green or red: a cactus, a mouth, a brick, a piece of turf.

This eclectic collection was finally presented to the public by the Wolfgang Ketterer Gallery in Munich. A catalogue itemized each piece and its asking price. At the auction that followed the lots were sold in a manner previously reserved for collections of fine art. Products made of foam rubber, plastic, or chrome were suddenly treated as valuable collector's pieces. Five thousand copies of the catalogue, *Italienisches Design* 1951–1984, were printed and immediately sold out. The auction was organized by Steven Cristea, the former director of Sotheby's Munich branch, and the bidders included numerous international museums, galleries, and collectors.

The auction took place on March 24, 1984, and attracted extensive media coverage in Germany and around the world; Italian design again appeared like a sleeping beauty kissed awake by a prince. The event marked the rediscovery of a limpid beauty achieved through a combination of experimentation, creative power, color, material, and ambition. Of course, it was also an opportunity for manufacturers to take a second look at their old products and, if possible, reintroduce them. This has created some confusion on the market. It often appears unclear whether products are new or reproductions, historic pieces or contemporary contributions—which, on second thought, may simply be an argument for the agelessness of Italian design.

Fulvio Ferrari

Argine chair by
Studio Libidarch for
Gruppo Ind. Busnelli, 1974

Page 87
Capitello chair
by Studio 65
for Gufram, 1972

Directory

From Abet Laminati to Zeus

ABET LAMINATI

Laminate manufacturer

In the 1960s and 1970s, Abet Laminati had worked with **Gio Ponti, Joe Colombo,** and **De Pas/D'Urbino/Lomazzi** in the development of innovative laminates like *Print, HPL Print,* and *Folden.* But the laminate manufacturer's real breakthrough didn't come until the early 1980s. The design groups **Alchimia** and **Memphis** had sparked a renewed interest in surfaces, and designers like **Ettore Sottsass** and **Michele De Lucchi** were creating such eye-straining patterns as *Bacterio, Spugnato, Fantastic,* and *Micidial* for the company. By using these laminates in spectacular furniture designs such as the *Carlton* shelf (fig. p. 12), they lent cachet to a material often dismissed as cheap and ugly. Abet caused a sensation a few years later, when it introduced the first translucent laminate, *Diafos.* The 1988 exhibition *Material Light* showcased Diafos's properties with applications designed by Sottsass, De Lucchi, James Irvine, **Antonio Citterio, Massimo Iosa Ghini,** and others. Today, Abet's laminates are used in furniture and trade show construction and in the design of building facades.

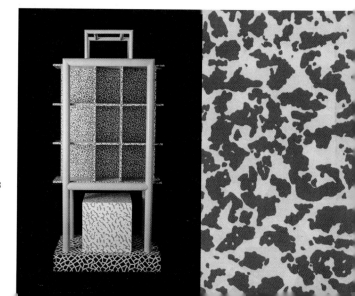

Regal *Union* by Marco Zanini, 1983
Laminat *Spugnato*
by Ettore Sottsass, 1979

Franco ALBINI

Architect and furniture designer

Franco Albini was already a well-known architect when a young **Anna Castelli Ferrieri** joined his Milan studio in 1942. Her first assignment was to draw his famous hanging shelves. The next day, she found a note on her desk, in which Albini instructed her to put the rulers in a tidy row and precisely align the triangles each night before leaving work. He demanded perfection.

Albini's minimalist, spare designs were far ahead of their time, which preferred a heavy, more stately look. His shelves of the 1940s—metal or wood-framed glass shelves suspended from metal chains—had reinvented a familiar product, giving it the dual functions of storage unit and room divider. Even before the war, he had presented a prototype for a transparent radio, whose components were housed between two rectangular panes of glass. (The radio never went into production.)

Alessandro Mendini once described Albini as "the greatest master of modern Italian architecture." And though architecture was his primary field, he was also one of the early heroes of

1905 born in Robbiate, Como

1929 graduates from
architecture school
in Milan

1930 opens architectural office

1945 publisher of *Casabella*
(until 1946)

1949 professor of architecture,
Venice and Turin (until 1963)

1950 renovation of *Palazzo
Bianco* and Museum
in Genoa
(with Franca Helg)

1952 works with **Franca Helg**;
*Museo del Tesoro di San
Lorenzo*, Genoa

1955 *Compasso d'oro*
(again in 1964)

1957 **La Rinascente** department
store, Rome (compl. 1961)

1958 *Premio Olivetti*
architecture prize

1962 works with **Antonio Piva**

1964 professor of architectural-
composition, Milan
Polytechnic (until 1977)

1965 works with **Marco Albini**

1977 dies in Milan

Luisa chair for Poggi, 1954

modern Italian design. His *Room for a Man,* shown at the 1936 **Triennale,** was a remarkably progressive object. It consisted of a tiny room in which each element had clear but multiple functions—a shelving unit featured a built-in desk; a ladder leading up to the bed also served as a coat rack; the bed provided the room's ceiling.

After the end of World War II, Albini's deep involvement in discussions about the social tasks of architecture and design was reflected in his various commitments as publisher of the journal *Casabella,* member of the Congresso Internazionale di Architettura Moderna (CIAM), and professor of architecture. But he also continued to work on architectural projects and furniture designs, applying the ideas he had formulated before the war under the influence of Modernism. The Luisa chair for **Poggi** (a company specializing in wood furniture, whose postwar production was largely designed by Albini), the *Margherita* wicker chair for **Bonacina,** and the *Fiorenza* chair for **Arflex** confirmed Albini's reputation as a master of restrained, but never bloodless, forms, who found ingenious solutions in the most diverse materials. One of his most complex projects still provides guidance to visitors of Milan— in the early sixties, together with his partner **Franca Helg** and the graphic artist **Bob Noorda,** he designed the subway stations and developed the signage system for Milan's Number 1 line.

ALCHIMIA

Gallery and design group

Page 93

top: *Ondoso* table by
Alessandro Mendini, 1979

left:. *Le strutture tremano* table
by Ettore Sottsass, 1979

right: single piece for *Robot
Sentimentale*, exhib. by
Alessandro Mendini, 1982

In 1976, **Alessandro Guerriero** invited a group of designers, including **Alessandro Mendini, Andrea Branzi, Ettore Sottsass, Michele Lucchi, Franco Raggi, and Paola Navone,** to create experimental designs for an exhibition in his Milan gallery. Freed from the constraints of industrial production processes, the designers used vernacular materials such as laminates, combining supposedly incompatible styles in various appropriations of design classics and in their own, wildly unconventional creations (fig. p. 14). "There is no more originality, declared Alchimia's chief theorist, Alessandro Mendini. Invention of forms has been supplanted by variations on decors, patterns, and surfaces— design as re-design. Designing is decorating." His manifesto challenged the doctrine of functionalism and, along with it, the dominance of Italian **Bel Design.**

In the exhibitions *Bau.Haus I* and *Bau.Haus II,* held in Milan in 1979 and 1980, respectively, Alchimia designers ironically commented on classic Bauhaus and period furniture by covering them with colorful laminates and quotes culled from the fine arts. For their *mobile infinito* (infinite furniture), presented during the 1981 Milan furniture fair, they asked prominent designers, architects, and artists, including Sandro Chia and Francesco Clemente, to design decorations, handles, lamps, and banners that could be applied to blank wooden objects. An almost infinite pool of patterns was provided for the object's surfaces; everyone could put together his or her own mobile. While such events did not gain Alchimia much of a clientele, the group was an important catalyst of **Nuovo Design** and a precursor of the much more commercially successful **Memphis** movement.

ALESSI

Housewares manufacturer

Alessi spa, Crusinallo

1921 founded by
Giovanni Alessi Anghini
as a foundry and metal
workshop

1924 first collection and
brand name, FAO
(Fratelli Omegna Alessi)

1932 Carlo Alessi joins the firm

1938 experiments with steel

1983 product line, *Officina
Alessi*, introduced

1986 collaboration with
Philippe Starck

1987 *Compasso d'oro*

1988 Casa della felicità
(designed by
Alessandro Mendini)
built on Lake Orta

1989 *Twergi* collection

1990 opening of *Centro Studi
Alessi* in Milan

1991 *Family follows
Fiction* collection

Page 95
Bird Kettle 9093 by
Michael Graves, 1985

Nuovo Milano silverware set
by Ettore Sottsass, 1989

Juicy Salif lemon juicer by Philippe
Starck, 1990

To the countless owners of the firm's housewares, the name Alessi is permanently wedded to the idea of design. In the 1980s, its association with illustrious designers, its sleek shiny products, and their playful takes on form, function, and color made Alessi the design company. The firm's design approach is neatly epitomized in Philippe Starck's famous *Juicy Salif* lemon juicer of 1990: everyone knows it, many own it, but no one uses it. A striking but barely functional "designer object," it is more commonly displayed as a status symbol.

In Alessi products, form follows not only function but also the designer's fancy, which has found expression in pieces like **Guido Venturini's** bulbous *Firebird* gas stove lighter, **Philippe Starck's** oblique *Hot Bertaa* tea kettle, the warbling little bird on **Richard Sapper's** kettle, and **Alessandro Mendini's** *Anna G.* corkscrew (fig. p. 44), modeled after the designer's companion. The path to this "anything goes" approach was paved in the early 1980s by groups like **Alchimia** and **Memphis**, whose products defied design's subservience to function. Alessi systematically applied this new design philosophy to mass-produced housewares.

But design is not just an effective marketing tool for Alessi; the firm been integrating innovative design into its products from its beginnings in the 1920s, when the firm's founder, Giovanni Alessi Anghini, designed coffee pots and trays in his metalshop. Since then, designers have always found ideal conditions to freely explore new ideas and forms at Alessi. In 1945, Carlo Alessi introduced his famous *Bombé* coffee set, and in the 1950s the firm produced its classic stainless-steel fruit bowls and breadbaskets. In the seventies, Alberto Alessi established relationships with Richard Sapper, **Ettore Sottsass,**

Achille Castiglioni, and Alessandro Mendini, who became the principal authors of today's Alessi design. At the beginning of the next decade, Mendini invited a group of international architects, including **Aldo Rossi,** Michael Graves, and **Paolo Portoghesi,** to design tea and coffee sets. With its collection of "miniature architectures," the project, known as *Tea and Coffee Piazza,* was an instant success, and led Alessi to split its production into separate divisions. While the mass production of stainless-steel housewares continues under the **Alessi** label (with espresso makers by Rossi and Sapper, pots by Massimo Morozzi, and silverware by Sottsass and Castiglioni), the new division, *Officina Alessi,* focuses on limited-edition products in various metals. Housewares made of turned wood have been marketed under t he *Twergi* label since 1989, and the *Family Follows Fiction* collection, introduced in 1991, comprises Alessi's colorful home accessories.

Products

1945 *Bombé* coffee set *by*
Carlo Alessi Anghini

1951 *826* wire basket

1952 *370* fruit basket
both by Ufficio
Tecnico Alessi

1970 *7690 Spirale* ashtray by
Achille Castiglioni

1978 *5070-5079* oil and vinegar
set by **Ettore Sottsass**

1984 *La conica* espresso maker

1988 *La Cupola* espresso maker
both by **Aldo Rossi**

1990 *Juicy Salif* lemon
juicer by **Philippe Starck**

1994 *Anna G.* corkscrew by
Alessandro Mendini

1997 *Cobán*
espresso maker by
Richard Sapper

Firebird gas lighter by
Guido Venturini, 1993

Page 97
top: *9091* teakettle by
Richard Sapper, 1983
left: *Pasta Set*
by Massimo Morozzi, 1986
right: *Il conico* series by
Aldo Rossi, 1989

ALFA ROMEO

Automobile manufacturer

Alfa Romeo
(now Fiat Auto spa), Turin

1910 founded as *Società Anonima Lombarda Fabbrica Automobili* (ALFA) in Portello near Milan

1915 Nicola Romeo joins the firm

1932 new organizational structure

1938 factory in Pomigliano d'Arco (Naples)

1963 Factory in Arese

1967 Construction of *Alfasud* factory

1987 acquired by **Fiat**

Page 99

top: *Giulietta Sprint* by Bertone, 1954

bottom: *1750 GT Veloce*, 1967

below left: *Montreal Coupé* by Bertone, 1967

below right: *Giulia 1600 T.I.*, 1962

According to company legend, Henry Ford once said that every time he saw an Alfa Romeo, he tipped his hat.

Alfa Romeo was founded in 1910, Italy's only major automobile manufacturer based in Milan rather than Turin. Initially, the Anonima Lombarda Fabbrica Automobili manufactured primarily utility vehicles and aircraft engines and compressors for the defense industry, which became an important client during the First and Second World Wars. But even in its earliest years, Alfa Romeo triumphed in the racing arena. Its *24 HP* racing model won the 1911 *Targa Florio*, establishing a precedent for the Alfa *RL's* great successes of the 1920s and the countless victories that followed.

For many years, the construction of racing engines drove Alfa's entire automobile output. Starting in the 1930s, though, the company hired renowned car-body makers to translate speed and power into more satisfying outer forms. For the 1937 *8 C 2900* B sports roadster, **Touring** created a body that seemed to have been poured into place; **PininFarina's** aerodynamic design for the *6 C 2300 Pescare Coupé* of 1936 displayed the car's power in aggressively swelling fenders and low-mounted headlights. With the end of the Second World War and Italy's rise to prosperity, Alfa Romeo gradually shifted into large-scale production. The elegant *Giulietta* series of the mid-1950s, for which both Bertone and Pinin Farina designed body variants, marked Alfa Romeo's successful breakthrough to a broader

Products

1910 *24HP* touring car

1927 *Typ RL* racing car

1937 *8 C 2900 B* roadster
by Touring

1939 *6 C 2300 B* convertible
by Pininfarina

1954 *Giulietta Sprint* sportscar
by Bertone

1960 *Giulietta Sprint Speciale*
sportscar

1962 *2600* sedan

1963 *Giulia Sprint GT Coupé*

1966 *1600 Spider
Duetto* convertible;
Giulia 1300 t.i. sedan

1972 *Alfasud* sedan

1998 *Alfa 156* sedan

market. In the fifties and sixties, the company succeeded internationally with models such as the Spider *1600 Duetto* of 1966 and Pinin Farina's Spider 1750 of 1969, both of which have since attained cult status. One of the most Alfas was the 1972 *Alfasud,* for whose production a new plant was built.

In the early 1970s the company slipped into a lingering financial crisis that led to Alfa Romeo's acquisition by Fiat in the mid-1980s. Under its new owner, Alfa Romeo has continued to produce cars noted for their sporty performance and design, such as the sleek *164 Berlina* of 1987, with its narrow taillight section, and the wedge-shaped *ES 30* of 1989. More recently, the Alfa *156* was voted Germany's Car of the Year, not least because of its beautiful design.

Alfa *156*, 1998

Furniture company

Alias's very first product, **Giandomenica Belotti's** 1979 *Spaghetti* chair, which featured a rubber-string seat, became an instant bestseller. The young company went on to translate the new creative freedom of **Nuovo Design** into an eclectic product line that reflected its designers' different approaches. Belotti remained a purist, while Mario Botta went for sculptural effects in his *Prima, Seconda, Quarta,* and *Quinta* chairs, and **Alberto Meda** focused on technological innovation with his ultra-lightweight seating designs such as *Armframe* and *Highframe.* Other designers associated with Alias include **Carlo Forcolini, Paolo Rizzatto,** Jasper Morrison, Häberli & Marchand, and Riccardo Blumer. The simple, transparent pieces are fabricated by selected manufacturers; Alias concentrates on development, marketing, and distribution. In 1991, the company became part of the **Artemide** group; since 1994 it has been distributing the **Danese** collection of housewares.

Alias srl,
Grumello del Monte
1979 founded by
**Giandomenico Belotti,
Carlo Forcolini** and
Enrico Baleri;
1991 Alias becomes part of
the **Artemide** group
1994 Alias takes over
Danese

Products
1979 *Bloomstick* series
by **Vico Magistretti**
1984 *Apocalypse Now* table
by **Carlo Forcolini**
1986 *Quinta* chair, *Tesi* table
by Mario Botta
1987 *Light Light* chair
by **Alberto Meda**
1994 *Longframe* chaise
and *Highframe* chair
by Alberto Meda;
Alpha bookcase by
Jasper Morrison
1997 *Sec* furniture system
by Häberli / Marchand;
Laleggera chair by
Riccardo Blumer

left: *Spaghetti* chair
by Giandomenico Belotti, 1979
right: *Seconda* chair by Mario
Botta, 1982

ARCHIZOOM

Design and architecture group

A sterile, air-conditioned, artificially lit, shopping-mall city determined only by the cycle of selling and buying—from today's perspective, the pessimistic science-fiction tableau Archizoom developed in the *No-Stop-City* project of 1970 seems rather prescient.

Founded in Florence in 1966 by the architects **Andrea Branzi, Paolo Deganello, Massimo Morozzi,** and Gilberto Coretti, Archizoom formulated its ideas in the context of the political protest and upheaval of the time. The young rebels, who had visited London, Branzi said," to see Carnaby Street and the grave of Karl Marx" took the work of the English architecture group Archigram as guiding inspiration. In manifestoes and contributions to exhibitions, they criticized design's blind faith in functionalism, its subservience to industrial interests, and its role as a status symbol. Most of their work consisted of drawings and texts, which were far better suited to their utopian concepts than concrete objects—a tendency characteristic of the entire **Radical Design** movement. Nonetheless, they realized a number of ideas, such as the *Mies* chair (fig. p. 35), which exaggerated the constructive elements of one of Mies van der Rohe's famous chairs to a degree that it looked unusable (though it really was not—one could comfortably sink into its steeply angled seat). And in their pompous *Dream Beds,* Archizoom used kitschy elements from Art Deco and Pop Art to undercut **Bel Design's** purist aesthetics: bad taste became part of their strategy. Archizoom dissolved in 1974, but the group's ideas, stripped of their explicitly political agenda, continued to be influential in the **Anti-Design** movement led by **Alchimia** and **Memphis.**

ARFLEX

Furniture manufacturer

Arflex International spa
(now Gruppo Seven
Italia), Giussano (MI)

1950 founded by **Pirelli**
managers Aldo Bai,
Pio Reggiani, Aldo Barassi

1994 Arflex becomes part of
Gruppo Seven

Products

1951 *Lady* chair by
Marco Zanuso

1952 *Fiorenza* chair by
Franco Albini

1954 *Elettra* bench and chair by
BBPR; *Martingala* chair
and *Sleep-o-matic* sofa
by Marco Zanuso

1959 *Airone* chair by
Alberto Rosselli

1964 *Fourline* chair by
Marco Zanuso

1971 *Serpentone* seating
system by **Cini Boeri**

1985 *Felix* chair and sofas by
Burkhard Vogtherr

1996 *Calea* chair by
Prospero Rasulo

Page 105

top left: *Bobo* by Cini Boeri, 1967

top right: *Lady* by Marco Zanuso,
1951

bottom: *Delfino* by Erberto Carboni,
1954

At the 1996 Cologne furniture fair, Arflex reintroduced its classic seating from the 1950s and 1960s, including **Marco Zanuso's** *Lady,* **Cini Boeri's** *Bobo,* **Erberto Carboni's** *Delfino,* and **Franco Albini's** *Fiorenza.* But the event was not completely steeped in nostalgia; it's title was "*Modern Times.*" Arflex, after all, had been Italy's most modern furniture company since its founding in 1951.

Unlike most of its competitors, which were rooted in Italy's long crafts tradition, Arflex was a child of big industry. It was started after the tire manufacturer Pirelli had developed a new kind of foam rubber, named "gommapiuma", and was looking for ways to use it in furniture. The company approached the young architect Marco Zanuso for advice, and he gave "gommapiuma" shape in his *Lady* chair. Not only the material was new in this piece; Zanuso had also replaced the traditional metal inner frame with a system of elastic bands. At the 1951 *Triennale,* the chair was cut open to reveal its innovative innards. *Lady* won the show's gold medal and went on to become a ubiquitous presence in the world's living rooms and a symbol of the organic style of the fifties.

Founded on the strength of the chair's success, Arflex continued to experiment with new materials and develop products noted for their modern design. Over the years, it has worked with an expanding circle of designers, which has included, among others, Burkhard Vogtherr, Paola Nava, and Prospero Rasulo. Marco Zanuso created a number of other pieces for the company, including the Martingala, Antropus, and Woodline chairs, and the convertible Sleep-o-matic sofa. The polyurethane Bobo chaise, designed by Cini Boeri in the late 1960s, was the first piece of furniture to dispense entirely with an inner frame, and Boeri's Serpentone (fig. p. 30) became an icon of progressive chic in the seventies.

Giorgio ARMANI

Fashion designer

There is a scene in the 1980 movie *American Gigolo* where Richard Gere spreads out his jackets, shirts, and ties on a bed. Some critics commented that the clothes could claim acting credits, and in a sense they did: the cinematic gigolo's workwear had been created by Giorgio Armani, Milan's master of casual understatement.

A medical school dropout and former buyer for the **La Rinascente** department store, Armani, born in 1934 in Piacenza, did not always seem destined to be a star. Starting out as a designer for Cerruti before striking out on his own, he first came to attention with his 1974 line of menswear and, a year later, a collection for women. With his men's jackets, Armani rebelled against the dominant style, which he called "Maoist." He discarded the then-popular shoulder pads and used luxurious fabrics for a loose, easy, and elegant fit. Soon women, too, began wearing these innovative jackets, Armani's sister being one of the first. This inspired Armani to liberate women from their stiff business suits. He "invented" the loose-fitting ladies' blazer, which could be coordinated with a wide range of clothes to fit almost any occasion. Today, the Armani-style blazer is a fixture in many women's wardrobes.

If Armani has revolutionized fashion, he has done it in a gentle manner. He shuns all lurid effects. His haute couture designs suggest, rather than reveal, the body's forms. His fashions are comfortable, their colors muted, their lines subtle, and their fabrics of exquisite quality. Armani's name stands for cool, sophisticated elegance aloof from shock and scandal.

ARTELUCE

Lighting manufacturer

When the high society of the 1950s took their after-dinner promenades on the luxury liners *Michelangelo* and *Raffaelo,* the decks were illuminated by Arteluce lights. The ballrooms of the Castello Sforzesco and the Palazzo Bianco in Genoa, the airports of Rome and Milan, the **Olivetti** building in Barcelona, even ordinary offices and schools used the firm's lighting. For private homes, the firm produced imaginative sconces, sculptural mobiles such as the models *2072* and *2097,* small table lamps in the typical fifties look, and also functional floor lamps.

The company was founded in 1939 by **Gino Sarfatti,** who designed almost all the early Arteluce products. An inexhaustible pioneer of lighting design, he developed the proper illumination for much of Italy's Modernist postwar architecture. Obsessed with light and its possibilities, the former aeronautics engineer

focused all his energy on his company, taking charge of everything from design to marketing and distribution. He kept his distance from Milan's cultural establishment and used the company's store on the city's Corso Matteotti as a place to meet young designers such as **Marco Zanuso, Franco Albini, Vittoriano Vigano´** or **Gianfranco Frattini,** who shared his enthusiasm for modern industrial design. The many awards his products won mattered little to him.

When Sarfatti realized in the early 1970s that his company needed to be restructured to remain economically viable, he sold it to his competitor *Flos*. Since 1974 *Arteluce* has been an independent product line within Flos, presenting the work of a younger generation of international designers, including **Matteo Thun, King-Miranda, Rodolfo Dordoni,** and Stephan Copeland. Many of Sarfatti's designs are also still being produced.

Products
1952 *187* wall lamps
1954 *1063* and *1064* floor lamps
1957 model *2097*
        all by Gino Sarfatti
1977 *Jill* lamp by **Perry A. King**
        and **Santiago Miranda**
1979 *Ring* desk lamp by
        Bruno Gecchelin
1989 *Tango* table lamp
        by Stephan Copeland
1991 *Corolle* floor lamp
        by Ezio Dodone;
        Pao floor lamp
        by **Matteo Thun**

From left
2133 lamp by Gino Sarfatti, 1976
Pao lamp by Matteo Thun, 1993
600 lamp by Gino Sarfatti, 1966
Low-voltage halogen table lamp,
model 607, by Gino Sarfatti,
1969/1971

ARTEMIDE

Lighting manufacturer

Artemide's catalogue reads like a list of design classics: **Vico Magistretti's** 1965 *Eclisse* lamp, with its pivoted reflector; **Richard Sapper's** perfectly balanced *Tizio* desk lamp of 1972; **Ettore Sottsass's** 1983 *Pausiana;* and **Michele De Lucchi** and Giancarlo Fassina's 1987 *Tolomeo* desk lamp (what architecture studio or ad agency doesn't have it?).

In the 1960s the company produced plastic furniture and accessories, including Magistretti's *Selene* and **Sergio Mazza's** *Toga* chairs (fig. p. 7). But before long, the company's energetic founder, **Ernesto Gismondi,** concentrated exclusively on lights. In addition to developing his own designs, which include the *Tebe, Utopia,* and *Aton* lamps, he has worked with **Carlo Forcolini, Rodolfo Dordoni, Gianfranco Frattini, Angelo Mangiarotti,** Hannes Wettstein and other well-known designers. Commercial lighting and a playful collection of Murano glass complement the product line. In recent years Gismondi, who sponsored the **Memphis** group in the early 1980s, has turned his company into a small design conglomerate by acquiring two related companies, **Alias** and Megalit.

Artemide spa,
Milan

1959 founded by
Ernesto Gismondi

1995 *Compasso d'oro*

1997 *European Design Prize*

Products

1969 *Selene* plastic chair by
Vico Magistretti

1972 *Tizio* desk lamp by
Richard Sapper

1979 *Tholos* desk and wall lamp
by Ernesto Gismondi

1985 *Icaro* wall lamp by
Carlo Forcolini

1992 *Orione* table lamp by
Rodolfo Dordoni

Dedolo umbrella stand by
Emma Schweinberger-
Gismondi, 1966

Page 111

top left: *Boalum* light tube by
Livio Castiglioni and
Gianfranco Frattini, 1969

top right: *Eclisse* lamp by
Vico Magistretti, 1965

bottom left: *Echos* floor lamp by
Jan van Lierde, 1998

bottom right: *Tolomeo* desk lamp by
Michele De Lucchi
and Giancarlo Fassina, 1987

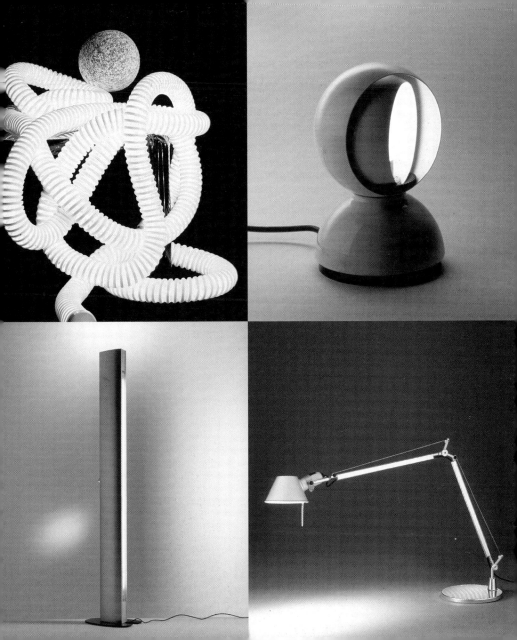

Sergio ASTI

Architect, furniture and product designer

Sergio Asti first made his mark as a designer in the mid-1950s with objects that perfectly embodied the **Linea italiana's** famous combination of organic forms and functional design. With its sleek, streamlined shape, his soda dispenser for Saccab is a perfect example of **Bel Design**. While thoroughly modern, Asti's designs were also informed by a sense of tradition, which is reflected in his preference for "old" materials such as glass, ceramics, and marble. When the **Neo-Liberty** movement emerged in northern Italy toward the end of the 1950s, Asti contributed to the rediscovery of pre-Modernist forms and traditions with pieces like his graciously curved wooden *Bertoli* table and his sculptural *Marco* vase for Salviati. Today, Asti designs furniture and exhibitions but is primarily known for elegant smaller objects, such as his bulbous *Daruma* table lamps made of hand-blown glass, and the *Profiterolle* line of silverware, vases, dishes, and faucets.

1926 born in Milan
1953 architectural office in Milan
1957 Gold medal at IX. *Triennale*
1962 *Compasso d'oro*

Products
1961 *Marco* glass vase for Salviati
1968 *Daruma* lamp for Candle
1969 *Navy* folding chair
1972 *Dada* tableware for Ceramica Revelli
1991 *Alice's* table for **Up&Up**

Soda dispenser for Saccab, 1956
Kilimandjaro table lamp for Raak Amsterdam, 1976

Antonia ASTORI

Furniture and exhibition designer

Antonia Astori, or the Search for the Perfect System: this could be the title for a book on the Milan designer, who throughout all the stylistic changes of the past thirty years has continuously come up with new systematic solutions. *Oikos,* developed in 1972 for her own company, **Driade,** uses a plain cube as the basic element of a complex architectural concept for the design of living rooms, workspaces, bedrooms, baths and kitchens. Nearly three decades later, *Oikos* stands as a classic of its genre on the strength of its clear geometry, high formal precision, and minimalist elegance. Among Astori's other successful furniture systems are *Kaos* from the 1980s and *Pantos,* introduced in 1993. She also designed numerous individual pieces of furniture for Driade and helped create the company's visual identity and graphics program. In addition, she has worked for international companies as a designer of trade show presentations, offices, and exhibitions.

1942 born in Melzo (Milan)

1968 cofounder of
Driade

1981 *Compasso d'oro* for
Driade identity and
marketing design

Products

1968 *Driade 1* system

1972 *Oikos I* system

1977 Bric system
with **Enzo Mari**

1980 *Oikos* II system

1986 *Kaos* system

1993 *Pantos* system
all for Driade

Elements from *Driade I* system,
1968

Gae AULENTI

Architect, furniture and lighting designer

As part of her project to design **Olivetti's** Paris office in the 1960s, Gae Aulenti created the flower-shaped *Pipistrello* lamp, which later went into commercial production. Indeed, most of her furniture and lighting designs developed out of larger architectural commissions. In the 1980s, when hired to transform the Gare d'Orsay in Paris into a museum and the Musée d'Art Moderne into the Centre Georges Pompidou, she not only reconceived the buildings' interior architecture but also designed display cases, lights, and all the other objects necessary to achieve "a complete harmony of all elements," as she describes it. Gae Aulenti had gotten her start as a furniture designer in the late 1950s in the context of the **Neo-Liberty** movement. With her *Sgarsul* (1962) for **Poltronova** she interpreted the quaint rocking chair as a nimble modern object.

Emphasizing the structure of her pieces, Aulenti achieved an elegant look, which in the 1960s and 1970s contributed to the international fame of Italian **Bel Design.** Among her memorable designs are the *April* folding chair (1972); the *Gaetano* glass table for **Zanotta** (1973); the crystal tables for **Fontana Arte** (1980, 1982, 1993) and the *3 Più* series of lights for Stilnovo. But her strongest impact was on architecture, with showroom designs for **Fiat** and Olivetti, the interior architecture for the Palazzo Grasso in Venice and the Catalan Museum in Barcelona, and a number of stage designs. Her writings have also been seminal in Italian architectural theory.

B & B ITALIA

Furniture manufacturer

An odd object made its appearance in furniture showrooms toward the end of the 1960s. When its tight wrapping was opened, an amorphous foam rubber blob popped out and expanded, as if by magic, into a rounded form. As unconventional as it appeared, **Gaetano Pesce's** *Up* chair series was the result of intensive research in the laboratories of C & B Italia. Founded in 1966 by Cesare Cassina and Piero Busnelli, the young company's furniture made of cold-foamed polyurethane quickly made it a trendsetter, and in 1968 it established a large research center headed by **Francesco Binfaré.** An illustrious group of graphic designers, including Enrico Trabacchi, **Bob Noorda,** Roberto Svegliado, **Pierluigi Cerri,** and **Oliviero Toscani** worked on B & B's strikingly clean-looking corporate identity. The company's name had changed to B & B Italia when Cassina left the company in 1973, but its approach has not, continuing to emphasize experimentation in design and innovative materials, if perhaps in slightly less flamboyant style. Among the company's current designers are **Afra** and **Tobia Scarpa, Antonio Citterio, Paolo Nava, Mario Bellini,** and **Vico Magistretti.** B & B Italia produces about 80 percent of the polyurethane seating sold globally, but also uses rattan, wood, and fiberglass in its products.

B&B Italia spa, Novedrate

1966 founded by
Cesare Cassina and
Piero Busnelli as
C&B Italia

1968 establishment of
reasearch and
development center

1973 Cesare **Cassina** leaves
company; renamed
B&B Italia

Products

1966 *Amanta* chair
by **Mario Bellini**

1969 *Up* seat by
Gaetano Pesce

1974 *Tema, Quartetto,
Sestetto, Coda* tables
by **Vico Magistretti**

1980 *Sity* sofa by
Antonio Citterio

1985 *Artona* chair by **Afra**
and **Tobia Scarpa**

Diesis sofa by Antonio Citterio
and Paolo Nava, 1980

Page 117
top *Alanda* table, 1982
bottom left: *Arcadia* chair, 1985
both by Paolo Piva
bottom right: *Le Bambole* chair
by Mario Bellini, 1972

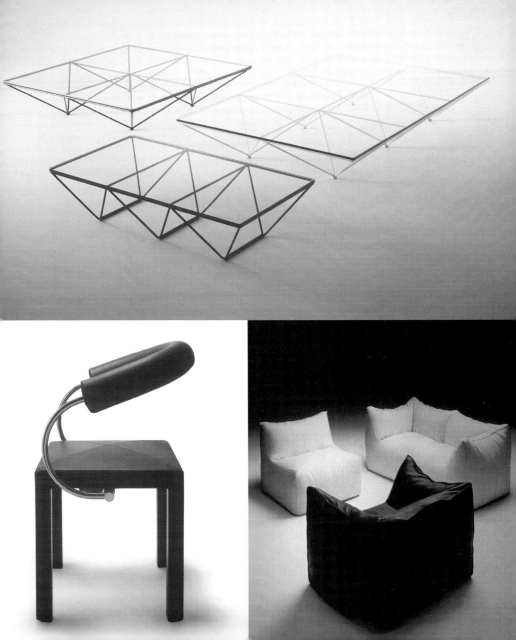

BALERI ITALIA

Furniture manufacturer

Baleri Italia was founded by **Enrico Baleri** and Marilisa Baleri Decimo in 1984 during a period of profound changes in the Milan design scene brought about by the rise of **Nuovo Design.** Enrico Baleri was already known as a trendsetter; he had been one of the founders of the cutting-edge furniture company **Alias** in 1979, and had also created pieces for **Gavina, Flos,** and Knoll. Some of his designs for Baleri Italia are committed to the kind of free experimentation evident in his minimalist, egg-shaped *Tato* chair, designed with **Denis Santachiara.** Others make reference to the Modernist heritage; with its austere lines, his *Molly* sofa is clearly in the tradition of Le Corbusier and Mies van der Rohe, while adapted to today's living environments.

The overall look of the company's furniture is not specifically Italian but reflects Baleri's international approach. Along with Italians like **Riccardo Dalisi, Angelo Mangiarotti,** and **Alessandro Mendini,** the Frenchman Philippe Starck, the Austrian Hans Hollein, and the Swiss Hannes Wettstein have all contributed pieces to the Baleri collection, which, while showing each designer's individual sensibility, generally maintains a purist line. In 1994 Baleri and Baleri Decimo founded a second company, the lighting manufacturer Gloria.

Baleri Italia Spa, Lallio (Bergamo)

1984 founded by **Enrico Baleri** and Marilisa Baleri Decimo

1994 Enrico Baleri and Marilisa Baleri Decimo found lighting company Gloria

Products

1985 *Richard III* chair by Philippe Starck

1986 *Bristol* sofa by Enrico Baleri

1994 *Bill Club* sofa by Hannes Wettstein

1996 *Ypsilon* shelf unit by **Angelo Mangiarotti**

1997 *Tato*, *Tatino*, and *Tatone* seats by Enrico Baleri and **Denis Santachiara**

T-table by Angelo Mangiarotti, 1998

Page 119
left: *Ad Iovis* lamp by Angelo Mangiarotti für Gloria, 1998
top right:.*Mama* chair by Denis Santachiara, 1995
bottom right: *Mimì* chair by Enrico Baleri, 1991

BARILLA

Pasta manufacturer

Barilla is a leading manufacturer of Italy's most common mass-produced design product: pasta. Pasta-making is a classic example of product design, a craft rooted in centuries-old traditions. Farfalle, penne, linguini, and spaghetti are just four of the more than 300 different kinds of pasta, many of which are made by Barilla. The design of each type follows culinary criteria: how it feels in the mouth and how its shape makes it more or less suitable for different kinds of sauces or recipes.

It is in the field of marketing and communications, though, that Barilla has won several important design awards. In the 1920s and 1930s, its postcards and calendars, many of them designed by **Erberto Carboni,** were sought-after collector's items. After the war, Carboni continued to shape Barilla's public image. His 1952 campaign, with the slogan *Con Pasta Barilla è sempre domenica* (With Barilla pasta, it's always Sunday), became a classic of Italian advertising. Carboni created the company's oval, red and white logo, and used simple, modern graphics for advertisements and packaging: images of noodles, silverware, and pots silhouetted on a blue background (fig. p. 37). In the 1960s and 1970s, Barilla hired celebrities such as playwright Dario Fo, the popular singer Mina, and Richard Lester, director of the Beatles movies, for its popular *Carosello* series of TV commercials. During the 1980s, campaigns by TBWA and Young & Rubicam and TV spots by filmmakers such as David Lynch, Ridley Scott, and Nikita Michalkoff were equally successful. Paired with effective management, such well-conceived publicity efforts made Barilla (which today consists of some thirty companies) Europe's largest pasta producer.

Barilla G. e R. F.lli spa, Holding of Barilla Group, Parma

1877 Pietro Barilla makes pasta and breads

1910 pasta factory

1952 *Golden Palm* advertising award for **Erberto Carboni's** *Con Pasta Barilla è sempre domenica* campaign

1964 *C'è una gran cuoca in voi e Barilla la rivela* (A great chef lies asleep in you and Barilla awakes her)

1987 *Golden Lion* for TV commercial at Cannes International Advertising Festival

Page 121

top left: *Farfalla, Fusillo, Penna*

top right: Advertisement by Erberto Carboni, 1956

bottom left: *Multicoloured Totem,* trade fair display by Erberto Carboni, 1957

bottom right: Advertisement by Erberto Carboni, 1952

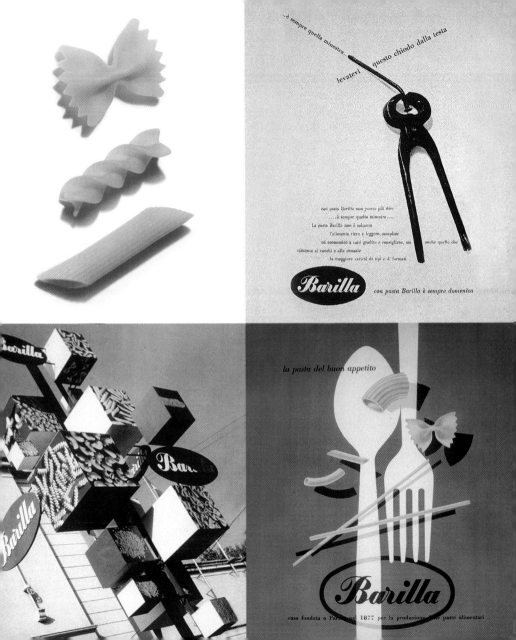

BBPR

Architecture and design studio

1932 founded in Milan by
Banfi, Belgiojoso,
Peressutti and Rogers

1936 development plan for
Aosta valley (compl. 1973);
interior design for
conference hall at VI.
Triennale

1946 memorial for victims of
German concentration
camps, Milan

1954 interior design for **Olivetti**
offices in New York

Products

1950 Electric clock for **Solari**

1954 *Urania* chair for **Arflex**

1955 TV set for CGE
Electric Co.

1960 *Arco* office furniture
system for Olivetti

One of the first commissions realized by BBPR after the Second World War was a monument to the victims of German concentration camps for Milan's Cimitero Monumentale. The history of the firm's principals made this a highly personal project: Gian Luigi Banfi, Lodovico Barbiano di Belgiojoso, Enrico Peressutti, and **Ernesto N. Rogers** had all fought in the anti-Fascist resistance movement; Banfi had died in a concentration camp. Their moral integrity and conviction that design and architecture had important social tasks to fulfill invested them with an authority that "made Italy's cultural world tremble," as **Alessandro Mendini** put it. Although the group developed numerous product designs (seating furniture for **Arflex**; *Spazio,* a flexible office furniture system for **Olivetti**; faucets for **Olivari**, and furniture for **Azucena**), their influence was strongest in architecture and theory. Rogers, who was editor-in-chief of *Domus* (1946–47, with **Marco Zanuso**) and *Casabella–continua* (1953–64), fought for the realization of the social ideas that had once informed Modern architecture and for the principle of "usefulness plus beauty."

Elettra side chair and club chair
for Arflex, 1954

Mario BELLINI

Architect, industrial and furniture designer

There is "a greater difference between a computer and a chair than there is between a chair and a cathedral," according to Mario Bellini. Machines have a short life span, due to continuous technological innovation, and their form always depends on the conditions of their use. Furniture, on the other hand, is tied to semantic values and integrated into the context of cultural traditions.

Throughout his career, however, Bellini has focused on both machines and furniture. The situation, which he feels can be "schizophrenic," has been a recurring theme in his theoretical writing, in general, and in his work as editor of *Domus* magazine (1986–91) in particular. In the field of "machine design," his work includes the *Totem* stereo system and the *Triangular TV* set for **Brionvega** in the 1960s, as well as the look and feel of numerous **Olivetti** products produced from the 1960s to the 1980s. For his *Divisumma 18* calculator of 1972 (fig. p. 16), the first pocket-sized device in a category hitherto full of clunky desktop boxes, he

1935 born in Milan

1959 graduates from architecture school in Milan; works at **La Rinascente's** design office (until 1961)

1962 architecture and design studio; *Compasso d'oro* (also in 1964, 1970, 1979, 1984)

1963 consultant for **Olivetti**

Cab chair for Cassina, 1977
Monitor 15 TV set for Brionvega, 1975

completely wrapped the sensitive inner works in a thin orange membrane. In addition to its practical function and the visual pleasure of its rounded shape, the *Divisumma* gave its user a tactile, vaguely erotic bonus in the softly yielding feel of its keys. Bellini also designed architectural, angular products like the *Logos* series of calculators and the *Lettera 92* typewriter for Olivetti, and the *TC 800* upright tape recorder for Yamaha.

Bellini applied the principle of wrapping to furniture as well. A leather cover was pulled over a skinny metal frame and then zipped tight for his famous 1978 *Cab* chair for **Cassina**. He designed numerous other pieces of furniture for Cassina and **B & B Italia**, including the sumptuously pliant *Le Bambole* chairs and the monumentally solid tables *Il Colonnato* and *La Basilica*.

Be it a calculator or a chair, Bellini rejects an overly functionalist doctrine: "Each design implies the possibility of other designs." In his products, clear function always goes hand in hand with emotional value. He is well aware of the cultural dimension of design and architecture, and he synthesizes both fields in an approach that aims at the design and reorganization of larger environments. His is a design with an architectural scope and vision—whether he develops office furniture for Vitra, cars for Renault, lights for **Artemide** and Erco, fountain pens, or espresso makers. In all of this, he has been undeniably successful: in 1987, Bellini was the first living designer since Charles Eames to be given a major retrospective at New York's Museum of Modern Art.

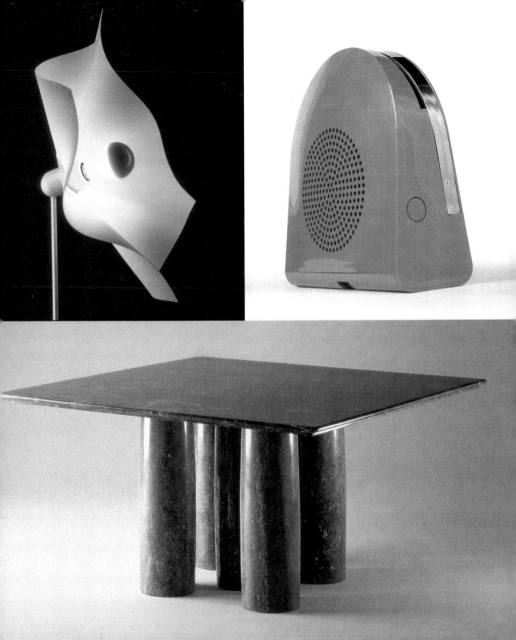

BENETTON

Clothing manufacturer

Benetton Group spa,
Ponzano (Treviso)

1966 founded by **Luciano Benetton** in Ponzano

1984 *All the Colors of the World* campaign

1990 *United Colors of Benetton* campaign

1992 *HIV Positive* campaign

1993 campaign with Bosnian soldier's blood-soaked t-shirt

1998 *Enemies* campaign

left: *Colors*, magazine cover, 1997
center, right: Advertisements, 1992

Images of racial discrimination, war, hunger, and AIDS are among the many prize-winning photos **Oliviero Toscani** has used in his advertising campaigns for Benetton since 1984. The one that won the most awards was a 1989 shot of a white baby suckling on a black woman's breast. Time and again, Toscani's campaigns have proved to be as controversial as the social issues they depict. On occasion, the company has even backed up its apparent commitment to social causes with actual activities: a few years ago, company owner Luciano Benetton distributed condoms in his stores; another time he appeared nude to collect clothes for needy people with the slogan, "Give Me Back My Clothes!" But the campaigns have also created remarkable publicity. It is questionable whether sweaters and sportswear alone would have made Benetton the corporate giant it is today; with annual sales of some 4.2 trillion lire, the Benetton group now owns well-known brands such as Rollerblade, Kästle, and Asolo, is active in Formula 1 racing, and in 1993 founded the **Fabrica** academy for thepromotion of art and design.

Furniture manufacturer

Bernini's history reaches back to 1904, when the company was founded as a cabinetmaking business in the Brianza region, then and now the center of Italy's furniture industry. The firm first made its mark in design in the 1960s with beautifully made, solid wood furniture, and through its elegant use of plastics and metal. The 1969 Maia desk, designed by **Giotto Stoppino**, has a double wooden top with compartments for writing materials in the back that can be concealed under a sliding cover. The desktop rests on a tubular steel frame, which is also used for the matching chairs.

Bernini's designs combine modern, sophisticated form with exquisite materials. Conceived as timeless, durable pieces, many of the company's table, chair, and bed designs have been in production for some thirty years. In the 1970s the firm proved its expertise in the manufacture of high-quality wood furniture when it produced a number of subtly elegant designs by the architect **Carlo Scarpa,** including the symmetrical Zibaldone

Bernini spa,
Carate Brianza

1904 founded as carpenter's workshop

1964 furniture with plastics

Products

1969 *Combicenter* by **Joe Colombo**

1971 *Quattro quarti 700* elements by **Rodolfo Bonetto**

Maia table and chairs by Giotto Stoppino, 1969

shelving unit. With its many intricately designed drawers, **Gianfranco Frattini's** 1981 *Practica* unit has an equally timeless, distinct beauty, coupled with a high degree of functionality and flexibility. The firm's successful designs of the 1990s include **Gaetano Pesce's** *543 Broadway* chair, which is made of transparent, iridescent plastic and has skinny legs ending in springs—giving the chair a somewhat shifty feeling under the weight of a body.

Designers who have worked for Bernini also include **Achille Castiglioni, Rodolfo Bonetto, Joe Colombo,** Toshiyuki Kita, **Paolo Nava, Ugo La Pietra,** and **Leila** and **Massimo Vignelli.**

Enzo BERTI

Artist and furniture designer

Enzo Berti's furniture for La Palma and Montina, and his kitchens for **Arc Linea** are purist designs. Born and educated as a fine artist in Venice, Berti pursues the "correct" synthesis of form and function. But his wood, leather, metal, and textile objects always contain an aesthetic punchline: instead of merely being "correct" they surprise us with disturbing details. Only a close look reveals the shimmering layer of sand under the glass top of Enzo Berti's *Dune* table, prompting a heightened appreciation of that "inferior" material's qualities. To the asymmetric edges of the modular *Zoom* shelving system, additional box elements can be attached, so that it can easily grow to any size. The wooden *Passepartout* chair subverts its own apparent simplicity with a geometric window in the backrest, which unexpectedly turns the chair into a minimalist sculpture.

1950 born in Venice
   studies at the Accademia delle Belle Arti di Venezia; studies industrial design in Venice

Products

1993 *Passepartout* chair for Montina;
   Nest chaise for Montina

1995 *Zoom* expandable shelf unit for La Palma;
   Dune metal table with glass and sand for La Palma

1996 *Cuba* stacking chair

1997 *Fenj* chair both for La Palma;
   Clubhouse furniture series for Montina

1998 *Up* folding chair for La Palma

Tables from *Club House* series for Montina, 1997

BERTONE

Car body designer

"If the car has a soul, the battle is almost won."

—Nuccio Bertone

Carozzeria Bertone spa,
Grugliasco (TO)

1912 Giovanni Bertone opens
workshop for car-body
parts

1934 his son, **Nuccio Bertone**
(1914–1997) joins the firm

Products

1921 **Fiat** *501* racing car
1954 **Alfa Romeo** *Giulietta Sprint*
1958 NSU *Prinz Coupé*
1961 Alfa Romeo *2600 Sprint*
1962 BMW *3200 CS*
1964 Fiat *850 Spider*
1966 **Lamborghini** *Miura*
1972 Fiat *X 1/9*;
Lamborghini *Countach*
1975 VW *Polo*
1982 Citroen *BX*
1985 Volvo *780 Coupé*
1994 Fiat *Punto Cabrio*
1999 BMW *C1* motorcycle

Along with his student **Giorgetto Giugiaro** and **Sergio Pininfarina, Nuccio Bertone,** who died in 1997, is one of the greats of Italian car design. He knew that the battles of the highly competitive automobile market are often decided by a car's impact on the emotions. So his primary goal was to overcome mediocrity, especially in sports cars. His **Lamborghinis**— the *Miura, Espada,* and *Countach*—**Ferrari** *Dino 308 GT 4,* **Alfa Romeo** *Carabo,* and **Lancia** *Stratos* zipped along racetracks and roads like arrows, with extremely pointed fronts and compact backsides.

Since the 1930s, Bertone had systematically turned the bodyshop opened by his father, Giovanni, in 1912 into a modern company, styling such luxury cars as the *Fiat 2800 Cabriolet.* His breakthrough came in 1954 with the modest but elegant Alfa Romeo *Giulietta Sprint* (fig. p. 36), which was originally designed for a limited series of 500 but went on to be in production for thirteen years. Other classic Bertone designs include the 1964 **Fiat** *Spider 850* and the low-slung, sporty 1972 *Fiat X1/9.* In more recent years Bertone's company designed the Opel *Kadett Cabrio* (1987), the Opel *Astra Cabrio* (1993), and the Fiat *Punto Cabrio* (1994).

Lamborghini *Miura*, 1966

Page 131
top: Fiat *2800* convertible, 1939
bottomright: Fiat *X 1/9*, 1972

Cini BOERI

Architect, furniture and lighting designer

The title of Cini Boeri's book, *Le dimensioni umane dell' abitazione* (The human dimension of habitation), defines her entire career. For more than four decades, her theoretical and practical work has centered on humans and their needs. Boeri's one of the few women acknowledged as major forces in Italian design. Interestingly, she says she learned more from her mentor, **Marco Zanuso,** than she ever did at architecture school.

Her product designs encompass a variety of fields but have several things in common: they make life easier in a casual, relaxed manner; are often modular and available in several variations; and are made to fit changing requirements. Her *Borgogna* easy chairs on castors of the early 1960s anticipated today's home office. The armrests accommodated writing utensils and a telephone and were fitted for a reading light and manuscript holder. A 1967 stainless-steel cart did multiple duty as

a serving tray, laundry basket, and sideboard. In the early 1970s, her *Serpentone* seating snake (fig. p. 30) for Arflex became famous. Based on a simple rubber module, it could be configured in any length or layout, fitting a cultural moment that had temporarily leveled the distinctions between sitting and lying down. For Arflex, Boeri also designed the frameless *Bobo* chair, made of polyurethane, which could be manufactured in different "degrees of softness," and the *Strips* seating units, which had conveniently removable zippered covers. In addition, Boeri has designed lights for **Artemide, Arteluce,** and Stilnuovo; door handles for Fusital; furniture for **Fiam;** and prefabricated houses. As an architect, she designed public and private buildings as well as showrooms for Knoll International in Milan (1984), **Arflex** in Tokyo (1981), and **Venini** in Frankfurt (1988).

Products

1964 *Borgogna* chair

1967 *Bobo* monoblock chair

1971 *Serpentone* seating system; all for **Arflex**

1973 *Lucetta* table lamp for Stilnovo

1976 *Talete* tables

1979 *Strips* chairs; both for Arflex

1982 *Tre B* door handle for Fusital; *Ditto* table lamp for Tronconi

1983 *Malibu* table for Arflex; prefabricated house for Misawa Homes, Tokyo; *Shadows* table series for ICF

1986 *Brontes* table lamp for **Artemide**

1987 *Voyeur* glass partition for **Fiam**

1988 *Palo Alto* table

1989 *Feltro* hanging lamp for **Venini**

From left
Cubotto-Bar, 1967
Serpentone seating system, 1971
Strips chair, 1979
all for Arflex

Studio BOGGERI

Graphic design studio

At the beginning of modern Italian graphic design there is a musician: Antonio Boggeri, was a trained violinist. As the founder of Studio Boggeri, though, he came to use photos and fonts instead of notes.

In 1924, Boggeri happened onto a job with the Milan printing establishment of Alfieri & Lacroix, where he deepened his knowledge of lithography and typography. After intensively studying the techniques and possibilities of photomontage, he decided in 1933 to set up his own studio, which quickly became a hotbed for up-and-coming graphic artists, including **Max Huber, Bob Noorda, Xanti Schawinsky, Bruno Monguzzi, Bruno Munari,** and **Erberto Carboni.** All of them contributed to the extraordinary reputation the studio gained, which peaked in the late 1950s and early 1960s. The cover for **Olivetti's** brochure on the *M 42* typewriter is an excellent example of the studio's principles:

1934 Brochure for *M40*

Huber superimposed technical sketches on typographic elements and added a silhouetted, colorized photograph of the typewriter and a photo of the office situation, in which it was to be used. The result was a multilayered design that put the advertised product in a meaningful context.

Boggeri once said that graphic art is like theater: it has to create the same surprise and fascination as a rising curtain. In this metaphoric scenario, he took the role of a theater principal who gave his directors all the artistic freedom they needed. Through Huber and Schawinsky, the Swiss school of graphic design and late Bauhaus typography had an indirect influence on the Studio's work for clients like Olivetti, Roche, Glaxo, Dalmine, and **Pirelli.** Throughout the 1960s, 1970s, and 1980s, the Swiss Bruno Monguzzi, in particular, distinguished himself with exceptional designs for Boggeri.

typewriter for **Olivetti** by **Xanti Schawinsky**

1936 *Bantam* poster for Cervo by **Erberto Carboni**

1945 Brochure cover for Studio Boggeri by **Max Huber**

1956 Logo for Olivetti (also 1970)

1962 *Guanti Satinati,* advertisement for **Pirelli** by **Bruno Monguzzi**

1972 Advertisements for Pirelli tennis balls by Bruno Monguzzi and **Roberto Sambonet**

1979 Logo for IGA 83 by Bruno Monguzzi

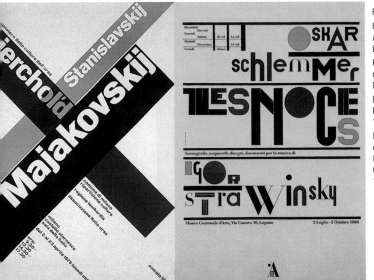

From left

Cover design for Olivetti's *M 42* typewriter, 1942, by Max Huber

Poster for Società Nazionale Gasometri by Fortunato Depero, 1934

Exhibition poster for the Milan department of culture, 1975, by Bruno Monguzzi

Poster for an exhibition on Oskar Schlemmer and Igor Stravinsky at the Museo Cantonale d'Arte. Lugano, 1988, by Bruno Monguzzi

Pierantonio BONACINA

Furniture manufacturer

Pierantonio Bonacina snc,
Lurago d'Erba
1898 founded

Products
1957 *Egg* suspended chair
by Nanna Ditzel
1960 *Martingala* chair
by **Marco Zanuso**
1963 *Continuum* chair
by **Gio Ponti**
1964 *Nastro* chair
by **Joe Colombo**
1988 *Atlantic* sofa
by Franco Bizzozzero
1991 *Flûte* wicker lamp
by Marco Agnoli
1993 *Cosy Ton* chair
by Giuseppe Viganò

Page 137
top l. *Continuum* chair
by Gio Ponti, 1963
top r. *Martingala* chair
by Marco Zanuso, 1960
bottom *Nastro* chair
by Joe Colombo, 1964

Pierantonio Bonacina is known for combining traditional and newer materials—rattan, rush, wood, leather, tubular steel, and fabrics—in decidedly modern designs. In the early 1960s, the firm began to cooperate with some of the biggest names in modern Italian furniture design. The architect and designer **Tito Agnoli,** in particular, became a central figure in its development. Approached by company owner Pierantonio Bonacina after his designs had won gold medals at the 1959 and 1961 wicker furniture expositions at Lurago d'Erba, where Bonacina is based, Agnoli helped transform the firm into a modern industrial manufacturing business and radically updated its aesthetics. His designs for Bonacina include the delicate *S.21* chair, with its finely-woven seat and backrest, and the cubic *S.23* chair.

During the early 1960s, Bonacina also worked with designers such as **De Pas/D'Urbino/Lomazzi** and **Joe Colombo,** whose uncompromisingly industrial aesthetics are evident in the boldly curved *Nastro* chair. **Gio Ponti** contributed the comfortable *Continuum* chair, with its gracefully curving armrests, and **Marco Zanuso** his famous *Martingala* wicker chair. Today, a number of younger designers, including Franco Bizzozzero, Joey Mancini, Marco Agnoli, and Giuseppe Viganò, continue to develop the firm's design strategy. Tables and lights have been added to Bonacina's elegant product line, though the priority is still on seating.

Rodolfo BONETTO

Industrial designer

Unlike Italy's numerous architect-designers, Rodolfo Bonetto has always focused exclusively on industrial design. And he came to the profession not from architecture school but after a career as an internationally successful jazz drummer. Few of his peers fought as passionately for their vision of a design culture as Bonetto did. His goal was nothing less than perfection: to achieve an entirely flawless design solution in cooperation with the client, and to invest the product with its own cultural dignity. It is not surprising that he considered **Marco Zanuso** and **Marcello Nizzoli** his spiritual teachers — they too had developed their concept of industrial culture in close collaboration with their corporate clients. His main focus was on the design process, which for him was firmly anchored in mass production.

Never a snob, Bonetto took on even seemingly unattractive projects, such as the design of measuring instruments, plumbing fixtures, and technical equipment. In the 1960s he became an indispensable consultant for **Olivetti's** instrument division; in **Fiat's** styling center he developed the *Fire engine* for the *Uno* subcompact; and for **Borletti Veglia** he designed gauges for cars as well as his first great popular success, the *Sfericlock* alarm clock. By the end of Bonetto's life, there was hardly a product that he hadn't worked on: his projects ranged from furniture to audio equipment and musical instruments. He particularly loved cars. Indeed, it was in **PininFarina's** car-body workshop that he had started his design career at the suggestion of his uncle, Felice Bonetto, who later died when his *Lancia 3300* crashed during the Carrera Messicana rally.

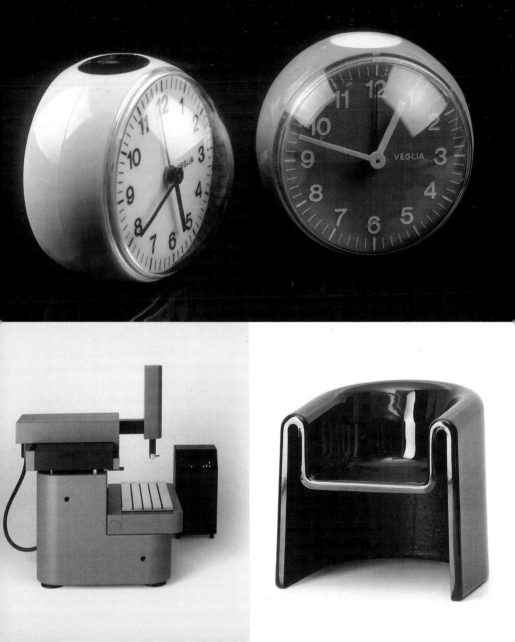

Renata BONFANTI

Textile designer

"I do not think that hand looms can only be used to make individual items for the arts and crafts market, that they have no business in industrial production," the textile designer Renata Bonfanti said in 1975. "I have always tried to organize my work in a way that makes use of both techniques, and my studio is consequently equipped with different kinds of looms." Based in the Italian province of Vicenza, Bonfanti has successfully straddled the worlds of fine art and industrial design. And with her unflagging commitment to experimentation, Bonfanti has continuously given fresh impulses to Italian textile design. Her work has been featured in international art exhibitions such as the 1961 show *Contemporary Italian Art,* which traveled from Oslo to Stockholm and Copenhagen. At the same time, she has been recognized as a great industrial designer; in 1962 she won a *Compasso d'oro* for her airy *JL fabric.*

Many of Bonfanti's textiles seem almost Scandinavian in their austere aesthetic. In fact, the designer spent some time in Norway in the early 1950s after graduating from art school in Venice. Studying at Kvinnelige Industriskole in Oslo, she was strongly influenced by Northern European techniques and formal ideas before returning to Italy. In 1961 she attracted attention with her *Algeria* series of rugs, whose amorphous fields of color were scattered across the fabric in powdery patches. Like many of her rugs, her 1974 *Bengal* series could be used on floors and walls alike.

Osvaldo BORSANI

Architect and furniture designer

At the tenth Milan **Triennale,** in 1954, Osvaldo Borsani introduced his *P 40* recliner, which could be adjusted to 486 different positions, thanks to a modular inner support structure and a patented mechanism that widened or narrowed the angle between seat and backrest in minute increments. This kind of seamless interplay between technology and design fascinated Borsani, who believed that good design was not so much a matter of brilliant inspiration, but primarily the result of intensive research and development. Each of his furniture designs was the solution to a concrete problem. His *D 70* sofa, for example, designed for a house on *Lago Maggiore,* could be flipped over so that its occupant could either look at the fireplace or enjoy the beautiful view on the opposite side.

Borsani worked exclusively for **Tecno,** a company he had founded; most of his furniture is still being produced. He also designed Tecno's factory building and the company's Milan offices, and was one of the founders of the journal Ottagono.

Sessel *P 40* für Tecno, 1954

Fabio BORTOLANI

Furniture and industrial designer

Fabio Bortolani has a special knack for receptacles and holders. He designs modest little objects like the *Semplice* ashtray, the low *Opus* tables, with their integrated compartments for pens and paper, and the colorful *Quaderno* sketchbooks for Authentics. His useful household items are extremely simple constructions, some of them bordering on non-design—his *Multiplos* toilet paper holder, for example, consists of a couple of joined wooden sticks. His most remarkable designs offer ingenious solutions to common problems: his *Bucatini* system for **Agape** consists of simple wall-mounted loops that can hold bathrooms utensils of different sizes, from toothbrushes to cups and bottles. In their stripped-down material aesthetics—raw wood, translucent plastic, and shiny metal prevail—Bortolani's products perfectly suit the purist tastes of the 1990s.

1957 born in Spilambert
studies design in Florence

1997 *Segreta,* exhibition at Victoria and Albert Museum, London

1998 *Intorno Alla Fotografia,* exhibition

Products

1991 *Terranea* bench for **Crassevig**

1996 *Semplice* ashtray

1997 *Clips* tables and teacart for Hoffmann

1998 *Quaderno* sketchbook for Authentics; *Opus* table for La Palma

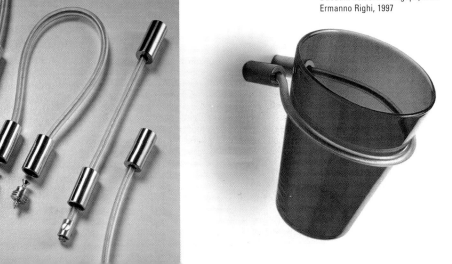

Bucatini holders for Agape, with Ermanno Righi, 1997

Andrea BRANZI
Architect, designer, and writer

Andrea Branzi has described design as a practical as well as philosophical task. As an independent thinker, mentor, critic, and exhibition organizer, he has been on the cutting edge of Italy's design discourse for the last three decades. He helped launch the Radical Design movement in 1966 as a cofounder of the Archizoom group, which humorously criticized the doctrine of functionalism with pieces like the oversized Dream-Beds and the wave-shaped Superonda crinkle leather sofa for Poltronova. And with his designs and writings he has put his stamp on virtually every important new movement that has followed. Emphasizing the aesthetic language of individual objects over stylistic dogmas, he contributed to the educational Global Tools project in the mid-1970s, and was among the founders of Alchimia and Memphis. Branzi has also worked for Cassina, Alessi, Zanotta, and Rossi & Arcandi, for whom he designed the popular Labrador gravy boat.

1938 born in Florence

1966 graduates from architecture school in Florence; cofounder of **Archizoom**

1971 editor at *Casabella* (until 1974)

1973 collaborates with **Massimo Morozzia** and **C.T. Castelli** (CDM) (until 1981); primary design and color concepts

1979 *Compasso d'oro* (also in 1987)

1983 director of Domus Academy (until 1987); editor in chief of *Modo* (until 1987)

1984 book, *La casa calda,* publ.

1987 *Compasso d'oro*

Products

1980 *Ginger* chair for **Alchimia**

1982 *Labrador* sauceboat

1986 *Berlino* chair and sofa for **Zanotta**

1992 *Mamma-ò* tea kettle for **Alessi**

Muzio console for Alchimia, 1979
Furniture sculpture from *Archi, fusi, e forcelle* series, 1988 (prototype for Cassina)

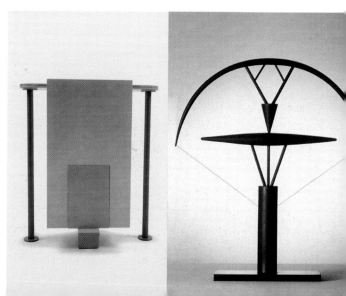

Home electronics manufacturer

There are noticeable parallels between Brionvega and the German electronics manufacturer Braun. Each company's distinct design aesthetic was developed in the 1960s, and each has produced stereo sets that have become objects of almost fetishistic veneration among high-tech connoisseurs. And Brionvega's slogan, "Technology in its most beautiful form," could easily have been invented by Braun. But unlike Braun's designs, Brionvega's products, while formally immaculate, also evoke playful instincts. There is something poetic in the way they make technology and function visible.

Brionvega's unmistakable look was developed by some of Italy's best designers, particularly the team of **Marco Zanuso** and **Richard Sapper,** the **Castiglioni** brothers, and **Mario Bellini.** They all started working for Brionvega in the early 1960s, formulating a consistent, adventurous design strategy which, along with innovative technology, catapulted a company that had been around since 1945 to the forefront of its industry. Brionvega dared

1945 founded as manufacturer
of radios

1952 production of TV sets

1970 *Compasso d'oro*

1992 Brionvega liquidated

Black ST 201 TV set by Marco Zanuso and Richard Sapper, 1969

Products

1962 *Doney* TV set

1964 *TS 502* radio; *Algol* TV set;
all by **Marco Zanuso**
and **Richard Sapper**

1966 *RR 126* stereo set by
Achille and **Pier Giacomo Castiglioni**

1969 *Black ST 201* TV set
by Marco Zanuso and
Richard Sapper;
Volans TV set

1970 *Astor 20* TV set

1979 *TVC 26* stereo system;
all by **Mario Bellini**

Page 147

Algol TV set by Marco Zanuso
and Richard Sapper, 1964

TS 502 radio by Marco Zanuso
and Richard Sapper, 1964

to break with established and seemingly normative forms, encouraging its designers to practically reinvent the TV set and the radio. The results were quite spectacular: the small *TS 502* radio by Marco Zanuso and Richard Sapper revealed its function only when snapped open; the team's compact 1962 *Doney* television set was Italy's first transistor-equipped TV and the precursor of the *Algol* models (fig. p. 4) in the Pop style of the 1960s and 1970s. In 1960 Zanuso and Sapper developed the *Black* TV set, a mysterious all-black cube that came to life when the screen lit up—slowly creating a contrast between solid frame and electronic image, a vivid demonstration of the magic of technology. Another successful Brionvega product was Achille and Pier Castiglioni's *RR 126* radio and turntable. An oblong box whose panel looked like a friendly cartoon face with raised eyebrows, it came on a stand with wheels. To save floor space, it was also equipped with mounts to which the speakers could be attached.

Brionvega gradually lost its competitive edge as the importance of design was eclipsed by the trend toward microelectronics, and in 1992 the company was liquidated.

Carlo BUGATTI

Cabinet maker

Carlo Bugatti's fame was on a more modest scale than that achieved by his son, Ettore, and grandson, Jean, two of the twentieth century's most celebrated car builders and race car drivers. Between 1880 and 1904, the elder Bugatti worked as a cabinetmaker, creating richly ornate pieces in a Moorish style, which gave way to Art Nouveau around the turn of the century. His style became so much in demand that it gave rise to a whole genre of "Bugatti furniture." The trade press praised his interiors, which included the "Snail Room," which featured parchment-covered furniture painted red and gold. The crowning event of Bugatti's career occurred at the 1902 *International Arts and Crafts Exhibition in Turin,* where he was given the first prize. His artful inlay work has secured him a place alongside such masters of the craft as Henry van de Velde, Antonio Gaudí, Charles Rennie Mackintosh, and Peter Behrens. In 1904 he gave up cabinetry to dedicate himself to painting and silverwork.

1856 born in Milan

1888 opens workshop; participates in crafts exhibition, Milan (and international exhib. in Antwerp, Amsterdam and Turin, 1894, 1895 and 1902)

1900 *Silver Medal* at Paris World's Fair

1902 participates in *International Arts and Crafts Exhibition*, Turin

1904 moves to Paris

1910 turns to painting

1940 dies in Dorlisheim (Bas-Rhin)

Products

1900 Furniture for the Khediven's palace in Istanbul

1902 "Snail Room," Turin

1904 Silverware

Bench made of wood, metal, and parchment, c. 1900

Architect, furniture, lighting, and product designer

Luigi Caccia Dominioni was not only an important architect but also a pioneer of modern Italian industrial design. His 1938 Caccia cutlery set, designed in collaboration with **Livio** and **Pier Giacomo Castiglioni,** was so far ahead of its time that **Alessi** added it to its product line decades later. Today, no one would guess that it is a design from the thirties. Caccia Dominioni and the Castiglionis' innovative Bakelite radio for Phonola, introduced at the 1940 Milan *Triennale,* marked a similarly radical departure from convention at a time when radios still resembled cabinets. After the war, Caccia Dominioni designed harmonically balanced furniture for **Azucena,** including his famous *Catilina* chair of 1949, with its supple leather cushion resting in a slender, rounded metal frame, and the simple *Sasso* and *Base Gisa* floor and table lamps. More recent designs include his symmetrical *Toro* sofa of the 1970s and the gracefully curved *Cristallo* door handle of the 1980s.

1913 born in Milan
1936 graduates from architecture school in Milan
1948 opens **Azucena** store in Milan with **I. Gardella** and C. Corradi Dell'Acqua
1960 *Compasso d'oro*
1970 Chase Manhattan Bank, Milan

Products
1938 *Caccia* silverware set
1959 School furniture for Palini; both with **Livio** and **Pier Giacomo Castiglioni**

Radio for Phonola with Livio and Pier Giacomo Castiglioni, 1939
Catilina chair for Azucena, 1949

CAPPELLINI

Furniture manufacturer

Cappellini spa, Arosio (CO)

1946 founded in Arosio, produces hand-crafted furniture

1960 refocuses on modern design

1987 establishment of subsidiary, **Mondo**; reproductions of classic furniture

Products

1970 *PC/3* S*ide 1* and *PC/6* S*ide 2* sideboards by Shiro Kuramata

1975 *Cenacolo Marmo* table by **Giulio Cappellini**

1977 *PC/8 Solaris,* object by Shiro Kuramata

1986 *Passepartout* shelf system by Giulio Cappellini and **Rodolfo Dordoni**

1988 *Thinking Man's Chair* by Jasper Morrison

Page 151
l. *S-Chair* by Tom Dixon, 1992
top right: *Embryo Chair* by Marc Newson, 1998
bottom right: *Satellite Table* by Konstantin Grcic, 1992

No furniture company celebrates design in quite the spectacular fashion as Cappellini. To own a Cappellini piece means to partake of its exclusive aura, to possess not simply a costly object but a sculpture. The firm's displays at furniture fairs attract crowds; its catalogues and brochures resemble lifestyle glossies. Shiro Kuramata's "dancing" *Side 1/Side 2* chest, Tom Dixon's sinuously curved *S Chair,* and Jasper Morrison's elegantly minimalist *Three Sofa System* have become design icons. With this rarefied philosophy Cappellini has touched on the sensibilities of a younger generation of affluent sophisticates to whom designers are stars and designed objects are fetishes.

Giulio Cappellini has a unique eye for talent. He has discovered promising young designers from all parts of Europe, and his firm has helped launch the careers of many of them. Among the designers working for Cappellini are Marc Newson, James Irvine, and Werner Aisslinger, as well as **Michele De Lucchi, Rodolfo Dordoni, Alberto Meda, Anna Gili,** and **Piero Lissoni.** The company, based in Arosio, seems to provide a particularly stimulating working environment, where designers feel free to fully realize their personal vision. Many Cappellini pieces look like ideas fully developed to their essential form. Though this implies certain risks for the company, since the market is not always receptive to experimental products, Cappellini has never let such considerations upset his design policy.

The company was founded in 1946 as a furniture manufacturer rooted in the crafts tradition. By 1970, Cappellini had transformed it into a high-powered design factory, organizing production in different workshops and coordinating everything from product development to marketing and distribution. The highest technological capabilities enable the company to produce furniture that tests the limits of manufacturing techniques.

1991 *Tonda* chair by **Anna Gili**

1992 *S-Chair* by Tom Dixon

1993 *Three Sofa System* by Jasper Morrison

1994 *ABC* aluminum shelf unit by **Alberto Meda**; *Eight Chair* by Ross Lovegrove

1995 *Alfabeto System* by Jasper Morrison and James Irvine; *Jaipur* and *Jodhpur* sofas by Jasper Morrison; *Statuette* plastic chair by Lloyd Schwan

1996 *Juli* chair by Werner Aisslinger

1998 *Embryo Chair* by Marc Newson

As diverse as the company's output is, a tendency toward minimalism is apparent in all its products, from Giulio Cappellini's own *Cenacolo* tables, alternatively made in marble or wood, whose special flair lies in the contrast between their stout legs and skinny top, to Jasper Morrison and James Irvine's *Alfabeto* shelving system, with its cubic modules. But Cappellini also challenges his designers to include divergent elements—the use of bold colors and curved lines is part of the overall repertoire, as Ross Lovegrove's *Eight Chair* and Christophe Pillet's *Y's Chair* show.

Jasper Morrison's *Thinking Man's Chair* is perhaps the best example of the Cappellini concept. The British designer redefined the classic lounge chair by replacing soft cushions with hard steel; an extremely long seat provides the necessary comfort. Radically simple in its materials, the chair looks by no means bloodless or sober, but conveys a sense of quiet, natural elegance.

In 1987 Cappellini, **Paola Navone,** and Rodolfo Dordoni founded a subsidiary, **Mondo,** to focus on reeditions of classic residential furniture and on reviving traditional manufacturing techniques, such as wire plaiting.

Page 153

top left: *Juli* chair by Werner Aisslinger, 1996

bottom left: *Thinking Man's Chair* by Jasper Morrison, 1988

right: *Pyramid* chiffonier by Shiro Kuramata, 1998

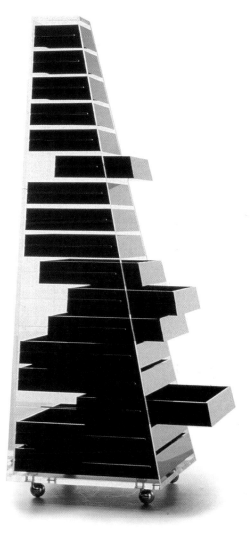

CASSINA

Furniture manufacturer

In 1957 Cassina produced the *Superleggera,* touted as the lightest chair in history. Its designer, **Gio Ponti,** had partially modeled it after chairs he had seen in the Italian fishing village of Chiavari. He kept those pieces' traditional materials—wickerwork and wood—but reduced the structural elements so drastically that the chair was ideally suited for mass production. A worldwide success, the *Superleggera* became a shining example of the new, modern Italian furniture design.

The *Superleggera* blended tradition and modernity on several levels. It is this special synthesis that has characterized the company since 1945, when it began to become a seminal design force. Cassina was founded in 1927 as a traditional manufacturer of upholstered furniture and developed a reputation for its high standards of craftsmanship. The Meda-based company has since evolved into a technologically advanced furniture producer, but the same dedication to quality still applies, and is one of the cornerstones of its success.

A sense of tradition is also important at Cassina; it's clearly present in the company's *I Maestri* series of classic furniture by Le Corbusier, Frank Lloyd Wright, Charles Rennie Macintosh, Gerrit Thomas Rietveld, and Gunnar Asplund. Introduced in the

Chair by Angelo Mangiarotti, 1963

Page 155
AEO chair by Paolo Deganello, 1973

mid-1960s, these reeditions now account for a third of Cassina's total sales and have solidified the firm's reputation as a guardian of the modern heritage. In its own designs, Cassina has been committed to innovation since the early 1950s, when it established close relationships with important contemporary designers such as **Franco Albini** and Gio Ponti. This embrace of modern design, which completely transformed the firm's profile, had been preceded by a large contract from the Italian shipbuilding industry. Between 1947 and 1952 Cassina furnished the luxury liners *Andrea Doria, Raffaelo,* and *Michelangelo.* The huge volumes this commission involved paved the way to mass production.

Cassina has continued to work with well-known designers, who today include **Mario Bellini, Vico Magistretti, Afra** and **Tobia Scarpa,** and Philippe Starck. But in the late 1960s, the company's energetic owner, Cesare Cassina, also started to search out young nonconformists like **Gaetano Pesce** and **Paolo Deganello** and to produce designs that defied convention. One radical example is Deganello's *AEO* chair of 1973, a literal deconstruction of a traditional upholstered chair. It easily disassembles into a base, cushions, two frames for the seat and backrest, and a tent-like slipcover. The form and look of Pesce's *Dalila* chair, made of polyurethane with a polyester cover, changed with every new production run; his *I Feltri* chair (fig. p. 25) has "wings" that can be spread out or pulled closer. In such projects, Pesce expressed his criticism of the uniformity of furniture design.

The company, now headed by Franco Cassina, has continued to be successful internationally; today, some 80 percent of its seating, tables, and shelving units are exported.

Anna CASTELLI FERRIERI

Architect and designer

In her book *Interfaces of Material,* published in 1991, Anna Castelli Ferrieri admonished designers to work responsibly and consider the environmental impact of the products they help create. But responsibility in design is not her only concern. She is also active in the human rights movement, with a particular focus on women's rights, and her ACF Officina group, an organization she founded in 1990, is committed to working with young designers.

One of the few successful women in Italian design, she first became known for her masterly use of plastics, a material closely associated with industrial technology. Castelli Ferrieri takes pride in designing highly functional objects for mass production; to her, market success means communicating with the user. In her mission to turn design into a more democratic practice that benefits many, she was strongly influenced by the strict minimalist **Franco Albini**. She gained her first working experience in his studio, and after the war joined him in his struggle to help build a democratic Italy through modern architecture and design. They also cooperated in promoting their ideas in the journal *Casabella-Costruzioni.*

From 1959 to 1973 Castelli Ferrieri and her partner, **Ignazio Gardella,** designed residential and office interiors. Even after she had become famous as an industrial designer she continued working as an architect on projects such as the **Kartell** Building in Binasco and the technical offices of **Alfa Romeo** in Arese, as well as homes, hospitals, churches, and industrial buildings. In 1966 she became a design consultant for Kartell, the company her husband, Giulio Castelli, had founded in 1949. Since then, Kartell's history has been inextricably linked to her work. For every new technology, she found an

Page 159

appropriate new form that perfectly reflected its properties. Her *4970/84* container system, for example, was an entirely new type of product made of a recently introduced material, ABS plastic. A small architectural exercise, it consisted of multiple elements that could be stacked without the use of screws or clamps. And her *4822/44* stool of 1979 was not only a bestseller but also a technological breakthrough: it was the first plastic stool that had long legs. Until then, no plastic compound had been sufficiently stable; Castelli Ferrieri used a new fiberglass-reinforced polypropylene foam into which metal pieces could be inserted to make the material as solid as cement. In the 1980s, she set out to design a chair that would be elegant, lightweight, and stackable as well as ergonomically shaped, elastic, durable, and inexpensive. The result, the *4870* polypropylene chair, won her the *Compasso d'oro*.

Almost all of Castelli Ferrieri's designs are still in production, proving that she reached one of her most important goals—to create successful designs for mass production. Besides working for Kartell, in recent years she has also designed products for other companies, including cutlery sets for **Sambonet,** upholstered furniture for **Arflex,** and the *Contralto* table for Ycami, whose legs taper from wide bases to narrow points under the tabletop, turning formal convention upside-down.

Achille & Pier Giacomo CASTIGLIONI

Architects; furniture, lighting, and industrial designers

Achille Castiglioni

1918 born in Milan

1944 graduates from architecture school in Milan

Pier Giacomo Castiglioni

1913 born in Milan

1937 graduates from architecture school in Milan

1968 dies in Milan

1945 collaboration

1947 design of *Mostre Nazionali della Radio e Televisione* in Milan

1953 Design of *National Housewares Exhibitions Italy* (until 1972)

1955 *Compasso d'oro* (also 1962, 1964, 1967, Achille Castiglioni alone, 1979, 1984, 1989)

Cumano tables for Zanotta, 1979

Page 163

Mezzadro tractor seat, 1957/1970

In 1957 a strange scene met visitors at the Villa Olmo in Como: iron bowls from the nineteenth century, a rocking bicycle seat (fig. p. 15), a stylized tractor chair, ceiling-mounted TV sets, abstract wall decorations, and portable radio telephones were casually arranged in a surreal mix of the past and the present. Achille and Pier Giacomo Castiglioni had titled this unusual exhibition of their own designs and found objects *Forme e colori nella casa di oggi* (Forms and colors in today's home). The message was clear: it is the quality and interplay of individual objects that creates ambiance, not the presumed harmony of a unified style. The Castiglioni brothers have stuck to this contextual design concept throughout their careers. (The bicycle and tractor seats have been produced by **Zanotta** since the 1970s, under the names *Sella* and *Mezzadro*.)

Their first important commission was the design of the radio exhibition at the seventh Milan *Triennale,* in 1940, to which Pier Giacamo Castiglioni, along with his elder brother **Livio** and **Luigi Caccia Dominioni**, also contributed an innovative Bakelite receiver whose form followed, rather than concealed, its technical makeup. After World War II, Pier Giacomo, Livio, and Achille produced a series of spectacular exhibits, some of which became famous events. Thousands of people came to see their perfectly choreographed shows for the Italian broadcasting company RAI, with audiovisual effects directed by Livio. (He went

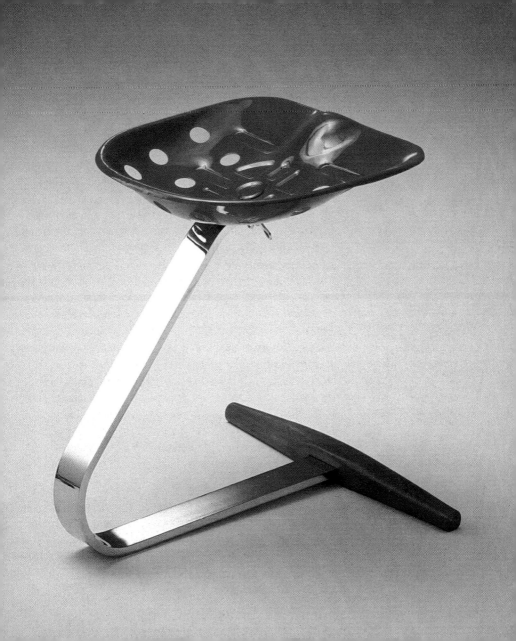

Collaborative products
1949 *Tubino* table lamp
1955 *Luminator* floor lamp
1956 *Spalter* vacuum cleaner
1957 *Sella* stool
prod. by **Zanotta** from 1983;
Mezzadro stool
prod.by Zanotta from 1970
1960 *San Luca* chair for **Gavina**
1961 *Splügenbräu* lamp
1962 *Taccia* table lamp;
Arco floor lamp;
Toio floor lamp;
all for **Flos**
1966 *RR 126* stereo
receiver for **Brionvega**

Products, A. Castiglioni
1970 *Primate* chair for Zanotta
1971 *Parentesi* light with Pio
Manzú
1972 *Noce* lamp
1975 *Potenusa* desk lamp
1978 *Frisbi* hanging lamp
all for Flos

his separate way in the early 1950s.) Exhibition design continued to be an important part of Achille Castiglioni's work after Pier Giacomo's premature death in 1968.

The two brothers also started to focus on industrial products at the beginning of the 1950s. They designed household appliances like the modest *Spalter* vacuum cleaner and their first lights, which included the simple *Luminator* floor lamp of 1955. In many cases they revised existing objects or put them in a new context; Achille Castiglioni has said that "design has always existed—one looks at objects and naturally comes up with ideas to improve them." By transposing art's ready-made concept into design they often created ironic comments on Italian **Bel Design** and on overly dogmatic versions of functionalism. The reflector of his *Toio* floor lamp for Flos, for example, was originally made for automobile headlights. Another successful example is his small *Cumano* table for Zanotta, which was modeled after French bistro tables. His improvement consisted in punching a small hole near the edge so the folded-up table could be hung up on the wall. Lined up in a row, they look like mounted insects, an amusing visual effect quite separate from their everyday function.

Electrical light and the techniques of its diffusion always attracted the Castiglioni brothers. Indeed, a review of their lamps and lights, most of which were developed for Flos, amounts to a lesson in modern lighting design. In 1962 they designed the *Arco* lamp, whose form was inspired by common streetlights, and the massive *Taccia* table lamp (fig. p. 2). Their lighting designs of the early 1970s include the rounded, unpretentious *Noce,* a variation on simple basement lights; *Parentesi,* the first halogen light movable along a suspended cord; and the *Frisbi* hanging lamp, with its two reflectors that focus light upward and diffuse it downward. Achille Castiglioni also designed the *Tubo* and *Ipotenusa* desk lamps, the birdlike *Gibigiano* floor lamp, and, in the 1990s, the elegant *Brera* and *Fucsia* hanging lamps.

While the Castiglioni's created an entire world of products, from their innovative 1966 *RR 126* stereo set for **Brionvega** to clocks and housewares for **Alessi** and numerous furniture designs for **De Padova, Gavina,** and Zanotta, it is almost impossible to discern a personal style that ties them all together. Their hallmarks, instead, are creative wit and a form that always follows the objects' inner logic. These qualities have won them seven *Compasso d'oro* awards.

1979 *Cumano* folding chair for Zanotta

1982 *Dry* silverware set for **Alessi**

1983 *Albero* flower stand for Zanotta

1991 *Sangirolamo* office furniture for **Olivetti** with **Michele de Lucchi**

1992 *Brera* lamp

1996 *Fucsia* hanging lamp both for Flos

From left:

Castiglietta chair for Zanotta, 1967

Parentesi for Flos, 1971, with Pio Manzú

Frisbi for Flos, 1978

Wall clock, 1965 (prod. 1996 by Alessi)

Linda plumbing fixtures

Trio for Interflex, 1991 with G. Pozzi

Page 166/167

Arco lamp for Flos, 1962

Antonio CITTERIO

Architect; furniture and lighting designer

Antonio Citterio is less concerned with putting his personal stamp on products than in fully realizing the design opportunities offered by new materials and technology. The best example of this is his 1994 *Mobil* container system for **Kartell**. Its drawer elements were made of translucent plastic (a striking novelty at the time) and were extremely restrained in their form, so the focus is entirely on the material's aesthetics. Citterio has also designed residential and commercial lighting, hospital beds, kitchens, and office furniture, an area where he has been particularly successful. His *Ad Hoc* office system, developed with Glen Oliver Loew for Vitra, consists of flexible elements that easily adapt to a constantly changing environment. He has also made a strong impact with his upholstered furniture, such as the *Sity* sofa for **B & B Italia**, which combines the traditional forms of sofa and chaise with additional cushions to create a sense of comfortable familiarity within a formal language of clean, simple lines.

Among the Italian designers of his generation, Citterio stands out as one of the most successful. The rise of **Nuovo Design** in the 1980s had little effect on his work; his style is timeless rather than of-the-moment, though he is able to give the Zeitgeist its due, as his store designs for the fashion retailer Esprit show.

1950 born in Meda

1973 studio with **Paolo Nava**
(until 1981)

1975 graduates from
architecture school

1987 *Compasso d'oro*
(also 1995)

Products

1978 *Aria* and *Pasodouble*
sofas for **Flexform**

1980 *Factory*
kitchen system for **Boffi**

1982 Showroom for **B&B Italia**

1985 Esprit stores in Milan
and Amsterdam

1986 *Sity* sofa for B&B Italia

1992 *Ephesos* office furniture
system for Olivetti
Synthesis

1996 Fausto Santini showroom
in Düsseldorf

1997 *Artusi* kitchen system for
Arc Linea

Page169

Mobil container system for Kartell,
1994

Elettra lighting system for Ansorg,
1993, with Glen Oliver Loew

Dolly folding chair for Kartell, 1997

AC Program office chair system for
Vitra, 1989, with Glen Oliver Loew

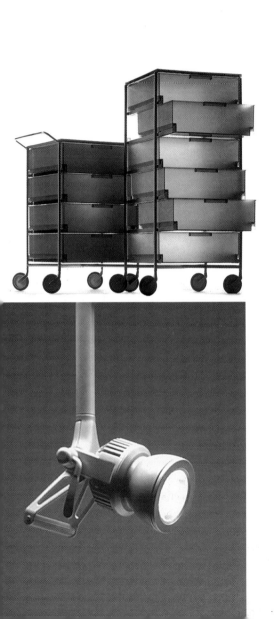

Joe COLOMBO

Furniture and lighting designer, painter, and sculptor

For Joe Colombo the designer was the "creatore dell'ambiente futuro," the creator of the future environment. To be preoccupied with mere furniture or decoration seemed backward to him, and he denounced most contemporary homes as "temples of self-glorification." He advanced his own visions and work in a career that lasted only a decade but left such a strong mark on Italian design that by the time of his early death in 1971, Colombo had become a legend.

Brimming with optimism, Colombo believed in the transforming power of design and in a civilization able to solve its problems through analytical processes and technology. The economic boom of the 1960s seemed to confirm his enthusiasm; he did not live to experience the disillusionment that followed the oil crisis, global recession, and mounting social problems of the seventies. During the 1960s, Colombo developed the idea of an "integral" design, in which each element in his product universe contributed to the overall shape. His reinterpretation of the living

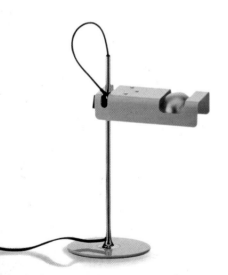

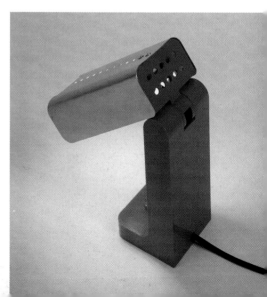

room led to complex solutions such as the 1970 Living Center, developed for Rosenthal, which consisted of lounges on wheels and a plastic unit, which looked like a spaceship's instrument panel and served as table, storage container, stereo cabinet, and minibar. The 1964 *Uomo/Donna* container system for **Arflex** held every conceivable living room accessory from ashtray, lighter, and pipe rack to lamp, books, and turntable. His 1963/64 *Carrellone Mini Kitchen* for **Boffi** integrated all necessary tools and appliances in one compact block on wheels. And the plastic living landscape he developed for Bayer in 1969 was a science-fiction utopia that epitomized the sensibilities of a generation shaped by Pop Art and a triumphant youth culture.

Colombo also expressed his enthusiasm for technology in the design of single products. His *Onda* hanging lamp is equipped with a reflector that directs the light upward as well as downward, encircling the object in a mysterious halo. His *Spider* table lamp resembles a small robot. His stackable *4867* chair,

Products

1963 *Carellone Mini-Kitchen* for **Boffi**

1963 *Elda* chair for Comfort

1964 *Uomo-Donna* modular containers for **Arflex**

1965 *Spider* lamp for **O Luce**

1966 *4801/5* plastic chair for **Kartell**

From left:
Spider lamp for O Luce , 1965
Vademecum lamp for Kartell, 1968
580 Birillo barstool for Zanotta, 1970
Poker table for Zanotta, 1968

Joe COLOMBO

introduced by **Kartell** in 1968, was one of the first chairs made entirely of plastic. Its design emphasized its production process by drawing attention to elements like the hole in the backrest, which was created when the chair was pulled out of the mold.

Colombo's designs for upholstered furniture broke with conventional ideas of refined living comfort. The *Elda* chair for Comfort, for example, was a leather-lined sitting machine on a massive base. And the *Additional System* for Sormani (fig. p. 18) had modules of varying heights that could be combined into different seating arrangements.

As passionate as Colombo was about technology, he had come to industrial design by way of fine art. As a painter and sculptor he had helped launch the Nuclear Painting movement in the 1950s, before taking up design in 1961. (In his own definition of his work, he was neither an artist nor a technologist but an "epistemologist.") His love of drawing found a new outlet in the minutely detailed construction plans he made for all his three-dimensional projects.

Unconditional faith in technology may have died years ago, but most of Colombo's creations are still in production. It is also worth noting that the things that most interested him, such as flexibility and multifunctionality, play a crucial part in much of today's furniture design.

Page 173
top left: *4867* stacking chair for Kartell, 1968
top right: *Elda 1005* chair for Comfort, 1963
bottom: Sessel *Tubo* chair for Flexform prima, 1969

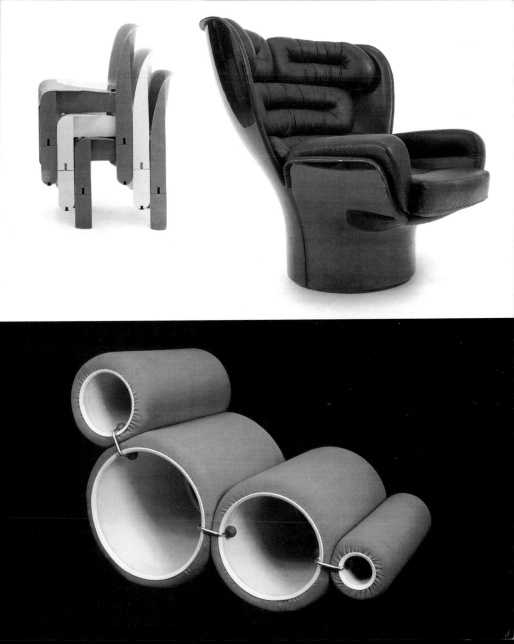

DANESE

Housewares manufacturer

Danese, Divisione di Alias,
Grumello del Monte

1957 founded by Bruno Danese
and Jacqueline Vodoz
Danese in Milan

1994 acquired by **Alias**

Products

1957 *Cubo* ashtray

1958 *Ponza* ashtray

1961 *Stromboli* candlestick;
all by **Bruno Munari**

1964 *Barbados* ashtray
by **Angelo Mangiarotti**

1969 *Bambú* vase

1970 *In attesa* waste-paper
basket;
both by **Enzo Mari**

1978 *Dattilo* lamp
by Bruno Munari

1983 *Paro* goblet
by **Achille Castiglioni**

1996 *Antipodi* bowls by
Marco Ferreri

Milo Tino concrete clock
by Kuno Prey, 1986

Page 175

Falkland lamp
by Bruno Munari, 1964

Formosa calendar
by Enzo Mari, 1962

Marmo H vase by Enzo Mari, 1964

When **Bruno Danese** and Jacqueline Vodoz founded their company in 1957, they wanted to produce "perfect objects." And they did achieve perfection in products such as Bruno Munari's *Cubo* ashtray, which completely swallows up cigarette butts and contains their smell, and **Enzo Mari's** *In attesa* wastebasket, whose built-up rim catches even clumsy throws. The Daneses found sympathetic designers in Munari and Mari and, later on, **Achille Castiglioni,** Kuno Prey, and **Angelo Mangiarotti.** Highly eclectic in their choice of materials, these designers developed an "industrial art" that today is considered timeless. Mari's table calendars, vases (fig. p. 47), and *Giglio* letter opener (a plain metal loop); Munari's *Falkland* lamp made of hosiery fabric stretched over a frame; and Prey's *Tino* table clock, in its concrete case, are such simple and obvious solutions that it seems amazing that no one had come up with them before. Besides housewares, Danese also produced artwork in multiple editions, including Munari's 1959 *Travel Sculpture* and *Air Machine,* and his games for children, before the company was acquired by **Alias** in 1994.

Today young designers such as **Marco Ferreri** (fig. p. 28), Alfredo Häberli, and Christophe Marchand continue to refine Danese's philosophy with new forms and materials.

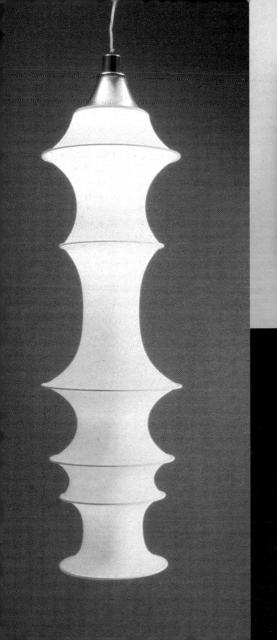

Michele DE LUCCHI

Architect, industrial and furniture designer

Michele De Lucchi started out as an **Anti-Design** rebel but wound up a modern design entrepreneur. Dressed up as a Napoleonic general, the young architecture student stood guard outside the 1973 Milan **Triennale** with a trash bag full of products to protest against the design establishment. A short time later, he was working for **Alchimia** and **Memphis,** designing furniture, accessories, and laminates that marked a radical departure from functionalism. His First chair of 1983, for example, transforms armrests and backrest into two balls and a bright blue disk fixed to the orbit of a metal hoop—functional elements became metaphor. Memphis disbanded in 1988, but according to De Lucchi, the group created "a new notion of what's valuable" that has remained "anchored in the consciousness of all designers working today." De Lucchi has since realized his own notions of value in numerous products. His best-selling *Tolomeo* desk lamp for **Artemide,** made of matte aluminum, marked a return to functional, elegant form.

1951 born in Ferrara

1973 cofounds *Cavart* group (until 1976); experimental architecture projects

1975 graduates from architecture school in Florence

1978 member, **Alchimia**

1979 design consultant for **Olivetti**

1981 founding member of **Memphis**

1988 opens Studio De Lucchi

1992 chief designer at Olivetti

1998 founds Studio aDML with Angelo Micheli

As early as 1979, **Olivetti** had hired the young dissident as a design consultant; since 1992 he has been heading the company's design department focusing on computers and other electronic appliances. In 1988, along with Angelo Micheli and Nicholas Bewick, he founded Studio De Lucchi, which has worked for large international service companies. Among other projects, the Studio developed a complete store-design program for **Mandarina Duck;** designed piazza-like interiors for branches of Deutsche Bank and for the Booking and Travel Center of Deutsche Bahn, Germany's railway company, in Frankfurt. Since 1987, De Lucchi has also realized a number of architectural projects in Japan and Europe.

De Lucchi's design philosophy emphasizes teamwork, simplicity, functionality, and consumer needs. Guided by these principles, he has turned his studio into one of Europe's most modern and successful design businesses.

Products
1981 *Oceanic* lamp;
Lido sofa;
both for Memphis
1987 *Tolomeo* desk lamp for **Artemide** with Giancarlo Fassina
1988 plastic desk set for **Kartell**
1993 branch offices for Deutsche Bank
1995 *OFX 1000* fax machine, *Echos 20* laptop PC;
both for Olivetti;
store design for **Mandarina Duck** with Geert Koster, **Mario Trimarchi** and Paolo De Lucchi

From left:
Deutsche Bahn travel center, Frankfurt, 1997, with N. Bewick
First chair for Memphis, 1983
Tre Forchette lamp, 1997
OFX 1000 fax machine for Olivetti, 1995

DE PADOVA

Furniture manufacturer

De Padova srl, Milano

1958 founded by Maddalena and Fernando De Padova as a furniture import business

Products
1983 *De Padova Edizioni*
1988 *Raffles* Sofa
1993 *Lousiana* chair with ottoman
1997 *Safran* sofa
all by **Vico Magistretti**

Scrittarello table
by Achille Castiglioni, 1996
Silver chair
by Vico Magistretti, 1989

Maddalena De Padova has always had a preference for essential, pure forms, a no-frills approach she found exemplified in Charles and Ray Eames's house in California and in Scandinavian design. In 1958, she and her husband founded a company to import Herman Miller furniture and Scandinavian products. In the mid-1980s the firm began marketing its own line of furniture, the *De Padova Edizioni.* Timeless in style, purist in its formal vocabulary, and meticulously crafted in precious woods, metal, and textiles, the collection includes **Vico Magistretti's** *Raffles* and *Saffran* sofas, *Louisiana* easy chair and ottoman, and aluminum *Silver* chair, as well as **Achille Castiglioni's** *Scrittarello* desk. Reeditions of American Shaker furniture and Maddalena De Padova's tableware, vases, and rugs round out the company's catalogue.

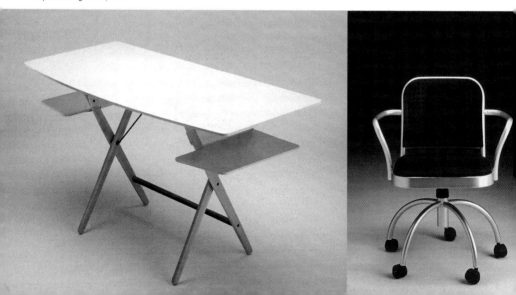

DE PAS / D'URBINO / LOMAZZI

Architects and designers

In 1997, a German design magazine called Jonathan De Pas, Donato D'Urbino, and Paolo Lomazzi "veterans of Pop." Though the trio's DDL studio is still very active on the Italian design scene (minus De Pas, who died in 1992), their names are permanently tied to two early products, the first of which gained them instant fame. Their inflatable *Blow* chair of 1967, produced by **Zanotta,** was the near-weightless messenger that carried Pop into countless living rooms and brought **Anti-** or **Radical Design** to public attention. In a 1974 retrospective of the movement, *Casabella* magazine described the chair as "Italy's first inflatable design object that was widely popular outside of strictly elite circles. "Tens of thousands were sold in the United States alone, at about ten dollars a piece. DDL repeated Blow's spectacular success with their 1970 *Joe* leather chair (fig. p. 46)

1966 collaboration in architecture, urban planning and design

1979 *Compasso d'oro*

Products

1967 *Blow* inflatable chair for **Zanotta** with Carla Scolari

1970 *Joe* chair for **Poltronova**; series of inflatable household furnishings for the Italian pavillion at the *Expo* in Osaka

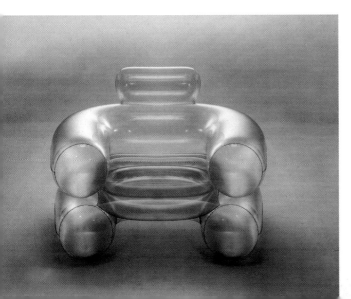

Blow chair for Zanotta, 1967

for **Poltronova.** Shaped like a giant baseball mitt, it was designed as an homage to Joe DiMaggio. Both chairs broke with conventional ideas of furniture, as they accommodated their era's relaxed posture and slouchy insouciance. The trio was similarly successful with its *Sciangai* coat rack, which consisted of eight wooden poles joined in the middle to resemble a jumble of chopsticks.

D'Urbino and Lomazzi have remained largely unimpressed by the market's supposedly binding laws. Their revolving *Giotto* stool of 1976 may look modest but works beautifully; the steel-and-black-leather *Onda* sofa of 1985 is a humorous variation on a famous Le Corbusier piece; and the coat racks, chairs, and tables they developed for Zerodisegno in the 1990s are as sly in their looks as they are smart in their functional design.

1973 *Flap* convertible chair for **B&B Italia**; *Sciangai* clothes tree
1975 *Giotto* stool; both for Zanotta
1985 candleholder for Jerusalem Museum
1990 *Abracadabra* shelf unit
1997 *Bikini* plastic chair for Zerodisegno; *Silverghost* closet system; both for Zerodisegno

Onda sofa for Zanotta, 1985
Zerone girder system for Quattrocchio, 1988

Paolo DEGANELLO

Architect, furniture designer, and essayist

In a 1997 speech, Paolo Deganello called for resistance to the dictates of the market, advocating instead smaller series of long-lasting products designed for niche markets. As a cofounder of **Archizoom,** Deganello has roots in the **Radical Design** movement of the 1960s, and his practical work has always been linked with theoretical considerations of contemporary design and its social functions. When he designed his best-known piece, the 1973 *AEO* chair for **Cassina,** he combined metal, a simple cotton fabri, and plastic. The chair's unusual form offered alternatives to both "beautiful" upholstered furniture and the raw **Anti-Design** look. He later designed the deliberately plain *Torso* sofa for Cassina. Deganello has also worked with **Driade** and **Zanotta,** for which he created the leather-and-wicker *Regina* chair, which features a peculiar, organically-shaped backrest.

1940 born in Este

1966 graduates from
architecture school in
Florence; cofounder of
Archizoom

1991 teaches at Isia (Istituto
Superiore Statale di
Disegno Industriale),
Florence

Products

1973 *AEO* chair for **Cassina**

1981 *Squash* sofa for **Driade**

1982 *Torso* sofa for Cassina

1987 *Documenta Chair*
for Vitra Edition

1991 *Regina* leather-and-wicker
chair for **Zanotta**

Regina chair for Zanotta, 1991
Documenta Chair
for Vitra Edition, 1987

DESIGN GROUP ITALIA

Industrial design studio

Among Italy's large industrial design studios, Design Group Italia is one of the most active, providing an international roster of clients with services from market analyses to product, graphic, and interface design. Formal versatility is part of the studio's conceptual basis. It has developed self-explanatory electrical control panels; user-friendly pharmaceutical devices such as the Jet inhaler for asthmatics and a contraceptive pill dispenser; functional writing utensils like the award-winning *Tratto pens* for Fila; housewares including the retractable *Amleto* ironing board; and futuristic racing seats, helmets, and sunglasses. Some of DGI's designs incorporate calculated ornamental details, such as the cut-out semicircle in the seat of the *Lyra* barstool for Magis; others, like the standard telephone for **Italtel,** are strikingly devoid of any decorative elements.

1968 founded in Milan, headed by Marco Del Corno, Edgardo Angelini, Ross De Salvo, Sigurdur Thorsteinsson

1979 *Compasso d'oro* (also 1991)

Products

1976 *Tratto Pen* for Fila

1989 corporate identity for ABB control panel systems

1991 *Freak* children's helmet for Uvex

1997 *Tecnic Advance* toothbrush for Elida Gibbs/Unilever

Lyra barstool for Magis, 1994
Standard telephone for Italtel, 1979

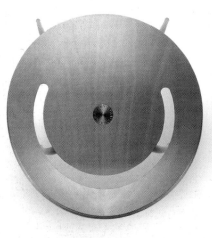

Rodolfo DORDONI

Architect; furniture and lighting designer

Rodolfo Dordoni has pioneered a friendlier rapport between design and its users. For Dordoni, the decisive questions in design are,"For whom and why?" Clean in their form and lovingly detailed, his products obligingly adapt to users' needs. His Fermo table system for **Driade,** for example, consists of inexpensive standard legs and medium density fiberboard tops that can be cut to any size. His *Paco* table lamp for **Arteluce,** whose light is filtered through a colored polycarbonate shade, features a glow-in-the-dark pull switch; the *Milo* table lamp for **Artemide** is similarly equipped. He has developed design solutions for **Cappelini, Fontana Arte,** Minotti, and **Moroso,** as well as designing interiors, including the **Dolce & Gabbana** showroom in Milan.

1954 born in Milan

1979 graduates from architecture school in Milan

Products

1986 *Cuba* sofa system for **Cappellini**

1992 *Arianna* chair for **Driade**; *Hall* sofa for Driade

1995 *Fermo* table for *Atlantide*

1998 *Braque, Delaunay, Leger, Villon, Duchamp* and *Gris* seats for Minotti

Orione table lamp for Artemide,1992
Delaunay chair for Minotti, 1998

DRIADE

Furniture manufacturer

Driade s.p.a, Fossadello di Caorso (Piacenza)

1968 founded in Piacenza
1981 *Compasso d'oro*
1996 first issue of *Driade Edizioni* magazine

Products

1968 *Driade*
system by **Antonia Astori**
1970 *Melaina* chair
by **Rodolfo Bonetto**;
Febo chair
by **Giotto Stoppino**
1972 *Oikos I* system
1980 *Oikos II* system
both by Antonia Astori
1982 *Sancarlo* chair by
Achille Castiglioni
1985 *Ubik* series
by Philippe Starck
1993 *Pantos* system
by Antonia Astori

Page 185

Delfina chair by Enzo Mari, 1974
Fermo tables by Rodolfo Dordoni
(*Atlantide*),1995
Oikos system by
Antonia Astori, 1972/1980

Lord Yo chair, Philippe Starck, 1994
Duecavalli chair by De Pas/
D'Urbino/Lomazzi, 1969/1995

When Driade debuted at the 1968 Milan furniture fair, the young company's peculiar Op-Art logo, designed by cofounder Adelaide Acerbi, attracted as much attention as its furniture designs. To this day, Driade is associated with the spectacular marketing efforts that accompany each product introduction. A few years ago, the company even started its own magazine, *Driade Edizioni.*

From the start, Driade's owners, Enrico and **Antonia Astori** and Acerbi, demonstrated a keen instinct for spotting trends. They made a strong early impression with Antonia Astori's pioneering modular solutions, such as the *Oikos* system, while also producing futuristic plastic furniture like **Rodolfo Bonetto's** chubby *Melaine* monoblock chair and **Enzo Mari's** slender *Delfina* chair. In the 1980s, under the influence of **Memphis,** Driade developed the landmark *Aleph* collection (1984), which included Philippe Starck's three-legged *Costes* bistro chair. The *Follies* series of accessories, also produced in the eighties, was typified by Borek Sipek's neo-Baroque, bombastic vessels. In the more modest 1990s, Driade introduced the *Atlantide* collection, for which designers such as **Marco Romanelli, Rodolfo Dordoni,** and Konstantin Grcic have created simple, straightforward products aimed at young, price-conscious buyers.

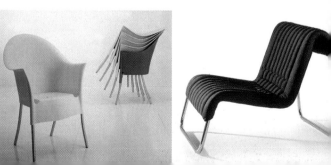

EDRA MAZZEI

Furniture manufacturer

Edra spa, Perignano (PI)
1987 founded in Perignano

Products
1988 *Wawy* seat by Zaha Hadid
1989 *Tatlin* sofa by Mario
Cananzi, Roberto Semprini
1990 *Fiori* chair series, incl.
Rose Chair by Masanori
Umeda
1991 *Topolone* sofa
by **Massimo Morozzi**
1993 *L'homme et la femme*
sofa by **Francesco Binfaré**
1994 *Island* seat
by **Alessandro Mendini**
1996 *Paesaggi*
italiani closet system;
Kasimir bookcase
both by Massimo
Morozzi

Pop singer Madonna was reportedly so taken with the bright red, helical *Tatlin* sofa that she bought one on the spot. Designed by Mario Cananzi and **Roberto Semprini** and manufactured by Edra Mazzei, the sofa is typical of a product line short on modest forms but rich in humor and visual trickery. It is not surprising that Edra furniture has been used as set pieces in such movies as *Wittgenstein, Star Trek,* and *Cosi Fan Tutte.* Most of the Tuscan manufacturer's chairs, sofas and wardrobes are legitimate descendants of early Pop furniture, designed not to blend in but to dominate their surroundings. Among the company's products are such eye-catching creations as Masanori Umeda's *Rose* Chair; and **Massimo Morrozzi's** *Paessaggi Italiani* closet system, whose cubic modules can be combined, Lego-like, to grow to any size or shape.

Ironic furniture's names (a sofa by **Francesco Binfaré** is called *L'homme et la femme*), product presentations with provocative titles such as *Sex for Angels,* and art director Massimo Morozzi's hypercharged marketing campaigns are all part of a philosophy that claims that "the public doesn't just want a nicely furnished home. It wants a dynamic, vivid, sensual, happy living environment."

Nuovo Domino sofa by
Massimo Morozzi, 1985 / 1998

Page 187
top left: *Rose Chair,* 1990
top right:. *Getsuen* chair, 1990;
both by Masanori Umeda
bottom: *Vermelha* chair by
Fernando and Humberto
Campagna, 1993 / 1998

Salvatore FERRAGAMO

Manufacturer of shoes, bags, and fashion accessories

Salvatore Ferragamo's biography reads like an Italian version of the American Dream. Born the eleventh of fourteen children in a small village near Naples, young Salvatore left school at the age of nine to become a shoemaker. After an apprenticeship in southern Italy, he emigrated to the United States in 1914. There he found employment in the flourishing movie industry, making cowboy boots, Egyptian sandals, and elegant pumps for stars like Gloria Swanson and Joan Crawford, who soon wore Ferragamo's shoes off the set as well as on camera. A few years before the Great Depression he returned to Italy and set up a business in Florence. When, in 1936, the League of Nations imposed sanctions on Fascist Italy and raw materials became scarce, Ferragamo made a virtue of necessity and, in place of leather, used materials such as thin metal threads, wood, transparent plastics, felt, and the raffia fibers typical of Florentine crafts. Careful craftsmanship and the use of unconventional materials became Ferragamo's trademarks. And unique designs such as the "invisible" high-heeled sandal of 1947 made him a legend in footwear. In 1950, his workshop contained rows upon rows of custom-made lasts modeled after the feet of clients like Greta Garbo, Sophia Loren, and Audrey Hepburn. Today, under the direction of Ferragamo's children, the company has expanded its product lines to include bags, leather accessories, ties, and scarves.

1889 Salvatore Ferragamo
born in Bonito
(near Naples)

1914 emigrates to U.S.
(returns in 1927)

1937 buys Palazzo Spini
Feroni in Florence

1960 Salvatore Ferragamo
dies; his children continue
to run the firm

1995 opening of Ferragamo
Museum in Florence

1996 Salvatore Ferragamo buys
Emanuel Ungaro

1997 joint venture with Bulgari
(perfume and cosmetics
products)

Page 189

top: Pump, 1962

bottom right: *Calipso* sandal , 1956,
and pump, 1934

Shoe, 1941

Uppers made of cellophane strings

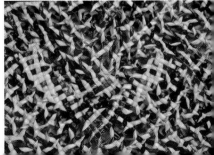

FERRARI

Automobile manufacturer

Shiny red metal, an aggressive radiator grill, and the famous bucking-horse logo are the images that come to mind when one hears the name Ferrari. And, of course, speed. Since the company was founded by Enzo Ferrari, a former race car driver, after the war, its cars have won more than 5,000 racing trophies. Ferrari's very first model, the twelve-cylinder *125* of 1946, became a benchmark for all sports cars that followed it. Unabashedly sexy in their design, Ferraris came to be used as symbols of erotic power in countless movies and TV series, from Miami Vice to Magnum, P.I. Their aura was not based on mere looks but on Ferrari's superior engines and the enormous success of its racing teams. Body design mattered, of course, and the cars' power was translated by **Pininfarina** into aerodynamic lines and sharply contoured details. In the 1950s and 1960s, rounded, organic forms characterized models such as the *250 GT SWB* (fig. p. 42/43), the *250 GTO* (dubbed a "phallus on wheels"), and the *365 GTB/4 "Daytona."* The cars became more angular in the 1970s. The only lapse in Ferrari's otherwise immaculate styling was the flashy *Testarossa,* now considered a symbol of the excesses of the 1980s.

Ferrari (now Fiat spa), Turin

1947 founded by Enzo Ferrari in Modena

1969 **Fiat** acquires a 50% stake in Ferrari

1988 increases stake to 90%

Models
1947 Type *125*
1953 *212 Inter*
1958 *250 GT Coupé*
1959 *Testarossa 250*
1960 *250 GT SWB*
1962 *250 GTO*
1967 *Dino 206 GT*
1968 *365 GTB/4 Daytona*
1975 *308 GTB*
1984 *Testarossa*
1987 *F 40 Berlinetta*

Ferrari *250 GT*, 1963

Page 191
top: Ferrari *Mythos*, 1989
bottom: Ferrari *328 GTB*, 1985;
all by Pininfarina

Gianfranco FERRÉ

Fashion designer

An Italian in the French shrine of couture—Gianfranco Ferré's appointment as Christian Dior's artistic director in 1989 caused quite a stir in fashion circles. Despite his critics' dire predictions, Ferré's ideas proved to be perfectly compatible with the house's venerable tradition, winning him the *Golden Thimble,* France's highest fashion award, in his first year at Dior. His sensuously elegant gowns typify his signature combination of simplicity and Mediterranean flair.

With a degree in architecture from Milan's polytechnic university, Ferré has an educational background shared by many Italian furniture designers, but few couturiers. After graduation he designed accessories, and in 1974 created his first collection for Baila. In 1978 he introduced his own label and eight years later joined the top ranks of fashion designers with his *Ferré Couture Collection,* which was discontinued after his appointment to Dior.

1944 born in Legnano near Milan

1969 graduates from architecture school in Milan

1978 founds company, Gianfranco Ferré, with Franco Mattiolo

1985 *Cutty Sark Men's Fashion Award*

1989 artistic director of Christian Dior, Paris (until 1996); *Golden Thimble*

Products

1984 perfume, *Gianfranco Ferré*

1986 men's perfume, *Gianfranco Ferré*; haute couture for women

1987 *Studio 000.1 by Ferré*

1993 *Pitti Immagine Uomo*

1990 *Lorenzo il Magnifico* award, Florence

1991 *Ferré by Ferré,* second women's perfume

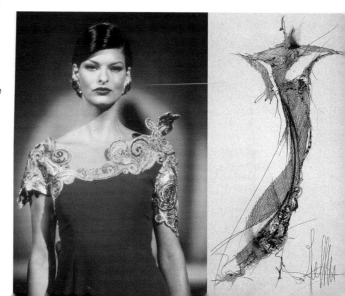

Dress from 1992/1993 collection
Drawing from 1998/1999 collection

Marco FERRERI

Architect, designer of furniture, accessories, and lighting

Price-consciousness and the exploration of new technologies and materials are important aspects of Marco Ferreri's design philosophy. "I'm interested in pushing the limits of materials," he says, explaining that his goal is "to produce something that is already inherent in the material and/or the construction process." This approach is exemplified in designs like the translucent *Antipodi* plastic bowls for **Danese,** with their organically swelling forms, and the *Less* chair for Nemo. Part of a furniture series titled *Less is More,* the chair's seat is made of Softwood, an experimental plywood-and-fabric compound. A thin sheet of wood is applied over a layer of cushioning material, so that the apparently hard surface yields, surprisingly, to the body's weight. One of Italy's most versatile designers, Ferreri has also created bathroom fixtures, faucets, and containers, such as the *Roll-Box* for garden waste.

1958 born in Imperia

1981 graduates from architecture school in Milan

1984 opens studio

Products

1990 *Zan-Zo* lamp for **Fontana Arte**

1993 *Less* stacking chair, *Is* stool, *More* table for Nemo/BPA International

1994 *Libro letto* cushion for Interflex with **Bruno Munari**; *O'Key* keychain for Robots; *O* bathroom faucets for **Agape**

1996 *Antipodi* bowls for **Danese**

1997 *Flirt* sofa for Adele C.

Antipodi bowls for Danese, 1996

Less chair for Nemo/ BPA International, 1993

FIAM

Furniture manufacturer

Fiam has liberated glass from its old, subordinate function and given it an autonomous role in furniture design. In 1984 the company achieved a technological breakthrough: the monolithic *Ragno,* designed by company founder Vittorio Livi, was the world's first table consisting of a single sheet of bent glass. Though is not that unusual for a manufacturer to focus on just one material, glass tends to follow its own rules. It is entirely due to Fiam's research and development efforts that it could be harnessed to realize designs like **Cini Boeri** and Tomu Katayanagi's throne-like *Ghost* chair, Danny Lane's sculptural *Shell* and *Atlas* tables, and **Massimo Morozzi's** *Hydra* table, which resembles a giant insect. Fiam is also the leading supplier of glass to the Italian furniture industry, with production capabilities ranging from glass-blowing to laser-cutting.

Fiam Italia spa, Tavullia
1973 founded by Vittorio Livi

Products
1984 *Ragno* glass table by **Vittorio Livi**

1987 *Ghost* glass chair by **Cini Boeri** and Tomu Katayanagi

1988 *Hydra* table by **Massimo Morozzi**; *Shell* and *Atlas* tables by Danny Lane

1992 *Illusion* table by Philippe Starck

1996 *Cler* glass cabinet by Ron Arad

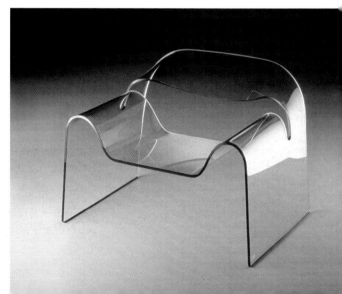

Ghost glass chair by Cini Boeri and Tomu Katayanagi, 1987

FIAT

Automobile manufacturer

If **Alfa Romeo** and **Ferrari** have made Italian cars famous for their luxurious, sporty design, Fiat has turned Italy into a nation of motorists. The Turin automobile manufacturer's *500* (fig. p. 48), developed by **Dante Giacosa,** was introduced in 1936 at a widely affordable price of 8,900 lire. With its thirteen-horsepower engine and light, 1,100 pound weight, the *"Topolino"* was the world's smallest car; by 1954 half a million had been sold. The popular model was twice relaunched in updated versions, first as the *Nuova 500* in 1957 and again in the 1990s as the *Cinquecento*.

The Fabbrica Italiana Automobili Torino was established in 1899. Like many other car manufacturers it concentrated on the production of expensive luxury vehicles and race cars during its early years. Giovanni Agnelli, one of the company's founders, quickly came to recognize the industry's broader potential, and in 1912 the Fiat Zero series went into production, Italy's answer to

Fiat Auto spa, Turin

1899 founded by Giovanni Agnelli and others in Turin

1919 Lingotto plant (until 1921)

1939 Mirafiori plant

1945 Senator Giovanni Agnelli dies

1958 Centro Stile design center established

1963 Giovanni Agnelli, Giovanni's grandson. becomes managing director and, in 1966, chairman

1968 City Taxi by **Pio Manzú** at Centro Stile

Fiat *Nuova 500* by Dante Giacosa, 1957 (mahogany model)

Ford's *Model T.* By the early 1930s Fiat had developed into Italy's leading car manufacturer and began to focus on an emerging mass market with family sedans like the 1932 *Balilla.* But Fiat also continued to make luxury cars, hiring car-body stylists like **Bertone** and **PininFarina** to design sleek sports cars such as the elegantly streamlined Fiat *1500* of 1935.

With the economic boom of the mid-1950s, a golden era began for the carmaker. In 1961, 90 percent of all cars sold in Italy were made by Fiat; between 1969 and 1973 the company more than doubled its output. After the 1974 oil crisis, low fuel consumption was suddenly as important as attractive design. Two hugely successful models were introduced in the eighties: the 1980 Fiat *Panda,* designed by **Giorgetto Giugiaro,** made a stir with its stripped-down look that emphasized the car's practical value. It was followed by Giugiaro's inexpensive 1983 Fiat *Uno,* which became the quintessential subcompact.

In recent decades, the Fiat group has taken over its former competitors **Lancia** and Alfa Romeo, and acquired a majority stake in Ferrari. In addition to cars, it manufactures trucks, buses, and utility vehicles, constructs dams, tunnels, satellites, and rocket engines, and develops pacemakers, lighting, robot technology, and computer systems for the health-care industry.

1969 acquisition of **Lancia** and **Ferrari**
1982 Lingotto plant is closed (turned into convention center)
1984 purchase of Palazzo Grassi in Venice; turned into museum
1987 Fiat buys **Alfa Romeo**

Models
1912 *Zero* subcompact
1932 *Balilla* sedan
1935 *1500* sportscar
1936 *500 Topolino* subcompact
1952 *8 V* racing car
1955 *600* subcompact
1957 *Nuova 500* subcompact
1959 *1800/1900* sedan
1964 *850* subcompact
1972 *X 1/9* convertible
1980 *Panda* subcompact
1988 *Tipo* compact car
1993 *Cinquecento* subcompact; *Seicento* subcompact

Fiat *124 Sport Spyder* by Pininfarina, 1966

Page 187
top: Fiat *Uno*, 1983
bottomright: Fiat *Punto*, 1993; both by Giorgetto Giugiaro

FIORUCCI

Fashion and accessories manufacturer

Fiorucci srl, Milan/
Edwin International Inc.,
Tokyo

1935 Elio Fiorucci born in Milan

1967 first Fiorucci store
in Milan

1974 opening of Fiorucci store
on Via Torino, Milan

1976 Fiorucci store in New York

1990 Fiorucci brand bought by
Edwin International Inc.,
Japan, Elio Fiorucci
continues as creative
director and PR manager

When Elio Fiorucci opened his first store in the Galleria Passarella in 1967, he gave Milan's teenagers their first taste of the street fashions of Swinging London. Fiorucci imported Ossi Clark's and Zandra Rhodes's mod styles to Milan and developed his own designs, which soon became wildly popular. With inexpensive jeans, T-shirts, and accessories, he created a distinctive look that was as sexy, romantic, and exuberantly colorful as the company logo's Raphaelite putti, while a slew of advertising brochures turned the Fiorucci style into an ongoing statement on Italian youth culture (fig. p. 26). The Fiorucci stores that opened all over the world in the 1970s were gigantic playgrounds, hedonistic temples to the joys of fashion and bric-a-brac, food, music, and art. As the prime exporter of a new, post-sixties Italian dolce vita, Fiorucci became a trendsetter in sportswear and successfully marketed his brand in international licensing deals. The brand was acquired by Edwin Inc. of Japan in 1990, but Elio Fiorucci has remained as head of its creative development and marketing departments.

Shoe from 1998 collection

Page 199
top left: Fiorucci's "Angels" logo
top right:, bottom right: 1997/1998
collection
bottom left: platform shoes, 1970s

FLOS

Lighting Manufacturer

From the tall *Arco* floor lamp, which curves to provide overhead lighting, to the ready-made aesthetic of the upright *Toio* lamp, with its car headlight mounted on a skinny pole; from the *Frisbi* ceiling light, which shoots direct light downward and diffused light outward, to the monumental *Taccia* table lamp, the list of **Achille** and **Pier Giacomo Castiglioni's** creations for Flos reads like a history of modern lighting design. The two brothers defined the profile of the company, which was founded in 1962 by **Dino Gavina** and Cesare **Cassina**. In recent years, Achille, whose brother died in 1968, has contributed such elegant designs as the Brera and Fuscia hanging lamps to the Flos collection.

Tobia Scarpa (occasionally in cooperation with his wife, **Afra**) and, more recently, Philippe Starck have also made designs for the company. Scarpa's designs are predominantly simple, airy constructions, like the *Ariette 1-2-3* ceiling light, with a shade of

Flos spa, Bovezzo
1962 founded by Dino **Gavina** and **Cesare Cassina**
1995 *Compasso d'oro*

Products
1961 *Splügenbräu* ceiling light
1962 *Taccia* table lamp;
 Arco floor lamp;
 Toio floor lamp;
 all by **Achille** and **Pier Giacomo Castiglioni**
1968 *Biagio* table lamp
 by **Tobia Scarpa**
1970 *Parentesi* lamp
1972 *Noce T* floor and table lamp
1976 *Ipotenusa* table lamp;
 all by Achille Castiglioni

Luminator floor lamp by Achille and Pier Giacomo Castiglioni for Gilardi and Bazarghi, 1954, now produced by Flos

Taraxacum 88 C-W lamp by Achille Castiglioni, 1988

semitransparent fabric that reveals the electrical cord above it when the light is switched on; and the Butterfly floor lamp, whose glass reflector resembles a paper accordion. Since the 1980s Starck has contributed a number of humorous interpretations of traditional forms, including the *Rosy Angelis* floor lamp, where a piece of fabric is casually thrown over the light source, and the inexpensive, solid-colored *Miss Sissy* lamp, which looks like a toy-town version of a bar lamp.

In 1974, Flos bought its competitor **Arteluce**, which had been founded by Gino **Sarfatti**. Today, *Arteluce by Flos* comprises an independent line of lighting by younger designers, including **Marc Sadler, Rodolfo Dordoni**, and **Matteo Thun**, as well as Gino Sarfatti's legendary models from the 1950s and 1960s. The company also produces the Flos Murano glassware line in a joint venture with **Venini**, commercial lighting under the *Flight* label, and the Arteluce Bagno lighting systems.

1988 *Arà* table lamp
1989 *Luci Fair* wall lamp
both by Philippe Starck
1990 *Pierrot* desk lamp by Afra and Tobia Scarpa
1991 *Miss Sissy* table lamp by Philippe Starck
1992 *Brera* lamp by Achille Castiglioni
1994 *Rosy Angelis* floor lamp by Philippe Starck
1996 *Fucsia* hanging lamp by Achille Castiglioni; *Romeo Moon* and *Romeo Babe* hanging lamps by Philippe Starck

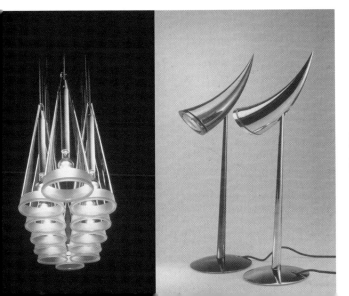

Fucsia hanging lamp
by Achille Castiglioni, 1996
Arà table lamp
by Philippe Starck, 1988

FONTANA ARTE

Lighting and furniture manufacturer

Fontana Arte has a long, if temporarily interrupted, tradition of design. The famous architect and designer **Gio Ponti** founded the firm in 1932 as the artistic arm of Luigi Fontana's glass factory. Ponti, as well as **Pietro Chiesa**, contributed high-quality glass furniture and lamps to the Fontana Arte collection. The company lost its distinctive profile when it was acquired, after the war, by the French St. Gobain group. In 1979, Carlo Guglielmi bought Fontana Arte and revived its former cachet by collaborating with a number of renowned designers. **Daniela Puppa** and **Franco Raggi** created exhibits for trade fairs; **Pierluigi Cerri** designed the visual communication, and **Gae Aulenti** was appointed art director. In the 1980s and '90s the company developed outstanding furniture and lighting collections that reaffirmed Fontana Arte's status as a leading force in Italian design. Its Schopenhauer collection comprises exquisite tables and chairs, including Aulenti's famous Tour glass table on wheels. In addition, Fontana Arte produces the Candle and Naskaloris lighting collections.

Fontana Arte spa, Corsico
1932 founded by **Gio Ponti**
1998 *Compasso d'oro*

Products
1931 *0024* hanging lamp
by Gio Ponti (reintrod.)
1967 *Pirellina* table and floor
lamp by Gio Ponti
1971 *Daruma* table lamp by
Sergio Asti (Candle)
1985 *Tea* hanging lamp by
Pierluigi Cerri
1989 *Franceschina*
table and hanging lamp by
Umberto Riva
1991 *2892 Small,
3064 Medium, 2850 XL*
table lamps by
Daniela Puppa
1992 *Piccola San* table lamp by
Daniela Puppa
1993 *Tour* table by **Gae Aulenti**
1996 *3094 Alzaia* hanging lamp
by **Vico Magistretti**

Glass table by Pietro Chiesa, 1932

Page 203
left: *Luminator 0556* floor lamp by
Pietro Chiesa, 1933
top right: *Congo* container by
Rodolfo Dordoni, 1998
lower right: *Bilia* lamp by Gio Ponti,
1931 (reintrod.)

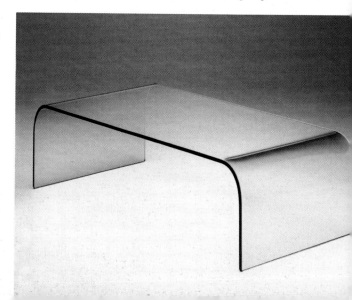

Piero FORNASETTI

Product and graphic designer, artist, and illustrator

Suns, fish, flowers, and architectural motifs populate the design world of Piero Fornasetti, a self-taught, all-around genius who covered every conceivable product—from plates and cups to vases, textiles, wallpaper and buttons—with his trompe l'oeil imagery. All told, Fornasetti, whose works transform the visible world into a magical realm of surrealistic effects and illusion, created more than 11,000 decorative designs.

Expelled from Milan's Brera art school because he wouldn't accept its educational ideas and values, Fornasetti went on to become a painter, sculptor, artisan and decorator, and a set, costume, exhibition, graphic, and product designer. Ironically, his rise to fame came in the 1950s, when the new functionalist Italian design experienced its first great successes. An especially fertile relationship developed between Fornasetti and **Gio Ponti,** whom he had met at the 1940 *Triennale* and who published his works in *Domus* magazine. Fornasetti decorated many of Ponti's furniture and interior designs with his motifs (fig. p. 39). In 1950, they cooperated in the design of the casino in San Remo.

A renewed interest in surfaces made Fornasetti popular once more in the 1980s. Since Fornasetti's death in 1988, his son, Barnaba, has carried on his work. Products in the typical Fornasetti style can be seen in his Milan showroom on Via Manzoni.

1913 born in Milan

1930 studies art at Accademia di Brera, Milan (expelled in 1932)

1950 interior of casino in San Remo with **Gio Ponti**

1951 interior of Dulciora bakery, Milan

1970 opens store in Milan

1988 dies in Milan

Products

1940 cover designs for *Domus* magazine

1951 *Architettura* series

1952 collaborates on interiors for cruise ship *Andrea Doria*

1954 twelve plates with Adam-and-Eve motifs

1955 *Stanza Metafisica* (until 1958)

Page 205

left: *Dedicato a Piero e Gio* by Barnaba Fornasetti, 1990

top right: Platter, c. 1950-55

bottom right: *Quattro stagioni* chair, c. 1955

Architettura coffee set, 1960s

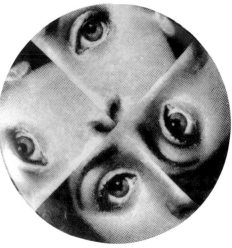

Gianfranco FRATTINI

Architect, furniture and lighting designer

Gianfranco Frattini's design philosophy crystallized in the 1950s under the influence of the Scandinavian school, which he greatly admired. He shares the Nordic designers' sense for detail and their love of carpentry—qualities apparent in his elegant wooden furniture for **Cassina** and **Bernini,** including the *804* bureau of 1961 and the wooden *Practica* bookcase of 1981.

Though they have sometimes been called unspectacular, Frattini's designs are more aptly described as deeply serious. He has consistently stuck to the conviction that the design process does not end with the completed drawing but continues until the final phase of production. With his thoughtful, meticulous approach, Frattini has also helped pioneer the use of industrial materials in innovative designs, such as his well-known set of plastic tables for Cassina and the *Boalum* snake light, a rather spectacular coil of luminescent tubing that he created for **Artemide** in collaboration with Livio Castiglioni.

1926 born in Padua

1952 collaboration with
Gio Ponti (until 1954)

1953 graduates from
architecture school in
Milan

1956 cofounder of **ADI**

Products

1961 *804* bureau for **Bernini**

1966 *780* set of tables
for **Cassina**;desk for
Bernini;*Damecuta* sofa and
chair for **C&B Italia**

1970 *Boalum*
light tube for **Artemide** mit
Livio Castiglioni

1974 *Kioto* table for Ghianda

1978 *Megaron* floor lamp
for Artemide

1980 office chair for **Fantoni**

1981 *Practica* shelf unit for
Bernini

1988 office system for Knoll

Kioto table for Ghianda, 1974

Page 207

Megaron Terra floor lamp
for Artemide, 1979

804 bureau for Bernini, 1961

Maestro table for Acerbis, 1996

Futurism was one of the most radical movements within the European avant-garde. In his seminal 1909 manifesto, Futurism's spokesman, Filippo Tommaso Marinetti, proclaimed its course: "We declare that the world's glories have been enriched by a new beauty: the beauty of speed. A racing car, its body adorned by great pipes like snakes with explosive breath . . . a roaring car that seems to run on grenades is more beautiful than the Nike of Samothrake." The Futurists rigorously denounced *"il passatismo,"* the adherence to the past and to the ossified educational and aesthetic ideals of the nineteenth century, and instead propagated free, unbridled inspiration. They enthusiastically embraced the age of the machine (including the machines of war, which made them spiritual fathers of Fascism) in a country that was still predominantly agrarian.

While the big city, with its crowds of people and ceaseless traffic, was its central theme, Futurism had little impact on architectural practice. The movement did have an architect in **Antonio Sant'Elia,** but while his 1914 study, *La nuova città,* shows towering high-rises, underpasses, and transparent glass-and-steel structures, its true focus is on the movement of traffic.

Futurism was also not a design movement—industrial design was still decades in the future. Still, the Futurists were interested

in utilitarian objects and their form. In his 1914 Futurist manifesto, **Fortunato Depero** wrote, "We must destroy traditional clothing . . . We must invent Futurist clothing." The garments he had in mind were supposed to be "dynamic," "aggressive," "violent," and "astounding." In 1914, the futurist painter **Giacomo Balla** presented clothing designs whose pointed shapes and sharply angular patterns were inspired by Cubism.

By the end of the First World War, Futurism was well past its prime, but Futurist ideas and stylistic aspects—such as the representation of dynamic processes—persisted in graphic design, advertising, and applied arts throughout the 1920s and 1930s. After 1919, Depero designed posters for **Campari** as well as toys, wallpaper, lamps, rugs, and rather rustic-looking wooden furniture. During those years, **Marcello Nizzoli** \and **Bruno Munari** also worked for Campari. After the Second World War, Futurism, with its ideological ties to Fascism, was passé.

A resurgence of Futurism's formal aesthetics occurred in the late 1980s, when the **Bolidismo** movement, formed around the designer **Massimo Iosa Ghini** and a group of architects from Bologna, appropriated its dynamic lines in their sofa and kitchen designs.

"From Futurism, Italian design has inherited the ability to continuously put objects in relationship to the metropolis, the ›metropolis‹ being a stage that gives meaning to the modern sign."

Andrea Branzi

From left:

Poster by von Fortunato Depero for Campari, 1920s

Vest by Fortunato Depero, 1924

If Rain Were Campari Bitter, poster for Campari, 1926

Tea set by Giacomo Balla, 1928

GAVINA

Furniture Manufacturer

Dino Gavina's once had business cards printed that read simply, "Dino Gavina-Revolutionary." A passionate art lover, Gavina founded a small furniture company in 1949 and used it to fight, with missionary zeal, for a modern, poetic design liberated from an overly rationalist straightjacket. Always open to experiment, Gavina enthusiastically embraced the new ideas formulated by such architects as Carlo Mollino, Carlo De Carli, Carlo Scarpa, and Franco Albini, whom he met in Milan in the early 1950s. Between 1955 and 1960 he produced furniture ranging from Achille and Pier Giacomo Castiglioni's San Luca chair in the Neo-Liberty style to Marco Zanuso's Milord chair. To find spiritual fellow travelers was always more important to him than commercial success. Success found him, however, when in 1962 Gavina reintroduced Marcel Breuer's tubular steel furniture to international acclaim. (That year he also cofounded another design company, the lighting manufacturer Flos, with Cesare Cassina.) He also produced Carlo Scarpa's furniture, including the nine-foot-long Doge table, made of flat steel and crystal. In 1968 Gavina sold his company to Knoll and established Simon International.

Sanluca chair by Achille and
Pier Giacomo Castiglioni, 1960

Romeo GIGLI

Fashion designer

Romeo Gigli is a stylistic globetrotter, a fashion designer whose poetic and sometimes cerebral creations, which often incorporate ethnic motifs, attest to his sensitivity to other cultures. After dropping out of architecture school, Gigli traveled throughout Asia, North Africa, and South America before becoming an apprentice at the studio of the New York couturier Dimitri. Upon his return to Italy he worked as a designer for Callaghan, and in 1984 created his first collection. In the late 1980s Gigli presented luxurious, gold-embroidered coats inspired by clothes worn by the Byzantine empress Theodora. And in 1989 he stirred up the Paris fashion crowd when he went against prevailing trends by eliminating shoulder pads in favor of a soft, feminine silhouette with unusual necklines and high waists. Gigli has since returned to simpler lines and cuts.

1950 born in Faenza
1979 works for Dimitri, New York
1985 Collaboration with Zamasport
1986 international breakthrough
1988 Spazio Romeo Gigli iopens in Milan
1989 Collaboration with Ermenegildo Zegna; presentation in Paris
1990 *Woolmark Award*
1997 Japanese investors support Gigli's company

Products
1984 first collection under Gigli
1986 first menswear collection
1989 perfume *Romeo di Romeo Gigli; Teodora* collection
1990 *G Gigli collection*

Donna collection 1989/90 (*Teodora*)

Stefano GIOVANNONI

Architect, furniture, and product designer

1954 born in La Spezia

1978 graduates from
architecture school in
Florence

1985 collaboration with **Guido
Venturini** in King-
Kong studio (until 1989)

Products

1986 *Iguana Jeans* for Levi's

1987 *Girotondo* series
with Guido Venturini

1993 *Fruit Mama* bowl;
Merdolino toilet brush;
Lilliput salt and pepper set
and *Nutty the cracker*
all for **Alessi**

1996 *Roller Ball* wristwatch
for Seiko

Girotondo series for Alessi, 1987,
with Guido Venturini

Bombo barstool for Magis, 1996

As a young boy, Stefano Giovannoni was so fascinated by the sea creatures he saw at the beaches and in the markets of his hometown, La Spezia, that he made them the subjects of small picture stories. Since the late 1980s he has created a similarly fanciful world of products that strike a peculiar balance between utilitarian function and a design vocabulary inspired by science fiction, movies, and comic strips. A nutcracker takes the form of a squirrel named *Nutty the Cracker;* his *Lilliput* salt and pepper shakers are egg-shaped homunculi; the *Merdolino* toilet brush (all for **Alessi**) sits in a flower pot; and a barstool for Magis comes with a Hula Hoop that serves as a footrest. Brightly colored, they appeal to playful instincts and reflect a design approach in which form follows fun. When Giovannoni worked with **Guido Venturini** in the 1980s, their studio was named **King-Kong**. "We were never afraid to be kitschy," Giovannoni has said. Their disrespect for the rules of good taste paid off. King-Kong's *Girotondo* series of kitchen utensils and tableware, decorated with a round dance of perforated little figures, became a huge success, selling more than a million pieces.

Giorgetto GIUGIARO

Automobile and industrial designer

Introduced in 1974, the Volkswagen *Golf* (called the Rabbit in the U.S. until 1985) quickly become one of the most successful German cars in history. It had been designed by Giorgetto Giugiaro, one of Italy's leading body makers. At the time, Giugiaro could already look back at an impressive career. As an automobile designer at **Fiat's** Centro Stile and later at **Bertone** and **Ghia,** he had specialized in luxury cars. In 1968 he established his own firm, **Italdesign,** with Aldo Mantovani. Italdesign ushered in a new era in automobile design—the company offered an unprecedented range of preproduction services, from the development of models and prototypes to the calculation of production schedules and processes to plans for automation and implementation. Since then, Italdesign has worked for BMW, Hyundai, Renault, and Audi and has developed such highly successful models as the *Alfasud,* Fiat *Panda,* Fiat *Uno,* VW *Passat,* and VW *Scirocco.*

In the early 1970s, Giugiaro realized that the market, suffering from the effects of the oil crisis and a general recession, was

1938 born in Garessio
Cuneo

1955 joins Centro Stile **Fiat** after graduating from school of art and technology, Turin

1959 joins **Bertone**

1965 becomes director at **Ghia**

1968 **Italdesign** founded

1981 **Giugiaro Design** founded; *Compasso d'oro* (also 1984, 1991, 1995)

1987 Giugiaro spa founded: accessories, clothing

Bugatti *EB 112,* 1993

ready for inexpensive small and mid-sized cars. And he has always held that the automobile industry, where large quantities of a very expensive object must be sold in a highly competitive market, needs to subject the design process to a continuous reality check. Giugiaro believes that "within a company's decision-making structure, the designer must have the courage to question whether it makes sense to launch a new product, whether it will appeal to the consumer. This may sound like marketing theory but without good design marketing is rarely successful."

His firm, **Giugiaro Design,** founded in 1981, is committed to functional, user-oriented products, and has developed cameras, watches, dishwashers, furniture, racing boats, trains, sewing machines, and even a new pasta shape. The firm emphasizes technological innovation; for example, its *F4* for Nikon, developed in 1988, was the first camera equipped with autofocus. The firm's work does not end with the development of a product but extends to naming, packaging, and promoting it. In recent years, Giugiaro has further broadened his scope by establishing Giugiaro spa, which produces clothing and accessories. His daughter, Laura, following in Giugiaro's footsteps, has recently introduced successful fashion and jewelry collections of her own.

GRUPPO (Cinelli/Columbus/Tecno Tubo Torino)

Manufacturer of bicycles and bicycle accessories

Gruppo spa, Caleppio
di Settala (MI)

1930 Columbus founded;
Cinelli founded
in 1940s

1961 Tecno Tubo Torino founded

1996 merger under new name,
Gruppo

Products

1991 *Laser Evoluzione* bicycle
(*Compasso d'oro*)

1995 *Rampichino* mountain bike

1996 *Spinaci,* handlebar
extension; all by Cinelli

Page 217
Laser Evoluzione bicycle, 1991
Spinaci handlebar extension, 1996

Soft Machine bicycle, 1998 (Cinelli)
Altec² Megatubes, 1998 (Columbus)

In Italy, **Cinelli** is synonymous with bicycling in the same way that Ferrari stands for car racing. Fidel Castro and Bruce Springsteen own bicycles by Cinelli; Simon Lessing used Cinelli handlebars in his successful run for the 1995 World Triathlon title, as did Chris Boardman when he set a new world record by riding 56.375 kilometers (34.95 miles) in one hour.

Founded in the early 1940s, Cinelli has continuously come up with technological innovations, such as its recently introduced *Aliante* bicycle frame, which weighs a mere three pounds. In 1985 the company introduced mountain biking to Italy with the sleek *Rampichino* model. A love of cycling and enthusiasm for design have always gone hand in hand at the Milan company, which has worked with designers like **Matteo Thun** and the **Alchimia** studio. The company won a *Compasso d'oro* in 1991 for the *Laser Evoluzione* racing bike, a true technological marvel; its *Spinaci* handlebar extension, which reduces the strain on riders' bodies, combines ergonomic form and function with a riot of colors and wild patterns. In 1996 Cinelli merged with **3 T (Tecno Tubo Torino),** Italy's leading producer of handlebars, and the frame manufacturer **Columbus** to form Gruppo. Gruppo produces racing, mountain, and touring bikes, though its backbone is its wide range of colorful accessories.

GRUPPO IND. BUSNELLI

Furniture manufacturer

The design historian Anty Pansera's once described Gruppo Industriale Busnelli as "200,000 square meters of seating." With its large-scale production of seating furniture, the company, whose methods are taken straight from automobile manufacturing, is the exception within a furniture industry characterized by smaller firms. Founded in 1953, the company is a conglomerate of 240 firms, ranging from textile and metal manufacturers to computer labs. In 1972 it moved to Misinto and has since been the leading player in the development of the surrounding region. Always open to technological innovation, Busnelli experimented with **Pirelli's** new steel-reinforced foam rubber in the 1950s and with plastics in the 1960s. *Argin,* an amorphous sculpture created in 1974 by Studio Libidarch, was among the more unusual results of the company's R&D efforts. Today, renowned designers such as **Bruno Gecchelin, Ugo La Pietra,** and **Giotto Stoppino** ensure the formal variety of Busnelli's products.

Gruppo Industriale
Busnelli spa, Misinto

1953 founded in Meda

1969 establishment of Centro
Studi e Ricerche; use of
plastics

1972 moves to Misinto

Products

1955 *Bilux* convertible sofa by
Augusto Managhi and
Alessandro Terzaghi

1966 *Miranda* chair
by **Bruno Gecchelin**

1984 *Flessuosa* sofa and chair
by **Ugo La Pietra**

1992 *Rock bergère* chair by
Giotto Stoppino

Libro chair by Gruppo DAM, 1970
Sessel *Fiocco* chair by G 14,
1970 (reintroduced in 1987)

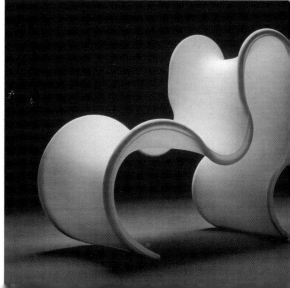

Furniture manufacturer

When furniture dealers started offering Gufram's *Multipli* objects around 1970, their shops and windows suddenly resembled surrealist landscapes. Customers marveled at the bright red *Bocca* "lip sofa," the *Pratone* polyurethane turf (fig. p. 20), the inflatable *Cactus* clothes tree, and the *Capitello* seat, which looked like the capital of a Greek column but was made of soft plastic. Produced in limited editions, these pieces were pure Pop design, inspired by the **Radical Design** movement of the 1960s. Far from being appropriate, sensible, elegant solutions, their forms were freely taken from contexts outside of design. The creative minds behind this strange furniture were a group of young Turin designers and artists, including Studio 65, **Gruppo Strum,** the design duo of **Guido Drocco** and **Franco Mello,** and Piero Gilardi. Since 1978, Gufram has also designed furniture for movie houses, theaters, hotels, and universities.

Gufram srl, Balangero (TO)

1966 founded

1968 production of *Multipli* design objects in limited editions

Products

1971 *Pratone* artificial turf by Ceretti, Derossi, Rossi; *Bocca* sofa by Studio 65

1972 *Cactus* clothes tree by **Guido Drocco/Franco Mello**; *Capitello* seat by Studio 65

1974 *Massolo* by Piero Gilardi

Cactus clothes tree by Guido Drocco/Franco Mello, 1972
Bocca sofa by Studio 65, 1971

Isao HOSOE

Furniture and industrial designer

Trained in Tokyo as an aerospace engineer, Isao Hosoe compares the design process with a tornado: though full of tempestuous force, it is calculable to a certain degree, and the energy ultimately gathers in one single point. It is this point, the ideal result, that Hosoe is seeking, with the close cooperation of his team of designers, clients, and students. There is no "Hosoe style"; his solutions always follow the project's specific requirements, though often with an unexpected twist. His small plastic ashtray for **Kartell,** for example, revolves and works from either side. And the *Heron* desk lamp is highly functional, but looks like a friendly bird, in order to brighten up the workday.

Hosoe has also designed public transportation, such as the *Spazio* bus for Iveco (with Antonio Barrese, Pietro Salmoiraghi, Angelo Torricelli, and Antonio Locatelli), furniture, and office solutions.

1942 born in Tokyo

1967 studies space technology in Tokyo

1970 *Compasso d'oro* (also 1979, 1998)

Products

1971 melamine ashtray for **Kartell**

1977 *Spazio* bus for Iveco Carozzeria Orlandi with Antonio Barrese, Pietro Salmoiraghi, Angelo Torricelli, Antonio Locatelli

1996 *Gyra* lamp for **Luxo Italia**

1997 *Cosmo* office chair for BIF, Korea

1998 *HOI* lamp for Luxo Italia with Peter Salomon

Flo TV stand for Tonelli, 1997

Interior of *Spazio* bus for Iveco Carozzeria Orlandi, 1977

Massimo IOSA GHINI

Architect, furniture and product designer

In his comic strips for the magazines *Frigidaire, Fashion News,* and *Vanity* in the early 1980s, Massimo Iosa Ghini depicted the adventures of a spy named Capitano Sillavengo in a futuristic urban landscape. It wasn't long before he turned his imagination toward real products. Ghini came to product and furniture design by way of television, for which he created studio sets and graphic inserts. He got his professional start with the **Memphis** group in 1986, at the same joining forces with other Bologna architects to invent **Bolidismo,** a style that borrowed freely from **Futurism** with additional flashbacks to the American streamline look and 1950s aesthetics. Curves, ellipses, and boldly receding lines characterized his first collection of upholstered furniture for Moroso, which was introduced under the title *Dinamic* in 1986 and made him instantly famous. Iosa Ghini has continued to work with **Moroso,** while also designing kitchens, sunglasses, and comprehensive corporate identity programs, as well as showrooms for **Fiorucci,** Renault, **Ferrari,** Maserati, and Ominitel.

1959 born in Bologna

1982 studies architecture in Florence and Milan

1985 works for RAI

1986 collaboration with **Memphis**/12 New; cofounder of Bolidismo in Bologna

Products

1989 *Newtone* collection for **Moroso**

1991 *Philips Design Edition*

1993 *Big Mama* chair for Moroso

1994 Showrooms for **Ferrari**

1998 store designs for Omnitel

Rodi screen for Lisar, 1991
Dinamic Collection for Moroso (bench, chair and table), 1986

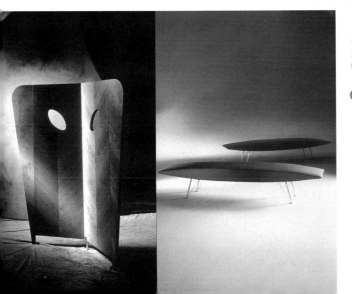

KARTELL

Manufacturer of plastic furniture and accessories

Kartell spa., Noviglio

1949 founded by Giulio Castelli in Milan

1953 production of small household objects

1958 establishment of Labware division

1964 experiments with furniture

1972 move to Noviglio near Milan

1979 *Compasso d'oro*

1988 Giulio Castelli leaves, Claudio Luti becomes new general manager

1993 acquisition of Standard e Casa Kit

In the mid-1990s a bookshelf appeared that sold by the running yard. Today, the brightly colored *Bookworm* can be spotted winding its way along the walls of trendy shops, apartments, offices and lobbies all over Europe. Its inventor, Ron Arad, is thrilled by how his invention has multiplied. Originally designed in steel, *Bookworm* became an overwhelming success when it was produced in thermoplastic polymer.

Plastic, of course, is as inexpensive as it is durable, but for a long time it was stigmatized as a cheap, inferior material. The fact that such perceptions have changed is in great part due to the pioneering work of Kartell and the vision of its founder, the chemist and engineer Giulio Castelli, who is still a vital force in his company's management. He once said, "if people are afraid of the new, give them something even newer." He has done just that. In 1953, his company, which had previously focused on car accessories, began bringing a fresh new look and bright colors to Italy's hopelessly dull housewares industry. Company designer **Gino Colombini** revolutionized the design of these small, inexpensive items, winning numerous awards for his attractive juicers, garbage cans, storage containers, and other kitchen utensils (fig. p. 23)

In the 1950s it was not yet possible to make plastic furniture, due to the material's softness, but by the early 1960s technological advances allowed the production of the first plastic chair. The cheerful *K 4999* polyethylene children's chair, designed in 1961 by **Marco Zanuso** and **Richard Sapper** and introduced in 1964, did not reveal the long hours of research that Kartell's laboratories had put into its development. Stackable, weather- and shock-resistant, it ushered in a decade when plastic furniture became the rage in Italy and soon the rest of the world.

Page 223

top left: *Bookworm* by Ron Arad, 1994

bottom left: *K 4999* children's chair by Marco Zanuso and Richard Sapper, 1964

right: *4970/84* container elements by Anna Castelli Ferrieri, 1967

KARTELL

As political protest movements and the emergent pop culture swept the Western world, traditional notions of a classic, elegant lifestyle eroded or at least gave room to fresh interpretations. Furniture makers—and consumers—freely experimented with new forms and colors, and plastic became the preferred material as it opened up entirely new possibilities for furniture design. Kartell laid the groundwork with a continuous output of innovative patented plastics and new products created by the best contemporary designers, including **Joe Colombo, Gae Aulenti, Vico Magistretti, Anna Castelli Ferrieri, Ignazio Gardella, Achille Castiglioni, Giotto Stoppini, Sergio Asti, Centrokappa,** among others. Colombo's *4867* of 1968 was one of the first large chairs made of ABS plastic. Chubby and stackable, it hit a nerve with the public and quickly became a bestseller.

Anna Castelli Ferrieri joined Kartell in the mid-1960s and remained the defining force behind the company's products well into the 1980s. For each new plastic the company developed, she found it an appropriate form. Her *4970/84* stacking containers of 1967, made of ABS plastic, worked without screws or braces. In 1976 she demonstrated how elegant and beautiful plastic salad servers could be; three years later she designed the first plastic stool with long legs—made possible through a unique combination of polypropylene and metal; and her *4870* and *4873* polypropylene chairs of 1985–86 offered a graceful alternative to the blandness of conventional white plastic patio furniture.

Plastics have become a sophisticated material. Since the 1980s, Kartell has added furniture by younger international design stars to its collections, including Philippe Starck's *Dr.*

Page 225

top left: *4822/26* stool, 1979
bottom left: *4870* chair, 1986
top and bottom right: *4310* table,
1983; all by Anna Castelli Ferrieri

KARTELL

Glob chair. More recently, the company has produced Starck's *Miss Tripp,* an inexpensive chair that jauntily combines wood with pastel-colored plastic and comes disassembled, to be put together at home. Arad's *Bookworm* and Antonio Citterio's elegant *Mobil* container system, made of translucent plastic, became design icons of the 1990s. But even the old masters of Italian design continue to explore new directions. Like most of Kartell's products, Vico Magistretti's molded *Maui* chair is available in many colors, and it seems set to become as popular as Arne Jacobsen's famous *Ant* chair, whose form it echoes.

From material to design—this formula has fueled Kartell's new, affordable solutions for more than five decades, a longevity that makes the company an exception in international furniture manufacturing. Kartell's current managing director, Claudio Luti, once called the firm's staff and designers "missionaries for plastic." Their commitment benefits not only the development of furniture and housewares—Kartell also produces supplies for laboratories and research institutions, which make up almost half of its total sales.

Page 227

top left: *Hi-Glob 4860* stool
by Philippe Starck, 1992

top right: ashtray
by Isao Hosoe, 1971

bottom: magazine rack
by Giotto Stoppino, 1971

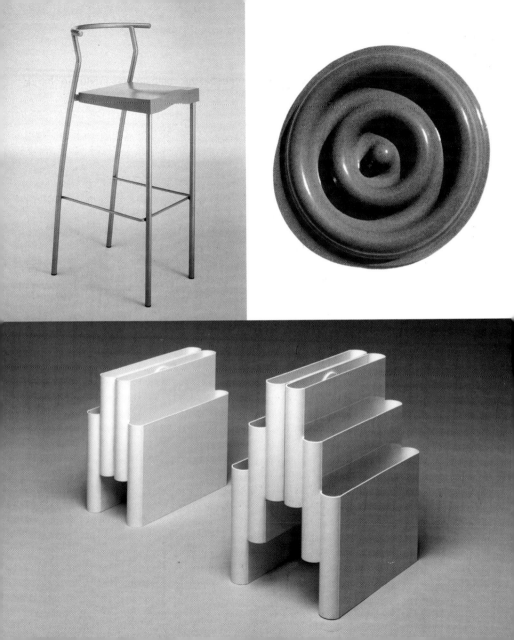

KING-MIRANDA

Industrial, furniture and lighting designers

1975 studio in Milan

1990 EDEN (European Designers Network) founded

Products

1974 *Type Face Design,* manifesto for **Olivetti**

1978 exhibition design for *Design Process Olivetti 1908–1979*

1980 corporate identity for **Arteluce**

1983 interfaces for Olivetti office machines

1984 dance club interior for *Sogno A* in Tokyo

1986 *Beato* chair for Disform

1990 *Sedia N* chair for Atelier International

1992 *Polo* fan for Elettro plastica Elettrodomestici

1995 cellphones for Ericsson

1996 *Borealis* lamp for Louis Poulsen; *Tam Tam* lamp for Sirrah

In 1996, for the first time in its history the renowned Danish lighting manufacturer Louis Poulsen turned to a non-Scandinavian studio to design a new outdoor light. Perhaps it was King-Miranda's mix of British understatement and Spanish temperament that prompted the decision. The result of the cooperation was a high-tech creation named *Borealis,* which now illuminates areas like the plaza in front of the La Défense arch in Paris.

The studio of Perry A. King and Santiago Miranda, which has been based in Milan since the mid-1970s, specializes in a combination of serious design research, a talent for presenting technology in a beguiling package, and the courage to use suggestive forms to satisfy emotional needs. King-Miranda have designed computer interfaces and photocopiers for Olivetti, as well as chairs and corporate identity programs. They are particularly fascinated by light; the best known of their many designs for Arteluce is probably the *Donald* desk lamp, a friendly homage to Disney's cartoon duck. In addition to their numerous research projects, they have also established the European Designers Network, EDEN.

GSM cellphone for Ericsson, 1995
Donald lamp for Arteluce, 1978

KRIZIA

Fashion designer

Mariuccia Mandelli took her professional alias, Krizia, from a Platonic dialogue that denounces the vanity of women. Interested in fashion from an early age, she followed her parents' wishes and became a teacher before designing her first practical clothes for young women in 1954. A decade later she became famous overnight when she won the *Critica della Moda* prize for her presentation at the Palazzo Pitti in Florence. In the 1960s she experimented with Op Art elements and in 1970 dressed her models in hot pants, which became a European fashion hit the following year.

One of Krizia's trademarks are animal motifs, which have accompanied her collections since the 1960s; every year a new animal shows up on her T-shirts, sweaters, or dresses as a good-luck charm. Krizia has consistently offered a range of designs from which any woman can chose pieces that suit her personal style. Her work has significantly contributed to the success of Italian ready-to-wear fashion.

1933 Mariuccia Mandelli born in Bergamo

1954 makes her first tops and skirts

1964 presents collection in Florence and wins *Critica della Moda* prize

1970 introduces hot pants

1971 *Tiberio d'oro* prize

1986 appointed *Commendatore della Repubblica Italiana*

1995 *Krizia. Una storia,* exhibition in Milan

Products

1964 Op-Art collection

1967 *Kriziamaglia* knitwear collection

1970 Hot pants

1978 pleated raincoats

1991 *Krizia Uomo* menswear collection

left: Dress from summer collection 1997

right: Dress, 1964, received the *Premio Pitti Critica della Moda*

Ugo LA PIETRA

Artist, architect, furniture and lighting designer

1938 born in Tirino (Pescara)

1964 graduates from architecture school in Milan

1973 cofounder of **Global Tools**

1979 *Compasso d'oro*

1981 editor at *Domus* (until 1985)

1985 art director for **Gruppo Industriale Busnelli**

Products

1969 *Uno sull'altro* bookcase

1975 *Telaio* bed with canopy

1983 *La casa telematica*, exhibit at Milan furniture fair

1984 *Pretenziosa* chair; *Agevole* chair; both for Gruppo Ind. Busnelli

1988 marble table for **Up&Up**

1997 *A bocca aperta* mirror

Plants shoot out of a tabletop; a vase, rather than serving as a vessel for cut flowers, offers a flat surface to grow a small garden. With "moral recklessness," in the words of Pierre Restany, Ugo La Pietra illustrates his conviction that art objects and utilitarian items have moved toward a synthesis outside the notion of "arts and crafts."

A designer, artist, filmmaker, exhibition organizer, critic, and philosopher, La Pietra describes himself as a researcher exploring the relationships between individuals and space, between humans and their urban context. His examination of the "system of immbalance" made an important contribution to the **Radical Design** of the 1960s and 1970s. La Pietra's "fantastic" objects and installations have indeed thrown the world of design off balance, serving as irritants that raise new questions and trigger new ways of looking at things. Many of his designs are mass-produced by **Zanotta, Gruppo Industriale Busnelli,** and **Poggi.**

Liquor cabinet for *Sellaro*, 1988
Agevole chair for Gruppo Ind. Busnelli, 1984

LA RINASCENTE

Department store chain

The history of La Rinascente, which today is Italy's largest department store chain, is closely associated with the birth of Italian industrial design in the 1950s. In 1954 the store instituted the *Compasso d'oro design* award to "encourage industrialists and artisans to improve their production on the technical as well as the aesthetic level," in the words of its owner, Aldo Borletti. Founded in 1865 by Ferdinando Coccone as Italy's first ready-made clothes emporium, the rapidly growing company was sold to Borletti, a businessman, in 1918. After the Second World War, La Rinascente became a creative hotbed for talented young designers. The graphic artists **Max Huber** and **Albe Steiner** developed the firm's new identity and advertising (fig. p. 45); such artists and designers as **Bruno Munari** and **Tomàs Maldonado** worked on window displays and special presentations; and many young industrial designers, including **Mario Bellini**, started their careers at the in-house design department. Even **Giorgio Armani** is among the store's alumni—he once worked as a buyer in its fashion department.

1865 Ferdinando Bocconi opens first Italian store for ready-to-wear clothes on Via Santa Radegonda in Milan. Four years later, store moves to Piazza del Duomo

1917 store is sold to Senatore Borletti; the poet Gabriele d'Annunzio invents new name, La Rinascente

1918 destroyed in fire

1921 reopening

1943 destroyed in bomb attack

1950 reopening

1954 La Rinascente institutes *Compasso d'oro*

1967 *Compasso d'oro*

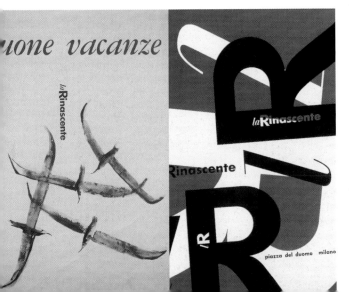

Buone Vacanze, poster by Roberto Sambonet, 1958

Advertisment by Max Huber, 1951

LANCIA

Automobile manufacturer

Lancia (now
Fiat Auto spa), Turin

1906 founded by Vincenzo
Lancia in Turin

1937 Vincenzo Lancia dies

1969 takeover by Fiat

Models

1921 *Lambda* sedan

1939 *Astura Cabriolet*

1951 *Aurelia Spider*

1959 *Flaminia Coupé*

1969 *Flavia Coupé 2000;*
last four cars by
Pininfarina

1971 *Stratos* sportscar
by **Bertone**

1975 *Beta Spider* by Pininfarina

1997 *Lancia k* sedan and station
wagon

While **Alfa Romeo's** cars project a fast, racy image, Lancias have always embodied a more sophisticated lifestyle. Favored by illustrious clients such as Prince Rainier of Monaco, Brigitte Bardot, and Marcello Mastroianni, the company's impeccably elegant models included the 1952 *Aurelia,* the 1954 *Aurelia B 24 Spider,* and the 1956 *Flaminia* luxury sedan, with its panoramic windshield.

The company was founded in 1906 by the race driver Vincenzo Lancia, and throughout the 1930s was highly successful in the Grand Prix and Rallye circuits while also developing an impressive roster of luxury automobiles. Lancia produced such milestones of automotive history as the 1921 *Lambda,* the first car with an integral body, and the 1937 *Aprilia,* with its flowing lines, which, in **Pininfarina's** coupé version, became an Italian answer to American streamline design. After the war, Lancia reclaimed its tradition of racing victories and its reputation for superior design by producing cars codeveloped with **Bertone,** Pininfarina, Touring, and Zagato. Lancia, which today is known for elegant mid-sized cars, was acquired by **Fiat** in 1969 but continues to exist as an independent brand.

Lancia *Lambda IV*, 1924

Page 233
top: Lancia *Aurelia Spider*, 1954
bottom: Lancia *Stratos* by Bertone, 1971

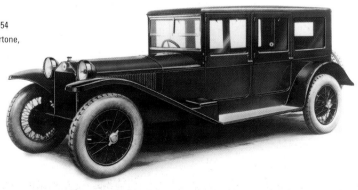

Piero LISSONI

Architect and furniture designer

1956 born in Seregno
studies architecture in
Milan

1977 collaborates with G14
studio, Milan (until 1984)

1984 opens studio in Milan

1998 showroom for **Cappellini**
in Milan

Products

1984 corporate image for
Molteni & C.

1989 *Esprit* kitchen for **Boffi**

1993 *Filoti* lamp for **Artemide**

1995 *Atlantic* bed and *Met*
sofa for **Cassina**

1996 *Bench-Sofa* for
Living Divani

Modern system for Porro, 1996

Piero Lissoni dislikes design's cult of personality and fetishistic celebration of objects. He finds most of the resulting products rather hard to live with. As an antidote, he creates products with a "silent quality." His comfortable *Frog* chair and restrained *Village* and *Box* sofas for Living Divani; his Basics bed and modular *Modern* wall cabinet system for Porro; the *Esprit, Works,* and *WK 6* kitchens for **Boffi**; and his sofas for **Cappellini** and **Cassina** are all impeccably simple and functional in their discreet use of the formal vocabulary.

Lissoni names Charles Eames, Ludwig Mies van der Rohe, and Eileen Gray as his historical touchstones. Like them, his goal is to reach an ideal synthesis of design, material, and construction. Lissoni describes his concept—an integral effort to design every aspect of a given project—as "medieval." His studio develops interior architecture and furniture as well as public relations programs for companies such as Boffi, Lema, Cappellini, and Units. In 1998 he also designed Cappellini's new showroom in Milan.

Lighting manufacturer

Visitors to Luceplan's factory at the edge of Milan seem to happen upon a dissection: the company's high-tech products are exhibited in a carefully disassembled state. The presentation is about transparency, a constructive principle shared by all the lighting products developed here. Everything at Luceplan looks up-to-the-minute: the technologically-oriented forms, the clean corporate identity, the bold presentations. The aesthetics are spare, though that does not exclude spectacular effects; at the 1996 *Euroluce* trade fair the firm showed technical drawings and two-dimensional studies but not one actual product.

Luceplan is one of the most advanced lighting laboratories of the 1990s, and its designers include some of the most promising talents of the last decade. Two of them, **Paolo Rizzatto** and the **Alberto Meda**—one trained as an architect, the other as an engineer—have worked with the company from its beginning and given its products their unmistakable look. Their designs include the iridescent *Titania* hanging lamp (fig. p. 38), with its

Luceplan spa, Milan
1978 founded by Riccardo Sarfatti, **Paolo Rizzatto** and Sandra Severi

Products
1980 *D 7* by Paolo Rizzatto
1985 *Berenice* by **Alberto Meda** and Paolo Rizzatto
1986 *Costanza* by Alberto Meda and Paolo Rizzatto
1987 *Lola* by Alberto Meda and Paolo Rizzatto

Berenice desk lamp by A. Meda and P. Rizzatto, 1985

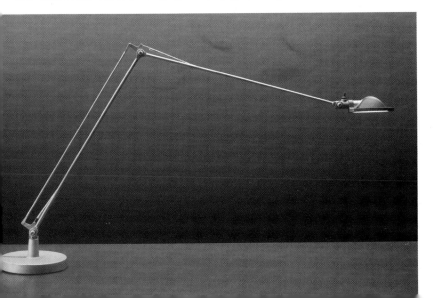

exchangeable color filters; the delicate *Berenice* desk lamp, a smart new take on traditional library lamps with a softly gleaming green or blue shade; and the geometric, radically simple *Costanza* table lamp. Jean Nouvel, Häberli & Marchand, Dante Donegani, **Denis Santachiara,** and Ross Lovegrove have also designed lighting for Luceplan.

One of the firm's newer products, Rizzatto's *Glassglass* hanging lamp, is equipped with a clever holding device. Different shades—colored or clear, round or pointed—can be snapped into an aluminum ring attached to a clamp that secures the electrical cord. The shades can be easily exchanged or cleaned, a design that is typical of Luceplan's commitment to offering flexible solutions for different needs and tastes. Despite their metallic aesthetic, the designs are far from frigid, and there is no shortage of bold colors.

Long, extensive research precedes the introduction of each new product, and there is a strong accent on teamwork. The company was founded in 1978 by three architects: Riccardo Sarfatti, the son of lighting pioneer **Gino Sarfatti;** Paolo Rizzatto; and Sandra Severi (Alberto Meda has since joined them as a partner). Architecture remains the central point of reference for the group, who made a name for themselves by planning the lighting for Milan's Linate and Malpensa airports before setting up their own design and manufacturing company. Commercial and architectural lighting are still an important part of Luceplan's business, as is the belief that good design is best combined with reasonable prices.

Page 237
top left: *On Off* table lamp, 1988
bottom left: Elements for *Titania* hanging lamp, 1989
right: *Lola* floor lamp, 1987

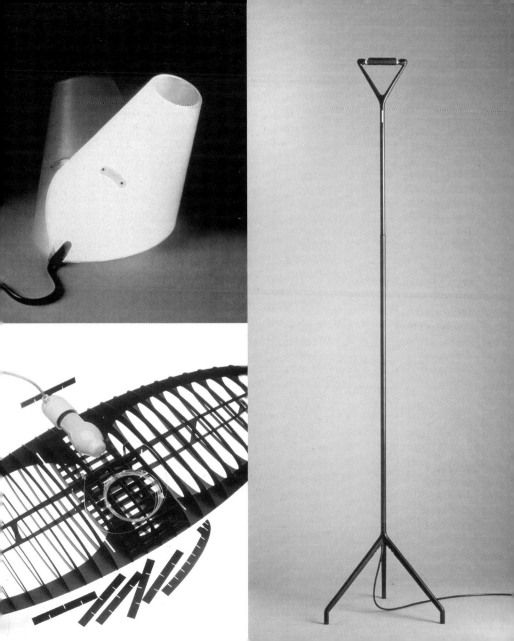

Italo LUPI

Graphic designer

Italo Lupi works on the border between art and communication. He has helped shape the profile of contemporary Italian graphic design without following accepted rules. He became extraordinarily successful with his designs for the Vatican Museums, the lighting company **bTicino,** and Italy's broadcasting company RAI, but is perhaps best known for his work as an art director for **Domus** and **Abitare** magazines.

Lupi's style is characterized by his refusal to use standardized grids. "One comes to realize that some graphic problems may have a three-dimensional solution," he says. In his layouts, he often presents complex, upbeat combinations of typography, drawings, and photographs, as in his 1991 calendar, whose pages are flooded with colorful numbers. He designs for alert, active users to whom chromatic finesse is more important than quick orientation.

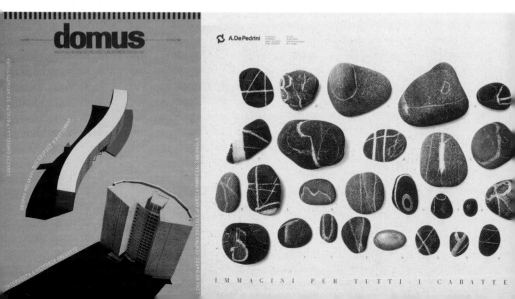

In 1996 Lupi designed the exhibition *Latin Lover* for the *Pitti Immiagine* fashion fair. Set in an abandoned railroad station, the show was a memorable success. "After the exhibition you are left not merely with a catalogue, but with memories of a spectacular act of communication," said **Achille Castiglioni,** one of the doyens of Italian design. Ironic and lusty, the presentation moved along an axis that ended in a pavilion dedicated to the quintessential Latin lover, Rudolph Valentino. That final destination was preceded by a gallery of the "Latin man per se,"shown in forty-eight photographs, which Lupi had "toppled"—they were lying on soft sand from Adriatic beaches, their "work base."

Lupi is currently the art director and managing editor of *Abitare* magazine. In 1998 he won the *Compasso d'oro* for his design of **Olivetti's** company magazine, *If.*

1986 art director of *Domus*

1989 art director of *International Design Conference* in Aspen, Colorado

1992 publisher and art director of *Abitare*

1998 *Compasso d'oro*

Projects

1988 poster for *Moda Italia*, exhibition, New York; design for *Triennale* with **Achille Castiglioni** and Paolo Ferrari; *Printed in Italy*, book project

1990 poster for Museo Di Storia Contemporanea, Milan

1996 exhibition design for *Latin Lover – a sud della passione* in Florence

From left:

Cover for *Domus* magazine, 1990

Poster for De Pedrini illustrating the alphabet, 1992

Two calandar pages for Grafiche Mariano (1991–1996)

Vico MAGISTRETTI

Architect and designer

"I have always tried to not produce any oddities," Vico Magistretti once said. His work avoids all formal excesses, fashionable trappings, and ephemeral ideas. Designers, he believes, need to develop lasting solutions.

An éminence grise of Italian postwar design, Magistretti is reserved as a person and as a designer. His works' subtle qualities gradually reveal themselves through daily use. Magistretti first made a name for himself in the late 1950s; inspired by rustic furniture, his wooden *Carimate* chair, with a woven raffia seat, marked the beginning of a fertile relationship with Cassina and earned him a reputation as a master of simple, austere forms. His many designs for **Cassina** include the cozy *Sinbad* seating furniture, which developed from the idea of a horse blanket thrown over a trestle.

In the 1960s, when the material properties of plastic inspired wild experiments, Magistretti decided to tackle the new possibilities with a distinctly different approach—an attempt to find elegant form for a material often denounced as tacky. In contrast to **Joe Colombo's** famous 4867 chair for **Kartell** (1968), which Magistretti thought "looked like an elephant," he set out to design a chair with slender legs, cast in one piece. The experiment proved successful: his *Selene* chair, which is still produced by **Artemide,** helped change the perception of plastic being an inferior material.

For Artemide, Magistretti also designed the small *Eclissi* lamp in 1965. Playful in appearance, it is cleverly designed with a simple but ingenious mechanism that allows the user to regulate the intensity of light by turning the curved shade to the "half moon," "full moon," and "new moon" positions. Magistretti has also designed lighting for **O Luce,** including the 1977 *Atollo* table lamp (fig. p. 34), a masterpiece of geometric composition that

1920 born in Milan

1945 graduates from architecture school, opens studio in Milan

1958 apartment buildings in Milan on Via San Gregorio (until 1959)

1960 begins designing products

1967 *Compasso d'oro* (also 1979, 1995)

Products

1960 *Carimate* chair for **Cassina**

1963 *Mania* wall lamp

1965 *Eclisse* lamp

1969 *Selene* plastic chair; all for **Artemide**

1972 *Tema* table for **B&B Italia**

1973 *Maralunga* sofa for Cassina

1977 *Atollo* table lamp for **O Luce**; *Nuvola rossa* shelf unit for Cassina

1978 *Nathalie* bed for **Flou**

Page 241
Selene chair for Artemide, 1969

1981 *Sindbad* suite for Cassina; *Pan* series for

features an illuminated hemisphere seemingly hovering over a cylinder, also illuminated. Since the mid-1980s, Magistretti has created many furniture designs for De Padova, a company that shares a preference for the classic, elegant lines epitomized in his aluminum-and-plastic *Silver* chair, a redesign of Marcel Breuer's 811 wooden chair for Thonet (1925). One of Magistretti's most successful recent designs is the *Maui* chair for Kartell, a plastic variation on the simple molded-wood chair perfected by Arne Jacobsen.

Magistretti began his career as an architect in the 1950s, and despite all his success in product design, architecture has remained his true passion. If it seems surprising that he continues to develop small, everyday objects, an explanation may be found in his understanding of design as a way of communicating with humanity at large.

Maralunga sofa
for Cassina, 1973

Page 243

Lousiana chair
for De Padova, 1993

Mezzachimera floor lamp
for Artemide, 1966

Golem chair for Poggi, 1970

MANDARINA DUCK

Manufacturer of bags and accessories

Plastimoda spa, Cadriano
di Granarolo Emilia (BO)

1968 founded in Bologna

1977 brand name Mandarina
Duck introduced

Products

1977 *Utility* collection

1981 *Tank* collection

1988 *Hera* collection

1994 *Wink* collection

Mandarina Duck is proof of the theory that acting against prevailing trends is often the key to success. In 1977, when natural materials and muted colors dominated the accessories industry, the company launched its exuberantly colorful, brazenly synthetic *Utility* line of bags. Today Mandarina Duck is Italy's market leader, and its bags and backpacks, from the casual *Tank* and elegant black *Hera* lines to the playful *Wink* collection, have become ubiquitous fashion statements among younger women. In a recent survey, the Bologna-based company's products were named as "quintessential objects," taking their place alongside Levi's 501s, the Fiat *500*, **Brionvega's** *TS 502* box radio (fig. p. 146), and the Coca-Cola bottle.

Mandarina Duck continuously researches and develops new materials and has registered some eighty patents. Close cooperation with renowned designers is central to the firm's success. For the corrugated-rubber look of the Tank collection, Richard Sapper borrowed a special inflation process from the automobile industry to stabilize the material. Under the direction of **Mario Trimarchi,** the **De Lucchi** studio developed the firm's graphic identity program; De Lucchi also designed the interiors of the company's stores. Mandarina Duck also produces timepieces, writing utensils, and textiles.

Suitcase for *Tank* series by Alberto
Meda, 1989

Page 245
top: *Linea Twice* bag, 1998
bottom left: *Wink* knapsack, 1994
bottom right: Store design
by Studio De Lucchi, 1996

Angelo MANGIAROTTI

Architect, furniture and product designer

"Material is to design what the brain is to thought," Angelo Mangiarotti says, explaining his highly considered use of wood, plastic, glass, and metal. For him, each design project is primarily a transformation of materials. In his opalescent *Lesbo* glass lamp for **Artemide** and in the *Eros* and *Fiorera* marble tables for **Skipper,** the *Chicago* fiberglass chair, and the *Ergonomica* flatware set, the final form did not follow the designer's fancy but rather the peculiar language of the material.

Mangiarotti has rarely mixed materials, almost obsessively insisting on keeping them pure. Technology, in his approach, provides the syntax while design controls the relationship between theme and variation. "The correctness of the design process is almost more important than the quality of the product," he says. Mangiarotti discovered his love of materials through architecture, which has remained the main focus of his career. But with his research into fabrication processes and materials, particularly plastics, he has been giving new directions to Italian design since the 1950s.

1921 born in Milan
1948 graduates from architecture school in Milan
1955 collaboration with **Bruno Morassutti** (until 1960)
1956 cofounder of **ADI**
1989 railroad stations Certosa and Rogoredo in Milan
1995 *Compasso d'oro*

Products

1955 *Multi-use* furniture (and 1964, 1977) with Bruno Morassutti
1960 *Section* table clock with Bruno Morassutti
1964 *T 11* table clock
1966 *Lesbo* lamp for Artemide
1971 *Eros* and *Fiorera* marble tables for **Skipper**
1981 *Estrual* shelf unit for Skipper
1998 *T-table* for **Baleri**

Eros marble table for Skipper, 1973

Page 247
Chicago fiberglass chair for Skipper, 1980
Clizia seats for Skipper, 1990
Incas stone table for Skipper, 1977
Askos pitcher for Colle Cristalleria, 1986

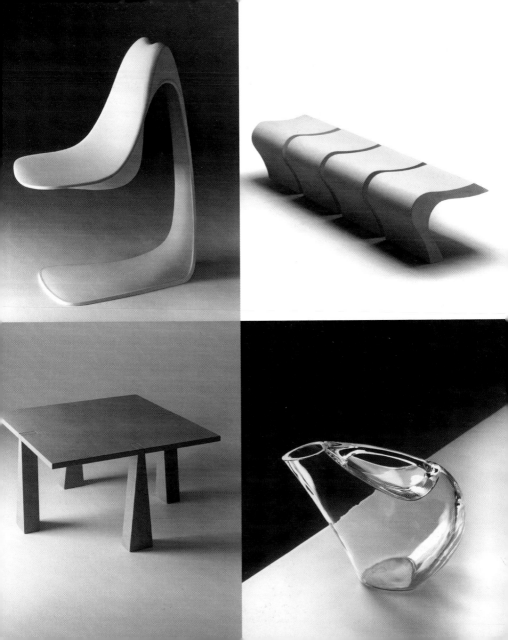

Enzo MARI

Artist, theorist, furniture and product designer

"When I have designed an object and people say to me, 'Oh, good job!' I cannot help but wonder, what did I do wrong? If everybody likes it, it means that I have affirmed reality as it exists, which is precisely what I do not want." Enzo Mari's position is a principled antithesis to the contemporary design industry, which he deplores for its excess production of useless, kitschy products.

Mari maintains a vision of design that is informed by Karl Marx's critique of capitalism and the French Revolution's ideal of equality. Trained as a fine artist, Mari published his first theoretical writings on the psychology of visual perception, aesthetics, and design in 1952, when he was just twenty years old. In his more than 1,400 objects and furniture designs, he has given his thinking material shape and formulated his demand for good, affordable design for everyone. His iron *Putrella* bowl, wooden games, and plastic objects for **Danese** (fig. p. 47) all take advantage of their material's properties to arrive at graceful formal solutions. Usefulness is always the ruling principle,

whether Mari is designing book covers, housewares, or tiles. The furniture he has developed for **Driade** and **Zanotta** includes such functional pieces as the lightweight *Delfina* stacking chair and the *Day-Night* sofa bed.

In 1993 Mari was appointed director of design at Berlin's venerable Royal Prussian Porcelain Manufactory, KPM. In close cooperation with the company's artisans he has been developing small numbers of archetypal forms, which are then produced in elegant variations. An idealist at heart, he has little tolerance for designers whose sights are trained on fame and fortune: "A designer's most important task is to define his own model of an ideal world," he says, "not to create an aesthetic one. If he doesn't have his own ideology he is a fool who only lends form to other people's ideas." Whether he has succeeded in realizing his ideas will ultimately be decided by the consumer—Mari's products are not among the least expensive, but certainly among the most beautiful.

Products

1958 *Putrella* bowl
1966 *Timor* table calendar;
both for **Danese**
1968 *Elementare* tiles
for **Gabbianelli**
1970 *In Attesa* waste-paper
basket for Danese
1971 *Sof-Sof* chair
1974 *Delfina* chair;
both for **Driade**
1984 *Giglio* letter opener;
Sixteen Fishes, game for children;
both for Danese
1996 *Berlin* tableware set for
KPM

From left:
Tonietta chair for Zanotta, 1985
Delos glass ashtray
for Danese, 1981
Putrella bowl for Danese, 1958

Sergio MAZZA, Giuliana GRAMIGNA
Architects, furniture and product designers

1961 Sergio Mazza and Giuliana Gramigna found SMC Architettura

Products

1969 Mazza:
Toga plastic chair for **Artemide**

1989 Gramigna:
Giuliana faucet for **Olivari**

1995 *Flamen* and *Flamina* lamps for Quattrifolio

Bacco plastic container for Artemide, 1967

Marlia lamp for Quattrifolio, 1989, both by Sergio Mazza

From furniture to lighting and faucets, Sergio Mazza and Giuliana Gramigna's designs come alive in the dynamic space between creative inspiration and industrial process. They see themselves as architectural designers who develop each object in the context of its environment. On this common conceptual basis, they work on individual or joint projects such as their numerous geometric lighting solutions for Quattrifoglio and their furniture for Cinova, Full, and Frau. Modernism and minimalism are unmistakable influences on their designs. Mazza's comfortable *Poker* chair, for example, consists of four identical pieces that serve as sides, back, and seat.

Mazza first made a name for himself as a pioneer of plastics technology with his throne-like 1969 *Toga* chair (fig. p. 7) for **Artemide,** an undisputed classic of Pop design. Gramigna is best known for her purist collection of faucets for **Olivari.**

Angelo MANGIAROTTI

Architect, furniture and product designer

"Material is to design what the brain is to thought," Angelo Mangiarotti says, explaining his highly considered use of wood, plastic, glass, and metal. For him, each design project is primarily a transformation of materials. In his opalescent *Lesbo* glass lamp for **Artemide** and in the *Eros* and *Fiorera* marble tables for **Skipper,** the *Chicago* fiberglass chair, and the *Ergonomica* flatware set, the final form did not follow the designer's fancy but rather the peculiar language of the material.

Mangiarotti has rarely mixed materials, almost obsessively insisting on keeping them pure. Technology, in his approach, provides the syntax while design controls the relationship between theme and variation. "The correctness of the design process is almost more important than the quality of the product," he says. Mangiarotti discovered his love of materials through architecture, which has remained the main focus of his career. But with his research into fabrication processes and materials, particularly plastics, he has been giving new directions to Italian design since the 1950s.

1921 born in Milan
1948 graduates from architecture school in Milan
1955 collaboration with **Bruno Morassutti** (until 1960)
1956 cofounder of **ADI**
1989 railroad stations Certosa and Rogoredo in Milan
1995 *Compasso d'oro*

Products
1955 *Multi-use* furniture (and 1964, 1977) with Bruno Morassutti
1960 *Section* table clock with Bruno Morassutti
1964 *T 11* table clock
1966 *Lesbo* lamp for Artemide
1971 *Eros* and *Fiorera* marble tables for **Skipper**
1981 *Estrual* shelf unit for Skipper
1998 *T-table* for **Baleri**

Eros marble table for Skipper, 1973

Page 247
Chicago fiberglass chair for Skipper, 1980
Clizia seats for Skipper, 1990
Incas stone table for Skipper, 1977
Askos pitcher for Colle Cristalleria, 1986

MANDARINA DUCK

Manufacturer of bags and accessories

Plastimoda spa, Cadriano
di Granarolo Emilia (BO)

1968 founded in Bologna
1977 brand name Mandarina
Duck introduced

Products
1977 *Utility* collection
1981 *Tank* collection
1988 *Hera* collection
1994 *Wink* collection

Mandarina Duck is proof of the theory that acting against prevailing trends is often the key to success. In 1977, when natural materials and muted colors dominated the accessories industry, the company launched its exuberantly colorful, brazenly synthetic *Utility* line of bags. Today Mandarina Duck is Italy's market leader, and its bags and backpacks, from the casual *Tank* and elegant black *Hera* lines to the playful *Wink* collection, have become ubiquitous fashion statements among younger women. In a recent survey, the Bologna-based company's products were named as "quintessential objects," taking their place alongside Levi's 501s, the Fiat *500*, **Brionvega's** *TS 502* box radio (fig. p. 146), and the Coca-Cola bottle.

Mandarina Duck continuously researches and develops new materials and has registered some eighty patents. Close cooperation with renowned designers is central to the firm's success. For the corrugated-rubber look of the Tank collection, Richard Sapper borrowed a special inflation process from the automobile industry to stabilize the material. Under the direction of **Mario Trimarchi,** the **De Lucchi** studio developed the firm's graphic identity program; De Lucchi also designed the interiors of the company's stores. Mandarina Duck also produces timepieces, writing utensils, and textiles.

Suitcase for *Tank* series by Alberto
Meda, 1989

Page 245
top: *Linea Twice* bag, 1998
bottom left: *Wink* knapsack, 1994
bottom right: Store design
by Studio De Lucchi, 1996

features an illuminated hemisphere seemingly hovering over a cylinder, also illuminated. Since the mid-1980s, Magistretti has created many furniture designs for De Padova, a company that shares a preference for the classic, elegant lines epitomized in his aluminum-and-plastic *Silver* chair, a redesign of Marcel Breuer's 811 wooden chair for Thonet (1925). One of Magistretti's most successful recent designs is the *Maui* chair for Kartell, a plastic variation on the simple molded-wood chair perfected by Arne Jacobsen.

Magistretti began his career as an architect in the 1950s, and despite all his success in product design, architecture has remained his true passion. If it seems surprising that he continues to develop small, everyday objects, an explanation may be found in his understanding of design as a way of communicating with humanity at large.

Maralunga sofa
for Cassina, 1973

Page 243

Lousiana chair
for De Padova, 1993

Mezzachimera floor lamp
for Artemide, 1966

Golem chair for Poggi, 1970

Alberto MEDA

Industrial and furniture designer

Unlike most Italian designers, Alberto Meda is not an architect but an engineer by training. His most important source of inspiration is modern technology, which he describes as a "supermarket of creative possibilities." For his design of the *Tank* luggage collection for **Mandarina Duck**, he adapted a blowing technology used in the automobile industry for producing gas tanks. (Meda worked as a consultant to **Alfa Romeo** for several years.) The resulting series of suitcases is not only extremely sturdy and pressure-resistant but also extraordinarily lightweight. Transparency is another central theme of Meda's work, particularly in furniture. In 1987 he designed the *Light Light* chair for Alias as a successor to Gio Ponti's 1957 *Superleggera,* once touted as the world's lightest chair. Made of carbon fibre and aluminum, the chair proves equal to its name with a weight of a little over two pounds.

Meda has consistently focused on exploring new material possibilities and giving them adequate form. He gathered much of

1945 born in Lenno Tremezzina (Como)

1969 graduates from engineering school in Milan, assistant at Magneti Marelli (until 1973)

1973 technical director at **Kartell** (until 1979)

1979 independent designer, collaboration with **Franco Raggi** and **Denis Santachiara**

1982 designs for **Alfa Romeo** (until 1986)

1984 collaboration with **Italtel**

1987 collaboration with **Alias** and **Luceplan**

1989 *Compasso d'oro* (also 1995)

Longframe chaise for Alias, 1994

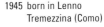

the requisite know-how in the 1970s as the technical director of **Kartell,** a company whose pioneering research and development of plastic materials has added several important chapters to the history of design. From this orientation toward technology, Meda has developed a poetic formal language. This is perhaps most strikingly evidenced in his lighting designs for **Luceplan,** which include such celebrated pieces as the *Lola, Berenice,* and *Metropolis* lights. His most successful design, the *Titania* hanging lamp (developed with **Paolo Rizzatto**), while uncompromisingly high-tech in its construction, is also reminiscent of a mysterious, hovering UFO (fig. p. 38).

From Charles Eames, Meda learned that the correct starting point for a project is a constructive idea, not a formal one. And his designs always appear simple and unpretentious, following his paradoxical statement that "the more complex a technology is, the better it is suited for simple utilitarian objects." This is beautifully demonstrated in the small *On-Off* table lamp, a lopsided object that is turned on or off by tilting it. The idea of creating light by a gesture has rarely been conveyed so well. The *Meda office* and *Conference chair* for Vitra, which has won the designer numerous awards, is a similarly pellucid solution to a far more complex technological challenge. His ability to humanize new technologies and translate them into light and simple forms has made Meda one of the most interesting designers of the 1990s.

Products

1986 *Berenice* desk lamp for **Luceplan** with **Paolo Rizzatto**

1987 *Light Light* chair;
Dry table;
both for Alias

1988 *On Off* lamp for Luceplan with **Franco Raggi, Denis Santachiara**

1989 *Tank* luggage for **Mandarina Duck**;
Titania hanging lamp for Luceplan with P. Rizzatto

1992 *Metropolis* for Luceplan

1993 crystal-and-titanium glasses for Compagnia Italiana del Cristallo

1994 *Frame* chair system for Alias

1997 *Meda Chair* for Vitra

Page 253
Meda Chair for Vitra, 1997
Metropoli light for Luceplan, 1992, with Paolo Rizzatto and Riccardo Sarfatti
Light Light chair for Alias, 1997

MEMPHIS

Design group; also name of collection and company

Memphis delivered a jolt that left the previously sedate world of design in turmoil. After seeing the group's first exhibition of furniture, hand-crafted objects and lights in Milan in 1981, the *Chicago Tribune's* design critic, Nancy Adams, wrote that whatever else the show may be called, it was the opposite of boring. A development that had been started by the **Radical Design** movement and the **Alchimia** group in the 1960s and 1970s suddenly erupted into wide popularity, with the media doing its best to fan the flames. The orthodoxy of functional beauty in design was called into question, and even appeared obsolete. But despite its revolutionary effects, Memphis did not share the overtly political agenda of the early design renegades.

In its first exhibition and in the many that followed it, Memphis presented multifunctional, colorful, ambiguous objects: shelf units that didn't look like shelves, such as **Ettore Sottsass's** *Carlton* (fig. p. 12) and *Casablanca;* lamps that were really illuminated toys, like Martine Bedin's *Super,* a small

1981 founded by **Ettore Sottsass** and **Michele De Lucchi;**
first Memphis exhibition in Milan

1982 second Memphis exhibition in Milan

1986 second Memphis generation, *Twelve New*

1988 group dissolves

Products

1981 *Carlton* shelf unit;
Tahiti table lamp;
Beverly sideboard ;
Casablanca shelf unit,
all by **Ettore Sottsass;**
Dublin sofa
by **Marco Zanini;**
Super lamp
by Martine Bedin;
Gritti shelf unit
by **Andrea Branzi**

Antares vase
by Michele De Lucchi, 1993

Danubio vase
by Matteo Thun, 1982

Page 255
Casablanca shelf unit
by Ettore Sottsass, 1981

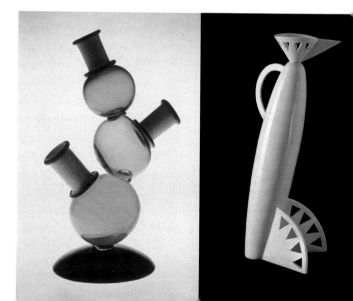

object on wheels equipped with colored bulbs; and vases, plates, and other housewares that broke with conventional forms. Everything seemed possible in Memphis's celebration of shapes, colors, and ideas. The design of surfaces took precedence over the commandment that form follow function. In close cooperation with **Abet Laminati,** Memphis designers created wild patterns for the company's plastic laminates, which provided their objects' signature look.

Ettore Sottsass was the central figure of Memphis, which formed as a loose association of international designers and architects, including **Michele De Lucchi, Andrea Branzi,** Michael Graves, **Aldo Cibic,** Nathalie du Pasquier, Hans Hollein, **George J. Sowden,** Shiro Kuramata, Javier Mariscal, **Marco Zanini,** and Daniel Weil. The group, which found an enthusiastic sponsor in **Ernesto Gismondi,** the head of **Artemide,** came upon its name by accident—Bob Dylan's "Memphis Blues" was played on the stereo during one of their informal meetings. They initially focused on producing objects in small series and questioned criteria such as feasibility, usability and profitability. But Memphis did not remain anti-industrial for long. The "Memphis style" was soon widely imitated and heavily marketed. More and more designers jumped on the bandwagon, and numerous furniture and lighting manufacturers began offering postmodernist conversation pieces. Before long, the original Memphis designers moved on, and in the late 1980s, the group dissolved, though the Memphis collection still exists. Still, by the time of its demise, Memphis had fundamentally changed international design culture and permanently undermined the blind faith in a rigid set of "correct" design parameters.

1982 *Lido* sofa
by **Michele De Lucchi**;
Alaska vase for Rossi & Arcandi by Ettore Sottsass; *Kenya, Gabon, Zaire, Zambia* fabrics for Rainbow by Nathalie Du Pasquier

1983 *Hollywood* table
by Peter Shire;
Palace chair
by **George J. Sowden**;
Volga vase
by **Matteo Thun**;
First chair
by Michele De Lucchi

1984 *Objects for the Electronic Age* by
George J. Sowden and Nathalie du Pasquier

Page 257

Ginza Robot cabinet
by Masanori Umeda, 1982

Sol bowl
by Ettore Sottsass, 1982

Cairo table
by Michele De Lucchi, 1996

Serpente laminate
for Abet Laminati, 1979

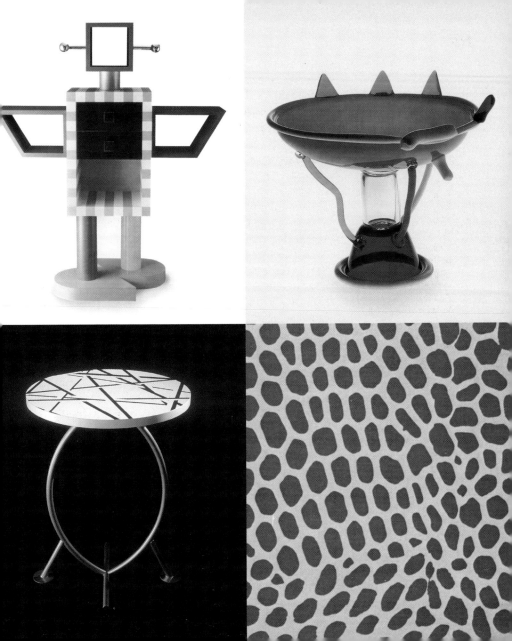

Alessandro MENDINI

Architect, designer, and theorist

In the 1960s no one would have expected that Alessandro Mendini, then a designer and architect at the serious-minded firm of **Nizzoli** Associati, would become one of the most flamboyant and controversial figures in alternative design. It was not until the early 1970s that he stepped forth to vigorously promote a design liberated from all industrial constraints. A tireless worker, he developed his ideas in a variety of forums and functions: as a writer of numerous essays for *Casabella, Modo,* and *Domus* magazines, as a sponsor of the **Global Tools** design school, founded in 1973, and as the head theorist of the **Alchimia** group.

Since the end of the 1970s, Mendini's name has been associated with the concepts of **Re-Design** and **Banal Design,** exemplified in his ironic alterations of classic Thonet and Bauhaus chairs, which he decorated with flags and ornaments. Decorative elements have continued to play an important part in Mendini's work. Ornament covers his portly *Poltrona di Proust* chair (fig. p. 14), the hand-crafted objects of his *Collezione*

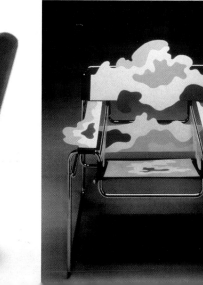

Privata, and the surfaces he designed for **Abet Laminati**. As an art director, Mendini also helped develop the product concept of the Swiss watch manufacturer Swatch. Since the 1980s, Mendini has worked as a consultant for **Alessi;** he restructured the housewares manufacturer's entire line, created the famous *Anna G.* corkscrew (fig. p. 44), and designed a house for Alberto Alessi, the *Casa della felicità* on Lago di Orta.

Mendini's designs often appear strange and impenetrable. Stylistically diverse, they have never conformed to the notion of functional design, but instead invite questions about design's meaning and purpose. In that respect, they serve a communicative function. In recent years Mendini, along with his brother Francesco, has dedicated more time to architectural projects. An antithesis to neutral exhibition spaces, his exuberant Groningen Museum, built in 1993, again raises many questions and is thus typical of his gently rebellious work.

1989 opens Studio Mendini in Milan with his brother, Francesco; Paradise Tower in Hiroshima with Yumiko Kabayashi

1993 museum in Groningen

Products

1978 *Poltrona di Proust* chair for **Alchimia** (reintrod. in 1993 by **Cappellini**)

1983 tea and coffee set for **Alessi**

1984 *Dorifora* chair for Zabro

1990 *Cosmesis* and *Metroscape* wristwatches for Swatch

1994 streetcar stop for *Busstop* project, Hanover; *Anna G.* corkscrew for Alessi

From left:
Scala chair for Mastrangelo, 1996
Vassilij chair for Alchimia, 1978
Kandissi sofa for Alchima, 1979

MISSONI

Fashion designer

"Who says there are only colors? There are also sounds!" legendary *Vogue* editor Diana Vreeland reportedly exclaimed when Rosita Missoni showed her a sampling of her creations she had brought along in a large trunk. Vreeland's enthusiastic comment proved a door opener for the Missonis; the 1969 meeting became a milestone in the history of one of Italy's most successful fashion houses.

Originally a cloth and knitwear factory based in Gallarate, the company had been owned by the Missoni family for decades when Rosita joined it in the early 1950s. Even before they met, her husband Ottavio Missoni, a successful track-and-field-athlete, had been interested in fashion. Together with a friend he had designed the official track suits for the Italian Olympic team of 1948. After their marriage, Ottavio and Rosita set up a studio in Milan and focused on creating knitwear.

The Missonis quickly established themselves with designs that were a far cry from knitwear's traditionally drab image. They initially produced fashions for the boutique Biki, then for the **La Rinascente** department store, before coming out with their own label in 1966.

With influences ranging from African cultures to Op Art, they designed youthful, casual knitwear with refined patterns and sophisticated color combinations—qualities that have remained hallmarks of the Missoni style. They became famous for their zigzag patterns, a recurrent theme in their fashions. Their sweaters, produced in relatively limited numbers, have become exclusive fashion statements popular with such celebrities as Tom Hanks and Luciano Pavarotti.

Carlo MOLLINO

Architect, engineer, photographer, and designer

When Carlo Mollino decided to learn to ski, he tackled the task with such determination and success that within a short time he was one of Italy's best skiers. He also became the director of the Italian Winter Sports Association and in 1951 published a pioneering book on modern skiing techniques. In the 1950s, Mollino turned his attention to motor sports and won numerous international car races, including several victories at Le Mans, while designing his own race cars, including the sleek *Bisiluro.* He distinguished himself as a passionate stunt pilot and airplane builder but also as a gifted photographer of nudes and other subjects. He designed elegant women's fashions and shoes, and as a successful inventor, registered some fifteen patents, including a control system that could be programmed for aerial stunt maneuvers. In addition, Mollino designed stage and movie sets and wrote numerous essays. Finally, he was one of Italy's most unusual architects and furniture designers. In the late 1940s, *Interiors* magazine described the highly personal style he had developed as "Turinese Baroque."

Mollino had nothing in common with the **rationalist** approach of the Milan designers. His specialty was a patented process for bending plywood at low temperatures. He had developed it himself and was not shy in exploring its possibilities. Swelling and tumid, meandering and sinuous, his organic forms were often dismissed as lapses of taste. He indulged in extravagant formal experiments such as three-legged, oddly curved chairs, and imitated the female anatomy with reckless abandon: the backs of his chairs echo female torsos; bipartite seats resemble luscious buttocks. Several of his table legs, some of which he dressed in stiletto-heeled shoes, were modeled after dancers at the *Crazy Horse* in Paris. If there is such a thing as "erotic design," Mollino was its most inspired representative. But in his furniture's visual language there are also reflections of ski tracks in the snow or aerobatic figures.

Mollino's life and work blended into an opulent synthesis. From his father Eugenio, a Turin architect, he inherited an urge for

perfection. In all its mannered splendor, Mollino's furniture follows precise constructive principles (fig. p. 31) that were often adopted from airplane and automobile design. However, his furniture was not made for mass-production—it was usually developed for a specific context, such as the Casa Orengo and Casa Minola in Turin, which Mollino furnished in the 1940s.

Mollino lived in Turin throughout his life, and in his work he expressed his love for the Baroque traditions and woodworking techniques of the surrounding Piemont region. For this he reaped small thanks: his hometown permitted the demolition of some of his most important buildings, including the Ippica Equestrian Club of 1937; his bold chairlift station on Lago Nero, built in 1946, was simply abandoned.

Products

1940   chair for Lisa and **Gio Ponti**

1949   interiors and furniture for Casa Orengo, Turin

1950   *Arabesque* furniture series

1953   red-velvet chair for RAI auditorium

1954   *Osca 1100* racing car

1955   *Bisuluro* racing car

1957   furniture for XI *Triennale* in Milan

1965   women's wear collection

Table from *Arabesque* series, 1949

MOROSO

Furniture manufacturer

From Ron Arad's amorphous organic bulks and Javier Mariscal's cheerful, fifties-style chairs and chaises to the cool elegance of **Massimo Iosa Ghini's** sofas, Moroso's collection mirrors the eclectic sensibilities of the 1990s. Working with internationally renowned younger designers, the company produces seating furniture for an upscale market with sophisticated tastes. That strategy evolved only in the 1980s, when Moroso shifted away from the traditional upholstered furniture it had produced since 1952. The high quality of its fabrics and craftsmanship remain the same, but are now ensured by advanced production technologies. Moroso, whose most important market is Germany, makes furniture for the home as well as for public buildings and offices.

Moroso spa,
Crespano del Grappa

1952 founded in Cavallico di
Tavagnacco (Udine)

Products

1986 *Dinamic Collection*
by **Massimo Iosa Ghini**

1989 *Saruyama*
by Toshiyuki Kita

1990 *Waiting Collection*
by **Rodolf Dordoni**

1991 *Spring Collection*
by Ron Arad

1993 *Gluon* by Marc Newson

1995 *Los mueblos amorosos*
by Javier Mariscal

1996 *Jules e Jim*
by **Enrico Franzolini**

Newtone sofas
by Massimo Iosa Ghini, 1989
The 21 Hotel chair
by Javier Mariscal, 1997

266

Massimo MOROZZI
Architect, furniture and product designer

"The problem is not to create useful things that are also beautiful. It is to create objects that possess beauty despite perhaps being ugly."

Massimo Morozzi has been on a mission to liberate design from aesthetic value judgments since 1966, when he cofounded **Archizoom,** a collective of Florentine architects who set out to break the functionalist dogma. During the 1970s, Morozzi conducted systematic design research, then focused once more on the design of furniture and objects for **Driade, Alessi,** and other companies in the 1980s. Many of his designs, including the meandering *Paesaggi Italiani* cabinet system for Edra Mazzei, are strikingly witty and colorful. But as fellow designer **Alessandro Mendini** notes, their crucial quality lies in the fact that Morozzi approaches each project by meticulously analyzing its specific requirements. In recent years, Morozzi, who in 1987 became the art director of **Edra Mazzei,** has increasingly focused on communication design.

1941 born in Florence
1966 cofounder of **Archizoom**
1967 graduates from architecture school in Florence
1972 moves to Milan; design research at Centro Design, Montefiore (until 1977)
1979 *Compasso d'oro* for design research
1982 opens Massimo Morozzi Design
1983 establishes O.T.E., a company specializing in medical instruments

1987 art director at **Edra Mazzei**

Products
1983 *Bibì Bibò* bed for **Driade;** *300 Tangram* table
1985 *950 Domino* sofa; both for **Cassina;** *Pasta Set* for **Alessi**
1986 *Orchidea* table for **Edra**
1990 *Vapor Set* for Alessi
1991 *Topolone* sofa for Edra

Paesaggi italiani closet system for Edra, 1996

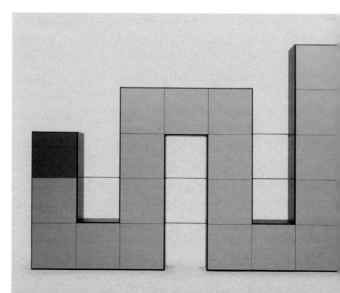

MOTO GUZZI

Motorcycle manufacturer

Moto Guzzi's success is based on a reliable line of large one-cylinder, classic V-2 engines, and on the thoroughly functional design of its motorcycles. In the 1920s, the company paved the way for the large-scale production of motorcycles when it broke from the traditional "motorized bicycle" look. For its committed fan base of "Guzzisti," a Moto Guzzi is the essential heavy road bike—as opposed to the stripped-down, aggressively racy models of the company's domestic competitor, **Ducati** (fig. p. 24). Nonetheless, it was the distinctive roar of its engines as well as its 3,329 racing victories that made the company famous. (It left the racing arena in 1957.) Some of its most notable models are the *Falcone* (1950s and 1960s), the powerful V7 (since the late 1960s), the sleek *Le Mans* and best-selling *California* (since 1970) series. Among the company's most loyal customers is the Italian police, who used the classic *Falcone* bikes throughout the 1950s and 1960s and, in the late 1960s, equipped its motorcycle units with V7s.

Moto Guzzi spa.,
Mandello del Lario

1921 founded by Carlo Guzzi and Giorgio Parodi in Mandello del Lario
1967 subsidized by Italian government
1997 annual production reaches 6,300 motorcycles

Models
1921 *Tipo Normale*
1925 *Tipo Sport*
1936 *Airone* (until 1957)
1939 *Alce* with sidecar (until 1945)
1954 *Falcone* (until 1967)
1967 introduction of *V7* series
1970 *California* series
1991 *Daytona*
1997 *California Anniversary*

850 Le Mans, 1978

Bruno MUNARI

Artist and designer

"Give me four stones and a sheet of tissue paper and I'll build you a wonderland," Bruno Munari once said. His poetic world includes *Useless Machines* and *Illegible Books,* cleverly designed lights and furniture and extensive studies on visual perception. When he died in 1998 at the age of ninety-one, the self-taught artist and designer had been giving given new impulses to Italy's cultural life for some seven decades. In addition to his many accomplishments in product design, he was one of Italy's most important representatives of Op Art (in 1962 he organized a large exhibition on kinetic art for **Olivetti**), a gifted poet, theorist, and teacher, and an innovative graphic artist known to a large audience for his groundbreaking children's books and games, which were designed to educate through playful experimentation.

Munari started out in the 1920s as a painter fascinated by **Futurism.** In 1930 he created his first three-dimensional object, a large red, white, and black mobile made of wood and metal. Titled *Macchina aerea,* it was designed to be set in motion by the slightest breeze. In 1933 he began working on his series of *Macchini inutili* (useless machines), which included a mobile constructed of painted cardboard (1934) and a sculpture made of wire and wooden balls. In their modest simplicity they stood in marked contrast to Futurism's bombastic celebrations of progress. For Munari, the *Macchine inutili* signaled his growing doubt in the traditional concept of art. After breaking with Futurism in the 1930s, he worked as a graphic artist, creating advertisements for such companies as Olivetti and **Campari** (which remained an important client after the war).

Munari's career as a product and environmental designer began in the postwar years, when he created such pieces as the sleek, formally immaculate *TMT* ice bucket (fig. p. 19) and

Page 269
Cubo ashtray
for Danese, 1957

designed exhibitions and store windows for retailers including **La Rinascente.** A particularly fertile relationship developed in 1957 between Munari and the housewares manufacturer **Danese,** for which he designed the legendary *Cubo* ashtray, a black cube into which a strip of aluminum is folded; the *Falkland* hanging lamp, consisting of nylon stocking fabric stretched over hoops of different sizes; and many other useful and beautiful objects. Danese also issued Munari's art multiples, games, and children's books, the first of which were created in 1943 and 1945. Innovative in their formal design, they used devices like fold-out pages to actively involve their readers in the stories they told. Munari's *Positive-Negative* Images and *Proiezioni dirette,* which had developed out of his research into sense perception, formed the basis of a 1959 game in which children could explore light and its effects with the help of transparent and semitransparent materials.

While his objects were usually not created for mass-production, Munari was an important figure for industrial design. In the early 1950s, he invented a small bendable toy monkey named *Zizi,* which made perfect use of **Pirelli's** new type of foam rubber. In the 1970s, he designed the *Abitacolo* steel unit for **Robots,** which combined the functions of bed, bench, and desk in a proposal for the redefinition of living space. Consistently following his own imagination, Munari always steered clear of the design industry's hustle and bustle. His objects are quiet, modest invitations to explore and contemplate the world that surrounds us.

Products
1930 *Macchina aerea*
1933 first *Macchine inutili* (useless machines)
1937 advertisements for **Campari**
1949 first *Libri illegibili* (illegible books)
1950 *Negative-Positive Images*
1954 fountain for the Biennale di Venezia; ice bucket for **Zani & Zani**
1964 *Falkland* lamp for **Danese**
1968 develops educational toys with **Giovanni Belgrando** (until 1976)
1971 *Abitacolo* furniture for Robots
1991 production of *Chair for Brief Visits* by **Zanotta** (designed in 1945)

Page 271
top left: *Vademecum* cart for Robots, 1974
top right: Advertisement for Campari, 1964
bottom left:. *Illegible Book*, 1953 (red-and-white pages)
bottom right: *Zizi* for Pigomma, 1953

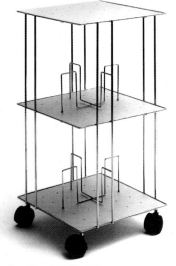

Marcello NIZZOLI

Painter, architect, graphic and industrial designer

When **Olivetti** introduced Marcello Nizzoli's *Lexikon 80* typewriter in 1948 it was instantly acclaimed as a classic. The curators of New York's Museum of Modern Art were so taken by its beauty that they immediately acquired an example for their permanent collection. Like the legendary *Vespa,* introduced the same year, the *Lexikon 80* had an independent shell that covered the mechanical innards like a removable dome. The combination of organic, sculptural form and functional design are a hallmark of Nizzoli's work.

Nizzoli was a consummate industrial designer. Meticulously developing each element of his designs with an eye to the manufacturing process, he put a distinctive aesthetic stamp on Olivetti's products of the 1950s. Nizzoli's machines, such as the portable *Lettera 22* typewriter and the *Tectactrys* calculator, reveal their symmetric perfection from every perspective and stand as defining examples of the **Linea italiana,** with its

1887 born in Boretto
(Reggio Emilia)

1913 graduates after studying art and architecture in Parma

1924 works as graphic artist and painter

1931 collaboration with **Giuseppe Terragni** and **Edoardo Persico** (until 1936)

1934 Parker showroom in Milan (with E. Persico)

1954 *Compasso d'oro* (also 1957)

1963 office building for **Olivetti** in Ivrea

1969 dies in Milan

Products

1926 Posters for **Campari** Bitter and Cordial

1940 *MC 4S Summa* calculator

1948 *Lexikon 80* typewriter

1950 *Lettera 22* portable typewriter

1952 *Studio 44* typewriter; all for Olivetti

1953 *Supernova BU* sewing machine for Necchi

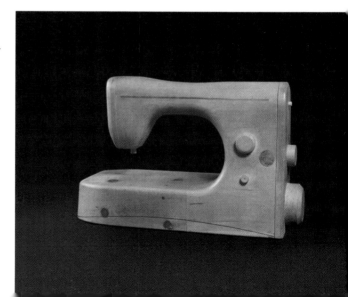

organically rounded forms. At the end of the decade Nizzoli made his first foray into a more angular look with the *Diaspron* typewriter, introduced in 1959.

Nizzoli had started out in the 1920s as an abstract painter and graphic designer influenced by **Futurism.** After designing posters for **Campari,** in 1938, Adriano Olivetti hired him to work in his company's advertising department, which at the time employed some of the best graphic artists in the world. In 1940, Nizzoli designed his first product, the *MC 4S Summa* calculator. But it was not until after the war that he came into his own as a product designer, working not only for Olivetti but also for the sewing machine manufacturer **Necchi,** for which he developed such lucid designs as the *Mirella* of 1957. And Nizzoli's accomplishments in product design should not obscure his significance as an architect: in the 1950s he designed workers' housing, and in the 1960s, office buildings for Olivetti.

1956 *Tectactrys* calculator for Olivetti

1957 *Mirella* sewing machine for Necchi

1959 lighters for Ronson; *Diaspron 82* typewriter for Olivetti

1960 gas pump for **Agip**

Wooden model of *Mirella* sewing machine for Necchi, 1957 (model built by Giovanni Sacchi)

Lexikon 80 typewriter for Olivetti, 1948

O LUCE

Lighting manufacturer

During the 1960s, O Luce established itself as one of Italy's leading lighting manufacturers. This success was largely due to the work of three very different designers. **Joe Colombo** contributed an experimental, cutting-edge sensibility with such creations as the boldly curved *281* Plexiglas light, the robot-like *Spider* lamp and, in 1971, the *626,* which was the first halogen floor lamp made in Italy. **Vico Magistretti** brought a more discreet, classic look. His geometric *Atollo* table lamp (fig. p. 36) has remained O Luce's best-known product, and his symmetrical *Snow* and *Sonora* hanging lamps have inspired countless copies. **Bruno Gecchelin** rounded out the collection with such restrained, ergonomically designed products as the arching *Dogale 512* desk lamp and the *Gemma* floor lamp.

Since the 1980s, O Luce has also worked with younger designers, including Hannes Wettstein, **Marco Romanelli** and **Marta Laudani, Riccardo Dalisi,** Sebastian Bergne, and Hans Peter Weidemann.

O Luce spa.,
San Giuliano Milanese
1948 founded in Milan

Products
1966 *Colombo 281; Spider;*
both by **Joe Colombo**
1974 *Snow* by **Vico Magistretti**
1976 *Sonora* by Vico
Magistretti (metal version)
1977 *Atollo* by Vico Magistretti;
Dogale 512 by **Bruno
Gecchelin**
1990 *Sister* floor and wall lamp
by **Riccardo Dalisi**
1992 *Gemma* floor lamp
by Bruno Gecchelin
1998 *Lid* hanging lamp by
Sebastian Bergne

Personal 230 desk lamp by Bruno
Gecchelin, 1988

Page 275

top left: *Lanterna* hanging lamp
by Marco Romanelli and Marta
Laudani, 1998

bottom left: *Colombo 281*
by Joe Colombo, 1966

right: *626* floor lamp
by Joe Colombo, 1971

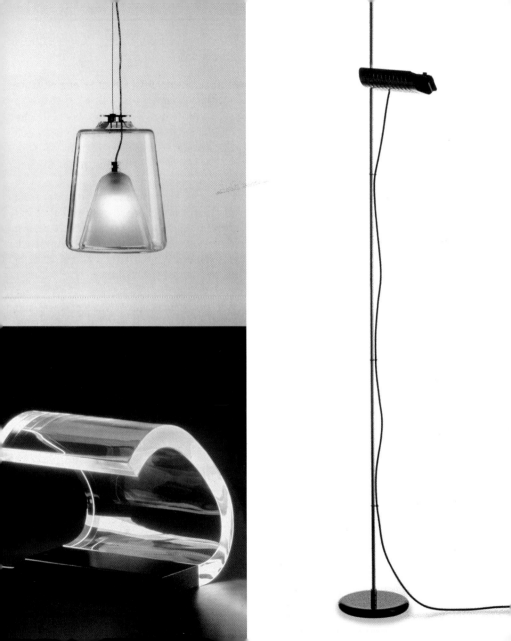

OLIVETTI

Manufacturer of office machines, computers and office furniture

"Typewriters shouldn't be parlor items with ornaments of questionable taste, but should look serious as well as elegant." Camillo Olivetti's simple verdict contains, in a nutshell, the design principle on which the company he had founded in 1908 rose to global prominence. Its consistent design philosophy not only ensured the success of its product lines but also made Olivetti a pioneer in the creation of a unified corporate culture.

The company's first product, the *M1,* designed by Camillo Olivetti in 1911, was also the very first typewriter made in Italy. Conceived with a view to American methods of standardized production, the typewriter's design did away with all superfluous elements—an early example of form following function. But it was Camillo's son, Adriano, who led the company to global fame in the 1930s with his energetic implementation of a comprehensive design strategy. A central component of his vision was Olivetti's advertising and development department, which was established in 1932 and attracted a staff of collaborators that included the Bauhaus artist **Xanti Schawinsky,** Renato Zveteremich, **Bruno Munari, Marcello Nizzoli, Studio Boggeri, Erberto Carboni, Franco Albini,** Giovanni Pintori, the Rationalist architects of the **BBPR** studio, **Luigi Figini,** and **Gino Pollini.** They all helped create a comprehensive corporate identity that encompassed the firm's functional product designs as well as modern advertising graphics, company magazines (including *Tecnica ed Organizzazione,* launched in 1937, and the architectural journals *Urbanistica* and *Zodiac*), and the starkly elegant look of its glass-and-steel production plants, designed by Figini and Pollini. Adriano Olivetti also created an extensive social infrastructure for his employees, providing them with housing, libraries, and day-care centers for their children. The basis of Olivetti's rapid growth and exemplary corporate culture was its

Olivetti spa, Ivrea

1908 founded by Camillo Olivetti in Ivrea

1925 Adriano Olivetti travels the U.S. before joining the firm in 1926

1932 establishment of advertising and development department

1933 Adriano Olivetti becomes general manager

1936 **Marcello Nizzoli** is hired

1937 **Giovanni Pintori** is hired to later become head of advert. dept.

1939 workers' housing and factory buildings by **Luigi Figini** and **Gino Pollini**

1943 Camillo Olivetti dies

1952 Olivetti exhibition at MoMA, New York

1954 Olivetti showroom in New York opens (designed by **BBPR**)

Page 277
top: *Lettera 22,* 1950
bottom left: *Divisumma 14,* 1948
bottom right: Poster for Diaspron, 1959; all by Marcello Nizzoli

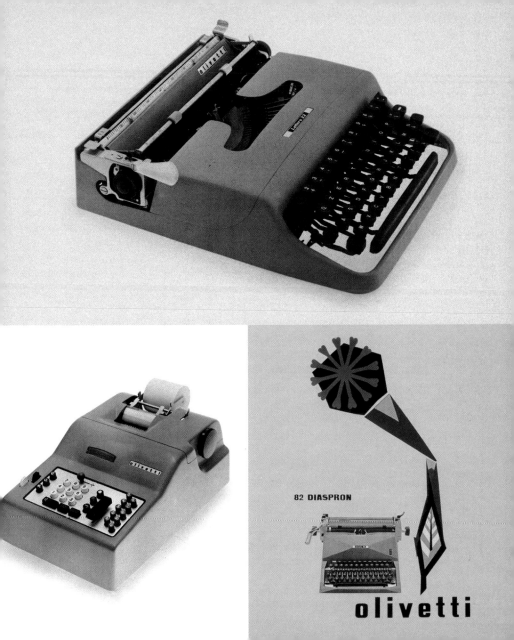

82 DIASPRON

olivetti

pioneering combination of functional design and efficient manufacturing processes, which resulted in highly successful products, such as the flat *MP1* portable typewriter of 1932, the *Studio 42* of 1935, and the *MC 4S Summa* calculator (fig. p. 32), designed by Marcello Nizzoli in 1940.

After the end of the Second World War, Nizzoli's organically-shaped typewriters and calculators defined the look of Olivetti. In 1948, he presented the groundbreaking *Lexikon 80* typewriter, whose top shell was the first to be entirely independent of the inner mechanical structure. He followed that in 1950 with the *Lettera 22,* a flat, lightweight, compact typewriter, which, in 1959, was chosen as the best industrial product of the last hundred years by an international jury of one hundred renowned designers.

With the industrial boom of those years, Olivetti became a household name, globally identified with outstanding design. Its ads lived up to the standards of Nizzoli's products. Headed by **Giovanni Pintori,** the company's advertising department became a forum for modern Italian graphic design in the 1950s. And the company was also known for its showrooms, designed by Studio BBPR, Franco Albini and **Franca Helg, Carlo Scarpa,** and **Gae Aulenti;** its growing international network of production plants; and its cultural center, which began organizing art exhibitions in 1950.

At the end of the 1950s, **Ettore Sottsass** replaced Nizzoli as Olivetti's chief design consultant. The appointment, made by Adriano Olivetti shortly before his death, brought in an energetic free spirit who led the company into a new, fruitful period of creative development. Sottsass's debut project was the spectacular *Elea 9003* mainframe computer, designed as an extremely user-friendly control room. In the 1960s, Sottsass created the elegant *Tekne 3* and *Praxis 48* (with Hans von Klier) and the unconventional red *Valentine* (with **Perry A. King**) typewriters,

---

1959 Olivetti acquires one-third of Underwood; enters computer business

1960 Adriano Olivetti dies

1962 Olivetti foundation established

1964 sale of electronics division to General Electric

1968 return to electronics business

1969 new corporate identity by **Hans von Klier**

1978 Carlo De Benedetti becomes general manager

1983 joint venture with AT&T

1994 top executives arrested on corruption charges

1998 Archivio Storico Olivetti in Ivrea opens

Page 279

top: *Spazio* office furniture system by BBPR, 1960

bottom left: *Valentine* portable typewriter by Ettore Sottsass and Perry A. King, 1969 (model)

bottom right: *Tekne 3* typewriter by Ettore Sottsass and Hans von Klier, 1963

as well as office furniture for the *Olivetti Synthesis* line. Hans von Klier took charge of the corporate identity in 1969. Together with C. Castelli and Perry A. King, he put together the legendary "Red Books," graphic standards manuals for all of Olivetti's publications, packaging, and products. In the mid-1960s, **Mario Bellini** joined the company's design team. One of his most striking ideas was to cover the innards of machines like the *Divisumma 18* calculator (fig. p. 16) with a thin orange "skin." He also developed the *Logos* series of calculators and the *ET 101* typewriter.

Despite the success of its designs, Olivetti slipped into a serious financial crisis in the 1970s. A new general manager, Carlo De Benedetti, hired in 1978, reversed the downward slide through rigorous restructuring measures. In the 1980s, the company successfully entered the new fields of office automation and telecommunications. **Michele De Lucchi** and his team created a sleek, technology-oriented look for its fax machines, laptop computers, and multimedia equipment. In 1993, though, the company was again shaken by a severe crisis; one year later several of its top executives were arrested on charges of corruption. Olivetti has since recovered and is now organized as a holding company with numerous international subsidiaries that include the telecommunications firm Oliman, a joint venture with the German Mannesmann group.

Terri PECORA

Fashion, furniture, and product designer

When Terri Pecora moved from California to Milan in the late 1980s, she brought with her a wide range of experience. Trained as a fashion designer, she had also created furniture and eyewear, areas she has continued to explore in her work for **Edra Mazzei,** Interflex, Silhouette, and L.A. Eyeworks.

Design in Pecora's understanding is akin to witchcraft, a magical process that conjures up solutions to everyday problems. Her firm, Plumcake Kids, founded in 1996 with Marian de Rond, focuses on products for children, a long-neglected niche market between design and fashion. "There are plenty of uncomfortable chairs for grown-ups," Pecora says. "It was time that someone designed warm and cozy chairs for smaller children." Other products include *Sleeping Bag,* which easily opens up into a blanket to play on, and a baby carrier that can be comfortably worn on the parent's body.

1958 born in Idaho, USA

studies fashion design at
Art Center College of
Design in
Pasadena, CA

1989 moves to Italy

1991 opens studio in Milan

1996 establishes Plumcake
Kids with Marian de Rond

Products

1987 *Gym* mirror for **Bieffeplast**

1989 *Angel Chair* for Bieffeplast

1991 *Chameleon* table for **Edra**

1993 *Tati* bed for Interflex

1994 *Mixo* children's bedroom
for Interflex with N.
Bewick

Eyewear for Silhouette
Children's blanket for Plumcake
Kids, 1997

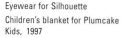

Gaetano PESCE

Artist, architect, furniture and product designer

"I believe that death makes us all alike, and that being alive means to be different. The objects that surround us during the short time of our existence should help us enjoy that prerogative." Gaetano Pesce, who switched from fine art to design in the 1960s, tries to encourage interaction between products and their users. In order to address each user's individuality, he has developed product lines with built-in variations. An emphasis on difference rather than standardization may not be the best qualification for an industrial designer, but Pesce was never eager to fit into that particular mold. He has always been far more interested in the meaning of his objects than in their mere function.

In the late 1960s, Pesce found a mentor in Cesare **Cassina,** who gave the young designer the opportunity to develop numerous experimental pieces. One of his first products became a milestone of design history: made of polyurethane foam, the 1969 *Up* chairs for **C & B Italia** popped out of their wrapping to spring into rounded,

1939 born in La Spezia

1959 cofounder of artists' group N

1961 contacts with Hochschule für Gestaltung, Ulm

1965 graduates from architecture school in Venice

1971 works for **Cassina**

1993 first large architectural project in Osaka, Japan

1996 Pesce exhibition at Centre Georges Pompidou, Paris

543 Broadway chair for Bernini, 1995

body-like shapes. Pesce instantly became one of the most exciting figures within the anti-functionalist **Radical Design** movement. He also designed the 1980 *Dalila* series for Cassina—slightly amorphous chairs, each of which differed from the next by minute formal peculiarities. That same year, Cassina introduced Pesce's *Sansone* synthetic resin tables, with tops whose color and form were decided, within a set spectrum, by the workers who fabricated them. Another notable design for Cassina was the *I Feltri* series of felt chairs (fig. p. 25), which had cloak-like backs. More figurative forms emerged with the 1987 *Green Street Chair* for **Vitra,** a spider-legged, dark-gray object that seemed to have sprung from a monster movie. In the 1990s, he continued to create ingenious surprises such as the aptly named *Umbrella Chair* and the *543 Broadway* chair, which moves slightly under the weight of the body, to remind the sitter of its presence.

Now based in Paris and New York, Pesce has focused on architecture in recent years. Commissioned in 1993 to design a building in Osaka, he created an "organic" structure whose blood-red facade is interspersed with giant containers filled with plants that fill the atmosphere with oxygen. "Over the last thirty years, I have tried to restore to architecture its ability to be meaningful," Pesce says. "I have done this by using recognizable, figurative images reflecting street life and popular culture, and by creating new typologies . . . I have tried to convey feelings of surprise, discovery, optimism, stimulation and originality."

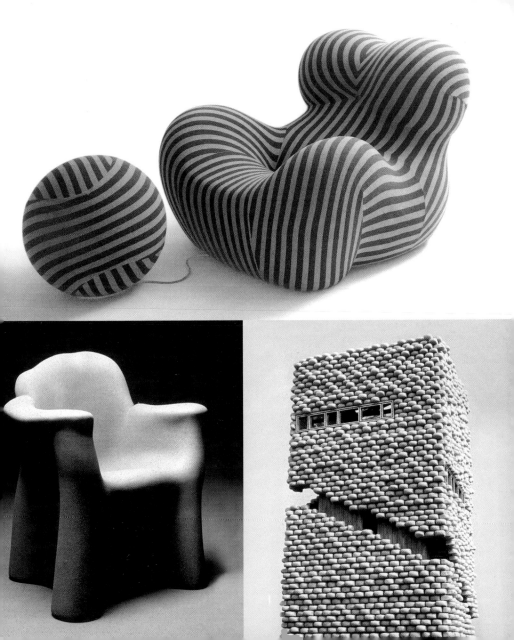

PININFARINA

Car-body designer

In 1995, Sergio Pininfarina received the *Compasso d'oro* for lifetime achievement. Pininfarina had "succeeded in applying a sense of continuity as well as innovative ideas to automobile design," the posthumous award speech declared. "With his designs for Ferrari he has also made a significant contribution to Italy's image in the world." Pininfarina in fact defined the entire look and style of **Ferrari's** sports cars, from the organically shaped *250 GT SWB* of 1960 (fig. pp. 42/43) and the *GTB4 "Daytona"* of 1968 to the flashy 1984 *Testarossa* and the futuristic *Mythos* of 1989.

Founded in 1930 by Sergio's father Battista "Pinin" Farina as a bodymaking workshop for luxury automobiles, the company today employs more than 2,000 people, but has essentially remained a family business. Sergio's children are now in charge of management. The overwhelming number of its designs for **Alfa Romeo, Lancia,** and Ferrari, and more recently for international manufacturers like Peugeot, Rolls-Royce, Audi, Cadillac, and Jaguar, were highly successful.

Pininfarina's early creations, such as the meticulously designed, streamlined Alfa Romeo *6 C 2300 "Pescara" Coupé* and the sleek, aerodynamic Lancia *Aprilia Coupé* from the 1930s are now celebrated as legends of luxury carmaking. After the Second World War, Battista Farina's *Cisitalia Coupé,* with his voluptuously rounded, flowing form, set a new standard for Italian car design. Battista's reputation reached such heights that, in 1961, Italy's president, Giovanni Gronchi, made his nickname official, changing the name of the family, and thus the firm, to "Pininfarina."

While Battista and Sergio were always the haute couturiers of car design, they also created such successful mass-produced models as the Lancia *Aurelia B 20 Berlinetta,* the *Peugeot 405*, and the *Alfa Giulietta Spider,* 27,000 of which were sold.

1930 Battista "Pinin" Farina forms company

1959 his son, Sergio, succeeds him as company head

1961 new company name, **Pininfarina**

1966 Battista "Pinin" Farina dies; Institute for Design Research founded

1979 *Compasso d'oro*

1995 *Compasso d'oro* for Sergio Pininfarina's lifetime achievements

Products

1937 **Lancia** *Aprilia Coupé*

1956 **Alfa Romeo** *Giulietta Spider*

1960 **Ferrari** *250 GT*

1966 **Fiat** *124 Spider*

1968 Ferrari *GTB4 "Daytona";* Peugeot *504*

1975 Ferrari *308 GTB*

1984 Ferrari *Testarossa*

1986 Cadillac *Allanté*

1994 Alfa Romeo *Spider* u. *GTV*

1996 Ferrari *550 Maranello*

Page 287

Lancia *Aurelia B 20*, 1951

Ferrari *330 GT*, 1966 (wooden model)

Pages 288/289: *Cisitalia Coupé*, 1947

PIRELLI

Manufacturer of tires and rubber products

Pirelli spa, Milan

1872 founded by Giovanni
Battista Pirelli

1938 Pirelli Holding S.A.
established

Products

1949 *Giocattolin Gommapiuma*,
toy figure with internal
metal skeleton by **Bruno
Munari**

1958 gas container by
Roberto Menghi

Design by Armando Testa, 1955
Poster by Bruno Munari, 1953

Founded in 1872 as a company "manufacturing and selling elastic rubber goods," Pirelli secured its place in design history not so much with its car tires and cable sheathing but with its modern advertising. **Albe Steiner, Bob Noorda,** and **Massimo Vignelli** were among the designers who created the company's promotional graphics in the 1950s and 60s, and **Armando Testa's** aggressive "elephant" poster and **Bruno Munari's** subtle geometric layouts have lost none of their visual power.

Another important innovation came when Pirelli manager Aldo Bai and his team asked **Marco Zanuso** to explore possible applications for their new foam rubber, *gommapiumo.* Zanuso used the material to develop his famous *Lady* chair, whose success led to the establishment of **Arflex** in 1951. Munari soon created toys out of *gommapiumo,* and **Gio Ponti** designed the Pirelli Tower in Milan (1954–56), one of the most important landmarks of modern Italian architecture.

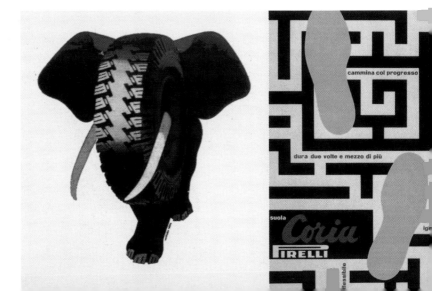

Furniture manufacturer

Poggi was founded over a hundred years ago as a traditional carpenter's workshop, and throughout its history, the quality of its woodworking has been the company's hallmark. Poggi initially specialized in building furniture for exclusive interiors designed by architects. The transformation from custom workshop to manufacturer came in the late 1940s, when Poggi began working with **Franco Albini,** one of the most important representatives of modern furniture design. With its geometric structure, Albini's *Luisa* chair of 1950 is typical of the minimalist look of Poggi's early products. Until 1968, the chairs, tables, and shelves the company built were all designed by Albini; in later years it also began producing designs by **Achille Castiglioni, Vico Magistretti,** and **Afra** and **Tobia Scarpa.** Poggi's output has always been small, its production capacity limited by choice rather than necessity. Proud of its history and committed to the highest standards of craftsmanship, the firm is a living example of the inspirational role traditional carpentry has played in Italian furniture design.

Poggi snc, Pavia
1890 founded

Products
1950 *Luisa* chair
1951 *Cavalletto* folding table
1952 folding chair
1956 *PS 16* chaise;
suspension shelves;
all by **Franco Albini**
1970 *Golem* chair by
Vico Magistretti

PL 19 chair by Franco Albini
and Franca Helg, 1957

POLTRONOVA

Furniture manufacturer

Poltronova srl, Montale
1957 founded

Products

1962 *Sgarsul* rocking chair
by **Gae Aulenti**

1964 *Saratoga* suite of chairs,
sofas and cabinets by
Massimo and **Lella
Vignelli**

1965 *Loto* table by **Ettore
Sottsass;**
Multi-use shelf unit by
Angelo Mangiarotti

1966 designs for laminate
furniture by Ettore
Sottsass

1967 *Superonda* seating
elements by **Archizoom**

1970 *Mobili Grigi* by Ettore
Sottsass

1971 *Joe* catcher's mitt chair

1976 *Insieme* suite;
both by **De Pas/
D'Urbino/Lomazzi**

1997 *Able* table
by Tim Power;
Nella chair by
Biagio Cisotti

According to **Radical Design** connoisseur Gianni Pettena, it was **Ettore Sottsass** who triggered the stylistic revolution at Poltronova, with his "lights and colors and the way he enlightened the world of design." Pettena refers to a moment in the 1960s when Sottsass presented his *Mobili grigi* (Gray furniture), which was indeed made of gray glass but bathed in the glaring light of colorful neon frames. Sottsass, who also experimented with laminates and ceramics, paved the way for other leaders of the Radical Design movement, who joined Poltronova in the late 1960s and early 1970s. The company's products of the period include such spectacular pieces as **De Pas/D'Urbino/Lomazzi's** *Joe* chair, which is in the shape of a giant baseball mitt (fig. p. 46); **Archizoom's** *Safari* seating landscape, arranged like a flower's petals but upholstered in leopard print; and **Superstudio's** altar-like *Desino* table. But there were also a number of classical, elegant pieces in Poltronova's collection: in 1962, **Gae Aulenti** had contributed the *Sgarsul* bentwood rocking chair; and **Massimo** and **Lella Vignelli's** purist *Saratoga* sitting-room suite, constructed of square and oblong elements, was introduced in 1964. In more recent years, Poltronova has produced designs by **Ron Arad, Prospero Rasulo, Michele De Lucchi,** and **Franco Raggi.**

Saratoga suite by
Massimo and Lella Vignelli, 1964

Architect, designer, and publisher

"Let us return to chair-chairs, house-houses, works without labels or adjectives, to real, true, natural, simple and spontaneous things," Gio Ponti wrote in his article *Senza aggettivi* (without adjectives), published in 1952 in *Domus* magazine. The chair-chair, which he designed the same year and which came onto the market in 1957, was the *Superleggera* for **Cassina**. Modeling his design after a simple chair he had seen in the fishing village of Chiavari, Ponti retained the vernacular's materials—wickerwork and wood—but reduced the structural elements so drastically that the result was a transparent, elegant piece ideally suited for mass production. Hailed at the time as the world's lightest chair, it also became one of the most famous.

As a bridge between past and present, the *Superleggera* epitomizes Ponti's design philosophy. While he was committed to Italy's traditions of artisanship, his interest in new technologies and manufacturing processes made him a pioneer of industrial design. He is often described as Italy's first product designer, a

1891 born in Milan

1921 graduates from architecture school; opens studio with Emilio Lancia and Mino Fiocchi

1923 artistic director at **Richard-Ginori** (until 1930); participates in *Biennale*, Monza (later director of 1933 *Triennale* in Milan)

1926 **Novecento** group founded

1928 *Domus* magazine founded (editor-in-chief until 1979, except 1941–44 and 1946–47)

Piatti in smalto del campo plates, 1957

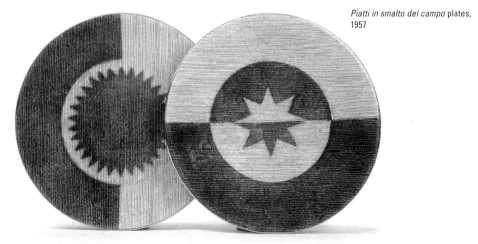

term that did not yet exist in the 1920s and 1930s, when Ponti was already fully engaged in the activity it came to describe. He designed fabrics for Vittorio Ferrari and interiors for trains as well as lighting and furniture for **Fontana Arte,** including the geometrically balanced *Bilia* table lamp, which consists of a globe resting on a cone, and the famous *0024* hanging lamp, with its glass-encased cylindrical shade. At the ceramics manufacturer, **Richard-Ginori,** he was in charge of what would today be called art direction, redesigning the entire product line and preparing it for large-scale production. For Ponti, there were no "good" or "bad" materials. Whether it was marble, wood and glass, or plastics and aluminum, he found them all *meraviglioso,* wonderful.

Design was only one of Ponti's many abilities. It was his architectural work that first brought him to international attention. **Alessandro Mendini** once called him the father of modern Italian architecture and ranked him alongside Le Corbusier, Alvar Aalto, and Oscar Niemeyer; his 1936 Montecatini building and 1954 **Pirelli** Tower in Milan are today considered landmarks. In his architecture as well as in his designs, Ponti tried to strike a balance between the contemporary and the traditional; he once said, "the past does not exist, everything is contemporary. In our culture only the present exists in the ideas we form of the past as well as in our anticipation of the future." In 1926 he was among the founders of the **Novecento** movement, which, unlike the adherents of **Rationalism,** integrated classical elements in their architecture. Ponti was never a radical modernist but always a modernizer of traditional values.

Ponti was also committed to communicating and discussing new ideas and developments. In 1928, he founded the architectural magazine *Domus,* still one of the most important international publications of its kind, and, with two brief

Gio PONTI

interruptions (1941–44 and 1946–47), served as its pub-lisher until his death in 1979. In *Domus,* he discussed new currents in modernism and published the works of international architects as well as Italian product designers like **Piero Fornasetti,** with whom he would later collaborate (fig. p. 39), and **Carlo Mollino.** After the Second World War it was Ponti who introduced the work of Charles Eames and other American designers to Italy.

Ponti's crucial contributions to Cassina's postwar collections included not only the *Superleggera* but also the *Distex* chair, with its distinctive, sloping armrests, as well as other seats. The range of his projects in the 1950s, 1960s and 1970s was as wide as it had been in the 1930s. He designed plumbing fixtures for **Ideal Standard;** chrome-plated espresso makers for **La Pavoni;** lamps and luminous objects for Arredoluce and Reggiani; elegant chairs and tables for Walter Ponti; ceramics, silverware, and glass objects for **Venini;** and numerous interiors.

"We wanted to bring into the house everything that had been left outside: calculated banality, willful vulgarity, urban elements, and vicious dogs," the members of the **Archizoom** group—**Andrea Branzi, Massimo Morozzi, Paolo Deganello,** and others—wrote about their overdone, "tasteless" *Dream* Beds of 1967. With a mixture of quotes from Art Deco, pure kitsch, and pompous clutter they and others railed against Italian **Bel Design,** which was at the peak of its success. Along with groups like **Superstudio** (with **Adolfo Natalini**), **UFO** (with **Lapo Binazzi**), and **Strum, Archizoom** was a driving force in the **Radical Design** movement, which emerged in the late 1960s as an offspring of Architettura Radicale (a term coined by Germano Celant in 1966). Against the backdrop of student protests and the radical changes in art marked by the advent of conceptual art and Arte Povera, the young rebels used a comprehensive critique of society to rigorously question the marriage of design and industry and to attack the dogmatic belief in the formal prescriptions of **Rationalism** and functionalism. (This antagonistic attitude was also dubbed **Anti-Design.**)

In their exhibition, *Italy: The New Domestic Landscape,* held at the Museum of Modern Art in New York in 1972, Superstudio presented a vision of a life without objects, shown in sketches, collages, and photomontages. This was typical of the movement,

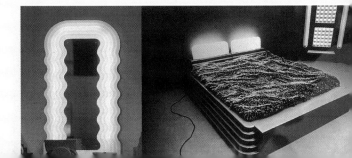

which took the city and urban planning as its main frame of reference. Consequently, much of Radical Design's work focused on developing alternative environments and living spaces rather than designing new products. **Ettore Sottsass,** who had questioned the unchanging cycle of production and consumption since the early 1960s, and artists like **Ugo La Pietra** and **Gaetano Pesce** also participated in the movement, which quickly became the dominant topic in the design world.

But there was also a more optimistic side to Radical Design's incendiary agenda. By opening up new formal possibilities, the movement set off a wave of joyful experimentation that resulted in designs like **Gatti/Paolini/Teodoro's** *Sacco* beanbag chair, **De Pas/D'Urbino/Lomazzi's** giant *Joe* baseball mitt, and **Gufram's** *Cactus* clothes tree and *Lip Sofa*. Pop design was born, and companies like **Cassina, C & B Italia,** and **Zanotta** had the courage to produce its innovative creations, which have since become icons of design.

By the mid-1970s Radical Design was past its peak, its hopes of social change through design and architecture unfulfilled. In hindsight, though, the movement paved the way for a new approach that led to Pop design, **Alchimia,** and **Memphis,** effecting a comprehensive renewal of Italian design.

"Every day, our industries produce cubic miles of city in the shape of mass-produced goods, and every day many of these molecular urban units are put in circulation to be consumed and transformed into trash within the cold, inert city of stone."
Andrea Branzi

From left:
Mirror and bed from *I Mobili grigi* by Ettore Sottsass for Poltronova, 1970
No-Stop-City project by Archizoom, 1970

Prospero RASULO

Artist, furniture and accessories designer

1953 born in Stigliato (MT)

1973 starts art school in Milan

1979 opens studio for painting, sculpture, interior architecture and set design in Milan

Products

1988 *Senso* vase for Bottega dei Vasai

1992 *She* chair for **Poltronova**

1993 *Gallery* collection for Poltronova; *Albera* coat rack for BRF

1995 *Mollys* bathroom system for Antonio Luoi

1996 *Orbis* table and *Obeo* trolley for Costantino; *Texo* table for **Zanotta**; *Calea* chair for **Arflex**

1997 *Charlotte* collection for **Fiam**

1998 *Souvenir* mirror for Glas

Page 301

Calea chair for Arflex, 1996

South Vietnam glass for Ritzenhoff, 1998, with Alessandro Mendini

Orbis table for Costantino, 1996

Element from *Mollys* bathroom collection for Antonio Lupi, 1995

In the 1970s **Alessandro Mendini** asked Prospero Rasulo to work with **Alchimia**, the laboratory of new Italian design. A sculptor at the time, Rasulo later said that the experience was "a liberation from the constraints of fine art." With a new sense of creative freedom he collaborated with Mendini in developing alternative design concepts, such as **Re-Design** and **Banal Design,** as well as furniture and accessories.

Rasulo has remained committed to Alchimia's lighthearted approach to form, color, and materials. Experimenting with porcelain for Costantino in 1996, he designed the *Orbis* shelf unit and the *Orbis Trolley,* using the material's inherent resistance to angular forms as an aesthetic element. "I was trained as an artist, which is perhaps the reason for my interest in the symbolic value of color and the power it can lend to even the most simple things," Rasulo says, describing the idea behind such vibrant objects as his graceful *Albera* clothes tree for BRF, the eccentric red *She* chair for **Poltronova,** and the colorful *Mollys* bathroom accessories for Antonio Lupi. "In the last few years the object has become the main attraction; it is trying to speak to us at all costs." Rasulo believes in the transformative power of the object, which is perhaps why an Italian magazine called him "the last romantic." In 1998, he and Mendini set up a tent outside the grounds of the Milan furniture fair to introduce their *Eco Mimetico Collection,* a series of glasses, vases, mirrors, furniture, and rugs covered in a camouflage print. It conveyed their belief that design could redirect meaning—in this case, changing camouflage from a signifier of war into a symbol for the return to living in harmony with nature.

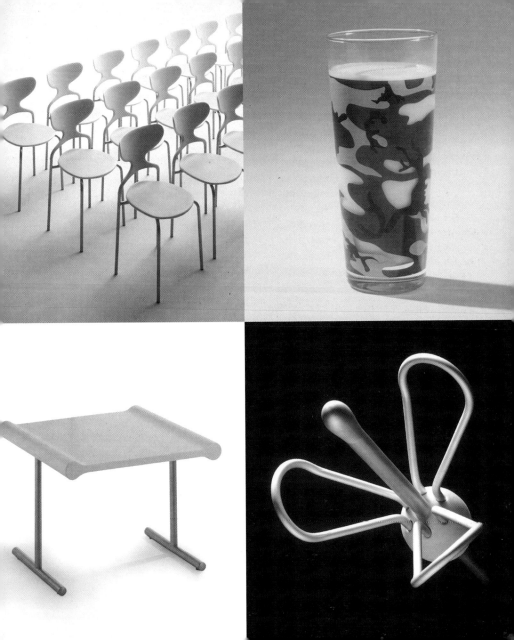

RATIONALISM

Rationalism was the Italian and Spanish version of European modernism. But as **Andrea Branzi** has pointed out, "there was one respect in which the Italian rationalists differed from their European counterparts: they were Fascists." While they may not have been among Fascism's leading proponents, the rationalists openly supported its goals in the 1920s and early 1930s. Mussolini, who came to power in 1926, attached great importance to architecture and the applied arts but didn't issue any formal or ideological directives for the development of a "Fascist style." So the rationalists and the more classically oriented Novecento movement entered into a fierce rivalry that came to head at the *Triennale* of 1933. In the mid-1930s, Mussolini finally took the side of the **Novecento** group, lauding their emphasis of genuinely "Italian" elements as opposed to rationalism's more "international" approach. In the process, many rationalists began to disassociate themselves from Fascism.

Rationalism began as an architectural movement. In 1926, its early proponents also included **Luigi Figini, Gino Pollini,** and **Giuseppe Terragni,** had formed the Gruppo 7. Terragni designed the Fascist Party's headquarters in Como, which was built in 1934–36. His design also included distinctly

Lira chair by Piero Bottoni, 1934 (prod. by Zanotta)

Olivetti factory in Ivrea by Luigi Figini and Gino Pollini, 1937

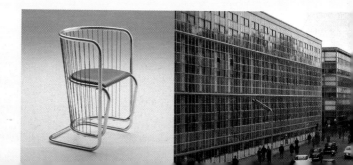

rationalist furniture, like the *Lariana* chair, constructed of a bent steel tube that holds the seat and backrest. (The chair is now produced by Zanotta.) In the 1930s, Figini and Pollini designed new factory buildings for Olivetti, boxy glass-and-steel structures without even a hint of ornament.

Out of the context of the new architecture, rationalist lighting and furniture designs began to emerge. **Piero Bottoni, Giuseppe Pagano,** Gino Levi Montalcini, and **Gabriele Mucchi** did away with the traditional stately look and, following the example of the German Bauhaus, experimented with new industrial materials such as tubular steel and chrome. In addition to metal furniture, rationalist designs also included such impressive objects as **Luciano Baldessari's** towering *Luminator* light column of 1929. However, many designs never went beyond the prototype stage, as the workshops were not equipped technically to realize them. After the Second World War, rationalist principles inspired an intellectual elite of leftist architects, among them the **BBPR** studio, **Franco Albini, Ignazio Gardella, Alberto Rosselli,** and a younger group that included **Marco Zanuso** and **Anna Castelli Ferrieri.** Postwar design remained rooted in the modernist tradition until the late 1960s when, in the wake of the Radical Design movement, a new generation began to question the functionalist dogma.

"Rationalism remains (...) highly significant as a reflection of Italy's internationalist ambitions at a time of strong nationalism, and as an expression of the complex relationship between politics and design that developed in Italy during those years."

Penny Sparke

Lariana chair by Giuseppe Terragni, 1936 (prod. by Zanotta)
MB 48 cabinet system by Franco Albini and Franca Helg, 1950s

Umberto RIVA

Architect, furniture and lighting designer

"I cannot design. I don't have a designer's mental structure. In my view a designer should be able to create a need, to invent an object that doesn't yet exist, and to enter it into the cycle of production. Designers in that sense are rare; it takes intelligence and a certain cleverness," Umberto Riva says.

Riva designs furniture and lighting only when his architectural work leaves him time; in many cases, the designs are by-products of architectural projects. "I always succeed in designing objects that don't sell," he says. Riva's products do not necessarily look expensive, but they usually are, due to his preference for costly materials; the *Veronese* lamp for Barovier & Toso, for example, is made of colored Murano glass.

A perpetual outsider, Riva is not interested in designing for contemporary tastes, which in the age of marketing-through-

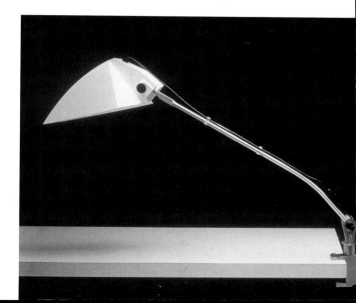

design must seem rather old-fashioned. That adjective, however, hardly applies to objects like Riva's *E 63* lamp, designed in 1963 for a competition organized by **Artemide.** Strikingly timeless in its clear proportions, the design went through a long odyssey before it was finally produced by **Fontana Arte** in 1991. For his Victor bureau for Schopenhauer/Fontana Arte, Riva used alder and beechwood. In its self-assured elegance, the piece recalls **Carlo Scarpa's** material aesthetics, while its pure, refined form is reminiscent of Scandinavian design. That can also be said of his *Agio* armchair for Bellato, with its geometric structure and segmented, blondewood frame. But Riva would never design a side chair—that, he says, is a difficult project, for which Thonet and Aalto have already found perfect solutions.

Products

1985 *Veronese*
and *Tesa* table lamps for
Barovier & Toso

1989 *Franceschina* table lamp

1991 *E 63* table lamp
(designed in 1963);
both for **Fontana Arte**

1992 *Ala* desk for **Driade**

1993 *Agio* chair and side table
for Bellato

1994 *Victor* bureau for
Fontana Arte (Schopen-
hauer)

From left:

Lem table lamp for Ve-Art, 1973 (re-edition by Fontana Arte as *Dilem*, 1991)

Tesa lamp for Barovier & Toso, 1985

E 63 lamp for Ve-Art, 1963
(re-edition by Fontana Arte, 1991)

Paolo RIZZATTO

Architect, furniture and lighting designer

Paolo Rizzatto and **Alberto Meda's** delicate *Berenice* desk lamp, made of glass, aluminum, and plastic for **Luceplan** (which is co-owned by Rizzatto) is a contemporary, technology-inspired interpretation of the classic library lamp. The principle of blending past and present is also apparent in Rizzatto's *Dakota* chair for **Cassina**, whose aluminum seat is upholstered in a combination of leather and polypropylene. "I don't have a problem with mixing different materials, styles, or approaches, nor do I care whether they are considered old or modern," he says. His furniture for **Alias** and **Molteni** and designs like the *Lola, D 7,* and *Titania* (fig. p. 38) lights for Luceplan often seem like highly condensed statements: simultaneously complex and minimal, they stand apart from loud postmodern experimentation and the anemic products of the fashionable new simplicity.

1941 born in Milan

1965 graduates from architecture school in Milan

1966 works for **Arteluce** (until 1977)

1968 opens studio

1972 daycare center in Segrate

1978 cofounder of **Luceplan**

1981 *Compasso d'oro* (also 1989 and 1995)

1986 town hall in Torricella Peligna

Products

1969 *265* lamp for Arteluce

1985 *Berenice* with **Alberto Meda**

1986 *Costanza* lamp

1989 *Titania* with Alberto Meda all for Luceplan

1995 *Dakota* chair for **Cassina**

1998 *Glassglass* hanging and wall lamp for Luceplan

Donald System for Joint, 1998, with Carlo Forcolini

Costanza table lamp for Luceplan, 1986

Marco ROMANELLI

Architect, furniture and lighting designer

One of the most active figures in Milan's design scene since the mid-1980s, Marco Romanelli has made a name for himself as a critic (for *Domus, Abitare,* and other magazines), exhibition organizer, and designer. Romanelli's designs reveal their high functionality in an almost casual way, creating a poetic balance between minimalist form and imaginative play. For **Up & Up** he created a washstand and console made of pale marble and airy wickerwork in a nimble, innovative interpretation of two traditional materials. For **Driade's** *Atlantide* collection, which reflects a younger generation's nomadic lifestyle, he designed wooden furniture on wheels and a wall cabinet with a front panel that comes as either a mirror or a blackboard. Working as **O Luce's** art director, he also developed, with his frequent collaborator Marta Laudani, the *Lanterna* lamp, whose Murano glass shade is contained, like a precious object or an exhibit, in a glass jar.

1958 born in Trieste

1983 graduates from architecture school in Genoa

1986 editor at *Domus* (until 1994)

1995 art director at **O Luce** editor at *Abitare*

1996 art director at **Montina**

Products

1988 *Trame* table for **Arflex** with Marta Laudani

1997 *Saudade* lamp for O Luce with Marta Laudani and Massimo Noceto

1998 *Lanterna* lamp for O Luce with Marta Laudani

Materco wall cabinet for Driade (*Atlantide*), 1996

Francescano shelf unit for Driade (*Atlantide*), 1995, with Marta Laudani

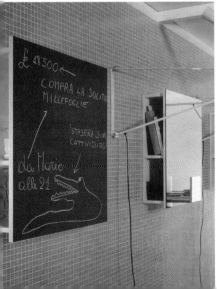

Alberto ROSSELLI

Architect and industrial designer

A theorist, architect, and designer, Alberto Rosselli thought of his work as a service to the new society that emerged from the ravages of the Second World War. He demonstrated his vision of modern, simple, beautiful, and inexpensive design in his 1951 *Kitchen for a Two-person Household.* Functional and efficient, it was a response to the cramped living quarters typical of those years.

Rosselli considered it vital to strengthen the cooperation between designers and manufacturers; when he founded a design magazine in 1953 he gave it the title, *Stileiundustria.* [TRANS. TK] Though the magazine occasionally fetishized industrial products, it was an important forum for contemporary design discourse before it folded in 1962. From the 1950s through the 1970s, Rosselli designed gas water heaters, electric hairdryers, plumbing fixtures, coffeemakers, clocks, and furniture. And together with **Isao Hosoe,** he developed the *Meteor* bus in 1970.

Jumbo chair for Saporiti, 1960

Aldo ROSSI

Architect and industrial designer

Aldo Rossi was singularly consistent in treating product design as architecture on a smaller scale. This is particularly apparent in his coffeepots for Alessi. Like Rossi's buildings they are composed of geometric forms: his *La Conica* pot is a cylindrical tower with a conical roof for the flat landscape of the coffee table; the *La Cupola* espresso maker of 1988 has a domed top. His chairs, like the *Capitolo* series for **Molteni** and the *Parigi* for **Unifor,** are also modeled after classic architectural forms.

Rossi's rigorous adherence to a restricted formal vocabulary was based on a theory he developed in his book, *L'architettura della città,* published in 1966. Contrasting his own model of an architecture reduced to archaic forms with organic and functionalist approaches, the book became a fundamental text in the debate over postmodern architecture.

Rossi's architectural projects include the town square and memorial fountain in Segrate, near Milan; the Il Palazzo Hotel in Fukuoka, Japan; and the Bonnefanten museum in Maastricht, the Netherlands.

1931 born in Milan

1955 editor at *Casabella* (until 1964)

1959 graduates from architecture school in Milan

1966 *L'architettura della città* published

1971 San Cataldo cemetary in Modena

1994 Bonnefanten Museum, Maastricht

1997 dies in Milan

La conica espresso maker for Alessi, 1994

Cartesio bookcase for Unifor, 1996/1996

Roberto SAMBONET

Painter, graphic and product designer

1924 born in Vercelli

1945 graduates from architecture school in Milan

1956 art director of *Zodiac* magazine (until1960); *Compasso d'oro* (also 1970, 1979, 1995); establishes Sambonet spa

1960 consultant for **La Rinascente**

1995 dies in Milan

Page 311

top left: *Center Line* bowls, 1965 (until 1971)

top right: Logo for Lombardy region, 1974, with Bob Noorda and Pino Tovaglia

bottom left: *Empilage* glasses for Baccarat, 1971

bottom right: Packaging for stainless-steel flatware for Sambonet, 1959

Pesciera fish platter, 1957

Many of Roberto Sambonet's elegant housewares, such as his *Center Line* set of stainless-steel bowls and crystal glasses for Baccara, can be stacked or nested, creating visual patterns that have often been photographed in extreme close-up views. Though influenced by his friend Alvar Aalto and by Frank Lloyd Wright, the main point of reference in his work as a graphic and product designer was not architecture but art. Sambonet believed in a fundamental relationship between art and design. He had staged successful exhibitions of his paintings and drawings in Europe and Brazil before he turned to product design. In the early 1950s he opened a design studio in Milan, and in 1956, founded his own company, Sambonet spa, transforming an existing traditional workshop into a modern manufacturer of sophisticated stainless-steel goods at a time when such products were still largely neglected by designers. The best known example of his organic, sculptural style is the *Pesciera* fish platter, which won numerous awards. For other firms he also designed glass, crystal, and porcelain objects. As a graphic artist, he collaborated with **Bruno Monguzzi, Max Huber** and **Bob Noorda** on the packaging for his company's products and other projects. He also created graphics for such clients as **La Rinascente, Pirelli, Alfa Romeo,** and the architectural magazine *Zodiac.*

Denis SANTACHIARA
Industrial, furniture, and lighting designer

Denis Santachiara's *Sister Chairs* for Vitra (1987) are peculiar creatures. *Timida* blushes when "she" is talked to, *Espansiva* puffs up when warmed by a person's body, and *Volubile* changes color on contact. Interaction between object and user and unconventional ways of using technology have always fascinated Santachiara, who says that "the more tricks a magician knows, the more he can amaze and delight his audience."

Unlike most of his peers, Santachiara didn't study at Milan's prestigious Polytechnic. Instead, he started out as a self-taught automobile designer in the mid-1960s, when he was sixteen years old. Motion is still a recurrent theme in his designs: he has developed a blow-dryer whose airstream can be precisely controlled (and is also fragrant); and his *Notturno Italiano* bed lamp provides first light and then help for insomniacs by projecting a procession of little sheep onto the wall. Many of Santachiara's

1951 born in Campagnola, Reggio Emilia

1966 opens design studio; works as self-taught car designer

1975 research into "soft technology"

1990 forms Domodinamica with Cesare Castelli

Products

1986 *Work Station*, prototype for **Italtel** Telematica with **Franco Raggi** and **Alberto Meda**; *Epsylon* dance club in Reggio Emilia

1987 *Mistral* ventilation aplliance for Dilmos; *Sister Chairs,* prototypes for Vitra Edition

1988 *Thunderstorm Kit* for Dilmos

designs have remained prototypes, small poetic creations not necessarily fit for mass production. Despite that, his work has been supported by companies like Italtel, for which Santachiara, along with **Franco Raggi** and **Alberto Meda,** developed a multifunctional *Workstation* in 1986. For Stil Resine he designed a *Plastic Bicycle,* equipped with a horn that plays tunes from five Verdi operas and a counter for calories burnt pedaling.

Santachiara's animated designs are not simply fun objects; they reveal different, unaccustomed aspects of familiar functions, and thus sharpen the perception for undiscovered possibilities. Or, as Santachiara puts it: "As a designer I am not interested in the material marvels of technology but in its immaterial extensions." One of his most recent inventions is the *Pisolò* ottoman, which, with the help of a built-in electric motor, turns into a bed-and-table unit.

1989 *Oxalis* chair for **Cidue**;
     Mama chair for **Baleri**;
     Astro seat for Campeggi;
     plastic bicycle for
     Stil Resine

1990 *Domodinamica*
     oggeti animari per la casa
     Collection

1993 *Notturno Italiano*
     lamp for Domodinamica

1997 *Pisolò* convertible ottoman
     for Campeggi

From left:
Sciuscia furniture
Trans chair for Campeggi
Bicycle for Stil Resine, 1989

Richard SAPPER

Industrial designer

1932 born in Munich

1955 graduates from Munich University with an engineering degree

1956 works in design dept. of Mercedes-Benz (until 1958)

1958 moves to Italy, works at **Gio Ponti's** studio, then at **La Rinascente** (1959-1961); collaboration with **Marco Zanuso** (until 1977)

1960 *Compasso d'oro* (also 1962, 1964, 1967, 1979, 1987, 1991, 1995, 1998)

1970 consultant for **Fiat** (until 1976)

1986 professor at Stuttgart art school (until 1998)

Products

1962 *Doney 14* TV set for **Brionvega** with M. Zanuso

1964 plastic children's chair for **Kartell** with M. Zanuso

1983 *Bollitore* tea kettle for **Alessi**

1995 *Zoombike* folding bicycle

Page 315

top: *Tizio* desk lamp for Artemide, 1972

bottom l.: *Cobán* espresso maker, 1997

bottom r.: *9090* espresso maker, 1979

both for Alessi

In 1970, **Artemide** owner **Ernesto Gismondi** received a call from Richard Sapper. "Remember when you asked me to design an extremely functional, innovative light?" the designer asked. Then he announced that he was ready to present his solution. The solution turned out to be the prototype for *Tizio,* one of the most famous lamps in design history. With its perfectly balanced system of weights and counterweights, the lamp could be adjusted with unprecedented ease and precision; it was also one of the first desk lamps equipped with a low-voltage halogen bulb, ideal for spotlighting specific areas.

Born in Germany and now based in Milan, Sapper has been a vital part of the Italian design world for the last forty years. He is an industrial designer in the fullest sense; the products he has developed range from furniture, clocks and espresso makers to faucets, cars, and bicycles. To him, designing means problem-solving with the goal of "giving meaning to form." In 1964, as a designer for **Kartell,** he explored plastic furniture production with his mentor, **Marco Zanuso.** He also designed some of the most compact and formally adventurous electronic equipment of the 1960s with Zanuso, including the *Black, Algol* (fig. p. 4), and *Doney* television sets and the *TS 502* box radio for **Brionvega.** More recently, Sapper won a *Compasso d'oro,* the ninth in his career, for his aluminum *Zoombike,* which can easily be folded and carried on trains or buses. While all his designs are impeccably functional, many of them come with an extra twist, like his famous teakettle for **Alessi,** which instead of a shrill whistle emits a pleasant chord.

SAWAYA & MORONI

Furniture and accessories manufacturer

When Beirut-born William Sawaya and Paolo Moroni founded their company in Milan in 1984, they invited such international architects as Michael Graves, Charles Jencks, Oswald Matthias Ungers, Zaha Hadid, and Jean Nouvel to design furniture and silverware. There were no further conditions or requirements, except that each architect follow his or her unique stylistic ideas.

Jean Nouvel contributed the *TBL Inox table,* an austere purist design, while **Toni Cordero's** velvet *Faia* chair, with arms made of blue cords, was an opulent, ironic commentary on the longing for the "good old days." Marcello Morandini designed his *Bine* chair (fig. p. 21) as a dizzying sculpture of black and white lines, and Sawaya himself created *Wienerin,* an homage to the classic Viennese café chair. He also designed the *Acqua di Fuoco* liquor cabinet, a dangerous-looking piece whose back panel aggressively thrusts up into the air. In addition, the collection

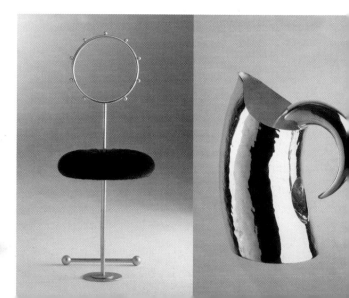

includes elegant silver objects such as Matthew Hilton's hand-shaped *Mano* ashtray and Zaha Hadid's *Tea and Coffee Set,* whose parts are reminiscent of rough-hewn crystals. Sawaya's glass objects take a special position in the company's program: his *Dialetti impossibili* and *Fleur Du Mal* vases are sumptuous, sensual creations that stretch limits of the material's possibilities. *Le Possedé* consists of an orb from which red glass tubes stretch out like greedy arms, and the milky body of his *Hymne à la beauté* is covered with bee-like clusters of ornaments.

Modesty is certainly not an attribute of Sawaya & Moroni's collection; instead, it is a bold statement on the stylistic diversity in architecture at the end of the twentieth century. In that sense, the company resembles a sophisticated design gallery rather than a conventional manufacturer.

1995 *I Dialetti Impossibili* glass vases by William Sawaya

1997 *Tea and Coffee Set* by Zaha Hadid

1998 *Spring* collection, incl. *MY 98* chair by Michael Young, *Povera* chair by William Sawaya and *Lintaro* furn. object by Makoto Kawamoto

From left:
Drum side table by Marco Mencacci, 1991
Santa chair by Luigi Serafini, 1990
Le Diable en Tête pitcher, 1995
Ex Libris bookcase, 1997
Patty Diffusa chair, 1993;
all by William Sawaya

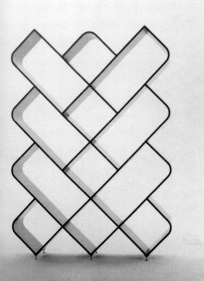

Afra & Tobia SCARPA

Architects, furniture and lighting manufacturer

"You don't instantly know whether a product really works. It must pass the test of time," Tobia Scarpa says. Longevity and a sensitive use of materials are crucial in the work of Tobia and Afra Scarpa, who met at architecture school in Venice. The couple's approach owes a debt to Tobia's father, **Carlo Scarpa,** who was famous for his masterly treatment of exquisite materials, and to Tobia's early experiences at the glass-blowing workshop of **Venini.** A gentle austerity characterizes all their products, like the *Biagio* lamp, which is cut by hand from a massive block of marble, and the airy *Ariette 1-2-3* ceiling light (both for **Flos**), with its diffuser made of a semitransparent piece of fabric. For their archaic-looking *Africa* chair for **B & B Italia** and the *Bastiano* sofa for **Gavina** (one of their earliest designs), they used massive pieces of wood. The Scarpas have also developed furniture for **Cassina** and **Molteni** and designed buildings for **Benetton** (1966) and **C & B Italia** (1968).

1960 design and architecture studio established in Montebelluna

1970 *Compasso d'oro*

Products

1961 *Bastiano* sofa for **Gavina** (now prod. by Knoll)

1962 *Vanessa* bed for Gavina; *Fantasma* floor lamp for **Flos**

1963 *Modell 917* chair for **Cassina**

1968 *Biagio* table lamp for **Flos**

1969 *Soriana* chair for Cassina

1970 *Bonanza* chair for **B&B Italia**

1984 *Poligonon* table series for B&B Italia

1986 *Marly* shelf unit for **Molteni**

Ariette 1-2-3 ceiling light for Flos, 1973 by Tobia Scarpa

Carlo SCARPA

Architect and furniture designer

In the 1930s, when the young Venetian architect Carlo Scarpa was fiercely attacked for his modernist restorations of historic buildings, he withdrew to the workshop of **Paolo Venini,** a close friend and seminal innovator of the art of glass-blowing. During those years of seclusion, Scarpa designed exquisite vases and bowls (fig. p. 27), reinterpreted traditional materials, and "invented" two new kinds of glass: one heavy and opaque, the other light and composed of two layers.

The love of precious materials, especially those with a long history, and a deep commitment to cultural traditions would later resurface in all Scarpa's projects. His most important works were in the field of architecture, although the academic world long refused to acknowledge their greatness. He made a name for himself as a brilliant exhibition designer with projects such as the Paul Klee retrospective at the 1948 *Biennale,* the 1957 **Olivetti** showroom in Venice, and the Venezuela pavilion on the grounds of the Biennale. In the early 1970s Scarpa also designed the family

1906 born in Venice

1926 graduates from architecture school in Venice

1931 Casa Asta, with the painter Mario De Luigi

1942 exhibition architect for *Biennale di Venezia*

1951 meets Frank Lloyd Wright in Venice

1956 **Olivetti** prize for architecture

1957 Olivetti showroom in Venice

1960 Frank Lloyd Wright exhibition in Milan

1978 dies in Sendai (Japan)

Murrine opache glass bowls for Venini, 1940

Products
1927 glass objects for
      Cappellin & C. (until 1930)
1933 glass objects for **Venini**
      (until 1947)
1940 *Tessuto* glass series
      for Venini
1969 *Doge* table
1972 *Valmarana* table
      both for Simon
      International
1974 *Zibaldone* shelving system
      for **Bernini**

Zibaldone shelving system for
Bernini, 1974

cemetery for the Brion family in Treviso. It wasn't until the late 1960s that Scarpa began designing objects for mass production. But he never really embraced its principles of scale and automation—they were simply too far removed from his own involvement with each material's aesthetics, his practice of developing designs out of a concrete context, and his commitment to meticulous workmanship.

Scarpa designed his furniture to last, possibly forever. There is an aura of permanence to pieces like the steel-and-crystal *Doge* table for Simon, a company owned by his friend, **Dino Gavina** (the table was originally designed for the dining room of the Zentner House in Zürich); the marble *Delfi* table (with Marcel Breuer); and the monumental *Valmarana* wooden table. In the 1970s, Scarpa also created designs for Bernini, including the *Zibaldone* bookcase, with doors made of crystal glass.

Furniture and textile designers

At Sigla, three key skills are embodied in the design studio's founders. Marina Bani used to be in charge of **Zanotta's** product development; Marco Penati still heads its technology department; and Patrizia Scarzella is an architect and journalist. They use their combined experience to develop functional, technically brilliant solutions. The *Wiz* desk for Penalto, to name one example, improves on a familiar design by putting a kidney-shaped top on two three-legged saw-horses made of tubular steel.

One of the studio's specialties is the development of new textiles. The *Spezie* upholstery fabric for Zanotta is made of natural fibers and has a strikingly rich texture. The studio also curates exhibitions, such as the 1997 show *Bello Quotidiano* (Everyday Beauty), on the history of Italian furniture design. Sigla also designs upholstered furniture for Zanotta, beds for **Flou,** and lighting for **Fontana Arte** and Barovier & Toso.

1994 studio established by
Marina Bani, Patrizia
Scarzella and
Marco Penati in Milan

Products
1995 *Ito* table series; *Nilo* table
both for **Arflex**
1997 *Est* sofa; *Nadir* sofa
1998 textile collection;
all for **Zanotta**;
Atlante bed for **Flou**

Upholstery fabric from *Spezie*
series for Zanotta
Wiz table for Desalto, 1997

Ettore SOTTSASS jr.

Architect, furniture and industrial designer

Page 323

Hanging lamp for Arredoluce, 1957

Fruit bowl, 1952

Svincolo floor lamp for Alchimia, 1979

As a young student of architecture in the 1930s, Ettore Sottsass Jr. experienced the great architectural movement of **Rationalism** in the office of his father, who was one of the modernist style's leading proponents. At the time there were no indications that, a few decades later, the son would be a central figure in a movement that first rigorously questioned rationalism, and finally replaced it with a completely new understanding of design.

In the early 1950s, Sottsass realized his first architectural projects in Milan. He became known to a wider public in 1959 when he designed the *Elea 9003,* the first Italian mainframe computer, for **Olivetti.** He arranged the computer's countless controls in a clear, user-friendly way, and color-coded them for easier orientation. Sottsass became Olivetti's chief consultant for office machines, and in the following years designed equipment such as the *Tekne 3,* the small red *Valentine,* and the *Praxis* typewriters, as well as office furniture. Still, he was never an organization man, either at Olivetti or in his later work for other employers.

Sottsass moved between the two poles of art and industry with great freedom. While he held his position at Olivetti, he also designed his *Ceramics of Darkness* and *Ceramics for Shiva,* which were inspired by a trip to India and marked an attempt to return to primal cultural forms.

By the beginning of the 1960s Sottsass had begun to dissociate himself from purely functional design. When **Radical Design** emerged in Italy, he was among those who harshly criticized design's dull formalism and subservience to industrial clients. He started experimenting with laminate-covered furniture, designing the *Mobili grigi* (Gray furniture) prototypes for **Poltronova**—a series of fiberglass beds and mirrors framed in glaring neon tubes. In 1972, he contributed a micro-environment consisting of variously combinable furniture units to the New York

1988 Bischofberger house,
Zürich (compl. 1989)

1990 gas stations for Italian oil
company ERG (until 1997)

1995 Malpensa 2000 airport
(public areas),
Milan (compl. 1998)

1996 urban planning studies in
Seoul (until 1998)

Products

1963 *Ceramics of Darkness*

1964 *Ceramics for Shiva*;
Praxis 48 typewriter;
Tekne 3 typewriter;

both typewriters for
Olivetti with **Hans von
Klier**

1965 *Loto* table for **Poltronova**

1969 *Valentine* portable
typewriter for Olivetti,
with **Perry A. King**

exhibition *Italy: The New Domestic Landscape*. In 1973 he was among the founders of the alternative design school **Global Tools,** and a short time later he created **Banal** and **Anti-Designs** for the **Alchimia** studio.

Then, in 1981, Sottsass founded the movement that made him famous—**Memphis.** His *Carlton* shelf unit (fig. p. 12), covered in colorful laminates, and numerous other furniture objects, lights, and accessories, defined the Memphis style and message, which declared that the form of a product is not its ultimate purpose, but rather a starting point from which to establish a relationship with its users. The first Memphis exhibition made a tremendous splash in the design world. "To me, designing doesn't mean to give shape to a more or less stupid product for a more or less indifferent industry. For me, design is a way to discuss life, social

relationships, politics, food, and even design itself," Sottsass wrote at the time. For an international group of mostly young architects and designers, Sottsass became a mentor, promoter, and central source of new ideas. In 1981 he founded Sottsass Associati, a professional studio for architecture and graphic and industrial design, which was joined by **Marco Zanini,** James Irvine, and Johanna Grawunder, among others.

Sottsass is still one of the most protean figures in international design. He continues to develop electronic appliances, lights, office furniture, writing instruments, and ceramics. And he has stuck to his belief that form is not an end in itself but a means for interaction with the consumer. Among his clients and friends are **Alessi, Artemide, Abet Laminati,** Vitra, Zumtobel, Siemens, Apple, and Yamagiwa.

1970 *Mobili grigi* (GrayFurniture); *Elledue* fiberglass bed and *Ultrafragola* fiberglass mirror, all for Poltronova

1979 *Le strutture tremano* table for **Alchimia**

1981 *Carlton* shelf unit for Memphis

1985 Esprit store in Cologne

1988 *Mobile giallo* for Design Gallery Milano

1992 wristwatches for Seiko with **Marco Zanini** and **Marco Susani**

From left:
Valentine typewriter for Olivetti, 1969, with Perry A. King
Summa 19 calculator for Olivetti, 1970
Callimaco floor lamp for Artemide, 1982
Sirio vase for Memphis, 1982
Camomilla fruit bowl, 1987

Albe STEINER

Graphic designer

From 1933, when he designed a brochure for the motorcycle manufacturer Atala, to his death in 1974, Albe Steiner gave important new directions to Italian graphic design. Steiner's work was always intertwined with his political commitment. He believed that "freedom is culture," and he fought for his convictions as a self-taught graphic designer and as an ardent communist who, along with his wife Lica, had joined the party in 1939 and worked in the anti-Fascist resistance movement. After the Second World War, Steiner served as the Italian Communist Party's secretary and helped shape its public image with his powerful poster and publication designs. He was also active as the director of the Scuola del Libro all'Umanitaria in Milan, the founder of the Italian artists' union, Sindacato Artisti, and a cofounder of the **ADI** and other designers' associations. As deep as his convictions ran, Steiner was flexible enough to work for large companies if they had a strong cultural identity or gave him the opportunity to create one for them. For the **La Rinascente**

mostra della

ricostruzior

i C.L.N. al lavoro

Carpi Castello dei Pio 14 ottobre 1973
Museo Monumento
al deportato politico e razziale
nei campi di sterminio nazisti

A cura del
Comitato di Liberazio
all'ex Arengario

department store, he designed posters (fig. p. 45), helped develop the corporate graphics program, and created the logo for the *Compasso d'oro* award, which La Rinascente instituted in 1954. With a clear graphic concept, he revolutionized the packaging design of the pharmaceutical company Pierrel; and in 1962 he created the retail identity for Italy's first supermarket, the Coop market in Reggio Emilia, convinced that this new type of store would raise the living standards of the masses. He also designed for **Pirelli, Olivetti,** Italy's broadcasting network, RAI, and several pharmaceutical manufacturers. Throughout his career, Steiner cooperated with magazines and book publishers in editorial and design projects. With his expressive, partly abstract and partly figurative book and poster art, he was a driving force in the formation of modern Italian graphic design.

1962 store design for first Italian supermarket

1968 poster for XIV. *Triennale*

1972 poster for thirty-sixth *Biennale di Venezia*

From left:

Poster for exhibition, *Museo Monumento al deportato politico e razziale nei campi di sterminio nazisti*, 1973

Poster for exhibition, *Mostra della Rico-struzione*, 1945

Detail from poster raising awareness for tumorous diseases, 1959

Poster for XIV. *Triennale*, 1968

Giotto STOPPINO

Architect, furniture, lighting, and industrial designer

1926 born in Vigevano

1951 graduates from architecture school in Milan

1968 opens studio

1979 *Compasso d'oro* (also 1991)

Products

1960 *Cavour* chair for S.I.M with **Vittorio Gregotti** and **Lodovico Meneghetti** (since 1988 prod. by **Poltrona Frau**)

1969 *Maia* table and chair series for **Bernini**

1971 magazine rack made of ABS plastic for **Kartell**

1977 *Sheraton* program

1984 *I Menhir* furniture system with **Lodovico Acerbis**; both for **Acerbis**

1989 *Alessia* door handle for **Olivari**

One of Giotto Stoppino's earliest successes was the art nouveau–inspired *Cavour* chair, with a bentwood frame. He had developed the piece with his partners, **Vittorio Gregotti** and **Lodovico Meneghetti,** in 1960, giving the **Neo-Liberty** movement one of its defining designs. A short time later, Stoppino began experimenting with virtually every material that was available. All of his designs, from furniture, lighting, and glasses to razors, bookends, and magazine racks have since shared one distinctive quality: the advanced technologies they are based on completely recede behind clear lines, smooth surfaces, and clever details to create an impression of perfect balance and harmony. This is evident in his small, three-legged stacking chairs made of ABS plastic, which he designed in the mid-1960s for **Kartell**; in the *Maia* tubular steel chair for Bernini, whose delicate look barely betrays its robust construction; and in the *Alessia* door handle for Olivari, which is solid where the hand grips it and hollow where it doesn't. His *Sheraton* sideboard for **Acerbis** is an exercise in symmetry, with a simple top that seems to hover contemplatively over a rectangular module.

Sheraton sideboard for Acerbis, 1977, with Lodovico Acerbis

SUPERSTUDIO

Architects and designers

Superstudio was one of the most important groups within the **Radical Design** movement, which set out to end the dogmatic functionalism and subservience to industrial needs that dominated design. Founded in 1966 in Florence by two young architects, **Adolfo Natalini** and Cristiano Toraldo di Francia (they were later joined by Piero Frassinelli and Roberto and Giancarlo Magris), Superstudio's utopian designs were proposals for new housing and living structures. In their 1968 project *Monumento continuo,* they overlaid cities and landscapes with an endless grid that was meant to replace existing structures and serve as a matrix for the construction of a new environment where everyone was assigned a neutral space free from objects and consumerist pressures. In 1971 they covered small tables with a black grid on white laminate. Again, the squares were essentially blanks to be filled in—the *Quaderno* (notebook) tables for **Zanotta,** like the 1977 *Desino* table for **Poltronova,** were reflections on an open-ended design.

1966 founded in Florence

1972 contribution to *Italy: The New Domestic Landscape,* MoMA, New York

1973 collaboration with **Global Tools** (until 1975)

1978 group dissolves

Products

1967 *Gherpe* table and floor lamp for **Poltronova**

1969 *Il monumento continuo* project

1971 *Quaderna* tables for **Zanotta**

1977 *Desino* table for Poltronova

Quaderna table
for Zanotta, 1971

TECNO

Furniture manufacturer

Tecno, the name **Osvaldo** and Fulgenzio **Borsani** decided on for the firm they had founded in 1953, is a reference to the Greek word "techne," which means art as well as technology. The word perfectly matched their ideas, which were translated by Osvaldo, who, for several decades, was the company's sole designer. His very first designs, the adjustable *P 40* chair and the *D 70* folding sofa, were true technical marvels. The brothers' father, Gaetano, had been a renowned furniture builder before the war and had taught them how to work with wood. From this base, they expanded their expertise into new materials including glass, plastics, and metal. In the 1950s and 1960s, Tecno developed sophisticated, comprehensive design solutions, such as the *Graphis* office furniture system of 1968. Now headed by Paolo and Valeria Borsani and specializing in furniture for offices and public buildings, the company has worked with such renowned international architects as Norman Foster and **Gae Aulenti.**

Tecno spa, Milan

1953 founded by **Osvaldo** and **Fulgenzio Borsani** in Milan

1984 *Compasso d'oro* (also 1987, 1988 and 1991)

1988 European Design Award

Products

1954 *P 40* chair; *D 70* sofa both by Osvaldo Borsani

1968 *Graphis* office furniture system by Osvaldo Borsani with Eugenio Gerli

1986 *Nomos* office furniture system by Norman Foster

1991 *Tlinkit* rattan chair by **Gae Aulenti**

P 40 chair and *D 70* sofa by Osvaldo Borsani, 1954

Matteo THUN

Architect, furniture, accessories, and product designer

"Less is more" is certainly not a principle that Matteo Thun would subscribe to, at least as far as his product design is concerned. Born in the alpine Alto Adige region of Italy, Thun is far more interested in the visually apparent than in the discreetly concealed: the grips of his *Hommage à Madonna* silverware set (1986) are decked out in rings, the stems of his *Tiffany Gin Gin* goblets are shaped like ornamental columns, and his **Memphis** coffeepots resemble cartoon animals. The antifunctionalist ideas Thun developed as a member of Memphis in the 1980s are aimed at establishing communication between user and object. His ceramic products for firms like Rosenthal, Villeroy & Boch, and Arzberg are a central part of his work. In addition to his housewares, lighting, and bathroom furnishings, Thun also designs much more functional office furniture and prefabricated houses, as well as retail identities for firms like Swatch, **Missoni,** and **Fiorucci,** and architectural exteriors for Coca-Cola, which play off the companies' overall identities.

1952 born in Bolzano

1975 graduates from architecture school in Florence

1981 member of Sottsass Associati (until 1984)

1984 opens studio in Milan

1990 art director for Swatch (until 1993)

Products

1982 *Corvus Corax* pitcher for **Memphis**

1987 *Le petit café* set for Arzberg; *Walking Coffee Pots* for WMF

1993 *Pao* table lamp for **Flos (Arteluce)**

1996 *O Sole Mio* cups for Rosenthal; *Sole Mio* prefab. house for Griffner Haus (compl. 1997)

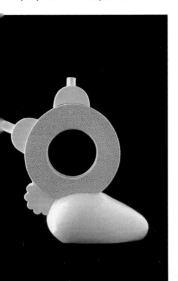

Chad ceramic for Memphis, 1982
Lola chair for Martin Stoll, 1993

Mario TRIMARCHI, Marco SUSANI
Architects and product designers

Mario Trimarchi and his partner, Marco Susani, belong to a new generation of Italian industrial designers who carry out a kind of poetic technology research. Instead of inventing new forms, they try to change everyday modes of behavior through their products. Their wardrobe-like piece of furniture, for example, with its wood fiber–cushioned panels and glass door, doesn't look at all like a fridge. It works like one, though: named *Keep-it-cool*, it needs no electricity, offers an attractive, stripped-down alternative to the customary metal behemoths, and keeps things chilled for up to two days, which is enough for most fresh products. "You don't need a Ferrari to go shopping, either," Marco Trimarchi says. He and Susani use technology to create new modes of interaction between appliances and their users. At the research center of the Domus Academy in Milan they directed the development of the *Movaid* robot, which helps people with disabilities perform household chores. Their *New Tools* for Philips, which include a juicer, an egg boiler, and a toaster, are equipped with storage batteries and a special recharging device to use electricity only as needed.

Keep-it-cool refrigerator, 1997

Office furniture manufacturer

In 1970, when the market for office furniture was defined by dull, unexciting uniformity, newcomer Unifor sounded a fresh note with its enormously successful *Modulo 3* program, designed by **Bob Noorda** and **Franco Mirenzi**. With its focus on technically sophisticated, high-quality products, the company has since followed up with other complex, formally reductive programs such as the *Master* and *Mats* office furniture by **Afra** and **Tobia Scarpa,** and Fernando Urquijo and Giorgio Macola's *Mood* system. Unifor's choice of designers reflects the company's commitment to functionality and elegance. Unifor has produced furniture by the architects Jean Nouvel, **Aldo Rossi,** and Renzo Piano and the technology-inspired industrial designer **Richard Sapper** as well as **Luca Meda,** a master of clear lines, and Angelo **Mangiarotti,** who is famous for his purist approach to materials. Unifor has furnished the offices of many large corporations, including IBM, Hewlett-Packard, Rank Xerox, Deutsche Bank, Hong Kong Telecom, and Volkswagen.

Unifor spa, Turate (CO)
1970 founded as division of **Molteni** group

Products
1989 *Mood* office furniture system by Fernando Urquijo and Giorgio Macola; *Parigi* chair by **Aldo Rossi**
1990 *Progetto 25* office furniture system by **Luca Meda**
1994 *Less* desk and cabinet by Jean Nouvel

Naos system by Pierluigi Cerri, 1993

VALENTINO

Fashion designer

The gown Jacqueline Kennedy wore at her wedding to Aristotle Onassis in 1968 was designed by Valentino. The master of Roman haute couture had been picked to design the bride's dress for the most glamorous wedding of the year, and he enthusiastically dedicated an entire new collection to her, the all-white *Collezione Bianca*.

Valentino had decided early on to devote his life to fashion, and after graduating from high school he studied fashion design in Milan and Paris. After working for Jean Dessès and Guy Laroche, he opened his own studio in 1959. His breakthrough occurred in 1962, when he made a splash with his elegant, luxuriously tailored designs at the Florence fashion shows at the Palazzo Pitti. Another crucial moment came when he was awarded the *Neiman Marcus* fashion prize in 1967, which confirmed his elevated rank among Italian designers, particularly within haute couture.

Valentino's trademark has been an elegant opulence that has made his haute couture presentations the climactic events of many *Alta Moda* shows in Milan. The basic components of Valentino's creative language are geometric cuts in black and white fabrics, animal prints, and especially a recurring shade of red that even many other designers now call "Valentino red." He is one of the most recognized living fashion designers; a 1994 exhibition of his work in New York attracted more than 70,000 visitors in two weeks. And for almost four decades he has dressed the rich and the beautiful, from Elizabeth Taylor and Audrey Hepburn to Sharon Stone.

1932 Valentino Garavani born in Voghera

1959 opens fashion studio in Rome (after working for Jean Dessès and Guy Laroche)

1967 *Neiman Marcus Prize*

1971 menswear boutique in Rome; Valentino Più boutique (fabrics, decoration)

1990 founds LIFE (assoc. against AIDS) with Giancarlo Giammetti

1996 appointed *Cavaliere del Lavoro*

Products

1962 first collection in Florence

1968 wedding dress for Jacqueline Kennedy; *Bianca* collection

1970 Prêt-à-porter collection

1984 clothes for Italian Olympic team

1994 costumes for *Dream of Valentino*, opera prod., New York

Page 335

left: Haute couture collection, 1994
right: Couture fall/winter 1993

Pages 335/337 from left:
Haute couture collection, 1985/1986, Couture 1967, Couture 1983

Gino VALLE

Architect and industrial designer

Gino Valle never reached celebrity status, but his products became part of the everyday lives of millions of people in the 1950s and 1960s. He designed timetable displays for train stations and airports and some of the first digital clocks, as well as household appliances. Although Valle saw himself primarily as an architect (he realized numerous important building and urban planning projects), he was also a committed industrial designer. His focus was never solely on the beautiful object—he repeatedly declared that he didn't intend to "fall in love with objects"—but always on the entire design process, from initial idea to mass production. His work with **Zanussi,** which continued from the 1950s to the 1970s, allowed him to fully develop his design concepts. While electric appliances had previously been unremittingly bland, he created a unified, simple, white design with clear controls, giving products like the *202* washer and the *170 TS* refrigerator a distinctive look and giving Zanussi a significant competitive advantage.

Valle's designs are always developed with the users' needs in mind. His appliances for Zanussi and his digital clocks for Solari have virtually redefined entire product categories. His *Cifra 3* desk clock of 1966, for example, became a bestseller that is still universally recognized. Valle, who studied art before switching to architecture, was among the pioneers who bridged the gap between design's formal goals and the requirements of an expanding manufacturing industry after the war. One of the first design consultants in the proper sense of the term, he applied his comprehensive vision not only to the design of new products but also to help define the corporate culture of his clients.

VENINI

Glass manufacturer

When **Paolo Venini** abandoned the practice of law in 1921 to open a glass-blowing workshop in Venice, he brought new style to an old craft. Compared to the overbearing pomp of conventional Murano glasswares, his vases, mosaics, and lamps looked like precious jewels in a sea of glittering baubles. With their restrained abstract forms and deliberate, bold use of color, his products made a strong impression at the 1923 *Biennale* in Monza—modernism had entered glass design. From those early days to his death in 1959, Venini, who also explored new manufacturing techniques, worked with designers who were known for their sensitive use of glass. In the 1920s and 1930s, his collaborators included Napoleone Marinuzzi, **Gio Ponti,** and **Carlo Scarpa,** who contributed to his *Tessuti* string glasses and artistic vases (fig. p. 27). After 1945 he also cooperated with Ken Scott, **Franco Albini,** and **Massimo Vignelli,** and later with **Alessandro Mendini, Tobia Scarpa,** and Tapio Wirkkala. Among Venini's most famous products are **Fulvio Bianconi's** 1952 *Pezzati* vases, made of a patchwork of small colored rectangles, and the *Vaso Fasoletto,* or "handkerchief vase," with its distinctive pinched corners.

1921 founded in Venice

1925 **Paolo Venini** becomes sole owner

1959 Paolo Venini dies; his son-in-law, Ludovico de Santillana, and widow succeed him at the head of the company

Products

1940 *Murrine opache* bowls by **Carlo Scarpa**

1946 *99.81.01.12* lamps by **Gio Ponti**

1952 *Pezzati Series* by **Fulvio Bianconi**

1955 *Fungo* table lamp by **Massimo Vignelli**

1956 bottle series by Gio Ponti

1995 *Geacolor* lamp by **Gae Aulenti**

Hand-blown *Flor Do Sul* vase by Marco Zanini, 1997

Vecchia Dama, Elisir and *Donna Campigliesca* bottles by Gio Ponti, 1956

Page 341
Decoro A Fili vase by Carlo Scarpa, 1942 (re-edition, 1993)

Gianni VERSACE

Fashion designer

News of Gianni Versace's violent death in 1997 cast a temporary pall over the entire fashion industry. It had lost a designer whose creative imagination had circled around the themes of power and eroticism in an entirely unprecedented way. Versace had fashioned himself into a modern Renaissance prince, with a medusa emblazoned on his coat of arms. The very lushness of his colors, forms and patterns, taken to near excess in his accessories and textiles for the home, reflected his preoccupation with, and extensive knowledge of, history and art.

In his hands, even the most unlikely combinations—leather and silk, lace and denim—turned into felicitous, exciting inventions. His book projects and numerous designs for opera and ballet productions by Maurice Béjart, Robert Wilson, and others testified to a creative freedom that knew few boundaries. His extravagant, exuberantly colorful clothes represented only one aspect of his work, which also extended to timeless evening gowns, often black and with elegantly austere lines.

Versace learned the basics of tailoring as a child in his mother's studio, and it wasn't long before he proved his skills in collections for Callaghan, **Genny,** and **Complice.** In 1978, he founded his own company, and by the early 1980s, Versace was a star in the international fashion scene. The most famous models and the best photographers were eager to add glamour to his collections. After Versace's death, his sister, Donatella, became the company's creative director, while his brother, Santo, has remained in charge of management.

1978 Gianni Versace establishes company for ladies' and menswear

1982 *Occhio d'Oro* (also 1984, 1990)

1983 *Cutty Sark Award* (also 1988)

1986 appointed *Commenda- tore della Repubblica Italiana*

1992 costumes for Elton John; *Versace: Signatures,* retrospective exhibition at Fashion Institute, New York

1997 Gianni Versace murdered in Miami

Products

1981 perfume, *Gianni Versace Donna*

1984 fragrance, *Versace l'Homme*

1989 introd. *Versus* line

1990 introd. *V 2 by Versace*

1991 perfume, *Versus*

1993 *Home Signature Collection*

Page 343
1991/1992 collection
table lamp from
Home Collection

Tureen from *Russian Dream* collection, 1998/1999

Massimo & Lella VIGNELLI

Industrial, furniture, and graphic designers

Red or black type on a white ground, often a combination of all three colors, set in large letters—whenever one encounters this distinctive look in logos (for Knoll International, Cinzano, or Milan's trade fair company, **Cosmit,** for example) or in promotional materials (such as the posters for Milan's Piccolo Teatro [fig. p. 22]), chances are that it was designed by Vignelli Associates. Massimo and Lella Vignelli's graphic work has always been characterized by a careful use of typography to establish a lucid structure and a reduced formal vocabulary to ensure clarity. As part of this overall concept they often use a classic book font, Bodoni. The Vignellis approach each design challenge with a strong historical consciousness—working for **Lancia,** for instance, they reinstituted the company's old logo instead of creating a new one.

Since the mid-1960s, the Vignellis have lived and worked in New York, putting their mark on many of its public spaces: they designed the way-finding system for the city's subway, and corporate identity programs for the International Design Center and Bloomingdale's, among others. Still, Europe, and especially Italy, has remained a focus of their activities. For **Poltronova** they designed the austere *Saratoga* furniture collection in the 1960s; in the 1980s they created the massive *Serenissimo* and *Creso* tables for **Acerbis**. For **Artemide** and **Poltrona Frau** they have designed exhibition booths and salesrooms as well as lighting and other products. Following **Ernesto N. Rogers'** dictum that the field of design should encompass everything "from spoons to cities," they have always approached design in terms of public service and social responsibility rather than mere embellishment.

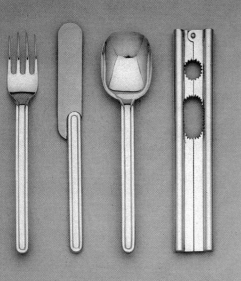

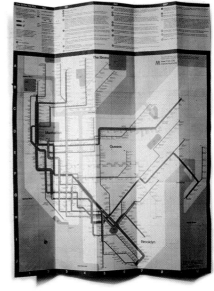

ZANI & ZANI

Housewares manufacturer

Zani & Zani's roots reach back to the nineteenth century, when Serafino Zani created exquisite silver tableware. Today, Zani & Zani is still a family business that caters to sophisticated tastes with elegantly functional table and kitchen products made of stainless steel and aluminum. Thanks to Franca and Luigi Zani's superior technical knowledge, the company is able to fabricate even the most difficult forms and is thus an ideal match for **Enzo Mari.** The designer is a master of fine small products; he created much of Zani & Zani's collection, including the *Smith e Smith* system of pots and other kitchen items, which are conveniently suspended from a rod. Mari's *Piuma* silverware, which hangs from a small stand, casually invites diners to help themselves. The company's products also include **Bruno Munari's** *TMT* ice bucket, made of aluminum and glass wool (fig. p 19), and a more recent line of tablecloths, aprons, and bathrobes in natural fabrics, as well as Claudio La Viola's soft vinyl vases.

Zani industria
dell'acciao spa,
Toscolano

1922 founded; crafts tradition
goes back to 19th century

1960 specializes in flatware and
other tableware

Products

1954 *TMT* ice bucket
by **Bruno Munari**

1976 *Roswita* silverware set by
Carla Nencioni, Armando
Moleri

1987 *Smith e Smith* kitchen
objects

1990 *Copernico* set of pots;

both by **Enzo Mari**

1993 *Vesuvio* espresso maker
by **Gaetano Pesce**

1995 *I Vasi Morbidi* (soft vinyl
vases) by Claudio La Viola

Opasis oil-and-vinegar set
by Enzo Mari, 1986

Page 347
Piuma silverware by Enzo Mari,
1992/1996

Chopping knife

Cheese grater; both from the *Smith
e Smith* series by Enzo Mari, 1987

ZANOTTA

Furniture manufacturer

Zanotta spa.,
Nova Milanese

1954 founded in Nova Milanese

Products

1968 *Blow* chair by **De Pas / D'Urbino / Lomazzi**; *Sacco* by **Gatti / Paolini / Teodoro**

1970 *Mezzadro* (design:1957)

1983 *Sella* (design: 1957); both by **Achille** and **Pier Giacomo Castiglioni**

1985 *Tonietta* chair

1994 *Novecento* glass cabinet both by **Enzo Mari**

1997 *Nadir* sofa by **Sigla**

Page 349

Albero flower stand by Achille Castiglioni, 1983

Lariana chair by Giuseppe Terragni, 1936, reprod. 1982

Giotto stool by De Pas/D'Urbino/Lomazzi, 1975/76

Servomuto table by Achille Castiglioni, 1974/1975

Pages 350/351: *Sciangai* clothes tree by De Pas/D'Urbino/Lomazzi, 1973/1974, and *Spiffero* screen by Bruno Munari, 1989

When Aurelio Zanotta, a ten-year veteran of furniture manufacturing, discovered Willie Landels's prototype of a frameless chair in London in 1965, it was the spark that ignited his passion for innovative design. Zanotta immediately decided to produce the unusual seat, giving it the name *Throw Away.* Since then, his firm has established itself as an open-minded platform for avant-garde design. **Emilio Ambasz,** who curated the 1972 New York exhibition Italy: *The New Domestic Landscape,* once remarked that "it would be impossible to write a history of Italian design without referring to the pieces produced by Zanotta." The list of the company's collaborators a Who's Who of contemporary furniture design, including the likes of **Achille** and **Pier Giacomo Castiglioni, Ettore Sottsass, Joe Colombo, Marco Zanuso, Enzo Mari, Alessandro Mendini,** and **Gae Aulenti.**

Never afraid to take risks, Zanotta produced, in the late 1960s, **Gatti/Paolini/Teodoro's** *Sacco* beanbag chair (fig. p. 40), which defied all notions of graceful home design and became an international bestseller. Equally unpredictable successes followed when Zanotta introduced the inflatable *Blow* chair and the bundle of oversize jackstraws that masqueraded as the *Sciangai* clothes tree (both by **De Pas/D'Urbino/Lomazzi**). Zanotta also produced two ready-mades Achille and Pier Giacomo Castiglioni had designed in the 1950s, the *Mezzadro* tractor seat and the *Sella* bicycle seat (fig. p. 15). Classic 1930s tubular steel furniture by **Giuseppe Terragni, Gino Levi Montalcini, Giuseppe Pagano,** and **Gabriele Mucchi** were later added to the collection, which has also come to include more traditionally styled upholstered furniture, tables, chairs, and accessories.

350

Marco ZANUSO

Architect, furniture and industrial designer

Asked once what his most important quality was, Marco Zanuso answered, "curiosity." Following his inquisitive spirit, the young architect gladly accepted an invitation from **Pirelli** to experiment with a new foam rubber. The result of his research was the *Lady* chair, with its now-famous kidney-shaped arms. Introduced in 1951, the chair was awarded a gold medal at the Milan **Triennale** and led to the formation of **Arflex,** a company for which Zanuso also designed other successful furniture, such as the 1954 *Sleep-o-matic* convertible sofa and the 1964 *Woodline* chair, made of bent plywood and leather.

In many respects, Zanuso is one of the founding fathers of Italian industrial design. In addition to his practical work, he became influential as a theorist and copublisher of *Domus* and *Casabella* magazines; along with the **BBPR** studio, **Alberto Rosselli, Marcello Nizzoli, Franco Albini,** and the **Castiglioni** brothers, he dominated the postwar discussion about the redefinition of modernism in design and architecture.

1916 born in Milan

1939 graduates from architecture school in Milan

1946 co-publisher of *Domus* (until 1947)

1952 co-publisher of *Casabella* (until 1954)

1955 **Olivetti** building in Buenos Aires (compl. 1957); Olivetti building in São Paulo

1956 cofounder of **ADI; *Compasso d'oro*** (also 1962, 1964, 1967, 1979, 1995)

1958 collaboration with **Richard Sapper** (until 1977)

1972 convention center in Grado (compl. 1974)

1974 IBM buildings in Italy (until 1982)

1978 waterworks in Reggio Emilia

Grillo telephone for Auso Siemens, 1966, with Richard Sapper

Zanuso's enthusiasm about new industrial technologies had been fostered early on by an uncle who had a passionate interest in obscure technical and astronomical instruments. At a time when large parts of Italy's industrial sector still consisted of traditional workshops, Zanuso demonstrated his special ability to translate new industrial possibilities into products with a distinctively modern look. Though trained as an architect, he was a "true" industrial designer for whom design had nothing to do with decoration but was all about "compact, precise, useful objects." With good-humored envy, **Alessandro Mendini** once described Zanuso's products as "so umimpeachably correct that it is downright irritating."

In the 1960s, Zanuso and his partner, **Richard Sapper,** created entirely new product types, such as the *Grillo* telephone, which integrated handset and dial in a single piece. For **Brionvega,** Zanuso and Sapper redefined the look of audio and video equipment with such revolutionary designs as the *TS 502* fold-up radio; the *Doney,* Italy's first transistor-equipped TV set; and the compact *Algol* (fig. p. 4), whose screen was tilted up to give it a somewhat pug-nosed profile. That piece was later followed by the *Black* TV set, a mysterious black cube that revealed its

Products

1951 *Lady* chair

1954 *Sleep-o-matic* sofa
both for **Arflex**

1956 *1100/2* sewing machine for Borletti

1958 *Lambda* chair for **Gavina**

1962 *Doney* TV set

1963 design for car's frontal part for **Alfa Romeo**

1964 *Algol* TV set;
both TV sets for **Brionvega**;
Woodline chair for Arflex;
K 4999 plastic children's chair for **Kartell**

1965 *TS 502* radio for Brionvega

1966 *Grillo* telephone for Auso Siemens;
last three with **Richard Sapper**

Algol TV set for Brionvega, 1964, with Richard Sapper

function only when the screen lit up. With this product, the designer was successful in two significant respects: he liberated an entire product category from its ponderous formal boundaries by rigorously reducing the equipment's size and emphasizing its communicative function, and he created an unmistakable corporate identity for Brionvega.

Zanuso also designed one of the first plastic chairs, the *K 4999* children's chair for **Kartell**; sewing machines for **Borletti Veglia**; coffee grinders; tiles; airplane seats; and car bodies. All his products were developed with an eye on the market but also with a strong sense that it is necessary to take risks in order to succeed. In recent years, Zanuso has concentrated primarily on architecture, saying that "design is something for young people." Among Zanuso's best-known architectural projects are the large factory buildings in Italy and South America he designed for **Olivetti** in the 1950s. He also designed production plants for IBM as well as museums and convention centers.

Fourline chair for Arflex, 1964

Manufacturer of home appliances

Today, Zanussi markets a "designer series" of products, such as the mint-green, paunchy and flat-footed *Oz* refrigerator, by the company's chief designer, Roberto Pezzetta, and the *Zoe* washing machine, whose rounded lines and minimalist control panel exude an equally friendly and comfortable aura. But while such self-conscious marketing may reflect current trends, the company, founded in 1914 by Antonio Zanussi as a repair shop for kitchen appliances, has pursued a clear design policy since the 1950s.

It began in 1954, when Lino Zanussi commissioned **Gino Valle** to design washing machines, refrigerators, and stoves that would stand out from the bland uniformity of conventional white "elettrodomestici." Valle restructured the company's product lines and developed a unified, clean look that emphasized controls. The results were so successful that in 1962 Zanussi for the first time outsold its German competitors, who had previously dominated the market. Valle's partner at Zanussi was Gastone Zanello, who headed the company's

Zanussi spa., Pordenone

1916 founded by Antonio Zanussi as a repair shop for home appliances in Pordenone, Zanussi soon starts producing his own "elettrodomestici"

1954 **Gino Valle** is hired as design consultant

1958 design dept. headed by **Gastone Zanello** (until 1981)

1960 production of TV sets

1976 Andries van Onck hired as design consultant (until 1989)

1981 *Compasso d'oro*

1982 **Roberto Pezzetta** succeeds Gastone Zanello

1984 merger with Electrolux

Stove from *700* program by Gastone Zanello, 1960

Black refrigerator from *Wizard* collection by Roberto Pezzetta, 1986

design department, which had been established in 1958, and developed the first modular built-in systems for kitchens. In the mid-1970s, Zanussi hired another external consultant, the Dutchman Andries van Onck, a graduate of the Ulm School of Design. Van Onck created distinctive design concepts for the company's growing number of products, which were now organized in *"family lines."* In the 1980s, a failed expansion into the stereo market caused a severe crisis, which ultimately led Zanussi to refocus on its core business and put a renewed emphasis on design. The results were mixed: Roberto Pezzeta's 1986 *Wizard* refrigerator, which looked like a miniature campanile with a pretentious little flag on top, was a commercial flop but won numerous design awards.

Oz refrigerator, 1995
Zoe washing machine, 1996

Design group and furniture manufacturer (Zeus Noto)

In 1984, Zeus, a group of young designers, introduced their first collection of furniture, which used a severely reduced vocabulary of archetypal and geometric forms. Roughly welded from black square-edged steel and laconically named *Sedia* (side chair), *Poltrona* (easy chair), *Sgabello* (stool), and *Savonarola*, **Maurizio Peregalli's** pieces used deliberate artlessness to communicate the group's opposition to **Memphis's** postmodern fireworks of form and color. "If the Memphis object is an affirmation of the transitory, the luxurious, the superficial, a costly and amoral object," wrote **Paolo Deganello,** "the Zeus object is a modest, moral object with transcendental tendencies. As such it reaffirms an absolute quality, which the industrial product has always had."

But even Peregalli, Zeus's art director, and his partners **Davide Mercatali** and Roberto Marcatti, have taken advantage of an expanded repertoire of forms and materials pioneered by Memphis,

Noto-Zeus srl, Milano

1984 founded by Sergio Calatroni, Roberto Marcatti, Ruben Mochi and **Maurizio Peregalli**

1988 Noto becomes production company of *Zeus Collection*

1989 *Sottosuolo* magazine launched

From left: *Golia* barstool by Maurizio Peregalli, 1993

Hotel Zeus TV stand by Ron Arad, 1992

MDF stool by M. Peregalli, 1993

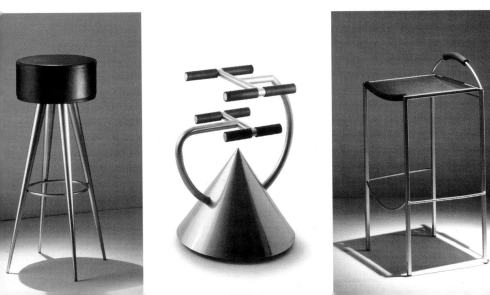

Products

1984 *Millepunte* furniture series
1986 *Musa* floor lamp,
     both by Maurizio Peregalli
1994 *Orb* stool series by
     Jasper Morrison;
     Crab stool series by
     Maurizio Peregalli;
     Anonimus stools and side
     tables by Ron Arad;
     Little Sister chairs
     by Andreas Brandolini
1995 *Anais Porta-*
     Abiti clothes rack by
     Robert Wettstein;
     Alice furniture series by
     Claudi Nardi;
     Artú table by Andreas
     Brandolini

including linoleum and Pirelli rubber flooring. Originally, the Zeus group also designed clothes, small objects, and graphics and showed their work in a small Milan gallery as part of an overall concept that stressed communication. They still publish their own newsletter, and Zeus's parties at the Milan furniture fair are annual get-togethers of the entire alternative design scene.

Since the mid-1980s, their furniture and lighting collections have been produced by Noto, while Zeus has become a forum for a small, select circle of young international designers, including Ron Arad, Jasper Morrison, Robert Wettstein, and Andreas Brandolini. The black and gray of the early years has given way to a broader color spectrum, and there is a greater formal variety in their designs. Nonetheless, Zeus continues to be a symbol of the post-Memphis generation's return to basics.

Chair and stool from *Millepunte* series by Maurizio Peregalli, 1984

Page 359
left: Donna collection, 1989/90 (*Teodora*)
right: Uomo collection, 1998/99 both by Romeo Gigli

Guide

Sites, Museums, Showrooms

Sights and Culture in the Milan Area

Although Milan is Italy's design capital, there is no museum devoted to collecting and showing design. There are, however, a number of smaller collections where visitors can get information on specific aspects of product history (in some cases, by appointment only), as well as several interesting institutions and galleries.

TRIENNALE

Palazzo dell'Arte, Via Alemagna 6, Milan. The Triennale is an institution that has made design history. Since 1933 it has regularly presented major product shows. Today it features exhibitions on architecture, design, urban planning and arts and crafts as well as large international expositions. The building was designed by Giovanni Muzio and completed in 1933. The new interiors were designed by architects including Umberto Riva, Cini Boeri and Gae Aulenti.

COLLEZIONE "GLI ANNI DI PLASTICA"

Montedison s.p.a., Foro Bonaparte 31, Milan. A private collection of historic plastic products, established by Montedison, one of Italy's largest chemical manufacturers (by appointment only).

COLLEZIONE LORENZI

Via Montepoleone 9, Milan. The collection includes 1,400 scissors, razors and knives from the 17th century to the present.

COLLEZIONE SAMBONET

Fondazione Sambonet, Foro Bonaparte 44/a, Milan. More than 4,000 pieces of silverware, including antique artifacts as well as contemporary products by Sambonet.

DESIGN GALLERY MILANO

Via Manzoni 46, Milan. Located in an old palazzo, the gallery features regular sales exhibitions of works by renowned designers.

ASSSOCIATION JACQUELINE VODOZ ET BRUNO DANESE Via S. Maria Fulcorina 17, Milan. Changing exhibitions on art and design in a beautiful old palazzo.

CIVICO MUSEO D'ARTE CONTEMPORANEO

Palazzo Reale, Piazza del Duomo, Milan. Opened in 1984, the museum has a collection of primarily Italian art from the 19th century to the present. Its main focus is on works by Futurists, such as Umberto Boccioni, and abstract art, but it also includes works by Giorgio Morandini and a selection of international artists.

PINOTECA DI BRERA

Via Brera 28, Milan. Milan's largest collection of paintings is housed in the 17th century Palazzo di Brera. In addition to major baroque paintings there are works by important modern Italian artists, incl. Boccioni or Carrà. The neighboring Accademia di Brera art academy counts among its alumni such designers as Enzo Mari, Joe Colombo and Piero Fornasetti.

MUSEO SIRM

Via Tirano 18, Palazzolo Milanese. This small museum of industry near Milan shows the world's largest collection of gas pumps and related objects. A metal-and-oil monument to industrial modernism, it is also an homage to Enrico Mattei, the legendary head of Agip who annoyed the Anglo-American oil giants in the 50s, turned Agip into a model company (with a corporate identity by Marcello Nizzoli) and died in a plane crash.

MUSEO STORICO ALFA ROMEO

Centro direzionale 1, Arese. Opened in 1976, the museum illuminates Alfa Romeo's company history, showing some seventy-five historical and contemporary automobiles.

COLLEZIONE CASSINA

Via Busnelli 1, Meda. Collection of over one hundred Cassina prototypes (not open to public).

COLLEZIONE CANDY

Via Eden Fumagalli, Brugherio. Documents the history of Candy's products and the development of electronic household appliances.

MUSEO DELLE PORCELLANE DI DOCCIA

Richard-Ginori s.p.a., Via Pratese 31, Sesto Fiorentino. Presents, on 13,000 square feet, the most important products of the venerable company Gio Ponti worked for in the 1920s.

COLLEZIONE STORICA KARTELL

Viale dell'Industria 1, Noviglio. Giulio Castelli founded this museum, which documents Kartell's product history (by appointment only).

MALPENSA 2000 AIRPORT
From Milan in the dir. of Varese/Switzerland. The airport is quite a drive from Milan, but the trip is rewarded by its impressively pleasant ambiance. The public areas were in large part designed by Ettore Sottsass.

METRO, LINE 1
Milan, inner city. The subway stations along the Nr. 1 line were designed by the architects Franco Albini and Franca Helg in the early 1960s. The wayfinding system is by Bob Noorda.

PIRELLI TOWER
Pirelli industrial park on Milan's northern periphery. Architect Gio Ponti saw this tower, which was built in 1954-1956, as his "tribute to work." Its spectacular shape, reminiscent of an upright knife, makes it one of the most significant landmarks of Italian modernist postwar architecture. Paolo Cevini described the building as an "extraordinary expression of capitalist industrial culture at its peak."

Showrooms in Milan/Furniture

Shopping at the source: Milan is the city with perhaps the highest density of design studios, furniture and lighting companies, fairs and showrooms in Europe. They are all located within a relatively small area that can easily be explored by foot. Here is a selection of the most interesting:

ARTEMIDE; Corso Monforte

B&B ITALIA; Corso Europa 2

BALERI ITALIA; Via Cavallotti 8

CAPPELLINI; Via Statuto

CASSINA; Via Durini 18

DA DRIADE; Via Manzoni 30

DE PADOVA; Corso Venezia 14

FLOS; Corso Monforte 9

KARTELL; Via Turati/Via Carlo Porta 1

MOROSO; Via Pontaccio 8/10

SAWAYA & MORONI; Via Manzoni 11

ZANOTTA; Via Durini 3

ZEUS; Corso S. Gottardo 21/9

Showrooms in Milan/Fashion

Milan is an international fashion capital. Virtually all major Italian fashion designers are based here and present their collections in elegant showrooms. Prada, Dolce&Gabbana Romeo Gigli, Gucci, Escada, Armani, Ferré and many others are all tightly clustered around the Piazza San Babila, on Via Montenapoleone and Via della Spiga.

MISSONI; Via T. Slavini 1

KRIZIA; Via Manin 19

DOLCE & GABBANA; Piazza Umanitaria 2

Stores in Milan

GALLERIA VITTORIO EMANUELE II
Main entrances on Piazza del Duomo and Piazza della Scala. Designed by Giuseppe Mengoni in the 19th century, this world-famous shopping gallery is called "il salotto di Milano," "Milan's salon," by the locals. Elegant boutiques (including the original Prada store), restaurants and cafés attract a fair share of the city's rich and beautiful. The steel-and-glass roof, topped by an enormous dome, was the first construction of its kind in Italy. Another impressive feature is the design of its floors with its mosaics and zodiac motifs.

CARLA SOZZANI
Corso Como 10. Owned by the sister of *Vogue* Italy's editor-in-chief, the store offers an ultrahip mix of ethno-pop, fashion and books. The upper-floor gallery shows changing exhibitions of art and design.

FORNASETTI IMMAGINAZIONE
Via Manzoni 45. This store exhibits and sells Piero Fornasetti's numerous designs – sun, animal, or architectural motifs on plates furniture and foulards.

LA RINASCENTE
Piazza Duomo. The flagship of the elegant department store chain with its impressive facade is right across from the Milan cathedral.

MH WAY
Via Durini 2, Bags, knapsacks and art supplies in a mix of

Italian and Japanese styles—Makio Hasuike has made quite a splash with his company and products over the last few years.

Sights and Culture in the Turin Area

FIAT FACTORY
Turin-Lingotto; The legendary Fiat factory from the 1920s hasn't been operating for many years but is definitely worth a visit for the spiral ramp that leads around the building and up to the rooftop test track. Today this landmark of industrial architecture serves as a cultural and convention center.

MUSEO DELL'AUTOMOBILE CARLO BISCARETTI DI RUFFA
Corso Unità d'Italia 40, Turin; One of the world's largest automobile museums; besides numerous models from all phases of automotive history, it features an extensive library.

MUSEO PININFARINA
Via Nazionale 30, Cambiano; Presentation of many of the bodymakers famous models for Alfa Romeo, Cisitalia, Ferrari and Lancia (by appointment only).

ASSOCIAZIONE ARCHIVIO STORICO OLIVETTI
Via delle Miniere, Ivrea; The Olivetti Archive was opened in 1998 in Ivrea, the company's traditional base near Turin. The firm's history is exhaustively documented in a large exhibit of products and graphics, a photographic archive, and an extensive library that includes books as well as video and audio material (by appointment only).

SALA DA BALLO
Via Stradelle, 10, Turin; Old public dance hall in Turin, still with its original interior designed by the famous architect Carlo Mollino.

Other Destinations in Italy

MUSEO ALESSI
Crusinallo (Como); Alessi's vast archive of prototypes, early products, drawings and documents, collected since the firm's establishment in 1921, has recently moved into this new building designed by Alessandro Mendini. The museum, with some 6,000 square feet of exhibition space, is located in Crusinallo, near idyllic Lago Maggiore. The collection will initially be open only to researchers and journalists. In neighboring Omegna another Alessi museum, also designed by Mendini, will soon be open to the general public.

COLLEZIONE LAGOSTINA
Via IV Novembre 45, Omegna; Housewares manufacturer's historical collection.

MUSEO MOTO GUZZI
Via Parodi 57, Mandello del Lario; Collection on the history of the motorcycle manufacturer.

COLLEZIONE GUZZINI
Località San Leopardo, Recanati; Collection of products by Fratelli Guzzini (not public).

Page 363

Cassina showroom in Milan

Gas pump, Italy, 1935. Museo Sirm

Galleria Ferrari, Maranello. Gateway by Massimo Losa Ghini

COLLEZIONE AEREI PIAGGIO
Piaggio, Via R. Piaggio, Finale Ligure. Aircraft museum documenting Piaggio's.aeronautical history since 1919 (by appointment only).

GALLERIA FERRARI
Via Dino Ferrari 1, Maranello; Automobile museum illustrates the exclusive carmaker's history with different Ferrari models, historical documents, trophies and curiosities. Some of the exhibits were designed by Massimo Iosa Ghini.

MUSEO DEGLI ARGENTI CONTEMPORANEI
Piazza L. da Breme 4, Sartirana; The museum, which opened in 1992, shows works of Italian silversmiths' from the 1970s to the present.

MUSEO DELL'ARREDO CONTEMPORANEO
S.S. San Vitale 253, Russi. Shows outstanding examples of contemporary Italian furniture and lighting production.

MUSEO DELLA CERAMICA
Palazzo Perabò, Laveno Mombello Cerro;. Opened in 1970, the museum documents Italian ceramics production from the middle of the 19th century to the postwar era.

PALAZZO GRASSI
Canale Grande, Venice; Fiat bought this Venetian palazzo and turned it into a gallery for outstanding art exhibitions. The interiors were designed in the 1980s by Gae Aulenti.

LA BIENNALE DI VENEZIA
Giardini, Venice; Renowned biennial art and architecture exhibition.

MUSEO SALVATORE FERRAGAMO
Via Tornabuoni 2, Florence; A magnificent building showcasing the ingenious creations of shoe designer Salvatore Ferragamo. The collection includes more than 10,000 historical shoes from the 1920s to the present.

Page 365
Oihos I System
by Antonia Astori
for Driade, 1973

Index

Designers, Companies, Terms

366 Boldface numbers refer to individual entries

ABET LAMINATI 88, 256, 259, 325

ABITARE Architecture and design mag.; founded 1962. Editorial focus on professional practice. Aimed at architects and designers as well as a wider readership interested in the subject. 238

ACERBIS Furniture manufacturer; founded 1870. Family-owned; modern furniture design since 1968. Acerbis collection (living room furniture); lower-priced *Morphos* collection for younger customers (since 1983), *Bed Side* collection (bedrooms). Designers: Giotto Stoppino, Lodovico and Marco Acerbis, Mario Bellini, Michele De Lucchi and Andrea Branzi. 328, 344

ADI (Associazione per il Disegno Industriale) Italian design association; founded 1956. Over 600 members, including industrial, furniture and graphic designers, design-oriented companies, journalists, writers and critics.). Mission is to promote industrial and graphic design by fostering contacts between designers and industry and cooperating with cultural institutions (exhibitions, conferences, seminars). Organizes the *Compasso d'oro* awards and exhibition. 64, 326

AGAPE Manufacturer of faucets and bathroom accessories; founded 1973; Mantua. Works with such designers as Giampaolo Benedini but also with a younger group incl. Fabio Bortolani, Marco Ferreri and Carlo Tinti. 143

AGIP (Azienda Generale Italiana dei Petroli) Govermt.-owned oil and energy company; founded 1926. Visual image defined by Marcello Nizzoli (electromechanical gas pump, 1950–52. 1952, company logo by Giuseppe Guzzi. In the 1970s, Unimark redesigned the corporate identity.

AGNOLI, Tito b. 1931, Peru. Painter, architect and product designer. Lamps for O Luce; beds for Rondo; chairs *(THF, Europa 80), 9000* modul. seating system for Arflex; seats and tables *(Boulevard, IDC)* for Poltrona Frau. Defined collection of furniture manuf. Pierantonio Bonacina. 136

ALBINI, Franco 89, 57, 60, 64, 104, 109, 156, 158, 210, 276, 291, 303, 340, 352

ALCHIMI 79, 88, **92,** 94, 102,144,176, 216, 254, 258, 299, 300, 324

ALESSI 78, **94,** 96, 144, 149, 165, 212, 259, 266, 314, 325

ALFA ROMEO 52, 54, 65, **98,** 130, 158, 195, 232,251, 286, 310

ALIAS 78, **101,** 110, 118, 174, 251, 306

AMBASZ, Emilio b. 1943, Argentina. Architect, furniture and lighting designer; 1970–77, curator at Mus. of Modern Art, NY *(Italy: The New Domestic Landscape,* exhib., 1972); 1977, indep. designer; 1981, studio in New York. Worked for Tecta, Castelli, Artemide and Erco. 1981, 1991 *Compasso d'oro.* 71

ANTI-DESIGN Design movement formed in the mid-1960's .in opposition to the doctrines of "good taste" and functionalism. Products incl. *Sacco* beanbag and *Joe* catcher's-mitt chairs by De Pas/D'Urbino/Lomazzi; *Blow* chair by Gatti/Paolini/Teodoro. Anti-Design and Radical Design are nearly conterminous, except for the added political agenda of Radical Design and its protagonists (incl. Archizoom, Superstudio). 102, 176, 179, 181, 298, 324

ARC LINEA Kitchen manufacturer; founded 1925 by Silvio Fortuna as a workshop. Company name "Arc Linea" since 1960. Italian market leader. First big success in 1963 with *Claudia* kitchen (first Italian kitchen with built-in electric appliances). Recent designs by Antonio Citterio. 129

ARCHITETTURA RADICALE 72, 298

ARCHIZOOM; 102, 144, 181, 266, 292, 298

ARFLEX; 62, 90, **104,** 122, 132, 160, 171, 290, 352

ARMANI, Giorgio 80, **106,** 231

AROLDI, Danilo and **Corrado** b. 1925 and 1936. Furniture and lighting designers. Joint studio in Milan. The Aroldi brothers are best known for their kitchens and lighting for Campi e Caligari, Luci, Pabis, Zetamobili, Tonon, and Delta.

ARTELUCE 63, **108,** 133, 183, 184, 228

ARTEMIDE 78, 101, **110,** 124, 133, 176, 183, 206, 240, 246, 250, 256, 305, 314, 325, 344

ASTI, Sergio 112, 224

ASTORI, Antonia113, 184

ATLANTIDE; 183, 184

AULENTI, Gae 66, **114,** 202, 224, 278, 292, 330, 348

AURORA Manufacturer of fountain pens; founded 1919. First Italian fountain pen. Combination of technical perfection and innovative design.

AZUCENA; Furniture and lighting manufact.; founded 1947 by Luigi Caccia Dominioni, Ignazio Gardella and Corrado Corradi Dell'Acqua. First furniture company focusing on modern design after World War II. Close cooperation with traditional workshops. Designs by Caccia Dominioni (*Imbuto* table lamp, 1953; *Catilina* chair, 1958; *Melanzana* door handle, 1960), Gardella/Corradi Dell'Acqua (*Coppa Vetro Chiusa* wall and floor lamp, 1954). 122, 149

B&B ITALIA 82, **116**, 124, 168, 318

BALDESSARI, Luciano 1896–1982. Architect, painter, graphic and set designer. Influenced by Futurism and Rationalism. 1929, *Luminator* lamp in rationalist. style. Famous for his dynamic exhibition designs of the 1950s. Worked with Le Corbusier, Walter Gropius, Alvar Aalto, Oskar Niemeyer. 303

BALERI, Enrico b. 1942. Furniture and lighting designer, entrepreneur. Founded companies Pluri (1968), Alias (1979), Baleri Italia (1984) and Gloria (c 1990); produced designs by Philippe Starck, Alessandro Mendini and Hans Hollein. Created design for Gavina, Flos, Knoll. 118

BALERI ITALIA 79, **118**

BALLA, Giacomo 1871–1958. Futurist. painter and product designer; 1915, interior design for Löwenstein house in Düsseldorf. In the 1920s ceramics and lamps. 53, 208

BANAL DESIGN refers to non-designed everyday objects. The term was coined in the 1970s by Alessandro Mendini who believed that banal forms could give impulses to design. 258, 300, 324

BARILLA 120

BARTOLI, Carlo b. 1931. Architect and furniture designer in Milan and Monza. 1959–81, architectural office. Designs for Arflex (*Gaia* chair, 1966), Arc Linea, Confalonieri, UCG, Con & Con, Kartell, Oscam, Rossi di Albizzate, Tisettanta.

BBPR 122, 276, 352, 303

BEL DESIGN Italy's "beautiful design," characterized by extraordinary formal and technological innovation. Bel Design's prime lasted from the beginning of the economic miracle in late 1950s when the industrial sector strove to differentiate its products through high functionality and formal beauty, until the 1970s, when these values were questioned by young design rebels (Radical Design, Global Tools, Alchimia). Numerous classics illustrate the Bel Design concept: Marco Zanuso's and Richard Sapper's TV- and radio sets for Brionvega and *Grillo* telephone for Siemens; Mario Bellini's typewriters and calculators for Olivetti and

chairs for Cassina; Vico Magistretti's *Selene* chair for Artemide and *Atollo* table lamp for O Luce are only a few distinguished examples. 66, 92, 102, 112, 114, 164, 298

BELLINI, Mario 116, **123**, 145, 156, 231, 280

BELOTTI, Giandomenico b. 1922. Architect, furniture designer and sculptor. One-family homes, industr. and public buildings. Has worked for Alias since 1979 (*Spaghetti* chair, *Hommage à Man Ray* chair, *Four Balls* table).

BENETTON 126, 318

BERCHICCI, Guglielmo b. 1957. Architect, product, furniture and lighting designer. Studio in Milan since 1986. Has worked for Kundalini (*Loto* lamp, 1997).

BERNINI 127, 206, 284, 320, 328

BERTI, Enzo 129

BERTONE; 65, 100, **130**, 196, 213, 232

BETTONICA, Franco Product and lighting designer; cofounder of Cini & Nils.

BIAGIOTTI, Laura b. 1943. Fashion designer. In 1962 started working in her mother's fashion studio in Rome (collections for Schuberth and Capucci). Since 1972 she has produced her own collections.

BIALETTI now Bialetti Industrie spa. Manufacturer of espresso makers. 1933 Alfonso Bialetti designed and produced the famous octagonal *Moka Express* stovetop-espresso maker,. 250 million of which have since been sold.

BIANCHI Bicycle manufacturer; founded 1885. In 1901 began producing automobiles and motorcycles. Stopped prod. of cars during World War II, of motorcycles in 1964. Has since concentrated exclusively on bicycles. Division of Piaggio since 1976.

BIANCONI, Fulvio b. 1915. Graphic designer and illustrator. Designed books, dust jackets, record covers, theater programs and advertisements for Fiat and Pirelli. Famous for his glasses (for Venini), drawings and lithographs.

BIEFFEPLAST Lighting and furniture manufacturer; founded around 1980 by Anna Anselmi; division of Bieffe. Works with metals and plastics; research focus on. CAD/CAM automation of furniture production. Designers: Michele de Lucchi, Rodney Kinsman and Matteo Thun. 78

BINAZZI, Lapo b. 1943. Product designer and author; representative of Radical Design. Cofounded Gruppo UFO. Opened studio for objects and architecture in Florence in 1975. Writes for *Domus* and *Modo;* produced videos and films; designed ceramics for Eschenbach and silverware for Pampaloni.

BINFARÉ, Francesco b. 1939. Architect and furniture designer. Headedf B&B Italia's research center (establ. 1968) for many years. Now designs for Edra Mazzei (*L'homme et la femme* sofa). 116, 186

BOERI, Cini 104, **132**, 194

BOFFI Manufacturer of kitchen and bathroom furniture; founded 1947. In the 1950s, modular kitchen systems. Produced pioneering solutions such as Joe Colombo's 1966 *Carrellona* compact kitchen or Antonio Citterio and Paolo Nava's 1980 *Factory* kitchen. Designers also include Marc Sadler (*Totem, Alu Kit)* Luigi Massoni, Piero Lissoni. 171, 234

BOGGERI 134

BOLIDISMO Design and architectural movement formed in 1986 by 15 young architects, incl. Massimo Iosa Ghini, in Bologna. The "Bolidistas" were interested in a flexible and "fast" lifestyle. They took their formal cues from Futurism, American streamline-style and 1950s aesthetics to create a boldly dynamic look (Iosa Ghini's *Dinamics Collection* for Moroso, 1986, and Bolido dance club in New York, 1986). Largely lost its relevance in the stylistically purist 1990s. 208, 221

BONACINA 90, **136**

BONETTO, Rodolfo 128, **138**, 184

BONFANTI, Renata 140

BORLETTI VEGLIA Manufacturer of clocks and measuring instruments; founded 1896. Temporarily manufacturer of sewing machines; worked with Marco Zanuso (*Superautomatica 1100/2* sewing machine, 1956), Rodolfo Bonetto (*Sfericlock* with graphics by *Max* Huber, dashboard displays for Fiat (*131, Ritmo, Cromo*) and Giorgetto Giugiaro. Owned by Citizen. 138, 354

BORSANI, Osvaldo 142, 330

BORTOLANI, Fabio 143

BOTTONI, Piero 1903–1973. Architect and furniture designer, cofounder of Movimento Italiano per l'Architettura Razionale (MIAR). *Lira* tubular steel chair, 1934 (prod. by Zanotta, 1986). *Curator of Triennale* 1946. 55, 61, 303

BRANZI, Andrea 77, 92, 102, **144**, 256, 298, 302

BREDA FERROVIE Large Italian railroad company; founded 1886. Important force in Italian industrialization in 19th century. In the 1930s, first electric, streamlined train, *Etr 200 Breda* by Giuseppe Pagano; in 1949, famous *Etr 300 Settebello* train.

BRIONVEGA 123, **145**, 165, 244, 314, 353

bTICINO Manufacturer of light switches.; founded c. 1950 as Bassani Ticino. Since the 1960s very design-oriented in product and communications strategy (*Magic* and *Living* series).

BUGATTI Automobile manufact.; founded by *legendary* car builder Ettore Bugatti (son of cabinetmaker Carlo Bugatti). Firm became famous for its racing models (*Typ 35*, 1924) and elegant touring cars. Gradual decline of the company after Ettore's death in 1947. Sold to Hispano-Suiza in 1963.

BUGATTI, Carlo 56, **148**

BUSNELLI 218

BYBLOS Fashion line by Genny.

C&B ITALIA 116, 283, 299, 318

CACCIA DOMINIONI Luigi **149**, 162

CAMPAGNOLO Bicycle manufacturer; founded 1933 by Tullio Campagnolo. The in-house design dept. received a *Compasso d'oro* for bicycle accessories in 1995.

CAMPARI Beverage company, Milan. Since the 1920s innovative advertising campaigns by renowned graphic designers and artists, incl. Futurist painter Fortunato Depero, Marcello Nizzoli, Bruno Munari. 209, 268, 273

CAMPI, Antonia b. 1921. Product and furniture designer. Designs for Richard-Ginori and Ermenegildo Collini. 1959, *Compasso d'oro* (for scissors).

CANDY Manufacturer of household appliances, incl. refrigerators and washers; founded 1945. Worked with Marco Zanuso (who introduced new conceptual priorities such as energy efficiency, durability, and sensitive pricing),

Rodolfo Bonetto (1972–1975), Mario Bellini (*Primato 440, Primato 971* washing machines, 1978), Giorgetto Giugiaro (aggressive graphics for *Domino* series, 1983).

CAPPELLINI 82, **150**, 183, 234

CAPPIELLO, Leonetto 1875–1942. Graphic designer. Numerous posters around 1900.

CAPRONI Aircraft manufacturer; founded 1910. During the World Wars production of war planes; in 1940, first Italian jet airplane.

CAPUCCI, Roberto b. 1930. Fashion designer. Opened studio in Rome in 1950; moved to Paris in 1962; returned to Italy in 1968.

CARBONI, Erberto b. 1899. Graphic and furniture designer. Designs for Montecatini, Agip, Campari, Motta, RAI, Barilla, Olivetti and Arflex (*Delfino* Sessel, 1954). Known for making abstract concepts vivid in his exhibition designs (Chemistry Exposition, 1952 in Milan). Coined the term "atomico" for the isolation of parts in a dynamic design concept. Numerous advertising awards. 104, 120, 134, 276

CARMINATI TOSELLI & C. Streetcar manufacturer, founded 1899. 1927, famous 1500 series aka *tipo 1928* by Giovanni Cuccoli; many of the streetcars built in 1928–31 are still in operation today.

CASABELLA Magazine; important forum of contemporary discussions in architecture and design, especially from the 1950s through the 1970s. Essays on a high theoretical level (former editors include Pierluigi Cerri, Anna Castelli Ferrieri, Marco Zanuso, Vittorio Gregotti, Aldo Rossi, Alessandro Mendini).

CASATI, Cesare Furniture and product designer. Student of Gio Ponti. Studio D.A. with Emanuele Ponzio; furniture for hotels, banks, convention centers. Designs for Phoebus, Nai Ponteur and Autovox.

CASSIA, Antonio Macchi b. 1937. Industrial designer. Worked for Studio Bonfanti-Macchi Cassia-Porta from 1968–70; from 1968–71, consultant for Olivetti and Steiner International. Designs for Olivetti (*Divisumma 18* and *28* calculators, *Copia 2000* copier, *M 20* personal computer), Arteluce, Stilnovo, Totalglas, Condor and Radiomarelli.

CASSINA 57, 63, 78, 124, 144, **154**, 181, 206, 234, 240, 283, 293, 299, 306, 318

CASTELLI Furniture manufacturer; founded 1877 by Cesare Castelli in Bologna. One of Europe's leading furniture companies; produces designs by Giancarlo Piretti (*Plia* Plexiglas chair, 1968), Rodolfo Bonetto and Richard Sapper. Development of modular office systems.

CASTELLI FERRIERI, Anna 89, **158**, 224, 303

CASTIGLIONI, Achille 61, 96, 128, 145, *162,* 174, 178, 200, 210, 224, 239, 291, 348

CASTIGLIONI, Livio 1911–1979. Architect and product designer; brother of Achille and Pier Giacomo. Joint projects with his brothers included audio-visual environments and exhibits for RAI. Single projects from 1952, incl. lighting and electronic appliances. Designs for Fiat, Olivetti and Brionvega. 54, 63, 149, 162

CASTIGLIONI, Pier Giacomo 54, 61, 63, 64, 145, 149, **162**, 200, 210, 348

CENTROKAPPA Independent creative division of Kartell. Worked for Kartell as well as other companies; dissolved in the late 1980s. 224

CERAMICA BARDELLI Tiles manufact.; founded 1962. Works by Gio Ponti (tiles series, 1966) and Piero Fornasetti (*Sole* and *Luna* tiles, 1990).

CERRI, Pierluigi b. 1939. Architect, graphic, furniture and lighting designer. Graphic and exhib. design with Gregotti Associati. Editor at *Casabella* and *Rassegna;* since 1982 artistic director of B&B Italia; Lighting and furniture for Poltrona Frau and Fontana Arte. 1995 *Compasso d'oro.* 202

CHIESA, Pietro 1892–1948. Opened glass workshop in 1921; founded, with Gio Ponti, furniture and lighting co. Fontana Arte as artistic division of Luigi Fontana in 1932; numerous furnture and lighting designs (incl. *0556* floor lamp, 1933). 202

CIBIC, Aldo b. 1955. Interior architect, furniture and product designer; student of Ettore Sottsass. Opened studio in 1991. Designs for Memphis (*Belvedere* sideboard, 1982); furniture systems (*Standard* program); watches for Tissot; Esprit stores. 256

CIDUE Furniture manufacturer; founded 1970. produces works by younger designers, incl. Rodolfo Dordoni and Roberto Lazzeroni.

370

CIMINI, Tommaso b. 1947. Lighting designer. Engineer at Artemide; founded his own company in 1978; best-known work is *Daphine* lamp (with M. de André) for Lumina.

CINELLI 216

CINI & NILS Lighting manufact.; founded 1969 by Mario Melocchi and Franco Bettonica. Packaging designer Melocchi initially produced objects inc. table sets and magazine racks; with Bettonica's *Cuboluce* cubic lamp (1972) shift of focus to lighting.

CITTERIO, Antonio 88, 116, **168**, 226

COLNAGO Bicycle manufacturer; founded 1954. Originally custom workshop with limited output; today production of racing and mountain bikes (1983, star-shaped *Master* frame, 1993, *C 35* bicycle).

COLOMBINI, Gino b. 1915. Designed formally varied, colorful plastic housewares in the 1950s. Since 1949 techn. director at Kartell. Multiple *Compasso d'oro*. 51, 64, 222

COLOMBO, Joe (Cesare) 88, 128, 136, **170**, 224, 240, 274, 348

COLUMBUS 216

COLUMBUS MOBILI Former furniture manufact.; founded 1919. Originally specialized in steel tubes for cars, bicycles and airplanes; in the 1930s produced high-quality tubular-steel furniture by Marcel Breuer and Italian Rationals, incl. Piero Bottoni, Lugi Figini, Gino Pollini and Giuseppe Terragni; Discontinued furn. prod. c. 1970. Part of Gruppo. **216**

COMPASSO D'ORO Prestigious Italian design award. Instituted in 1954 by La Rinascente department store on the suggestion of Gio Ponti. Awarded by prominent ADI-appointed panel in irregular intervals since 1959 for outstanding products, services and research projects. 51, 64

COMPLICE Fashion line by Genny. 342

COPPOLA, Silvio 1920–1986. Architect, product and graphic designer. Designed furniture, faucets and spoons, winning numerous awards. Consultant for Bayer Italia, Monteshell, Montecatini, Cinzano and Laminati Plastici.

CORDERO, Toni b. 1937. Architect, lighting and furniture designer. 1985, Alpine stadium, 1987, Automobile museum in Turin. Designs for Artemide, Driade and Sawaya & Moroni.

COSMIT Milan trade show company, which organizes furniture, office furniture and lighting fairs.

CRASSEVIG Furniture manufacturer since 1960s. Specializes in bent solid wood. Collaboration with designers incl. Gigi Sabadin, Rodolfo Dordoni, Enrico Franzolini, Carlo Bartoli and Fabio Bortolani.

CUNEO, Marcello b. 1933. Architect, industrial and product designer. Designed office buidings, dept. stores, government buildings, museums and churches. Diverse product designs, incl. lighting for Gabbianelli, furniture for Arflex and Cassina.

DALISI, Riccardo b. 1931. Architect, product designer and theorist; Radical Design. Lives, teaches and works in Naples; was member of Mitglied of Global Tools; realized projects for Alchimia; designed furniture for Zanotta and Baleri and coffee makers for Alessi; *Compasso d'oro* 1981. 118, 274

DANESE 101, **174**, 193, 248, 270

D'ASCANIO, Corradino 1891-1981. Engineer and aircraft engineer. Designed legendary *Vespa* scooter for Piaggio (produced in 1946) and built helicopters after designs by Leonardo da Vinci. 59

DDN (Design Diffusion News). Large-sized furniture magazine aimed at dealers, producers and other business insiders.

DE CARLI, Carlo 1910–1971. Architect and furniture designer. In the 1950s, innovative furniture designs with new materials for Cassina and others. 210

DE LUCCHI, Michele 77, 88, 92, 110, 150, **176**, 244, 256, 280, 292

DE PADOVA 178, 242

DE PAS / D'URBINO / LOMAZZI 179, 136, 292,299, 348

DE PAS, Jonathan; 1932–1991; Architekt und Möbeldesigner. 88, 136, **179**, 292, 299, 348

D'URBINO, Donato b. 1935. Architect and furniture designer. 88, 136, **179**, 292, 299, 348

DE VECCHI Silverware manufacturer; founded 1962. Company founder Gabriele De Vecchi designed *T8* candleholder (Gold medal at *Triennale* 1947); in the 1950s, works by Piero Bottoni, Guglielmo Ulrich and Gio Ponti, later by Sergio Asti, Ugo La Pietra, Enzo Mari.

DEGANELLO, Paolo 82, 102, 156, **181**, 298, 357

DEPERO, Fortunato 1892–1960; Painter, graphic designer,

author, set and textile designer. 1914, member of Roman Futurists (*Futurist Reconstruction of the Universe, manifesto).* Designed stage sets, book illustrations, posters, interiors and furniture. 208

DESIGN GROUP ITALIA 182

DIULGHEROFF, Nicolai Bulgarian, 1901–1982. Painter, ceramic and furniture designer. Studied at Bauhaus. Went to Italy in 1920s; Futurist in Turin.

DOLCE & GABBANA Milan fashion company; founded 1985 by Domenico Dolce and Stefano Gabbana. Quotes from Italian fashion and cultural history. 1990–1994, designs for Complice. 80, 183

DOMODINAMICA 312

DOMUS Magazine for urban planning, architecture, art and design; founded 1928 by Gio Ponti, who was editor-in-chief until 1979, with few interruptions (other editors in chief included Mario Bellini, Vittorio Magnano Lampugnani, François Burkhardt). Highly influential publication. 1970 *Compasso d'oro.* 238

DOMUS ACADEMY Private sachool for advanced training; founded in 1982 in Milan. Courses in Industrial and fashion design.

DORDONI, Rodolfo 82, 109, 110, 150, **183**, 184, 201

DORFLES, Gillo b. 1910. Univ. professor and influential art and design critic; prominent scholar of Italian design history. 1956, member of ADI; professor of aesthetics in Trieste. Spokesman of International Congress of Industrial Designers (ICSID). Speaker at numerous conventions. 1970 *Compasso d'oro.*

DRIADE 78, 113, 181, 183, **184**, 249, 266, 307

DROCCO, Guido b. 1942. Furniture designer; Radical Design. Known for multifunctional furniture (*Cactus* clothes treee for Gufram, 1972). Worked with Franco Mello. 219

DUCATI Motorcycle manufact.; founded. 1926 by Antonio Cavalieri Ducati and family. Initially produced portable radios, then, after World War II, calculators, electric razors, film cameras, and finally motorcycles. Known for stripped-down, high-tech motorcycle design. New Logo by Massimo Vignelli in 1996. 267

EDEN (European Designers Network); founded 1990 by BRS Premsala Vonk (Amsterdam), MetaDesign (Berlin), Elene Design (Kopenhagen) and King -Miranda (Milan). 228

EDRA MAZZEI 79, **186,** 266, 282

ELAM Manufacturer of upholstered furniture; founded 1954. Clear design strategy from the 1950s, then long hiatus in creative output until the mid-1990s when the company began presenting new functional designs (by Gae Aulenti, Michele De Lucchi, Alessandro Mendini and others).

FANTONI Furniture manufacturer based in Osoppo near Udine; founded 1882 as a workshop for period furniture. Rapid growth from 1950s. Fantoni was the first European company to produce medium density fiberboard. Focus on office furniture since the 1970s. Designers include Gino Valle (who also built Fantoni factory), Herbert Ohl. 1998 *Compasso d'oro.*

FERRAGAMO, Salvatore 56, **188**

FERRARI 65, 130, **190,** 195, 221, 286

FERRÉ, Gianfranco 192

FERRERI, Marco 174, **193**

FIAM 83, 133, **194**

FIAT 52, 54, 65, 114, 130, 138, **195,** 213, 232

FIGINI, Luigi b. 1903. Architect and industrial designer; was member of Gruppo Sette and Movimento Italiano l'Architettura Razionale. Worked with Gino Pollini. 1935–57 at Olivetti (*Studio 42* portable typewriter with Alexander Schawinsky). Designed offices, industrial buildings and church in Milan. 53, 276, 302

FILA (Fabbrica Italiana Lapis e Affini). Manufacturer of writing instruments; founded 1920 in Florence, now based in Milan. Since the 1970s collaboration with renowned designers, incl. Design Group Italia (*Tratto Pen* and *Tratto Clip,* 1977 and 1978).

FIORUCCI 198, 221, 331

FLEXFORM Furniture manufacturer; founded 1959 by Romeo, Agostino, and Pietro Galimberti. Upholstered furniture. Designers: Antonio Citterio, Paolo Nava, Cini Boeri, Joe Colombo, Sergio Asti and Gabriele Mucchi.

FLOS 118, **200**, 210, 318

FLOU Bed manufacturer; founded 1978 in Meda. Company

produces beds in a variety of sizes and finishes; c. 160 different styles. Designer: Vico Magistretti. 321

FONTANA ARTE 114,183, **202**, 294, 305, 321

FORCOLINI, Carlo b. 1947. Painter, furniture and lighting designer. 1979, cofounder of Alias; lighting for Artemide and Alias (Icaro wall lamp, *Apokalypse Now* table); owner of furniture and lighting company. Nemo (founded. 1993). 78, 101, 110

FORNASETTI, Piero 62, **204**, 296

FRANCO TOSI Machine manufacturer; founded 1881. Initially steam engines, later ship's engines and electrical units.

FRANZOLINI, Enrico b. 1952. Artist, restorer, architect and product designer. 1972, artistic contribution to *Biennale di Venezia*. Sofas and shelving units for Cappellini *(Londra, Vienna, Light-Box cabinet system)*. Furn. designs for Moroso (*Jules e Jim* sofa), Alias, Crassevig, Montina and Knoll.

FRATTINI, Gianfranco 109, 110, 128, **206**

FRONZONI, A.G. b. 1923. Architect, graphic and furniture designer. 1945, office in Brescia, later Milan, 1965–67, publisher and art director at *Casabella;* 1978, founded Istituto di Communicazione Visiva in Milan. His work is characterized by strict reduction to graphic elements in black and white for Galli (1964 *Serie 64).*

FUTURISM 208, 268

GABBIANELLI Ceramics manufacturer; founded 1939 in Milan. In the 1950s and 60s between trad. crafts and design. Objects by Sergio Asti (*Omaggio ad Alvar Aalto* and *Turbante basso* vases, 1967), Gio Ponti, Makio Hasuike, Marcello Cuneo, Gianfranco Frattini and Enzo Mari. Part of Gruppe Ceramica Bardell since 1996.

GABETTI, Roberto Turin-based architect, partner of Aimaro Isola. 67

GABETTI, Roberto/ISOLA, Aimaro b. 1925/1928. Turn-based architects and designers. Numerous architectural projects; furniture inspired by trad. crafts, incl. famous drop-shaped hanging lamp, 1956; and wooden chairs, often with boldly curved shapes. 67

GAGGIA Manufacturer of espresso makers; founded 1948. Produced first commercial espresso makers for bars, etc.; equipped with milk steamers. From 1968 collaboration with designers (*Tell 70* model by Giuseppe de Goetzen; *Baby Gaggia* by Makio Hasuike, 1977).

GAP CASA Magazine for interior architecture and furniture design; founded 1980. Aims at dealers, designers and manufacturers.

GARDELLA, Ignazio b. 1905. Architect, product designer and writer. Rationalist. Architecture; buildings for Olivetti, Kartell and Alfa Romeo. In the 1950s experimental designs, incl. furniture for his company Azucena (founded 1947 with Luigi Caccia Dominioni in Milan). Designs with Anna Castelli Ferrieri for Kartell and Gavina (*Diagramm* chair, 1957). 60, 64, 224, 303

GARELLI Motorcycle manufacturer; founded 1919 (*Mosquito,* 1945). Since 1962 part of Agrati di Monticello.

GARIBOLDI, Giuseppe Product designer. Designs for Richard Ginori (plumbing fixtures and tableware). 1954 *Compasso d'oro.*

GATTI/PAOLINI/TEODORO Design studio; founded 1965 by architects Piero Gatti, Cesare Poilini and Franco Teodoro in Turin. Graphic and industrial design, urban planning; known for *Sacco* beanbag chair (1969 for Zanotta). 299, 348

GAVINA 118, 165, 200, **210**, 318, 320

GECCHELIN, Bruno b. 1939. Architect and Product designer. Lamps for O Luce, furniture for Busnelli and Frau, gas heaters and refrigerators for Indesit, glassware for Venini, typewriters and computers for Olivetti. 1989 and 1991 *Compasso d'oro.* 218, 274

GEDY Manufacturer of bathroom accessories; founded 1953 (*Cucciolo* toilet brush by Makio Hasuike, 1979). Designs by Matteo Thun.

GENNY Fashion company; founded 1961 by Arnaldo Girombell (run by his wife, Donatella, since 1980). *Genny* collection, *Byblos* (1973) and *Complice* lines (1975). Designers have included Versace, Claude Montana, Domenico Dolce and Stefano Gabbana. 342

GHIA Car-body maker; founded 1915 by Giacinto Ghia in Turin. Extravagant single designs. Known for VW *Karmann-Ghia* (1955); car bodies for Chrysler. Luxury car, *Ghia L. 6.4* with Osi. Bought by Ford in 1972. 213

GHIA, Giacinto Car-body designer and entrepreneur. Legendary company for car design, Carozzeria Ghia; founded 1915 in Turin. Known for luxury cars (Maserati *Ghibli,* 1968). Company was bought by Ford in 1972 (1974, *Capri Ghia,* 1975, *Mark II Escort*).

GIACOSA, Dante b. 1905. Engineer and car designer. Worked for Fiat for fifty years (1936, *500 A* aka *Topolino,* 1948, *500 B,* 1957, *Nuova 500;* and Fiat *124, 128* and *130*). 1959 *Compasso d'oro.* 66, 195

GIGLI, Romeo 80, **211**

GILI, Anna b. 1960. Explores new applications for known materials in single products and small series. Designs furniture and living accessories often characterized by symbolic, figurative vocabulary. 150

GIO' STYLE Manufacturer of plastic housewares (with in-house R&D dept.); founded c. 1950. Annual production of some 2.5 billion plates, glasses, forks, knives, etc.

GIORGETTI Furniture manufacturer; founded 1898 in Meda. Family-owned business. Designers incl. Massimo Morozzi, Anna Castelli Ferrieri and Gianfranco Frattini.

GIOVANNONI, Stefano 79, **212**

GISMONDI, Ernesto b. 1931. Lighting designer, rocket engineer and entrepreneur. Founded Artemide with Sergio Mazza and was president and sponsor of Memphis group. Under the pseudonym "Örni Halloween" and later under his own name he designed, for Artemide, the *Ator* floor lamp and the *Pilade* table lamp. 110, 256, 314

GIUGIARO, Giorgetto 81, 100, 130, 196, **213**

GIUGIARO DESIGN 214

GLOBAL TOOLS Design project and design school (1973–75). Founders incl. Ettore Sottsass, Ugo La Pietra, Alessandro Mendini, Gaetano Pesce, Archizoom, Gruppo 9999 and Superstudio. Planned as design laboratories for free experimentation, Global Tools spawned Alchimia and Memphis. 144, 258, 324

GLORIA Lighting manufacturer. 118

GRAMIGNA, Giuliana b. 1929. Architect, furniture and product designer. **250**

GREGOTTI, Vittorio b. 1927. Architect and writer, one of Italy's most important design theorists. Editor at numerous magazines (1952–60, *Casabella*); 1974–1976, director of fine arts and architecture dept. at *Biennale di Venezia.* Author (*Il Disegno del Prodotto Industriale,* 1982). 1952–67, with Ludovico Meneghetti and Giotto Stoppino Architetti Associati, with offices in Novara and Milan (in late 1950s, cofounder of Neoliberty movement), 1968–74 with Pierluigi Carri and Hiromichi Matsui Gregotti Associati. *Compasso d'oro* 1967. 328

GRUPPO 216

GRUPPO INDUSTRIALE BUSNELLI 218, 230

GRUPPO STRUM Group of architects and designers (Piero Derossi, Giorgio Ceretti, Carlo Giammarco, Riccardo Rosso, Maurizio Vogliazzo); founded 1971 in Turin. Architettura Radicale/Radical Design (pop furniture for Gufram; *Pratone* plastic turf, 1971). Contribution to 1972 exhib., *Italy: The New Domestic Landscape.* 219, 298

GRUPPO 9999 Design group; founded 1967 in Florence by the architects Giorgio Birelli, Carlo Caldini, Fabrizio Fiumi and Paolo Galli. Radical Design. Contribution to 1972 exhib., *Italy: The New Domestic Landscape.*

GRUPPO UFO Group of designers and architects; founded 1967 by Lapo Binazzi, Carlo Bachi, Riccardo Foresi, Patrizia Cammeo, Vittorio Maschietto and Sandro Gioli in Florence. Radical Design. Urban visions, in which architecture blended with art, design and literature. From 1972 Binazzi was the group's central figure. 298

GUCCI Fashion company; founded 1904 by saddlemaker Guccio Gucci as a producer of exclusive leather goods in Milan. 1960, success with Gucci *Loafers;* from 1978 women's prêt-à-porter. After a severe financial crisis, American designer Tom Ford was hired and gave the company a new image. Today, Gucci is one of Italy's most influential fashion companies along with Prada. Known for references to fashion history and for use of new materials. 81

GUERRIERO, Alessandro b. 1943. Architect and design theorist. In 1976, with his sister, Adriana, founded Alchimia studio, which was later joined by Alessandro Mendini and Giorgio Gregori. 1982, cofounder of Domus Academy; since 1983, copublisher, with Pierre Restany, of *Decoration International* magazine, Paris. Films, videos, books and numerous exhibitions. 92

GUFRAM 219, 299

HAMEL, Maria Christina b. 1958 in New Delhi. Product designer, lived in India, Thailand and Austria before settling in Milan in 1973. Was Alessandro Mendini's assistant at Alchimia in the 1980s; designs lamps, small furniture as well as suggestively colorful vases and ceramics. Works for Alessi, Swatch, Rado and other companies.

HASUIKE, Makio b. 1938 in Tokyo; based in Italy since the 1960s. Designs incl. ceramic objects for Gabbianelli, espresso makers for Gaggia and *Cucciolo* toilet brush for Gedy (1979, permanent collection of Museum of Modern Art, New York). In 1982 cofounded bags and accessories manufacturer MH Way.

HELG, Franca 1920-1989. Architect and furniture designer. From 1951 worked with Franco Albini and after his death ran his studio with Antonio Piva and Marco Albini. 90, 278

HOSOE, Isao 220, 308

HUBER, Max 1919-1992. Swiss graphic designer; art director at Studio Boggeri. Moved to Milan in 1945. 1950, corp. ID for La Rinascente; exhibition concepts (*La forma dell'utile, Milan Triennale* 1951 with Achille and Pier G. Castiglioni). Famous posters for car races with characteristic combination of abstract color planes and silhouetted photographs. 1954 *Compasso d'oro.* 134, 231, 310

ICE; (Istituto Nazionale per il Commercio Estero). Italian foreign trade office; founded 1926 for promoting exports, partcularly for small and mid-sized firms. 1989 *Compasso d'oro.*

IDEAL STANDARD Manufacturer of bathroom furniture; founded 1909 in Milan. Rapid growth in 1950s though 1970s. Designs by Achille Castiglioni (*Aquatonda* Series, 1971), Mario Bellini (*Class* faucet, 1990), Gae Aulenti, Paolo Tilche, Enzo Mari. 296

iGUZZINI Lighting manufacturer; founded 1963. Produces sophisticated lighting systems, using materials such as die-cast aluminum and plastics. Designs by Rodolfo Bonetto, Pier Giacomo Castiglioni, Pierluigi Molinari, Bruno Gecchelin and others.

INNOCENTI LAMBRETTA car and motor scooter manufacturer.; founded 1931 by Ferdinando Innocenti in Milan. Best known for its motor scooters; At 1961 Turin car show presented the *Innocenti 950* roadster designed by Ghia. In 1965 the company developed the *Mini Minor* for which took over Lambretta in 1972. Bought by Fiat in 1989.

INTERNI Magazine for interior architecture; founded 1954. Reports on designers, products and applications.

IOSA GHINI, Massimo 78, 88, 209, **221**, 265

ITALDESIGN 100, 196, 213

ITALTEL Telephone manufacturer; founded in 1921 as Siemens S.A.. in Milan. In the 1950s designs by Roberto Menghi (1966, *Grillo* compact telephone by Marco Zanuso and Richard Sapper), Giorgetto Giugiaro. Achille Castilgioni, Design Group Italia. 182

ISOLA, Aimaro Turin architect. Gabetti/Isola office with Roberto Gabetta.

JOINT Furniture and accessories manufacturer, Milan. Colorful objects incl. mirrors, bookcases and clothes trees. *Joker* by Carlo Forcolini. Außerdem shelves (incl. *Metro* system), stools and other small furniture.

KARTELL 64, 158, 172, 220, *222,* 240, 252, 314, 328, 354

KING-MIRANDA 228, 109

KING, Perry A. b. 1938 London. Product and furniture designer. *228,* 280

KING-KONG; Design Studio 1985-89; founded by Stefano Giovannoni and Guido Venturini. Arbeiten für Alessi. 212

KLIER, Hans von b. 1934, Czechoslovakia. Graphic and product designer. Graduated from Hochschule für Gestaltung, Ulm; worked for Ettore Sottsass 1960-68. Wooden toys for children. From 1969 corp. ID for Olivetti. 1970 *Compasso d'oro.*

KRIZIA 229

LA CIMBALI Manufacturer of espresso makers; founded 1912. Since 1962 collaboration with designers, incl. Achille and Pier Giacomo Castiglioni (model *Pitagora),* Rodolfo Bonetto (model *M 15,* 1970, model *M 20,* 1979). The *ET* of 1983 was the first "superautomatica" machine, which at the push of a button did everything from grinding the coffee to pouring it.

LA PAVONI Manufacturer of espresso makers; founded

1905. Invented espresso making with *Ideale* model. *La Cornuta* by Gio Ponti, 1949. *La Diamante* by Bruno Munari and Enzo Mari, 1957. Machines are still crafted partly by hand . 296

LA PIETRA, Ugo 128, 218, **230**, 299

LA RINASCENTE 106, **231**, 260, 270, 310, 327

LAGOSTINA Housewares manufacturer; founded 1901 in Omegna. One of the leading manuf. of high-quality pots, pans and silverware. Designs by, among others, Paolo Zani and Giugiaro Design (*Modia* pots and *Atmosphere* pressure cooker); also in-house design dept.

LAMBORGHINI Automobile manufacturer; founded by Ferruccio Lamborghini. Originally tractor manuf.; then competed with Ferrari. (*350 GTV,* 1964; Lamborghini *Miura,* 1966; *Countach* by Bertone with angular, futuristic look, in production since 1972.) Company was temporarily owned by Indonesian investor, bought in 1998 by VW. 130

LANCIA 52, 54, 130, 196, **232**, 286, 344

LAZZARINI, Claudio b. 1953. Architect and furniture designer. (First design project: *Dormusa* program). From 1988, collaboration with Carl V. Pickering. Interior design of offices and stores in Rome and Milan, and design of exhibition spaces, landscapes and boats.

LAZZERONI, Roberto b. 1950. Architect and product designer. Radical Design. Designs for Acerbis.

LIBERTY Italian term for Art Nouveau. In the arts and crafts, Carlo Bugatti was the most inspired representative of "Stile Liberty". The name refers to the London store of Liberty & Co., which was founded in 1875 by Arthur Lasenby Liberty and had relationships with Italy in the late 19th century. A climactic event for Stile Liberty was the 1902 *International Arts and Crafts Exhibition* in Turin. 56, 68

LINEA ITALIANA The specifically Italian formal language developing from the late 1940s onward: organic forms and flowing, elegant lines combined with functional product design. Famous examples include the *Lexicon 80* typewriter for Olivetti (1948), the *Vespa* (1946), and Marco Zanuso's *Lady* chair for Arflex (1951). 60, 83, 112, 273

LISSONI, Piero 150, **234**

LOEW, Glen Oliver Longtime collaborator of Antonio Citterio; jointly designed office furniture for Vitra and others.

LOMAZZI, Paolo b. 1936Architect and furniture designer. 88, 136, **179**, 292, 299, 348

LORENZO RUBELLI see RUBELLI

LUCEPLAN 82, **235**, 252, 306

LUMINA Lighting manufacturer; founded 1976 by Tommaso Cimini and Ermanno Prosperi. Produces primarily halogen lights. Designers: Ricardo Blumer and Yaacov Kaufman.

LUPI, Italo 238

LUXOTTICA GROUP Eyewear manufacturer; founded 1961 by Leonardo del Vecchio in Agordo. In addition to lines like *Persol,* the company produces designs by Giorgio Armani, Giugiaro, Ferragamo, Genny, Byblos and Yves Saint-Laurent.

MAGISTRETTI, Vico 61, 110, 116, 156, 178, 224, **240**, 274, 291

MALDONADO, Tomàs b. 1922, Argentina. Industrial designer and theorist; publisher of Argentine magazine *Nueva Vision* and *Casabella* (1976-81). Director of design schools in Ulm (1954-66), Princeton, USA (1968-70), Bologna (1971-83) and Milan. 1967-1969, pres. of Intern. Council of Societies of Industrial Design. Consultant for La Rinascente. 231

MANDARINA DUCK 177, **244**, 251

MANDELLI, Mariuccia 229

MANGIAROTTI, Angelo 110, 118, 174, **246**, 333

MANZU, Pio 1939-1969. Car and product designer, author. Worked for Olivetti, since 1968 for Fiat (City Taxi, tractors and *127*). *Parentesi* light for Flos, compl. after his death by Achille Castiglioni (*Compasso d'oro* 1979).

MARCARTRÉ Office furniture manufacturer; founded 1975. Works with Mario Bellini, Achille Castiglioni (*Solone* office furniture series), Paolo Deganello and King-Miranda.

MARI, Enzo 174, 184, **248**, 346, 348

MARTINELLI, Elio b. 1922. Interior architect, lighting designer and entrepreneur. In 1942 began working in his father's lighting company (Martinelli Luce) in Lucca; in the 1950s interiors for offices and hotels.

MARZANO, Stefano b. 1950. Product designer; in 1972 joined Makio Hasuike's Milan studio; 1978 Philips Design Center in Eindhoven; 1989 Vice President for corp. ID at Whirlpool International; since 1991 Senior Director of Philips Design;

1998 *Compasso d'oro*. 83

MASERATI Automobile manufacturer. Legendary racing and sportscars. Had its peak in the 1960s and 70s. (Maserati *Ghibli*, 1966, design by Giorgetto Giugiaro, who also designed other Maserati models). In 1998, successful comeback with *3200 GT* coupe by Giorgetto Giugiaro's Italdesign.

MASSONI, Luigi b. 1930. Industrial designer and author. In 1972 appointed president of design dept. of A&D, with commissions from Boffi, Poltrona Frau and Fratelli Guzzini. Publisher of *Forme* and other design and photography magazines. Founded Mabilia studio for furniture and industrial design.

MAZZA, Sergio b. 1931. Architect, furniture and product designer. 110, **250**

MEDA, Alberto 101, 150, 235, 244, **251**, 306, 313

MEDA, Luca b. 1936. Architect and furniture designer. From 1961, architectural projects and interiors with Aldo Rossi (1985 *Biennale di Venezia*). Since the 1960s, furniture and mass-produced articles, for Molteni, Unifor and others. 333

MEGALIT 110

MELLO, Franco Furniture designer. *Cactus* clothes tree with Guido Drocco, 1972 for Gufram. 219

MELOCCHI, Mario b. 1931. Entrepreneur, packaging and lighting designer; cofounder of Cini & Nils.

MEMPHIS 77, 88, 92, 94, 102, 110, 144, 176, 184, 221, **254**, 299, 324, 331

MENDINI, Alessandro 79, 90, 92, 94, 118, 122, **258**, 266, 294, 300, 340, 348, 353

MENEGHETTI, Lodovico b. 1926. Architect and product designer. Since 1953 partner in Architetti Associati with Vittorio Gregotti and Giotto Stoppino. 328

MENGHI, Roberto b. 1920. Architect and industrial designer. In the 1950s, worked with Marco Zanuso, Anna C. Ferrieri, Ignazio Gardella and Franco Albini. One of the first designers to use plastic (gas container for Pirelli). Designed glassware and elctr. appliances. Clients incl. Arflex, Fontana, Siemens and Venini. 1956 and 1957 *Compasso d'oro*.

MERCATALI, Davide b. 1948. Product designer. *Nomade* furniture system with Maurizio Dallasta, 1974-77. 1982-87, collaboration with Paolo Pedrizetti; intelligent household objects (*Giotto* can opener). Founder of Zeus group, 1984.

MH WAY Manufacturer of bags, backpacks and office accessories; founded 1982 by Makio Hasuike (*Piuma* translucent plastic suitcase, 1983; purist, pressure-resistant *Impronta* backpack).

MICHELOTTI, Giovanni 1921-1980. Car designer. Worked for Pininfarina, Triumph in England (1959, Triumph *Herald*) und Datsun in Japan (1961, Datsun *Prince Skyline*).

MINOLETTI, Giulio b. 1910. Architect and industrial designer. Urban planning for Milan. Designs incl. *Etr 300 Settebello* train (1949 for Breda *Ferroviarie*) and *Better Living* bathroom (1949).

MIRANDA, Santiago b. 1947 Sevilla. **228**

MIRENZI, Franco b. 1942. Furniture and industrial designer; Interiors for exhibition and office spaces for Fiat, Brionvega and Zanussi. Has worked primarily for Unimark. In addition to furniture and technical objects, has also designed corp. ID programs.

MISSONI 260, **331**

MODO Design magazine; founded 1977 by Alessandro Mendini (who was its first editor-in-chief). Background reports and news from furniture, industrial and exhibition design.

MOLINARI, Pierluigi b. 1938. Furniture and product designer. Started his career in 1961 working for Guzzini, Ampaglas and Fedegari. 1988-91, president of ADI.

MOLLINO, Carlo 62, 210, **262**, 296, 348

MOLTENI Furniture manufacturer. The Molteni group owns several companies: Molteni & C. produces furniture for residential and public use; Unifor specializes in office furn.; Dada in kitchens; Citterio in closet systems. Important designer: Luca Meda.

MONGUZZI, Bruno b. 1941. Graphic designer. Studied in Geneva and London. Worked with Studio Boggeri 1961-63 ; opened his own studio in Milan in 1968. Combines influences from Swiss design with photographic elements. (1986, poster announcing the opening of Musée d'Orsay). 134, 310

MONDO 152

MONTECATINI Chemical company; founded 1888. In the 1930s worked with Gio Ponti and Marcello Nizzoli. 1964, *Algol*

TV set by Marco Zanuso and Richard Sapper for Brionvega with *Montecatini* technology. 1965, merger between Montecatini und Edison (largest industrial merger in Italian history) ; company name since 1996, Montedison.

MORASSUTTI, Bruno b. 1920. Architect and industrial designer. 1949-50, worked in Frank Lloyd Wright's Studio, 1955-60, collaboration with Angelo Mangiarotti; 1968, collaboration with Mario Memoli, Giovanna Gussoli and Gabriella Benevento in Milan.

MOROSO 83, 183, 221, **265**

MOROZZI, Massimo 102, 186, 194, **266,** 298

MOSCHINO, Franco 1950-1994. Fashion designer. Studied art in Milan, 1968-71. Independent illustrator; ad campaigns for Versace. 1983, first collection (*Couture*); ironic take on fashion world.

MOTO GUZZI 267

MUCCHI, Gabriele b. 1899. Architect, engineer and furniture designer; representative of Rationalism. Early tubular steel furn. (*S5* chair). Worked for furn. manuf. Emilio Pino, 1934-45. 303, 348

MUNARI, Bruno 134, 174, 231, 209, **268,** 276, 290, 346

MURATORE, Remo 1912-1983. Graphic designer. Worked for Studio Boggeri.

NATALINI, Adolfo b. 1941. Architect and furniture designer. 1966, cofounder of Superstudio. In addition to his practical design work, focuses on architectural theory. With Superstudio cofounded Global Tools in 1973; later artistic director of Up & Up. Furniture for Arflex, Sawaya & Moroni and Driade. 298, 329

NAVA, Paolo b. 1943. Furniture and industrial designer. 1972, studio with Antonio Citterio (*Aria* and *Pasodoble* seats for Flexform, *Toscano* table series for Boffi). Begins collaborating with B&B Italia in 1973 (1975, *Baia* sofa; 1977, *345* office chair). 104, 116, 128

NAVONE, Paola b. 1950. Architect, design consultant and author. Worked at Kartell's creative dept., Centrokappa, 1974-78. Editor at *Domus;* Studio Alchimia; consultant for Abet Laminati, Fiat, Renault and Moroso. 1987, appointed creative director of Mondo, a subsidiary of Cappellini. 92, 152

NEO-LIBERTY Term for short-lived, heterogeneous stylistic movement in Italian design at the end of the 1950s. At one time or another the movement included Gae Aulenti, Roberto Gabetti, Aimaro Isola, Aldo Rossi, Vittorio Gregotti, Lodovico Meneghetti, and Giotto Stoppino. Borrowing from Art Nouveau (Stile Liberty), the movement criticized blind adherence to Modernism and functionalism. Well-known designs include the *Cavour* chair with voluptuously curved armrests (by Gregotti, Stoppino and Meneghetti), and the red *San Luca* chair by Achille und Pier Giacomo Castiglioni for Gavina (1960). 68, 112, 114, 210, 328

NIZZOLI, Marcello 53, 64, 138, 209, 258, **272,** 276, 352

NOORDA, Bob b. 1927, Netherlands. Graphic designer. Studied in Amsterdam; since 1952 based in Italy. Developed pictographic systems and corp. ID programs (1962-64 signage system for Milan subway). 1961, artistic director at Pirelli. 1979, 1984, 1995 *Compasso d'oro.* 90, 116, 134, 290, 310, 333

NOVECENTO Architectural movement founded in 1926. Members included Gio Ponti, Emilio Lancia, Giovanni Muzio, Pietro Chiesa, Guido Andloviz, Michele Marelli, Giuseppe De Finetti. They favored a formally reduced, neoclassicist style, inspired, in part, by the Viennese Workshops. Their goal was to create an "Italian" style. They used *Domus* magazine as their main forum. Their influence was felt in architecture (monumental buildings) arts and crafts and commercial art. 55, 57, 296, 302

NUOVO DESIGN "New design" emerged in Italy in opposition to a purely functionalist design concept. The ground was prepared by the Anti- and Radical Design movements (late 1960s and 1970s). The breakthrough for Nuovo Design came in the 1980s with the success of Memphis, which opened the door for a playful, antifunctionalist design. 79, 92, 101, 118, 168, 256, 299

O LUCE; 242, **274,** 307

OFFREDI, Giovanni b. 1927. Architect and Product designer. Worked for Ultravox, Bazzani, Bandi Line and Saporiti (sales center and exhibition booths).

OLIVARI Manufacturer of door handles; founded 1911 by Battista Olivari. Designers include Gio Ponti, Angelo Mangiarotti, Giotto Stoppino and Sergio Asti. 122, 250, 328

OLIVERI, Mario b. 1921 Industrial designer. 1952, beginning of collaboration with Marcello Nizzoli; 1965-71 partner at

Nizzoli Associati in Milan. Gas station design for Ceccato;, spark plugs for Lombardini; cover designs for *L'Architettura* magazine.

OLIVETTI 51, 52, 53, 57, 59, 64, 65, 108, 114, 122, 123, 134, 138, 177, 228, 239, 268, 272, **276**, 320, 322, 327

OTTAGONO Magazine for industrial design; founded 1966 by Osvaldo Borsani. Focuses on theoretical and historical subjects.

PAGANO, Giuseppe (Giuseppe Pagano Pogatschnig) 1896–1945. Architect, furniture designer, author. In the 1930s, furn. designer; representative of Rationalism; editor at *Casabella* and *Domus*. An antifascist, he was interned and killed in a German camp.. 303, 348

PALLUCCO Furniture manufacturer; founded 1980 by Paolo Pallucco. In addition to its founder's designs, the firm produces works by young designers and reeditions by Gio Ponti and others. Renamed Palluccoitalia, the firm has been run by Mino Bellato since 1989.

PAMIO, Roberto b. 1937. Architect, furniture and lighting designer. Worked with Renato Toso; furniture and lights for Arflex, Art Linea, Cidue, Leucos and Zanussi.

PECORA, Terri 282

PEDRIZZETTI, Paolo b. 1947. Architect, product designer and author. 1982-88, studio with Davide Mercatali (experiments with plastic, metal and other materials). Opened new studio in 1988; publisher of *Blu & rosso* and *Bagno & Bagni*.

PENATI, Marc 321

PEREGALLI, Maurizio b. 1951. Architect, entrepreneur and furniture designer. Worked with Giorgio Armani, whose stores in Italy, London and New York he designed. 1984, cofounder of Zeus. 357

PERSICO, Edoardo died 1939. Architect, graphic designer, lawyer and author. Rationalist. architect; wrote about architecture and design. 1935-36, co-publisher of *Casabella*.

PESCE, Gaetano 116, 128, 156, **283**, 299

PIACENTINI, Marcello 1881-1960. Architect and urban planner. 1927, exemplary planning of town center of Bergamo (classical and modern elements). Received important architect. commissions from Fascist government. (1928, court house in Messina; 1931-39, in Milan).

PIAGGIO Motor scooter manufacturer. Before World War II aircraft manufacturer The 1946 *Vespa* by airplane engineer Corradino d'Ascanio, was a new type of vehicle with an integral body and "aeronautic" look. In the 1950s, it became a symbol of Italian Dolce Vita. 59

PIERANTONIO BONACINA 136

PININFARINA/PININ FARINA 65, 98, 130, 138, 190, 196, 213, 232, **286**

PINTORI, Giovanni b. 1912. Graphic designer and artist. Worked primarily for Olivetti (1947, Logo). Best known for his posters for *Lettera 22* and *Elettrosumma 22*. Headed Olivetti's graphic design dept. from 1967. 278

PIRELLI 62, 104, 135, 218, 270, **290**, 294, 310, 327, 352

PIRETTI, Giancarlo b. 1940. Furniture designer. Head of research & design dept at Castelli. Ergonom. furniture for mass prod. (1969, *Plia* folding chair made of Plexiglas, which was frequently copied). Later worked for Open Ark and, from 1984, for Castilia. 1981 and 1991, *Compasso d'oro*.

PIVA, Paolo b. 1950. Architect, product designer and author (1980, Ambassador to Kuweit in Quatar). Furniture and products for B & B Italia, Poliform, Stilnovo and Giovannetti.

POGGI 90, 230, **291**

POLITECNICO DI MILANO Architecture school of Milan University. Almost all famous Italian designers studied here, many of them have also taught at the school. Since 1994 the Politecnico also has an industrial design dept.

POLLINI, Gino b. 1903; Architect and product designer. 1926, cofounder of Gruppo Sette, which advocated Rationalist architecture. 1930-1946, Italian delegate to International Congress for Modern Architecture (CIAM). Collaborated with Luigi Figini (1934-1935, Olivetti building in Ivrea; 1935, *Studio 42* typewriter with Alexander Schawinsky). 53, 276, 302

POLTRONA FRAU Furniture manufacturer; founded 1912 by Renzo Frau in Turin. Specializing in upholstered furniture, the company furnished salons and luxury liners in the 1920s. After 1945 it switched to industrial production, working with designers incl. Gio Ponti, Marco Zanuso, Pierluigi Cerri, Gae Aulenti and Mario Bellini. Today it also produces airplane seats and furniture for public/commercial use. 344

POLTRONOVA 114, 144, 179, **292**, 300, 324, 329, 344

PONTI, Gio 57, 63, 88, 136, 154, 202, 204, 251, 290, **293**, 340

PORTOGHESI, Paolo b. 1931. Architect, author, teacher, furniture and product designer. Co-publisher of trade magazines and author of numerous books on architecture. Designs for Poltrona Frau, Alessi and Ritzenhoff. 96

POZZI-GINORI Ceramics manufacturer; founded 1906 as Ceramica Pozzi spa. Specializes in bathroom fixtures. Designs by Gae Aulenti, Matteo Thun, Makio Hasuike. 1976, merger with Richard-Ginori.

PRADA, Miuccia b. 1950. Fashion designer. Studied political science and theater. In 1980 joined her uncle Mario's leathergoods company in Milan. First collection 1985 (waterproof nylon knapsack). Minimalist. Frequent use of unusual patterns, synthetic materials. 81

PUCCI, Emilio 1914–1992. Fashion designer. 1947, ski clothes. Pucci influenced fashions of the 1960s with silk jersey dresses and blouses in colorful, wild patterns influenced by Pop Art and Op-Art. Also known for his capri pants and bodysuits.

PUPPA, Daniela b. 1947. Author, furniture and fashion designer. Worked for Nizzoli Associati, 1970-74;1972-76, at *Casabella;* 1977-83 at *Modo.* Designs for Fontana Arte, Cappellini, Ligne Roset, Alchimia and Gianfranco Ferré. 202

RADICAL DESIGN 102, 144, 179, 181, **298**, 219, 230, 254, 284, 292, 322, **329**

RAGGI, Franco b. 1945. Architect, furniture and lighting designer and critic. Worked for *Casabella,* 1971-75. From 1977-1983 publisher of *Modo.* Theorist of Radical Design; active in Global Tools. With Daniela Puppa designed lamps and chairs for Fontana Arte and Cappellini. 92, 202, 292, 313

RASULO, Prospero 104, 292, **300**

RATIONALISM 55, 276, 296, 298, **302**, 322

RE-DESIGN Term used in Italy to describe reinterpretations of existing products. Raymond Loewy was an early, prominent representative of the concept with his restyling work on cars and other objects. It was picked up by Alessandro Mendini in the 1970s as part of Alchimia's design project. Claiming that invention of new forms was not possible anymore, Mendini ironically reinterpreted classic Bauhaus and Thonet chairs by covering pieces like Marcel Breuer's *Wassily* chair with patterns or adding little flags. 258, 300

REXITE Manufacturer of small furniture and accessories; founded 1968. Since 1978 Raul Barbieri has been in charge of design, often collaborating with Giorgio Marianelli (joint designs incl. *Babele* letter tray, 1995, over one million sold. Also *Cribbio* series with umbrella stand). Designs by Giotto Stoppino (c. 1990, *Biblio* cassette holder), Julian Brown, Gabriella Montaguti.

RICHARD-GINORI Ceramics manufacturer; founded 1873 in Milan. Gio Ponti artistic dir. from 1923 (vases and vessels); succeeded by Giovanni Gariboldi in the 1940s and 50s (1954, *Ulpia* tea set); and later by Gae Aulenti. 1976, merger with Ceramiche Pozzi. 56, 294

RIMA (Rinaldi Mario) Furniture manufacturer; founded 1946 by Rinaldi family of hardware dealers in Milan. After World War II, production of metal furniture; combination of iron with rubber and plastic.

RINALDI, Gastone b. 1920. Architect and furniture designer. Designed numerous delicate, elegant pieces of metal furniture, incl. *DU 10* (1951), *DU 30* and *DU 43* (1953), *DU 57* (1956) chairs, most of them for RIMA, founded by his father, Mario. In the 1970 s, *Ondalunga* sofa and *Dafne* folding chair.

RIVA, Umberto 304

RIZZATTO, Paolo 101, 235, 252, **306**

ROGERS, Ernesto Nathan 1909–1969. Architect, furniture designer and author. 1932, cofounder of BBPR. 1946-1947, publisher of *Domus;* 1953-1964, *Casabella- Continuità.* From 1962, teacher at Milan polytechnic. Was important influence on development of Italian design in the 1950s. 51, 122

ROMANELLI, Marco 82, 184, 274, **307**

ROSSELLI, Alberto 303, 352, **308**

ROSSI, Aldo 79, 96, **309**, 333

RUBELLI Renowned textile company founded 1858 in Venice. Produces high-quality decorative fabrics, incl. heavy gold and velvet materials, but also airy cloths in natural colors. Also hand-woven velvet fabrics (*Soprarizzi*) using techniques from the 16th century.

SABADIN, Gigi b. 1930. Not a designer or architect, Sabadin is a traditional artisan specializing in wood and metal. Designs furniture primarily for Crassevig. Well-known pieces include wooden cradle for Stilwood.

SABATTINI, Lino b. 1925. Silversmith and product designer. Leitete Headed design dept of Christofle. 1956-1963. Founded Argenteria Sabattini in 1964. Works for Rosenthal and Zani & Zani.

SACCHI, Giovanni Model builder. Italy's best-known model builder, worked for Richard Sapper, Marcello Nizzoli, Brionvega and Olivetti. 1998 *Compasso d'oro* for lifetime achievement.

SACCO, Bruno b. 1934. Car designer. Joined Mercedes-Benz in 1958; in 1975 became head of styling dept. (1991, new *S-Class,* later *E-* and *C-Class*).

SADLER, Marc French industrial designer based in Venice. Sadler specializes in plastics and new technologies and has worked for Boffi (*Alukit* kitchen). 201

SALOCCHI, Claudio b. 1934. Architect, furniture and industrial designer. From 1965, designs in plastics (1965, *Palla* armchair). Member of Ricerche non finalizzate group. Designs for Skipper, Alberti Cucine, Besana and Desozzi.

SAMBONET, Roberto 160, **310**

SAN LORENZO Silverware manufacturer; founded. 1970 in Milan. Designers incl. Franco Albini and Franca Helg (1971 *Pannocchia* bowls), Antonio Piva, Afra and Tobia Scarpa, (1979, silverware set; 1990, *Moretta* carafe), Lella and Massimo Vignelli.

SANTACHIARA, Denis 118, 236, **312**

SANT'ELIA, Antonio 1888-1916. Architect and theorist. In 1914 wrote Manifesto of Futurist architecture; designs for *La città nuova.* Influential in architecture and urban planning.

SAPORITI Furniture manufacturer; founded 1949. Designers: Alberto Rosselli and Giorgio Raimondi.

SAPPER, Richard 94, 110, 145, 222, **314**, 333, 353

SARFATTI Gino 1912-1985. Aeronautics engineer and lighting designer. Pioneer of modern Italian lighting design. Founded Arteluce in 1939. Important designs in 1940s and 50s. 63, 108, 201, 236

SARFATTI Riccardo Architect. Son of Gino Sarfattis; cofounder of lighting manuf. Luceplan. 236

SAWAYA & MORONI 83, **316**

SCARPA, Afra b. 1937. Furniture designer and architect. 116, 156, 200, 291, **318**, 333

SCARPA, Carlo 63, 128, 210, 278, 305, 318, **319**, 340

SCARPA, Tobia b. 1935. Furniture designer and architect. 116, 156, 200, 291, **318**, 333, 340

SCARZELLA, Patrizia 321

SCHAWINSKY, Alexander "Xanti" 1904-1979. Swiss-born product and graphic designer and artist. Studied at Bauhaus. 1933-1936, designed advertisements and brochures at Studio Boggeri for clients incl. Motta, Cinzano and Olivetti. In the 1930s joined Olivetti's advertising dept. Typewriters for Olivetti (1936, *Studio 42*). In 1936 emigrated to U.S. where he worked primarily as a painter and teacher. 53, 134

SCHIAPARELLI, Elsa 1890-1973. Italian fashion designer. Went to U.S. early on and in 1922 moved to Paris. In the 1930s highly successful with surrealist, avant garde designs (collaboration with Salvador Dali, Jean Cocteau) 1937, *Music* collection; 1938, *Circus* collection. Retired from fashion design in mid-1950s.

SCHUBERTH, Emilio 1904-1972. Fashion designer. Roman. couturier who created exclusive evening gowns for the rich and the beautiful, from Sophia Loren to Soraya.

SCUOLA POLITECHNICA DI DESIGN Private design school in Milan; founded 1954. (Not to be confused with Politecnico). Offers courses in industrial, furniture, public and visual design. 1995 *Compasso d'oro.*

SEEGATZ / EIFLER Design studio; founded 1994 by Claus Eifler, Andreas Seegatz, Ludolf von Alvensleben and Tom Keller in Milan/ Berlin. Architecture, graphic and product design, cultural projects (1996, *World interiors* project in Cologne and Milan).

SEMPRINI, Roberto b. 1959 Architect and furniture designer. Belonged to Bolidismo movement. In 1988 worked with Massimo Iosa Ghini for RAI TV network (set designs for *Fuori Orario*). Bolidò dance club with Iosa Ghini in New York. Furniture for Disform, Fiam, Ferrart, Sigla and Edra-Mazzei (1989, *Tatlin* sofa with Mario Cananzi). 186

SIGLA 321

SILVESTRIN, Danilo b. 1942. Architect, furniture and product designer. Master of simple form. Designs for ClassiCon, Lambert, Rosenthal, Up & Up and WMF.

SKIPPER Furniture manufacturer; founded 1968. Since 1973 producer of different collections, incl. *Comput* (office furniture), *B. Ardani* (residential furn.), *Green* (outdoor furn.). Designers incl. Ettore Sottsass, Bruno Gecchlin and Angelo Mangiarotti. 246

SMC ARCHITETTURA Studio of Sergio Mazza and Giuliana Gramigna. **250**

SMEG Manufacturer of electric appliances; founded 1948 in Guastalla. Stoves, washing machines and dishwashers in classically elegant, functional designs.

SOTTSASS, Ettore 61, 65, 77, 88, 92, 96, 110, 254, 278, 292, 299, **322**, 348

SOWDEN, George James b. 1942, England. Architect, furniture and industrial designer. From 1970 collaborated with Ettore Sottsass. Computer systems and office work stations as well as research into ergonomics for Olivetti. Cofounder of Memphis (1982, *Luxor* closet). Designs for Ritzenhoff and Rasch.

STEINER, Albe 231, 290, **326**

STILEINDUSTRIA Magazine founded in 1953 by Alberto Rosselli to promote exchange between industry and design. Folded in 1962. Unsuccessful relaunch in the 1990s. 1970 *Compasso d'oro.*

STOPPINO, Giotto 127, 218, 224, **328**

STUDIO ALCHIMIA 88, **92**, 94, 102, 144, 176, 216, 254, 258, 300, 324

STUDIO BOGGERI 134, 276

SUPERSTUDIO 292, 298, **329**

SUSANI, Marco b. 1956. Studied architecture in Milan. **332**

TAKAHAMA, Kazuhide b. 1930, Japan. Architect and furniture designer. Opened studio in Bologna in 1963. Designs for B&B Italia, Simon International and lighting manuf. Sirrah.

TECNO 142, **330**

TECNO TUBO TORINO 216

TERRAGNI, Guiseppe 1904-1943. Architect and furniture designer; Rationalist. (1934-36, Fascist part headquarters in Como). Used industrial materials; designed early serial products (1936, *Lariana* tubular-steel chair; produced by Zanotta since 1982). 55, 302, 348

TESTA, Armando 1917-1992. Graphic designer. One of the most influential figures in Italian graphics and advertising. Opened in Turin in 1946. Founded successful advertising agency in 1956. Best-known for poster for 1960 Olympics in Rome and advertisements for Pirelli. 290

THUN, Matteo 77, 109, 201, 216, **331**

TOSCANI, Oliviero b. 1942. Fashion photographer and art director. Spectacular advertising campaigns for Benetton. Developed modern corp. ID for Fiorucci and Esprit; visual communication for B&B Italia. 116, 126

TOURING Car-body maker; founded 1926. 1931, legendary aerodynamic *Flying Star,* 1937, Alfa *8 C 2900 B Superleggera;* 1939, Alfa *6 C 2500 SS Duxia;* 1957, Lancia *3500 GT;* 1959, Lancia *Flaminia.* 1967 dissolved. 98, 232

TOVAGLIA, Pino 1923-1977. Graphic designer. Advertisements for Pirelli, Logos for Ottagono and Alfa Romeo. Founder of Art Director's Club Milan. Consultant for La Rinascente and Flos; directed course in corp. ID at Scuola Politecnica di Design in Milan; 1998 *Compasso d'oro* for lifetime achievement.

TRIENNALE Influential international exhibition of architecture and design. Since 1933, held in three-year intervals (with interruptions) at Palazzo dell'Arte in Milan (designed by Giovanni Muzio). Precursors were the *Biennali* in Monza (I through IV) of the 1920s, which showed primarily arts and crafts and interior architecture. The shows, each focusing on a particular subject, have had an eventful history: V. and VI. *Triennale,* 1933 and 1936, were so-called "direction Triennales" (Rationalism vs. Novecento); VII. *Triennale* 1940; VIII. *Triennale* 1947 (subject, "L'abitazione", living and furniture); IX. to XI. *Triennale* 1951, 1954, 1957 devoted to new discipline of industrial design; XII. *Triennale* 1960; XIII. *Triennale* 1964 (subject "Il tempo libero," leisure time); IVX. *Triennale* 1968 (occupied by adherents of Radical Design); XV. *Triennale* 1973; XVI. *Triennale* 1982; XVII. *Triennale* 1983–1988 (exhibition cycle); XVIII. *Triennale* 1992; XIX. *Triennale* 1994 (subject, "Identità e differenze"). One of the most important institutions for the promotion of design for many years, its significance has gradually been diminishing since the late 1960s. 1967 *Compasso d'oro*. 54, 57, 64, 90, 142, 162, 176, 204, 352

TRIMARCHI, Mario b. 1958, Messina. Studied architecture in Reggio Calabria. 44, **332**

TRUSSARDI Fashion company; founded 1910 in Bergamo, now in Milan. Initially glovemaker's workshop, later complete line of leather goods. Headed since 1970 by Nicola Trussardi. 1983, ladies' wear; 1984, menswear. Since 1991 also haute couture. Produces accessories, furniture, tableware; popular leather jackets and coats.

UFO see Gruppo UFO

ULTIMA EDIZIONE Furniture manufacturer; founded 1986. Specializes in working in old marble. Designers incl. Gae Aulenti, Ettore Sottsass, Marco Zanuso, Marco Zanini, Vico Magistretti.

UNIFOR 309, **333**

UP&UP Manufacturer of tables, flooring, bathroom fixtures, fireplaces; founded 1986; specializes in marble. Designs by Aldo Rossi, Marco Romanolli and Marta Laudani, Achille Castiglioni, Adolfo Natalini, Marco Zanini. 307

VALENTINO 334

VALLE, Gino 338, 355

VENINI 132, 201, 296, **340**

VENINI, Paolo 1895-1959. Glass designer and entrepreneur. 1921, cofounder of Venini, of of Venice's most renowned glass manufacturers. Sole owner from 1925. Venini revived old techniques and developed them further. Designers incl. Gio Ponti, Carlo Scarpa. 296, 319, 318, 340

VENTURINI, Guido b. 1957. Product designer. Representative of Bolidismo. Worked with Stefano Giovannoni for King-Kon, 1985-1989. Designs for Alessi, Ultima Edizione, Twergy and Bianchi & Bruni. 94, 212

VERSACE, Donatella 80, 342

VERSACE, Gianni 342

VIGANÓ, Vittoriano b. 1919. Architect and Product designer. Early experiments with new materials. Worked with Gio Ponti and at BBPR. Communicated Le Corbusier's ideas. Influential in the 1950s with his steel, glass and plywood furniture. Designs for Arteluce. 60, 109

VIGNELLI, Lella b. 1936. Architect, furniture and graphic designer. Studied at MIT Cambridge and in Venice. 128, 292, **344**

VIGNELLI, Massimo b. 1931. Architect, furniture and graphic designer. Studied architecture in Milan and Venice. 128, 290, 292, 340, **344**

VIGO, Nanda Architect, artist and product designer. Worked for Lucio Fontana and Gio Ponti. In addition to architectural and art projects, furniture and lighting for Driade, Gabbianelli and Glass Design.

VORTICE Manufacturer of electric appliances; founded 1954. Well-known poroducts incl. Marco Zanuso's innovative 1977 *Ariante* fan housed in a "box."

ZANI & ZANI 346

ZANINI, Marco b. 1954. Architect, furniture, glass and lighting designer. Worked for Sottsass Associati; known for designs for Memphis (1986, *Roma* chair) and glass objects for Venini. 77, 256, 325

ZANOTTA 55, 78, 114, 144, 162, 179, 181, 230, 299, 321, 329, **348**

ZANUSO, Marco 61, 62, 63, 104, 109, 122, 132, 136, 138, 145, 222, 290, 314, 348, **352**

ZANUSO, Marco jr. b. 1954. Architect, furniture and lighting designer. Lighting for his own firm, Oceano Oltreluce; furniture for Memphis; architectural projects in Europe. 303

ZANUSSI 65, 338, **355**

ZEUS 81, **357**

ZUCCHETTI RUBINETTERIA manufacturer of faucets; founded 1929 by Alfredo Zucchetti. 1975, collaboration with Studio Nizzoli (*Zetamix 6000*), later with Raul Barbieri and Giorgio Marianelli.

The author wishes to thank

Markus Schuler, Cologne,
without whose help this book would not exist. I am greatly indebted to him for
his enthusiastic, expert research and knowledgeable, inspired editing of the
sections on graphic and fashion design.

Fulvio Ferrari, Turin, for giving generous access to his photographic archive.

Jan Strathmann, Cologne, for his careful editing of the text.

Helge Aszmoneit and the German Design Council, Frankfurt, for their valuable
research assistance.

Donatella Cacciola, Rome and Bonn, for her tireless help in compiling
photographic material.

Giulio Castelli, Milan, and ADI for assisting our photographic research efforts;
with special thanks to Alessandra Fossati.

Uta Brandes, Cologne. ICE, Istituto Nazionale per il Commercio Estero,
Düsseldorf (Dr. Andrea Ferrari, Mariana Lopper, Dr. Tommaso Maria Gliozzi).
Michael Erlhoff, Cologne. Galerie Ulrich Fiedler, Cologne (Ulrich Fiedler and
Katharina Evers). Thomas Hauffe and Elisabeth Knoll, DuMont Buchverlag,
Cologne. Bruno Mocci, Cultural Representative of the Italian Embassy, Bonn.
Peter Pfeiffer, Milan. Marco Romanelli, Milan. Heike Tekampe, Cologne.

Paolo Antonelli, Peter Boragno, Guido Boragno, Robin Davy, Klaus Thomas
Edelmann, Ruth Hanisch-Raddatz and Wolfgang Raddatz, Dr. Hans Höger,
Christoph Johannsson, Michael Junker, Olaf Kriszio, Antonia Lahmé, Ines Lu-
sche, Manu Lange, Julia Lenz, Kathrin Luz, Anne Marburger, Alexandra Maus,
Susan Neumann, Eleonore Neumann, Ingeborg Polster, Udo Schliemann,
Klaus Schmidt-Lorenz, Ulrike Stiefelhagen, Ute von Elsen.

Thanks to all the firms and designers who graciously supported me in my
research efforts.

And special thanks to Mandy, Bernd and Olaf.

Cover: photo of a Vespa PK 50 S.
Vespa is a registered trademark of Piaggio & C. SpA.

This edition published in
Great Britain in 1999
by PAVILION BOOKS LIMITED
London House, Great Eastern Wharf
Parkgate Road, London SW11 4NQ

© 1999 Howard Buch Produktion
Bonn, Germany

Concept and realization:
Howard Buch Produktion
editor: Bernd Polster
art director: Olaf Meyer

English translation
© 1999 Universe Publishing

A CIP catalogue record for this book
is available from the British Library.

ISBN 1 86205 312 X

Printed in Italy
10 9 8 7 6 5 4 3 2 1

This book can be ordered direct
from the publisher. Please contact
the Marketing Department.
But try your bookshop first.

Photographs and illustrations that are not listed separately are reprinted by courtesy of the designers and companies.

Unless otherwise indicated, the copyrights are with the respective designers and companies. In a few cases it was not possible to identify the copyright holders. Legitimate claims will be settled according to customary agreements.

Fulvio Ferrari: 14, 18, 30, 35, 53 (l., c.), 55 (l.), 57 (l.), 61 (c.), 63 (c., r.), 65 (c.), 67 (c.), 71 (c., r.), 72 (l., c.), 74 (l.), 75 (l., c.), 92 (top, bottom r.), 104 (b.), 104 (t.r.), 105 (t.r.), 142, 144 (l.), 149 (l.), 164 (l.), 170 (r.), 173 (r., b.), 175 (b.r.), 210, 219 (l.), 263, 279 (t.), 285 (t.), 293, 297 (t.l., b.l.), 323 · **Studio Aldo Ballo:** 7, 19, 111 (t.l., t.r.), 125 (t.l.), 132 (l.), 139 (b.l.), 155, 156 (t.r., b.l.), 162 (r.), 171 (l., r.), 207 (t.r.), 241, 250 (l.), 295, 316 (r.), 325 (l.), 346, 347, 349 (b.r.) · **Andreas Jung / Galerie Ulrich Fiedler, Cologne:** 4, 31, 66 (c.), 91 (b.), 109, 279 (b.l.), 297 (b.r.) · **ADI Archive, Milan:** 33, 34, 62 (r.), 64 (c.), 65 (l.), 67 (l.), 68, 69 (c., r.), 71 (l.), 72 (r.), 78 (l.), 79 (r.), 103 (t.), 146, 147, 156 (b.r.), 165 (c.), 173 (t.l.), 179, 208, 246, 271 (t.l., u.r.), 273, 311 (b.r.), 315 (t.), 318, 330, 339 (t.), 352, 353, 354 · **Gio Ponti Photo Archives, Salvatore Licitra:** 39, 54 (c.), 62 (c.) · **Studio Masera:** 40, 114 (r.), 163, 329, 349 (t.l.) · **Archivio Storico of Olivetti, Ivrea, Italy:** 51 (r.), 52 (l.), 55 (l.), 67 (r.), 139, 277, 279 (b.r.), 281 · **Robin Davy:** 2 · **M. Ramazzotti:** 15 · **Ramazzotti & Stucchi:** 302, 303 (l.), 349 (b.l.), 349 (t.r.), 351 · **Nucera / Casa Vogue:** 21 · **Miro Zagnoli:** 111 (u.l., u.r.), 169 (o.l.), 316 (m.) · **Notarianni:** 316 (l.) · **Victor Mendini:** 317 (l.) · **Santi Caleca:** 317 (r.) · **Centrokappa:** 161 (b.l.) · **Bella & Ruggeri:** 25, 156 (t.l.), 250 (r.) · **Roberto Sellitto:** 243 (b.r.), 193 (r.) · **Luciano Soave:** 54 (b.r.) · **Salvador Liderno:** 38, 237 (b.l.) · **Gionata Xerra:** 237 (r.) · **Studio Azurro:** 235 · **Bruno Di Bello:** 253 (b.l.) · **Archiv Albe Steiner:** 45, 326, 327 · **Leo Torri:** 180 (r.), 306 (b.r.) · **Bruno Stefani:** 61 (b.l.) · **Serge Libiszewski:** 310, 311 (t.l.) · **Hans Hansen:** 168 · **Bernd Mayer:** 169 (b.l.) · **Axel Siebmann:** 106 · **Anghinelli:** 206 · **Paolo Roversi:** 229 (l.) · **Mici Toniolo:** 282 (b.r.) · **Franco Manfrotto:** 141 (b.) · **P. Bramati:** 306 (b.l.) · **Guy Marineau:** 335 (r.) · **Piero Biasion:** 335 (l.) · **Beppe Caggi:** 343 (t.r.) · **Abbattista:** 343 (t.l.) · **R. Tecchio:** 359 (r.)